The Norton Reader

THIRD EDITION / SHORTER

D0066727

The Norton Reader

An Anthology of Expository Prose

THIRD EDITION

Arthur M. Eastman, *General Editor*
CARNEGIE-MELLON UNIVERSITY

Caesar R. Blake
UNIVERSITY OF TORONTO

Hubert M. English, Jr.
UNIVERSITY OF MICHIGAN

Alan B. Howes
UNIVERSITY OF MICHIGAN

Robert T. Lenaghan
UNIVERSITY OF MICHIGAN

Leo F. McNamara
UNIVERSITY OF MICHIGAN

James Rosier
UNIVERSITY OF PENNSYLVANIA

Shorter Edition

W · W · NORTON & COMPANY · INC · *New York*

Library of Congress Cataloging in Publication Data
Eastman, Arthur M   1918–   ed.
    The Norton reader; an anthology of expository prose.
    "Shorter edition."
    1. College readers. I. Title.
[PE1122.E3 1973b]   808'.04275   72-11776
ISBN 0-393-09370-0

PRINTED IN THE UNITED STATES OF AMERICA

4 5 6 7 8 9 0

ACKNOWLEDGMENTS

Maya Angelou: from *I Know Why the Caged Bird Sings,* copyright © 1969 by Maya Angelou. Reprinted by permission of Random House, Inc.

Carl Becker: from *Modern Democracy.* Copyright 1941 by Yale University Press. Reprinted by permission of the Press.

Ronald Blythe: from *Akenfield: Portrait of an English Village,* published by Penguin Press, 1969. Reprinted by permission of David Higham Associates, Ltd.

William Bondeson: from *The New York Times.* Copyright © 1971 by The New York Times Company. Reprinted by permission of The New York Times Company and the author.

Jacob Bronowski: "The Reach of Imagination," from *American Scholar,* Spring 1967. Reprinted by permission of The American Academy of Arts and Letters and the author.

Dee Brown: from *Bury My Heart at Wounded Knee,* copyright © 1970 by Dee Brown. Reprinted by permission of Holt, Rinehart and Winston, Inc.

Jerome S. Bruner, from *Partisan Review,* Summer 1956, Vol. XXIII, No. 3. Copyright 1956 by Partisan Review. Reprinted by permission of *Partisan Review* and the author.

Anthony Burgess: from *The New York Times Magazine,* November 7, 1971. Copyright © 1971 by The New York Times Company. Reprinted by permission.

H. J. Campbell: from *Smithsonian,* October 1971, Vol. II, No. 7. Copyright © 1971 by Smithsonian National Associates. Reprinted by permission.

Edward Hallett Carr: from *What Is History?* Copyright © 1961 by Edward Hallett Carr. Reprinted by permission of Alfred A. Knopf, Inc., and The Macmillan Company Ltd. of Canada.

Joyce Cary: from *Highlights of Modern Literature,* copyright © 1949 by The New York Times Company. Reprinted by permission.

Kenneth Clark: from *Encounter,* January 1963. Reprinted by permission of the author and *Encounter.*

Eldridge Cleaver: from *Soul on Ice,* copyright © 1968 by Eldridge Cleaver. Reprinted by permission of McGraw-Hill Book Company.

Henry Sloane Coffin: from *The Meaning of the Cross.* Copyright 1931 by Charles Scribner's Sons; renewal copyright © 1959 by Dorothy Prentice Coffin. Reprinted with the permission of Charles Scribner's Sons.

Robert Coles: from *The Middle Americans* by Robert Coles and Jon Erikson, copyright © 1971 by Robert Coles. Reprinted by permission of Atlantic–Little, Brown and Co.

Bernadette Devlin: from *The Price of My Soul,* copyright © 1969 by Bernadette Devlin. Reprinted by permission of Alfred A. Knopf, Inc., and Andre Deutsch Ltd.

Malcolm L. Diamond: from *The New York Times.* Copyright © 1971 by The New York Times Company. Reprinted by permission of The New York Times Company and the author.

Joan Didion: from *Slouching Towards Bethlehem,* copyright © 1967, 1968 by Joan Didion. Reprinted by permission of Farrar, Straus & Giroux, Inc.

W. E. B. Du Bois: from *W. E. B. Du Bois Speaks,* edited by Philip S. Foner, copyright © 1970 by Philip S. Foner and Shirley Graham Du Bois. Reprinted by permission of Philip S. Foner.

Ralph Ellison: from *Shadow and Act,* copyright © 1955 by Ralph Ellison. Reprinted by permission of Random House, Inc.

Erik H. Erikson and Huey P. Newton: from *In Search of Common Ground,* edited by Kai T. Erikson and J. Herman Blake. Copyright © 1973 by Rikan Enterprises Ltd., Kai T. Erikson, and Stronghold Consolidated Productions, Inc. Reprinted by permission of W. W. Norton & Company, Inc.

Jim Essenson: from *The New York Times.* Copyright © 1971 by The New York Times Company. Reprinted by permission of The New York Times Company.

Robert Frost: "Education by Poetry." All rights reserved. Reprinted by permission of the Estate of Robert Frost and Holt, Rinehart and Winston, Inc.

Christopher Fry: from *Vogue,* January 1951, copyright 1951 by Christopher Fry. Reprinted by permission of ACTAC Limited, 16 Cadogan Lane, London, S.W. 1.

Northrop Frye: from *The Educated Imagination.* Reprinted by permission of Indiana University Press and the Canadian Broadcasting Corporation. This essay was one of a series of Massey Lectures given by Northrop Frye on the Canadian Broadcasting Corporation's radio network. The series is published in Canada by CBC Publications under the title *The Educated Imagination.*

Garrett Hardin: from *Science,* No. 162, December 13, 1968. Copyright © 1968 by the American Association for the Advancement of Science. Reprinted by permission of the author and the publisher.

Eric Hoffer: from *The Ordeal of Change* (1963). Copyright © 1952 by Eric Hoffer. Reprinted by permission of Harper & Row, Publishers.

John Holt: from *Redbook,* November 1967. Copyright © 1967 by McCall Corporation. Reprinted by permission of the publishers and the author. John Holt is the author of *How Children Fail* and *How Children Learn,* both published by Pitman Publishing Corporation.

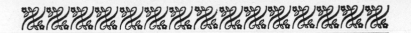

Contents

ON RELIGION

Preface to the Shorter Edition

THIRD EDITION

This Shorter Edition of the Third Edition of *The Norton Reader* contains some forty new selections, a marked increase in material by women and black authors, and a new Prose Forms section on Oral History. The section formerly entitled On Civilization, now called Signs of the Times, is totally new, containing selections by such contemporary authors as Verta Mae, Adrienne Rich, Eldridge Cleaver, Peter Schrag, and Anthony Burgess. Selections by Toni Morrison, John Updike, and Tom Wolfe are among those that have updated An Album of Styles. On Politics has been retitled On Politics and Government—with a corresponding change in its contents.

Such additions have been purchased at the expense of a large number of selections which the editors have removed because they seemed to have served their turn, because reports from the field indicated that they were receiving scant attention, or because other good things crowded them out. The Prose Forms sections on Letters and Characters are gone for want of use, though some of the best of their material has been transplanted to other places in the text. In this Shorter Edition the sections On Language and On Ethics will no longer be found, though Orwell's "Politics and the English Language" appears in On Politics and Government and material of significant ethical import is scattered throughout the book. Still, a large number of selections continue from the past. In the opinion of the editors and their colleagues around the country, the essays by Stegner, White, Holt, Thoreau, Bronowski, Frye, Frost, and Clark—to name a few—deserve to remain. Users of earlier editions will find an abundance of tried and proven material among the newer entries.

As in the past, the essays in the Reader are gathered into sections titled according to major fields of human concern—Education, Mind, Literature and the Arts, etc. The ordering remains unchanged—unobtrusive, we think, minimal, yet reflective of the individual's enlarging experience. Teachers who wish to work by topic can use its divisions. On gaining familiarity with the text, moreover, they will discover thematic links between the different sections. For

example, Adrienne Rich's "When We Dead Awaken: Writing as
Re-Vision" appears in Signs of the Times because its primary con-
cern is with the awakening of the consciousness of modern women,
but it ties in nicely with essays under On Literature and the Arts.
B. F. Skinner's "What Is Man?" sets forth a view of man's nature
central to one kind of scientific exploration and so appears in On
Science, but it links with Jerome Bruner's essay "Freud and the
Image of Man," which is under On Mind, and with Simone Weil's
"Spiritual Autobiography," which is under On Religion.

Teachers who prefer to organize their courses rhetorically will
find useful, we trust, the Index of Essays Illustrative of Rhetorical
Modes and Devices that appears at the beginning of the book and,
at the end, the Notes on Composition, which directs attention to
rhetorical principles as exemplified in the text. Study questions,
attached to approximately half of the essays, are offered diffidently
for those who care to use them.

It is a pleasure to acknowledge again the perceptive help we
received, while the First Edition was in the making, of Professors
Hulon Willis of Bakersfield College, James H. Broderick of Bryn
Mawr College, Cecil M. McCulley of the College of William and
Mary, Harold D. Kelling of the University of Colorado, Scott Elledge
of Cornell University, John Doebler of Dickinson University, Fred
A. Tarpley of East Texas University, Harris W. Wilson of the University of Illinois, Don L. Cook and Donald J. Gray of the University
of Indiana, Fabian Gudas of Louisiana State University, Eugene
Hardy of the University of Nebraska, J. R. Gaskin of the University
of North Carolina, Frederick Candelaria of the University of Oregon,
Robert D. Bamberg of the University of Pennsylvania, W. Donald
Head of San Jose State College, David J. DeLaura of the University
of Texas, Joseph P. Roppolo of Tulane University, and John P. Cutts
of Wayne State University. Their counsel was augmented in the
Second Edition by Professors Byron Patterson of American River
College; Hulon Willis of Bakersfield College; A. G. Medlicott, Jr.,
of the University of Connecticut; Charles B. Ruggless of Humboldt
State College; Scott Elledge, Donald J. Gray, and James W. Gro-
shong of Oregon State University; Carl E. Stenberg of Rhode Island
College; James Wheatley of Trinity College; and Donald L. Cross
of Upsala College.

For their tireless efforts in bringing to this Third Edition more
selections by and about women, the editors gratefully acknowledge
the assistance of Dr. Joan E. Hartman of Staten Island Community
College and Dr. Carol Ohmann of Wesleyan University. Thanks
are also extended to the many teachers who, by drawing on their
classroom experiences with *The Norton Reader*, have offered a
wealth of ideas and suggestions for its improvement. These include:
Denis M. Murphy, Allegheny College; Anne Wiggins and Ella Mae

York, Arizona Western College; Thomas Boghosian, Atlantic Community College; Dale K. Boyer, Boise State College; Don Norton, Brigham Young University; Robert R. Gross, Bucknell University; Louis E. Murphy, J. Michael Pilz, Katherine Rankin, and Judith A. Switzer, Bucks County Community College; D. E. James, University of California at Riverside; Thomas Miles, Carnegie-Mellon University; David Noveshen, Catonsville Community College; Barbara Horgan and Rachel Meyerholtz, Clayton Junior College; Margaret W. Freeman, College of William and Mary; Raymond G. McAll, College of Wooster; Jack Brown, Columbus College; Ronald Migaud, Compton College; George T. Bush, William Devlin, Mrs. E. P. Johnston, Cornelia Rathke, and Alice M. Rusbar, Delgado Junior College; William G. Johnston, University of Denver; William Fisher, Detroit Institute of Technology; S. J. Kozikowski, Elms College; Peter Martin, Florida Atlantic University; Charles Gillespie, Florida Keys Community College; Marguerite del Mastro, Fordham University; James Lawrence, Framingham State College; George Haich, Richard L. Hall, and Susan Passler, Georgia State University; Martin Newitz and R. C. Ridenour, Golden West College; Georgiana Goldberg, Green River Community College; Charles Ruggless, Humboldt State College; Helen W. Krueger and Edwina Patton, Huntington College; Ceary E. Danihy, Prem Kumar, and James F. O'Callaghan, University of Idaho; John Bell, University of Illinois Circle Campus; Terrance B. Kearns and Ronald Sommer, Indiana University; Judith Cushman, Ethel Deutsch, and Theresa Lenora Drew, Indiana University Northwest; S. D. Rowe and Daniel S. Grubb, Indiana University of Pennsylvania; Paul A. Parrish, Indiana University at South Bend; Mary W. Schneider, Kansas State University; Donald Stuart, Longwood College; Ira Hindman, Mansfield State College; Richard M. Judd, Marlboro College; William Kemp, Mary Washington College; John J. Lavelle, Monmouth College; Bernice Katz and Grant E. Strickland, Monroe Community College; Paul Benson, Mountain View College; Gary Lane, Muhlenberg College; Clarence S. Johnson, Newark College of Engineering; Daniel O'Day, Jr., Newark State College; Michael Spitzer, New York Institute of Technology; Arnold Bartini, North Adams State College; Edward Boucher, Mary L. Brittain, L. R. Early, James Evans, Ruth C. Hege, and Marvin Weaver, University of North Carolina at Greensboro; Martha L. Adams, Northeast Louisiana University; Maureen Edison, Dorothy Havens, Nancy Lee, Benjamin A. Little, and Harvey Vetstein, Northeastern University; Ely Liebow, Northeastern Illinois University; David Allen, Northland College; John P. Cutts, Oakland University; Rose D'Agostino and James Tarvin, Orange County Community College; Richard Woods, Pasadena City College; William E. Lucas, Peninsula College; Joseph M. Paradin and David Snyder, University of Pennsylvania; N. R. Brown,

Charles Dewees, Jr., and Lee L. Snyder, Philadelphia College of Textiles and Science; Alex M. Baumgartner, Robert Fox, and Frederick Wilbur, Rider College; Anthony Amberg and Joseph Paris, Roosevelt University; Joel Magid, Rutgers University; Robert Noreen, San Fernando Valley State College; Richard A. Alden, Kenneth Cooney, and Lee Leonard, Shasta College; Stan Smith, Sierra Junior College; Robert Weisberg, Skidmore College; Charles White, Southeastern Massachusetts University; Lila R. Fink, Juanita Mantovani, Tom Patty, and Jay Thompson, University of Southern California; George Gleason, Southwest Missouri State College; Karen Petz, State University of New York at Geneseo; Stanley M. Vogel, Suffolk University; William D. Stewart, Francis Thompson, and Earl Melton Williams, University of Tampa; Harry Ebert, Jr., Urbana College; I. R. Adams, University of Virginia; Shirley Borel, L. E. Seits, Mary Shesgreen, and James Zemek, Waubonsee Community College; W. Nicholas Knight, Wesleyan University; Sharon L. Taylor, Western State College; and Carol Metzger, West Los Angeles College.

Arthur M. Eastman

An Index of Essays
Illustrative of Rhetorical
Modes and Devices

THESIS[1]

1. The section headings of this index are treated more fully in the Notes on Composition, p. 477.

STYLE

The Norton Reader

Shorter Edition

THIRD EDITION

Personal Report

WALLACE STEGNER
The Town Dump

The town dump of Whitemud, Saskatchewan, could only have been a few years old when I knew it, for the village was born in 1913 and I left there in 1919. But I remember the dump better than I remember most things in that town, better than I remember most of the people. I spent more time with it, for one thing; it has more poetry and excitement in it than people did.

It lay in the southeast corner of town, in a section that was always full of adventure for me. Just there the Whitemud River left the hills, bent a little south, and started its long traverse across the prairie and international boundary to join the Milk. For all I knew, it might have been on its way to join the Alph: simply, before my eyes, it disappeared into strangeness and wonder.

Also, where it passed below the dumpground, it ran through willowed bottoms that were a favorite campsite for passing teamsters, gypsies, sometimes Indians. The very straw scattered around those camps, the ashes of those strangers' campfires, the manure of their teams and saddle horses, were hot with adventurous possibilities.

It was as an extension, a living suburb, as it were, of the dumpground that we most valued those camps. We scoured them for artifacts of their migrant tenants as if they had been archaeological sites full of the secrets of ancient civilizations. I remember toting around for weeks the broken cheek strap of a bridle. Somehow or other its buckle looked as if it had been fashioned in a far place, a place where they were accustomed to flatten the tongues of buckles for reasons that could only be exciting, and where they made a habit of plating the metal with some valuable alloy, probably silver. In places where the silver was worn away the buckle underneath shone dull yellow: probably gold.

It seemed that excitement liked that end of town better than

1

our end. Once old Mrs. Gustafson, deeply religious and a little raddled in the head, went over there with a buckboard full of trash, and as she was driving home along the river she looked and saw a spent catfish, washed in from Cypress Lake or some other part of the watershed, floating on the yellow water. He was two feet long, his whiskers hung down, his fins and tail were limp. He was a kind of fish that no one had seen in the Whitemud in the three or four years of the town's life, and a kind that none of us children had ever seen anywhere. Mrs. Gustafson had never seen one like him either; she perceived at once that he was the devil, and she whipped up the team and reported him at Hoffman's elevator.

We could hear her screeching as we legged it for the river to see for ourselves. Sure enough, there he was. He looked very tired, and he made no great effort to get away as we pushed out a half-sunken rowboat from below the flume, submerged it under him, and brought him ashore. When he died three days later we experimentally fed him to two half-wild cats, but they seemed to suffer no ill effects.

At that same end of town the irrigation flume crossed the river. It always seemed to me giddily high when I hung my chin over its plank edge and looked down, but it probably walked no more than twenty feet above the water on its spidery legs. Ordinarily in summer it carried about six or eight inches of smooth water, and under the glassy hurrying of the little boxed stream the planks were coated with deep sun-warmed moss as slick as frogs' eggs. A boy could sit in the flume with the water walling up against his back, and grab a cross brace above him, and pull, shooting himself sledlike ahead until he could reach the next brace for another pull and another slide, and so on across the river in four scoots.

After ten minutes in the flume he would come out wearing a dozen or more limber black leeches, and could sit in the green shade where darning needles flashed blue, and dragonflies hummed and darted and stopped, and skaters dimpled slack and eddy with their delicate transitory footprints, and there stretch the leeches out one by one while their sucking ends clung and clung, until at last, stretched far out, they let go with a tiny wet *puk* and snapped together like rubber bands. The smell of the river and the flume and the clay cutbanks and the bars of that part of the river was the smell of wolf willow.

But nothing in that end of town was as good as the dumpground that scattered along a little runoff coulee dipping down toward the river from the south bench. Through a historical process that went back, probably, to the roots of community sanitation and distaste for eyesores, but that in law dated from the Unincorporated Towns

Ordinance of the territorial government, passed in 1888, the dump was one of the very first community enterprises, almost our town's first institution.

More than that, it contained relics of every individual who had ever lived there, and of every phase of the town's history.

The bedsprings on which the town's first child was begotten might be there; the skeleton of a boy's pet colt; two or three volumes of Shakespeare bought in haste and error from a peddler, later loaned in carelessness, soaked with water and chemicals in a house fire, and finally thrown out to flap their stained eloquence in the prairie wind.

Broken dishes, rusty tinware, spoons that had been used to mix paint; once a box of percussion caps, sign and symbol of the carelessness that most of those people felt about all matters of personal or public safety. We put them on the railroad tracks and were anonymously denounced in the *Enterprise*. There were also old iron, old brass, for which we hunted assiduously, by night conning junkmen's catalogues and the pages of the *Enterprise* to find how much wartime value there might be in the geared insides of clocks or in a pound of tea lead carefully wrapped in a ball whose weight astonished and delighted us. Sometimes the unimaginable outside world reached in and laid a finger on us. I recall that, aged no more than seven, I wrote a St. Louis junk house asking if they preferred their tea lead and tinfoil wrapped in balls, or whether they would rather have it pressed flat in sheets, and I got back a typewritten letter in a window envelope instructing me that they would be happy to have it in any way that was convenient for me. They added that they valued my business and were mine very truly. Dazed, I carried that windowed grandeur around in my pocket until I wore it out, and for months I saved the letter as a souvenir of the wondering time when something strange and distinguished had singled me out.

We hunted old bottles in the dump, bottles caked with dirt and filth, half buried, full of cobwebs, and we washed them out at the horse trough by the elevator, putting in a handful of shot along with the water to knock the dirt loose; and when we had shaken them until our arms were tired, we hauled them off in somebody's coaster wagon and turned them in at Bill Anderson's pool hall, where the smell of lemon pop was so sweet on the dark pool-hall air that I am sometimes awakened by it in the night, even yet.

Smashed wheels of wagons and buggies, tangles of rusty barbed wire, the collapsed perambulator that the French wife of one of the town's doctors had once pushed proudly up the planked sidewalks and along the ditchbank paths. A welter of foul-smelling feathers and coyote-scattered carrion which was all that remained of somebody's dream of a chicken ranch. The chickens had all got some mysterious pip at the same time, and died as one, and the dream lay out there with the rest of the town's history to rustle to the empty sky on the border of the hills.

There was melted glass in curious forms, and the half-melted office safe left from the burning of Bill Day's Hotel. On very lucky days we might find a piece of the lead casing that had enclosed the wires of the town's first telephone system. The casing was just the right size for rings, and so soft that it could be whittled with a jackknife. It was a material that might have made artists of us. If we had been Indians of fifty years before, that bright soft metal would have enlisted our maximum patience and craft and come out as ring and metal and amulet inscribed with the symbols of our observed world. Perhaps there were too many ready-made alternatives in the local drug, hardware, and general stores; perhaps our feeble artistic response was a measure of the insufficiency of the challenge we felt. In any case I do not remember that we did any more with the metal than to shape it into crude seal rings with our initials or pierced hearts carved in them; and these, though they served a purpose in juvenile courtship, stopped something short of art.

The dump held very little wood, for in that country anything burnable got burned. But it had plenty of old iron, furniture, papers, mattresses that were the delight of field mice, and jugs and demijohns that were sometimes their bane, for they crawled into the necks and drowned in the rain water or redeye that was inside.

If the history of our town was not exactly written, it was at least hinted, in the dump. I think I had a pretty sound notion even at eight or nine of how significant was that first institution of our forming Canadian civilization. For rummaging through its foul purlieus I had several times been surprised and shocked to find relics of my own life tossed out there to rot or blow away.

The volumes of Shakespeare belonged to a set that my father had bought before I was born. It had been carried through successive moves from town to town in the Dakotas, and from Dakota to Seattle, and from Seattle to Bellingham, and Bellingham to Redmond, and from Redmond back to Iowa, and from there to Saskatchewan. Then, stained in a stranger's house fire, these volumes had suffered from a house-cleaning impulse and been thrown away for me to stumble upon in the dump. One of the Cratchet girls had borrowed them, a hatchet-faced, thin, eager, transplanted Cockney girl with a frenzy, almost a hysteria, for reading. And yet somehow, through her hands, they found the dump, to become a symbol of how much was lost, how much thrown aside, how much carelessly or of necessity given up, in the making of a new country. We had so few books that I was familiar with them all, had handled them, looked at their pictures, perhaps even read them. They were the lares and penates, part of the skimpy impedimenta of household gods we had brought with us into Latium.[1] Finding those three thrown away was a little like finding my own name on a gravestone.

And yet not the blow that something else was, something that impressed me even more with the dump's close reflection of the town's intimate life. The colt whose picked skeleton lay out there was mine. He had been incurably crippled when dogs chased our mare, Daisy, the morning after she foaled. I had labored for months to make him well; had fed him by hand, curried him, exercised him, adjusted the iron braces that I had talked my father into having made. And I had not known that he would have to be destroyed. One weekend I turned him over to the foreman of one of the ranches, presumably so that he could be cared for. A few days later I found his skinned body, with the braces still on his crippled front legs, lying on the dump.

Not even that, I think, cured me of going there, though our parents all forbade us on pain of cholera or worse to do so. The place fascinated us, as it should have. For this was the kitchen midden of all the civilization we knew; it gave us the most tantalizing glimpses into our lives as well as into those of the neighbors. It gave us an aesthetic distance from which to know ourselves.

The dump was our poetry and our history. We took it home with us by the wagonload, bringing back into town the things the town had used and thrown away. Some little part of what we gathered, mainly bottles, we managed to bring back to usefulness, but most of our gleanings we left lying around barn or attic or cellar until in some renewed fury of spring cleanup our families carted them off to the dump again, to be rescued and briefly treasured by some other boy with schemes for making them useful. Occasionally something we really valued with a passion was snatched from us in horror and returned at once. That happened to the mounted head of a white mountain goat, somebody's trophy from old times and the far Rocky Mountains, that I brought home one day in transports of delight. My mother took one look and discovered that his beard was full of moths.

I remember that goat; I regret him yet. Poetry is seldom useful, but always memorable. I think I learned more from the town dump than I learned from school: more about people, more about how life is lived, not elsewhere but here, not in other times but now. If I were a sociologist anxious to study in detail the

1. In Roman families the lares and penates were the ancestral, household gods; they came to embody the con- tinuity of the family. Cf. Virgil, *Aeneid* I. 1-7.

life of any community, I would go very early to its refuse piles. For a community may be as well judged by what it throws away —what it has to throw away and what it chooses to—as by any other evidence. For whole civilizations we have sometimes no more of the poetry and little more of the history than this.

QUESTIONS

1. Stegner begins his reminiscence of the town dump by saying that it had "poetry and excitement" in it. In what ways does he seek to convey those qualities to the reader?
2. Is Stegner's description of the dump and its surroundings vivid? Where does his writing directly appeal to the senses, and which senses are called into play?
3. In his second paragraph Stegner speaks of the Alph, the "sacred river" of Coleridge's poem "Kubla Khan." Why? How does allusion to that poem help him convey the strangeness and wonder he then felt?
4. In paragraphs 5-8 Stegner departs, as he had departed to a lesser degree in the two preceding paragraphs, from his description of the dump. Explain how that departure is justified and whether the writing there is appropriate to the essay as a whole.
5. Why does Stegner say (p. 5) that finding the three volumes of Shakespeare in the dump was "a little like finding my own name on a gravestone"? What is the purpose and effect of his allusion to Virgil's Aeneid in the sentence just before that?
6. Through what particular details does Stegner portray the dump as a record of his childhood? How is it shown to be also a record of the brief history of the town? In what respects does it reflect and suggest more widely yet, European and American history and culture and, ultimately, the ancient past, the foundations of civilization? Explain how and to what effect Stegner's focus on the dump enables these considerations to widen in scope but remain associated.

MAYA ANGELOU

High School Graduation[1]

The children in Stamps[2] trembled visibly with anticipation. Some adults were excited too, but to be certain the whole young population had come down with graduation epidemic. Large classes were graduating from both the grammar school and the high school. Even those who were years removed from their own day of glorious

1. Chapter 23 of *I Know Why the Caged Bird Sings*, 1970.   2. A town in Arkansas.

release were anxious to help with preparations as a kind of dry run. The junior students who were moving into the vacating classes' chairs were tradition-bound to show their talents for leadership and management. They strutted through the school and around the campus exerting pressure on the lower grades. Their authority was so new that occasionally if they pressed a little too hard it had to be overlooked. After all, next term was coming, and it never hurt a sixth grader to have a play sister in the eighth grade, or a tenth-year student to be able to call a twelfth grader Bubba. So all was endured in a spirit of shared understanding. But the graduating classes themselves were the nobility. Like travelers with exotic destinations on their minds, the graduates were remarkably forgetful. They came to school without their books, or tablets or even pencils. Volunteers fell over themselves to secure replacements for the missing equipment. When accepted, the willing workers might or might not be thanked, and it was of no importance to the pregraduation rites. Even teachers were respectful of the now quiet and aging seniors, and tended to speak to them, if not as equals, as beings only slightly lower than themselves. After tests were returned and grades given, the student body, which acted like an extended family, knew who did well, who excelled, and what piteous ones had failed.

Unlike the white high school, Lafayette County Training School distinguished itself by having neither lawn, nor hedges, nor tennis court, nor climbing ivy. Its two buildings (main classrooms, the grade school and home economics) were set on a dirt hill with no fence to limit either its boundaries or those of bordering farms. There was a large expanse to the left of the school which was used alternately as a baseball diamond or basketball court. Rusty hoops on swaying poles represented the permanent recreational equipment, although bats and balls could be borrowed from the P.E. teacher if the borrower was qualified and if the diamond wasn't occupied.

Over this rocky area relieved by a few shady tall persimmon trees the graduating class walked. The girls often held hands and no longer bothered to speak to the lower students. There was a sadness about them, as if this old world was not their home and they were bound for higher ground. The boys, on the other hand, had become more friendly, more outgoing. A decided change from the closed attitude they projected while studying for finals. Now they seemed not ready to give up the old school, the familiar paths and classrooms. Only a small percentage would be continuing on to college —one of the South's A & M (agricultural and mechanical) schools, which trained Negro youths to be carpenters, farmers, handymen, masons, maids, cooks and baby nurses. Their future rode heavily on their shoulders, and blinded them to the collective joy that had pervaded the lives of the boys and girls in the grammar school graduating class.

Parents who could afford it had ordered new shoes and ready-made clothes for themselves from Sears and Roebuck or Montgomery Ward. They also engaged the best seamstresses to make the floating graduating dresses and to cut down secondhand pants which would be pressed to a military slickness for the important event.

Oh, it was important, all right. Whitefolks would attend the ceremony, and two or three would speak of God and home, and the Southern way of life, and Mrs. Parsons, the principal's wife, would play the graduation march while the lower-grade graduates paraded down the aisles and took their seats below the platform. The high school seniors would wait in empty classrooms to make their dramatic entrance.

In the Store I was the person of the moment. The birthday girl. The center. Bailey[3] had graduated the year before, although to do so he had had to forfeit all pleasures to make up for his time lost in Baton Rouge.

My class was wearing butter-yellow piqué dresses, and Momma launched out on mine. She smocked the yoke into tiny crisscrossing puckers, then shirred the rest of the bodice. Her dark fingers ducked in and out of the lemony cloth as she embroidered raised daisies around the hem. Before she considered herself finished she had added a crocheted cuff on the puff sleeves, and a pointy crocheted collar.

I was going to be lovely. A walking model of all the various styles of fine hand sewing and it didn't worry me that I was only twelve years old and merely graduating from the eighth grade. Besides, many teachers in Arkansas Negro schools had only that diploma and were licensed to impart wisdom.

The days had become longer and more noticeable. The faded beige of former times had been replaced with strong and sure colors. I began to see my classmates' clothes, their skin tones, and the dust that waved off pussy willows. Clouds that lazed across the sky were objects of great concern to me. Their shiftier shapes might have held a message that in my new happiness and with a little bit of time I'd soon decipher. During that period I looked at the arch of heaven so religiously my neck kept a steady ache. I had taken to smiling more often, and my jaws hurt from the unaccustomed activity. Between the two physical sore spots, I suppose I could have been uncomfortable, but that was not the case. As a member of the winning team (the graduating class of 1940) I had outdistanced

3. The author's brother.

unpleasant sensations by miles. I was headed for the freedom of open fields.

Youth and social approval allied themselves with me and we trammeled memories of slights and insults. The wind of our swift passage remodeled my features. Lost tears were pounded to mud and then to dust. Years of withdrawal were brushed aside and left behind, as hanging ropes of parasitic moss.

My work alone had awarded me a top place and I was going to be one of the first called in the graduating ceremonies. On the class-room blackboard, as well as on the bulletin board in the audito-rium, there were blue stars and white stars and red stars. No absences, no tardinesses, and my academic work was among the best of the year. I could say the preamble to the Constitution even faster than Bailey. We timed ourselves often: "WethepeopleoftheUnited Statesinordertoformamoreperfectunion . . ." I had memorized the Presidents of the United States from Washington to Roosevelt in chronological as well as alphabetical order.

My hair pleased me too. Gradually the black mass had length-ened and thickened, so that it kept at last to its braided pattern, and I didn't have to yank my scalp off when I tried to comb it.

Louise and I had rehearsed the exercises until we tired out our-selves. Henry Reed was class valedictorian. He was a small, very black boy with hooded eyes, a long, broad nose and an oddly shaped head. I had admired him for years because each term he and I vied for the best grades in our class. Most often he bested me, but instead of being disappointed I was pleased that we shared top places between us. Like many Southern Black children, he lived with his grandmother, who was as strict as Momma and as kind as she knew how to be. He was courteous, respectful and soft-spoken to elders, but on the playground he chose to play the roughest games. I admired him. Anyone, I reckoned, sufficiently afraid or suf-ficiently dull could be polite. But to be able to operate at a top level with both adults and children was admirable.

His valedictory speech was entitled "To Be or Not to Be." The rigid tenth-grade teacher had helped him write it. He'd been work-ing on the dramatic stresses for months.

The weeks until graduation were filled with heady activities. A group of small children were to be presented in a play about butter-cups and daisies and bunny rabbits. They could be heard through-out the building practicing their hops and their little songs that sounded like silver bells. The older girls (nongraduates, of course) were assigned the task of making refreshments for the night's festiv-ities. A tangy scent of ginger, cinnamon, nutmeg and chocolate wafted around the home economics building as the budding cooks made samples for themselves and their teachers.

In every corner of the workshop, axes and saws split fresh timber as the woodshop boys made sets and stage scenery. Only the graduates were left out of the general bustle. We were free to sit in the library at the back of the building or look in quite detachedly, naturally, on the measures being taken for our event.

Even the minister preached on graduation the Sunday before. His subject was, "Let your light so shine that men will see your good works and praise your Father, Who is in Heaven." Although the sermon was purported to be addressed to us, he used the occasion to speak to backsliders, gamblers and general ne'er-do-wells. But since he had called our names at the beginning of the service we were mollified.

Among Negroes the tradition was to give presents to children going only from one grade to another. How much more important this was when the person was graduating at the top of the class. Uncle Willie and Momma had sent away for a Mickey Mouse watch like Bailey's. Louise gave me four embroidered handkerchiefs. (I gave her crocheted doilies.) Mrs. Sneed, the minister's wife, made me an undershirt to wear for graduation, and nearly every customer gave me a nickel or maybe even a dime with the instruction "Keep on moving to higher ground," or some such encouragement.

Amazingly the great day finally dawned and I was out of bed before I knew it. I threw open the back door to see it more clearly, but Momma said, "Sister, come away from that door and put your robe on."

I hoped the memory of that morning would never leave me. Sunlight was itself young, and the day had none of the insistence maturity would bring it in a few hours. In my robe and barefoot in the backyard, under cover of going to see about my new beans, I gave myself up to the gentle warmth and thanked God that no matter what evil I had done in my life He had allowed me to live to see this day. Somewhere in my fatalism I had expected to die, accidentally, and never have the chance to walk up the stairs in the auditorium and gracefully receive my hard-earned diploma. Out of God's merciful bosom I had won reprieve.

Bailey came out in his robe and gave me a box wrapped in Christmas paper. He said he had saved his money for months to pay for it. It felt like a box of chocolates, but I knew Bailey wouldn't save money to buy candy when we had all we could want under our noses.

He was as proud of the gift as I. It was a soft-leather-bound copy of a collection of poems by Edgar Allan Poe, or, as Bailey and I called him, "Eap." I turned to "Annabel Lee" and we walked up and down the garden rows, the cool dirt between our toes, reciting the beautifully sad lines.

Momma made a Sunday breakfast although it was only Friday. After we finished the blessing, I opened my eyes to find the watch on my plate. It was a dream of a day. Everything went smoothly and to my credit. I didn't have to be reminded or scolded for anything. Near evening I was too jittery to attend to chores, so Bailey volunteered to do all before his bath.

Days before, we had made a sign for the Store, and as we turned out the lights Momma hung the cardboard over the doorknob. It read clearly: CLOSED. GRADUATION.

My dress fitted perfectly and everyone said that I looked like a sunbeam in it. On the hill, going toward the school, Bailey walked behind with Uncle Willie, who muttered, "Go on, Ju." He wanted him to walk ahead with us because it embarrassed him to have to walk so slowly. Bailey said he'd let the ladies walk together, and the men would bring up the rear. We all laughed, nicely.

Little children dashed by out of the dark like fireflies. Their crepe-paper dresses and butterfly wings were not made for running and we heard more than one rip, dryly, and the regretful "uh uh" that followed.

The school blazed without gaiety. The windows seemed cold and unfriendly from the lower hill. A sense of ill-fated timing crept over me, and if Momma hadn't reached for my hand I would have drifted back to Bailey and Uncle Willie, and possibly beyond. She made a few slow jokes about my feet getting cold, and tugged me along to the now-strange building.

Around the front steps, assurance came back. There were my fellow "greats," the graduating class. Hair brushed back, legs oiled, new dresses and pressed pleats, fresh pocket handkerchiefs and little handbags, all homesewn. Oh, we were up to snuff, all right. I joined my comrades and didn't even see my family go in to find seats in the crowded auditorium.

The school band struck up a march and all classes filed in as had been rehearsed. We stood in front of our seats, as assigned, and on a signal from the choir director, we sat. No sooner had this been accomplished than the band started to play the national anthem. We rose again and sang the song, after which we recited the pledge of allegiance. We remained standing for a brief minute before the choir director and the principal signaled to us, rather desperately I thought, to take our seats. The command was so unusual that our carefully rehearsed and smooth-running machine was thrown off. For a full minute we fumbled for our chairs and bumped into each other awkwardly. Habits change or solidify under pressure, so in our state of nervous tension we had been ready to follow our usual assembly pattern: the American national anthem, then the pledge of allegiance, then the song every Black person I knew called the

Negro National Anthem.[4] All done in the same key, with the same passion and most often standing on the same foot.

Finding my seat at last, I was overcome with a presentiment of worse things to come. Something unrehearsed, unplanned, was going to happen, and we were going to be made to look bad. I distinctly remember being explicit in the choice of pronoun. It was "we," the graduating class, the unit, that concerned me then.

The principal welcomed "parents and friends" and asked the Baptist minister to lead us in prayer. His invocation was brief and punchy, and for a second I thought we were getting on the high road to right action. When the principal came back to the dais, however, his voice had changed. Sounds always affected me profoundly and the principal's voice was one of my favorites. During assembly it melted and lowed weakly into the audience. It had not been in my plan to listen to him, but my curiosity was piqued and I straightened up to give him my attention.

He was talking about Booker T. Washington, our "late great leader," who said we can be as close as the fingers on the hand, etc. . . . Then he said a few vague things about friendship and the friendship of kindly people to those less fortunate than themselves. With that his voice nearly faded, thin, away. Like a river diminishing to a stream and then to a trickle. But he cleared his throat and said, "Our speaker tonight, who is also our friend, came from Texarkana to deliver the commencement address, but due to the irregularity of the train schedule, he's going to, as they say, 'speak and run.' " He said that we understood and wanted the man to know that we were most grateful for the time he was able to give us and then something about how we were willing always to adjust to another's program, and without more ado—"I give you Mr. Edward Donleavy."

Not one but two white men came through the door off-stage. The shorter one walked to the speaker's platform, and the tall one moved to the center seat and sat down. But that was our principal's seat, and already occupied. The dislodged gentleman bounced around for a long breath or two before the Baptist minister gave him his chair, then with more dignity than the situation deserved, the minister walked off the stage.

Donleavy looked at the audience once (on reflection, I'm sure that he wanted only to reassure himself that we were really there), adjusted his glasses and began to read from a sheaf of papers.

He was glad "to be here and to see the work going on just as it was in the other schools."

At the first "Amen" from the audience I willed the offender to immediate death by choking on the word. But Amens and Yes, sir's began to fall around the room like rain through a ragged umbrella.

4. "Lift Every Voice."

He told us of the wonderful changes we children in Stamps had in store. The Central School (naturally, the white school was Central) had already been granted improvements that would be in use in the fall. A well-known artist was coming from Little Rock to teach art to them. They were going to have the newest microscopes and chemistry equipment for their laboratory. Mr. Donleavy didn't leave us long in the dark over who made these improvements available to Central High. Nor were we to be ignored in the general betterment scheme he had in mind.

He said that he had pointed out to people at a very high level that one of the first-line football tacklers at Arkansas Agricultural and Mechanical College had graduated from good old Lafayette County Training School. Here fewer Amen's were heard. Those few that did break through lay dully in the air with the heaviness of habit.

He went on to praise us. He went on to say how he had bragged that "one of the best basketball players at Fisk sank his first ball right here at Lafayette County Training School."

The white kids were going to have a chance to become Galileos and Madame Curies and Edisons and Gauguins, and our boys (the girls weren't even in on it) would try to be Jesse Owenses and Joe Louises.

Owens and the Brown Bomber were great heroes in our world, but what school official in the white-goddom of Little Rock had the right to decide that those two men must be our only heroes? Who decided that for Henry Reed to become a scientist he had to work like George Washington Carver, as a bootblack, to buy a lousy microscope? Bailey was obviously always going to be too small to be an athlete, so which concrete angel glued to what country seat had decided that if my brother wanted to become a lawyer he had to first pay penance for his skin by picking cotton and hoeing corn and studying correspondence books at night for twenty years?

The man's dead words fell like bricks around the auditorium and too many settled in my belly. Constrained by hard-learned manners I couldn't look behind me, but to my left and right the proud graduating class of 1940 had dropped their heads. Every girl in my row had found something new to do with her handkerchief. Some folded the tiny squares into love knots, some into triangles, but most were wadding them, then pressing them flat on their yellow laps.

On the dais, the ancient tragedy was being replayed. Professor Parsons sat, a sculptor's reject, rigid. His large, heavy body seemed devoid of will or willingness, and his eyes said he was no longer with us. The other teachers examined the flag (which was draped stage right) or their notes, or the windows which opened on our now-famous playing diamond.

Graduation, the hush-hush magic time of frills and gifts and congratulations and diplomas, was finished for me before my name was called. The accomplishment was nothing. The meticulous maps, drawn in three colors of ink, learning and spelling decasyllabic words, memorizing the whole of *The Rape of Lucrece*—it was for nothing. Donleavy had exposed us.

We were maids and farmers, handymen and washerwomen, and anything higher that we aspired to was farcical and presumptuous.

Then I wished that Gabriel Prosser and Nat Turner[5] had killed all whitefolks in their beds and that Abraham Lincoln had been assassinated before the signing of the Emancipation Proclamation, and that Harriet Tubman[6] had been killed by that blow on her head and Christopher Columbus had drowned in the *Santa Maria*.

It was awful to be a Negro and have no control over my life. It was brutal to be young and already trained to sit quietly and listen to charges brought against my color with no chance of defense. We should all be dead. I thought I should like to see us all dead, one on top of the other. A pyramid of flesh with the whitefolks on the bottom, as the broad base, then the Indians with their silly toma-hawks and teepees and wigwams and treaties, the Negroes with their mops and recipes and cotton sacks and spirituals sticking out of their mouths. The Dutch children should all stumble in their wooden shoes and break their necks. The French should choke to death on the Louisiana Purchase (1803) while silkworms ate all the Chinese with their stupid pigtails. As a species, we were an abomi-nation. All of us.

Donleavy was running for election, and assured our parents that if he won we could count on having the only colored paved playing field in that part of Arkansas. Also—he never looked up to acknowl-edge the grunts of acceptance—also, we were bound to get some new equipment for the home economics building and the workshop.

He finished, and since there was no need to give any more than the most perfunctory thank-you's, he nodded to the men on the stage, and the tall white man who was never introduced joined him at the door. They left with the attitude that now they were off to something really important. (The graduation ceremonies at Lafay-ette County Training School had been a mere preliminary.)

The ugliness they left was palpable. An uninvited guest who wouldn't leave. The choir was summoned and sang a modern arrangement of "Onward, Christian Soldiers," with new words per-taining to graduates seeking their place in the world. But it didn't work. Elouise, the daughter of the Baptist minister, recited "Invic-tus," and I could have cried at the impertinence of "I am the master of my fate, I am the captain of my soul."

5. Leaders of Virginia slave rebellions in 1800 and 1831 respectively.
6. Nineteenth-century black abolition-ist, a "conductor" on the Underground Railroad.

My name had lost its ring of familiarity and I had to be nudged to go and receive my diploma. All my preparations had fled. I neither marched up to the stage like a conquering Amazon, nor did I look in the audience for Bailey's nod of approval. Marguerite Johnson, I heard the name again, my honors were read, there were noises in the audience of appreciation, and I took my place on the stage as rehearsed.

I thought about colors I hated: ecru, puce, lavender, beige and black.

There was shuffling and rustling around me, then Henry Reed was giving his valedictory address, "To Be or Not to Be." Hadn't he heard the whitefolks? We couldn't *be*, so the question was a waste of time. Henry's voice came out clear and strong. I feared to look at him. Hadn't he got the message? There was no "nobler in the mind" for Negroes because the world didn't think we had minds, and they let us know it. "Outrageous fortune"? Now, that was a joke. When the ceremony was over I had to tell Henry Reed some things. That is, if I still cared. Not "rub," Henry, "erase." "Ah, there's the erase." Us.

Henry had been a good student in elocution. His voice rose on tides of promise and fell on waves of warnings. The English teacher had helped him to create a sermon winging through Hamlet's soliloquy. To be a man, a doer, a builder, a leader, or to be a tool, an unfunny joke, a crusher of funky toadstools. I marveled that Henry could go through with the speech as if we had a choice.

I had been listening and silently rebutting each sentence with my eyes closed; then there was a hush, which in an audience warns that something unplanned is happening. I looked up and saw Henry Reed, the conservative, the proper, the A student, turn his back to the audience and turn to us (the proud graduating class of 1940) and sing, nearly speaking,

> "Lift ev'ry voice and sing
> Till earth and heaven ring
> Ring with the harmonies of Liberty ..."

It was the poem written by James Weldon Johnson. It was the music composed by J. Rosamond Johnson. It was the Negro national anthem. Out of habit we were singing it.

Our mothers and fathers stood in the dark hall and joined the hymn of encouragement. A kindergarten teacher led the small children onto the stage and the buttercups and daisies and bunny rabbits marked time and tried to follow:

> "Stony the road we trod
> Bitter the chastening rod
> Felt in the days when hope, unborn, had died.
> Yet with a steady beat
> Have not our weary feet
> Come to the place for which our fathers sighed?"

Each child I knew had learned that song with his ABC's and along with "Jesus Loves Me This I Know." But I personally had never heard it before. Never heard the words, despite the thousands of times I had sung them. Never thought they had anything to do with me.

On the other hand, the words of Patrick Henry had made such an impression on me that I had been able to stretch myself tall and trembling and say, "I know not what course others may take, but as for me, give me liberty or give me death."

And now I heard, really for the first time:

> "We have come over a way that with tears
> has been watered,
> We have come, treading our path through
> the blood of the slaughtered."

While echoes of the song shivered in the air, Henry Reed bowed his head, said "Thank you," and returned to his place in the line. The tears that slipped down many faces were not wiped away in shame.

We were on top again. As always, again. We survived. The depths had been icy and dark, but now a bright sun spoke to our souls. I was no longer simply a member of the proud graduating class of 1940; I was a proud member of the wonderful, beautiful Negro race.

Oh, Black known and unknown poets, how often have your auctioned pains sustained us? Who will compute the lonely nights made less lonely by your songs, or the empty pots made less tragic by your tales?

If we were a people much given to revealing secrets, we might raise monuments and sacrifice to the memories of our poets, but slavery cured us of that weakness. It may be enough, however, to have it said that we survive in exact relationship to the dedication of our poets (include preachers, musicians and blues singers).

BERNADETTE DEVLIN

Politics in the University[1]

* * *

I went up to university with some vague notion of being able, one day, to improve some aspect of life in Northern Ireland. In my last years at school I had toyed with the idea of becoming a teacher for the gypsies, and later I thought of joining either the Ministry of Health and Social Services or the Ministry of Education, to work

1. From Chapter 5 of *The Price of My Soul*, 1969.

from within the citadel. But it seemed a long process, waiting to get into a position where I could have an impact on the system. Without any clear idea of what I planned to do with it, I started an Honours Celtic degree course. It seemed a natural choice: Celtic had been my best subject at school, and I was very interested in all the Celtic languages—from a cultural, not a political, point of view. I joined the Irish Democratic Club at Queen's, which trotted round the country to festivals and competitions, producing plays in the Irish language. But my main interest was in the Gaelic Society, which held Irish debates. Very soon I became irritated by the Gaelic Society. It was a small, inward-looking group, making very little attempt to reach anybody outside the converted, and boring people like myself to death. We produced an Irish-language newspaper called *An Scathan* (The Reflection), and there were eternal arguments over articles printed in it, over who was editor, over failures to sell the newspaper, over the fact that pamphlets and papers sent by organizations in the South hadn't been distributed by the society. In my second year at Queen's, when I gave up Celtic Studies in favor of Psychology, I become secretary of the Gaelic Society, and at the end of that year I resigned my office and my membership with a disillusioned farewell speech: until such time as they were interested in culture as culture, instead of who was leader of the group, I was bailing out.

However I was still keen on debating and used to attend meetings of the "Literific"—the Literary and Scientific Society—which organized debates just for the fun of debating, not to press any point of view, political or otherwise. In its day, the Literific had been a good forum for discussion, but by 1965 it had degenerated into nothing more than student obscenity. You could get up and shout, "Spit on the Vice-Chancellor!" without any further explanation, and be sure of applause. My friends enjoyed this frivolity but I didn't, and I never spoke at a Queen's debate in my first year. My second year saw the birth of the Union Debating Society. I had no hand in its formation, but I was one of many who saw in it a chance of discussing something worth talking about. I should have liked serious discussion on such subjects as the university structure, the relations between students and lecturer, or between student and tutor. The most obvious thing about the tutorials I attended was the credibility gap between the idea that this was an informal discussion group and the respectful attitude of the students toward the tutor. The relationship was one of teacher and pupil, there was no equal communication of ideas, and people accepted that what the lecturers said should be reproduced in examinations.

The first debate I spoke at was on the motion: Free love is too expensive. As far as I was concerned, this could be treated with a certain amount of humor, but it was a serious subject of concern to every student present. However, it degenerated into a lot of double-meaning jokes on the comparative cost of prostitutes in Amsterdam and San Francisco and about the price of contraceptives on the black market in Southern Ireland, making it cheaper to conduct your affairs in Ulster. Everybody thought it was just so amusing. Well, I sat through this for about two hours, until I couldn't resist standing up any longer, and then I told them that not only were they ignorant of the basic sexual morality of their own society, but they were also still so much part of their environment that they were incapable of rising above the situation and looking at it without embarrassment: hence all the bravado and the doubtful jokes. My own opinion was, I said, that while society had a double attitude, tolerating free love but not tolerating illegitimate children, free love *was* too expensive. We should be talking about the moral and social cost of individual independence and we were talking about contraceptives. I proposed that the motion should not be put until every student had gone out and troubled to learn a bit more about the society he or she was living in.

Everybody felt very uncomfortable when I accused them of ignorance of their own sexual morality, but when I used the word "bastard," the tension was broken, and this so-called intellectual gathering came down in an uproar of laughing and giggling. I finished off my speech by saying, "You may find the word bastard amusing. You may find free love is not expensive, if in fact it can be had for two-and-ninepence in Sandy Row (a poor area of Belfast). But how many people here can stand up without blushing and say without any qualms on the matter, 'I am a bastard'?" Nobody stood up and everything went dead quiet. Then tittering broke out and several people stood up and said, "I am a bastard." Finally a young fellow got up. "It is quite obvious," he said, "that none of those people has ever seriously been called a bastard. I have, and I understand the point you are making." But the debate broke up because people couldn't face serious discussion on it. Such was the mentality of Queen's at the time: people consciously played at being students, carrying briefcases about and looking intellectual.

Over the course of my first two years at university, I attended meetings of all the political parties. I felt I needed some ideology, so off I went on my round of the parties in search of one. There was then at Queen's a Tory Club, the Young Liberals, the Labour group that had risen and fallen over the years, the National Democrats, who were a new group, and the Young Socialists, who weren't actually part of the university at all. They were all little gatherings of initiates, but there was also the New Ireland Society, which was large and loosely structured, attracting people of different tendencies. In none of the political parties could I find anything to believe in. They all had a sort of self-importance, as if their interest in politics raised them above the level of ordinary people, and they all went in for an intellectual type of discussion that had no relevance to any kind of society I knew. They tried to be very sophisticated, working out policies and inviting guest speakers down; but they weren't *real*. You got the impression that they really didn't care what went on outside the university, so long as they had plenty to talk about. There was more real politics in the Folk Music Society than in any of the parties. They sang black civil-rights songs in the Folk Music Society before anybody else in Queen's was interested in the race problem, and they were singing songs about unemployment in Belfast long before the civil-rights movement took it up. That was a good society. It had a strong American influence in it, but because of this there was another section that was determined to keep Irish influence, so you had the best of both American protest songs and traditional Irish folk music.

What made student politics all the more absurd at that time was that Queen's was basically a nine-to-six university. None of us was the kind of independent, twenty-four-hours-a-day student that you get at colleges in England. We went home for tea. You were a student during the day, but your mother asked you where you were going at eight o'clock at night.

For a moment in my third year, it looked as if there might·be some excitement. The Minister of Home Affairs issued an order banning Republican Clubs. These had been allowed to continue throughout Northern Ireland, though the Republican Party itself had always been illegal. Immediately the ban was announced, a Republican Club was formed in Queen's and I joined it. We had a peaceful little demonstration against the ban, carried a coffin to the Minister's house, mourned the death of democracy and so forth, and went back to the university. But then the steam went out of the Republican Club. It didn't seem to have anything other than an existence.

So, disenchanted with Queen's politics, I moved to the do-good organizations. These were Catholic societies who visited the poor, decorated houses for old people, did voluntary work at hospitals, and so on. I stayed with them for a while until I decided they were just perpetuating aspects of the system I didn't like. When we visited old people in their homes, we were letting off the neighbors and relatives who should have done it and who, instead of saying, "Those people are doing it—why don't we?" were saying, "Those people are doing it—we don't need to." By carol-singing at Christmas to collect money for coal for poor families, we were relieving the local authorities of their responsibility. They just budgeted our contribution into what they spent and cut down on their own spending.

For a while after that I wandered about by myself, making terrorist plans. I've often wondered why the IRA is so keen on blowing up bridges, when Northern Ireland offers much greater possibilities for disruption and international publicity. In Derry there is an American communications base that is used as a look-out post for the rest of Europe and whose strategic importance has never been appreciated by people in Northern Ireland. This base, it seemed to me, was custom-built for causing an international crisis and bringing Northern Ireland to the attention of the world, and I developed a very nasty plan for its destruction. The first thing to do was to set fire to Gortin Forest Park in County Tyrone. It always closes in the evening, so nobody would be in it by about nine o'clock at night, and since it is in the middle of the wilderness, you wouldn't endanger any houses. Once Gortin Forest Park was burning nicely, all the fire brigades in Ulster would come storming around to deal with it, blaming the IRA; and while everybody was putting out that fire, you could set fire to Tullamore Forest Park on the other side of the country. With the entire country running around putting out fires it would take no more than half a dozen hand grenades lobbed over the wall of the communications base to create a very nasty diplomatic incident. It would involve the British, because this was British territory and they were supposed to be guarding it. It would involve the Americans, because it belonged to them. And it would raise the question of why the United States had a base in Northern Ireland at all.

I never told anybody this idea because, quite honestly, it terrified me. As theoretical terrorism, it was great, but I couldn't reconcile myself to the thought that maybe, against all the probabilities, someone might be in Gortin Forest Park when it went up in flames. Another idea I had was to send an ultimatum to every fly-by-night foreign firm who invested money in Northern Ireland, giving them a breakdown of the short-term profits to them, and the long-term inefficiency to us, of their operation. Such firms are attracted to Northern Ireland by government building grants and short-term tax concessions. But when the tax concessions run out, so do they, leaving behind an empty factory and another couple of hundred unemployed. I planned to send them a warning: "You have three years to promise you will remain here more than ten years, or we'll blow your little factory out of the ground." Those were my militant Republican days. But I got over these dreams of violence, and told myself it didn't matter if the people who kept us in poverty were called British or not. It wasn't simply getting Britain out of Ireland that mattered: it was the fact that we were economically depressed, and I couldn't see terrorism solving that.

STANLEY SANDERS
I'll Never Escape the Ghetto

I was born, raised and graduated from high school in Watts. My permanent Los Angeles home address is in Watts. My father, a brother and sister still live in Watts. By ordinary standards these are credentials enough to qualify one as coming from Watts.

But there is more to it than that. I left Watts. After I was graduated from the local high school I went away to college. A college venture in Watts terms is a fateful act. There are no retractions or future deliverances. Watts, like other black ghettos across the country, is, for ambitious youths, a transient status. Once they have left, there is no returning. In this sense, my credentials are unsatisfactory. To some people, I am not from Watts. I can never be.

The Watts-as-a-way-station mentality has a firm hold on both those who remain and those who leave. Such as it is, the ghetto is regarded as no place to make a career for those who have a future. Without exception, the prime American values underscore the notion. Negroes, inside it or out, and whites too, behave toward the ghetto like travelers.

Accordingly, I was considered one of the lucky ones. My scholarship to college was a ticket. People did not expect me to return. Understanding this, I can understand the puzzlement in the minds of those in Watts when I was home last summer, working in the local poverty program. Rumors spread quickly that I was an FBI agent. I was suspect because I was not supposed to return. Some people said I was either a federal agent or a fool, for no reasonable man, they said, returns to Watts by choice. Outside of Watts, reports stated that I had "given up" a summer vacation to work in Watts. For my part, I had come home to work in my community, but to some people I could not come home to Watts. To them I was no longer from Watts.

My own state of mind, when I left Watts eight years ago to take up the freshman year at Whittier College, was different. It was to me less of a departure; it was the stepping-off point of an Odyssey that was to take me through Whittier College and Oxford University, to Yale Law School, and back to Watts. I had intended then, as now, to make Watts my home.

A career in Watts had been a personal ambition for many years. In many ways the career I envisioned was antithetical to ghetto life. In the ghetto, a career was something on the outside. In Los Angeles, this meant a pursuit founded in a world beyond Alameda street, at a minimum in the largely Negro middle-class Westside of Los Angeles. The talk among the ambitious and future-minded youth in

Watts was on getting out so that careers could begin. And they did just that. The talented young people left Watts in droves. The one skill they had in common was the ability to escape the ghetto.

I was especially intrigued by a career in Watts because it was supposed to be impossible. I wanted to demonstrate that it could be done more than anything else. I recall a moment during a city-wide high school oratorical contest when one of the judges asked whether anything good could come out of Watts. Our high school won the contest. We showed that judge. I saw that achievement as a possible pattern for the entire ghetto. I was pleased.

I had not realized in leaving for Whittier College that, however worthy my intention of returning was, I was nevertheless participating in the customary exodus from Watts. It was not long after leaving that my early ambitions began to wear thin. The stigma of Watts was too heavy to bear. I could easily do without the questioning looks of my college classmates. I did not want my being from Watts to arouse curiosity.

I followed the instructions of those who fled Watts. I adopted the language of escape. I resorted to all the devices of those who wished to escape. I was from South Los Angeles, thereafter, not Watts. "South Los Angeles," geographically identical to Watts, carried none of the latter's stigma. South Los Angeles was a cleaner—safer—designation. It meant having a home with possibilities.

It never occurred to me at the time what I was doing. I thought of it only as being practical. It was important to me to do well in college. Community identity was secondary, if a consideration at all. Somehow, the Watts things interfered with my new college life. Moreover, Negro college youth during those undergraduate years had none of its present mood. Its theme was campus involvement. Good grades, athletics, popularity—these were the things that mattered. The word "ghetto" had not even entered the lexicon of race relations. Students were not conscious of the ghetto as a separate phenomenon. Civil rights, in the Southern sense, was academically fashionable. But the ghetto of the North was not. The concern for the ghetto was still in the future.

It was to occur to me later, at the time of the Watts riots, two years after I graduated from college, if my classmates at Whittier realized that the epochal conflagration taking place was in the home of one of their very own student body presidents. They had no reason to think it was. I had never told them that I was from Watts.

A lot of things changed during the two years at Oxford. My attitude toward home was one of them. It was there, ironically enough, that the Odyssey turned homeward. Those years were bound to be meaningful as a Yankee foreign student or Rhodes Scholar. I knew that much. But I would never have imagined when receiving the award that Oxford would be significant as a Negro experience. After all, it was part of the faith gained during four years at Whittier that everything concerning me and Watts would remain conveniently buried.

It emerged in an odd context. England then, for the most part, was free of the fine distinctions between blacks and whites traditionally made in America. Except for some exclusive clubs in London, there were few occasions where racial lines were drawn. The color-blindness of England was especially true in the student life at Oxford. (This relatively mild racial climate in England during the last three years has, with the large influx of blacks from the West Indies and Southern Asia, adopted some very American-like features.) It was in such a relaxed racial atmosphere that all my defenses, about race and home, came down. At Oxford, I could reflect on the American black man.

My ghetto roots became crucially important in this examination. Englishmen were not concerned about the distinctions I was making in my own mind, between Watts and "South Los Angeles," between Watts and Whittier. They were not imagined distinctions. I was discovering that I could not escape the ghetto after all. A fundamental change was taking place in the ghettos, the Wattses, across the country. These changes were making the distinction. I realized I was a part of them, too.

By far the most traumatic of the new changes was ghetto rioting. I was studying at the University of Vienna, between semesters at Oxford, during the summer of 1964. News of Harlem rioting jolted the multi-national student community there. The typical European response was unlike anything I had seen before. They had no homes or businesses to worry about protecting. They wanted to know why Negroes did not riot more often. As the only Negro in the summer session I felt awkward for a time. I was being asked questions about the black man in America that no one had ever asked me before. I was embarrassed because I did not have any answers.

My own lack of shame in the rioting then taking place in America surprised me. In one sense, I was the archetype of the ghetto child who through hard work and initiative was pulling himself toward a better life. I was the example, the exception. It was my life that was held up to Watts youth to emulate.

In another sense, however, my feelings toward the rioting were predictable. I had always been bothered by the passivity of the ghetto. The majority of black men in the North had remained outside the struggle. Nothing was happening in the ghettos. No one was making it happen. Ghetto rioting then was the first representation I perceived of movement and activity among the mass of Negroes in the North. It marked a break with the passive tradition of dependency and indifference. The ghetto was at least no longer content with its status as bastard child of urban America. The currents set in motion had a hopeful, irreversible quality about them. The ghetto wanted legitimation. That was a beginning.

The parallel between a single individual's success and the bootstrap effort of the mass of ghetto youth is and remains too tenuous to comport with reality. This was made clear to me during the discussions of the Harlem riots on those hot summer days in Vienna. It shattered the notion that my individual progress could be hailed as an advance for all Negroes. Regrettably, it was an advance only for me. Earlier I had thought the success I had won satisfied an obligation I had to all Negroes. It is part of the lip service every successful Negro is obliged to pay to the notion of race progress whenever he achieves. In the face of mass rioting, the old shibboleths were reduced to embarrassing emptiness. I was enjoying the privileges of studying at the world's finest universities; Negroes at home were revolting against their miserable condition. To them, my experience and example were as remote as if I had never lived or been there. At best, only the top students could identify with my example—but they were few. And besides, the top students were not the problem.

When I returned to Oxford in the fall, following a spate of summer rioting in Eastern cities, I was convinced that some momentous changes had been wrought for all Negroes, not just those in the ghetto. It certainly meant a new militancy and a militancy of action, not the passive fulminations of the demi-militants. This was for Watts.

I returned home in August, 1965, from two years at Oxford just in time for the beginning of the Watts riots. As I walked the streets I was struck by the sameness of the community. There were few changes. Everything seemed to be in the same place where I had last seen it. It was unsettling for me to recall so easily the names of familiar faces I saw on the street. It was that feeling one gets when he feels he has done this one same thing before.

Streets remained unswept; sidewalks, in places, still unpaved. During this same time the growth rate in the rest of Southern California had been phenomenal, one of the highest in the country. L. A. suburbs had flourished. Watts, however, remained an unacknowledged child in an otherwise proud and respectable family of new towns.

The intellectual journey back to Watts after the Vienna summer and during the last year at Oxford had partly prepared me for what was soon to erupt into revolutionary-scale violence. My first reaction after the riot began was to have it stopped. But I was not from Watts for the past six years. I, nor anyone outside of Watts, was in no moral position to condemn this vicious expression of the ghetto.

I enrolled in Yale Law School in the fall after the riots. This time I did not leave Watts. Nor did I wish to leave Watts. Watts followed me to Yale. In fact, Watts was at Yale before I was. The discussions about riots and ghettos were more lively and compelling than the classroom discussions on the law. There were no word games or contrived problems. The questions raised were urgent ones.

Not surprisingly, Watts, too, was in the throes of painful discussion about the riots. It was beginning to look as though the deepest impact of the riots was on the people of Watts themselves. Old attitudes about the community were in upheaval. There were no explanations that seemed complete. No one knew for sure how it all began. There was no agreement on how it was continued as long as it was—and why. We only knew it happened. What I had often mistaken for pointless spoutings was in reality a manifestation of this desperate search for a truth about the riots.

The new intellectual climate in Watts was hard-wrought. It was rich enough to support even a communist bookstore. Writers, poets, artists flourished. I was handed full manuscripts of unpublished books by indigenous writers and asked to criticize them. I have not seen during eight years of college life as many personal journals kept and sketches written as in Watts since the 1965 riots. A new, rough wisdom of the street corner was emerging.

I suspected at the time and now realize that the riots were perhaps the most significant massive action taken by Northern Negroes. It was a watershed in the ghetto's history. Before the riots, the reach of the Negro movement in America seemed within the province of a small civil rights leadership. Now Watts, and places like Watts, were redefining the role of black men in their city's life.

I have affectionate ties to Watts. I bear the same mark as a son of Watts now that I did during that oratorical contest in high school. I may be personally less vulnerable to it today, but I am nevertheless influenced by it. While a group in Whittier, Calif., may regard it as unfortunate that its college's first Rhodes Scholar comes from Watts, I, for my part, could not feel more pride about that than I do now. I feel no embarrassment for those who think ill of Watts. I had once felt it. Now I only feel the regret for once having been embarrassed. "South Los Angeles" is a sour memory. Watts is my home.

Then I have my logical ties to Watts, too. My interest in the law stems from a concern for the future of Watts. The problem of the poor and of the city in America, simplified, is the problem of the ghetto Negro. I regard it as *the* problem of the last third of this century. Plainly, Watts is where the action is. The talents and leadership which I saw leave Watts as a child are the very things it needs most today. Many of the ghetto's wandering children are choosing a city to work in. My choice was made for me—long ago.

There is a difference between my schooling and the wisdom of the street corner. I know the life of a black man in Watts is larger than a federal poverty program. If there is no future for the black ghetto, the future of all Negroes is diminished. What affects it, affects me, for I am a child of the ghetto. When they do it to Watts, they do it to me, too. I'll never escape from the ghetto. I have staked my all on its future. Watts is my home.

JOAN DIDION
On Going Home

I am home for my daughter's first birthday. By "home" I do not mean the house in Los Angeles where my husband and I and the baby live, but the place where my family is, in the Central Valley of California. It is a vital although troublesome distinction. My husband likes my family but is uneasy in their house, because once there I fall into their ways, which are difficult, oblique, deliberately inarticulate, not my husband's ways. We live in dusty houses ("D-U-S-T," he once wrote with his finger on surfaces all over the house, but no one noticed it) filled with mementos quite without value to him (what could the Canton dessert plates mean to him? how could he have known about the assay scales, why should he care if he did know?), and we appear to talk exclusively about people we know who have been committed to mental hospitals, about people we know who have been booked on drunk-driving charges, and about property, particularly about property, land, price per acre and C-2 zoning and assessments and freeway access. My brother does not understand my husband's inability to perceive the advantage in the rather common real-estate transaction known as "sale-leaseback," and my husband in turn does not understand why so many of the people he hears about in my father's house have recently been committed to mental hospitals or booked on drunk-driving charges. Nor does he understand that when we talk about sale-leasebacks and right-of-way condemnations we are talking in code about the things we like best, the yellow fields and the cotton-woods and the rivers rising and falling and the mountain roads closing when the heavy snow comes in. We miss each other's points, have another drink and regard the fire. My brother refers to my husband, in his presence, as "Joan's husband." Marriage is the classic betrayal.

Or perhaps it is not any more. Sometimes I think that those of us who are now in our thirties were born into the last generation to carry the burden of "home," to find in family life the source of all tension and drama. I had by all objective accounts a "normal" and a "happy" family situation, and yet I was almost thirty years old before I could talk to my family on the telephone without crying after I had hung up. We did not fight. Nothing was wrong. And yet some nameless anxiety colored the emotional charges between me and the place that I came from. The question of whether or not you could go home again was a very real part of the sentimental and largely literary baggage with which we left home in the fifties; I suspect that it is irrelevant to the children born of the fragmentation after World War II. A few weeks ago in a San Francisco bar I saw a pretty young girl on crystal take off her clothes and dance for the cash prize in an "amateur-topless" contest. There was no particular sense of moment about this, none of the effect of romantic degradation, of "dark journey," for which my generation strived so assiduously. What sense could that girl possibly make of, say, *Long Day's Journey into Night?* Who is beside the point?

That I am trapped in this particular irrelevancy is never more apparent to me than when I am home. Paralyzed by the neurotic lassitude engendered by meeting one's past at every turn, around every corner, inside every cupboard, I go aimlessly from room to room. I decide to meet it head-on and clean out a drawer, and I spread the contents on the bed. A bathing suit I wore the summer I was seventeen. A letter of rejection from *The Nation*, an aerial photograph of the site for a shopping center my father did not build in 1954. Three teacups hand-painted with cabbage roses and signed "E.M.," my grandmother's initials. There is no final solution for letters of rejection from *The Nation* and teacups hand-painted in 1900. Nor is there any answer to snapshots of one's grandfather as a young man on skis, surveying around Donner Pass in the year 1910. I smooth out the snapshot and look into his face, and do and do not see my own. I close the drawer, and have another cup of coffee with my mother. We get along very well, veterans of a guerrilla war we never understood.

Days pass. I see no one. I come to dread my husband's evening call, not only because he is full of news of what by now seems to me our remote life in Los Angeles, people he has seen, letters which require attention, but because he asks what I have been doing, suggests uneasily that I get out, drive to San Francisco or Berkeley. Instead I drive across the river to a family graveyard. It has been vandalized since my last visit and the monuments are broken, overturned in the dry grass. Because I once saw a rattlesnake in the grass I stay in the car and listen to a country-and-Western station. Later I drive with my father to a ranch he has in the foothills. The man who runs his cattle on it asks us to the roundup, a week from Sunday, and although I know that I will be in Los Angeles I say, in the oblique way my family talks, that I will come. Once home I mention the broken monuments in the graveyard. My mother shrugs.

I go to visit my great-aunts. A few of them think now that I am my cousin, or their daughter who died young. We recall an anecdote about a relative last seen in 1948, and they ask if I still like living in New York City. I have lived in Los Angeles for three years, but I say that I do. The baby is offered a horehound drop, and I am slipped a dollar bill "to buy a treat." Questions trail off, answers are abandoned, the baby plays with the dust motes in a shaft of afternoon sun.

It is time for the baby's birthday party: a white cake, strawberry-marshmallow ice cream, a bottle of champagne saved from another party. In the evening, after she has gone to sleep, I kneel beside the crib and touch her face, where it is pressed against the slats, with mine. She is an open and trusting child, unprepared for and unaccustomed to the ambushes of family life, and perhaps it is just as well that I can offer her little of that life. I would like to give her more. I would like to promise her that she will grow up with a sense of her cousins and of rivers and of her great-grandmother's teacups, would like to pledge her a picnic on a river with fried chicken and her hair uncombed, would like to give her *home* for her birthday, but we live differently now and I can promise her nothing like that. I give her a xylophone and a sundress from Madeira, and promise to tell her a funny story.

E. B. WHITE

Once More to the Lake (August 1941)

One summer, along about 1904, my father rented a camp on a lake in Maine and took us all there for the month of August. We all got ringworm from some kittens and had to rub Pond's Extract on our arms and legs night and morning, and my father rolled over in a canoe with all his clothes on; but outside of that the vacation was a success and from then on none of us ever thought there was any place in the world like that lake in Maine. We returned summer after summer—always on August 1st for one month. I have since become a salt-water man, but sometimes in summer there are days when the restlessness of the tides and the fearful cold of the sea water and the incessant wind which blows across the afternoon and into the evening make me wish for the placidity of a lake in the woods. A few weeks ago this feeling got so strong I bought myself a couple of bass hooks and a spinner and returned to the lake where we used to go, for a week's fishing and to revisit old haunts.

I took along my son, who had never had any fresh water up his nose and who had seen lily pads only from train windows. On the journey over to the lake I began to wonder what it would be like. I wondered how time would have marred this unique, this holy spot— the coves and streams, the hills that the sun set behind, the camps and the paths behind the camps. I was sure the tarred road would have found it out and I wondered in what other ways it would be desolated. It is strange how much you can remember about places like that once you allow your mind to return into the grooves which lead back. You remember one thing, and that suddenly reminds you of another thing. I guess I remembered clearest of all the early mornings, when the lake was cool and motionless, remembered how the bedroom smelled of the lumber it was made of and of the wet woods whose scent entered through the screen. The partitions in the camp were thin and did not extend clear to the top of the rooms, and as I was always the first up I would dress softly so as not to wake the others, and sneak out into the sweet outdoors and start out in the canoe, keeping close along the shore in the long shadows of the pines. I remembered being very careful never to rub my paddle against the gunwale for fear of disturbing the stillness of the cathedral.

The lake had never been what you would call a wild lake. There were cottages sprinkled around the shores, and it was in farming country although the shores of the lake were quite heavily wooded. Some of the cottages were owned by nearby farmers, and you would live at the shore and eat your meals at the farmhouse. That's what our family did. But although it wasn't wild, it was a fairly large and undisturbed lake and there were places in it which, to a child at least, seemed infinitely remote and primeval.

I was right about the tar: it led to within half a mile of the shore. But when I got back there, with my boy, and we settled into a camp near a farmhouse and into the kind of summertime I had known, I could tell that it was going to be pretty much the same as it had been before—I knew it, lying in bed the first morning, smelling the bedroom, and hearing the boy sneak quietly out and go off along the shore in a boat. I began to sustain the illusion that he was I, and therefore, by simple transposition, that I was my father. This sensation persisted, kept cropping up all the time we were there. It was not an entirely new feeling, but in this setting it grew much stronger. I seemed to be living a dual existence. I would be in the middle of some simple act, I would be picking up a bait box or laying down a table fork, or I would be saying something, and suddenly it would be not I but my father who was saying the words or making the gesture. It gave me a creepy sensation.

We went fishing the first morning. I felt the same damp moss covering the worms in the bait can, and saw the dragonfly alight on the tip of my rod as it hovered a few inches from the surface of the water. It was the arrival of this fly that convinced me beyond any doubt that everything was as it always had been, that the years were a mirage and there had been no years. The small waves were the same, chucking the rowboat under the chin as we fished at anchor, and the boat was the same boat, the same color green and the ribs broken in the same places, and under the floor-boards the same fresh-water leavings and débris—the dead helgramite,[1] the wisps of moss, the rusty discarded fishhook, the dried blood from yesterday's catch. We stared silently at the tips of our rods, at the dragonflies that came and went. I lowered the tip of mine into the water, tentatively, pensively dislodging the fly, which darted two feet away, poised, darted two feet back, and came to rest again a little farther up the rod. There had been no years between the ducking of this dragonfly and the other one—the one that was part of memory. I looked at the boy, who was silently watching his fly, and it was my hands that held his rod, my eyes watching. I felt dizzy and didn't know which rod I was at the end of.

We caught two bass, hauling them in briskly as though they were mackerel, pulling them over the side of the boat in a businesslike manner without any landing net, and stunning them with a blow on the back of the head. When we got back for a swim before lunch, the lake was exactly where we had left it, the same number of inches from the dock, and there was only the merest suggestion of a breeze. This seemed an utterly enchanted sea, this lake you could leave to its own devices for a few hours and come back to, and find that it had not stirred, this constant and trustworthy body of water. In the shallows, the dark, water-soaked sticks and twigs, smooth and old, were undulating in clusters on the bottom against the clean ribbed sand, and the track of the mussel was plain. A school of minnows swam by, each minnow with its small individual shadow, doubling the attendance, so clear and sharp in the sunlight. Some of the other campers were in swimming, along the shore, one of them with a cake of soap, and the water felt thin and clear and unsubstantial. Over the years there had been this person with the cake of soap, this cultist, and here he was. There had been no years.

Up to the farmhouse to dinner through the teeming, dusty field, the road under our sneakers was only a two-track road. The middle track was missing, the one with the marks of the hooves and the splotches of dried, flaky manure. There had always been three tracks to choose from in choosing which track to walk in; now the choice was narrowed down to two. For a moment I missed terribly the middle alternative. But the way led past the tennis court, and something about the way it lay there in the sun reassured me; the tape had loosened along the backline, the alleys were green with plantains and other weeds, and the net (installed in June and removed in

1. The nymph of the May-fly, used as bait.

September) sagged in the dry noon, and the whole place steamed
with midday heat and hunger and emptiness. There was a choice of
pie for dessert, and one was blueberry and one was apple, and the
waitresses were the same country girls, there having been no passage
of time, only the illusion of it as in a dropped curtain—the waitresses
were still fifteen; their hair had been washed, that was the only
difference—they had been to the movies and seen the pretty girls
with the clean hair.

Summertime, oh summertime, pattern of life indelible, the
fade-proof lake, the woods unshatterable, the pasture with the
sweetfern and the juniper forever and ever, summer without end;
this was the background, and the life along the shore was the design,
the cottagers with their innocent and tranquil design, their tiny
docks with the flagpole and the American flag floating against the
white clouds in the blue sky, the little paths over the roots of the
trees leading from camp to camp and the paths leading back to the
outhouses and the can of lime for sprinkling, and at the souvenir
counters at the store the miniature birch-bark canoes and the post
cards that showed things looking a little better than they looked.
This was the American family at play, escaping the city heat, wondering whether the newcomers in the camp at the head of the cove
were "common" or "nice," wondering whether it was true that the
people who drove up for Sunday dinner at the farmhouse were
turned away because there wasn't enough chicken.

It seemed to me, as I kept remembering all this, that those times
and those summers had been infinitely precious and worth saving.
There had been jollity and peace and goodness. The arriving (at the
beginning of August) had been so big a business in itself, at the
railway station the farm wagon drawn up, the first smell of the
pine-laden air, the first glimpse of the smiling farmer, and the great
importance of the trunks and your father's enormous authority in
such matters, and the feel of the wagon under you for the long
ten-mile haul, and at the top of the last long hill catching the first
view of the lake after eleven months of not seeing this cherished
body of water. The shouts and cries of the other campers when they
saw you, and the trunks to be unpacked, to give up their rich burden.
(Arriving was less exciting nowadays, when you sneaked up in your
car and parked it under a tree near the camp and took out the bags
and in five minutes it was all over, no fuss, no loud wonderful fuss
about trunks.)

Peace and goodness and jollity. The only thing that was wrong
now, really, was the sound of the place, an unfamiliar nervous sound
of the outboard motors. This was the note that jarred, the one thing
that would sometimes break the illusion and set the years moving.
In those other summertimes all motors were inboard; and when
they were at a little distance, the noise they made was a sedative,

an ingredient of summer sleep. They were one-cylinder and two-cylinder engines, and some were make-and-break and some were jump-spark,[2] but they all made a sleepy sound across the lake. The one-lungers throbbed and fluttered, and the twin-cylinder ones purred and purred, and that was a quiet sound too. But now the campers all had outboards. In the daytime, in the hot mornings, these motors made a petulant, irritable sound; at night, in the still evening when the afterglow lit the water, they whined about one's ears like mosquitoes. My boy loved our rented outboard, and his great desire was to achieve singlehanded mastery over it, and authority, and he soon learned the trick of choking it a little (but not too much), and the adjustment of the needle valve. Watching him I would remember the things you could do with the old one-cylinder engine with the heavy flywheel, how you could have it eating out of your hand if you got really close to it spiritually. Motor boats in those days didn't have clutches, and you would make a landing by shutting off the motor at the proper time and coasting in with a dead rudder. But there was a way of reversing them, if you learned the trick, by cutting the switch and putting it on again exactly on the final dying revolution of the flywheel, so that it would kick back against compression and begin reversing. Approaching a dock in a strong following breeze, it was difficult to slow up sufficiently by the ordinary coasting method, and if a boy felt he had complete mastery over his motor, he was tempted to keep it running beyond its time and then reverse it a few feet from the dock. It took a cool nerve, because if you threw the switch a twentieth of a second too soon you would catch the flywheel when it still had speed enough to go up past center, and the boat would leap ahead, charging bull-fashion at the dock.

We had a good week at the camp. The bass were biting well and the sun shone endlessly, day after day. We would be tired at night and lie down in the accumulated heat of the little bedrooms after the long hot day and the breeze would stir almost imperceptibly outside and the smell of the swamp drift in through the rusty screens. Sleep would come easily and in the morning the red squirrel would be on the roof, tapping out his gay routine. I kept remembering everything, lying in bed in the mornings—the small steamboat that had a long rounded stern like the lip of a Ubangi, and how quietly she ran on the moonlight sails, when the older boys played their mandolins and the girls sang and we ate doughnuts dipped in sugar, and how sweet the music was on the water in the shining night, and what it had felt like to think about girls then. After breakfast we would go up to the store and the things were in the same place—the minnows in a bottle, the plugs and spinners disarranged and pawed over by the youngsters from the boys' camp, the fig newtons and the Bee-

2. Methods of ignition timing.

man's gum. Outside, the road was tarred and cars stood in front of the store. Inside, all was just as it had always been, except there was more Coca-Cola and not so much Moxie and root beer and birch beer and sarsaparilla. We would walk out with a bottle of pop apiece and sometimes the pop would backfire up our noses and hurt. We explored the streams, quietly, where the turtles slid off the sunny logs and dug their way into the soft bottom; and we lay on the town wharf and fed worms to the tame bass. Everywhere we went I had trouble making out which was I, the one walking at my side, the one walking in my pants.

One afternoon while we were there at that lake a thunderstorm came up. It was like the revival of an old melodrama that I had seen long ago with childish awe. The second-act climax of the drama of the electrical disturbance over a lake in America had not changed in any important respect. This was the big scene, still the big scene. The whole thing was so familiar, the first feeling of oppression and heat and a general air around camp of not wanting to go very far away. In midafternoon (it was all the same) a curious darkening of the sky, and a lull in everything that had made life tick; and then the way the boats suddenly swung the other way at their moorings with the coming of a breeze out of the new quarter, and the premonitory rumble. Then the kettle drum, then the snare, then the bass drum and cymbals, then crackling light against the dark, and the gods grinning and licking their chops in the hills. Afterward the calm, the rain steadily rustling in the calm lake, the return of light and hope and spirits, and the campers running out in joy and relief to go swimming in the rain, their bright cries perpetuating the deathless joke about how they were getting simply drenched, and the children screaming with delight at the new sensation of bathing in the rain, and the joke about getting drenched linking the generations in a strong indestructible chain. And the comedian who waded in carrying an umbrella.

When the others went swimming my son said he was going in too. He pulled his dripping trunks from the line where they had hung all through the shower, and wrung them out. Languidly, and with no thought of going in, I watched him, his hard little body, skinny and bare, saw him wince slightly as he pulled up around his vitals the small, soggy, icy garment. As he buckled the swollen belt suddenly my groin felt the chill of death.

QUESTIONS

1. White had not been back to the lake for many years. What bearing has this fact on the experience which the essay describes?
2. What has guided White in his selection of the details he gives about the trip? Why, for example, does he talk about the road, the dragonfly, the bather with the cake of soap?

3. How do the differences between boats of the past and boats of today relate to or support the point of the essay?

4. What is the meaning of White's last sentence? What relation has it to the sentence just preceding? How has White prepared us for this ending?

5. How would the narrative differ if it were told by the boy? What details of the scene might the boy emphasize? Why? Show what point the boy's selection of details might make.

Prose Forms: Journals

[Occasionally a man catches himself having said something aloud, obviously with no concern to be heard, even by himself. And all of us have overheard, perhaps while walking, a solitary person muttering or laughing softly or exclaiming abruptly. For oneself or another, something floats up from the world within, forces itself to be expressed, takes no real account of the time or the place, and certainly intends no conscious communication.

With more self-consciousness, and yet without a specific audience, a man sometimes speaks out at something that has momentarily filled his attention from the world without. A sharp play at the ball game, the twist of a political speech, an old photograph—something from the outer world impresses the mind, stimulates it, focuses certain of its memories and values, interests and needs. Thus stimulated, the man may wish to share his experience with another, to inform or amuse him, to rouse him to action or persuade him to a certain belief. Often, though, the man experiencing may want most to talk to himself, to give a public shape in words to his thoughts and feelings but for the sake of a kind of private dialogue with himself. Communication to another may be an ultimate desire, but the immediate motive is to articulate the experience for himself.

To articulate, to shape the experience in language for his own sake, one may keep a journal. Literally a day-book, the journal enables one to write down something about the experiences of a day which for a great variety of reasons may have been especially memorable or impressive. The journal entry may be merely a few words to call to mind a thing done, a person seen, a menu enjoyed at a dinner party. It may be concerned at length with a political crisis in the community, or a personal crisis in the home. It may even be as noble as it was with some pious men in the past who used the journal to keep a record of their consciences, a periodic reckoning of their moral and spiritual accounts. In its most public aspect, the idea of a journal calls to mind the newspaper or the record of proceedings like the Congressional Record. In its most closely private form, the journal becomes the diary.

For the person keeping a journal, whatever he experiences and wants to hold he can write down. But to get it down on paper begins another adventure. For he has to focus on what he has experienced,

35

and to be able to say what, in fact, the experience is. What of it is new? What of it is remarkable because of associations in the memory it stirs up? Is this like anything I—or others—have experienced before? Is it a good or a bad thing to have happened? And why, specifically? The questions multiply themselves quickly, and as the journalist seeks to answer the appropriate ones, he begins to know what it is he contemplates. As he tries next to find the words that best represent his discovery, the experience becomes even more clear in its shape and meaning. We can imagine Emerson going to the ballet, being absorbed in the spectacle, thinking casually of this or that association the dancer and the movements suggest. When he writes about the experience in his journal, a good many questions, judgments, and speculations get tied up with the spectacle, and it is this complex of event and his total relation to it that becomes the experience he records. The simple facts of time, place, people, and actions drop down into a man's consciousness and set in motion ideas and feelings which give those facts their real meaning to that man.

Once this consciousness of events is formulated in words, the journal-keeper has it, not only in the sense of understanding what he has seen or felt or thought, but also in the sense of having it there before him to contemplate long after the event itself. When we read a carefully kept journal covering a long period and varied experiences, we have the pleasure of a small world re-created for us in the consciousness of one who experienced it. Even more, we feel the continuity, the wholeness, of the person himself. Something of the same feeling is there for the person who kept the journal: a whole world of events preservẹd in the form of their experienced reality, and with it the persistent self in the midst of that world. That world and that self are always accessible on the page, and ultimately, therefore, usably real.

Beyond the value of the journal as record, there is the instructive value of the habit of mind and hand journal keeping can assure. One begins to attend more carefully to what happens to him and around him. To have discovered, like Katherine Mansfield, that so apparently simple a thing as a pigeon sitting proudly on a tree can bring to mind the profoundest questions about the relation of God to His creatures, is to be thereafter a little more sensitive to all kinds of "simple" experience. Fact begins to be related to fact more readily, apparently dissimilar experiences may not be entirely different, the more and the less important begin to be discriminated. Even in so unlikely a situation for calm contemplation as war is, it is possible, like Pearce, to achieve that moment of detachment which focuses the immediate scene or event for what it is by seeing how it matters in relation to ideas or meanings beyond the battle or the beleaguered city or the desolated church. One begins to see what he is looking at, if he becomes accustomed to the characteristic method and form of the journal entry. All the while, one is learning the resources of language as a means of representing what he sees, and gaining skill and certainty in doing justice to experience and to his own consciousness when he writes.

The journal represents a discipline. It brings together an individual and a complex environment in a relation that teaches the individual something of himself, something of his world, and something of the meaning of their relation. There is scarcely a moment in a person's life when he is not poised for the lesson. When it comes with the promise of special force, there is the almost irresistible temptation to catch the impulse, give it form, make it permanent, assert its meaning. And so one commits himself to language. To have given up one's experience to words is to have begun marking out the limits and potential of its meaning. In the journal that meaning is developed and clarified to oneself primarily. When the whole intention of the development and the clarification is the consideration of another reader, the method of the journal redirects itself to become that of the essay.]

HENRY DAVID THOREAU: *from* Journal

As the least drop of wine tinges the whole goblet, so the least particle of truth colors our whole life. It is never isolated, or simply added as treasure to our stock. When any real progress is made, we unlearn and learn anew what we thought we knew before. [1837]

Not by constraint or severity shall you have access to true wisdom, but by abandonment, and childlike mirthfulness. If you would know aught, be gay before it. [1840]

It is the man determines what is said, not the words. If a mean person uses a wise maxim, I bethink me how it can be interpreted so as to commend itself to his meanness; but if a wise man makes a commonplace remark, I consider what wider construction it will admit. [1840]

Nothing goes by luck in composition. It allows of no tricks. The best you can write will be the best you are. Every sentence is the result of a long probation. The author's character is read from title-page to end. Of this he never corrects the proofs. We read it as the essential character of a handwriting without regard to the flourishes. And so of the rest of our actions; it runs as straight as a ruled line through them all, no matter how many curvets about it. Our whole life is taxed for the least thing well done; it is its net result. How we eat, drink, sleep, and use our desultory hours, now in these indifferent days, with no eye to observe and no occasion [to] excite us, determines our authority and capacity for the time to come. [1841]

What does education often do? It makes a straight-cut ditch of a free, meandering brook. [1850]

All perception of truth is the detection of an analogy; we reason from our hands to our head. [1851]

To set down such choice experiences that my own writings may inspire me and at last I may make wholes of parts. Certainly it is a distinct profession to rescue from oblivion and to fix the sentiments and thoughts which visit all men more or less generally, that the contemplation of the unfinished picture may suggest its harmonious completion. Associate reverently and as much as you can with your loftiest thoughts. Each thought that is welcomed and recorded is a nest egg, by the side of which more will be laid. Thoughts accidentally thrown together become a frame in which more may be developed and exhibited. Perhaps this is the main value of a habit of writing, of keeping a journal—that so we remember our best hours and stimulate ourselves. My thoughts are my company. They have a certain individuality and separate existence, aye, personality. Having by chance recorded a few disconnected thoughts and then brought them into juxtaposition, they suggest a whole new field in which it was possible to labor and to think. Thought begat thought. [1852]

It is pardonable when we spurn the proprieties, even the sanctities, making them stepping-stones to something higher. [1858]

There is always some accident in the best things, whether thoughts or expressions or deeds. The memorable thought, the happy expression, the admirable deed are only partly ours. The thought came to us because we were in a fit mood; also we were unconscious and did not know that we had said or done a good thing. We must walk consciously only part way toward our goal, and then leap in the dark to our success. What we do best or most perfectly is what we have most thoroughly learned by the longest practice, and at length it falls from us without our notice, as a leaf from a tree. It is the *last* time we shall do it—our unconscious leavings. [1859]

The expression "a *liberal* education" originally meant one worthy of freemen. Such is education simply in a true and broad sense. But education ordinarily so called—the learning of trades and professions which is designed to enable men to earn their living, or to fit them for a particular station in life—is *servile.* [1859]

DONALD PEARCE: *from* Journal of a War

December 28. We have been patroling the Rhine and guarding the bridge across it at Nijmegen continuously for so long now that they have begun to acquire a positive hold over our minds and imaginations. Our thoughts seem polarized by them, and turn to them like compasses to a magnet. This bridge is the only one over the Rhine left intact for a hundred miles, and we must keep it that way for our own no doubt imminent invasion of Germany. At the same time, if Jerry decides to counter-attack in force through here, and there has been a good deal of fresh evidence that he's getting ready to do just that, the bridge would become just as important to him. A really ambiguous prize. But he keeps sending explosives downstream at it. Damn strange. We shoot into the river at everything that moves, sometimes exploding mines tied to boards, or logs, or branches. Our engineers have run a huge net across the river about fifty yards upstream from the bridge to catch whatever floats downstream; but things get through or under the net somehow and that's what we shoot at. New rumor: German frogmen have been attempting to swim under the net; also, they have small one-man submarines in the river. Probably fairy lore.

But I was going to say—the bridge and river no longer appear ordinary to us, but seem to have acquired personalities, or to have been endowed with them. Sometimes the river seems less the watched one than the watcher, reflecting back our searchlight beams, and breaking the half-moon into a thousand yellow eyes as we steal along the edge on night patrols. The bridge's single span is unmistakably a high, arched eyebrow over an invisible eye peering across the Rhine. Everything we do here revolves around the bridge and river. As we go back for a rest or, as recently, for Christmas dinner, miles from the line, we cross the iced-flats that follow along the curving windswept dykes, and the great iron eyebrow is right behind us, lifting higher and higher above the mist, in a kind of inscrutable surmise, and as we return to those god-awful flats again, the eyebrow and invisible eye are at it again, staring back at us, watching the Rhine. Perhaps someone should put on a campaign to establish the ordinariness of this bridge and river, put up signs. But it would do no good, I tell myself, because this was Caesar's Rhine, Siegfried's Rhine, Wagner's Rhine, and you can't silence all that mystery. I hate it here.

Whipping the company jeep at top speed along a mile-long windswept section of one of the dykes that stretches between our company and the next is one of the low diversions we have worked out. It's completely exposed and utterly bare; so for two minutes you are an A-number one moving target. An insane game, but we play it. Once I heard the loud, flat snap of a bullet going past my head on one of these mad runs. We are, as they say, very definitely under observation.

* * *

March 3 [1945]. The city[1] was quite heavily defended. First, a steep, raw, anti-tank ditch completely girdling the city had to be negotiated, with continuous covering fire from both flanks. Then we ran into a connected system of crawl- and weapons-trenches forming a secondary ring about the interior. Our covering artillery fire was practically saturational; so he resisted only lightly till we were more than halfway in. There followed some sporadic street fighting and house clearing, nothing very spectacular, and the city fell to us shortly after daybreak; i.e., they simply pulled out and disappeared at about 4:00 A.M.

I had a couple of close ones during this show. On the way in, my platoon was evidently silhouetted against the night sky, and was fired on four times at a range of maybe 300 yards by an eighty-eight. (This is a notorious and vicious gun. The velocity of the shell is so

1. Udem, in The Netherlands.

high that you hear it pass or explode near you almost at the same
instant that you hear the sound of its being fired. You really can't
duck it. Also, it's an open-sights affair—you are aimed at particularly; not, as with mortars, aimed at only by approximation.)
Anyway, they went past me about an arm's length above or in front
of me, I don't know which. We hit the ditches. After pointing a
few more, the gun was forced off by our return tank fire.

During the house-clearing phase, at one spot, I walked instead of
ran from one house to another and got my helmet spun around on
my head with a close shot. There was an extremely loud, flat
"snap," like two hands clapped together hard beside my ear; that
was all. Plus a crease in my helmet, which gave me immense prestige with the men all morning.

We had two tanks along with us, and their support made the
assignment 100 per cent easier. At one point a handful of German
snipers, who were perched in the attic of a three-story house at a
bend in the main street, held up the battalion for over an hour.
They were finally silenced by one of the tanks. In the half-dark, we
circled around behind their house during the tank fire and cut off
their escape route. Presently they came out through the back
garden, dangling in front of them white cloths on long poles. It
was vastly disconcerting. Instead of a squad of Nazi supermen in
shiny boots, and packing Lugers, we were confronted by five of
the most unkempt, stunted, scrubby specimens I have ever had the
pleasure of capturing. Two of them couldn't have been more than
fourteen on their next birthday. Possibly they were on some kind of
dope; at least they acted that way, a little dazed, grinning, and
rather immune to voice control. One of them had nearly shot me a
few hours earlier in the dark before dawn. At the time, I remember, I had thought it wasn't any more than I had expected; but
later on, seeing them, I felt that it would have been an unfortunate
end to my life. I am obviously getting choosy. What I mean is that
I would simply like to be well killed, if killed I am to be. I came to
the conclusion that they were from the bottom of Germany's
recruiting barrel.

The men in the platoon seemed to think so too, for I caught
them in the middle of a queer performance. They had lined the
five of them up against a schoolhouse wall and were pretending,
quite ceremoniously, that they were going to shoot them. The prisoners certainly believed they were about to be shot; three of them
had their hands on their heads and their faces turned to the wall,
as for execution; the other two were pleading desperately with three
or four of our men. I was astonished to find my best corporal in the
thick of this business. I stopped it, of course. Not that they would
have carried out the execution; I feel sure of that.

We passed through the town and seized a road-and-rail junction about 800 yards past the outskirts and dug in under moderate shelling. A child would know that that junction would become a hot target—which it very shortly did. We sat it out. He sent several salvos of rockets in on us. These you always hear coming, if it's any comfort. The first salvo was the best, but there was time for my sergeant and me to flatten out in a shallow ditch alongside the track. One rocket hit about four or five feet from us, practically shattering my hearing; it chewed up a couple of railway ties, took two or three chunks out of the rails, and turned me over from my stomach to my back. The blast stung my whole left side. Nothing more really close happened there all night.

Next day, I went back to have a look at Udem. In daylight it seemed in worse condition than I remembered it from the night before. Enemy shelling accounted for much of the destruction; but looters, busy rooting around before daybreak, accounted for some too. The houses that had not been shelled were practically turned inside out by our troops. I came across one soldier telling an admiring group about his morning exploits: "First I took a hammer and smashed over 100 plates, and the cups along with them. Then I took an ax to the china cabinets and buffets. Next I smashed all the furniture and pulled the stuffing out of the big chairs. Then I took the hammer again and smashed all the elements on two electric stoves and broke the enamel off the stove fronts and sides. Then I put a grenade in the big piano, and after that I poured a jar of molasses into it. I broke all the French doors and all the doors with mirrors in them and threw the lamps out into the street. I was so mad."

I turned him over to the Provost Corps in the afternoon.

Udem had a large church made of red stone with high twin towers. German artillery scouts had stationed themselves in these towers in order to direct fire onto our positions five miles away. So the church had to be "neutralized," as they say. We engaged it with 17-pounders for about an hour, I believe successfully. Anyway, I went in to see what we had done. It was full of gaping holes; the stone pillars had even been shot off far within the building. The only unharmed thing I saw was the font. The walls had had blue and gold paintings of religious scenes extending all around the interior; these were mostly peeled or ripped off. One painting was of the Descent from the Cross. It had come loose from its frame and seemed heading for a nosedive; the pale belly of Christ had a group of machine-gun bullets through it. The Germans had made a brief stand at the church and had obviously used, it as a temporary strongpoint. As I left, engineers were already laying dynamite charges at critical points along the foundations, with the intention of using the stones as rubble for roads, almost the only reasonable use left for it.

On the way back, I met a number of civilians carrying bundles. Most of them were covered with mud from head to foot. They were staggering along rather than walking, and started every time a gun went off far away or close up. One tall thin man was leading two small children, one by each hand. The children were around his back. The man limped; I saw that he was weeping. My limited German enabled me to discover that he was wounded in a couple of places, that his wife had been killed by shrapnel in the morning, and that he didn't know what to do with his tiny children who were wet, cold, and hungry. I took them down into our cellar where the stretcher bearer dressed his wounds and evacuated him. I offered the two children food—chocolate, bread and jam, biscuits. They only tightened their lips and refused. So I tried a sort of game with the names of the articles of furniture in the cellar, deliberately making silly mistakes, and after a while they laughed at my stupidity. I kept this up, and before long they gobbled whatever I put in front of them. I would like to have done more; but instead I turned them over to the Civil Affairs people, not without complicated feelings of concern and regret. I will never know what happened to them.

Kept rummaging around in the town. Went to the place where I was nearly shot, stood on the exact spot, in fact, and determined the window at the end of the street where the shots had come from. An impulse sent me inside the house itself, where I climbed to the upper room. The machine gun was there on its heavy mounting, still pointing out the window and down the street. I sat behind it and took aim on the doorway I had disappeared into at the moment I was fired on, and waited for someone to pass the spot just to see how I must have looked through his sights. No one came and I got tired of the melodrama and went back to our forward positions.

* * *

March 4. When will it all end? The idiocy and the tension, the dying of young men, the destruction of homes, of cities, starvation, exhaustion, disease, children parentless and lost, cages full of shivering, staring prisoners, long lines of hopeless civilians plodding through mud, the endless pounding of the battle line. I can scarcely remember what it is like to be where explosions are not going off around me, some hostile, some friendly, all horrible; an exploding shell is a terrible sound. What keeps this war going, now that its end is so clear? What do the Germans think of us, and we of them? I do not think we think of them at all, or much. Do they think of us? I can think of their weapons, their shells, their machine guns, but not of the men behind them. I do not feel as if I were fighting against men, but against machines. I need to go up in an airplane and actually see German transport hauling guns and ammunition, see their actual armies; for everything that happens merely comes from a vague beyond, and I cannot visualize the people who are fighting against me. The prisoners that come over hills with their hands up, or who come out of houses with white cloths waving—they have no relation, almost, to anything for me. I can't connect them with the guns they have just laid down, it seems like forcing something to do so. It is becoming hard for me not to feel sometimes that both sides are the common victims of a common terror, that everybody's guns are against everybody ultimately.

These are times when I feel that every bit of fighting is defensive. Self defense. If a machine-gun nest is attacked and wiped out by us, by my own platoon, I do not feel very aggressive, as if I had attacked somebody. It is always that I have defended myself against something that was attacking me. And how often I have thought that there might be a Rilke out there in a German pill box. If I could only see them, as in battles long ago, at close range, before engaging them. In our wars, the warring sides are getting farther and farther apart and war is getting more and more meaningless for the field warriors, and more meaningful for the domestic warriors in factories and homes. Will there come a time when hundreds of miles separate the warring fronts? When long-range weapons and the ghastly impersonality of air attacks are the means of war? It is already a very impersonal thing. When a soldier is killed or wounded his buddies, shaking their heads, merely say, "Poor old Joe. He just got it. Just as he was going up that hill, he got it." As if to imply that he was merely in the wrong place at the wrong time, and that life and death are only matters of luck and do not depend on the calculations of human beings at the other end of an S.P. gun. When we were in our static positions around Wyler Meer and Nijmegen, the enemy became real to me for the first time. I watched him for weeks, saw him dig, run, hide, fire, walk. And when I went on patrols into his territory, there was meaning in that, too, for I knew where he was, I knew his habits. So that while we were probing the cuticle of the enemy, so to speak, he was real; but now when we are ripping into his body, he has disappeared and has turned into something read about in the papers. But the guns remain, manned by soldiers who are so meaningless to us that when they shoot a fellow, all we can say is, "He got it."

Once I could say you cannot be disgusted with the war, because it is too big for disgust, that disgust is too shallow an emotion for something involving millions of people. But I am disgusted now, and I know what I am saying. Once I used to get quite a thrill out of seeing a city destroyed and left an ash heap from end to end. It gave me a vicarious sense of power. I felt the romantic and histrionic emotion produced by seeing "retribution" done; and an aesthetic emotion produced by beholding ruins; and the childish emotion that comes from destroying man-made things. But it is not that way any more. All I experience is revulsion every time a fresh city is taken on. I am no longer capable of thinking that the systematic destruction of a city is a wonderful or even a difficult thing, though some seem to think it even a heroic thing. Well, how is it done? Dozens upon dozens of gun crews stationed some two or three miles away from the city simply place shell after shell into hundreds of guns and fire away for a few hours—the simplest and most elementary physical and mental work—and then presently the firing stops, the city has been demolished, has become an ash heap, and great praise is bestowed on the army for the capture of a new city.

I am not suggesting that cities shouldn't be captured in this way; actually it saves lives. But it fills me with disgust because it is all so abysmally foolish, so lunatic. It has not the dramatic elements of mere barbarism about it; it is straight scientific debauchery. A destroyed city is a terrible sight. How can anyone record it?—the million smashed things, the absolutely innumerable tiny tragedies, the crushed life-works, the jagged homes, army tanks parked in living rooms—who could tell of these things I don't know; they are too numerous to mention, too awful in their meanings. Perhaps everyone should be required to spend a couple of hours examining a single smashed home, looking at the fragmentation of every little thing, especially the tiniest things from kitchen to attic, if he could find an attic; be required, in fact, to list the ruined contents of just one home; something would be served, a little sobriety perhaps honored.

It is disgusting (that it should be necessary, is what galls me to the bones) that a towering cathedral, built by ages of care and effort, a sweet labor of centuries, should be shot down by laughing artillerymen, mere boys, because somebody with a machine gun is hiding in a belfry tower. When I see such a building, damaged perhaps beyond repair after one of these "operations," I know only disgust. The matter of sides in this war temporarily becomes irrelevant, especially if someone at my elbow says, like a conquering hero: "Well, we sure did a job on the old church, eh?"

A job has been done on Europe, on the world, and the resulting trauma will be generations long in its effects. It is not just the shock of widespread destruction, of whole cities destroyed, nor the shock which the defeated and the homeless must have suffered, that I am thinking of: it is even more the conqueror's trauma, the

habit of violence, the explosion of values, the distortion of relations, the ascending significance of the purely material, the sense of
power, and the pride of strength. These things will afflict the vic-
tors as profoundly and for quite as long a time as the other things
will afflict the victims; and of the two I am not sure that a crass
superiority complex is the more desirable. Perhaps I underestimate
our ability to return to normal again.

EDWARD WESTON: *from* The Daybooks[1]

March 20 [1927] * * * The shells I photographed were so marvellous one could not do other than something of interest. What I
did may be only a beginning—but I like one negative especially. I
took a proof of the legs recently done of Bertha, which Miss Shore[2]
was enthusiastic over.

April 1. Nudes of ———— again. Made two negatives,—variation
on one conception.

I am stimulated to work with the nude body, because of the
infinite combinations of lines which are presented with every move.
And now after seeing the shells of Henrietta Shore, a new field has
been presented.

* * *

April 24. What have I, that bring these many women to offer
themselves to me? I do not go out of my way seeking them,—I am
not a stalwart virile male, exuding sex, nor am I the romantic,
mooning poet type some love, nor the dashing Don Juan bent on
conquest. Now it is B.

April 28. Every day finds me working, or at least thinking of work
for myself,—and with more enthusiasm, surety and success than
ever before. Another shell negative,—another beginning of something, from yesterday.

One of these two new shells when stood on end, is like a magnolia
blossom unfolding. The difficulty has been to make it balance on
end and not cut off that important end, nor show an irrelevant
base. I may have solved the problem by using another shell for the
chalice, but I had the Devil's own time trying to balance those two
shells together. In the first negative, they slipped just a hair's

1. The "daybooks" are the journal of
Edward Weston, one of America's great
photographers. The first published volume is entitled *The Daybooks: Mexico,
1923–1927;* the second, from which the
present excerpts are drawn, *The Daybooks: California,* covers the years
1927–1934. When publication was proposed, Weston went through the journals
with a razor, cutting out names and
comments; hence annotation cannot be
complete. Both volumes were edited by
Nancy Newhall.
2. Henrietta Shore, a painter, and
friend of Weston's.

breadth,—and after a three hour exposure! The second attempt is technically good.

And then the dancing nudes of B.

I feel that I have a number of exceedingly well seen negatives,— several which I am sure will live among my best.

B. left me a record of one of Chopin's *Preludes* played by Casals.[3] Starting a tender, plaintive melody, it suddenly breaks, quite without warning into thundering depths, and then in a flash rises to electrifying heights, which makes my scalp tingle.

* * *

[*Undated*] . . . I think the Chambered Nautilus has one of the most exquisite forms, to say nothing of color and texture, in nature.

I was awakened to shells by the painting of Henry.[4] I never saw a Chambered Nautilus before. If I had, my response would have been immediate! If I merely copy Henry's expression, my work will not live. If I am stimulated and work with real ecstasy it will live.

Henry's influence, or stimulation, I see not just in shell subject matter, it is in all my late work,—in the bananas and the nudes. I feel it not as an extraneous garnish but as a freshened tide swelling from within my self.

* * *

Monday morning. I worked all Sunday with the shells,—literally all day. Only three negatives made and two of them were done as records of movement to repeat again when I can find suitable backgrounds. I wore myself out trying every conceivable texture and tone for grounds: Glass, tin, cardboard,—wool, velvet, even my rubber rain coat! I did not need to make these records for memory's sake,—no, they were safely recorded there. I did wish to study the tin which was perfect with the lens open; but stopped down I could not see sufficiently to tell, but was positive the surface would come into focus and show a net work of scratches—it did. My first photograph of the Chambered Nautilus done at Henry's was perfect all but the too black ground: yesterday the only available texture was white. Again I recorded to study at leisure the contrast. The feeling of course has been quite changed,—the luminosity of the shell seen against black, gone; but the new negative has a delicate beauty of its own. I had heart failure several times yesterday when the shells, balanced together, slipped. I must buy a Nautilus, for to break Henry's would be tragic.

Thursday, May 12. B. danced for me! This time I was spectator, —not photographer. A definite feeling is not always easy to put down in definite words, but I know I was privileged to have her dance for me,—to me. The work I do today must be finer than that

3. Pablo Casals, the cellist.   4. I.e., Henrietta Shore.

of yesterday because of B. dancing: she has added to my creative strength. B. danced nude. What a pity all dancing cannot be in the nude: or no!—some dances may well be covered for illusion's sake — — —

I have my work room barricaded,—for there, are two shells delicately balanced together awaiting the afternoon light. My first version of the combination was done Sunday: Monday a slight turn of one shell, and I gained strength: Wednesday the second proof decided me to try a lighter ground with the same arrangement,— but desiring to repeat, I again saw more clearly.

Wednesday, after developing. I thought—before putting away the shells I will see what a still lighter ground does, in fact a white ground. Seeing, I knew at once that now I had what I was fighting for! But the hour was late, the light failing, I could not expose another film. So there stands my camera focussed, trained like a gun, commanding the shells not to move a hair's breadth. And death to the person who jars out of place what I know shall be a *very important* negative.

* * *

May 13. After watching my shell arrangement all day,—repeatedly warning Brett[5] to walk lightly,—even keeping the windows shut for fear of a slight breeze, though the day was hot,—a cardboard background slipped, fell onto the shells, and completely disarranged them. I was literally on the verge of tears from disappointment, knowing the impossibility of repeating anything absolutely.

But now I see the Gods meant well. I took off my shirt, for the room was like an oven, and half indifferently, half rebelliously, retired under the focussing cloth. After twenty minutes' struggle in which I tried to register my previous negative over the ground glass image,—almost but not quite succeeding, I suddenly realized that the slight change was an improvement! I shall remember the making of this negative.

In the morning I enlarged the first five positives of B.—dancing nudes. They appear to advantage blown up. I am pleased with my day's work.

Saturday, May 14. I must do the shells again! That is the last combination. If I did not have the third proof to compare I would be very happy with the last: in some ways it is better, but one important upright line is not quite as fine. Henry agrees, though she thinks I have done a very important negative. Also she responded fully to six of my last dancing nudes. Says they are among the finest photographs I have ever done.

Four of the six I shall enlarge: two I shall try to improve by doing the impossible—repeating.

5. Weston's second son.

* * *

Tuesday, May 17. I could not be at peace until I had made the fifth attempt to improve the shell arrangement by a fifth negative. The result has been that I have printed my fourth negative, and am quite pleased. Also printed two former shell negatives, worthy recording if not so important. The fig tree done at Palm Springs is at last printed and the first of the dancing nudes: the former comes close to being fine,—the latter is fine,—a kneeling figure cut at the shoulder, but kneeling does not mean it is passive,—it is dancing quite as intensely as if she were on her toes! I am in love with this nude — — —

Late in the afternoon I took out the Chambered Nautilus thinking to improve on the first negatives: instead there came to me a new group over which I am absolutely enthusiastic! It was too late for an exposure so I must be patient until this afternoon. I find myself, every so often, looking at my ground glass as though the unrecorded image might escape me! I can see that I am to have days of struggle with the later group also. There are so many slight variations I can make. The last negative is better in most ways,— just one line I'm not so sure of. Also the background might be varied. But I shall enjoy the struggle!

* * *

Wednesday, June 15. Twice I have repeated the shell group,— the latest, which is one of the strongest, but blurred from slight movement. Monday I got a perfect negative and an improved arrangement: but Chandler[6] was using my cardboard backgrounds to press flowers between, so finding nothing else, I used a square of black velvet, which I knew was too black,—and proved so. Why I went ahead I don't know! Yesterday, I tried again: result, movement! The exposure was 4½ hours, so to repeat was no joy, with all the preoccupation of keeping quiet children and cats,—but I went ahead and await development.

Saturday, June 18. The shells again moved! It must be the heavy trucks that pass jar the building ever so slightly. Anyway I have quit trying: I can afford no more film.

The money question is disturbing me mentally.

* * *

Sunday morn. June 26. I have had very bad luck: Chandler lost a five dollar bill, just given him for groceries. This was part of ten dollars received from a print sale,—one of the first nudes of B. Five dollars!—Enough for *me* to live on a week!

I shall work with new shells to forget this tragedy! Three shells and a piece of coral came as a present: fine material for much thought. * * *

6. Weston's eldest son.

July 7—"Last evening Orozco was here. I got out the shell prints. Well, in a few words, he liked them better than all your collection put together. Of one he said, 'This suggests much more the "Hand of God" than the hand Rodin made.' It is the one that has made everybody, including myself, think of the sexual act."[7]

From the above quotations it will be seen that I have created a definite impression, but from an angle which surprised me!

Why were all these persons so profoundly affected on the physical side?

For I can say with absolute honesty that not once while working with the shells did I have any physical reaction to them; nor did I try to record erotic symbolism. I am not sick and I was never so free from sexual suppression,—which if I had, might easily enter into my work, *as it does* in Henry's painting.

I am not blind to the sensuous quality in shells, with which they combine the deepest spiritual significance: indeed it is this very combination of the physical and spiritual in a shell like the Chambered Nautilus, which makes it such an important abstract of life.

No! I had no physical thoughts,—never have. I worked with clearer vision of sheer aesthetic form. I knew that I was recording from within, my feeling for life as I never had before. Or better, when the negatives were actually developed, I realized what I felt, —for when I worked, I was never more unconscious of what I was doing.

No! The Shells are too much a sublimation of all my work and life to be pigeonholed. Others must get from them what they bring to them: evidently they do!

* * *

Saturday, March 8 [1930]. Yesterday I made photographic history: for I have every reason and belief that two negatives of kelp done in the morning will someday be sought as examples of my finest expression and understanding. Another is almost as good, and yet another might be considered a very strong example of a more usual viewpoint: this latter several steps beyond the salon type of photograph. But my two best,—they are years beyond.

I had found the kelp the evening before, almost at the foot of Ocean Avenue, washed there by the recent storm, the heavy sea. I knew it would not stay put, perhaps not even the night, so early next morning I walked down to see what the tides had done: and there it lay unchanged, twisted, tangled, interwoven, a chaos of convulsed rhythms, from which I selected a square foot, organized the apparently complex maze, and presented it, a powerful integration.

7. Weston is quoting from a letter written him by Tina Modotti—friend, pupil, and model of his in Mexico—in reaction to the shell photographs. José Clemente Orozco was an important Mexican painter, Auguste Rodin the French sculptor.

This was done of course with no manual arrangement,—the selection was entirely my viewpoint as seen through the camera. I get a greater joy from finding things in Nature, already composed, than I do from my finest personal arrangements. After all, selection is another way of arranging: to move the camera an eighth of an inch is quite as subtle as moving likewise a pepper.

These kelp negatives are as strong as any of my rocks: indeed I think they are stronger. A few of my rock details have lace-like delicacy. How little subject matter counts in the ultimate reaction!

* * *

July 10. * * * Herb Klein who bought my favorite kelp, wrote, —"interweaving like a Bach fugue, yet keeping its dynamic tension through the complexity."

Whenever I can feel a Bach fugue in my work I know I have arrived.

July 19. * * * Since my last entry, much has happened. I have worked with summer squash,—one afternoon, making some very beautiful and strong negatives: the squash nearly white in the sun, a grey ground, and intense black shadow,—the simple massing of the three values, most satisfying.

And I have worked with peppers again, surprising myself! Sonya[8] brought several home, and I could not resist, though I thought to have finished with peppers. But peppers never repeat themselves: shells, bananas, melons, so many forms, are not inclined to experiment,—not so the pepper, always excitingly individual. So I have three new negatives, and two more under way. One of these, and they are already printed along with the squash, is extraordinarily fine and different. It is the most exquisite one I have done; the former negatives [were] usually powerful. This slender, delicate pepper, I placed on a green-glazed oval dish,—it might be a strange tropical plant in itself, spiraling up from the roots, partly unfolded at the top like a fern. It has a mystic significance.

* * *

August 1. * * * The glorious new pepper Sonya brought me has kept me keyed up all week and caused me to expose eight negatives: —I'm not satisfied yet! These eight were all from the same viewpoint: rare for me to go through this. I started out with an underexposure—by the time I had developed the light had failed, and though I tripled my time again I undertimed! Again I tried, desperately determined to get it because I could ill afford the time. Giving an exposure of 50 minutes at 5:00 I timed correctly, but during exposure the fire siren shrieked, and promptly the fire truck roared by followed by every car in town: the old porch trembled, my

8. Sonia Noskowiak, a student and partner of Weston's.

wobbly old camera wobbled, the pepper shimmied, and I developed a moved negative. Next morning I went at it again: interruptions came, afternoon came, light weak, prolonged exposures necessary;— result, one negative possible, but possible also to improve upon it.

I tried the light from the opposite side in the next morning light, —brilliant sun through muslin. Better! A reason for my failures. Three negatives made, on a new angle so different as to be another pepper. And more failures, this time sheer thoughtlessness: a background of picture backing was placed too close and came into focus when stopped down which I could not see but should have realized, the corrugations plainly show and spoil the feeling. The one exposure from a new angle was perfect. So I have made eight negatives from the same angle and yet must go on. Today it is foggy and I am faced with an entirely new approach.

All this work has been done between moments of greeting tourists, printing, mounting, etc. Small wonder I have failed.

But the pepper is well worth all time, money, effort. If peppers would not wither, I certainly would not have attempted this one when so preoccupied. I must get this one today: it is beginning to show the strain and tonight should grace a salad. It has been suggested that I am a cannibal to eat my models after a masterpiece. But I rather like the idea that they become a part of me, enrich my blood as well as my vision. Last night we finished my now famous squash, and had several of my bananas in a salad.

* * *

August 3. Sonya * * * keeps tempting me with new peppers! Two more have been added to my collection. While experimenting with one of these, which was so small that I used my 21 cm. Zeiss to fill the 8 x 10 size, I tried putting it in a tin funnel for background. It was a bright idea, a perfect relief for the pepper and adding reflected light to important contours. I still had the pepper which caused me a week's work, I had decided I could go no further with it, yet something kept me from taking it to the kitchen, the end of all good peppers. I placed it in the funnel, focussed with the Zeiss, and, knowing just the viewpoint, recognizing a perfect light, made an exposure of six minutes, with but a few moments' preliminary work,—the real preliminary was done in hours passed. I have a great negative,—by far the best!

August 4. * * * In the late afternoon I made three more peppers in funnel, all with the Zeiss [lens], all very close, filling entire plate. The one great objection to the Zeiss is that I cannot stop down as far as I am used to.

* * *

On Education

JOHN HOLT
How Teachers Make Children Hate Reading

When I was teaching English at the Colorado Rocky Mountain School, I used to ask my students the kinds of questions that English teachers usually ask about reading assignments—questions designed to bring out the points that I had decided *they* should know. They, on their part, would try to get me to give them hints and clues as to what I wanted. It was a game of wits. I never gave my students an opportunity to say what they really thought about a book.

I gave vocabulary drills and quizzes too. I told my students that every time they came upon a word in their book they did not understand, they were to look it up in the dictionary. I even devised special kinds of vocabulary tests, allowing them to use their books to see how the words were used. But looking back, I realize that these tests, along with many of my methods, were foolish.

My sister was the first person who made me question my conventional ideas about teaching English. She had a son in the seventh grade in a fairly good public school. His teacher had asked the class to read Cooper's *The Deerslayer*. The choice was bad enough in itself; whether looking at man or nature, Cooper was superficial, inaccurate and sentimental, and his writing is ponderous and ornate. But to make matters worse, this teacher had decided to give the book the microscope and x-ray treatment. He made the students look up and memorize not only the definitions but the derivations of every big word that came along—and there were plenty. Every chapter was followed by close questioning and testing to make sure the students "understood" everything.

Being then, as I said, conventional, I began to defend the teacher, who was a good friend of mine, against my sister's criticisms. The argument soon grew hot. What was wrong with making sure that children understood everything they read? My sister answered that until this class her boy had always loved reading, and had read

53

a lot on his own; now he had stopped. (He was not really to start again for many years.)

Still I persisted. If children didn't look up the words they didn't know, how would they ever learn them? My sister said, "Don't be silly! When you were little you had a huge vocabulary, and were always reading very grown-up books. When did you ever look up a word in a dictionary?"

She had me. I don't know that we had a dictionary at home; if we did, I didn't use it. I don't use one today. In my life I doubt that I have looked up as many as fifty words, perhaps not even half that.

Since then I have talked about this with a number of teachers. More than once I have said, "according to tests, educated and literate people like you have a vocabulary of about twenty-five thousand words. How many of these did you learn by looking them up in a dictionary?" They usually are startled. Few claim to have looked up even as many as a thousand. How did they learn the rest?

They learned them just as they learned to talk—by meeting words over and over again, in different contexts, until they saw how they fitted.

Unfortunately, we English teachers are easily hung up on this matter of understanding. Why should children understand everything they read? Why should anyone? Does anyone? I don't, and I never did. I was always reading books that teachers would have said were "too hard" for me, books full of words I didn't know. That's how I got to be a good reader. When about ten, I read all the D'Artagnan stories and loved them. It didn't trouble me in the least that I didn't know why France was at war with England or who was quarreling with whom in the French court or why the Musketeers should always be at odds with Cardinal Richelieu's men. I didn't even know who the Cardinal was, except that he was a dangerous and powerful man that my friends had to watch out for. This was all I needed to know.

Having said this, I will now say that I think a big, unabridged dictionary is a fine thing to have in any home or classroom. No book is more fun to browse around in—*if* you're not made to. Children, depending on their age, will find many pleasant and interesting things to do with a big dictionary. They can look up funny-sounding words, which they like, or words that nobody else in the class has ever heard of, which they like, or long words, which they like, or forbidden words, which they like best of all. At a certain age, and particularly with a little encouragement from parents or teachers, they may become very interested in where words came from and when they came into the language and how their meanings have changed over the years. But exploring for the fun of it is very different from looking up words out of your reading because you're going to get into trouble with your teacher if you don't.

While teaching fifth grade two years or so after the argument with my sister, I began to think again about reading. The children in my class were supposed to fill out a card—just the title and author and a one-sentence summary—for every book they read. I was not running a competition to see which child could read the most books, a competition that almost always leads to cheating. I just wanted to know what the children were reading. After a while it became clear that many of these very bright kids, from highly literate and even literary backgrounds, read very few books and deeply disliked reading. Why should this be?

At this time I was coming to realize, as I described in my book *How Children Fail*, that for most children school was a place of danger, and their main business in school was staying out of danger as much as possible. I now began to see also that books were among the most dangerous things in school.

From the very beginning of school we make books and reading a constant source of possible failure and public humiliation. When children are little we make them read aloud, before the teacher and other children, so that we can be sure they "know" all the words they are reading. This means that when they don't know a word, they are going to make a mistake, right in front of everyone. Instantly they are made to realize that they have done something wrong. Perhaps some of the other children will begin to wave their hands and say, "Ooooh! O-o-o-oh!" Perhaps they will just giggle, or nudge each other, or make a face. Perhaps the teacher will say, "Are you sure?" or ask someone else what he thinks. Or perhaps, if the teacher is kindly, she will just smile a sweet, sad smile—often one of the most painful punishments a child can suffer in school. In any case, the child who has made the mistake knows he has made it, and feels foolish, stupid, and ashamed, just as any of us would in his shoes.

Before long many children associate books and reading with mistakes, real or feared, and penalties and humiliation. This may not seem sensible, but it is natural. Mark Twain once said that a cat that sat on a hot stove lid would never sit on one again—but it would never sit on a cold one either. As true of children as of cats. If they, so to speak, sit on a hot book a few times, if books cause them humiliation and pain, they are likely to decide that the safest thing to do is to leave all books alone.

After having taught fifth-grade classes for four years I felt quite sure of this theory. In my next class were many children who had had great trouble with schoolwork, particularly reading. I decided to try at all costs to rid them of their fear and dislike of books, and to get them to read oftener and more adventurously.

One day soon after school had started, I said to them, "Now I'm going to say something about reading that you have probably never heard a teacher say before. I would like you to read a lot of books this year, but I want you to read them only for pleasure. I am not going to ask you questions to find out whether you understand the books or not. If you understand enough of a book to enjoy it and want to go on reading it, that's enough for me. Also I'm not going to ask you what words mean.

"Finally," I said, "I don't want you to feel that just because you start a book, you have to finish it. Give an author thirty or forty pages or so to get his story going. Then if you don't like the characters and don't care what happens to them, close the book, put it away, and get another. I don't care whether the books are easy or hard, short or long, as long as you enjoy them. Furthermore I'm putting all this in a letter to your parents, so they won't feel they have to quiz and heckle you about books at home."

The children sat stunned and silent. Was this a teacher talking? One girl, who had just come to us from a school where she had had a very hard time, and who proved to be one of the most interesting, lively, and intelligent children I have ever known, looked at me steadily for a long time after I had finished. Then, still looking at me, she said slowly and solemnly, "Mr. Holt, do you really mean that?" I said just as solemnly, "I mean every word of it."

Apparently she decided to believe me. The first book she read was Dr. Seuss's *How the Grinch Stole Christmas*, not a hard book even for most third graders. For a while she read a number of books on this level. Perhaps she was clearing up some confusion about reading that her teachers, in their hurry to get her up to "grade level," had never given her enough time to clear up. After she had been in the class six weeks or so and we had become good friends, I very tentatively suggested that, since she was a skillful rider and loved horses, she might like to read *National Velvet*. I made my sell as soft as possible, saying only that it was about a girl who loved and rode horses, and that if she didn't like it, she could put it back. She tried it, and though she must have found it quite a bit harder than what she had been reading, finished it and liked it very much.

During the spring she really astonished me, however. One day, in one of our many free periods, she was reading at her desk. From a glimpse of the illustrations I thought I knew what the book was. I said to myself, "It can't be," and went to take a closer look. Sure enough, she was reading *Moby Dick*, in the edition with woodcuts by Rockwell Kent. When I came close to her desk she looked up. I said, "Are you really reading that?" She said she was. I said, "Do you like it?" She said, "Oh, yes, it's neat!" I said, "Don't you find parts of it rather heavy going?" She answered "Oh, sure, but I just skip over those parts and go on to the next good part."

This is exactly what reading should be and in school so seldom is—an exciting, joyous adventure. Find something, dive into it, take the good parts, skip the bad parts, get what you can out of it, go on to something else. How different is our mean-spirited, picky insistence that every child get every last little scrap of "understanding" that can be dug out of a book.

For teachers who really enjoy doing it, and will do it with gusto, reading aloud is a very good idea. I have found that not just fifth graders but even ninth and eleventh graders enjoy it. Jack London's "To Build a Fire" is a good read-aloud story. So are ghost stories, and "August Heat," by W. F. Harvey, and "The Monkey's Paw," by Saki (H. H. Munro), are among the best. Shirley Jackson's "The Lottery" is sure-fire, and will raise all kinds of questions for discussion and argument. Because of a TV program they had seen and that excited them, I once started reading my fifth graders William Golding's *Lord of the Flies*, thinking to read only a few chapters, but they made me read it to the end.

In my early fifth-grade classes the children usually were of high IQ, came from literate backgrounds and were generally felt to be succeeding in school. Yet it was astonishingly hard for most of those children to express themselves in speech or in writing. I have known a number of five-year olds who were considerably more articulate than most of the fifth graders I have known in school. Asked to speak, my fifth graders were covered with embarrassment; many refused altogether. Asked to write, they would sit for minutes on end, staring at the paper. It was hard for most of them to get down a half page of writing, even on what seemed to be interesting topics or topics they chose themselves.

In desperation I hit on a device that I named the Composition Derby. I divided the class into teams, and told them that when I said, "Go," they were to start writing something. It could be about anything they wanted, but it had to be about something—they couldn't just write "dog dog dog dog" on the paper. It could be true stories, descriptions of people or places or events, wishes, made-up stories, dreams—anything they liked. Spelling didn't count, so they didn't have to worry about it. When I said, "Stop," they were to stop and count up the words they had written. The team that wrote the most words would win the derby.

It was a success in many ways and for many reasons. The first surprise was that the two children who consistently wrote the most words were two of the least successful students in the class. They were bright, but they had always had a very hard time in school. Both were very bad spellers, and worrying about this had slowed down their writing without improving their spelling. When they were free of this worry and could let themselves go, they found hidden and unsuspected talents.

One of the two, a very driven and anxious little boy, used to write long adventures, or misadventures, in which I was the central character—"The Day Mr. Holt Went to Jail," "The Day Mr. Holt Fell Into the Hole," "The Day Mr. Holt Got Run Over," and so on. These were very funny, and the class enjoyed hearing me read them aloud. One day I asked the class to write a derby on a topic I would give them. They groaned; they liked picking their own. "Wait till you hear it," I said. "It's 'The Day the School Burned Down.' "

With a shout of approval and joy they went to work, and wrote furiously for 20 minutes or more, laughing and chuckling as they wrote. The papers were all much alike; in them the children danced around the burning building, throwing in books and driving me and the other teachers back in when we tried to escape.

In our first derby the class wrote an average of about ten words a minute; after a few months their average was over 20. Some of the slower writers tripled their output. Even the slowest, one of whom was the best student in the class, were writing 15 words a minute. More important, almost all the children enjoyed the derbies and wrote interesting things.

Some time later I learned that Professor I. S. Hayakawa, teaching freshman English, had invented a better technique. Every day in class he asked his students to write without stopping for about half an hour. They could write on whatever topic or topics they chose, but the important thing was not to stop. If they ran dry, they were to copy their last sentence over and over again until new ideas came. Usually they came before the sentence had been copied once. I use this idea in my own classes, and call this kind of paper a Non-Stop. Sometimes I ask students to write a Non-Stop on an assigned topic, more often on anything they choose. Once in a while I ask them to count up how many words they have written, though I rarely ask them to tell me; it is for their own information. Sometimes these papers are to be handed in; often they are what I call private papers, for the students' eyes alone.

The private paper has proved very useful. In the first place, in any English class—certainly any large English class—if the amount the students write is limited by what the teacher can find time to correct, or even to read, the students will not write nearly enough. The only remedy is to have them write a great deal that the teacher does not read. In the second place, students writing for themselves will write about many things that they would never write on a paper to be handed in, once they have learned (sometimes it takes a while) that the teacher means what he says about the papers' being private. This is important, not just because it enables them to get things off their chest, but also because they are most likely to write well, and to pay attention to how they write, when they are writing about something important to them.

Some English teachers, when they first hear about private papers, object that students do not benefit from writing papers unless the papers are corrected. I disagree for several reasons. First, most students, particularly poor students, do not read the corrections on their papers; it is boring, even painful. Second, even when they do read these corrections, they do not get much help from them, do not build the teacher's suggestions into their writing. This is true even when they really believe the teacher knows what he is talking about.

Third, and most important, we learn to write by writing, not by reading other people's ideas about writing. What most students need above all else is practice in writing, and particularly in writing about things that matter to them, so that they will begin to feel the satisfaction that comes from getting important thoughts down in words and will care about stating these thoughts forcefully and clearly.

Teachers of English—or, as some schools say (ugh!), Language Arts—spend a lot of time and effort on spelling. Most of it is wasted; it does little good, and often more harm than good. We should ask ourselves, "How do good spellers spell? What do they do when they are not sure which spelling of a word is right?" I have asked this of a number of good spellers. Their answer never varies. They do not rush for a dictionary or rack their brains trying to remember some rules. They write down the word both ways, or several ways, look at them and pick the one that looks best. Usually they are right.

Good spellers know what words look like and even, in their writing muscles, feel like. They have a good set of word images in their minds, and are willing to trust these images. The things we do to "teach" spelling to children do little to develop these skills or talents, and much to destroy them or prevent them from developing.

The first and worst thing we do is to make children anxious about spelling. We treat a misspelled word like a crime and penalize the misspeller severely; many teachers talk of making children develop a "spelling conscience," and fail otherwise excellent papers because of a few spelling mistakes. This is self-defeating. When we are anxious, we don't perceive clearly or remember what we once perceived. Everyone knows how hard it is to recall even simple things when under emotional pressure; the harder we rack our brains, the less easy it is to find what we are looking for. If we are anxious enough, we will not trust the messages that memory sends us. Many children spell badly because although their first hunches about how to spell a word may be correct, they are afraid to trust

them. I have often seen on children's papers a word correctly
spelled, then crossed out and misspelled.

There are some tricks that might help children get sharper word
images. Some teachers may be using them. One is the trick of air
writing; that is, of "writing" a word in the air with a finger and
"seeing" the image so formed. I did this quite a bit with fifth graders, using either the air or the top of a desk, on which their fingers
left no mark. Many of them were tremendously excited by this. I
can still hear them saying, "There's nothing there, but I can see
it!" It seemed like black magic. I remember that when I was little I
loved to write in the air. It was effortless, voluptuous, satisfying,
and it was fun to see the word appear in the air. I used to write
"Money Money Money," not so much because I didn't have any as
because I liked the way it felt, particularly that y at the end, with
its swooping tail.

Another thing to help sharpen children's image-making machinery is taking very quick looks at words—or other things.
The conventional machine for doing this is the tachistoscope. But
these are expensive, so expensive that most children can have few
chances to use them, if any at all. With some three-by-five and
four-by-eight file cards you can get the same effect. On the little
cards you put the words or the pictures that the child is going to
look at. You hold the larger card over the card to be read, uncover
it for a split second with a quick wrist motion, then cover it up
again. Thus you have a tachistoscope that costs one cent and that
any child can work by himself.

Once when substituting in a first-grade class, I thought that the
children, who were just beginning to read and write, might enjoy
some of the kind of free, nonstop writing that my fifth graders had.
One day about 40 minutes before lunch, I asked them all to take
pencil and paper and start writing about anything they wanted to.
They seemed to like the idea, but right away one child said anxiously, "Suppose we can't spell a word."

"Don't worry about it," I said. "Just spell it the best way you
can."

A heavy silence settled on the room. All I could see were still
pencils and anxious faces. This was clearly not the right approach.
So I said, "All right, I'll tell you what we'll do. Any time you want
to know how to spell a word, tell me and I'll write it on the
board."

They breathed a sigh of relief and went to work. Soon requests
for words were coming fast; as soon as I wrote one, someone asked
me another. By lunchtime, when most of the children were still
busily writing, the board was full. What was interesting was that

most of the words they had asked for were much longer and more complicated than anything in their reading books or workbooks. Freed from worry about spelling, they were willing to use the most difficult and interesting words that they knew.

The words were still on the board when we began school next day. Before I began to erase them, I said to the children, "Listen, everyone. I have to erase these words, but before I do, just out of curiosity, I'd like to see if you remember some of them."

The result was surprising. I had expected that the child who had asked for and used a word might remember it, but I did not think many others would. But many of the children still knew many of the words. How had they learned them? I suppose each time I wrote a word on the board a number of children had looked up, relaxed yet curious, just to see what the word looked like, and these images and the sound of my voice saying the word had stuck in their minds until the next day. This, it seems to me, is how children may best learn to write and spell.

What can a parent do if a school, or a teacher, is spoiling the language for a child by teaching it in some tired way? First, try to get them to change, or at least let them know that you are eager for change. Talk to other parents; push some of these ideas in the PTA; talk to the English department at the school; talk to the child's own teacher. Many teachers and schools want to know what the parents want.

If the school or teacher cannot be persuaded, then what? Perhaps all you can do is try not to let your child become too bored or discouraged or worried by what is happening in school. Help him meet the school's demands, foolish though they may seem, and try to provide more interesting alternatives at home—plenty of books and conversation, and a serious and respectful audience when a child wants to talk. Nothing that ever happened to me in English classes at school was as helpful to me as the long conversations I used to have every summer with my uncle, who made me feel that the difference in our ages was not important and that he was really interested in what I had to say.

At the end of her freshman year in college a girl I know wrote home to her mother, "Hooray! Hooray! Just think—I never have to take English any more!" But this girl had always been an excellent English student, had always loved books, writing, ideas. It seems unnecessary and foolish and wrong that English teachers should so often take what should be the most flexible, exciting, and creative of all school courses and make it into something that most children can hardly wait to see the last of. Let's hope that we can and soon will begin to do much better.

QUESTIONS

1. What are the major indictments Holt makes and what alternatives does he propose?
2. Here are two accounts of a young boy's going to school, the second a summary or précis of the first. Determine what has been removed from the original in the summary. Then write a short comparison of original and summary from Holt's educational point of view, as it can be inferred from his essay.

His days were rich in formal experience. Wearing overalls and an old sweater (the accepted uniform of the private seminary), he sallied forth at morn accompanied by a nurse or a parent and walked (or was pulled) two blocks to a corner where the school bus made a flag stop. This flashy vehicle was as punctual as death: seeing us waiting at the cold curb, it would sweep to a halt, open its mouth, suck the boy in, and spring away with an angry growl. It was a good deal like a train picking up a bag of mail. At school the scholar was worked on for six or seven hours by half a dozen teachers and a nurse, and was revived on orange juice in midmorning. In a cinder court he played games supervised by an athletic instructor, and in a cafeteria he ate lunch worked out by a dietitian.

—E. B. White, "Education"

His days followed a set routine. He wore overalls and an old sweater, as everyone else did in his school. In the morning, a parent or nurse walked the two blocks with him to the corner where he met the school bus. The bus was always on time. During the six or seven hours of the school day, he had six teachers. The school also employed a nurse and a dietitian. Games were supervised. The children ate in the cafeteria. Orange juice was served during the morning session.

—End-of-Year Examinations in English for college bound students grades 9-12, Commission on English.

HENRY F. OTTINGER
In Short, Why Did the Class Fail?[1]

And now, like it or not, I'd like to say a few parting words.

As you know, I began the semester in a way that departed from the manner in which I had taught composition classes in the past. Much of my attitude at that time was influenced by Jerry Farber's book, *The Student as Nigger*. On the first day of class, I read to you the following:

School is where you let the dying society put its trip on you. Our schools may seem useful: to make children into doctors, sociologists, engineers— to discover things. But they're poisonous as well. They exploit and enslave students; they petrify society; they make democracy unlikely. And it's not *what* you're taught that does the harm, but *how* you're taught. Our schools teach you by pushing you around, by stealing your will and your sense of power, by making timid, apathetic slaves of you—authority addicts.

That sounded like a breath of fresh air back in February—and I suggested that we try to break the mold, that we could write papers on any subject we wanted, that we could spend class time discussing things either "the burning issues of the day," or otherwise. You seemed to agree, and we spent a lot of time agreeing together that indeed Farber had *the* word and we would do what we could to break out of the mold.

As you know, things went from initial ecstasy to final catastrophe. And recently, I fell back—no, you forced me back—into assigning general topics. As a result of that action, and several other factors, this semester has been the worst I've ever taught. In fact, I even debated with myself whether or not to go on teaching next year. But in some ways the semester was valuable because I learned something, if you didn't.

Let me share with you some of the things I learned: and keep in mind that this does not apply to all of you, but it does to the majority.

I learned that all this bull about "getting it together" or "working together" (be it for peace or a grade) is just that—bull. The 1950's were labled by pop sociologists the "silent generation." I assure you they have nothing on you. Ten years ago, the people around the fountains wore saddle shoes and chinos, and had crewcuts. Now they're barefoot, wear Army fatigues, and have long hair. Big revelation: it's the same bunch of people.

Generally, this class has been the most silent, reticent, paranoid

1. This article was derived from a final lecture delivered in 1972 by Henry F. Ottinger, an instructor of English and a doctoral candidate at the University of Missouri. The text has been revised slightly by the author for this reprinting.

bunch of people in a group I have ever experienced. If you are indicative of the generation that's supposed to change things, good luck. Change is predicated on, among other things, communication between people, "which in your case," as the poem "Naming of Parts" goes, "you have not got."

You had an opportunity to exchange ideas (which it often turned out, "you have not got,") and you were too embarrassed to do so.

You had an opportunity to find out about each other—you didn't. (Or perhaps you found out some of the same things I did: if so, congratulations: the semester has not been a waste for you.)

You had an opportunity to find out something about yourselves. This, by the way, is the crux of education. And, as far as I can see, you found out very little.

You had an opportunity to explore ideas—on your own—and didn't. Most of the papers hashed over the usual cliché-ridden topics: abortion, the SST, the population explosion. One person went so far as to churn out a masterpiece on the pros and cons of fraternities, a topic that was really hot back around 1956.

Most of all, you had the opportunity to be free—free from the usual absurdities of a composition class where topics are assigned, thesis statements are submitted, and so on. You also had freedom of thought, as long as it was confined to the standards of formal English. You had the opportunity to be free—to be responsible to yourselves—and you succeeded in proving to me and to yourselves that Freedom is Slavery, a line from 1984 which I hope, for the sake of all of us, isn't prophetic.

But you protest! (Oh, how I wished you would): "We're incapable of handling all this freedom at once. You see, Mr. Ottinger, we've been conditioned; we're not used to all this!"

Well, I read that in Farber, too, and it's bull. Rats and dogs are conditioned, and are usually incapable of breaking that conditioning. Human beings *can* break conditioning, if it's to their advantage. But here, it's too good an excuse to say "I'm conditioned." Obviously, then, it's to your advantage *not* to break out of the mold.

Why is it to your advantage not to break the mold? In short, why did the class fail?

It failed because, as Dostoevski's "Underground Man" pointed out, thinking causes pain. And, like good little utilitarians, you want to avoid pain. No, it's much easier to come up with instant aesthetics, instant solutions, instant salvation, instant thoughts. After all, instant things, like breakfasts and TV dinners, are easily digestible —and easily regurgitated—and not terribly nourishing.

One of the more atrocious remarks I've heard this semester is, "Gosh, college is no fun," or, when an idea is presented, "it doesn't turn me on."

If you don't believe that knowledge for its own sake is a valid and valuable goal, then you are in the wrong place, and you'd do much better in a vocational school, studying how to be a plumber or a beautician. And if you don't believe, along with Ezra Pound, that "real education must ultimately be limited to men who INSIST on knowing," you are definitely in the wrong place. You are merely clutter.

Granted, there are problems within the University itself—serious problems—that, despite what you may think, show some sign of possible solution. One step they could take (but probably won't) is to limit enrollment, and keep the forty-five percent of you out who don't belong here, because it's no fun.

Well, it's time, I suppose, to bring this to a halt, and let you go over to the Union, or wherever. Until then, I invite you to listen to the lyrics of the Beatles' "Nowhere Man," and if it fits, take it to heart.

Last, I will bid a good-bye (until the final) and say that if at any time some sly hint, or clue, or (God forbid) a half-truth slipped out of my unconscious and slid out the corner of my mouth and, pardon the expression, "turned one of you on," then we have not failed, you and I.

And, to paraphrase Theodore Roethke: I love you for what you might be; I'm deeply disturbed by what you are.

Was It the Class, or Was It the Teacher— Who Failed?: Responses to Mr. Ottinger

WILLIAM BONDESON: The Romance of Teaching[1]

When a lover is spurned by his love, all the brightness is taken away and disillusionment sets in. I sense that is what has happened to you. I can't help but feel that you really do love those half-formed, recalcitrant, and ignorant young minds. And that passion is absolutely necessary for education. But like most lovers, and like all romantic educators, you have views about the objects of your love, those students of yours and mine, which are partially true but partially false as well. You believe that good educational intentions, simply of themselves, will produce similarly good intentions in others. You believe that spontaneity and impulse are exactly the same as freedom. You believe that every student has a self which, waiting loaded with potentialities and direction, requires only to be left alone in order to grow.

---

1. William Bondeson is director of the honors college and associate professor of philosophy at the University of Missouri.

Like most good things, a reply should begin with Plato. He says that when the young student of philosophy is to be educated, the first thing *not* to do is to expose him to the highest and most important principles, or, to use Plato's own analogy, it is unreasonable to expect someone who has long lived in darkness to immediately operate effectively when he is first exposed to broad daylight.

And this is just what you did when you tried to put those romantic half-truths into practice. In the name of freedom, you apparently abolished all structure, all restraint, and put the terrible burden of education upon the students themselves. In the ideal case there is much validity in doing this, but that's just the trouble with romantics. They assume that every case is the ideal case, act accordingly, and then become disillusioned when it turns out not to be that way. You seem to have forgotten that your composition course is required; that sets up some resistance to it automatically. If students are freed of one requirement, when all the others are retained, it is unreasonable to expect them to use that one bit of freedom in any other way than to spend more time doing the other required things.

Since I am not an expert in the teaching of English Composition I cannot give you any more suggestions, but I can point to a romantic principle which does not seem to be a part of your philosophy or at least one which you did not seem to put into effect. And this one is derived from Plato also. Romantics believe in the uniqueness and value of each individual; I suggest that you did not take that concept very seriously. If you had, you would not have imposed either radical authority or radical freedom on the members of your classes. You would have instead realized that college students are not all alike, that they come to college with very different reasons for being here and with consequently different expectations.

What about the seekers of instant gratification whom you so deservedly put down? First, they are not all the young; they are not even a major fraction of the young. But they are appreciated, if not emulated, by a very large number of our students. With you, I find it quite distressing that these students believe in the proposition "if it feels good, it's true." This is anti-intellectualism at its worst and is partly the result of their faulty concept of individualism.

JIM ESSENSON: A Student Describes the Slave System[2]

The student is probably the most intellectually conditioned animal in existence, and he suspects it least. In the same way that a small child is rewarded with an ice cream cone for being good, an

2. Jim Essenson is a student at New York University.

adept student quickly learns to "find out what the teacher wants" or expects from him in terms of work and intellectual participation (i.e., thinking).

The larger question which now presents itself is why are people interested solely in good grades. This query has wide sociological implications. American society is success, achievement, career oriented. Careers mean college, then graduate school with good grades as the catalyst. Unfortunately, this often means playing ball with the educational system and stifling individual initiative. You learn to find out what the teacher wants, to think it, to write it out, and to commit it to memory for the brief span of an examination period en route to that "A" and that graduate career.

You memorize information which has a staying power of thirty-six hours; you learn the intricacies of multiple-choice test-taking; you learn to question only in so far as the teacher demands or accepts it; you learn to interpret and to think only from your lecture notes.

Yes, Mr. Ottinger, we are slaves: slaves to SAT's, Regents, Merits, Co-ops, admissions tests and preconceived notions of success and fulfillment which permeate American society. When a student has all his academic life dealt with "cliché-ridden topics," as you call them, and has been told what to write, how many words, what aspect, and where to put his name on the paper, you cannot very well expect him to respond automatically to a plea of "O.K., here's the freedom you have asked for all along—write me a paper on anything."

MALCOLM L. DIAMOND: Self-Examination Must Begin with the Faculty[3]

The recent contribution from Mr. Ottinger was a sad example of faculty backlash. In teaching his composition course, he responded to what he felt to be current student desires by giving them complete freedom. Dispensing with a list of standard topics, he told them to write on anything that interested them. At the end of the term, he was utterly disillusioned. The students hadn't thought, and they hadn't been turned on.

In the context Mr. Ottinger's tough talk to his students is moralistic, like the tough talk of a father who tells a child with a handwashing compulsion to cut out that nonsense and get down to work. Mr. Ottinger writes as though he had never heard of Freud, Marx and other thinkers who have helped us to understand our conditioning.

3. Malcolm L. Diamond is professor of religion at Princeton.

As for self-knowledge, students may be reluctant to take a hard look at themselves, but so are faculty. The motivation of teachers is complex. It involves such laudable features as curiosity about the world and the desire to help students to learn about it. It also involves such natural drives as the search for status and other rewards of a successful career. One of these rewards is turning students on. Mr. Ottinger was clearly frustrated because he was open to students, gave them freedom, and still failed to turn them on.

Even in a stable period when students passively accept what is handed to them, faculty may tend to become disenchanted. This is even more likely when student agitation leads to faculty innovations. Mr. Ottinger's essay shrieks its message of betrayal.

Castigating students for unimaginativeness, laziness, and irresponsibility doesn't help education. It only encourages the students to play the same game of name-calling. They, in turn, castigate their professors for being smug, status-conscious and opportunistic.

PATRICIA REINFELD: The Instructor's Role Is to Guide Students[4]

When a teacher—supposedly older and wiser than his students —blames *them* en masse and in print for the failure of a class, that is very sad—for the teacher.

Has Mr. Ottinger never learned, in all his courses leading to the doctorate, that the *instructor* is the one responsible for the success —or failure—of a class? Surely he did not really believe that by totally freeing his composition students to talk and write about "any subject we wanted," they would know what to do or how to do it well?

Has Mr. Ottinger never learned about directed, or guided, freedom in the classroom through which the teacher unobtrusively moves things in the direction through which they must go? He blames his students for not thinking; it sounds on the contrary as if *he* took the vacation. And is it so horrible to assign general topics to (I assume) freshmen students, who need to become acquainted with, if not to master, particular kinds of writing?

Of course, it is much *easier* to say, in effect, "OK, kids, it's all yours"—and then blame those same kids when they don't make the class as stimulating and instructive as it should have been made *by the teacher.* This procedure also obviates the need for lesson planning and for sequential writing development. My goodness, Mr. Ottinger must have had so much free time this semester, once he put the responsibility on the students, that I wonder why he's complaining now.

4. Patricia Reinfeld is assistant professor of humanities at Gloucester County College, N.J.

HARVEY A. THOMSON: Teachers Must Create
Conditions for Growth[5]

Mr. Ottinger apparently attempted to design an English composition course in which students had complete responsibility for choosing what to work on and how to use class time during the term. The class failed and the article contains the substance of the instructor's final lecture, a ringing denunciation of the students. This article had a powerful impact on me because it was honest, expressed feelings, and described the author's actual experience rather than being abstract polemic.

Our methods of teaching rest on implicit assumptions about the nature of the students we teach. Mr. Ottinger experimented with a method which assumed that students were motivated toward achievement and knowledge, were responsible, and could regulate themselves to achieve the course objectives. The fact that they were Mr. Ottinger's objectives and not the students' limits the extent to which they were really "free," but that is not the main reason for the failure of the design.

My own experience with teaching this type of course is similar to Mr. Ottinger's. Most students have a great deal of difficulty handling this degree of autonomy in the classroom. But more important than this fairly predictable result is the way Mr. Ottinger and the class dealt with this problem.

Both parties seemed to feel frustrated and inadequate ("I even debated with myself whether or not to go on teaching next year") and responded by projecting the blame onto the other (or the "system" in the case of the students). While both parties probably have a point, I can't help feeling, from Mr. Ottinger's own account, that he bears a large part of the responsibility for the polarization that took place. He seems to be totally unaware of the ways in which he failed to be effective in the classroom and hence his own responsibility for what happened.

Classroom dynamics can be described in terms of teacher and student roles. Acceptable role behavior is normally agreed upon implicitly by both parties. However, the change in the ground rules in Mr. Ottinger's course meant that both students and the instructor had to learn to play their roles differently than they had been used to in the past.

5. Harvey A. Thomson is assistant professor of organization behavior at McGill University.

On Mind

HENRY DAVID THOREAU
Observation

There is no such thing as pure *objective* observation. Your observation, to be interesting, *i.e.* to be significant, must be *subjective*. The sum of what the writer of whatever class has to report is simply some human experience, whether he be poet or philosopher or man of science. The man of most science is the man most alive, whose life is the greatest event. Senses that take cognizance of outward things merely are of no avail. It matters not where or how far you travel—the farther commonly the worse—but how much alive you are. If it is possible to conceive of an event outside to humanity, it is not of the slightest significance, though it were the explosion of a planet. Every important worker will report what life there is in him. It makes no odds into what seeming deserts the poet is born. Though all his neighbors pronounce it a Sahara, it will be a paradise to him; for the desert which we see is the result of the barrenness of our experience. No mere willful activity whatever, whether in writing verses or collecting statistics, will produce true poetry or science. If you are really a sick man, it is indeed to be regretted, for you cannot accomplish so much as if you were well. All that a man has to say or do that can possibly concern mankind, is in some shape or other to tell the story of his love—to sing, and, if he is fortunate and keeps alive, he will be forever in love. This alone is to be alive to the extremities. It is a pity that this divine creature should ever suffer from cold feet; a still greater pity that the coldness so often reaches to his heart. I look over the report of the doings of a scientific association and am surprised that there is so little life to be reported; I am put off with a parcel of dry technical terms. Anything living is easily and naturally expressed in popular language. I cannot help suspecting that the life of these learned professors has been almost as inhuman and wooden as a rain-gauge or self-registering magnetic machine. They communicate no fact which rises to the temperature of blood-heat. It doesn't all amount to one rhyme.

JACOB BRONOWSKI

The Reach of Imagination

For three thousand years, poets have been enchanted and moved and perplexed by the power of their own imagination. In a short and summary essay I can hope at most to lift one small corner of that mystery; and yet it is a critical corner. I shall ask, What goes on in the mind when we imagine? You will hear from me that one answer to this question is fairly specific: which is to say, that we can describe the working of the imagination. And when we describe it as I shall do, it becomes plain that imagination is a specifically *human* gift. To imagine is the characteristic act, not of the poet's mind, or the painter's, or the scientist's, but of the mind of man.

My stress here on the word *human* implies that there is a clear difference in this between the actions of men and those of other animals. Let me then start with a classical experiment with animals and children which Walter Hunter thought out in Chicago about 1910. That was the time when scientists were agog with the success of Ivan Pavlov in forming and changing the reflex actions of dogs, which Pavlov had first announced in 1903. Pavlov had been given a Nobel prize the next year, in 1904; although in fairness I should say that the award did not cite his work on the conditioned reflex, but on the digestive gland.

Hunter duly trained some dogs and other animals on Pavlov's lines. They were taught that when a light came on over one of three tunnels out of their cage, that tunnel would be open; they could escape down it, and were rewarded with food if they did. But once he had fixed that conditioned reflex, Hunter added to it a deeper idea: he gave the mechanical experiment a new dimension, literally—the dimension of time. Now he no longer let the dog go to the lighted tunnel at once; instead, he put out the light, and then kept the dog waiting a little while before he let him go. In this way Hunter timed how long an animal can remember where he has last seen the signal light to his escape route.

The results were and are staggering. A dog or a rat forgets which one of three tunnels has been lit up within a matter of seconds—in Hunter's experiment, ten seconds at most. If you want such an animal to do much better than this, you must make the task much simpler: you must face him with only two tunnels to choose from. Even so, the best that Hunter could do was to have a dog remember for five minutes which one of two tunnels had been lit up.

I am not quoting these times as if they were exact and universal: they surely are not. Hunter's experiment, more than fifty years old now, had many faults of detail. For example, there were too few animals, they were oddly picked, and they did not all behave consistently. It may be unfair to test a dog for what he *saw*, when he commonly follows his nose rather than his eyes. It may be unfair to test any animal in the unnatural setting of a laboratory cage. And there are higher animals, such as chimpanzees and other primates, which certainly have longer memories than the animals that Hunter tried.

Yet when all these provisos have been made (and met, by more modern experiments) the facts are still startling and characteristic. An animal cannot recall a signal from the past for even a short fraction of the time that a man can—for even a short fraction of the time that a child can. Hunter made comparable tests with six-year-old children, and found, of course, that they were incomparably better than the best of his animals. There is a striking and basic difference between a man's ability to imagine something that he saw or experienced, and an animal's failure.

Animals make up for this by other and extraordinary gifts. The salmon and the carrier pigeon can find their way home as we cannot: they have, as it were, a practical memory that man cannot match. But their actions always depend on some form of habit: on instinct or on learning, which reproduce by rote a train of known responses. They do not depend, as human memory does, on calling to mind the recollection of absent things.

Where is it that the animal falls short? We get a clue to the answer, I think, when Hunter tells us how the animals in his experiment tried to fix their recollection. They most often pointed themselves at the light before it went out, as some gun dogs point rigidly at the game they scent—and get the name *pointer* from the posture. The animal makes ready to act by building the signal into its action. There is a primitive imagery in its stance, it seems to me; it is as if the animal were trying to fix the light on its mind by fixing it in its body. And indeed, how else can a dog mark and (as it were) name one of three tunnels, when he has no such words as *left* and *right*, and no such numbers as *one, two, three?* The directed gesture of attention and readiness is perhaps the only symbolic device that the dog commands to hold on to the past, and thereby to guide himself into the future.

I used the verb *to imagine* a moment ago, and now I have some ground for giving it a meaning. *To imagine* means to make images and to move them about inside one's head in new arrangements.

When you and I recall the past, we imagine it in this direct and homely sense. The tool that puts the human mind ahead of the animal is imagery. For us, memory does not demand the preoccupation that it demands in animals, and it lasts immensely longer, because we fix it in images or other substitute symbols. With the same symbolic vocabulary we spell out the future—not one but many futures, which we weigh one against another.

I am using the word *image* in a wide meaning, which does not restrict it to the mind's eye as a visual organ. An image in my usage is what Charles Peirce called a *sign*, without regard for its sensory quality. Peirce distinguished between different forms of signs, but there is no reason to make his distinction here, for the imagination works equally with them all, and that is why I call them all images.

Indeed, the most important images for human beings are simply words, which are abstract symbols. Animals do not have words, in our sense: there is no specific center for language in the brain of any animal, as there is in the human being. In this respect at least we know that the human imagination depends on a configuration in the brain that has only evolved in the last one or two million years. In the same period, evolution has greatly enlarged the front lobes in the human brain, which govern the sense of the past and the future; and it is a fair guess that they are probably the seat of our other images. (Part of the evidence for this guess is that damage to the front lobes in primates reduces them to the state of Hunter's animals.) If the guess turns out to be right, we shall know why man has come to look like a highbrow or an egghead: because otherwise there would not be room in his head for his imagination.

The images play out for us events which are not present to our senses, and thereby guard the past and create the future—a future that does not yet exist, and may never come to exist in that form. By contrast, the lack of symbolic ideas, or their rudimentary poverty, cuts off an animal from the past and the future alike, and imprisons him in the present. Of all the distinctions between man and animal, the characteristic gift which makes us human is the power to work with symbolic images: the gift of imagination.

This is really a remarkable finding. When Philip Sidney in 1580 defended poets (and all unconventional thinkers) from the Puritan charge that they were liars, he said that a maker must imagine things that are not. Halfway between Sidney and us, William Blake said, "What is now proved was once only imagined." About the same time, in 1796, Samuel Taylor Coleridge for the first time distinguished between the passive fancy and the active imagination, "the living Power and prime Agent of all human Perception." Now we see that they were right, and precisely right: the human gift is the gift of imagination—and that is not just a literary phrase.

Nor is it just a literary gift; it is, I repeat, characteristically human. Almost everything that we do that is worth doing is done in the first place in the mind's eye. The richness of human life is that we have many lives; we live the events that do not happen (and some that cannot) as vividly as those that do; and if thereby we die a thousand deaths, that is the price we pay for living a thousand lives. (A cat, of course, has only nine.) Literature is alive to us because we live its images, but so is any play of the mind—so is chess: the lines of play that we foresee and try in our heads and dismiss are as much a part of the game as the moves that we make. John Keats said that the unheard melodies are sweeter, and all chess players sadly recall that the combinations that they planned and which never came to be played were the best.

I make this point to remind you, insistently, that imagination is the manipulation of images in one's head; and that the rational manipulation belongs to that, as well as the literary and artistic manipulation. When a child begins to play games with things that stand for other things, with chairs or chessmen, he enters the gateway to reason and imagination together. For the human reason discovers new relations between things not by deduction, but by that unpredictable blend of speculation and insight that scientists call induction, which—like other forms of imagination—cannot be formalized. We see it at work when Walter Hunter inquires into a child's memory, as much as when Blake and Coleridge do. Only a restless and original mind would have asked Hunter's questions and could have conceived his experiments, in a science that was dominated by Pavlov's reflex arcs and was heading toward the behaviorism of John Watson.

Let me find a spectacular example for you from history. What is the most famous experiment that you had described to you as a child? I will hazard that it is the experiment that Galileo is said to have made in Sidney's age, in Pisa about 1590, by dropping two unequal balls from the Leaning Tower. There, we say, is a man in the modern mold, a man after our own hearts: he insisted on questioning the authority of Aristotle and St. Thomas Aquinas, and seeing with his own eyes whether (as they said) the heavy ball would reach the ground before the light one. Seeing is believing.

Yet seeing is also imagining. Galileo did challenge the authority of Aristotle, and he did look at his mechanics. But the eye that Galileo used was the mind's eye. He did not drop balls from the Leaning Tower of Pisa—and if he had, he would have got a very doubtful answer. Instead, Galileo made an imaginary experiment in his head, which I will describe as he did years later in the book he wrote after the Holy Office silenced him: the *Discorsi . . . intorno a due nuove scienze*, which was smuggled out to be printed in the Netherlands in 1638.

Suppose, said Galileo, that you drop two unequal balls from the tower at the same time. And suppose that Aristotle is right— suppose that the heavy ball falls faster, so that it steadily gains on the light ball, and hits the ground first. Very well. Now imagine the same experiment done again, with only one difference: this time the two unequal balls are joined by a string between them. The heavy ball will again move ahead, but now the light ball holds it back and acts as a drag or brake. So the light ball will be speeded up and the heavy ball will be slowed down; they must reach the ground together because they are tied together, but they cannot reach the ground as quickly as the heavy ball alone. Yet the string between them has turned the two balls into a single mass which is heavier than either ball—and surely (according to Aristotle) this mass should therefore move faster than either ball? Galileo's imaginary experiment has uncovered a contradiction; he says trenchantly, "You see how, from your assumption that a heavier body falls more rapidly than a lighter one, I infer that a (still) heavier body falls more slowly." There is only one way out of the contradiction: the heavy ball and the light ball must fall at the same rate, so that they go on falling at the same rate when they are tied together.

This argument is not conclusive, for nature might be more subtle (when the two balls are joined) than Galileo has allowed. And yet it is something more important: it is suggestive, it is stimulating, it opens a new view—in a word, it is imaginative. It cannot be settled without an actual experiment, because nothing that we imagine can become knowledge until we have translated it into, and backed it by, real experience. The test of imagination is experience. But then, that is as true of literature and the arts as it is of science. In science, the imaginary experiment is tested by confronting it with physical experience; and in literature, the imaginative conception is tested by confronting it with human experience. The superficial speculation in science is dismissed because it is found to falsify nature; and the shallow work of art is discarded because it is found to be untrue to our own nature. So when Ella Wheeler Wilcox died in 1919, more people were reading her verses than Shakespeare's; yet in a few years her work was dead. It had been buried by its poverty of emotion and its trivialness of thought: which is to say that it had been proved to be as false to the nature of man as, say, Jean Baptiste Lamarck and Trofim Lysenko[1] were false to the nature of inheritance. The strength of the imagination, its enriching power and excitement, lies in its interplay with reality— physical and emotional.

I doubt if there is much to choose here between science and the

1. Lamarck was a French biologist (1744–1829) who held that character- istics acquired by experience were bio- logically transmittable. Lysenko is a Russian biologist (1898–   ) who has held that hereditary properties of or- ganisms could be changed by manipu- lating the environment.

arts: the imagination is not much more free, and not much less free, in one than in the other. All great scientists have used their imagination freely, and let it ride them to outrageous conclusions without crying "Halt!" Albert Einstein fiddled with imaginary experiments from boyhood, and was wonderfully ignorant of the facts that they were supposed to bear on. When he wrote the first of his beautiful papers on the random movement of atoms, he did not know that the Brownian motion which it predicted could be seen in any laboratory. He was sixteen when he invented the paradox that he resolved ten years later, in 1905, in the theory of relativity, and it bulked much larger in his mind than the experiment of Albert Michelson and Edward Morley[2] which had upset every other physicist since 1881. All his life Einstein loved to make up teasing puzzles like Galileo's, about falling lifts and the detection of gravity; and they carry the nub of the problems of general relativity on which he was working.

Indeed, it could not be otherwise. The power that man has over nature and himself, and that a dog lacks, lies in his command of imaginary experience. He alone has the symbols which fix the past and play with the future, possible and impossible. In the Renaissance, the symbolism of memory was thought to be mystical, and devices that were invented as mnemonics (by Giordano Bruno, for example, and by Robert Fludd) were interpreted as magic signs. The symbol is the tool which gives man his power, and it is the same tool whether the symbols are images or words, mathematical signs or mesons. And the symbols have a reach and a roundness that goes beyond their literal and practical meaning. They are the rich concepts under which the mind gathers many particulars into one name, and many instances into one general induction. When a man says *left* and *right*, he is outdistancing the dog not only in looking for a light; he is setting in train all the shifts of meaning, the overtones and the ambiguities, between *gauche* and *adroit* and *dexterous*, between *sinister* and the sense of right. When a man counts *one, two, three*, he is not only doing mathematics; he is on the path to the mysticism of numbers in Pythagoras and Vitruvius and Kepler, to the Trinity and the signs of the Zodiac.

I have described imagination as the ability to make images and to move them about inside one's head in new arrangements. This is the faculty that is specifically human, and it is the common root from which science and literature both spring and grow and flourish together. For they do flourish (and languish) together; the great ages of science are the great ages of all the arts, because in

2. This was an experiment designed to measure the drag exerted on the passage of light by a hypothetical stationary medium. Its negative results eliminated the concept of a motionless, measurable ether and cleared the way for the development of the theory of relativity.

them powerful minds have taken fire from one another, breathless and higgledy-piggledy, without asking too nicely whether they ought to tie their imagination to falling balls or a haunted island. Galileo and Shakespeare, who were born in the same year, grew into greatness in the same age; when Galileo was looking through his telescope at the moon, Shakespeare was writing *The Tempest* and all Europe was in ferment, from Johannes Kepler to Peter Paul Rubens, and from the first table of logarithms by John Napier to the Authorized Version of the Bible.

Let me end with a last and spirited example of the common inspiration of literature and science, because it is as much alive today as it was three hundred years ago. What I have in mind is man's ageless fantasy, to fly to the moon. I do not display this to you as a high scientific enterprise; on the contrary, I think we have more important discoveries to make here on earth than wait for us, beckoning, at the horned surface of the moon. Yet I cannot belittle the fascination which that ice-blue journey has had for the imagination of men, long before it drew us to our television screens to watch the tumbling astronauts. Plutarch and Lucian, Ariosto and Ben Jonson wrote about it, before the days of Jules Verne and H. G. Wells and science fiction. The seventeenth century was heady with new dreams and fables about voyages to the moon. Kepler wrote one full of deep scientific ideas, which (alas) simply got his mother accused of witchcraft. In England, Francis Godwin wrote a wild and splendid work, *The Man in the Moone*, and the astronomer John Wilkins wrote a wild and learned one, *The Discovery of a New World*. They did not draw a line between science and fancy; for example, they all tried to guess just where in the journey the earth's gravity would stop. Only Kepler understood that gravity has no boundary, and put a law to it—which happened to be the wrong law.

All this was a few years before Isaac Newton was born, and it was all in his head that day in 1666 when he sat in his mother's garden, a young man of twenty-three, and thought about the reach of gravity. This was how he came to conceive his brilliant image, that the moon is like a ball which has been thrown so hard that it falls exactly as fast as the horizon, all the way round the earth. The image will do for any satellite, and Newton modestly calculated how long therefore an astronaut would take to fall round the earth once. He made it ninety minutes, and we have all seen now that he was right; but Newton had no way to check that. Instead he went on to calculate how long in that case the distant moon would take to round the earth, if indeed it behaves like a thrown ball that falls in the earth's gravity, and if gravity obeyed a law of inverse squares. He found that the answer would be twenty-eight days.

In that telling figure, the imagination that day chimed with nature, and made a harmony. We shall hear an echo of that harmony on the day when we land on the moon, because it will be not a technical but an imaginative triumph, that reaches back to the beginning of modern science and literature both. All great acts of imagination are like this, in the arts and in science, and convince us because they fill out reality with a deeper sense of rightness. We start with the simplest vocabulary of images, with *left* and *right* and *one, two, three*, and before we know how it happened the words and the numbers have conspired to make a match with nature: we catch in them the pattern of mind and matter as one.

QUESTIONS

1. How does the Hunter experiment provide Bronowski with the ground for defining the imagination?
2. Bronowski discusses the work of Galileo and Newton in the middle and at the end of his essay; what use does he make of their work? Does it justify placing them in the central and final positions?
3. On page 73 Bronowski attributes the imagination to a "configuration" in the brain. Configuration seems vague here; what else shows uncertainty about exactly what happens in the brain? Does this uncertainty compromise the argument of this essay?
4. What function is given to the mind by the title metaphor of reaching (later extended to symbols on page 76)? What words does Bronowski use to indicate the objects reached for? What is the significance of his selecting these words?

H. J. CAMPBELL

Pleasure-Seeking Brains: Artificial Tickles, Natural Joys of Thought

For some years now it has been known that animals will choose to press a lever repeatedly when the only thing that happens for their trouble is that they receive a very small amount of electricity in certain regions of the brain.

Rats engaged in this intracranial self-stimulation will press the lever so frequently and for so long that they drop to the floor of the cage with fatigue. After a little sleep, they awaken and immediately start to press the lever again.

When the electricity, by means of indwelling electrodes and a simple stimulator, goes to parts of the brain within what has been called the limbic system, the animal seems to want nothing else out of life. If it is a hungry animal, it will choose a lever for brain stimulation rather than a lever which it knows will provide food. More significantly, it will do this even if made thirsty, selecting brain stimulation rather than a source of water. Many other tests have shown that this kind of brain stimulation takes priority in the animal's behavior over any other kind of reward. It is not surprising, then, that the brain regions involved have been named the pleasure areas and that the lever-pressing is called pleasure-seeking.

I am a physiologist, concerned with normal functions, and the terrible compulsiveness of this pleasure-seeking behavior bothered me very much. It has led me, as I will show, to a new theory for explaining all behavior—or at least the behavior of animals ranging from fish to Man himself.

The presence of pleasure areas in the brain was discovered accidentally in 1954 by James Olds and Peter Milner in Canda. Since then many workers have demonstrated the same phenomenon in a variety of species—cats, dogs, sheep, dolphins, goldfish, monkeys and Man. The humans were mental patients o. Dr. Robert G. Heath at Tulane University School of Medicine. They were provided with a button they could press if they wanted to. And they did want to, often. When asked why they were pressing the button, the patients replied that it made them "feel good" and gave them a "happy feeling."

Notice especially that there is no question of an electric shock to the brain, in the ordinary sense of the term. The amount of electricity supplied is intended to be of the same order of magnitude as the charges naturally developed in the brain by cellular activity. A considerable amount of interesting and provocative theorizing has been going on about the meaning of intracranial self-stimulation responses. For me, the thought of humans acting this way engendered unease. When all is done and said about intracranial self-stimulation as a means of seeking pleasure, we are left with the persistent thought that this is not like any pleasure that we have experienced yet.

I have no doubt at all that experiments using the method of intracranial self-stimulation are of great value. But I do not believe that it is a *natural* form of behavior. It is unlikely that anyone else thinks it is natural, either. Yet no one seems to have asked what to me was a very obvious question—namely, how do the pleasure areas become activated in normal life?

Not only was the question obvious. So, too, was the answer. The way in which the pleasure areas of animals, including Man, are activated is via the senses. Clearly, nerve impulses that are generated at peripheral receptors pass into the central nervous system and reach (among other places) the limbic pleasure areas, thereby causing electrical activity in those regions. A quick ruffle through the anatomical literature showed that neural pathways which could subserve such a mechanism do indeed exist. The wires, so to speak, have been shown to be there, but nobody knew what they were for.

If those wires, those neural links between peripheral sense organs and limbic regions, were concerned in the production of pleasure, then certain things would inevitably follow. Almost by immediate inference, one could say that if I were right, then animals would press a lever (or do some other task) at their own volition, purely in order to obtain stimulation of peripheral sense organs. It should be possible to demonstrate peripheral self-stimulation. No electrodes in the brain, no electric currents to the brain, just stimulation of the eye or the ear or the skin or whatever.

The modern term for this sort of idea is almost certainly "way out." So I did the initial experiments at home, all alone, using an aquarium of tropical fish. I made a set of electrodelike goalposts that went into the water of the aquarium. A beam of light passed between the electrodes and fell upon a photocell. The photocell was rigged as a switch to a stimulator that would send a small pulse of electricity into the electrodes when the light beam was obscured. The electricity would, of course, pass through whatever was cutting off the light.

My hope was that the fish would, definitively, cut off the light. And this they did. Within minutes of setting up the apparatus, fish were swimming repetitively back and forth through the beam, getting each time a quantum of—what would you call it, stroking, tickling, caressing?

It was certainly not the light beam which attracted the fish, for when this was left on while the stimulator was switched off the animals swam through the beam no more than a chance number of times. Also, when the water contained a local anesthetic, they showed no interest in the apparatus even though the light and the stimulator were on. Would *you* enjoy being kissed after a tooth extraction with procaine?

These preliminary experiments encouraged me to go ahead with the project, using more sophisticated apparatus and a wider range of animals. I moved on to amphibians and reptiles, and found that newts and terrapins would seek out a source of electric current in the water. Most impressive, though, was the crocodile, for these creatures are well-known to be among the most sluggish kind.

The crocodile in my laboratory spends its time—for many hours on end—lying motionless on a stone slab. But when the goalpost-electrode assembly is put into its tank, the creature lumbers backwards and forwards between the electrodes about 50 times in 15 minutes. Sometimes, due to its largely immobile life, the crocodile becomes coated with green algae. It will not then respond to the electrodes until after its exterior has been scrubbed. The algae would seem to be forming an insulating layer over the skin receptors.

My next step was mammals, and I found that rabbits would press a lever for a longish flash of bright light. Moving on to primates, I tried the squirrel monkey. We have a capacitance rod, which looks and feels just like a piece of metal but is in fact a switch. This is connected to a stimulator that will activate a lamp whenever the rod is touched. The light goes out after five seconds unless the rod is released and touched again. When totally undeprived squirrel monkeys have had the rod pushed through the bars of their cage for a day or two for 15 minutes each day, they begin to reach through the bars and grab the rod before we can slide it in. As soon as they see the rod they begin to make happy, anticipatory chirping noises. They then touch the rod about 500 times in 15 minutes when a 750-watt bulb is the stimulus. With no light they touch the rod only about 20 times.

These experiments all show that peripheral and intracranial self-stimulation have much in common. One feature, however, is very different—and of great significance. It has been pointed out in many studies that a characteristic feature of intracranial self-stimulation is a lack of satiation: The animal never wants to stop pressing the lever. But with peripheral self-stimulation, all the animals tested, from fish to monkey, show a gradual decline in response rate down to zero when allowed the possibility to stimulate themselves indefinitely. This, surely, is much more like what happens in normal life.

While demonstrating the fact of peripheral self-stimulation from fish to monkey, I thought about its implications. There seemed no need to carry out any experiments with the highest primate: Even a brief glance at much human behavior reveals that it consists of a search for stimulation of the senses. Stimulus-seeking is by no means a new idea in psychology, or philosophy, but I developed a theory which establishes a neurological basis for stimulus-seeking—and indeed, I believe, for all animal behavior, at least from fish to Man.

We have seen that when the pleasure areas have electrodes in them, the animal is disinclined to engage in any behavior except lever-pressing for electrical stimulation of its brain. In peripheral self-stimulation, the animal obtains electrical activity in its pleasure areas by ensuring that sense organs generate nerve impulses which travel from the receptors to the limbic system. With this "natural" method, the animal does not continue indefinitely to ensure stimulation of a set of receptors. It does not, for example, go on and on eating, in order to make its taste buds act like electrodes in its brain.

We may ask why the animal reaches satiation. The answer is simply that all receptors exhibit a property known as "adaptation," which means that they cease to discharge impulses after a while even though the stimulus continues. Because of this property there comes a point in any pleasurable activity where continuance of the stimulus will *not* cause activation of the limbic pleasure areas. What seemed important to me about satiation, and which does not appear to have been given attention by other scientists, is that when an animal reaches satiation it does not stop behaving; it changes its behavior. Whereas intracranial self-stimulation is just one damned thing, peripheral self-stimulation (that is, natural behavior) is just one damned thing after another.

Thus it seems that we have here a neurological basis for the daily round of behavior—if we make just one assumption, which, sadly, can never be proved. The assumption is that in the course of evolution, when the nervous system reached a certain degree of complexity (at the moment we must start with the fish brain), the way in which it was put together demanded that the *pleasure areas be kept active*. Was this the "program" for the ancestral brain computer? If so, then much that has been vague and ill-defined about the animal kingdom and its history becomes readily explainable.

If we assume that animals, at least from fish to Man, *must*, in the sense defined, keep the limbic areas of the brain electrically activated, then we now know why animals behave and plants do not. We can explain Behavior as well as specific kinds of behavior, and we can now see the material basis of evolution, survival and extinction. In evolution, random genetic mutations have brought about gradual improvement of the motor system and nervous system, so that animals have become more competent at finding and manipulating the sensory stimuli available in the environment. Some animals found pleasure (that is, activation of parts of the limbic system) by stimulating their receptors in ways which were biologically disadvantageous: They became *extinct*. Others were spawned in an environment that, in a sense, was akin to the intracranial electrodes, conforming in near-perfection to the ancestral command, the intrinsic "program." Such animals exhibit remarkably slow evolution; why should they change their form or seek new sensory pastures? Still other animals chose advantageous means of seeking pleasure and also survived. From them evolved humankind, an animal with no fixed ecological niche, still motivated to wander and spread and explore the sensory surroundings and still, let us hope, to evolve.

But with the evolution of the human brain a very significant advance occurred. Few people doubt that Man is the highest animal. Fewer still could say in realistic, nonemotional terms why they believe this. Theories such as the notion of Man as the only creature to make tools on a systematic basis have fallen by the wayside, plagued with qualifications.

Many would take refuge in saying that the human brain shows the most complex structure, having that enormous amount of convoluted cerebral cortex. Numerous others would point to Man's works, his institutions, laws, religions and his overwhelmingly superior power to tamper with his environment. Caught up in both of these concepts is a rather tremulous adumbration of Man's uniqueness in being rational. Those who closely live and work with lower animals, especially but not exclusively with primates (do you own a dog?), have grave cause to doubt Man's prerogative of reasoning. And, pitifully, many who work closely with people doubt it too. What, then, is *human* behavior?

According to many experts, the experiments on peripheral self-stimulation carried out so far leave no sensible doubt that the neural mechanism of pleasure-seeking, of activating these limbic areas, requires no more complexity than the very simple brain of a fish. Obviously, with such a simple brain, there can be only simple pleasures. Equally obviously, even with a much more complex brain and much more complex sensory pleasures, the essential fundamental mechanism of action must be the same as that of a fish or a terrapin or a crocodile.

When people engage in a behavior that is a source of pleasure solely, or predominantly, because it stimulates their sense organs, then they are using their complex brains, that "enormous amount of convoluted cortex" to enable them to do what a fish or a crocodile does, only to do it much better—though possibly more expensively and harmfully. Should there be any people whose behavior is totally sensorially oriented, then they are not human, inasmuch as their behavior is, stripping off the technological veneer, the same as my monkeys or my fish. It is unlikely that such people exist. In the real world, we can say that the extent to which an individual's pleasure is obtained solely from the senses is the extent to which that individual is subhuman. Hard words. But these are hard times and we must face what seems to be the truth.

What behavior, then, is uniquely human? My theory is this, and you may take it or leave it at your own peril. It was said previously that a very significant advance occurred in the evolution of the human brain. It is this advance, and this advance only, which distinguishes some people almost all of the time and most people some of the time from the lower animals.

Neuroanatomists and some electrophysiologists have demonstrated that neural pathways exist between the cortical thinking regions of the brain and the limbic system and that nerve impulses flow downwards from the higher to the lower regions. We can now draw a distinct materialistic, nonreligious, nonphilosophical line between human and nonhuman behavior. Human behavior—meaning that not found in lower animals—is behavior that causes activation of the limbic pleasure regions of the brain, *not* as a result, primarily, of the sense organs, but primarily as activity of the brain's thinking regions. We all know that some people derive pleasure from non-sensory activity. Some of us are fortunate enough to be among the group who can have fun with mathematics or philosophy or science or languages or chess or crossword puzzles or reveries or anticipation or anything else that prompts us to behave without actually stimulating the sense organs, except, perhaps, adventitiously, as in music. When we are doing those things, those *thinking* kinds of things, we are being human. For, as far as we now know, the lower animals do not engage in behavior such that the process of thought is the reward. Only in the human brain can thinking activate the limbic pleasure areas.

It is pleasure-by-thinking that separates humans from lower animals. It is not true that the apes are nearest to us, unless we are overawed by anatomy. When a man is drinking bourbon he is no nearer to the ape than the fish. And whatever the ape does, he is as near to fish as to Man.

Usually it will be found upon analysis that unsuitable human behavior is firmly based upon materialistic, sensory objectives. Magic evolved into religion because of this. The main teaching of all major religions is, in effect, to moderate the sensory pleasures and give more importance to thinking, to be less subhuman and more human. In Oriental religions contemplation takes pride of place. Legal systems, which are uniquely human institutions, are essentially involved with reducing, by penalty, behavior based upon sensory pleasure-seeking.

Sexual mores in their multiplicity reflect the gigantic role that sexual behavior plays in the lives of people, as compared with lower animals. Whereas with lower animals sex is merely a part of life, it often dominates the human scene, so that some subscribe to the Freudian idea that "everything is sex." Since Man can turn his superior sensorimotor abilities to great account, he has made sex the most potent source of sensory pleasure, involving many more kinds of peripheral receptors than any animal uses. It is unlikely that any other form of behavior focuses so great a barrage of nerve impulses into the limbic areas of the brain.

There are many other implications of this theory which throw light upon the present state of Man. The direction of the arts towards abstraction, classical music towards mathematical design, architecture towards rhythmic functionalism; the occurrence of psychedelic predilections in the immature, the rise of vandalism and delinquency among juveniles, the mass hypnosis of the sensory communication media—all of these would bear an appraisal from the point of view of the new theory. But what of the future? Is the new theory one which implies hope or doom?

If I am right, evolution is moving with its traditional unalterable irrevocability towards a thinking organism rather than a feeling organism. Gradually, Man's brain structure and function are slowly changing, independently of his institutions, political systems and ideologies. Survival of the fittest applies, now, not to the sensorimotor people but to the thinking people. Natural selection is working in favor of mind, not muscle. Therefore Man's biological destiny is eventually to be fully distinguishable from the lower animals, by virtue of his behavior being totally directed to activating the limbic pleasure areas by exercising his capacity for thought, using his sense organs as ancillaries to mental phenomena. Each of us must decide whether that is cause for hope or despair.

If we take hope in it, then we do not have to wait for random mutations. The brain can be changed by experience as well. By recognizing what is human and what is subhuman behavior we can exert pressures upon ourselves and upon those around us, especially our children, to choose the human way of doing things. If we teach that the destruction of property—in the name of whatever freedom—is apelike sensation-seeking, if we show by preaching and preeminently by example that the rich store of human civilized treasures of the mind form the birthright of human people—if we do all this and more of its kind, we might well speed the course of Man's evolution. For whether or not a given *individual* is human or subhuman depends upon what has happened to him, not upon his genes. It depends upon the values and philosophy of life built into the potentially human brain with which he was born, wherever he happened to be born, whatever his color.

The laws of biology, I believe, are taking care of Man's evolution, with or without his help. But if we are really going to take the future seriously, it would be erroneous to continue with our totally man-centered anxieties alone. We have seen that the basic mechanism of behavior is present in the simple neural organization of the fish brain. There is no reason to believe that there is anything special about fish. Even lower animals, the invertebrates, seek their simple pleasures. We cannot rationally believe that the evolutionary processes that resulted in Man are not also at work in other animal hierarchies.

What will happen, do you suppose, when, millennia from now, some kind of activity in the higher centers causes activation of the pleasure areas in the brain of the octopus? We are not alone upon this planet. Nor has evolution ceased.

JEROME S. BRUNER
Freud and the Image of Man

By the dawn of the sixth century before Christ, the Greek physicist-philosophers had formulated a bold conception of the physical world as a unitary material phenomenon. The Ionians had set forth a conception of matter as fundamental substance, transformation of which accounted for the myriad forms and substances of the physical world. Anaximander was subtle enough to recognize that matter must be viewed as a generalized substance, free of any particular sensuous properties. Air, iron, water or bone were only elaborated forms, derived from a more general stuff. Since that time, the phenomena of the physical world have been conceived as continuous and monistic, as governed by the common laws of matter. The view was a bold one, bold in the sense of running counter to the immediate testimony of the senses. It has served as an axiomatic basis of physics for more than two millennia. The bold view eventually became the obvious view, and it gave shape to our common understanding of the physical world. Even the alchemists rested their case upon this doctrine of material continuity and, indeed, had they known about neutron bombardment, they might even have hit upon the proper philosopher's stone.

The good fortune of the physicist—and these matters are always relative, for the material monism of physics may have impeded nineteenth-century thinking and delayed insights into the nature of complementarity in modern physical theory—this early good fortune or happy insight has no counterpart in the sciences of man. Lawful continuity between man and the animal kingdom, between dreams and unreason on one side and waking rationality on the other, between madness and sanity, between consciousness and unconsciousness, between the mind of the child and the adult mind, between primitive and civilized man—each of these has been a cherished discontinuity preserved in doctrinal canons. There were voices in each generation, to be sure, urging the exploration of continuities. Anaximander had a passing good approximation to a theory of evolution based on natural selection; Cornelius Agrippa offered a plausible theory of the continuity of mental health and disease in terms of bottled-up sexuality. But Anaximander did not prevail against Greek conceptions of man's creation nor did Cornelius Agrippa against the demonopathy of the *Malleus Maleficarum*.[1] Neither in establishing the continuity between the varied states of man nor in pursuing the continuity between man and animal was there conspicuous success until the nineteenth century.

1. A notorious book about demons and witchcraft.

I need not insist upon the social, ethical, and political significance of an age's image of man, for it is patent that the view one
takes of man affects profoundly one's standard of dignity and the
humanly possible. And it is in the light of such a standard that we
establish our laws, set our aspirations for learning, and judge the
fitness of men's acts. Those who govern, then, must perforce be jeal-
ous guardians of man's ideas about man, for the structure of government rests upon an uneasy consensus about human nature and
human wants. Since the idea of man is of the order of *res publica*,[2]
it is an idea not subject to change without public debate. Nor is it
simply a matter of public concern. For man as individual has a deep
and emotional investment in his image of himself. If we have
learned anything in the last half-century of psychology, it is that
man has powerful and exquisite capacities for defending himself
against violation of his cherished self-image. This is not to say that
Western man has not persistently asked: "What is man that thou
art mindful of him?" It is only that the question, when pressed,
brings us to the edge of anxiety where inquiry is no longer free.

Two figures stand out massively as the architects of our present-
day conception of man: Darwin and Freud. Freud's was the more
daring, the more revolutionary, and in a deep sense, the more poetic
insight. But Freud is inconceivable without Darwin. It is both
timely and perhaps historically just to center our inquiry on Freud's
contribution to the modern image of man. Darwin I shall treat as a
necessary condition for Freud and for his success, recognizing, of
course, that this is a form of psychological license. Not only is it the
centenary of Freud's birth;[3] it is also a year in which the current of
popular thought expressed in commemoration of the date quickens
one's awareness of Freud's impact on our times.

Rear-guard fundamentalism did not require a Darwin to slay it in
an age of technology. He helped, but this contribution was trivial in
comparison with another. What Darwin had done was to propose a
set of principles unified around the conception that all organic species had their origins and took their form from a common set of circumstances—the requirements of biological survival. All living creatures were on a common footing. When the post-Darwin era of
exaggeration had passed and religious literalism had abated into a
new nominalism, what remained was a broad, orderly, and unitary
conception of organic nature, a vast continuity from the monocellu-
lar protozoans to man. Biology had at last found its unifying principle in the doctrine of evolution. Man was not unique but the inher-
itor of an organic legacy.

As the summit of an evolutionary process, man could still view
himself with smug satisfaction, indeed proclaim that God or Nature
had shown a persistent wisdom in its effort to produce a final, per-

2. The state.   3. 1956.

88 · *Jerome S. Bruner*

fect product. It remained for Freud to present the image of man as the unfinished product of nature: struggling against unreason, impelled by driving inner vicissitudes and urges that had to be contained if man were to live in society, host alike to seeds of madness and majesty, never fully free from an infancy anything but innocent. What Freud was proposing was that man at his best and man at his worst is subject to a common set of explanations: that good and evil grow from a common process.

Freud was strangely yet appropriately fitted for his role as architect of a new conception of man. We must pause to examine his qualifications, for the image of man that he created was in no small measure founded on his painfully achieved image of himself and of his times. We are concerned not so much with his psychodynamics, as with the intellectual traditions he embodies. A child of his century's materialism, he was wedded to the determinism and the classical physicalism of nineteenth-century physiology so boldly represented by Helmholtz. Inded, the young Freud's devotion to the exploration of anatomical structures was a measure of the strength of this inheritance. But at the same time, as both Lionel Trilling and W. H. Auden have recognized with much sensitivity, there was a deep current of romanticism in Freud—a sense of the role of impulse, of the drama of life, of the power of symbolism, of ways of knowing that were more poetic than rational in spirit, of the poet's cultural alienation. It was perhaps this romantic's sense of drama that led to his gullibility about parental seduction and to his generous susceptibility to the fallacy of the dramatic instance.

Freud also embodies two traditions almost as antithetical as romanticism and nineteenth-century scientism. He was profoundly a Jew, not in a doctrinal sense but in his conception of morality, in his love of the skeptical play of reason, in his distrust of illusion, in the form of his prophetic talent, even in his conception of mature eroticism. His prophetic talent was antithetic to a Utopianism either of innocence or of social control. Nor did it lead to a counsel of renunciation. Free oneself of illusion, of neurotic infantilism, and "the soft voice of intellect" would prevail. Wisdom for Freud was neither doctrine nor formula, but the achievement of maturity. The patient who is cured is the one who is now free enough of neurosis to decide intelligently about his own destiny. As for his conception of mature love, it has always seemed to me that its blend of tenderness and sensuality combined the uxorious imagery of the Chassidic tradition and the sensual quality of the Song of Songs. And might it not have been Freud rather than a commentator of the Haftorahs[4] who said, "In children it was taught, God gives humanity a chance to make good its mistakes." For the modern trend of

4. The Old Testament Prophets.

permissiveness toward children is surely a feature of the Freudian legacy.

But for all the Hebraic quality, Freud is also in the classical tradition—combining the Stoics and the great Greek dramatists. For Freud as for the Stoics, there is no possibility of man disobeying the laws of nature. And yet, it is in this lawfulness that for him the human drama inheres. His love for Greek drama and his use of it in his formulation are patent. The sense of the human tragedy, the inevitable working out of the human plight—these are the hallmarks of Freud's case histories. When Freud, the tragic dramatist, becomes a therapist, it is not to intervene as a directive authority. The therapist enters the drama of the patient's life, makes possible a play within a play, the transference, and when the patient has "worked through" and understood the drama, he has achieved the wisdom necessary for freedom. Again, like the Stoics, it is in the recognition of one's own nature and in the acceptance of the laws that govern it that the good life is to be found.

Freud's contribution lies in the continuities of which he made us aware. The first of these is the continuity of organic lawfulness. Accident in human affairs was no more to be brooked as "explanation" than accident in nature. The basis for accepting such an "obvious" proposition had, of course, been well prepared by a burgeoning nineteenth-century scientific naturalism. It remained for Freud to extend naturalistic explanation to the heart of human affairs. The *Psychopathology of Everyday Life* is not one of Freud's deeper works, but "the Freudian slip" has contributed more to the common acceptance of lawfulness in human behavior than perhaps any of the more rigorous and academic formulations from Wundt to the present day. The forgotten lunch engagement, the slip of the tongue, the barked shin could no longer be dismissed as accident. Why Freud should have succeeded where the novelists, philosophers, and academic psychologists had failed we will consider in a moment.

Freud's extension of Darwinian doctrine beyond Haeckel's theorem that ontogeny recapitulates phylogeny is another contribution to continuity. It is the conception that in the human mind, the primitive, infantile, and archaic exist side-by-side with the civilized and evolved.

Where animals are concerned we hold the view that the most highly developed have arisen from the lowest. . . . In the realm of mind, on the other hand, the primitive type is so commonly preserved alongside the transformations which have developed out of it that it is superfluous to give instances in proof of it. When this happens, it is usually the result of a bifurcation in development. One quantitative part of an attitude or an impulse has survived unchanged while another has undergone further development. This brings us very close to the more general problem of conservation in the mind. . . . Since the time when we recognized the

error of supposing that ordinary forgetting signified destruction or annihilation of the memory-trace, we have been inclined to the opposite view
that nothing once formed in the mind could ever perish, that everything
survives in some way or other, and is capable under certain conditions
of being brought to light again . . . (Freud, *Civilization and Its Discon-
tents*, pp. 14–15).

What has now come to be common sense is that in everyman there
is the potentiality for criminality, and that these are neither accidents nor visitations of degeneracy, but products of a delicate balance of forces that, under different circumstances, might have produced normality or even saintliness. Good and evil, in short, grow
from a common root.

Freud's genius was in his resolution of polarities. The distinction
of child and adult was one such. It did not suffice to reiterate that
the child was father to the man. The theory of infantile sexuality
and the stages of psychosexual development were an effort to fill the
gap, the latter clumsy, the former elegant. Though the alleged progression of sexual expression from the oral, to the anal, to the phal-
lic, and finally to the genital has not found a secure place either in
common sense or in general psychology, the developmental continuity of sexuality has been recognized by both. Common sense honors
the continuity in the baby-books and in the permissiveness with
which young parents of today resolve their doubts. And the research
of Beach and others has shown the profound effects of infantile
experience on adult sexual behavior—even in lower organisms.

If today people are reluctant to report their dreams with the
innocence once attached to such recitals, it is again because Freud
brought into common question the discontinuity between the
rational purposefulness of waking life and the seemingly irrational
purposelessness of fantasy and dream. While the crude symbolism
of Freud's early efforts at dream interpretation has come increasingly to be abandoned—that telephone poles and tunnels have an
invariant sexual reference—the conception of the dream as representing disguised wishes and fears has become common coin. And
Freud's recognition of deep unconscious processes in the creative
act, let it also be said, has gone far toward enriching our understanding of the kinship between the artist, the humanist, and the man of
science.

Finally, it is our heritage from Freud that the all-or-none distinction between mental illness and mental health has been replaced
by a more humane conception of the continuity of these states. The
view that neurosis is a severe reaction to human trouble is as revolutionary in its implications for social practice as it is daring in formulation. The "bad seed" theories, the nosologies of the nineteenth
century, the demonologies and doctrines of divine punishment—

none of these provided a basis for compassion toward human suffering comparable to that of our time.

One may argue, at last, that Freud's sense of the continuity of human conditions, of the likeness of the human plight, has made possible a deeper sense of the brotherhood of man. It has in any case tempered the spirit of punitiveness toward what once we took as evil and what we now see as sick. We have not yet resolved the dilemma posed by these two ways of viewing. Its resolution. is one of the great moral challenges of our age.

Why, after such initial resistance, were Freud's views so phenomenally successful in transforming common conceptions of man?

One reason we have already considered: the readiness of the Western world to accept a naturalistic explanation of organic phenomena and, concurrently, to be readier for such explanation in the mental sphere. There had been at least four centuries of uninterrupted scientific progress, recently capped by a theory of evolution that brought man into continuity with the rest of the animal kingdom. The rise of naturalism as a way of understanding nature and man witnessed a corresponding decline in the explanatory aspirations of religion. By the close of the nineteenth century, religion, to use Morton White's phrase, "too often agreed to accept the role of a non-scientific spiritual grab-bag, or an ideological know-nothing." The elucidation of the human plight had been abandoned by religion and not yet adopted by science.

It was the inspired imagery, the proto-theory of Freud that was to fill the gap. Its success in transforming the common conception of man was not simply its recourse to the "cause-and-effect" discourse of science. Rather it is Freud's imagery, I think, that provides the clue to this ideological power. It is an imagery of necessity, one that combines the dramatic, the tragic, and the scientific views of necessity. It is here that Freud's intellectual heritage matters so deeply. Freud's is a theory or a proto-theory peopled with actors. The characters are from life: the blind, energic, pleasure-seeking id; the priggish and punitive super-ego; the ego, battling for its being by diverting the energy of the others to its own use. The drama has an economy and a terseness. The ego develops canny mechanisms for dealing with the threat of id impulses: denial, projection, and the rest. Balances are struck between the actors, and in the balance is character and neurosis. Freud was using the dramatic technique of decomposition, the play whose actors are parts of a single life. It is a technique that he himself had recognized in fantasies and dreams, one he honored in "The Poet and the Daydream."

The imagery of the theory, moreover, has an immediate resonance with the dialectic of experience. True, it is not the stuff of superficial conscious experience. But it fits the human plight, its conflictedness, its private torment, its impulsiveness, its secret and frightening urges, its tragic quality.

Concerning its scientific imagery, it is marked by the necessity of the classical mechanics. At times the imagery is hydraulic: suppress this stream of impulses, and perforce it breaks out in a displacement elsewhere. The system is a closed and mechanical one. At times it is electrical, as when cathexes are formed and withdrawn like electrical charges. The way of thought fitted well the common-sense physics of its age.

Finally, the image of man presented was thoroughly secular; its ideal type was the mature man free of infantile neuroticism, capable of finding his own way. This freedom from both Utopianism and asceticism has earned Freud the contempt of ideological totalitarians of the Right and the Left. But the image has found a ready home in the rising, liberal intellectual middle class. For them, the Freudian ideal type has become a rallying point in the struggle against spiritual regimentation.

I have said virtually nothing about Freud's equation of sexuality and impulse. It was surely and still is a stimulus to resistance. But to say that Freud's success lay in forcing a reluctant Victorian world to accept the importance of sexuality is as empty as hailing Darwin for his victory over fundamentalism. Each had a far more profound effect.

Can Freud's contribution to the common understanding of man in the twentieth century be likened to the impact of such great physical and biological theories as Newtonian physics and Darwin's conception of evolution? The question is an empty one. Freud's mode of thought is not a theory in the conventional sense, it is a metaphor, an analogy, a way of conceiving man, a drama. I would propose that Anaximander is the proper parallel: his view of the connectedness of physical nature was also an analogy—and a powerful one. Freud is the ground from which theory will grow, and he has prepared the twentieth century to nurture the growth. But far more important, he has provided an image of man that has made him comprehensible without at the same time making him contemptible.

Signs of the Times

VERTA MAE
The Kitchen Crisis

AUTHOR'S NOTE:
i do not consider myself a writer, i am a rapper. therefore do not read this piece silently . . . rap it aloud.

there is confusion in the kitchen!
we've got to develop kitchen consciousness or we may very well see the end of kitchens as we now know them. kitchens are getting smaller. in some apts the closet is bigger than the kitchen. something that i saw the other day leads me to believe that there may well be a subversive plot to take kitchens out of the home and put them in the street. i was sitting in the park knitting my old man a pair of socks for next winter when a tall well dressed man in his mid thirties sat next to me.
i didnt pay him no mind until he went into his act.
he pulled his irish linen hankie from his lapel, spread it on his lap, opened his attache case, took out a box, popped a pill, drank from his thermos jug, and turned and offered the box to me. thank you no said i. "i never eat with strangers."
that would have been all except that i am curious black and i looked at the label on the box, then i screamed. the box said INSTANT LUNCH PILL: (imitation ham and cheese on rye, with diet cola, and apple pie flavor). i sat frozen while he did his next act. he folded his hankie, put it back in his lapel, packed his thermos jug away, and took out a piece of yellow plastic and blew into it, in less than 3 minutes it had turned into a yellow plastic castro convertible couch.
enough is enough i thought to myself. so i dropped the knitting and ran like hell. last i saw of that dude he was stretched out on the couch reading portnoys complaint.
the kitchens that are still left in the home are so instant they might as well be out to lunch.
instant milk, instant coffee, instant tea, instant potatoes, instant old

93

fashioned oatmeal, everything is preprepared for the unprepared woman in the kitchen. the chicken is pre cut. the flour is pre measured, the rice is minute, the salt is pre seasoned, and the peas are pre buttered. just goes to show you white folks will do anything for their women. they had to invent instant food because the servant problem got so bad that their women had to get in the kitchen herself with her own two little lily white hands. it is no accident that in the old old south where they had slaves that they was eating fried chicken, coated with batter, biscuits so light they could have flown across the mason dixon line if they had wanted to. they was eating pound cake that had to be beat 800 strokes. who do you think was doing this beating?

it sure wasnt missy. missy was beating the upstairs house nigger for not bringing her mint julep quick enough.

massa was out beating the field niggers for not hoeing the cotton fast enough. meanwhile up in the north country where they didnt have no slaves to speak of they was eating baked beans and so called new england boiled dinner.

it aint no big thing to put everything in one pot and let it cook. missy wasnt about to go through changes and whup no pound cake for 800 strokes.

black men and black women have been whipping up fine food for centuries and outside of black bottom pie and nigger toes there is no reference to our contribution and participation in and to the culinary arts.

when they do mention our food they act like it is some obscure thing that niggers down south made up and dont nobody else in the world eat it.

food aint nothing but food.

food is universal.

everybody eats.

a potato is a patata and not irish as white folks would have you believe. watermelons is prehistoric and eaten all ober de world.

the russians make a watermelon beer. in the orient they dry and roast and salt the seeds. when old chris got here the indians was eating hominy grits. and before he "discovered" this country the greeks and romans were smacking on collard greens. blackeyed peas aint nothing but dried cow peas whose name in sanskrit traces its lineage back to the days before history was recorded. uh ah excuse me boss, means befo you-all was recording history. uh ah i know this is hard for you to believe suh but i got it from one of yo history books and i know you-all wouldnt talk with no forked tongue about history.

the cooking of food is one of the highest of all the human arts. we need to develop food consciousness.

so called enlightened people will rap for hours about jean paul sartre, campus unrest, the feminine mystique, black power, and tania, but mention food and they say, rather proudly too, "i'm a bad cook." some go so far as to boast "i cant even boil water without burning it."

that is a damn shame.

bad cooks got a bad life style.

food is life.

food changes up into blood, blood into cells, cells into energy, energy changes up into the forces which make up your life style.

so if one takes a creative, imaginative, loving, serious attitude toward life everything one does will reflect one attitude hence when one cooks this attitude will be served at the table. and it will be good.

so bad cooks got a bad life style and i dont mean bad like we (blacks) mean bad i mean bad bad.

come on give a damn. anybody can get it together for vacation. change up and daily walk through kitchen life like you was on an endless holiday. aint no use to save yourself for vacation. it's here now.

make every and each moment count like time was running out. that will cool out that matter of guess who is coming to dinner and make it a fact that DINNER IS SERVED.

one of the best meals i was ever served was at my friend bella's. bella served an elegant meal in her two room cold water tub in kitchen six story walk up flat. she had a round oak table with carved legs, covered with a floor length off white shaker lace tablecloth. in the center was a carved african gourd filled with peanuts, persimmons, lemons and limes. to start off we had fresh squeezed tangerine juice in chilled champagne glasses. then scrambled eggs, sliced red onions marinated in lemon juice and pickapeppa sauce, fried green tomatoes, on cobalt blue china plates. hot buttermilk biscuits with homemade apple jelly on limoges saucers (bella got them from goodwill for 10 cent a piece) and fresh ground bustelo coffee served in mugs that bella made in pottery class at the neighborhood anti poverty pro community cultural workshop for people in low socio economic ethnic groups.

you are what you eat.

i was saying that a long time before the movie came out but it doesnt bother me that they stole my line. white folks are always stealing and borrowing and discovering and making myths. you take terrapins. diamondback terrapins. the so called goremays squeal with epicurean delight at the very mention of the word. there is a mystique surrounding the word. diamondback terrapins.

are you ready for the demystification of diamondback terrapins???????? they ain't nothing but salt water turtles.

slaves on the eastern shores used to eat them all the time. the slaves was eating so many that a law was passed to making it a crime to feed slaves terrapins more than 3 times a week.

white folks discovered terrapins, ate them all up and now they are all but extinct (terrapins).

oh there are a few left on terrapin reservations but the chances of seeing one in your neighborhood is not likely.

in my old neighborhood (fairfax s.c.) we always talk about how folks in new york will give you something to drink but nothing to eat. after having lived for several years in fun city i understand how the natives got into this.

with the cost of living as high as it is here i understand how you can become paranoid and weird about your food. i understand where they are coming from but i thank the creator that there is still a cultural gap between me and the natives. on the other hand you cant be no fool about it. it dont make sense to take food out your childrens mouths to give to the last lower east side poet who knocks on your door but you can give up a margarine sandwich and a glass of water. cant you? eating is a very personal thing.

some people will sit down and eat with anybody.

that is very uncool. you cant eat with everybody.

you got to have the right vibrations.

if you dont get good vibrations from someone, cancel them out for eating. (other things too.)

that is the only way to keep bad kitchen vibes at a minimum. tell those kind of folks that you will meet them in a luncheonette or a bar.

even at the risk of static from family and friends PRO TECT YO KITCH'N. it's hard though. sometimes look like in spite of all you do and as careful as you try to be a rapscallion will slip right in your kitchen. i cant stand rapscallions. among other things they are insensitive. you ask them "may i offer you something" "some coffee tea juice water milk juice or maybe an alcoholic beverage."

they always answer "nah nutin for me" or else they say "i'll have tea if you got tea bags" or "coffee if it is instant i dont want to put you through no trouble." check that out! talking about not going to any trouble. hell they already in your house and that is trouble and personal. what the rapscallions are really saying is dont go to any trouble for me cause i wouldnt go to none for you. rapscallions dont mind taking the alcoholic drink because it is impersonal. nothing of you is in that. all you got to do is pour from a bottle. they dont feel that you have extended yourself for them so they wont have to do no trouble for you in return. in most other cultures when you enter a persons home you and the host share a moment together by partaking of something. rapscallions love to talk about culture but their actions prove they aint got none. they dont understand that it is about more than the coffee tea or drink of water.

it's about extending yourself.
so watch out for rapscallions. they'll mess up your kitchen vibes.
PROTECT YOUR KITCHEN

ADRIENNE RICH

When We Dead Awaken: Writing as Re-Vision

Ibsen's *When We Dead Awaken* is a play about the use that the male artist and thinker—in the process of creating culture as we know it—has made of women, in his life and in his work; and about a woman's slow struggling awakening to the use to which her life has been put. Bernard Shaw wrote in 1900 of this play: "[Ibsen] shows us that no degradation ever devized or permitted is as disastrous as this degradation; that through it women can die into luxuries for men and yet can kill them; that men and women are becoming conscious of this: and that what remains to be seen as perhaps the most interesting of all imminent social developments is what will happen 'when we dead awaken.' "[1]

It's exhilarating to be alive in a time of awakening consciousness; it can also be confusing, disorienting, and painful. This awakening of dead or sleeping consciousness has already affected the lives of millions of women, even those who don't know it yet. It is also affecting the lives of men, even those who deny its claims upon them. The argument will go on whether an oppressive economic class system is responsible for the oppressive nature of male/female relations, or whether, in fact, the sexual class system is the original model on which all the others are based. But in the last few years connections have been drawn between our sexual lives and our political institutions which are inescapable and illuminating. The sleepwalkers are coming awake, and for the first time this awakening has a collective reality; it is no longer such a lonely thing to open one's eyes.

Re-vision—the act of looking back, of seeing with fresh eyes, of entering an old text from a new critical direction—is for us more than a chapter in cultural history: it is an act of survival. Until we can understand the assumptions in which we are drenched we cannot know ourselves. And this drive to self-knowledge, for woman, is more than a search for identity: it is part of her refusal of the destructiveness of male-dominated society. A radical critique of literature, feminist in its impulse, would take the work first of all as a clue to how we live, how we have been living, how we have been led to imagine ourselves, how our language has trapped as well as liberated us; and how we can begin to see—and therefore live—

1. G. B. Shaw, *The Quintessence of Ibsenism* (New York: Hill & Wang, 1959), p. 139.

afresh. A change in the concept of sexual identity is essential if we are not going to see the old political order reassert itself in every new revolution. We need to know the writing of the past, and know it differently than we have ever known it; not to pass on a tradition but to break its hold over us.

For writers, and at this moment for women writers in particular, there is the challenge and promise of a whole new psychic geography to be explored. But there is also a difficult and dangerous walking on the ice, as we try to find language and images for a consciousness we are just coming into, and with little in the past to support us. I want to talk about some aspects of this difficulty and this danger.

Jane Harrison, the great classical anthropologist, wrote in 1914 in a letter to her friend Gilbert Murray: "By the by, about 'Women,' it has bothered me often—why do women never want to write poetry about Man as a sex—why is Woman a dream and a terror to man and not the other way around? . . . Is it mere convention and propriety, or something deeper?"[2] I think Jane's question cuts deep into the myth-making tradition, the romantic tradition; deep into what women and men have been to each other; and deep into the psyche of the woman writer. Thinking about that question, I began thinking of the work of two twentieth-century women poets, Sylvia Plath and Diane Wakoski. It strikes me that in the work of both Man appears as, if not a dream, a fascination, and a terror; and that the source of the fascination and the terror is, simply, Man's power —to dominate, tyrannize, choose or reject the woman. The charisma of Man seems to come purely from his power over her, and his control of the world by force; not from anything fertile or life-giving in him. And, in the work of both these poets, it is finally the woman's sense of *herself*—embattled, possessed—that gives the poetry its dynamic charge, its rhythms of struggle, need, will and female energy. Convention and propriety are perhaps not the right words, but until recently this female anger, this furious awareness of the Man's power over her, were not available materials to the female poet, who tended to write of Love as the source of her suffering, and to view that victimization by Love as an almost inevitable fate. Or, like Marianne Moore and Elizabeth Bishop, she kept human sexual relationships at a measured and chiselled distance in her poems.

One answer to Jane Harrison's question has to be that historically men and women have played very different parts in each others' lives. Where woman has been a luxury for man, and has served as the painter's model and the poet's muse, but also as comforter, nurse, cook, bearer of his seed, secretarial assistant, and copyist of

2. Jessie G. Stewart, *Jane Ellen Harrison: A Portrait from Letters* (London: Merlin Press, 1959), pp. 140–41.

manuscripts, man has played a quite different role for the female artist. Henry James repeats an incident which the writer Prosper Mérimée described, of how, while he was living with George Sand,

> he once opened his eyes, in the raw winter dawn, to see his companion, in a dressing-gown, on her knees before the domestic hearth, a candle-stick beside her and a red *madras* round her head, making bravely, with her own hands, the fire that was to enable her to sit down betimes to urgent pen and paper. The story represents him as having felt that the spectacle chilled his ardor and tried his taste; her appearance was unfortunate, her occupation an inconsequence, and her industry a reproof—the result of all of which was a lively irritation and an early rupture.[3]

I am suggesting that the specter of this kind of male judgment, along with the active discouragement and thwarting of her needs by a culture controlled by males, has created problems for the woman writer: problems of contact with herself, problems of language and style, problems of energy and survival.

In rereading Virginia Woolf's A Room of One's Own for the first time in some years, I was astonished at the sense of effort, of pains taken, of dogged tentativeness, in the tone of that essay. And I recognized that tone. I had heard it often enough, in myself and in other women. It is the tone of a woman almost in touch with her anger, who is determined not to appear angry, who is *willing* herself to be calm, detached, and even charming in a roomful of men where things have been said which are attacks on her very integrity. Virginia Woolf is addressing an audience of women, but she is acutely conscious—as she always was—of being overheard by men: by Morgan and Lytton and Maynard Keynes and for that matter by her father, Leslie Stephen. She drew the language out into an exacerbated thread in her determination to have her own sensibility yet protect it from those masculine presences. Only at rare moments in that essay do you hear the passion in her voice; she was trying to sound as cool as Jane Austen, as Olympian as Shakespeare, because that is the way the men of the culture thought a writer should sound.

No male writer has written primarily or even largely for women, or with the sense of women's criticism as a consideration when he chooses his materials, his theme, his language. But to a lesser or greater extent, every woman writer has written for men even when, like Virginia Woolf, she was supposed to be addressing women. If we have come to the point when this balance might begin to change, when women can stop being haunted, not only by "convention and propriety" but by internalized fears of being and saying themselves, then it is an extraordinary moment for the woman writer—and reader.

I have hesitated to do what I am going to do now, which is to

3. Henry James, *Notes on Novelists*, 1897.

use myself as an illustration. For one thing, it's a lot easier and less dangerous to talk about other women writers. But there is something else. Like Virginia Woolf, I am aware of the women who are not with us here because they are washing the dishes and looking after the children. Nearly fifty years after she spoke, that fact remains largely unchanged. And I am thinking also of women whom she left out of the picture altogether—women who are washing other people's dishes and caring for other people's children, not to mention women who went on the streets last night in order to feed their children. We seem to be special women here, we have liked to think of ourselves as special, and we have known that men would tolerate, even romanticize us as special, as long as our words and actions didn't threaten their privilege of tolerating or rejecting us according to *their* ideas of what a special woman ought to be. An important insight of the radical women's movement, for me, has been how divisive and how ultimately destructive is this myth of the special woman, who is also the token woman. Every one of us here in this room has had great luck; our own gifts could not have been enough, for we all know women whose gifts are buried or aborted. Our struggles can have meaning only if they can help to change the lives of women whose gifts—and whose very being— continues to be thwarted.

My own luck was being born white and middle-class into a house full of books, with a father who encouraged me to read and write. So for about twenty years I wrote for a particular man, who criticized and praised me and made me feel I was indeed "special." The obverse side of this, of course, was that I tried for a long time to please him, or rather, not to displease him. And then of course there were other men—writers, teachers—the Man, who was not a terror or a dream but a literary master and a master in other ways less easy to acknowledge. And there were all those poems about women, written by men: it seemed to be a given that men wrote poems and women frequently inhabited them. These women were almost always beautiful, but threatened with the loss of beauty, the loss of youth—the fate worse than death. Or, they were beautiful and died young, like Lucy and Lenore. Or, the woman was like Maud Gonne, cruel and disastrously mistaken, and the poem reproached her because she had refused to become a luxury for the poet.

A lot is being said today about the influence that the myths and images of women have on all of us who are products of culture. I think it has been a peculiar confusion to the girl or woman who tries to write, because she is peculiarly susceptible to language. She goes to poetry or fiction looking for *her* way of being in the world, since she too has been putting words and images together; she is looking eagerly for guides, maps, possibilities; and over and over in the "words' masculine persuasive force" of literature she comes up against something that negates everything she is about: she meets the image of Woman in books written by men. She finds a terror and a dream, she finds a beautiful pale face, she finds La Belle Dame Sans Merci, she finds Juliet or Tess or Salomé, but precisely what she does not find is that absorbed, drudging, puzzled, sometimes inspired creature, herself, who sits at a desk trying to put words together.

So what does she do? What did I do? I read the older women poets with their peculiar keenness and ambivalence: Sappho, Christina Rossetti, Emily Dickinson, Elinor Wylie, Edna Millay, H.D. I discovered that the woman poet most admired at the time (by men) was Marianne Moore, who was maidenly, elegant, intellectual, discreet. But even in reading these women I was looking in them for the same things I had found in the poetry of men, because I wanted women poets to be the equals of men, and to be equal was still confused with sounding the same.

I know that my style was formed first by male poets: by the men I was reading as an undergraduate—Frost, Dylan Thomas, Donne, Auden, MacNiece, Stevens, Yeats. What I chiefly learned from them was craft. But poems are like dreams: in them you put what you don't know you know. Looking back at poems I wrote before I was twenty-one, I'm startled because beneath the conscious craft are glimpses of the split I even then experienced between the girl who wrote poems, who defined herself in writing poems, and the girl who was to define herself by her relationships with men. "Aunt Jennifer's Tigers," written while I was a student, looks with deliberate detachment at this split.

> Aunt Jennifer's tigers stride across a screen,
> Bright topaz denizens of a world of green.
> They do not fear the men beneath the tree,
> They pace in sleek chivalric certainty.
>
> Aunt Jennifer's fingers, fluttering through her wool,
> Find even the ivory needle hard to pull.
> The massive weight of Uncle's wedding-band
> Sits heavily upon Aunt Jennifer's hand.
>
> When Aunt is dead, her terrified hands will lie
> Still ringed with ordeals she was mastered by.
> The tigers in the panel that she made
> Will go on striding, proud and unafraid.

In writing this poem, composed and apparently cool as it is, I thought I was creating a portrait of an imaginary woman. But this woman suffers from the opposition of her imagination, worked out in tapestry, and her life-style, "ringed with ordeals she was mastered by." It was important to me that Aunt Jennifer was a person as distinct from myself as possible—distanced by the formalism of the poem; by its objective, observant tone; even by putting the woman in a different generation.

In those years formalism was part of the strategy—like asbestos gloves, it allowed me to handle materials I couldn't pick up barehanded. (A later strategy was to use the persona of a man, as I did in "The Loser.")

A man thinks of the woman he once loved: first, after her wedding, and then nearly a decade later.

I

I kissed you, bride and lost, and went
home from that bourgeois sacrament,
your cheek still tasting cold upon
my lips that gave you benison
with all the swagger that they knew—
as losers somehow learn to do.

Your wedding made my eyes ache; soon
the world would be worse off for one
more golden apple dropped to ground
without the least protesting sound,
and you would windfall lie, and we
forget your shimmer on the tree.

Beauty is always wasted: if
not Mignon's song sung to the deaf,
at all events to the unmoved.
A face like yours cannot be loved
long or seriously enough.
Almost, we seem to hold it off.

II

Well, you are tougher than I thought.
Now when the wash with ice hangs taut
this morning of St. Valentine,
I see you strip the squeaking line,
your body weighed against the load,
and all my groans can do no good.

Because you still are beautiful,
though squared and stiffened by the pull
of what nine windy years have done.
You have three daughters, lost a son.
I see all your intelligence
flung into that unwearied stance.

My envy is of no avail.
I turn my head and wish him well
who chafed your beauty into use
and lives forever in a house
lit by the friction of your mind.
You stagger in against the wind.[4]

1958

I finished college, published my first book by a fluke, as it seemed
to me, and broke off a love-affair. I took a job, lived alone, went on
writing, fell in love. I was young, full of energy, and the book
seemed to mean that others agreed I was a poet. Because I was also
determined to have a "full" woman's life, I plunged in my early
twenties into marriage and had three children before I was thirty.
There was nothing overt in the environment to warn me: these
were the fifties, and in reaction to the earlier wave of feminism, middle-class women were making careers of domestic perfection, working to send their husbands through professional schools, then retir-
ing to raise large families. People were moving out to the suburbs,
technology was going to be the answer to everything, even sex; the
family was in its glory. Life was extremely private; women were isolated from each other by the loyalties of marriage. I have a sense
that women didn't talk to each other much in the fifties—not
about their secret emptinesses, their frustrations. I went on trying to
write, my second book and first child appeared in the same month.
But by the time that book came out I was already dissatisfied with
those poems, which seemed to me mere exercises for poems I hadn't
written. The book was praised, however, for its "gracefulness"; I had
a marriage and a child. If there were doubts, if there were periods of
null depression or active despairing, these could only mean that I
was ungrateful, insatiable, perhaps a monster.

About the time my third child was born, I felt that I had either
to consider myself a failed woman and a failed poet, or try to find
some synthesis by which to understand what was happening to me.
What frightened me most was the sense of drift, of being pulled
along on a current which called itself my destiny, but in which I
seemed to be losing touch with whoever I had been, with the girl
who had experienced her own will and energy almost ecstatically at
times, walking around a city or riding a train at night or typing in a
student room. In a poem about my grandmother, I wrote (of
myself): "A young girl, thought sleeping, is certified dead."[5] I was
writing very little, partly from fatigue, that female fatigue of suppressed anger and the loss of contact with her own being; partly
from the discontinuity of female life with its attention to small
chores, errands, work that others constantly undo, small children's

4. "The Losers," in *Snapshots of a Daughter-in-Law* (New York: W. W. Norton, 1956), pp. 15–16.

5. "Halfway," in *Necessities of Life* (New York: W. W. Norton, 1966), p. 34.

constant needs. What I did write was unconvincing to me; my anger and frustration were hard to acknowledge in or out of poem, because in fact I cared a great deal about my husband and my children. Trying to look back and understand that time I have tried to analyze the real nature of the conflict. Most, if not all, human lives are full of fantasy—passive daydreaming which need not be acted on. But to write poetry or fiction, or even to think well, is not to fantasize, or to put fantasies on paper. For a poem to coalesce, for a character or an action to take shape, there has to be an imaginative transformation of reality which is in no way passive. And a certain freedom of the mind is needed—freedom to press on, to enter the currents of your thought like a glider pilot, knowing that your motion can be sustained, that the buoyancy of your attention will not be suddenly snatched away. Moreover, if the imagination is to transcend and transform experience it has to question, to challenge, to conceive of alternatives, perhaps to the very life you are living at that moment. You have to be free to play around with the notion that day might be night, love might be hate; nothing can be too sacred for the imagination to turn into its opposite or to call experimentally by another name. For writing is re-naming. Now, to be maternally with small children all day in the old way, to be with a man in the old way of marriage, requires a holding-back, a putting-aside of that imaginative activity, and seems to demand instead a kind of conservatism. I want to make it clear that I am *not* saying that in order to write well, or think well, it is necessary to become unavailable to others, or to become a devouring ego. This has been the myth of the masculine artist and thinker; and I repeat, I do not accept it. But to be a female human being trying to fulfill traditional female functions in a traditional way *is* in direct conflict with the subversive function of the imagination. The word *traditional* is important here. There must be ways, and we will be finding out more and more about them, in which the energy of creation and the energy of relation can be united. But in those earlier years I always felt the conflict as a failure of love in myself. I had thought I was choosing a full life: the life available to most men, in which sexuality, work and parenthood could coexist. But I felt, at twenty-nine, guilt toward the people closest to me, and guilty toward my own being.

I wanted, then, more than anything, the one thing of which there was never enough: time to think, time to write. The fifties and early sixties were years of rapid revelations: the sit-ins and marches in the South, the Bay of Pigs, the early anti-war movement raised large questions—questions for which the masculine world of the academy around me seemed to have expert and fluent answers. But I needed desperately to think for myself—about pacifism and dissent and violence, about poetry and society and about my own relationship to all these things. For about ten years I was reading in fierce snatches, scribbling in notebooks, writing poetry in fragments; I was looking desperately for clues, because if there were no clues then I thought I might be insane. I wrote in a notebook about this time: "Paralyzed by the sense that there exists a mesh of relationships—e.g. between my anger at the children, my sensual life, pacifism, sex, (I mean sex in its broadest significance, not merely sexual desire)—an interconnectedness which, if I could see it, make it valid, would give me back myself, make it possible to function lucidly and passionately. Yet I grope in and out among these dark webs." I think I began at this point to feel that politics was not something "out there" but something "in here" and of the essence of my condition.

In the late fifties I was able to write, for the first time, directly about experiencing myself as a woman. The poem was jotted in fragments during children's naps, brief hours in a library, or at 3 A.M. after rising with a wakeful child. I despaired of doing any continuous work at this time. Yet I began to feel that my fragments and scraps had a common consciousness and a common theme, one which I would have been very unwilling to put on paper at an earlier time because I had been taught that poetry should be "universal," which meant, of course, non-female. Until then I had tried very much *not* to identify myself as a female poet. Over two years I wrote a ten-part poem called "Snapshots of A Daughter-in-Law," in a longer, looser mode than I've ever trusted myself with before. It was an extraordinary relief to write that poem. It strikes me now as too literary, too dependent on allusion; I hadn't found the courage yet to do without authorities, or even to use the pronoun *I*—the woman in the poem is always *she*. One section of it, 2, concerns a woman who thinks she is going mad; she is haunted by voices telling her to resist and rebel, voices which she can hear but not obey.

2.

Banging the coffee-pot into the sink
she hears the angels chiding, and looks out
past the raked gardens to the sloppy sky.
Only a week since They said: *Have no patience.*

The next time it was: *Be insatiable.*
Then: *Save yourself; others you cannot save.*
Sometimes she's let the tapstream scald her arm,
a match burn to her thumbnail,

or held her hand above the kettle's snout
right in the woolly steam. They are probably angels,
since nothing hurts her any more, except
each morning's grit blowing into her eyes.[6]

6. "Snapshots of a Daughter-in-Law," in *Snapshots of a Daughter-in-Law*, p. 21.

The poem "Orion," written five years later, is a poem of reconnection with a part of myself I had felt I was losing—the active principle, the energetic imagination, the "half-brother" whom I projected, as I had for many years, into the constellation Orion.

Far back when I went zig-zagging
through tamarack pastures
you were my genius, you
my cast-iron Viking, my helmed
lion-heart king in prison.
Years later now you're young

my fierce half-brother, staring
down from that simplified west
your breast open, your belt dragged down
by an oldfashioned thing, a sword
the last bravado you won't give over
though it weighs you down as you stride

and the stars in it are dim
and maybe have stopped burning.
But you burn, and I know it;
as I throw back my head to take you in
an old transfusion happens again:
divine astronomy is nothing to it.

Indoors I bruise and blunder,
break faith, leave ill enough
alone, a dead child born in the dark.
Night cracks up over the chimney,
pieces of time, frozen geodes
come showering down in the grate.

A man reaches behind my eyes
and finds them empty
a woman's head turns away
from my head in the mirror
children are dying my death
and eating crumbs of my life.

Pity is not your forte.
Calmly you ache up there
pinned aloft in your crow's nest,
my speechless pirate!
You take it all for granted
and when I look you back

it's with a starlike eye
shooting its cold and egotistical spear
where it can do least damage.
Breathe deep! No hurt, no pardon
out here in the cold with you
you with your back to the wall.[7]

7. "Orion," in *Leaflets* (New York: W. W. Norton, 1969), pp. 11–12.

It's no accident that the words *cold and egotistical* appear in this poem, and are applied to myself. The choice still seemed to be between "love"—womanly, maternal love, altruistic love—a love defined and ruled by the weight of an entire culture—and egotis—a force directed by men into creation, achievement, ambition, often at the expense of others, but justifiably so. For weren't they men, and wasn't that their destiny as womanly love was ours? I know now that the alternatives are false ones—that the word *love* is itself in need of re-vision.

There is a companion poem to "Orion," written three years later, in which at last the woman in the poem and the woman writing the poem become the same person. It is called "Planetarium," and it was written after a visit to a real planetarium, where I read an account of the work of Caroline Herschel, the astronomer, who worked with her brother William, but whose name remained obscure, as his did not.

(Thinking of Caroline Herschel, 1750–1848, astronomer, sister of William; and others)

A woman in the shape of a monster
a monster in the shape of a woman
the skies are full of them

a woman   'in the snow
among the Clocks and instruments
or measuring the ground with poles'

in her 98 years to discover
8 comets

she whom the moon ruled
like us
levitating into the night sky
riding the polished lenses

Galaxies of women, there
doing penance for impetuousness
ribs chilled
in those spaces   of the mind

An eye,
        'virile, precise and absolutely certain'
        from the mad webs of Uranisborg

                        encountering the NOVA

every impulse of light exploding
from the core
as life flies out of us

Tycho whispering at last
'Let me not seem to have lived in vain'

What we see, we see
and seeing is changing

the light that shrivels a mountain
and leaves a man alive

Heartbeat of the pulsar
heart sweating through my body

The radio impulse
pouring in from Taurus

I am bombarded yet   I stand

I have been standing all my life in the
direct path of a battery of signals
the most accurately transmitted most
untranslatable language in the universe
I am a galactic cloud so deep   so invo-
luted that a light wave could take 15
years to travel through me   And has
taken   I am an instrument in the shape
of a woman trying to translate pulsations
into images   for the relief of the body
and the reconstruction of the mind.[8]

In closing I want to tell you about a dream I had last summer. I
dreamed I was asked to read my poetry at a mass women's meeting;
but when I began to read, what came out were the lyrics of a blues
song. I share this dream with you because it seemed to me to say a
lot about the problems and the future of the woman writer, and
probably of women in general. The awakening of consciousness is
not like the crossing of a frontier—one step, and you are in another
country. Much of women's poetry has been of the nature of the
blues song: a cry of pain, of victimization, or a lyric of seduction.
And today, much poetry by women—and prose for that matter—is
charged with anger. I think we need to go through that anger, and
we will betray our own reality if we try, as Virginia Woolf was
trying, for an objectivity, a detachment; that would make us sound
more like Jane Austen or Shakespeare. We know more than Jane
Austen or Shakespeare knew: more than Jane Austen because our
lives are more complex, more than Shakespeare because we know
more about the lives of women, Jane Austen and Virginia Woolf
included.

8. "Planetarium," in *The Will to* 1971), pp. 11–12.
Change (New York: W. W. Norton,

Both the victimization and the anger experienced by women are real, and have real sources, everywhere in the environment, built into society. They must go on being tapped and explored by poets, among others. We can neither deny them, nor can we rest there. They are our birth-pains, and we are bearing ourselves. We would be failing each other as writers and as women, if we neglected or denied what is negative, regressive or Sisyphean in our inwardness.

We all know that there is another story to be told. I am curious and expectant about the future of the masculine consciousness. I feel in the work of the men whose poetry I read today a deep pessimism and fatalistic grief; and I wonder if it isn't the masculine side of what women have experienced, the price of masculine dominance. One thing I am sure of: just as woman is becoming her own midwife, creating herself anew, so man will have to learn to gestate and give birth to his own subjectivity—something he has frequently wanted woman to do for him. We can go on trying to talk to each other, we can sometimes help each other, poetry and fiction can show us what the other is going through; but women can no longer be primarily mothers and muses for men: we have our own work cut out for us.

QUESTIONS

1. *A typical male-chauvinist cliché is that women take everything too personally, that they lack the larger (i.e. male) perspective. Does this article tend to confirm or deny that belief?*
2. *In the eighth paragraph, Rich asserts that "no male writer has written primarily or even largely for women, or with the sense of women's criticism as a consideration when he chooses his materials, his theme, his language." How can she know this? Do you think she is right? How do you know?*

ELDRIDGE CLEAVER

Convalescence[1]

. . . just as in childhood I envied Negroes for what seemed to me their superior masculinity, so I envy them today for what seems to me their superior physical grace and beauty. I have come to value physical grace very highly, and I am now capable of aching with all my being when I watch a Negro couple on the dance floor, or a Negro playing baseball or basketball. *They are on the kind of terms with their own bodies that I should like to be on with mine, and for that precious quality they seem blessed to me.* [Italics added]

—Norman Podhoretz, "My Negro Problem—And Ours,"
Commentary, February 1963

1. From *Soul on Ice*, 1968.

Why envy the Negro his grace, his physical skills? Why not ask what it is that prevents grace and physical skill from becoming a general property of the young? Mr. Podhoretz speaks of middle-class, white respectability—what does this mean but being cut off from the labor process, the work process, the creative process, as such? *The solution is thus not the direct liquidation of the color line, through the liquidation of color; but rather through a greater physical connectedness of the whites; and a greater intellective connectedness of the blacks . . ."* [Italics added]
—Irving Louis Horowitz,
Chairman, Department of Sociology,
Hobart and William Smith Colleges, Geneva, New York,
Commentary, June 1963

If the separation of the black and white people in America along the color line had the effect, in terms of social imagery, of separating the Mind from the Body—the oppressor whites usurping sovereignty by monopolizing the Mind, abdicating the Body and becoming bodiless Omnipotent Administrators and Ultrafeminines; and the oppressed blacks, divested of sovereignty and therefore of Mind, manifesting the Body and becoming mindless Supermasculine Menials and Black Amazons—if this is so, then the 1954 U.S. Supreme Court decision in the case of *Brown v. Board of Education*, demolishing the principle of segregation of the races in public education and striking at the very root of the practice of segregation generally, was a major surgical operation performed by nine men in black robes on the racial Maginot Line which is imbedded as deep as sex or the lust for lucre in the schismatic American psyche. This piece of social surgery, if successful, performed without benefit of any anesthetic except God and the Constitution, in a land where God is dead and the Constitution has been in a coma for 180 years, is more marvelous than a successful heart transplant would be, for it was meant to graft the nation's Mind back onto its Body and vice versa.

If the foregoing is true, then the history of America in the years following the pivotal Supreme Court edict should be a record of the convalescence of the nation. And upon investigation we should be able to see the Omnipotent Administrators and Ultrafeminines grappling with their unfamiliar and alienated Bodies, and the Supermasculine Menials and Amazons attempting to acquire and assert *a mind of their own*. The record, I think, is clear and unequivocal. The bargain which seems to have been struck is that the whites have had to turn to the blacks for a clue on how to swing with the Body, while the blacks have had to turn to the whites for the secret of the Mind. It was Chubby Checker's mission, bearing the Twist as *good news*, to teach the whites, whom history had taught to forget, how to shake their asses again. It is a skill they surely must once have possessed but which they abandoned for puritanical dreams of escaping the corruption of the flesh, by leaving the terrors of the Body to the blacks.

In the swift, fierce years since the 1954 school desegregation decision, a rash of seemingly unrelated mass phenomena has appeared on the American scene—deviating radically from the prevailing Hot-Dog-and-Malted-Milk norm of the bloodless, square, superficial, faceless Sunday-Morning atmosphere that was suffocating the nation's soul. And all of this in a nation where the so-called molders of public opinion, the writers, politicians, teachers, and cab drivers, are willful, euphoric liars or zip-dam ostriches and owls, a clique of undercover ghosts, a bunch of Walter Jenkinses;[2] a lot of coffee-drinking, cigarette-smoking, sly, suck-assing, status-seeking, cheating, nervous, dry-balled, tranquillizer-gulched, countdown-minded, out-of-style, slithering snakes. No wonder that many "innocent people," the manipulated and the stimulated, some of whom were game for a reasonable amount of mystery and even adventure, had their minds scrambled. These observers were not equipped to either *feel* or *know* that a radical break, a revolutionary leap out of their sight, had taken place in the secret parts of this nation's soul. It was as if a driverless vehicle were speeding through the American night down an unlighted street toward a stone wall and was boarded on the fly by a stealthy ghost with a drooling leer on his face, who, at the last detour before chaos and disaster, careened the vehicle down a smooth highway that leads to the future and life; and to ask these Americans to understand that they were the passengers on this driverless vehicle and that the lascivious ghost was the Saturday-night crotchfunk of the Twist, or the "Yeah, Yeah, Yeah!" which the Beatles highjacked from Ray Charles, to ask these Calvinistic profligates to see the logical and reciprocal links is more cruel than asking a hope-to-die Okie Music buff to cop the sounds of John Coltrane.

In the beginning of the era came a thief with a seven-year itch who knew that the ostriches and the owls had been bribed with a fix of Euphony, which is their kick. The thief knew that he need not wait for the cover of night, that with impunity he could show his face in the marketplace in the full light of the sun, do his deed, scratch his dirt, sell his loot to the fence while the ostriches and owls, coasting on Euphony, one with his head in a hole—any hole—and the other with his head in the clouds, would only cluck and whisper and hear-see-speak no evil.

So Elvis Presley came, strumming a weird guitar and wagging his tail across the continent, ripping off fame and fortune as he scrunched his way, and, like a latter-day Johnny Appleseed, sowing seeds of a new rhythm and style in the white souls of the white

2. Former White House aide; arrested in 1964 on a morals charge.

youth of America, whose inner hunger and need was no longer satisfied with the antiseptic white shoes and whiter songs of Pat Boone.
"You can do anything," sang Elvis to Pat Boone's white shoes, "but
don't you step on my Blue Suede 'Shoes!"

During this period of ferment and beginnings, at about the same
time that the blacks of Montgomery, Alabama, began their historic
bus boycott (giving birth to the leadership of Martin Luther King,
signifying to the nation that, with this initiative, this first affirmative step, somewhere in the universe a gear in the machinery had
shifted), something, a target, came into focus. The tensions in the
American psyche had torn a fissure in the racial Maginot Line and
through this fissure, this tiny bridge between the Mind and Body,
the black masses, who had been silent and somnolent since the '20s
and '30s, were now making a break toward the dimly seen light that
beckoned to them through the fissure. The fact that these blacks
could now take such a step was perceived by the ostriches and owls
as a sign of national decay, a sign that the System had caved in at
that spot. And this gave birth to a fear, a fear that quickly became a
focus for all the anxieties and exasperations in the Omnipotent
Administrators' minds; and to embody this perceived decay and act
as a lightning rod for the fear, the beatniks bloomed onto the American scene.

Like pioneers staking their claims in the no-man's land that lay
along the racial Maginot Line, the beatniks, like Elvis Presley
before them, dared to do in the light of day what America had long
been doing in the sneak-thief anonymity of night—consorted on a
human level with the blacks. Reviled, cursed, held in contempt by
the "molders of public opinion," persecuted by the police, made
into an epithet of derision by the deep-frozen geeks of the Hot-
Dog-and-Malted-Milk set, the beatniks irreverently refused to go
away. Allan Ginsberg and Jack Kerouac ("the Suzuki rhythm boys,"
James Baldwin called them, derisively, in a moment of panic, "tired
of white ambitions" and "dragging themselves through the Negro
streets at dawn, looking for an angry fix"; "with," as Mailer put it,
"the black man's code to fit their facts"). Bing Crosbyism, Perry
Comoism, and Dinah Shoreism had led to cancer, and the vanguard
of the white youth knew it.

And as the spirit of revolt crept across the continent from that
wayward bus in Montgomery, Alabama, seeping like new life into
the cracks and nooks of the northern ghettos and sweeping in
furious gales across the campuses of southern Negro colleges, erupt-
ing, finally, in the sit-ins and freedom rides—as this swirling mael-
strom of social change convulsed the nation, shocking an unsuspect-
ing American public, folk music, speaking of fundamental verities,
climbed slowly out of the grave; and the hip lobe of the national
ear, twitching involuntarily at first, began to listen.

From the moment that Mrs. Rosa Parks, in that bus in Montgomery, Alabama, resisted the Omnipotent Administrator, contact, however fleeting, had been made with the lost sovereignty—the Body had made contact with its Mind—and the shock of that contact sent an electric current throughout this nation, traversing the racial Maginot Line and striking fire in the hearts of the whites. The wheels began to turn, the thaw set in, and though Emmett Till and Mack Parker[3] were dead, though Eisenhower sent troops to Little Rock,[4] though Autherine Lucy's token presence at the University of Alabama was a mockery—notwithstanding this, it was already clear that the 1954 major surgical operation had been successful and the patient would live. The challenge loomed on the horizon: Africa, black, enigmatic, and hard-driving, had begun to parade its newly freed nations into the UN; and the Islam of Elijah Muhammad, amplified as it was fired in salvos from the piercing tongue of Malcolm X, was racing through the Negro streets with Allen Ginsberg and Jack Kerouac.

Then, as the verbal revolt of the black masses soared to a cacophonous peak—the Body, the Black Amazons and Supermasculine Menials, becoming conscious, shouting, in a thousand different ways, *"I've got a Mind of my own!"*; and as the senator from Massachusetts was saving the nation from the Strangelove grasp of Dirty Dick, injecting, as he emerged victorious, a new and vivacious spirit into the people with the style of his smile and his wife's hairdo; then, as if a signal had been given, as if the Mind had shouted to the Body, "I'm ready!"—the Twist, superseding the Hula Hoop, burst upon the scene like a nuclear explosion, sending its fallout of rhythm into the Minds and Bodies of the people. The fallout: the Hully Gully, the Mashed Potato, the Dog, the Smashed Banana, the Watusi, the Frug, the Swim. The Twist was a guided missile, launched from the ghetto into the very heart of suburbia. The Twist succeeded, as politics, religion, and law could never do, in writing in the heart and soul what the Supreme Court could only write on the books. The Twist was a form of therapy for a convalescing nation. The Omnipotent Administrator and the Ultrafeminine responded so dramatically, in stampede fashion, to the Twist precisely because it afforded them the possibility of reclaiming their Bodies again after generations of alienated and disembodied existence.

The stiff, mechanical Omnipotent Administrators and Ultrafeminines presented a startling spectacle as they entered in droves onto the dance floors to learn how to Twist. They came from every level

---

3. Emmett Till, a fourteen-year-old youth, kidnapped and killed for whistling at a white woman in Mississippi in August 1955; Mack Parker, lynched in Poplarville, Mississippi, while awaiting trial on a rape charge, April 1959.

4. Troops sent to Little Rock, Arkansas, in 1957 in support of a court order to integrate Little Rock schools.

of society, from top to bottom, writhing pitifully though gamely about the floor, feeling exhilarating and soothing new sensations, release from some unknown prison in which their Bodies had been encased, a sense of freedom they had never known before, a feeling of communion with some mystical root-source of life and vigor, from which sprang a new awareness and enjoyment of the flesh, a new appreciation of the possibilities of their Bodies. They were swinging and gyrating and shaking their dead asses like petrified zombies trying to regain the warmth of life, rekindle the dead limbs, the cold ass, the stone heart, the stiff, mechanical, disused joints with the spark of life.

This spectacle truly startled many Negroes, because they perceived it as an intrusion by the Mind into the province of the Body, and this intimated chaos; because the Negroes knew, from the survival experience of their everyday lives, that the system within which they were imprisoned was based upon the racial Maginot Line and that the cardinal sin, crossing the line—which was, in their experience, usually initiated from the black side—was being committed, *en masse*, by the whites. The Omnipotent Administrators and Ultrafeminines were storming the Maginot Line! A massive assault had been launched without parallel in American history, and to Negroes it was confusing. Sure, they had witnessed it on an individual scale: they had seen many ofays destroy the Maginot Line in themselves. But this time it had all the appearances of a national movement. There were even rumors that President Kennedy and his Jackie were doing the Twist secretly in the White House; that their Number One Boy had been sent to the Peppermint Lounge in disguise to learn how to Twist, and he in turn brought the trick back to the White House. These Negroes knew that something fundamental had changed.

"Man, what done got into them ofays?" one asked.

"They trying to get back," said another.

"Shit," said a young Negro who made his living by shoplifting. "If you ask me, I think it must be the end of the world."

"Oooo-weee!" said a Negro musician who had been playing at a dance and was now standing back checking the dancers. "Baby, I don't dig this action at all! Look here, baby, pull my coat to what's going down! I mean, have I missed it somewhere? Where've I been? Baby, I been blowing all my life and I ain't never dug no happenings like this. You know what, man, I'm gon' cut that fucking weed aloose. Oooo-weee! Check that little bitch right there! What the fuck she trying to do? Is she trying to shake it or break it? Oooo-weee!"

A Negro girl said: "Take me home, I'm sick!"

Another one said: "No, let's stay! This is too much!"

And a bearded Negro cat, who was not interested in learning how to Twist himself, who felt that if he was interested in doing it, he could get up from the table right now and start Twisting, he said, sitting at the table with a tinsel-minded female: "It ain't nothing. They just trying to get back, that's all."

"Get back?" said the girl, arching her brows quizzically, "Get back from where?"

"From wherever they've been," said the cat, "where else?"

"Are they doing it in Mississippi is what I want to know," said a tall, deadly looking Negro who had a long razor line down his left cheek and who had left Mississippi in a hurry one night.

And the dancers: they were caught up in a whirl of ecstasy, swinging like pendulums, mechanical like metronomes or puppets on invisible strings being manipulated by a master with a sick sense of humor. "They look like Chinese doing communal exercise," said a Negro. "That's all they're doing, calisthenics!"

"Yeah," said his companion. "They're trying to get in shape."

But if at first it was funny and confusing, it was nonetheless a breakthrough. The Omnipotent Administrators and Ultrafeminines were discovering new aspects of the Body, new possibilities of rhythm, new ways to move. The Hula Hoop had been a false start, a mechanized, theatrical attempt by the Mind to supply to itself what only the Body can give. But, with the Twist, as last they knew themselves to be swinging. The forces acting upon the world stage in our era had created, in the collective psyche of the Omnipotent —and the Hula Hoop and Twist offered socially acceptable ways to Administrators and Ultrafeminines, an irresistible urge—to just stand up and shake the ice and cancer out of their alienated white asses—the Hula Hoop and Twist offered socially acceptable ways to do it.

Of course, not all the whites took part in these joyful experiments. For many, the more "suggestive" a dance became—i.e., the more it became pure Body and less Mind—the more scandalous it seemed to them; and their reaction in this sense was an index to the degree of their alienation from their Bodies. But what they condemned as a sign of degeneracy and moral decay was actually a sign of health, a sign of hope for full recovery. As Norman Mailer prophesied: ". . . the Negro's equality would tear a profound shift into the psychology, the sexuality, and the moral imagination of every white alive." Precisely because the Mind will have united with the Body, theory will have merged with practice.

It is significant that the Twist and the Hula Hoop came into the scene in all their fury at the close of the Eisenhower and the dawn of the Kennedy era. It could be interpreted as a rebellion against the vacuous Eisenhower years. It could also be argued that the same collective urge that gave rise to the Twist also swept Kennedy into office. I shudder to think that, given the closeness of the final vote in 1960, Richard Nixon might have won the election in a breeze if he had persuaded one of his Ultrafeminine daughters, not to mention Ultrapat, to do the Twist in public. Not if Kennedy had stayed on the phone a week sympathizing with Mrs. Martin Luther King, Jr., over the fact that the cat was in jail, would he have won. Even as I am convinced that Luci Baines Johnson, dancing the Watusi in public with Killer Joe Piro,[5] won more votes for her old man in 1964 than a whole boxcar full of his hog-calling speeches ever did.

When the Birmingham Revolt erupted in the summer of 1963 and President Kennedy stepped into the void and delivered his unprecedented speech to the nation on civil rights and sent his bill to Congress, the foundation had been completed. Martin Luther King, Jr., giving voice to the needs of the Body, and President Kennedy, speaking out the needs of the Mind, made contact on that day. The Twisters, sporting their blue suede shoes, moved beyond the ghost in white shoes who ate a Hot Dog and sipped Malted Milk as he danced the mechanical jig of Satan on top of Medgar Evers' tomb.[6] In vain now would the murderers bomb that church and slaughter grotesquely those four little black girls[7] (what did they hope to kill? were they striking at the black of the skin or the fire of the soul? at history? at the Body?). In vain also the assassins' bullets that crashed through the head of John Kennedy, taking a life, yes, but creating a larger-than-life and failing utterly to expunge from the record the March on Washington and its truth: that this nation—bourgeois or not, imperialist or not, murderous or not, ugly or not—its people, somewhere in their butchered and hypocritical souls, still contained an epic potential of spirit which is its hope, a bottomless potential which fires the imaginations of its youth. It was all too late. It was too late because it was time for the blacks ("I've got a *Mind* of my own!') to riot, to sweep through the Harlem night like a wave of locusts, breaking, screaming, bleeding, laughing, crying, rejoicing, celebrating, in a jubilee of destruction, to regurgitate the white man's bullshit they'd been eating for four hundred years; smashing the windows of the white man's stores, throwing bricks they wished were bombs, running, leaping whirling like a cyclone through the white man's Mind, past his backlash, through the night streets of Rochester, New Jersey, Philadelphia. And even though the opposition, gorging on Hot Dogs and Malted Milk, with blood now splattered over the white shoes, would still strike out in the dark against the manifestations of the turning, showing the protocol of Southern Hospitality reserved for Niggers and Nigger Lovers—SCHWERNER–CHANEY–GOODMAN[8]

5. Discothèque dance teacher.
6. Evers was killed by a sniper in Jackson, Mississippi, in June 1963.
7. The bombing took place in Birmingham, Alabama, in September 1963.

8. Michael Schwerner, James Chaney, and Andrew Goodman, civil rights workers, were killed near Philadelphia, Mississippi, in June 1964.

—it was still too late. For not only had Luci Baines Johnson danced the Watusi in public with Killer Joe, but the Beatles were on the scene, injecting Negritude by the ton into whites, in this post-Elvis Presley-beatnik era of ferment.

Before we toss the Beatles a homosexual kiss—saying, "If a man be ass enough to reach for the bitch in them, that man will kiss a man, and if a woman reaches for the stud in them, that woman will kiss a woman"—let us marvel at the genius of their image, which comforts the owls and ostriches in the one spot where Elvis Presley bummed their kick: Elvis, with his *unfunky* (yet mechanical, alienated) bumpgrinding, was still too much Body (too soon) for the strained collapsing psyches of the Omnipotent Administrators and Ultrafeminines; whereas the Beatles, affecting the caucasoid crown of femininity and ignoring the Body on the visual plane (while their music on the contrary being full of Body), assuaged the doubts of the owls and ostriches by presenting an incorporeal, cerebral image.

Song and dance are, perhaps, only a little less old than man himself. It is with his music and dance, the recreation through art of the rhythms suggested by and implicit in the tempo of his life and cultural environment, that man purges his soul of the tensions of daily strife and maintains his harmony in the universe. In the increasingly mechanized, automated, cybernated environment of the modern world—a cold, bodiless world of wheels, smooth plastic surfaces, tubes, pushbuttons, transistors, computers, jet propulsion, rockets to the moon, atomic energy—man's need for affirmation of his biology has become that much more intense. He feels need for a clear definition of where his body ends and the machine begins, where man ends and the *extensions* of man begin. This great mass hunger, which transcends national or racial boundaries, recoils from the subtle subversions of the mechanical evironment which modern technology is creating faster than man, with his present savage relationship to his fellow men, is able to receive and assimilate. This is the central contradiction of the twentieth century; and it is against this backdrop that America's attempt to unite its Mind with its Body, to save its soul, is taking place.

It is in this connection that the blacks, personifying the Body and thereby in closer communion with their biological roots than other Americans, provide the saving link, the bridge between man's biology and man's machines. In its purest form, as adjustment to the scientific and technological environment of our era, as purgative and lullaby-soother of man's soul, it is the jazz issuing from the friction and harmony of the American Negro with his environment that captured the beat and tempo of our times. And although modern science and technology are the same whether in New York, Paris, London, Accra, Cairo, Berlin, Moscow, Tokyo, Peking, or São Paulo, jazz is the only true international medium of communication current in the world today, capable of speaking creatively, with equal intensity and relevance, to the people in all those places.

The less sophisticated (but no less Body-based) popular music of urban Negroes—which was known as Rhythm and Blues before the whites appropriated and distilled it into a product they called Rock 'n Roll—is the basic ingredient, the core, of the gaudy, cacophonous hymns with which the Beatles of Liverpool drive their hordes of Ultrafeminine fans into catatonia and hysteria. For Beatle fans, having been alienated from their own Bodies so long and so deeply, the effect of these potent, erotic rhythms is electric. Into this music, the Negro projected—as it were, *drained off*, as pus from a sore—a powerful sensuality, his pain and lust, his love and his hate, his ambition and his despair. The Negro projected into his music his very Body. The Beatles, the four long-haired lads from Liverpool, are offering up as their gift the Negro's Body, and in so doing establish a rhythmic communication between the listener's own Mind and Body.

Enter the Beatles—soul by proxy, middlemen between the Mind and the Body. A long way from Pat Boone's White Shoes. A way station on a slow route traveled with all deliberate speed.

QUESTIONS

1. What racial differences does Cleaver assume? Would you respond differently to these assumptions if they had been implicit in a piece by, say, a southern white racist politician?
2. Does Cleaver establish any connection between the Supreme Court decision he discusses in his introduction and the song and dance he focuses on in the body of the essay? Do you think the "convalescence" could have occurred without that particular piece of surgery? What other influences may have served to graft mind and body? What others may have impeded the convalescence?
3. This piece abounds with figures of speech. How many can you find? What purposes do they serve? Do they clarify Cleaver's argument? Or do they becloud the issues?
4. Cleaver's sentences are long, with ins and outs and round-abouts—and many internal interruptions. How would he do at Time or Newsweek?
5. Are Cleaver's long lists of appositives and adjectives of substantive importance? Or are they mere gimmicks?
6. Are you persuaded by Cleaver's pronouncements on how things are—or were?

PETER SCHRAG
The Forgotten American

There is hardly a language to describe him, or even a set of social statistics. Just names: racist-bigot-redneck-ethnic-Irish-Italian-Pole-Hunkie-Yahoo. The lower middle class. A blank. The man under whose hat lies the great American desert. Who watches the tube, plays the horses, and keeps the niggers out of his union and his neighborhood. Who might vote for Wallace (but didn't). Who cheers when the cops beat up on demonstrators. Who is free, white and twenty-one, has a job, a home, a family, and is up to his eyeballs in credit. In the guise of the working class—or the American yeoman or John Smith—he was once the hero of the civics book, the man that Andrew Jackson called "the bone and sinew of the country." Now he is "the forgotten man," perhaps the most alienated person in America.

Nothing quite fits, except perhaps omission and semi-invisibility. America is supposed to be divided between affluence and poverty, between slums and suburbs. John Kenneth Galbraith begins the foreword to *The Affluent Society* with the phrase, "since I sailed for Switzerland in the early summer of 1955 to begin work on this book ..." But *between* slums and suburbs, between Scarsdale and Harlem, between Wellesley and Roxbury, between Shaker Heights and Hough, there are some eighty million people (depending on how you count them) who didn't sail for Switzerland in the summer of 1955 or at any other time, and who never expect to. Between slums and suburbs: South Boston and South San Francisco, Bell and Parma, Astoria and Bay Ridge, Newark, Cicero, Downey, Daly City, Charlestown, Flatbush. Union halls, American Legion posts, neighborhood bars and bowling leagues, the Ukrainian Club and the Holy Name. Main Street. To try to describe all this is like trying to describe America itself. If you look for it, you find it everywhere: the rows of frame houses overlooking the belching steel mills in Bethlehem, Pennsylvania; two-family brick houses in Canarsie (where the most common slogan, even in the middle of a political campaign, is "curb your dog"); the Fords and Chevies with a decal American flag on the rear window (usually a cut-out from the *Reader's Digest*, and displayed in counter-protest against peaceniks and "those bastards who carry Vietcong flags in demonstrations"); the bunting on the porch rail with the inscription, "Welcome Home, Pete." The gold star in the window.

When he was Under Secretary of Housing and Urban Development, Robert C. Wood tried a definition. It is not good, but it's the best we have:

He is a white employed male . . . earning between $5,000 and $10,000. He works regularly, steadily, dependably, wearing a blue collar or white collar. Yet the frontiers of his career expectations have been fixed since he reached the age of thirty-five, when he found that he had too many obligations, too much family, and too few skills to match opportunities with aspirations.

This definition of the "working American" involves almost 23 million American families.

The working American lives in the gray area fringes of a central city or in a close-in or very far-out cheaper suburban subdivision of a large metropolitan area. He is likely to own a home and a car, especially as his income begins to rise. Of those earning between $6,000 and $7,500, 70 per cent own their own homes and 94 percent drive their own cars.

94 per cent have no education beyond high school and 43 per cent have only completed the eighth grade.

He does all the right things, obeys the law, goes to church and insists—usually—that his kids get a better education than he had. But the right things don't seem to be paying off. While he is making more than he ever made—perhaps more than he ever dreamed—he's still struggling while a lot of others—"them" (on welfare, in demonstrations, in the ghettos)—are getting most of the attention. "I'm working my ass off," a guy tells you on a stoop in South Boston. "My kids don't have a place to swim, my parks are full of glass, and I'm supposed to bleed for a bunch of people on relief." In New York a man who drives a Post Office trailer truck at night (4:00 P.M. to midnight) and a cab during the day (7:00 A.M. to 2:00 P.M.), and who hustles radios for his Post Office buddies on the side is ready, as he says, to "knock somebody's ass." "The colored guys work when they feel like it. Sometimes they show up and sometimes they don't. One guy tore up all the time cards. I'd like to see a white guy do that and get away with it."

What Counts

Nobody knows how many people in America moonlight (half of the eighteen million families in the $5,000 to $10,000 bracket have two or more wage earners) or how many have to hustle on the side. "I don't think anybody has a single job anymore," said Nicholas Kisburg, the research director for a Teamsters Union Council in New York. "All the cops are moonlighting, and the teachers; and there's a million guys who are hustling, guys with phony social-security numbers who are hiding part of what they make so they don't get kicked out of a housing project, or guys who work as guards at sports events and get free meals that they don't want to pay taxes on. Every one of them is cheating. They are underground people— *Untermenschen*. . . . We really have no systematic data on any of this. We have no ideas of the attitudes of the white worker. (We've been too busy studying the black worker.) And yet he's the source of most of the reaction in this country."

The reaction is directed at almost every visible target: at integration and welfare, taxes and sex education, at the rich and the poor, the foundations and students, at the "smart people in the suburbs." In New York State the legislature cuts the welfare budget; in Los Angeles, the voters reelect Yorty after a whispered racial campaign against the Negro favorite. In Minneapolis a police detective named Charles Stenvig, promising "to take the handcuffs off the police," wins by a margin stunning even to his supporters: in Massachusetts the voters mail tea bags to their representatives in protest against new taxes, and in state after state legislatures are passing bills to punish student demonstrators. ("We keep talking about permissiveness in training kids," said a Los Angeles labor official, "but we forget that these are our kids.")

And yet all these things are side manifestations of a malaise that lacks a language. Whatever law and order means, for example, to a man who feels his wife is unsafe on the street after dark or in the park at any time, or whose kids get shaken down in the school yard, it also means something like normality—the demand that everybody play it by the book, that cultural and social standards be somehow restored to their civics-book simplicity, that things shouldn't be as they are but as they were supposed to be. If there is a revolution in this country—a revolt in manners, standards of dress and obscenity, and, more importantly, in our official sense of what America is—there is also a counter-revolt. Sometimes it is inarticulate, and sometimes (perhaps most of the time) people are either too confused or apathetic—or simply too polite and too decent—to declare themselves. In Astoria, Queens, a white working-class district of New York, people who make $7,000 or $8,000 a year (sometimes in two jobs) call themselves affluent, even though the Bureau of Labor Statistics regards an income of less than $9,500 in New York inadequate to a moderate standard of living. And in a similar neighborhood in Brooklyn a truck driver who earns $151 a week tells you he's doing well, living in a two-story frame house separated by a narrow driveway from similar houses, thousands of them in block after block. This year, for the first time, he will go on a cruise—he and his wife and two other couples—two weeks in the Caribbean. He went to work after World War II ($57 a week) and he has lived in the same house for twenty years, accumulating two television sets, wall-to-wall carpeting in a small living room, and a basement that he recently remodeled into a recreation room with the help of two moonlighting firemen. "We get fairly good salaries, and this is a good neighborhood, one of the few good ones left. We have no smoked Irishmen around."

Stability is what counts, stability in job and home and neighborhood, stability in the church and in friends. At night you watch television and sometimes on a weekend you go to a nice place—maybe a downtown hotel—for dinner with another couple. (Or maybe your sister, or maybe bowling, or maybe, if you're defeated, a night at the track.) The wife has the necessary appliances, often still being paid off, and the money you save goes for your daughter's orthodontist, and later for her wedding. The smoked Irishmen—the colored (no one says black; few even say Negro)—represent change and instability, kids who cause trouble in school, who get treatment that your kids never got, that you never got. ("Those fucking kids," they tell you in South Boston, "raising hell, and not one of 'em paying his own way. Their fucking mothers are all on welfare.") The black kids mean a change in the rules, a double standard in grades and discipline, and—vaguely—a challenge to all you believed right. Law and order is the stability and predictability of established ways. Law and order is equal treatment—in school, in jobs, in the courts—even if you're cheating a little yourself. The Forgotten Man is Jackson's man. He is the vestigial American democrat of 1840: "They all know that their success depends upon their own industry and economy and that they must not expect to become suddenly rich by the fruits of their toil." He is also Franklin Roosevelt's man —the man whose vote (or whose father's vote) sustained the New Deal.

There are other considerations, other styles, other problems. A postman in a Charlestown (Boston) housing project: eight children and a ninth on the way. Last year, by working overtime, his income went over $7,000. This year, because he reported it, the Housing Authority is raising his rent from $78 to $106 a month, a catastrophe for a family that pays $2.20 a day for milk, has never had a vacation, and for which an excursion is "going out for ice cream." "You try and save for something better; we hope to get out of here to someplace where the kids can play, where there's no broken glass, and then something always comes along that knocks you right back. It's like being at the bottom of the well waiting for a guy to throw you a rope." The description becomes almost Chaplinesque. Life is humble but not simple; the terrors of insolent bureaucracies and contemptuous officials produce a demonology that loses little of its horror for being partly misunderstood. You want to get a sink fixed but don't want to offend the manager; want to get an eye operation that may (or may not) have been necessitated by a military injury five years earlier, "but the Veterans Administration says I signed away my benefits"; want to complain to someone about the teenagers who run around breaking windows and harassing women but get no response either from the management or the police. "You're afraid to complain because if they don't get you during the day they'll get you at night." Automobiles, windows, children, all become hostages to the vague terrors of everyday life; everything is vulnerable. Liabilities that began long ago cannot possibly be liquidated: "I never learned anything in that school except how to fight. I got tired of being caned by the teachers so at sixteen I quit and joined the Marines. I still don't know anything."

At the Bottom of the Well

American culture? Wealth is visible, and so, now, is poverty. Both have become intimidating clichés. But the rest? A vast, complex, and disregarded world that was once—in belief, and in fact—the American middle: Greyhound and Trailways bus terminals in little cities at midnight, each of them with its neon lights and its cardboard hamburgers; acres of tar-paper beach bungalows in places like Revere and Rockaway; the hair curlers in the supermarket on Saturday, and the little girls in the communion dresses the next morning; pinball machines and the *Daily News,* the *Reader's Digest* and Ed Sullivan; houses with tiny front lawns (or even large ones) adorned with statues of the Virgin or of Sambo welcomin' de folks home; Clint Eastwood or Julie Andrews at the Palace; the trotting tracks and the dog tracks—Aurora Downs, Connaught Park, Roosevelt, Yonkers, Rockingham, and forty others—where gray men come not for sport and beauty, but to read numbers, to study and dope. (If you win you have figured something, have in a small way controlled your world, have surmounted your impotence. If you lose, bad luck, shit. "I'll break his goddamned head.") Baseball is not the national pastime; racing is. For every man who goes to a major-league baseball game there are four who go to the track and probably four more who go to the candy store or the barbershop to make their bets. (Total track attendance in 1965: 62 million plus another 10 million who went to the dogs.)

There are places, and styles, and attitudes. If there are neighborhoods of aspiration, suburban enclaves for the mobile young executie and the aspiring worker, there are also places of limited expectation and dead-end districts where mobility is finished. But even there you can often find, however vestigial, a sense of place, the roots of old ethnic loyalties, and a passionate, if often futile, battle against intrusion and change. "Everybody around here," you are told, "Pays his own way." In this world the problems are not the ABM or air pollution (have they heard of Biafra?) or the international population crisis; the problem is to get your street cleaned, your garbage collected, to get your husband home from Vietnam alive; to negotiate installment payments and to keep the schools orderly. Ask anyone in Scarsdale or Winnetka about the schools and they'll tell you about new programs, or about how many are getting into Harvard, or about the teachers; ask in Oakland or the North Side of Chicago, and they'll tell you that they have (or haven't) had trouble. Somewhere in his gut the man in those communities knows that mobility and choice in this society are limited. He cannot imagine any major change for the better; but he can imagine change for the worse. And yet for a decade he is the one who has been asked to carry the burden of social reform, to integrate his schools and his neighborhood, has been asked by comfortable people to pay the social debts due to the poor and the black. In Boston, in San Francisco, in Chicago (not to mention Newark or Oakland) he has been telling the reformers to go to hell. The Jewish schoolteachers of New York and the Irish parents of Dorchester have asked the same question: "What the hell did Lindsay (or the Beacon Hill Establishment) ever do for us?"

The ambiguities and changes in American life that occupy discussions in university seminars and policy debates in Washington, and that form the backbone of contemporary popular sociology, become increasingly the conditions of trauma and frustration in the middle. Although the New Frontier and Great Society contained some programs for those not already on the roll of social pathology—federal aid for higher education, for example—the public priorities and the rhetoric contained little. The emphasis, properly, was on the poor, on the inner cities (*e.g.*, Negroes) and the unemployed. But in Chicago a widow with three children who earns $7,000 a year can't get them college loans because she makes too much; the money is reserved for people on relief. New schools are built in the ghetto but not in the white working-class neighborhoods where they are just as dilapidated. In Newark the head of a white vigilante group (now a city councilman) runs, among other things, on a platform opposing pro-Negro discrimination. "When pools are being built in the Central Ward—don't they think white kids have got frustration? The white can't get a job; we have to hire Negroes first." The middle class, said Congressman Roman Pucinski of Illinois, who represents a lot of it, "is in revolt. Everyone has been generous in supporting anti-poverty. Now the middle-class American is disqualified from most of the programs."

"Somebody Has to Say No . . ."

The frustrated middle. The liberal wisdom about welfare, ghettos, student revolt, and Vietnam has only a marginal place, if any, for the values and life of the working man. It flies in the face of most of what he was taught to cherish and respect: hard work, order, authority, self-reliance. He fought, either alone or through labor organizations, to establish the precincts he now considers his own. Union seniority, the civil-service bureaucracy, and the petty professionalism established by the merit system in the public schools become sinecures of particular ethnic groups or of those who have learned to negotiate and master the system. A man who worked all his life to accumulate the points and grades and paraphernalia to become an assistant school principal (no matter how silly the requirements) is not likely to relinquish his position with equanimity. Nor is a dock worker whose only estate is his longshoreman's card. The job, the points, the credits become property:

> Some men leave their sons money [wrote a union member to the *New York Times*], some large investments, some business connections, and some a profession. I have only one worthwhile thing to give: my trade. I hope to follow a centuries-old tradition and sponsor my sons for an apprenticeship. For this simple father's wish it is said that I discriminate against Negroes. Don't all of us discriminate? Which of us . . . will not choose a son over all others?

Suddenly the rules are changing—all the rules. If you protect your job for your own you may be called a bigot. At the same time it's perfectly acceptable to shout black power and to endorse it. What does it take to be a good American? *Give the black man a position because he is black, not because he necessarily works harder or does the job better.* What does it take to be a good American? Dress nicely, hold a job, be clean-cut, don't judge a man by the color of his skin or the country of his origin. What about the demands of Negroes, the long hair of the students, the dirty movies, the people who burn draft cards and American flags? Do you have to go out in the street with picket signs, do you have to burn the place down to get what you want? What does it take to be a good American? *This is a sick society, a racist society, we are fighting an immoral war.* ("I'm against the Vietnam war, too," says the truck driver in Brooklyn. "I see a good kid come home with half an arm and a leg in a brace up to here, and what's it all for? I was glad to see *my kid* flunk the Army physical. Still, somebody has to say no to these demonstrators and enforce the law.") What does it take to be a good American?

The conditions of trauma and frustration in the middle. What does it take to be a good American? Suddenly there are demands for Italian power and Polish power and Ukrainian power. In Cleveland the Poles demand a seat on the school board, and get it, and in Pittsburgh John Pankuch, the seventy-three-year-old president of the National Slovak Society, demands "action, plenty of it to make up for lost time." Black power is supposed to be nothing but emulation of the ways in which other ethnic groups made it. But have they made it? In Reardon's Bar on East Eighth Street in South Boston, where the workmen come for their fish-chowder lunch and for their rye and ginger, they still identify themselves as Galway men and Kilkenny men; in the newsstand in Astoria you can buy *Il Progresso*, *El Tiempo*, the *Staats-Zeitung*, the *Irish World*, plus papers in Greek, Hungarian, and Polish. At the parish of Our Lady of Mount Carmel the priest hears confession in English, Italian, and Spanish and, nearby, the biggest attraction is not the stickball game, but the *boccie* court. Some of the poorest people in America are white, native, and have lived all of their lives in the same place as their fathers and grandfathers. The problems that were presumably solved in some distant past, in that prehistoric era before the textbooks were written—problems of assimilation, of upward mobility—now turn out to be very much unsolved. The melting pot and all: millions made it, millions moved to the affluent suburbs; several million—no one knows how many—did not. The median income in Irish South Boston is $5,100 a year but the community-action workers have a hard time convincing the local citizens that any white man who is not stupid or irresponsible can be poor. Pride still keeps them from applying for income supplements or Medicaid, but it does not keep them from resenting those who do. In Pittsburgh, where the members of Polish-American organizations earn an estimated $5,000 to $6,000 (and some fall below the poverty line), the Poverty Programs are nonetheless directed primarily to Negroes, and almost everywhere the thing called urban backlash associates itself in some fashion with ethnic groups whose members have themselves only a precarious hold on the security of affluence. Almost everywhere in the old cities, tribal neighborhoods and their styles are under assault by masscult. The Italian grocery gives way to the supermarket, the ma-and-pa store and the walk-up are attacked by urban renewal. And almost everywhere, that assault tends to depersonalize and to alienate. It has always been this way, but with time the brave new world that replaces old patterns becomes increasingly bureaucratized, distant, and hard to control.

Yet beyond the problems of ethnic identity, beyond the problems of Poles and Irishmen left behind, these are others more pervasive and more dangerous. For every Greek or Hungarian there are a dozen American-Americans who are past ethnic consciousness and who are as alienated, as confused, and as angry as the rest. The obvious manifestations are the same everywhere—race, taxes, welfare, students—but the threat seems invariably more cultural and psychological than economic or social. What upset the police at the Chicago convention most was not so much the politics of the demonstrators as their manners and their hair. (The barbershops in their neighborhoods don't advertise Beatle Cuts but the Flat Top and the Chicago Box.) The affront comes from middle-class people —and their children—who had been cast in the role of social exemplars (and from those cast as unfortunates worthy of public charity) who offend all the things on which working class identity is built: "hippies [said a San Francisco longshoreman] who fart around the streets and don't work"; welfare recipients who strike and march for better treatment; "all those [said a California labor official] who challenge the precepts that these people live on." If ethnic groups are beginning to organize to get theirs, so are others:

police and firemen ("The cop is the new nigger"); schoolteachers; lower-middle-class housewives fighting sex education and busing; small property owners who have no ethnic communion but a passionate interest in lower taxes, more policemen, and stiffer penalties for criminals. In San Francisco the Teamsters, who had never been known for such interests before, recently demonstrated in support of the police and law enforcement and, on another occasion, joined a group called Mothers Support Neighborhood Schools at a school-board meeting to oppose—with their presence and later, apparently, with their fists—a proposal to integrate the schools through busing. ("These people," someone said at the meeting, "do not look like mothers.")

Which is not to say that all is frustration and anger, that anybody is ready "to burn the country down." They are not even ready to elect standard model demagogues. "A lot of labor people who thought of voting for Wallace were ashamed of themselves when they realized what they were about to do," said Morris Iushewitz, an officer of New York's Central Labor Council. Because of a massive last-minute union campaign, and perhaps for other reasons, the blue-collar vote for Wallace fell far below the figures predicted by the early polls last fall.[1] Any number of people, moreover, who are not doing well by any set of official statistics, who are earning well below the national mean ($8,000 a year), or who hold two jobs to stay above it think of themselves as affluent, and often use that word. It is almost as if not to be affluent is to be un-American. People who can't use the word tend to be angry; people who come too close to those who can't become frightened. The definition of affluence is generally pinned to what comes in, not to the quality of life as it's lived. The $8,000 son of a man who never earned more than $4,500 may, for that reason alone, believe that he's "doing all right." If life is not all right, if he can't get his curbs fixed, or his streets patrolled, if the highways are crowded and the beaches polluted, if the schools are ineffectual he is still able to call himself affluent, feels, perhaps, a social compulsion to do so. His anger, if he is angry, is not that of the wage earner resenting management—and certainly not that of the socialist ideologue asking for redistribution of wealth—but that of the consumer, the taxpayer, and the family man. (Inflation and taxes are wiping out most of the wage gains made in labor contracts signed during the past three years.) Thus he will vote for a Louise Day Hicks in Boston who promises to hold the color line in the schools or for a Charles Stenvig calling for law enforcement in Minneapolis but reject a George Wallace who seems to threaten his pocketbook. The danger is that he will identify with the politics of the Birchers and other middle-class reaction-

1. The presidential campaign of 1968.

aries (who often pretend to speak for him) even though his income and style of life are far removed from theirs; that taxes, for example, will be identified with welfare rather than war, and that he will blame his limited means on the small slice of the poor rather than the fat slice of the rich.

If you sit and talk to people like Marjorie Lemlow, who heads Mothers Support Neighborhood Schools in San Francisco, or Joe Owens, a house painter who is president of a community-action organization in Boston, you quickly discover that the roots of reaction and the roots of reform are often identical, and that the response to particular situations is more often contingent on the politics of the politicians and leaders who appear to care than on the conditions of life or the ideology of the victims. Mrs. Lemlow wants to return the schools to some virtuous past; she worries about disintegration of the family and she speaks vaguely about something that she can't bring herself to call a conspiracy against American-ism. She has been accused of leading a bunch of Birchers, and she sometimes talks Birch language. But whatever the form, her sense of things comes from a small-town vision of national virtues, and her unhappiness from the assaults of urban sophistication. It just so happens that a lot of reactionaries now sing that tune, and that the liberals are indifferent.

Joe Owens—probably because of his experience as a Head Start parent, and because of his association with an effective community-action program—talks a different language. He knows, somehow, that no simple past can be restored. In his world the villains are not conspirators but bureaucrats and politicians, and he is beginning to discover that in a struggle with officials the black man in the ghetto and the working man (black or white) have the same problem. "Every time you ask for something from the politicians they treat you like a beggar, like you ought to be grateful for what you have. They try to make you feel ashamed."

When Hope Becomes a Threat

The imponderables are youth and tradition and change. The civics book and the institution it celebrates—however passé—still hold the world together. The revolt is in their name, not against them. And there is simple decency, the language and practice of the folksy cliché, the small town, the Boy Scout virtues, the neighbor-hood charity, the obligation to support the church, the rhetoric of open opportunity: "They can keep Wallace and they can keep Alabama. We didn't fight a dictator for four years so we could elect one over here." What happens when all that becomes Mickey Mouse? Is there an urban ethic to replace the values of the small town? Is there a coherent public philosophy, a consistent set of

beliefs to replace family, home, and hard work? What happens
when the hang-ups of upper-middle-class kids are in fashion and
those of blue-collar kids are not? What happens when Doing Your
Own Thing becomes not the slogan of the solitary deviant but the
norm? Is it possible that as the institutions and beliefs of tradition
are fashionably denigrated a blue-collar generation gap will open to
the Right as well as to the Left? (There is statistical evidence, for
example, that Wallace's greatest support within the unions came
from people who are between twenty-one and twenty-nine, those,
that is, who have the most tenuous association with the liberalism of
labor.) Most are politically silent; although SDS has been trying to
organize blue-collar high-school students, there are no Mario Savios
or Mark Rudds—either of the Right or the Left—among them. At
the same time the union leaders, some of them old hands from the
Thirties, aren't sure that the kids are following them either. Who
speaks for the son of the longshoreman or the Detroit auto worker?
What happens if he doesn't get to college? What, indeed, happens
when he does?

Vaguely but unmistakably the hopes that a youth-worshiping
nation historically invested in its young are becoming threats. We
have never been unequivocal about the symbolic patricide of Ameri-
canization and upward mobility, but if at one time mobility meant
rejection of older (or European) styles it was, at least, done in the
name of America. Now the labels are blurred and the objectives
indistinct. Just at the moment when a tradition-bound Italian
father is persuaded that he should send his sons to college—that
education is the only future—the college blows up. At the moment
when a parsimonious taxpayer begins to shell out for what he considers an extravagant state university system the students go on
strike. Marijuana, sexual liberation, dress styles, draft resistance,
even the rhetoric of change become monsters and demons in a
world that appears to burn old virtues upside down. The paranoia
that fastened on Communism twenty years ago (and sometimes still
does) is increasingly directed to vague conspiracies undermining the
schools, the family, order and discipline. "They're feeding the kids
this generation-gap business," says a Chicago housewife who grinds
out a campaign against sex education on a duplicating machine in
her living room. "The kids are told to make their own decisions.
They're all mixed up by situation ethics and open-ended questions.
They're alienating children from their own parents." They? The
churches, the schools, even the YMCA and the Girl Scouts, are
implicated. But a major share of the villainy is now also attributed
to "the social science centers," to the apostles of sensitivity training, and to what one California lady, with some embarrassment,
called "nude therapy." "People with sane minds are being altered
by psychological methods." The current major campaign of the

John Birch Society is not directed against Communists in government or the Supreme Court, but against sex education.

(There is, of course, also sympathy with the young, especially in poorer areas where kids have no place to play. "Everybody's got to have a hobby," a South Boston adolescent told a youth worker. "Ours is throwing rocks." If people will join reactionary organizations to protect their children, they will also support others: community-action agencies which help kids get jobs; Head Start parent groups, Boys Clubs. "Getting this place cleaned up" sometimes refers to a fear of young hoods; sometimes it points to the day when there is a park or a playground or when the existing park can be used. "I want to see them grow up to have a little fun.")

Can the Common Man Come Back!

Beneath it all there is a more fundamental ambivalence, not only about the young, but about institutions—the schools, the churches, the Establishment—and about the future itself. In the major cities of the East (though perhaps not in the West) there is a sense that time is against you, that one is living "in one of the few decent neighborhoods left," that "if I can get $125 a week upstate (or downstate) I'll move." The institutions that were supposed to mediate social change and which, more than ever, are becoming priesthoods of information and conglomerates of social engineers, are increasingly suspect. To attack the Ford Foundation (as Wright Patman has done) is not only to fan the embers of historic populism against concentrations of wealth and power, but also to arouse those who feel that they are trapped by an alliance of upper-class Wasps and lower-class Negroes. If the foundations have done anything for the blue-collar worker he doesn't seem to be aware of it. At the same time the distrust of professional educators that characterizes the black militants is becoming increasingly prevalent among a minority of lower-middle-class whites who are beginning to discover that the schools aren't working for them either. ("Are all those new programs just a cover-up for failure?") And if the Catholic Church is under attack from its liberal members (on birth control, for example) it is also alienating the traditionalists who liked their minor saints (even if they didn't actually exist) and were perfectly content with the Latin Mass. For the alienated Catholic liberal there are other places to go; for the lower-middle-class parishioner in Chicago or Boston there are none.

Perhaps, in some measure, it has always been this way. Perhaps none of this is new. And perhaps it is also true that the American lower middle has never had it so good. And yet surely there is a difference, and that is that the common man has lost his visibility and, somehow, his claim on public attention. There are old liberals and socialists—men like Michael Harrington—who believe that a new alliance can be forged for progressive social action:

> From Marx to Mills, the Left has regarded the middle class as a stratum of hyprocritical, vacillating rear-guarders. There was often sound reason for this contempt. But is it not possible that a new class is coming into being? It is not the old middle class of small property owners and entre-preneurs, nor the new middle class of managers. It is composed of scien-tists, technicians, teachers, and professionals in the public sector of the society. By education and work experience it is predisposed toward plan-ning. It could be an ally of the poor and the organized workers—or their sophisticated enemy. In other words, an unprecedented social and political variable seems to be taking shape in America.
>
> The American worker, even when he waits on a table or holds open a door, is not servile; he does not carry himself like an inferior. The openness, frankness, and democratic manner which Tocqueville described in the last century persists to this very day. They have been a source of rudeness, contemptuous ignorance, violence—and of a creative self-confidence among great masses of people. It was in this latter spirit that the CIO was organized and the black freedom movement marched.

There are recent indications that the white lower middle class is coming back on the roster of public priorities. Pucinski tells you that liberals in Congress are privately discussing the pressure from the middle class. There are proposals now to increase personal income-tax exemptions from $600 to $1,000 (or $1,200) for each dependent, to protect all Americans with a national insurance sys-tem covering catastrophic medical expenses, and to put a floor under all incomes. Yet these things by themselves are insufficient. Nothing is sufficient without a national sense of restoration. What Pucinski means by the middle class has, in some measure, always been repre-sented. A physician earning $75,000 a year is also a working man but he is hardly a victim of the welfare system. Nor, by and large, are the stockholders of the Standard Oil Company or U.S. Steel. The fact that American ideals have often been corrupted in the cause of self-aggrandizement does not make them any less impor-tant for the cause of social reform and justice. "As a movement with the conviction that there is more to people than greed and fear," Harrington said, "the Left must . . . also speak in the name of the historic idealism of the United States."

The issue, finally, is not *the program* but the vision, the angle of view. The huge constituency may be coming up for grabs, and there considerable evidence that its political mobility is more sensitive is than anyone can imagine, that all the sociological determinants are not as significant as the simple facts of concern and leadership. When Robert Kennedy was killed last year, thousands of working-class people who had expected to vote for him—if not hundreds of thousands—shifted their loyalties to Wallace. A man who can change from a progressive democrat into a bigot overnight deserves attention.

JOHN F. KERRY
I Would Like to Tell You Something

I would like to tell you something about what veterans are doing in this country, and about our feelings now that we've come back from a war we didn't really want to fight.

A little over a week ago we held an investigation in Detroit where over 150 honorably discharged veterans, many of them highly decorated, testified to war crimes committed in Indochina—not isolated incidents, but crimes committed on a day-to-day basis with the full awareness of officers at all levels of command.

It's impossible to accurately describe to you the emotion in that room in Detroit, but these veterans relived the absolute horror of their experiences and told of the times that they had personally raped, cut off ears, taped wires from portable phones to human genitals and turned up the power, cut off limbs, blown up bodies, randomly shot at civilians, razed villages in a fashion reminiscent of Genghis Khan, shot cattle for fun, poisoned wells and foodstock, and on and on.

The investigation was not staged so that veterans could spill out their hearts or purge their souls; it was done to prove that the policy of the United States in Indochina is tantamount to genocide, and that not only the soldiers are responsible for what is happening, but that everyone here in America who has allowed the brutalization and depersonalization to go on is responsible. It was done also to show that you don't start making things right by prosecuting William Calley, no matter how guilty he may be; you also prosecute the men who encouraged the situation. It was done to show that there is not just one Mylai but countless Mylais and they are continuing every single day. There was an almost total press blackout on the testimony of those veterans.

But this isn't new to those of us who were in the war. I can remember traveling to Saigon and trying to talk to the admiral who commanded the naval forces to tell him that what we were doing was wrong. I remember going to a writer for a national magazine and telling him this was a story the American people should hear. He agreed, but said it would never get by his desk because the Army would rescind the magazine's accreditation to cover the war, and if you don't cover the war you don't sell magazines, and if you don't sell magazines then nothing happens because that's the American way.

But the press isn't the only party in this country that's guilty of this rampant insensitivity. When I went to the chairman of the board of a large New York-based firm and asked him for money to help us get transcripts of the testimony to present to each member of Congress so that we can press our demands for open hearings, I was told in seriousness: "I don't think you can market war crimes —it's a marketing question, you know." And then in the next breath to his executive vice president: "Hell, we used to do that in World War II. Christ, what's new?"

We all know that this de-sensitizing started a long time ago in this country, but it is carried out in a far more vicious way with the soldier. At boot camp he's presented with a poster in his barracks of a crucified Vietnamese and underneath it says, "Kill the gooks." The message begins to sink in. During training, calisthenics are done to a four-count, and at the end of the four-count everybody jumps up and yells "Kill!" For the Marines at Camp Pendleton, before they depart for Vietnam, there's a very special treat: the sergeant takes a live rabbit and skins it, tearing it open, pulling out the entrails to throw at the assembled soldiers, saying, "That's how it's done in Nam; go get 'em Marines!"

And so we're suddenly faced with a sickening situation in this country. There's no longer any moral indignation. And if there is, it comes from people who are almost exhausted from past indignities inflicted on them. The country seems to be lying down and accepting something as serious as Laos, just as before we dismissed the loss of 700,000 lives in Pakistan, the so called greatest disaster of all time. Well, I think we're in the midst of the greatest disaster of all time right now, because they are still dying over there every day. And I don't just mean American boys.

And the mass of people in this country literally don't give a damn. After all, you can switch off the TV news and put on Dick Van Dyke. We're not on food rationing; people can still charge prostitutes on credit cards; so what if a few lives are used to save American face in an unsaveable situation? It should not be hard for people in this country to admit there is no difference between a ground troop and a helicopter troop; yet we have accepted a differentiation fed us by the Administration. No ground troops are in Laos, so it's all right to kill Laotians as long as it's done by remote control. Believe me, the helicopter crews fill the same body bags as the ground troops, and they do the same damage to the Vietnamese countryside and the Laotian people. It's absolutely incredible that this country is ready to accept this kind of hypocrisy.

But what this country doesn't know is that America has created a monster in the form of millions of fighting men who have been taught to deal in violence, and who have been given a chance to die for the biggest nothing in history. We have returned to this country with a sense of anger and betrayal which nobody has yet grasped. We're angry about the same things you are in terms of policy—a little angrier because our lives were the things used to test those policies.

But we're angry also because of statements like the one Vice President Agnew made when he spoke at West Point in 1970. He spoke of how some people glamorize the criminal misfits of society while the best men die in Asian rice paddies to preserve the freedoms that those misfits abuse. Support the boys in Vietnam. But for us, those boys in Vietnam whom the country is supposed to support, this is a terrible distortion from which we draw only the deepest revulsion.

It's a distortion because we in no way considered ourselves the "best men" in this country, because those he called misfits were standing up for us in a way nobody else in this country dared to, because we know that so many who died would have come back to join the misfits, and because so many of us have actually returned to this country to demand an immediate withdrawal from Vietnam. And because so many of those "best men" have returned as amputees and quadraplegics to lie in rancid hospitals which fly the flag that Mr. Agnew holds so close.

And one can't consider us "best men" when we were ashamed of and hated what we were called on to do in Asia. And to attempt to justify the loss of one American life in Vietnam, Cambodia, Laos or anywhere in Indochina, or anywhere in the world, or even here in America, by saying that that kind of loss of life is linked to the preservation of freedom, is to play exactly the kind of criminal hypocrisy that has torn this country apart.

Our anger goes beyond the simple policy matters. It goes into the fact that all the things we were told about Vietnam we found untrue when we got there. We found that too often American men were dying in those rice paddies from want of support from our so-called allies. We saw first-hand the money—your taxes—squandered by a corrupt dictatorial regime. We saw that Agnew had a one-sided idea of who was kept free by the flag, as blacks provided the highest percentage of casualties.

We saw Vietnam ravaged equally by American bombs and search-and-destroy missions and by Viet Cong terrorists, and we listened while America blamed it all on the Viet Cong. We watched while we rationalized destroying villages to save them, while we saw America lose her sense of morality as she coolly accepted a Mylai and refused to give up the image of American soldiers handing out chewing gum and chocolate bars.

We watched while pride allowed unimportant battles to be escalated into the most important stands of the war—because we couldn't lose and we couldn't retreat and because it didn't matter how many American bodies were provided to prove that point. Now we are told that we have to watch quietly while more American lives are lost so that we can exercise the incredible arrogance of Vietnamizing the Vitnamese.

The problem of the veteran doesnt just end with his anger. One out of every 10 of the unemployed in this country today is a Vietnam veteran. That's 22.5 per cent of all the veterans who are unemployed. Thirty-three per cent of these are black. We have veterans who practically have to sue the Veterans Administration to get their artificial limbs. Fifty-seven per cent of those entering hospitals have thought about suicide and 27 per cent have tried it. Sixty-eight per cent of the troops in Vietnam are on dope, and the addicts who return receive little if any care.

We're going to do something about this situation. On April 19,[1] members of Vietnam Veterans Against the War, now numbering 7,000 men and growing, are marching on Washington—in uniform, wearing medals. We're paying homage to the dead in Arlington. We are then marching with veterans of other wars, with families of the deceased, families of prisoners of war, whoever will join us, on the Capitol. And we're camping and we're staying there to demand that our needs be met. But more important, we won't move until they set a date for withdrawal of troops from Vietnam.

We will also be returning our war medals to Congress and be demanding that the judiciary of this country rule on the Massachusetts bill which calls for the declaration that the Vietnam war is unconstitutional. We're asking for the support of all sections of the peace movement because we do not feel that this is a time to be dormant. The war is part and parcel of everything that we're trying to communicate to people of this country. The problem of Vietnam is not just the problem of war and diplomacy; it's a problem of the very basic American idealism that we're trying to question.

An American Indian friend of mine, a veteran, a member of the Indian Nation of Alcatraz, put it to me very succinctly: he told me how, as a boy on the Indian reservation, he had watched televison and cheered the cowboys who killed the Indians in an ambush. Then suddenly one day he woke up in Vietnam and he found himself doing to the Vietnamese exactly what had been done to his people and what he had been conditioned by America to applaud. I think that that says it all. The veteran has been used horribly.

But now he's going to to do something about it. He's going to take all the goodness of his uniform, all the apple pie and motherhood and medals in the service of his country, and he's going to place it before the people of this country, telling it like it really is.

1. 1971

ANTHONY BURGESS
Is America Falling Apart?

I am back in Bracciano, a castellated town about 13 miles north of Rome, after a year in New Jersey. I find the Italian Government still unstable, gasoline more expensive than anywhere in the world, butchers and bank clerks and tobacconists (which also means salt-sellers) ready to go on strike at the drop of a *cappello*, neo-Fascists at their dirty work, the hammer and sickle painted on the rumps of public statues, a thousand-lire note (officially worth about $1.63) shrunk to the slightness of a dollar bill.

Nevertheless, it's delightful to be back. People are underpaid but they go through an act of liking their work, the open markets are luscious with esculent color, the community is more important than the state, the human condition is humorously accepted. The *tramontana* blows viciously today, and there's no central heating to turn on, but it will be pleasant when the wind drops. The two television channels are inadequate, but next Wednesday's rerun of an old Western, with Gary Cooper coming into a saloon saying *"Ciao, ragazzi,"* is something to look forward to. Manifold consumption isn't important here. The quality of life has nothing to do with the quantity of brand names. What matters is talk, family, cheap wine in the open air, the wresting of minimal sweetness out of the long-known bitterness of living. I was spoiled in New Jersey. The Italian for *spoiled* is *viziato*, cognate with *vitiated*, which has to do with vice.

Spoiled? Well, yes. I never had to shiver by a fire that wouldn't draw, or go without canned kraut juice or wild rice. America made me develop new appetites in order to make proper use of the supermarket. A character in Evelyn Waugh's *Put Out More Flags* said that the difference between prewar and postwar life was that, prewar, if one thing went wrong the day was ruined; postwar, if one thing went right the day would be made. America is a prewar country, psychologically unprepared for one thing to go wrong. Now everything seems to be going wrong. Hence the neurosis, despair, the Kafka feeling that the whole marvelous fabric of American life is coming apart at the seams. Italy is used to everything going wrong. This is what the human condition is about.

Let me stay for a while on this subject of consumption. American individualism, on the face of it an admirable philosophy, wishes to manifest itself in independence of the community. You don't share things in common; you have your own things. A family's strength is signalized by its possessions. Herein lies a paradox. For the desire for possessions must eventually mean dependence on possessions.

Freedom is slavery. Once let the acquisitive instinct burgeon (enough flour for the winter, not just for the week), and there are ruggedly individual forces only too ready to make it come to full and monstrous blossom. New appetites are invented; what to the European are bizarre luxuries become, to the American, plain necessities.

During my year's stay in New Jersey I let my appetites flower into full Americanism except for one thing. I did not possess an automobile. This self-elected deprivation was a way into the nastier side of the consumer society. Where private ownership prevails, public amenities decay or are prevented from coming into being. The wretched run-down rail services of America are something I try, vainly, to forget. The nightmare of filth, outside and in, that enfolds the trip from Springfield, Mass., to Grand Central Station would not be accepted in backward Europe. But far worse is the nightmare of travel in and around Los Angeles, where public transport does not exist and people are literally choking to death in their exhaust fumes. This is part of the price of the metaphysic of individual ownership.

But if the car owner can ignore the lack of public transport, he can hardly ignore the decay of services in general. His car needs mechanics, and mechanics grow more expensive and less efficient. The gadgets in the home are cheaper to replace than repair. The more efficiently self-contained the home, primary fortress of independence, seems to be, the more dependent it is on the great impersonal corporations, as well as a diminishing army of servitors. Skills at the lowest level have to be wooed slavishly and exorbitantly rewarded. Plumbers will not come. Nor, at the higher level, will doctors. And doctors and dentists, in a nation committed to maiming itself with sugar and cholesterol, know their scarcity value and behave accordingly.

Americans are at last realizing that the acquisition of goods is not the whole of life. Consumption, on one level, is turning insipid, especially as the quality of the artifacts themselves seems to be deteriorating. Planned obsolescence is not conducive to pride in workmanship. On another level, consumption is turning sour. There is a growing guilt about the masses of discarded junk—rusting automobiles and refrigerators and washing machines and dehumidifiers— that it is uneconomical to recycle. Indestructible plastic hasn't even the grace to undergo chemical change. America, the world's biggest consumer, is the world's biggest polluter. Awareness of this is a kind of redemptive grace, but it doesn't appreciably lead to repentance and a revolution in consumer habits. Citizens of Los Angeles are horrified by that daily pall of golden smog, but they don't noticeably clamor for a decrease in the number of owner-vehicles. There is no worse neurosis than that which derives from a consciousness of guilt and an inability to reform.

America is anachronistic in so many ways, and not least in its clinging to a belief—now known to be unviable—in the capacity of the individual citizen to do everything for himself. Americans are admirable in their distrust of the corporate state—they have fought both Fascism and Communism—but they forget that there is a use for everything, even the loathesome bureaucratic machine. America needs a measure of socialization, as Britain needed it. Things—especially those we need most—don't always pay their way, and it is here that the state must enter, dismissing the profit element. Part of the present American neurosis, again, springs from awareness of this but inability to do anything about practical implementation. Perhaps only a country full of bombed cities feels capable of this kind of social revolution.

It would be supererogatory for me to list those areas in which thoughtful Americans feel that collapse is coming. It is enough for me to concentrate on what, during my New Jersey stay, impinged on my own life. Education, for instance, since I have a 6-year-old son to be brought up. America has always despised its teachers and, as a consequence, it has been granted the teachers it deserves. The quality of first-grade education that my son received, in a New Jersey town noted for the excellence of its public schools, could not, I suppose, be faulted on the level of dogged conscientiousness. The principal had read all the right pedagogic books, and was ready to quote these in the footnotes to his circular exhortations to parents. The teachers worked rigidly from the approved rigidly programed primers, ensuring that school textbook publication remains the big business it is.

But there seemed to be no spark; no daring, no madness, no readiness to engage the individual child's mind as anything other than raw material for statistical reductions. The fear of being unorthodox is rooted in the American teacher's soul: you can be fired for treading the path of experimental enterprise. In England, teachers cannot be fired, except for raping girl students and getting boy students drunk. In consequence, there is the kind of security that breeds eccentric genius, the capacity for firing mad enthusiasms.

I know that American technical genius, and most of all the moon landings, seems to give the lie to too summary a condemnation of the educational system, but there is more to education than the segmental equipping of the mind. There is that transmission of the value of the past as a force still miraculously fertile and moving—mostly absent from American education at all levels.

Of course, America was built on a rejection of the past. Even the basic Christianity which was brought to the continent in 1620 was

of a novel and bizarre kind that would have nothing to do with the
great rank river of belief that produced Dante and Michelangelo.
America as a nation has never been able to settle to a common
belief more sophisticated than the dangerous naiveté of the Declaration of Independence. "Life, liberty and the pursuit of happiness,"
indeed. And now America, filling in the vacuum left by the lique-
fied British Empire, has the task of telling the rest of the world that
there's something better than Communism. The something better
can only be money-making and consumption for its own sake. In
the name of this ghastly creed the jungles must be defoliated.

No wonder the guilt of the thoughtful Americans I met in Princeton and New York and, indeed, all over the Union tended to express itself as an extravagant masochism, a desire for flagellation.
Americans want to take on all the blame they can find, gluttons for
punishment. "What do Europeans really think of us?" is a common
question at parties. The expected answer is: "They think you're a
load of decadent, gross-lipped, potbellied, callous, overbearing
neoimperialists." Then the head can be bowed and the chest smit-
ten: "*Nostra culpa, nostra maxima culpa. . . .*" But the fact is that
such an answer, however much desired, would not be an honest
one. Europeans think more highly of Americans now than they ever
did. Let me try to explain why.

When Europe, after millennia of war, rapine, slavery, famine,
intolerance, had sunk to the level of a sewer, America became the
golden dream, the Eden where innocence could be recovered. Original sin was the monopoly of that dirty continent over there; in
America man could glow in an aura of natural goodness, driven
along his shining path by divine reason. The Declaration of Independence itself is a monument to reason. Progress was possible, and
the wrongs committed against the Indians, the wildlife, the land
itself, could be explained away in terms of the rational control of
environment necessary for the building of a New Jerusalem. Right
and wrong made up the moral dichotomy; evil—that great eternal
inextirpable entity—had no place in America.

At last, with the Vietnam war and especially the Mylai horror,
Americans are beginning to realize that they are subject to original
sin as much as Europeans are. Some things—the massive crime
figures, for instance—can now be explained only in terms of absolute evil. Europe, which has long known about evil and learned to
live with it (*live* is *evil* spelled backwards), is now grimly pleased
to find that America is becoming like Europe. America is no longer
Europe's daughter nor her rich stepmother: she is Europe's sister.
The agony that America is undergoing is not to be associated with
breakdown so much as with the parturition of self-knowledge.

It has been assumed by many that the youth of America has

been in the vanguard of the discovery of both the disease and the cure. The various copping-out movements, however, from the Beats on, have committed the gross error of assuming that original sin rested with their elders, their rulers, and that they themselves could manifest their essential innocence by building little neo-Edens. The drug culture could confirm that the paradisal vision was available to all who sought it. But instant ecstasy has to be purchased, like any other commodity, and, in economic terms, that passive life of pure being involves parasitism. Practically all of the crime I encountered in New York—directly or through report—was a preying of the opium-eaters on the working community. There has to be a snake in paradise. You can't escape the heritage of human evil by building communes, usually on an agronomic ignorance that, intended to be a rejection of inherited knowledge, that suspect property of the elders, does violence to life. The American young are well-meaning but misguided, and must not themselves be taken as guides.

The guides, as always, lie among the writers and artists. And Americans ought to note that, however things may seem to be falling apart, arts and the humane scholarship are flourishing here, as they are not, for instance, in England. I'm not suggesting that Bellow, Mailer, Roth and the rest have the task of finding a solution to the American mess, but they can at least clarify its nature and show how it relates to the human condition in general. Literature, that most directly human of the arts, often reacts magnificently to an ambience of unease or apparent breakdown. The Elizabethans, to whose era we look back as to an irrecoverable Golden Age, were far more conscious than modern Americans of the chaos and corruption and incompetence of the state. Shakespeare's period was one of poverty, unemployment, ghastly inflation, violence in the streets. Twenty-six years after his death there was a bloody civil war, followed by a dictatorship of religious fanatics, followed by a calm respite in which the seeds of a revolution were sown. England survived. America will survive.

I'm not suggesting that Americans sit back and wait for a transient period of mistrust and despair to resolve itself, like a disease, through the unconscious healing forces which lie deep in organic nature. Man, as Thornton Wilder showed in *The Skin of Our Teeth*, always comes through—though sometimes only just. Americans living here and now have a right to an improvement in the quality of their lives, and they themselves, not the remote governors, must do something about it. It is not right that men and women should fear to go on the streets at night, and that they should sometimes fear the police as much as the criminals, both of whom sometimes look like mirror images of each other. I have had too much evidence, in my year in New Jersey, of the police behaving like the "Fascist pigs" of the revolutionary press. There are too

many guns about, and the disarming of the police should be a
natural aspect of the disarming of the entire citizenry.

American politics, at both the state and the Federal levels, is too
much concerned with the protection of large fortunes, America
being the only example in history of a genuine timocracy. The
wealth qualification for the aspiring politician is taken for granted; a
governmental system dedicated to the promotion of personal wealth
in a few selected areas will never act for the public good. The time
has come, nevertheless, for citizens to demand, from their government, a measure of socialization—the provision of amenities for the
many, of which adequate state pensions and sickness benefits, as
well as nationalized transport, should be priorities.

As for those remoter solutions to the American nightmare—only
an aspect, after all, of the human nightmare—an Englishman must
be diffident about suggesting that America made her biggest mistake
in becoming America—meaning a revolutionary republic based on a
romantic view of human nature. To reject a limited monarchy in
favor of an absolute one (which is, after all, what the American
Presidency is) argues a trust in the disinterestedness of an elected
ruler which is, of course, no more than a reflection of belief in the
innate goodness of man—so long as he happens to be American
man. The American Constitution is out of date. Republics tend to
corruption. Canada and Australia have their own problems, but
they are happier countries than America.

This *Angst* about America coming apart at the seams, which
apparently is shared by nearly 50 per cent of the entire American
population, is something to rejoice about. A sense of sin is always
admirable, though it must not be allowed to become neurotic. If
electric systems break down and gadgets disintegrate, it doesn't
matter much. There is always wine to be drunk by candlelight,
uniced. If America's position as a world power collapses, and the
Union dissolves into independent states, there is still the life of the
family or the individual to be lived. England has survived her own
dissolution as an imperial power, and Englishmen seem to be happy
enough. But I ask the reader to note that I, an Englishman, no
longer live in England, and I can't spend more than six months at a
stretch in Italy—or any other European country, for that matter. I
home to America as to a country more stimulating than depressing.
The future of mankind is being worked out there on a scale typically American—vast, dramatic, almost apocalyptical. I brave the
brutality and the guilt in order to be in on the scene. I shall be
back.

QUESTIONS

1. What would Burgess say of the Whole Earth Catalogue: is it a
rejection of consumerism or a surrender to it?

2. In what respects is the substance of Burgess' argument similar to those of Eldridge Cleaver (above, pp. 109–118) and George Jackson (below, pp. 254–267)? Compare the language used by the three to articulate the similar substance; is the language of any one more basic than that of the other two?

3. Burgess' observation about the Italian word for spoiled implies a concern for etymology and precision of language. Is there evidence of that concern in his choice of English words?

Prose Forms: Oral History

[But what did he say?" is a question listeners would sometimes like to ask when they have been told what another person meant, or intended, or implied, or even thought. It is not a matter of distrusting the reporter's account, nor necessarily of merely wishing to hear the report put differently. It may be that in order to get the direct, unmediated, uninterpreted utterance, the listener will ask for the authentic—and authoritative—words as they were said. Does the listener therefore get a greater measure of truth or a clearer sense of meaning from the original utterance than from a report of it? He may not, of course; but he may in many instances, if the "truth" and "meaning" of the utterance depend as much on the personality and character of the speaker as they do on the occasion about which he speaks.

The kind of occasion is important here. If it is generally familiar in its outline because widely known or frequently encountered (either directly in one's own experience or indirectly through reading, study, or the communications and entertainment media), it is public and therefore familiarly accessible to our immediate understanding. The relation of a specific personality to that occasion, his perception of it, is as telling as the public occasion itself seen independently of its private effect on specific individuals—and frequently much more interesting because the coming together of the private and the public not only particularizes the relation but indeed humanizes the occasion.

The range of possibility in oral history encompasses the closely reasoned interchange between Huey Newton and Erik Erikson on the meaning of "armed love" and James Thurber's thoughts on his—and others'—methods as artists, on the one hand, and the simple declarations with complex implications of a police sergeant, on the other. The oral historian keeps us strictly in touch with the privately, personally human sieve of public experience.

All history was once oral, and out of it grew poetry as well as formal history as we now know it. One of the things which modern oral history preserves for us is the element of the poetic, if we understand that term to mean, in this broad context, the sense of private vision articulated in language which points toward both the public object or occasion and the unique sensibility perceiving it. In addition, it often arises freely, unpremeditated, almost unstructured except for loose chronology and the vagaries of association. It may not be logical, depending instead on a kind of psycho-logic which has its own meaning, usually evident in the style, the peculiar flavor of a distinct mind and personality apparent in the language of the recital.

And it is direct and honest, seeking usually no end except to express itself. We tend to minimize the factual errors, the mistaken vocabulary, the flamboyant rhetoric, the preposterous judgments of people and events in "Doc Graham," even as we are totally fascinated by him and his ruminations on crime, the Depression, and his own career in both. Uncensored, unrepressed, confined only by a sense of his own authority and confidence, Doc Graham's history wells up and flows out spontaneously, honestly, authentically. All around the edges of his remarks and appearing dramatically in the midst of them are "facts," public events and personalities and occasions which we know about independently. They are unsullied in our minds even if they are mangled in Doc Graham's, but the power and grandeur of his posture, his style as a man and as a speaker, ring marvelous subtleties on those facts without destroying them. He literally brings them to life, his life, in a way instructive to both. Private and public, person and events are the mixture. History of a very real and useful kind is the issue.]

STUDS TERKEL: Doc Graham[1]

A mutual acquaintance, Kid Pharaoh, insisted that we meet. Doc Graham had obviously seen better days.

My introduction to Chicago was when a guy got his head blowed off right across from where I went to stay. In that neighborhood where I gravitated, there was every kind of character that was ever invented. Con men, heist men, burglars, peet men: you name it, they had it.

These are highly sophisticated endeavors. To be proficient at it —well, my God, you spent a lifetime. And then you might fall, through not being sophisticated enough. You may have committed a common error, leaving fingerprints. . . .

I was a caged panther. It was jungle. Survival was the law of the land. I watched so many of my partners fall along the way. I decided the modus operandi was bad. Unavailing, non-productive. After spending ten Saturdays in jail, one right after another, I changed my modus operandi.

What were you in jail for?

Various allegations. All alleged. I been a con man, a heist man— you name it.

How does a heist man differ from a con man?

One is by force and the other is by guile. Very few people have encompassed both. I was very daring. When I came to the city and seen groceries on the sidewalk, I swore I'd never be hungry again. My family was extremely poor. My father was an unsuccessful gambler, and my mother was a missionary. Not much money was connected with either profession.

A family conflict . . . ?

Yes, slightly. He threw the Bible in the fire. He was right, incidentally. [Laughs.] My mother didn't see it that way.

I'm sixty-one, and I have never held a Social Security card. I'm not knocking it. I have been what society generally refers to as a parasite. But I don't think I'd be a nicer fellow if I held two jobs.

My teacher was Count Victor Lustig. He was perhaps the greatest con man the United States has ever known. Lustig's outstanding achievement was getting put in jail and paying a Texas sheriff off with $30,000 counterfeit. And the sheriff made the penitentiary also. He got to be a believer. And he went into the counterfeit profession.

Another teacher was Ace Campbell.[2] He was the greatest card

1. From *Hard Times: An Oral History of the Great Depression*, 1970.
2. A pseudonym for a celebrated gambler of the twenties and early thirties. He is still alive [Terkel's note].

mechanic that ever arrived on the scene. Nick the Greek[3] wouldn't
make him a butler. A footman. He couldn't open the door for him.
Ace played the crimp. A crimp is putting a weave in a card that
you'd need a microscope to see it. I know the techniques, but
having had my arm half removed, I had to switch left-handed, deal
left-handed. I'm ambidexterous.

An accident . . . ?

With a colored North American. The twenties and early thirties
was a jungle, where only the strong survived and the weak fell by
the wayside. In Chicago, at the time, the unsophisticated either
belonged to the Bugs Moran mob or the Capone mob. The fellas
with talent didn't bother with either one. And went around and
robbed both of 'em.

We were extremely independent. Since I'm Irish, I had a working affiliate with Bugs Moran's outfit. In case muscle was needed
beyond what I had, I called on Moran for help. On the other hand,
Moran might use me to help in one of his operations.

The nature of one operation was: if you had a load of whiskey
hijacked, we went over and reloaded it on a truck, while several surrounded the place with machine guns, sawed-off shotguns, etcetera.

Did you find yourself in ticklish situations on occasion . . . ?

Many of them. You see this fellow liquidated, that fellow disposed of. Red McLaughlin had the reputation of being the toughest
guy in Chicago. But when you seen Red run out of the drainage
canal, you realized Red's modus operandi was unavailing. His associates was Clifford and Adams. They were set in Al's doorway in his
hotel in Cicero. That was unavailing. Red and his partners once
stole the Checker Cab Company. They took machine guns and
went up and had an election, and just went and took it over. I
assisted in that operation.

What role did the forces of law and order play?

With a $10 bill, you wasn't bothered. If you had a speaking
acquaintance with Mayor Thompson,[4] you could do no wrong.
[Laughs.] Al spoke loud to him.

There was a long period during the Depression where the police
were taking scrip. Cash had a language all of its own. One night in
particular, I didn't have my pistol with me, and the lady of the evening pointed out a large score to me. [Laughs.] A squad car came
by, which I was familiar with. A Cadillac, with a bell on it. I knew
all the officers. I borrowed one of their pistols and took the score.
Then I had to strip and be searched by the policemen, keeping
honest in the end, as we divided the score. They wanted the right
count. They thought I might be holding out on 'em. They even
went into my shoes, even.

3. Another renowned gambler of the time [Terkel's note].

4. William Hale Thompson, three-term mayor of Chicago [Terkel's note].

Oh, many policemen in that era were thieves. Legal thieves. I accepted it as such and performed accordingly. We didn't have no problems. It was an era where there was no bread on the table. So what was the difference whether I put the bread on the table by my endeavor or they put the bread? I performed with a hundred policemen in my time. I can't say nothin' for 'em, nothin' against 'em. I would say they were opportunists. I would say that they were merely persons that didn't perhaps have the courage to go on and do what I did. Nevertheless, they were willing to be a part of it. A minor part, that is.

The era of the times led into criminality, because of the old precept and concepts were destroyed against everyday reality. So when a policeman or a fireman was not being paid, how in the name of God could you expect him to enforce what he knew as the concept of law and order, when you see the beer barons changing hundred-dollar bills, and the pimp and the whorehouse guy had hundred-dollar bills, and the guy digging the sewers couldn't pay his bills? So how could you equate these things?

A good example is Clyde Barrow and Bonnie Parker. They were a product of the era. Dillinger—it wasn't that he was really a tough. No, he was just a product of survival. Actually, Dillinger was a country bumpkin. He realized the odds were stacked against him and performed accordingly. I knew Dillinger. Yeah, I met him on the North Side. And Dillinger was nothing like people wrote about him. The times produced Dillinger. Pretty Boy Floyd. Baby Face Nelson.

They were dedicated heist men and in the end were killed, to achieve their purpose. By themselves, they didn't need an army.

Al Capone sublet the matter. Capone quickly removed himself from the danger zone, aside from murdering Anselmi and Scalisi with a baseball bat. Bugs Moran to the end—he died for a bank heist in Ohio. They were from two different bolts of cloth. One was a dedicated thief. And one was an intriguing Mediterranean product of guile, etcetera. So you'd have to say that Moran was dedicated while Capone was an opportunist.

How did you get along during those hard times?

By every way known to the human brain. All my brothers were in the penitentiary. I had one brother in Jefferson City, another one in San Quentin, another one in Leavenworth, another one in Louisiana. At that time I am a fighter. I started boxing in 1925. Fourteen years till 1939. And it's a bloodthirsty thing.

How'd you become a boxer?

Gravitation. Being on the road simulated that fate, trying to grab a buck and so forth. Five different years, *Ring* magazine rated me the most devastating puncher in the profession, pound for pound.

What was it like, being a boxer in those days . . . ?

Survival. If it worked out that you were on top, you made a living. And if you were three or four shades below the top, you scuffled for a buck. Fighters were very, very hungry.

I made some pretty big scores. But I spent it practically all on getting my brothers out of penitentiaries around the country. At that time, the one in San Quentin stood me thirty thousand, the one in Jefferson City stood me twenty-five thousand. Those were big give-ups in those days.

I lived from the bottom to the top. I lived as good as you could live. I run the gamut of having a butler and a chauffeur to a flop joint, into an open car overnight.

He describes the boxing "combination" of those days; the fix; the refusal of his manager and himself to "play ball"; the boxer as an investment, cut up "like a watermelon."

I had many injuries in between. My hands, you can see. [He holds out his gnarled, broken knuckles.] In the meantime, I had to step out and make a dollar otherwise. It was never with the law.

I've switched craps, I've run up the cards, I do the complete bit. Every way known to the human brain. I'm probably a rare species that's left.

Was muscle always involved?

Muscle if you hope to leave with the money. Muscle everywhere, yes. Because for some unknown reason, muscle has been going on since the Roman Army conquered the field with a way of life.

When you enter an endeavor unsuccessfully, then the planning was incorrect. The risk was above the gains, and you stumble along the way. And the windup is a rude awakening with numbers strung out over your back. Unsuccessful in your modus operandi. Sagacity, ingenuity, planning . . . it involves much weighing, odds against failure, odds against gain—if you care to be in a free society.

I spent much time in jail. That's why I'm a student of the matter.

(At this point, Kid Pharaoh and he conducted a vigorous and somewhat arcane debate concerning the relative dishonesty of Hoover and Roosevelt. The Kid insisted it was Hoover who, by clout, was saved from "the bucket." Doc was equally certain it was F.D.R. who should have had "numbers strung out over his shoulders.")
Do you recall your biggest haul during the thirties?

It was alleged—

Who alleged . . . ?

The newspaper report came out as $75,000. We took eight and were happy about the whole thing.

What was your role during Prohibition?

I was a cheater. After studying under Count Lustig and Ace Campbell, I considered it beneath my dignity delivering a barrel of beer. Although I drink beer. I hustled with crap mobs, on the

crimp, the weave, the holdout—the reason I didn't do the rum running is you can hire a mooch with muscle. But can you hire brains?
Big firms have not succeeded in doing this.

I have met only several proficient men in my time. On of them
was Jack Freed. [Cups hand over mouth, whispers.] D-e-a-d. He
worked right up to the edge of his demise. This is in the evening,
when you are not at home. He was dedicated to his labor. He spent
half his lifetime in the penitentiaries. One of my closest friends. I,
of course, assisted him, from time to time. He accused me of rat-
tling my coat one night, making entrance. I, who have endeavored
in every participation known to the human brain, where art, subterfuge and guile is involved.

I take it you were caught a few times—

Incarcerated. Nothing proven substantially. I was a victim of circumstances. What they were, I didn't say. Yes, I spent a year in
Salinas, California, amongst other places. The highlight was when I
was nineteen. If I get convicted, I'm going out to join my brother in
San Quentin. My brother was doing twenty years there. If I'm not
convicted, I'm going up to visit him. I'm going to San Quentin, one
way or the other.

And you did?

I did. As a free man. I was fortunate enough in having one of the
greatest criminal lawyers of all time defending me.

*For someone engaging in your varied skills, do you sense a differ-
ence between the thirties and today?*

It's so different today, it's unfathomable. You can't conjure what
the difference is. Today everything is a robot. Today everything is
mechanical. There is very little ingenuity. Everything today is no-
personal, there is no personality whatsoever. Everything today is
ipso facto, fait accompli. In my era they had to prove their point.
Today, you don't have to prove your point.

Back then Ace Campbell steered Arnold Rothstein,[5] with Nigger
Nate Raymond, into one of maybe the biggest card games was ever
involved. I was a small feature of it in the Park Central Hotel in
New York. Ace changed the weave [laughs], and when Rothstein
wound up a half-a-million loser, he said he was cheated. Rothstein
became jaded after he lost the half a million, no longer had any
interest. No interest in life. After the card game broke up, he said
he was no longer interested in this, that or the other. He refused to
pay off. So Nigger Nate Raymond held court with him. And that
was the end of that.

Held court . . . ?

The S&W people[6] had the implements that they held court with.

---

5. A gambler and fixer of reknown.
He was involved in the Black Sox scan-
dal of 1919.

6. Smith & Wesson, revolver manufacturers.

That's all. Rothstein didn't have to pay off. You understand what I mean? I know, because I assisted in the operation with Ace. But let that be as it may. It was unfortunate, yes. But that was his demise.
Were the S&W people popular those days?
Naturally, it was part of your wearing apparel.
Aren't some of the survivors in legitimate enterprises today?
One of the fellows who was a pimp in Chicago is the boss of one of the grandest hotels in Las Vegas. I assisted him in a few small matters. But true to all pimping, he forgot me entirely as he advanced into the autumn of life.
After Prohibition, what did the guys do?
The ones that were adroit enough branched into other fields. If they didn't have any knowledge, they fell by the wayside. I achieved some small success in race tracks. Machine Gun Jack McGurn[7] couldn't stand the traffic. He got his brains blown out, branching into other fields.
The night Prohibition was repealed, everybody got drunk. It was the only decent thing Roosevelt ever did in his Administration. I was not one of his admirers. I tried to fire him on four different occasions. If I ever had a person work for me that displeased me, it was Roosevelt. I voted against him four times.
What was it about him you didn't like?
Him being a con man, taking advantage of poor, misguided, gibbering idiots who believed in his fairy tales. The New Deal, the various gimmicks, the NRA ... the complete subterfuge, artifice and guile. ...
Some say Roosevelt saved our society. ...
I dare say it would have been saved if Roosevelt's mother and father had never met.
Many people were on relief ... on WPA. ...
I didn't have a thing to do with that, because I was above that. Nevertheless, the people that were involved in it did it merely to get some meat on the plates, some food in the kitchen. It was no more, no less. Survival. None of the connotations of social dissent that has crept in since then. Merely an abstract way of eating. ...
What do you think would happen if there were a big Depression today?
Very simple. They'd commit suicide today. I don't think they're conditioned to stand it. We were a hardier race then. We'd win wars. We didn't procrastinate. We'd win them or lose them. Today we're a new race of people. They'll quit on a draw—if they see any feasible way to see their way out to quit with any dignity, they'll

7. It was alleged that he was one of Capone's executioners in the St. Valentine's Day Massacre. He was killed in a bowling alley in 1936, on the eve of St. Valentine's Day.

quit. Back then, you had a different breed of people. You got $21 a month going into the army or the navy. So them guys, they went to win the war. There's been an emancipated woman since the beginning of the war, also.

KID PHARAOH *interjects. "The American woman during the Depression was domesticated. Today, as we move into the late sixties, if you go into any high school, you don't see any classes of cooking any more. You don't see any classes at all in sewing. None of them can boil water. They're all today in business in competition to the male animal. Why should a Playboy bunny make $200 a week? If a veteran goes to war, puts his life up . . . can't raise a family."*

DOC: *". . . a lot of country bumpkins in the city wanting to look at poor, misguided, gibbering idiot waitresses. That they've stripped down like a prostitute, but hasn't sense enough to know that it's on her alleged sex allure that the poor misguided chump is in the place. In the end it amounts to absolutely nothing. A hypothesis of silly nothingness . . . undressed broads serving hootch, that cannot fulfill. . . ."*

KID PHARAOH: *" . . . his dick directs him, like radar, to the Playboy Club. In a high moral society—in Russia—guys like Hugh Hefner would be working in the library."*

During the Depression . . . if a guy had a few drinks with a girl . . .?

If she had two drinks with him, and she didn't lay her frame down, she was in a serious matter. She could have one, and explain she made a mistake by marrying some sucker that she was trying to fulfill her marriage commitment. But in the thirties, if you had a second drink and she didn't make the commitment where she's going to lay her frame down for you, the entire matter was resolved quickly to the point and could end in mayhem. She was in a serious matter.

In the thirties, then, the individual con man, the heist man, had an easier time with it—all around?

Oh yes, it was much easier then. The Federal Government now has you on practically anything you do. They make a conspiracy whether you accomplish the matter or not. Today, it's fraught with much peril, any type of endeavor you engage in. A nefarious matter. It constantly comes under the heading of a federal statute. The Federal Government then collected taxes, and just a few interstate things, as white slavery, and that was about it.

Today, the Federal Government has expanded into every field. If you use a telephone, as an example, and you put slugs in it, that's a penitentiary offense. Strange as that may seem. So that will give you an idea how far the Federal Government has encroached on a citizen's prerogative.

You think Roosevelt had a role to play in this?

Definitely. He was perhaps the lowest human being that ever held public office. He, unfortunately, was a despot. I mean, you get an old con man at a point in high office, he begins to believe the platitudes that are expounded by the stupid populace about him.

What about the young people, during the Depression . . . ?

The young people in the Depression respected what laws there were. If they'd steal, they tried to do it with dignity. And what not. They respected the policeman. They looked at him with forebearance, that he was a necessary part of society. But, nevertheless, he didn't impede the mere fact of gain.

No, he didn't stop 'em.

The young today are feminized, embryo homosexuals. Stool pigeons.

What about the young dissenters?

If you gave 'em a push, they'd turn into a homosexual. When the German hordes fifty years ago surrounded Paris, Marshall Pétain brought out the pimps, whores, thieves, underground operators, he says: Our playground is jeopardized by the German Hun. Well, all Paris, every thief, burglar, pimp, he come out and picked up a musket. Stopped the German hordes.

Today you don't see any kind of patriotism like that. They're trying to tear down the courthouse, they try to throw paint on Johnson's car. How can you compare that era, coming into this? Those were men, and today you've got to question whether they're homosexual or whether they're not.

Since the Depression, manhood has been lost—the manhood that I knew. Where four or five guys went on an endeavor, they died trying to take the endeavor off. It was no big deal if they did die. If it didn't come off right, there was no recrimination. Everybody put skin off what they set on.

Today, the foible of our civilization is to attack the policeman with a rotten egg, throwing it at him. Or walking around with a placard, that they're against whatever the present society advocates as civilized. Those people today—the Fall of Rome could be compared with it. Because they were the strongest nation on earth, and they disinterrogated into nothing. Through debauchery, through moral decay.

They need a narcotic to do anything, they can't do it on their own. They need a drug. Back in my era, we could cold-bloodedly do it.

RONALD BLYTHE: Leonard Thompson, Aged Seventy-one, Farm-Worker[1]

You went to the verge, you say, and come back safely?
Some have not been so fortunate—some have fallen.
Conrad Aiken, *Prelude XIV*

* * *

In my four months' training with the regiment I put on nearly a stone in weight and got a bit taller. They said it was the food but it was really because for the first time in my life there had been no strenuous work. I want to say this simply as a fact, that village people in Suffolk in my day were worked to death. It literally happened. It is not a figure of speech. I was worked mercilessly. I am not complaining about it. It is what happened to me.

We were all delighted when war broke out on August 4th. I was now a machine-gunner in the Third Essex Regiment. A lot of boys from the village were with me and although we were all sleeping in ditches at Harwich, wrapped in our greatcoats, we were bursting with happiness. We were all damned glad to have got off the farms. I had 7s. a week and sent my mother half of it. If you did this, the government would add another 3s. 6d.—so my mother got 7s. My father died early this year and my mother lived on this 7s. a week for the whole of the war, adding a scrap to it by doing washing, and weeding in the fields. Neither of my parents lived long enough to draw the Old Age Pension. I can remember, when work was short, a group of unemployed young men coming to where some old men were sugar-beeting, which is the worst job there is, and shouting, 'Now that you grandfathers have got the pension'—it was 5s. a week—'why don't you get out of the field and give us a chance?' These 'old' men were only in their fifties but the hardness of their lives had made them ancient.

All this trouble with the village fell behind us now. I was nineteen and off to the Dardanelles, which is the Hellespont, I discovered. I had two boys from the village with me. We'd heard a lot about France so we thought we'd try Turkey. The band played on the banks of the river as we pulled out of Plymouth and I wondered if we would ever come home again. We were all so patriotic then and had been taught to love England in a fierce kind of way. The village wasn't England; England was something better than the village. We got to Gib and it was lovely and warm. Naked Spanish boys dived round us for coins. There were about fifty nurses on the top deck and they threw tanners.[2] You could see they were having

---

1. From Chapter 1 of *Akenfield: Portrait of an English Village*, 1969.　　2. Sixpence pieces.

an eye-opener. We stopped to coal-up. The dust blew all over the decks and all over us. We were packed like sardines and eating rubbish again. Water and salt porridge for breakfast. Beans and high salt pork for dinner. The pork was too bad for land-men to eat so we threw it into the coaldust and the coolies snatched it up and thrust it into their mouths, or put it into sacks to take home for their families.

We arrived at the Dardanelles and saw the guns flashing and heard rifle-fire. They heaved our ship, the *River Clyde* right up to the shore. They had cut a hole in it and made a little pier, so we were able to walk straight off and on to the beach. We all sat there —on the Hellespont!—waiting for it to get light. The first things we saw were big wrecked Turkish guns, the second a big marquee. It didn't make me think of the military but of the village fêtes. Other people must have thought like this because I remember how we all rushed up to it, like boys getting into a circus, and then found it all laced up. We unlaced it and rushed in. It was full of corpses. Dead Englishmen, lines and lines of them, and with their eyes wide open. We all stopped talking. I'd never seen a dead man before and here I was looking at two or three hundred of them. It was our first fear. Nobody had mentioned this. I was very shocked. I thought of Suffolk and it seemed a happy place for the first time.

Later that day we marched through open country and came to within a mile and half of the front line. It was incredible. We were there—at the war! The place we had reached was called 'dead ground' because it was where the enemy couldn't see you. We lay in little square holes, myself next to James Sears from the village. He was about thirty and married. That evening we wandered about on the dead ground and asked about friends of ours who had arrived a month or so ago. 'How is Ernie Taylor?'—'Ernie?—he's gone.' 'Have you seen Albert Paternoster?'—'Albert?—he's gone.' We learned that if 300 had 'gone' but 700 were left, then this wasn't too bad. We then knew how unimportant our names were.

I was on sentry that night. A chap named Scott told me that I must only put my head up for a second but that in this time I must see as much as I could. Every third man along the trench was a sentry. The next night we had to move on to the third line of trenches and we heard that the Gurkhas were going over and that we had to support their rear. But when we got to the communication trench we found it so full of dead men that we could hardly move. Their faces were quite black and you couldn't tell Turk from English. There was the most terrible stink and for a while there was nothing but the living being sick on to the dead. I did sentry again that night. It was one-two-sentry, one-two-sentry all along the trench, as before. I knew the next sentry up quite well. I remembered him in Suffolk singing to his horses as he ploughed. Now he fell back with a great scream and a look of surprise—dead. It is quick, anyway, I thought. On June 4th we went over the top. We took the Turks' trench and held it. It was called Hill 13. The next day we were relieved and told to rest for three hours, but it wasn't more than half an hour before the relieving regiment came running back. The Turks had returned and recaptured their trench. On June 6th my favourite officer was killed and no end of us butchered, but we managed to get hold of Hill 13 again. We found a great muddle, carnage and men without rifles shouting '*Allah! Allah!*', which is God's name in the Turkish language. Of the sixty men I had started out to war from Harwich with, there were only three left.

We set to work to bury people. We pushed them into the sides of the trench but bits of them kept getting uncovered and sticking out, like people in a badly made bed. Hands were the worst; they would escape from the sand, pointing, begging—even waving! There was one which we all shook when we passed, saying, 'Good morning', in a posh voice. Everybody did it. The bottom of the trench was springy like a mattress because of all the bodies under-neath. At night, when the stench was worse, we tied crêpe round our mouths and noses. This crêpe had been given to us because it was supposed to prevent us being gassed. The flies entered the trenches at night and lined them completely with a density which was like a moving cloth. We killed millions by slapping our spades along the trench walls but the next night it would be just as bad. We were all lousy and we couldn't stop shitting because we had caught dysentery. We wept, not because we were frightened but because we were all so dirty.

* * *

ROBERT COLES: A Police Sergeant[1]

* * *

Is he an "ordinary cop," as he once called himself? Is he a "boss," a "sergeant boss," as he refers to himself sometimes with mixed pride and embarrassment? Is he a "fascist pig," as he is called, among other things, by bright, vocal college students who are taking courses in sociology and psychology and political science and economics and urban affairs and law—and who prompt from him a wider range of responses than they might believe possible, for all their unquestionable awareness and sharpness of mind? It is, of

---

1. From *The Middle Americans*, 1971.

course, possible to list those responses, and yet somehow no list, however well drawn up and accurately phrased, quite seems to render truthfully a man's ideas as they come tumbling out in the course of talk after talk—all of which is rather obvious not only to "investigators" and "observers" doing their "research" but those very able and sensitive and strong-minded and independent and mean-spirited and inefficient and awkward and generous and sullen and lighthearted and callous and kind people who are "interviewed."

More than anything else the police sergeant resents "propaganda" about the police, his way of describing "those articles about our problems." He is tired of them, tired of "dumb reporters" doing "quickie stories on the cops," and tired of "smart-aleck graduate students and their professors" who are always going to police headquarters and wanting to interview someone on the force. Can't they simply go strike up a conversation with a cop, buy him a beer, get to know him, learn "whatever in hell it is" they want to know *that way?* Can't they do anything without those folders and the questions, dozens and dozens of questions? Life for him is too complicated for a questionnaire. Life for him is hard to put into any words, "even your own, never mind someone else's." It is easy to argue with him, or applaud him because he says what seems eminently sensible and correct. It is more important, perhaps, for all of us to understand that he is not so much against one or another "method" of research as he is doubtful that "a policeman or a fireman or a man who works on an assembly line of a factory" is going to get the compassion and fair treatment he deserves from people who make it their business to be known as compassionate and fair-minded: "The worst insults the police get is from the liberals and the radicals. A suburban housewife called up the other day and demanded to speak with 'the lieutenant.' She said she belonged to some committee, I didn't catch the name. She said we were the worst people in America, and if a Hitler ever took over here, we'd be marching people into concentration camps. Now, you know, that's not the first time I've heard that. Every time we get called to a college campus we get told things like that; and not only by the kids. Their teachers can be just as bad. I'd like to give each of them a jab to the stomach and a jab to the jaw. But I can't. And I tell my men that *they* can't either.

"Very few people know what it's like to have the radicals shouting at you from one direction and the Negro people in the slums looking at you as if you hate each and every one of them, and the people in between, most white people, claiming you've failed them, too, because there's crime all over, and it's the fault of the police, *the police.* I go to work some days and tell myself I'm going to quit. The men all say that. I don't know a policeman who feels he's being treated right. We don't get nearly the money we should, considering the fact that every hour we take risks all the time and could be killed almost every minute of the working day. And even our best friends and supporters don't know what we do—the calls' that come in for our help, the duties we have. You go and ask the average Negro in a Negro neighborhood about the police, and he won't talk the way the civil rights people do. They call us all the time, Negroes do. I used to work in one of their districts. The switchboard was busy all day and all night. They fight and squabble with each other. They drink a lot. They lose themselves on drugs. They rob and steal from each other. They take after each other and kill. Then people say it's us, the police, the white man, that's to blame.

"I know I keep telling you all that, but people don't understand. I have one wish. I wish I could take some of those student radicals and send them out with some of my men that work in the Negro sections. I think it would open up their eyes, the students—that is, if anything can. They'd see that if you pulled the police out of the Negro sections, like the white radicals say you should—*they* don't live there—then the ones who would suffer would be the poor, innocent colored people. They're always the ones to suffer. A lot of Negroes are like a lot of white folks—good people, real good people.

"I hear my men talking. They say what I do. I have a brother who's a fireman. He says the same thing: it's not the average colored man who's to blame for all the trouble we're having in this country. It's a handful; well, it's more than a handful of trouble-makers. There are the crazy agitators, and the college crowd, the students and the teachers, and worst of all, if you ask me, are the rich people who support them all, and come into the city to march and demonstrate and wave their signs. Maybe it's all for the good, though. I've given up figuring out the answers. There's a whole lot of injustice in America. I know that. I can't afford for anyone in my family to get sick, least of all myself. The rich get richer and the poor ordinary man, he can barely buy his food and pay his rent. I feel sorry for the Negroes, I really do. People are prejudiced, most people are. You're almost born that way, don't you think? People like to stick together. The Irish want to live near the Irish. The same with the Italians or the others. Jews always stick together, even when they get rich, and a lot of them do. The poor Negroes, they want to get away from each other. They want to break out. I don't blame them. But when they break out what will they find? They'll see that the Irish are no good, and the Italians and Jews and everyone. We're all no good. I believe you should know the man, not where his grandfather came from. I mean, people like their own, but that isn't the way it should be. My son comes home and tells me that his teacher says the world is always changing. Well, you know it *is* always changing. I can remember a different world, the one I grew up in. That's gone, that world. A Negro boy born today is growing up in a country really worried over his people. I think everyone accepts the fact that we've got to end poverty and give people an even break, whether their skin is black or brown or whatever color it is.

"When I was a kid of twenty-five, I used to patrol a Negro section of this city. All was quiet then, no riots and no talk of revolution, and all the rest. I knew a lot of Negro people. They were poor, but they were polite and friendly. I'd get dozens of offers of coffee or a drink. We could talk, easy, real easy, with each other. Now all I hear is how no white man is trusted over there in that section. So, I asked one of my buddies who's a sergeant like me, and over in the district I used to be in—I asked him how he could stand it over there. He said he was surprised at me talking that way. I said I was surprised at *him* talking that way. He said it wasn't the same all the time, because they'd had a small riot or two, but it was the same as it always was most of the time: women who have to be rushed to the hospital to deliver their babies, and fires, and robberies, and fights to help settle, and kids caught on a roof or hurt playing who need to go to the emergency ward—you know, a cop's job. Then I thought to myself that I was a real fool for not thinking like that in the first place. You let those news stories go to your head, and you forget that most Negro people are too busy for demonstrations; they go to work, like the rest of us.

"I'd like to see more Negro policemen. I have nothing against them. But I don't believe in hiring a man just because he's colored or white or Chinese or anything else. If a man is going to be a policeman these days he's got to be tough. The world is tough; it's tougher than it ever was. Sometimes I look at my kids and hope they'll be all right when they grow up. I hope they'll have a world to live in."

JAMES THURBER: Writers at Work
The *Paris Review* Interviews

The Hôtel Continental, just down from the Place Vendôme on the Rue Castiglione. It is from here that Janet Flanner (Genêt) sends her Paris letter to The New Yorker, *and it is here that the Thurbers usually stay while in Paris. "We like it because the service is first-rate without being snobbish."*

Thurber was standing to greet us[1] in a small salon whose cold European formality had been somewhat softened and warmed by well-placed vases of flowers, by stacks and portable shelves of Ameri-

---

1. George Plimpton and Max Steele.

can novels in bright dust jackets, and by pads of yellow paper and bouquets of yellow pencils on the desk. Thurber impresses one immediately by his physical size. After years of delighting in the shy, trapped little man in the Thurber cartoons and the confused and bewildered man who has fumbled in and out of some of the funniest books written in this century, we, perhaps like many readers, were expecting to find the frightened little man in person. Not at all. Thurber by his firm handgrasp and confident voice and by the way he lowered himself into his chair gave the impression of outward calmness and assurance. Though his eyesight has almost failed him, it is not a disability which one is aware of for more than the opening minute, and if Thurber seems to be the most nervous person in the room, it is because he has learned to put his visitors so completely at ease.

He talks in a surprisingly boyish voice, which is flat with the accents of the Midwest where he was raised and, though slow in tempo, never dull. He is not an easy man to pin down with questions. He prefers to sidestep them and, rather than instructing, he entertains with a vivid series of ancedotes and reminiscences.

Opening the interview with a long history of the bloodhound, Thurber was only with difficulty persuaded to shift to a discussion of his craft. Here again his manner was typical—the anecdotes, the reminiscences punctuated with direct quotes and factual data. His powers of memory are astounding. In quoting anyone—perhaps a conversation of a dozen years before—Thurber pauses slightly, his voice changes in tone, and you know what you're hearing is exactly as it was said.

THURBER: Well, you know it's a nuisance—to have memory like mine—as well as an advantage. It's . . . well . . . like a whore's top drawer. There's so much else in there that's junk—costume jewelry, unnecessary telephone numbers whose exchanges no longer exist. For instance, I can remember the birthday of anybody who's ever told me his birthday. Dorothy Parker—August 22, Lewis Gannett—October 3, Andy White—July 9, Mrs. White—September 17. I can go on with about two hundred. So can my mother. She can tell you the birthday of the girl I was in love with in the third grade, in 1903. Offhand, just like that. I got my powers of memory from her. Sometimes it helps me out in the most extraordinary way. You remember Robert M. Coates? Bob Coates? He is the author of *The Eater of Darkness*, which Ford Madox Ford called the first true Dadaist novel. Well, the week after Stephen Vincent Benét died—Coates and I had both known him—we were talking about Benét. Coates was trying to remember an argument he had had with Benét some fifteen years before. He couldn't remember. I said, "I can." Coates told me that was impossible since I hadn't been there. "Well," I said, "you happened to mention it in passing about twelve years ago. You were arguing about a play called *Swords*." I was right, and Coates was able to take it up from there. But it's strange to reach a position where your friends have to be supplied with their own memories. It's bad enough dealing with your own.

INTERVIEWERS: Still, it must be a great advantage for the writer. I don't suppose you have to take notes.

THURBER: No. I don't have to do the sort of thing Fitzgerald did with *The Last Tycoon*—the voluminous, the tiny and meticulous notes, the long descriptions of character. I can keep all these things in my mind. I wouldn't have to write down "three roses in a vase" or something, or a man's middle name. Henry James dictated notes just the way that I write. His note writing was part of the creative act, which is why his prefaces are so good. He dictated notes to see what it was they might come to.

INTERVIEWERS: Then you don't spend much time prefiguring your work?

THURBER: No. I don't bother with charts and so forth. Elliott Nugent, on the other hand, is a careful constructor. When we were working on *The Male Animal* together, he was constantly concerned with plotting the play. He could plot the thing from back to front—what was going to happen here, what sort of situation would end the first-act curtain, and so forth. I can't work that way. Nugent would say, "Well, Thurber, we've got our problem, we've got all these people in the living room. Now what are we going to do with them?" I'd say that I didn't know and couldn't tell him until I'd sat down at the typewriter and found out. I don't believe the writer should know too much where he's going. If he does, he runs into old man blueprint—old man propaganda.

INTERVIEWERS: Is the act of writing easy for you?

THURBER: For me it's mostly a question of rewriting. It's part of a constant attempt on my part to make the finished version smooth, to make it seem effortless. A story I've been working on —"The Train on Track Six," it's called—was rewritten fifteen complete times. There must have been close to 240,000 words in all the manuscripts put together, and I must have spent two thousand hours working at it. Yet the finished version can't be more than twenty thousand words.

INTERVIEWERS: Then it's rare that your work comes out right the first time?

THURBER: Well, my wife took a look at the first version of something I was doing not long ago and said, "Goddamn it, Thurber, that's high-school stuff." I have to tell her to wait until the seventh draft, it'll work out all right. I don't know why that should be so, that the first or second draft of everything I write reads as if it was turned out by a charwoman. I've only written one piece quickly. I wrote a thing called "File and Forget" in one afternoon—but only because it was a series of letters just as one would ordinarily dictate. And I'd have to admit that the last letter of the series, after doing all the others that one afternoon, took me a week. It was the end of the piece and I had to fuss over it.

INTERVIEWERS: Does the fact that you're dealing with humor slow down the production?

THURBER: It's possible. With humor you have to look out for traps. You're likely to be very gleeful with what you've first put down, and you think it's fine, very funny. One reason you go over and over it is to make the piece sound less as if you were having a lot of fun with it yourself. You try to play it down. In fact, if there's such a thing as a *New Yorker* style, that would be it—playing it down.

INTERVIEWERS: Do you envy those who write at high speed, as against your method of constant revision?

THURBER: Oh, no, I don't, though I do admire their luck. Hervey Allen, you know, the author of the big best-seller *Anthony Adverse*, seriously told a friend of mine who was working on a biographical piece on Allen that he could close his eyes, lie down on a bed, and hear the voices of his ancestors. Furthermore there was some sort of angel-like creature that danced along his pen while he was writing. He wasn't balmy by any means. He just felt he was in communication with some sort of metaphysical recorder. So you see the novelists have all the luck. I never knew a humorist who got any help from his ancestors. Still, the act of writing is either something the writer dreads or actually likes, and I actually like it. Even rewriting's fun. You're getting somewhere, whether it seems to move or not. I remember Elliot Paul and I used to argue about rewriting back in 1925 when we both worked for the *Chicago Tribune* in Paris. It was his conviction you should leave the story as it came out of the typewriter, no changes. Naturally, he worked fast. Three novels he could turn out, each written in three weeks' time. I remember once he came into the office and said that a sixty-thousand-word manuscript had been stolen. No carbons existed, no notes. We were all horrified. But it didn't bother him at all. He'd just get back to the typewriter and bat away again. But for me—writing as fast as that would seem too facile. Like my drawings, which I do very quickly, sometimes so quickly that the result is an accident, something I hadn't intended at all. People in the arts I've run into in France are constantly indignant when I say I'm a writer and not an artist. They tell me I mustn't run down my drawings. I try to explain that I do them for relaxation, and that I do them too fast for them to be called art.

INTERVIEWERS: You say that your drawings often don't come out the way you intended?

THURBER: Well, once I did a drawing for *The New Yorker* of a naked woman on all fours up on top of a bookcase—a big bookcase. She's up there near the ceiling, and in the room are her husband and two other women. The husband is saying to one of the women, obviously a guest, "This is the present Mrs. Harris. That's my first wife up there." Well, when I did the cartoon originally I meant the naked woman to be at the top of a flight of stairs, but I lost the sense of perspective and instead of getting in the stairs when I drew my line down, there she was stuck up there, naked, on a bookcase.

Incidentally, that cartoon really threw the *New Yorker* editor,
Harold Ross. He approached any humorous piece of writing, or
more particularly a drawing, not only grimly but realistically. He
called me on the phone and asked if the woman up on the bookcase was supposed to be alive, stuffed, or dead. I said, "I don't
know, but I'll let you know in a couple of hours." After a while
I called him back and told him I'd just talked to my taxidermist,
who said you can't stuff a woman, that my doctor had told me a
dead woman couldn't support herself on all fours. "So, Ross,"
I said, "she must be alive." "Well then," he said, "what's she
doing up there naked in the home of her husband's second wife?"
I told him he had me there.

INTERVIEWERS: But he published it.

THURBER: Yes, he published it, growling a bit. He had a fine understanding of humor, Ross, though he couldn't have told you
about it. When I introduced Ross to the work of Peter de Vries,
he first said, "He won't be good; he won't be funny; he won't
know English." (He was the only successful editor I've known
who approached everything like a ship going on the rocks.) But
when Ross had looked at the work he said, "How can you get this
guy on the phone?" He couldn't have said why, but he had that
bloodhound instinct. The same with editing. He was a wonderful
man at detecting something wrong with a story without knowing
why.

INTERVIEWERS: Could he develop a writer?

THURBER: Not really. It wasn't true what they often said of him
—that he broke up writers like matches—but still he wasn't the
man to develop a writer. He was an unread man. Well, he'd read
Mark Twain's *Life on the Mississippi* and several other books he
told me about—medical books—and he took the Encyclopedia
Britannica to the bathroom with him. I think he was about up to
H when he died. But still his effect on writers was considerable.
When you first met him you couldn't believe he was the editor
of *The New Yorker* and afterward you couldn't believe that anyone else could have been. The main thing he was interested in was
clarity. Someone once said of *The New Yorker* that it never contained a sentence that would puzzle an intelligent fourteen-year-
old or in any way affect her morals badly. Ross didn't like that,
but nevertheless he was a purist and perfectionist and it had a
tremendous effect on all of us: it kept us from being sloppy. When
I first met him he asked me if I knew English. I thought he meant
French or a foreign language. But he repeated, "Do you know
English?" When I said I did he replied, "Goddamn it, nobody
knows English." As Andy White mentioned in his obituary, Ross
approached the English sentence as though it was an enemy,
something that was going to throw him. He used to fuss for an
hour over a comma. He'd call me in for lengthy discussions about
the Thurber colon. And as for poetic license, he'd say, "Damn
any license to get things wrong." In fact, Ross read so carefully
that often he didn't get the sense of your story. I once said: "I

wish you'd read my stories for pleasure, Ross." He replied he hadn't time for that.

INTERVIEWERS: It's strange that one of the main ingredients of humor—low comedy—has never been accepted for *The New Yorker*.

THURBER: Ross had a neighbor woman's attitude about it. He never got over his Midwestern provincialism. His idea was that sex is an incident. "If you can prove it," I said, "we can get it in a box on the front page of *The New York Times*." Now I don't want to say that in private life Ross was a prude. But as regards the theater or the printed page he certainly was. For example, he once sent an office memorandum to us in a sealed envelope. It was an order: "When you send me a memorandum with four-letter words in it, *seal it*. There are women in this office." I said, "Yah, Ross, and they know a lot more of these words than you do." When women were around he was very conscious of them. Once my wife and I were in his office and Ross was discussing a man and woman he knew much better than we did. Ross told us, "I have every reason to believe that they're s-l-e-e-p-i-n-g together." My wife replied, "Why, Harold Ross, what words you do spell out." But honest to goodness, that was genuine. Women are either good or bad, he once told me, and the good ones must not hear these things.

Incidentally, I'm telling these things to refresh my memory. I'm doing a short book on him called "Ross in Charcoal." I'm putting a lot of this stuff in. People may object, but after all it's a portrait of the man and I see no reason for not putting it in.

INTERVIEWERS: Did he have much direct influence on your own work?

THURBER: After the seven years I spent in newspaper writing, it was more E. B. White who taught me about writing, how to clear up sloppy journalese. He was a strong influence, and for a long time in the beginning I thought he might be too much of one. But at least he got me away from a rather curious style I was starting to perfect—tight journalese laced with heavy doses of Henry James.

INTERVIEWERS: Henry James was a strong influence, then?

THURBER: I have the reputation for having read all of Henry James. Which would argue a misspent youth *and* middle age.

INTERVIEWERS: But there were things to be learned from him?

THURBER: Yes, but again he was an influence you had to get over. Especially if you wrote for *The New Yorker*. Harold Ross wouldn't have understood it. I once wrote a piece called "The Beast in the Dingle" which everybody took as a parody. Actually it was a conscious attempt to write the story as James would have written it. Ross looked at it and said: "Goddamn it, this is too literary; I got only fifteen per cent of the allusions." My wife and I often tried to figure out which were the fifteen per cent he could have got.

You know, I've occasionally wondered what James would have

done with our world. I've just written a piece—"Preface to Old Friends," it's called—in which James at the age of a hundred and four writes a preface to a novel about our age in which he summarizes the trends and complications, but at the end is so completely lost he doesn't really care enough to read it over to find his way out again.

That's the trouble with James. You get bored with him finally. He lived in the time of four-wheelers, and no bombs, and the problems then seemed a bit special and separate. That's one reason you feel restless reading him. James is like—well, I had a bulldog once who used to drag rails around, enormous ones—six-, eight-, twelve-foot rails. He loved to get them in the middle and you'd hear him growling out there, trying to bring the thing home. Once he brought home a chest of drawers—without the drawers in it. Found it on an ash-heap. Well, he'd start to get these things in the garden gate, everything finely balanced, you see, and then *crash*, he'd come up against the gate posts. He'd get it through finally, but I had that feeling in some of the James novels: that he was trying to get that rail through a gate not wide enough for it.

INTERVIEWERS: How about Mark Twain? Pretty much everybody believes him to have been the major influence on American humorists.

THURBER: Everybody wants to know if I've learned from Mark Twain. Actually I've never read much of him. I did buy *Tom Sawyer*, but dammit, I'm sorry, I've not got around to reading it all the way through. I told H. L. Mencken that, and he was shocked. He said America had produced only two fine novels: *Huck Finn* and *Babbitt*. Of course it's always a matter of personal opinion—these lists of the great novels. I can remember calling on Frank Harris—he was about seventy then—when I was on the *Chicago Tribune*'s edition in Nice. In his house he had three portraits on the wall—Mark Twain, Frank Harris, and I think it was Hawthorne. Harris was in the middle. Harris would point up to them and say, "Those three are the best American writers. The one in the middle is the best." Harris really thought he was wonderful. Once he told me he was going to live to be a hundred. When I asked him what the formula was, he told me it was very simple. He said, "I've bought myself a stomach pump and one half-hour after dinner I pump myself out." Can you imagine that? Well, it didn't work. It's a wonder it didn't kill him sooner.

INTERVIEWERS: Could we ask you why you've never attempted a long work?

THURBER: I've never wanted to write a long work. Many writers feel a sense of frustration or something if they haven't, but I don't.

INTERVIEWERS: Perhaps the fact that you're writing humor imposes a limit on the length of a work.

THURBER: Possibly. But brevity in any case—whether the work is supposed to be humorous or not—would seem to me to be desirable. Most of the books I like are short books: *The Red Badge of Courage*, *The Turn of the Screw*, Conrad's short stories, A

Lost Lady, Joseph Hergesheimer's *Wild Oranges*, Victoria Lincoln's *February Hill*, *The Great Gatsby*. . . . You know Fitzgerald once wrote Thomas Wolfe: "You're a puttier-inner and I'm a taker-outer." I stick with Fitzgerald. I don't believe, as Wolfe did, that you have to turn out a massive work before being judged a writer. Wolfe once told me at a cocktail party I didn't know what it was to be a writer. My wife, standing next to me, complained about that. "But my husband *is* a writer," she said. Wolfe was genuinely surprised. "He is?" he asked. "Why, all I ever see is that stuff of his in *The New Yorker*." In other words, he felt that prose under five thousand words was certainly not the work of a writer . . . it was some kind of doodling in words. If you said you were a writer, he wanted to know where the books were, the great big long books. He was really genuine about that.

I was interested to see William Faulkner's list not so long ago of the five most important American authors of this century. According to him Wolfe was first, Faulkner second—let's see, now that Wolfe's dead that puts Faulkner up there in the lead, doesn't it?— Dos Passos third, then Hemingway, and finally Steinbeck. It's interesting that the first three are putter-inners. They write expansive novels.

INTERVIEWERS: Wasn't Faulkner's criterion whether or not the author dared to go out on a limb?

THURBER: It seems to me you're going out on a limb these days to keep a book short.

INTERVIEWERS: Though you've never done a long serious work you have written stories—"The Cane in the Corridor" and "The Whippoorwill" in particular—in which the mood is far from humorous.

THURBER: In anything funny you write that isn't close to serious you've missed something along the line. But in those stories of which you speak there was an element of anger—something I wanted to get off my chest. I wrote "The Whippoorwill" after five eye operations. It came somewhere out of a grim fear in the back of my mind. I've never been able to trace it.

INTERVIEWERS: Some critics think that much of your work can be traced to the depicting of trivia as a basis for humor. In fact, there's been some criticism—

THURBER: Which is trivia—the diamond or the elephant? Any humorist must be interested in trivia, in every little thing that occurs in a household. It's what Robert Benchley did so well—in fact so well that one of the greatest fears of the humorous writer is that he has spent three weeks writing something done faster and better by Benchley in 1919. Incidentally, you never got very far talking to Benchley about humor. He'd do a take-off of Max Eastman's *Enjoyment of Laughter*. "We must understand," he'd say, "that all sentences which begin with W are funny."

INTERVIEWERS: Would you care to define humor in terms of your own work?

THURBER: Well, someone once wrote a definition of the difference between English and American humor. I wish I could re-member his name. I thought his definition very good. He said that the English treat the commonplace as if it were remarkable and the Americans treat the remarkable as if it were common-place. I believe that's true of humorous writing. Years ago we did a parody of *Punch* in which Benchley did a short piece depicting a wife bursting into a room and shouting "The primroses are in bloom!"—treating the commonplace as remarkable, you see. In "The Secret Life of Walter Mitty" I tried to treat the remarkable as commonplace.

INTERVIEWERS: Does it bother you to talk about the stories on which you're working? It bothers many writers, though it would seem that particularly the humorous story is polished through retelling.

THURBER: Oh, yes. I often tell them at parties and places. And I write them there too.

INTERVIEWERS: You write them?

THURBER: I never quite know when I'm not writing. Sometimes my wife comes up to me at a party and says, "Dammit, Thurber, stop writing." She usually catches me in the middle of a para-graph. Or my daughter will look up from the dinner table and ask, "Is he sick?" "No," my wife says, "he's writing something." I have to do it that way on account of my eyes. I still write occa-sionally—in the proper sense of the word—using black crayon on yellow paper and getting perhaps twenty words to the page. My usual method, though, is to spend the mornings turning over the text in my mind. Then in the afternoon, between two and five, I call in a secretary and dictate to her. I can do about two thousand words. It took me about ten years to learn.

INTERVIEWERS: How about the new crop of writers? Do you note any good humorists coming along with them?

THURBER: There don't seem to be many coming up. I once had a psychoanalyst tell me that the depression had a considerable effect—much worse than Hitler and the war. It's a tradition for a child to see his father in uniform as something glamorous—not his father coming home from Wall Street in a three-button sack suit saying, "We're ruined," and the mother bursting into tears—a catastrophe that to a child's mind is unexplainable. There's been a great change since the thirties. In those days students used to ask me what Peter Arno did at night. And about Dorothy Parker. Now they want to know what my artistic credo is. An element of interest seems to have gone out of them.

INTERVIEWERS: Has the shift in the mood of the times had any effect on your own work?

THURBER: Well, *The Thurber Album* was written at a time when in America there was a feeling of fear and suspicion. It's quite different from *My Life and Hard Times*, which was written earlier and is a funnier and better book. The *Album* was kind of an escape—going back to the Middle West of the last century and the beginning of this, when there wasn't this fear and hysteria.

I wanted to write the story of some solid American characters, more or less as an example of how Americans started out and what they should go back to—to sanity and soundness and away from this jumpiness. It's hard to write humor in the mental weather we've had, and that's likely to take you into reminiscence. Your heart isn't in it to write anything funny. In the years 1950 to 1953 I did very few things, nor did they appear in *The New Yorker*. Now, actually, I think the situation is beginning to change for the better.

INTERVIEWERS: No matter what the "mental climate," though, you would continue writing?

THURBER: Well, the characteristic fear of the American writer is not so much that as it is the process of aging. The writer looks in the mirror and examines his hair and teeth to see if they're still with him. "Oh my God," he says, "I wonder how my writing is. I bet I can't write today." The only time I met Faulkner he told me he wanted to live long enough to do three more novels. He was fifty-three then, and I think he *has* done them. Then Hemingway says, you know, that he doesn't expect to be alive after sixty. But he doesn't look forward *not* to being. When I met Hemingway with John O'Hara in Costello's Bar five or six years ago we sat around and talked about how *old* we were getting. You see it's constantly on the minds of American writers. I've never known a woman who could weep about her age the way the men I know can.

Coupled with this fear of aging is the curious idea that the writer's inventiveness and ability will end in his fifties. And of course it often does. Carl Van Vechten stopped writing. The prolific Joseph Hergesheimer suddenly couldn't write any more. Over here in Europe that's never been the case—Hardy, for instance, who started late and kept going. Of course Keats had good reason to write, "When I have fears that I may cease to be Before my pen has glean'd my teeming brain." That's the great classic statement. But in America the writer is more likely to fear that his brain may cease to teem. I once did a drawing of a man at his typewriter, you see, and all this crumpled paper is on the floor, and he's staring down in discouragement. "What's the matter," his wife is saying, "has your pen gleaned your teeming brain?"

INTERVIEWERS: In your case there wouldn't be much chance of this?

THURBER: No. I write basically because it's so much fun—even though I can't see. When I'm not writing, as my wife knows, I'm miserable. I don't have that fear that suddenly it will stop. I have enough outlined to last me as long as I live.

ERIK H. ERIKSON AND HUEY P. NEWTON: Armed Love[1]

JHB: . . . I would like to . . . go back to a matter that Erik has always been interested in: maybe it's time to talk about the gun.

EHE: Well, actually, that fits right in here. You see, when I started to talk in New Haven I reminded the students of the traditional image which Huey used to represent and which still appears on the cover of the Panther paper—the young Black man with the gun. All of this became more dialectical in our conversations when you, Huey, began to speak about arms and love. I thought I understood what you meant to some extent because of something that became clear to Gandhi as he developed his non-violent method—namely, that most people seem to feel that to be non-violent means not to *have* any gun and not to *want* any gun because one would not want to use it or would not know how to use it anyway. But there is an intermediary step between violence and non-violence where you have a gun but use it only in the most disciplined way—in part, at least, to show up the absurdity of particular kinds of armed violence. This, I think, you did on several important occasions which really created your original public image. I hope you see now what I mean. You were not afraid to carry that gun. Now I would understand armed love to mean that one can really love only if one knows that one could and would defend one's dignity, for only two people of equal dignity can love each other. There is no use trying to love somebody who denies you dignity or to whom you deny it. In this sense, then, there is a dialectical relation between violence and non-violence, and the last thing I would want to imply here is that your earlier image is inconsistent with the things you are saying and doing now. Both together make up an historical step and (I would assume) a very personal step, and you needed the one for the other. I don't know whether you would agree to that. You would now accept the gun-carrying image, wouldn't you, as historically necessary and valid?

HPN: I think it served a strategic purpose—although I imagine historians are going to make a lot out of it.

EHE: You mean as I just did?

HPN: No, no. It's just that so much has been written about the whole business of the armed self-defense of the community, and

1. Reprinted from *In Search of Common Ground*, edited by Kai T. Erikson and J. Herman Blake, 1973. This book is the record of two conversations which took place in early 1971 between Huey P. Newton, the Black Panther Party leader, and Erik H. Erikson, the renowned psychoanalyst and author of *Gandhi's Truth, Young Man Luther*, and many other books. The first conversation was in a formal conference setting at Yale University before a largely academic audience; the second took place around a small breakfast table in Newton's Oakland, California, apartment. Also participating in the dialogues are Kai T. Erikson, Erik's son, who teaches sociology at Yale, and J. Herman Blake, who teaches sociology at the University of California at Santa Cruz and is a member of the Black Panther Party. The excerpt reprinted here is taken from the first day of conversation in Oakland.

I haven't seen one thing that's accurate. I'm not talking about you, Erik; I think your interpretation is fair. But I just sort of shiver whenever I see books written on the matter.

EHE: For example, Bobby Seale describes some of the things you two did in the early days of the Party that, to me, seemed to amount to a parallel with the Gandhi technique—although I assume you didn't know about it then or, at any rate, it was not uppermost in your mind. When you faced down those policemen, for example —not threatening them with your guns or indicating with gestures that you would shoot first, but daring them to shoot first. That was a very important psychological condition you created there. You gave them the initiative and said, "Okay, you shoot first." All of this is probably related somehow to the old western frontier scenario, where the cowboys used to make this kind of confrontation a supreme test as to who would be quicker on the trigger. But you made something very different and, in a way, very revolutionary out of it when you made it clear that you didn't come to shoot them, but if they had come to shoot you, then they should come out with it. You paralyzed them morally, don't you think?

HPN: Well, I would agree that they were paralyzed at least.

KTE: But why were they paralyzed?

HPN: They had never been required to cope with a situation like that one. Because of their own racism, their own misconception of the Black community and the Black psyche, they did not know how to deal with the fact that we were not afraid of them, you see? And they were very provocative.

EHE: This kind of transvaluation can be a historical act, and Bobby Seale has a very good sense of how to describe such things—with humor, too. For example, how you would stand there with a few of your men and would confront those policemen and all the armed power they had behind them. Now, of course, you shouldn't be surprised if they afterwards should feel endangered in their essence. It has often been said about Gandhi that he could only have done what he did with the British and not anyone else. All of that fits rather well into what you refer to as the dialectical development of empires. You see, Gandhi met the British head-on with their own ideas of fairness, ideas they had widely established as an ideal, and when he faced them down with that they simply had to accept it as a lesson. It could well be that a policeman whose background does not include any kind of experience with this kind of thing would simply say to himself, "Okay, to hell with it, I'll sure get him some other time." What I learned in studying Gandhi was how he could give to a concrete object— and this is what I meant to apply to the gun in your case—some endless symbolic meaning. For example, Gandhi announced that he was going to the Indian Ocean, and that he was going to take salt out of it, salt that the British were taxing, no matter what they would say or do. It is perfectly obvious that he picked salt for many reasons. It is absolutely necessary in the tropics, for one thing, but it has great symbolic value too. Now my feeling is that, in principle, what you tried to do with the gun might have had something of the same concrete and symbolic meaning, and that you did it at the right historical moment. Does that make sense or not?

JHB: It makes perfect sense to me. I wish you would just be more specific, though. You used as a subtitle for the Gandhi book an expression like "the origins of militant non-violence," and I think the concept of non-violence as utilized by Americans with respect to Blacks is quite different from what I hear you saying. It seems to me that non-violence here has always meant acquiescence to whatever power is used against one in one's attempt to gain justice. Some moral force would come from somewhere and overcome the violent application of force. I'm not so sure that is what you are saying.

EHE: Not exactly. In fact, there is a similarity here which I brought out in the Gandhi book. It would be very easy to say that Black people have to remain non-violent because they'll never learn to fight anyway, and some people would say, "Well, non-violence fits their inborn meekness and their religious orientation." Now the case is very similar with India because there you have one military caste that had done virtually all the fighting, so that the great masses of people in India never learned to use weapons at all until the British came along and drafted them into the Army. Those crack Indian troops in the British Army that we heard so much about all came from warrior castes whose job on earth, decreed by heaven, was to fight. The rest of the Indians didn't know how to fight, had never had any experience with weapons, and made it a point of religious observance to do no harm to anyone. Now Gandhi (and his friends did not like him for it) would sometimes support the British demand that Indians be drafted, because he felt that Indians would have to learn to fight before they could *choose* to be non-violent. That's what you meant in part, isn't it? That it makes no sense for a meek person to call himself non-violent, because, sure, what else can he be?

HPN: I think it would be wrong to compare other situations to Gandhi's action. You have to leave it in context and regard it in terms of the particular contradictions involved. Now I would have agreed with the notion that Indians join the British Army in order to get the training necessary to oppose the Army: I can understand that at some point it is worthwhile to play upon the weakness of the oppressor. Gandhi did this knowing the character of the British quite well, but I think he would have acted differently here. People here who tried to act the same way he did, I think, missed the mark and were not realistic.

JHB: Most people would say that the apostle of non-violence in this country with respect to Blacks was Martin Luther King. He had a clearly stated philosophy and openly expressed a debt to Gandhi. Now I would suspect that most people, not understanding the context in which you are speaking, would expect to see a very strong clash between your [Erikson's] views and Huey's views on this particular subject. And I would like to see that cleared up, because I've always argued that there have to be certain social bases for non-violence. . . .

EHE: Look, the last thing I would wish to do is advocate non-violence outside of a concrete situation, particularly since it makes exploited people all the more vulnerable. Unless one is very careful, the whole non-violent point of view could be used against people rather than for them. I gave a seminar at MIT once, and somebody brought Tom Mboya to one of the meetings. The students and I had just been discussing Gandhi, so we asked Mboya what he thought about non-violence. Well, he said, you can use it with the British but you can't use it with the Belgians. No two historical situations are ever identical in this sense. What Mboya may have also meant is that Gandhi had become something of a Britisher himself. He had been educated in England, of course, and so he knew where he could count on the British to react to non-violence in a certain way. I guess that is really all I have to say. I just have a feeling that you [Newton] are not an advocate of violence as such, you know.

HPN: No, I don't advocate violence. I advocate non-violence. If I really had a choice, I would prefer the non-antagonistic kind of contradictions because they usually can be resolved in a peaceful way. But of course we have to deal with concrete conditions and the reality of the situation at this time is that there are many contradictions that probably can only be resolved in antagonistic ways and will probably result in violence—and this will probably be the case until man and society develop to the point where contradictions will no longer be antagonistic. So I am working for the day when antagonisms will no longer exist. And this will probably be only after people commonly own and share things.

JHB: Erik, you were saying the other day that the Panthers may understand non-violence better than anyone else because they understand violence so well. And I was thinking about that in connection with Huey's statement that we advocate the abolition of war. We say that power grows out of the barrel of a gun, Chairman Mao's words; but we also say that the purpose of picking up the gun is to get rid of it. Now most people in this society pick up the gun for the purpose of maintaining control, and they do not understand that someone else might pick it up in order to abolish control.

HPN: Use violence in order to eliminate it.

JHB: Right. Right.

EHE: The point is that you cannot step from undisciplined violence to non-violence. In India, Gandhi failed mostly where he could not restrain people from rioting, and you remember (I remember, at least) how he called off some of his non-violent campaigns because rioting broke out. Now the Panthers have actually opposed violence for its own sake, isn't that right?

HPN: Non-disciplined violence, yes.

EHE: Only a very self-disciplined use of force can lead to disciplined non-violence and the abolition of violence. And, of course, it also takes a pretty high set of moral aspirations for leaders to make people understand all of that. . . .

On Literature and the Arts

SUSANNE K. LANGER

Expressiveness[1]

When we talk about "Art" with a capital "A"—that is, about any or all of the arts: painting, sculpture, architecture, the potter's and goldsmith's and other designers' arts, music, dance, poetry, and prose fiction, drama and film—it is a constant temptation to say things about "Art" in this general sense that are true only in one special domain, or to assume that what holds for one art must hold for another. For instance, the fact that music is made for performance, for presentation to the ear, and is simply not the same thing when it is given only to the tonal imagination of a reader silently perusing the score, has made some aestheticians pass straight to the conclusion that literature, too, must be physically heard to be fully experienced, because words are originally spoken, not written; an obvious parallel, but a careless and, I think, invalid one. It is dangerous to set up principles by analogy, and generalize from a single consideration.

But it is natural, and safe enough, to ask analogous questions: What is the function of sound in music? What is the function of sound in poetry? What is the function of sound in prose composition? What is the function of sound in drama?" The answers may be quite heterogeneous; and that is itself an important fact, a guide to something more than a simple and sweeping theory. Such findings guide us to exact relations and abstract, variously exemplified basic principles.

At present, however, we are dealing with principles that have proven to be the same in all the arts, when each kind of art—plastic, musical, balletic, poetic, and each major mode, such as literary and dramatic writing, or painting, sculpturing, building plastic

---

1. Chapter 2 of *Problems of Art*, 1957.

shapes—has been studied in its own terms. Such candid study is more rewarding than the usual passionate declaration that all the arts are alike, only their materials differ, their principles are all the same, their techniques all analogous, etc. That is not only unsafe, but untrue. It is in pursuing the differences among them that one arrives, finally, at a point where no more differences appear; then one has found, not postulated, their unity. At that deep level there is only one concept exemplified in all the different arts, and that is the concept of Art.

The principles that obtain wholly and fundamentally in every kind of art are few, but decisive; they determine what is art, and what is not. Expressiveness, in one definite and appropriate sense, is the same in all art works of any kind. What is created is not the same in any two distinct arts—this is, in fact, what makes them distinct—but the principle of creation is the same. And "living form" means the same in all of them.

A work of art is an expressive form created for our perception through sense or imagination, and what it expresses is human feeling. The word "feeling" must be taken here in its broadest sense, meaning *everything that can be felt*, from physical sensation, pain and comfort, excietment and repose, to the most complex emotions, intellectual tensions, or the steady feeling-tones of a conscious human life. In stating what a work of art is, I have just used the words "form," "expressive," and "created"; these are key words. One at a time, they will keep us engaged.

Let us consider first what is meant, in this context, by a *form*. The word has many meanings, all equally legitimate for various purposes; even in connection with art it has several. It may, for instance—and often does—denote the familiar, characteristic structures known as the sonnet form, the sestina, or the ballad form in poetry, the sonata form, the madrigal, or the symphony in music, the contredance or the classical ballet in choreography, and so on. This is not what I mean; or rather, it is only a very small part of what I mean. There is another sense in which artists speak of "form" when they say, for instance, "form follows function," or declare that the one quality shared by all good works of art is "significant form," or entitle a book *The Life of Forms in Art*, or *Search for Form*. They are using "form" in a wider sense, which on the one hand is close to the commonest, popular meaning, namely just the *shape* of a thing, and on the other hand to the quite unpopular meaning it has in science and philosophy, where it designates something more abstract; "form" in its most abstract sense means structure, articulation, a whole resulting from the relation of mutually dependent factors, or more precisely, the way that whole is put together.

The abstract sense, which is sometimes called "logical form," is involved in the notion of expression, at least the kind of expression that characterizes art. That is why artists, when they speak of achieving "form," use the word with something of an abstract connotation, even when they are talking about a visible and tangible art object in which that form is embodied.

The more recondite concept of form is derived, of course, from the naive one, that is, material shape. Perhaps the easiest way to grasp the idea of "logical form" is to trace its derivation.

Let us consider the most obvious sort of form, the shape of an object, say a lampshade. In any department store you will find a wide choice of lampshades, mostly monstrosities, and what is monstrous is usually their shape. You select the least offensive one, maybe even a good one, but realize that the color, say violet, will not fit into your room; so you look about for another shade of the same shape but a different color, perhaps green. In recognizing this same shape in another object, possibly of another material as well as another color, you have quite naturally and easily abstracted the concept of this shape from your actual impression of the first lampshade. Presently it may occur to you that this shade is too big for your lamp; you ask whether they have *this same shade* (meaning another one of this shape) in a smaller size. The clerk understands you.

But what is *the same* in the big violet shade and the little green one? Nothing but the interrelations among their respective various dimensions. They are not "the same" even in their spatial properties, for none of their actual measures are alike; but their shapes are congruent. Their respective spatial factors are put together in the same way, so they exemplify the same form.

It is really astounding what complicated abstractions we make in our ordinary dealing with forms—that is to say, through what twists and transformations we recognize the same logical form. Consider the similarity of your two hands. Put one on the table, palm down, superimpose the other, palm down, as you may have superimposed cut-out geometric shapes in school—they are not alike at all. But their shapes are *exact opposites*. Their respective shapes fit the same description, provided that the description is modified by a principle of application whereby the measures are read one way for one hand and the other way for the other—like a timetable in which the list of stations is marked: "Eastbound, read down; Westbound, read up."

As the two hands exemplify the same form with a principle of reversal understood, so the list of stations describes two ways of moving, indicated by the advice to "read down" for one and "read up" for the other. We can all abstract the common element in these two respective trips, which is called the *route*. With a return ticket we may return only by the same route. The same principle relates a mold to the form of the thing that is cast in it, and establishes their formal correspondence, or common logical form.

So far we have considered only objects—lampshades, hands, or regions of the earth—as having forms. These have fixed shapes; their parts remain in fairly stable relations to each other. But there are also substances that have no definite shapes, such as gases, mist, and water, which take the shape of any bounded space that contains them. The interesting thing about such amorphous fluids is that when they are put into violent motion they do exhibit visible forms, not bounded by any container. Think of the momentary efflorescence of a bursting rocket, the mushroom cloud of an atomic bomb, the funnel of water or dust screwing upward in a whirlwind. The instant the motion stops, or even slows beyond a certain degree, those shapes collapse and the apparent "thing" disappears. They are not shapes of things at all, but forms of motions, or dynamic forms.

Some dynamic forms, however, have more permanent manifestations, because the stuff that moves and makes them visible is constantly replenished. A waterfall seems to hang from the cliff, waving streamers of foam. Actually, of course, nothing stays there in mid-air; the water is always passing; but there is more and more water taking the same paths, so we have a lasting shape made and maintained by its passage—a permanent dynamic form. A quiet river, too, has dynamic form; if it stopped flowing it would either go dry or become a lake. Some twenty-five hundred years ago, Heracleitos was struck by the fact that you cannot step twice into the same river at the same place—at least, if the river means the water, not its dynamic form, the flow.

When a river ceases to flow because the water is deflected or dried up, there remains the river bed, sometimes cut deeply in solid stone. That bed is shaped by the flow, and records as graven lines the currents that have ceased to exist. Its shape is static, but it *expresses* the dynamic form of the river. Again, we have two congruent forms, like a cast and its mold, but this time the congruence is more remarkable because it holds between a dynamic form and a static one. That relation is important; we shall be dealing with it again when we come to consider the meaning of "living form" in art.

The congruence of two given perceptible forms is not always evident upon simple inspection. The common *logical* form they both exhibit may become apparent only when you know the principle whereby to relate them, as you compare the shapes of your hands not by direct correspondence, but by correspondence of opposite parts. Where the two exemplifications of the single logical form are unlike in most other respects one needs a rule for matching up the relevant factors of one with the relevant factors of the other; that is to say, a *rule of translation*, whereby one instance of the logical form is shown to correspond formally to the other.

The logical form itself is not another thing, but an abstract concept, or better an *abstractable* concept. We usually don't abstract it deliberately, but only use it, as we use our vocal cords in speech without first learning all about their operation and then applying our knowledge. Most people perceive intuitively the similarity of their two hands without thinking of them as conversely related; they can guess at the shape of the hollow inside a wooden shoe from the shape of a human foot, without any abstract study of topology. But the first time they see a map in the Mercator projection—with parallel lines of longitude, not meeting at the poles—they find it hard to believe that this corresponds logically to the circular map they used in school, where the meridians bulged apart toward the equator and met at both poles. The visible shapes of the continents are different on the two maps, and it takes abstract thinking to match up the two representations of the same earth. If, however, they have grown up with both maps, they will probably see the geographical relationships either way with equal ease, because these relationships are not *copied* by either map, but *expressed*, and expressed equally well by both; for the two maps are different *projections* of the same logical form, which the spherical earth exhibits in still another—that is, a spherical—projecton.

An expressive form is any perceptible or imaginable whole that exhibits relationships of parts, or points, or even qualities or aspects within the whole, so that it may be taken to represent some other whole whose elements have analogous relations. The reason for using such a form as a symbol is usually that the thing it represents is not perceivable or readily imaginable. We cannot see the earth as an object. We let a map or a little globe express the relationships of places on the earth, and think about the earth by means of it. The understanding of one thing through another seems to be a deeply intuitive process in the human brain; it is so natural that we often have difficulty in distinguishing the symbolic expressive form from what it conveys. The symbol seems to be the thing itself, or contain it, or be contained in it. A child interested in a globe will not say: "This means the earth," but: "Look, this is the earth." A similar identification of symbol and meaning underlies the widespread conception of holy names, of the physical efficacy of rites, and many other primitive but culturally persistent phenomena. It has a bearing on our perception of artistic import; that is why I mention it here.

The most astounding and developed symbolic device humanity has evolved is language. By means of language we can conceive the intangible, incorporeal things we call our *ideas*, and the equally inostensible elements of our perceptual world that we call *facts*. It is

178 · Susanne K. Langer

by virtue of language that we can think, remember, imagine, and finally conceive a universe of facts. We can describe things and represent their relations, express rules of their interactions, speculate and predict and carry on a long symbolizing process known as reasoning. And above all, we can communicate, by producing a serried array of audible or visible words, in a pattern commonly known, and readily understood to reflect our multifarious concepts and percepts and their interconnections. This use of language is *discourse*; and the pattern of discourse is known as *discursive* form. It is a highly versatile, amazingly powerful pattern. It has impressed itself on our tacit thinking, so that we call all systematic reflection "discursive thought." It has made, far more than most people know, the very frame of our sensory experience—the frame of objective facts in which we carry on the practical business of life.

Yet even the discursive pattern has its limits of usefulness. An expressive form can express any complex or conceptions that, via some rule of projection, appears congruent with it, that is, appears to be of that form. Whatever there is in experience that will not take the impress—directly or indirectly—of discursive form, is not discursively communicable or, in the strictest sense, logically thinkable. It is unspeakable, ineffable; according to practically all serious philosophical theories today, it is unknowable.

Yet there is a great deal of experience that is knowable, not only as immediate, formless, meaningless impact, but as one aspect of the intricate web of life, yet defies discursive formulation, and therefore verbal expression: that is what we sometimes call the *subjective aspect* of experience, the direct feeling of it—what it is like to be waking and moving, to be drowsy, slowing down, or to be sociable, or to feel self-sufficient but alone; what it feels like to pursue an elusive thought or to have a big idea. All such directly felt experiences usually have no names—they are named, if at all, for the outward conditions that normally accompany their occurrence. Only the most striking ones have names like "anger," "hate," "love," "fear," and are collectively called "emotion." But we feel many things that never develop into any designable emotion. The ways we are moved are as various as the lights in a forest; and they may intersect, sometimes without cancelling each other, take shape and dissolve, conflict, explode into passion, or be transfigured. All these inseparable elements of subjective reality compose what we call the "inward life" of human beings. The usual factoring of that life-stream into mental, emotional, and sensory units is an arbitrary scheme of simplification that makes scientific treatment possible to a considerable extent; but we may already be close to the limit of its usefulness, that is, close to the point where its simplicity becomes an obstacle to further questioning and discovery instead of the revealing, ever-suitable logical projection it was expected to be.

Whatever resists projection into the discursive form of language is, indeed, hard to hold in conception, and perhaps impossible to communicate, in the proper and strict sense of the word "communicate." But fortunately our logical intuition, or form-perception, is really much more powerful than we commonly believe, and our knowledge—genuine knowledge, understanding—is considerably wider than our discourse. Even in the use of language, if we want to name something that is too new to have a name (e.g., a newly invented gadget or a newly discovered creature), or want to express a relationship for which there is no verb or other connective word, we resort to metaphor; we mention it or describe it as something else, something analogous. The principle of metaphor is simply the principle of saying one thing and meaning another, and expecting to be understood to mean the other. A metaphor is not language, it is an idea expressed by language, an idea that in its turn functions as a symbol to express something. It is not discursive and therefore does not really make a statement of the idea it conveys; but it formulates a new conception for our direct imaginative grasp.

Sometimes our comprehension of a total experience is mediated by a metaphorical symbol because the experience is new, and language has words and phrases only for familiar notions. Then an extension of language will gradually follow the wordless insight, and discursive expression will supersede the non-discursive pristine symbol. This is, I think, the normal advance of human thought and language in that whole realm of knowledge where discourse is possible at all.

But the symbolic presentation of subjective reality for contemplation is not only tentatively beyond the reach of language—that is, not merely beyond the words we have; it is impossible in the essential frame of language. That is why those semanticists who recognize only discourse as a symbolic form must regard the whole life of feeling as formless, chaotic, capable only of symptomatic expression, typified in exclamations like "Ah!" "Ouch!" "My sainted aunt!" They usually do believe that art is an expression of feeling, but that "expression" in art is of this sort, indicating that the speaker has an emotion, a pain, or other personal experience, perhaps also giving us a clue to the general kind of experience it is—pleasant or unpleasant, violent or mild—but not setting that piece of inward life objectively before us so we may understand its intricacy, its rhythms and shifts of total appearance. The differences in feeling-tones or other elements of subjective experience are regarded as differences in quality, which must be felt to be appreciated. Furthermore, since we have no intellectual access to pure subjectivity, the only way to study it is to study the symptoms of the person who is having subjective experiences. This leads to physiological psychology—a very important and interesting field. But it tells us nothing about the phenomena of subjective life, and sometimes simplifies the problem by saying they don't exist.

Now, I believe the expression of feeling in a work of art—the function that makes the work an expressive form—is not symptomatic at all. An artist working on a tragedy need not be in personal despair or violent upheaval; nobody, indeed, could work in such a state of mind. His mind would be occupied with the causes of his emotional upset. Self-expression does not require composition and lucidity; a screaming baby gives his feeling far more release than any musician, but we don't go into a concert hall to hear a baby scream; in fact, if that baby is brought in we are likely to go out. We don't want self-expression.

A work of art presents feeling (in the broad sense I mentioned before, as everything that can be felt) for our contemplation, making it visible or audible or in some way perceivable through a symbol, not inferable from a symptom. Artistic form is congruent with the dynamic forms of our direct sensuous, mental, and emotional life; works of art are projections of "felt life," as Henry James called it, into spatial, temporal, and poetic structures. They are images of feeling, that formulate it for our cognition. What is artistically good is whatever articulates and presents feeling to our understanding.

Artistic forms are more complex than any other symbolic forms we know. They are, indeed, not abstractable from the works that exhibit them. We may abstract a shape from an object that has this shape, by disregarding color, weight and texture, even size; but to the total effect that is an artistic form, the color matters, the thickness of lines matters, and the appearance of texture and weight. A given triangle is the same in any position, but to an artistic form its location, balance, and surroundings are not indifferent. Form, in the sense in which artists speak of "significant form" or "expressive form," is not an abstracted structure, but an apparition; and the vital processes of sense and emotion that a good work of art expresses seem to the beholder to be directly contained in it, not symbolized but really presented. The congruence is so striking that symbol and meaning appear as one reality. Actually, as one psychologist who is also a musician has written, "Music sounds as feelings feel." And likewise, in good painting, sculpture, or building, balanced shapes and colors, lines and masses look as emotions, vital tensions and their resolutions feel.

An artist, then, expresses feeling, but not in the way a politician blows off steam or a baby laughs and cries. He formulates that elusive aspect of reality that is commonly taken to be amorphous and chaotic; that is, he objectifies the subjective realm. What he expresses is, therefore, not his own actual feelings, but what he knows about human feeling. Once he is in possession of a rich symbolism, that knowledge may actually exceed his entire personal experience. A work of art expresses a conception of life, emotion, inward reality. But it is neither a confessional nor a frozen tantrum; it is a developed metaphor, a non-discursive symbol that articulates what is verbally ineffable—the logic of consciousness itself.

NORTHROP FRYE

The Keys to Dreamland[1]

* * * Suppose you're walking down the street of a North American city. All around you is a highly artificial society, but you don't think of it as artificial: you're so accustomed to it that you think of it as natural. But suppose your imagination plays a little trick on you of a kind that it often does play, and you suddenly feel like a complete outsider, someone who's just blown in from Mars on a flying saucer. Instantly you see how conventionalized everything is: the clothes, the shop windows, the movement of the cars in traffic, the cropped hair and shaved faces of the men, the red lips and blue eyelids that women put on because they want to conventionalize their faces, or "look nice," as they say, which means the same thing. All this convention is pressing toward uniformity or likeness. To be outside the convention makes a person look queer, or, if he's driving a car, a menace to life and limb. The only exceptions are people who have decided to conform to different conventions, like nuns or beatniks. There's clearly a strong force making toward conformity in society, so strong that it seems to have something to do with the stability of society itself. In ordinary life even the most splendid things we can think of, goodness and truth and beauty, all mean essentially what we're accustomed to. As I hinted just now in speaking of female makeup, most of our ideas of beauty are pure convention, and even truth has been defined as whatever doesn't disturb the pattern of what we already know.

When we move on to literature, we again find conventions, but this time we notice that they are conventions, because we're not so used to them. These conventions seem to have something to do with making literature as unlike life as possible. Chaucer represents people as making up stories in ten-syllable couplets. Shakespeare uses dramatic conventions, which means, for instance, that Iago has to smash Othello's marriage and dreams of future happiness and get him ready to murder his wife in a few minutes. Milton has two nudes in a garden haranguing each other in set speeches beginning with such lines as "Daughter of God and Man, immortal

1. Chapter 4 in *The Educated Imagination*, 1964.

Eve"—Eve being Adam's daughter because she's just been
extracted from his ribcase. Almost every story we read demands
that we accept as fact something that we know to be nonsense:
that good people always win, especially in love; that murders are
complicated and ingenious puzzles to be solved by logic, and so on.
It isn't only popular literature that demands this: more highbrow
stories are apt to be more ironic, but irony has its conventions too.
If we go further back into literature, we run into such conventions
as the king's rash promise, the enraged cuckold, the cruel mistress
of love poetry—never anything that we or any other time would
recognize as the normal behavior of adult people, only the mad-
dened ethics of fairyland.

Even the details of literature are equally perverse. Literature is a
world where phoenixes and unicorns are quite as important as
horses and dogs—and in literature some of the horses talk, like the
ones in *Gulliver's Travels*. A random example is calling Shakespeare
the "swan of Avon"—he was called that by Ben Jonson. The town
of Stratford, Ontario, keeps swans in its river partly as a literary
allusion. Poets of Shakespeare's day hated to admit that they were
writing words on a page: they always insisted that they were producing music. In pastoral poetry they might be playing a flute (or
more accurately an oboe), but every other kind of poetic effort was
called song, with a harp, a lyre or a lute in the background, depending on how highbrow the song was. Singing suggests birds, and so
for their typical songbird and emblem of themselves, the poets
chose the swan, a bird that can't sing. Because it can't sing, they
made up a legend that it sang once before death, when nobody was
listening. But Shakespeare didn't burst into song before his death:
he wrote two plays a year until he'd made enough money to retire,
and spent the last five years of his life counting his take.

So however useful literature may be in improving one's imagination or vocabulary, it would be the wildest kind of pedantry to use it
directly as a guide to life. Perhaps here we see one reason why the
poet is not only very seldom a person one would turn to for insight
into the state of the world, but often seems even more gullible and
simple-minded than the rest of us. For the poet, the particular literary conventions he adopts are likely to become, for him, facts of
life. If he finds that the kind of writing he's best at has a good deal
to do with fairies, like Yeats, or a white goddess, like Graves, or
a life-force, like Bernard Shaw, or episcopal sermons, like T. S.
Eliot, or bullfights, like Hemingway, or exasperation at social hypo-
crisies, as with the so-called angry school, these things are apt to
take on a reality for him that seems badly out of proportion to his
contemporaries. His life may imitate literature in a way that may
warp or even destroy his social personality, as Byron wore himself

out at thirty-four with the strain of being Byronic. Life and literature, then, are both conventionalized, and of the conventions of literature about all we can say is that they don't much resemble the
conditions of life. It's when two sets of conventions collide that we
realize how different they are.

In fact, whenever literature gets too probable, too much like life,
some self-defeating process, some mysterious law of diminishing
returns, seems to set in. There's a vivid and expertly written novel
by H. G. Wells called *Kipps*, about a lower-middle-class, inarticulate, very likeable Cockney, the kind of character we often find in
Dickens. Kipps is carefully studied: he never says anything that a
man like Kipps wouldn't say; he never sounds the "h" in home or
head; nothing he does is out of line with what we expect such a
person to be like. It's an admirable novel, well worth reading, and
yet I have a nagging feeling that there's some inner secret in bringing him completely to life that Dickens would have and that Wells
doesn't have. All right, then, what would Dickens have done?
Well, one of the things that Dickens often does do is write *badly*.
He might have given Kipps sentimental speeches and false heroics
and all sorts of inappropriate verbiage to say; and some readers
would have clucked and tut-tutted over these passages and
explained to each other how bad Dickens's taste was and how
uncertain his hold on character could be. Perhaps they'd be right
too. But we'd have had Kipps a few times the way he'd look to
himself or the way he'd sometimes wish he could be: that's part of
his reality, and the effect would remain with us however much we
disapproved of it. Whether I'm right about this book or not, and
I'm not at all sure I am, I think my general principle is right.
What we'd never see except in a book is often what we go to books
to find. Whatever is completely lifelike in literature is a bit of a
laboratory specimen there. To bring anything really to life in literature we can't be lifelike: we have to be literaturelike.

The same thing is true even of the use of language. We're often
taught that prose is the language of ordinary speech, which is
usually true in literature. But in ordinary life prose is no more the
language of ordinary speech than one's Sunday suit is a bathing
suit. The people who actually speak prose are highly cultivated and
articulate people, who've read a good many books, and even they
can speak prose only to each other. If you read the beautiful sentences of Elizabeth Bennett's conversation in *Pride and Prejudice*,
you can see how in that book they give a powerfully convincing
impression of a sensible and intelligent girl. But any girl who talked
as coherently as that on a street car would be stared at as though
she had green hair. It isn't only the difference between 1813 and
1962 that's involved either, as you'll see if you compare her speech

with her mother's. The poet Emily Dickinson complained that everybody said "What?" to her, until finally she practically gave up trying to talk altogether, and confined herself to writing notes.

All this is involved with the difference between literary and other kinds of writing. If we're writing to convey information, or for any practical reason, our writing is an act of will and intention: we mean what we say, and the words we use represent that meaning directly. It's different in literature, not because the poet doesn't mean what he says too, but because his real effort is one of putting words together. What's important is not what he may have meant to say, but what words themselves say when they get fitted together. With a novelist it's rather the incidents in the story he tells that get fitted together—as D. H. Lawrence says, don't trust the novelist; trust his story. That's why so much of a writer's best writing is or seems to be involuntary. It's involuntary because the forms of literature itself are taking control of it, and these forms are what are embodied in the conventions of literature. Conventions, we see, have the same role in literature that they have in life: they impose certain patterns of order and stability on the writer. Only, if they're such different conventions, it seems clear that the order of words, or the structure of literature, is different from the social order.

The absence of any clear line of connection between literature and life comes out in the issues involved in censorship. Because of the large involuntary element in writing, works of literature can't be treated as embodiments of conscious will or intention, like people, and so no laws can be framed to control their behavior which assume a tendency to do this or an intention of doing that. Works of literature get into legal trouble because they offend some powerful religious or political interest, and this interest in its turn usually acquires or exploits the kind of social hysteria that's always revolving around sex. But it's impossible to give legal definitions of such terms as obscenity in relation to works of literature. What happens to the book depends mainly on the intelligence of the judge. If he's a sensible man we get a sensible decision; if he's an ass we get that sort of decision, but what we don't get is a legal decision, because the basis for one doesn't exist. The best we get is a precedent tending to discourage cranks and pressure groups from attacking serious books. If you read the casebook on the trial of *Lady Chatterley's Lover*, you may remember how bewildered the critics were when they were asked what the moral effect of the book would be. They weren't putting on an act: they didn't know. Novels can only be good or bad in their own categories. There's no such thing as a morally bad novel: its moral effect depends entirely on the moral quality of its reader, and nobody can predict what that will be. And if literature isn't morally bad it isn't morally good either. I suppose one reason why *Lady Chatterley's Lover* dramatized this question so vividly was that it's a rather preachy and self-conscious book: like the Sunday-school novels of my childhood, it bores me a little because it tries so hard to do me good.

So literature has no consistent connection with ordinary life, positive or negative. Here we touch on another important difference between structures of the imagination and structures of practical sense, which include the applied sciences. Imagination is certainly essential to science, applied or pure. Without a constructive power in the mind to make models of experience, get hunches and follow them out, play freely around with hypotheses, and so forth, no scientist could get anywhere. But all imaginative effort in practical fields has to meet the test of practicability, otherwise it's discarded. The imagination in literature has no such test to meet. You don't relate it directly to life or reality: you relate works of literature to each other. Whatever value there is in studying literature, cultural or practical, comes from the total body of our reading, the castle of words we've built, and keep adding new wings to all the time.

So it's natural to swing to the opposite extreme and say that literature is really a refuge or escape from life, a self-contained world like the world of the dream, a world of play or make-believe to balance the world of work. Some literature is like that, and many people tell us that they only read to get away from reality for a bit. And I've suggested myself that the sense of escape, or at least detachment, does come into everybody's literary experience. But the real point of literature can hardly be that. Think of such writers as William Faulkner or François Mauriac, their great moral dignity, the intensity and compassion that they've studied the life around them with. Or think of James Joyce, spending seven years on one book and seventeen on another, and having them ridiculed or abused or banned by the customs when they did get published. Or of the poets Rilke and Valéry, waiting patiently for years in silence until what they had to say was ready to be said. There's a deadly seriousness in all this that even the most refined theories of fantasy or make-believe won't quite cover. Still, let's go along with the idea for a bit, because we're not getting on very fast with the relation of literature of life, or what we could call the horizontal perspective of literature. That seems to block us off on all sides.

The world of literature is a world where there is no reality except that of the human imagination. We see a great deal in it that reminds us vividly of the life we know. But in that very vividness there's something unreal. We can understand this more clearly with pictures, perhaps. There are trick-pictures—*trompe l'oeil*, the French call them—where the resemblance to life is very strong. An

American painter of this school played a joke on his bitchy wife by painting one of her best napkins so expertly that she grabbed at the canvas trying to pull it off. But a painting as realistic as that isn't a reality but an illusion: it has the glittering unnatural clarity of a hallucination. The real realities, so to speak, are things that don't remind us directly of our own experience, but are such things as the wrath of Achilles or the jealousy of Othello, which are bigger and more intense experiences than anything we can reach—except in our imagination, which is what we're reaching with. Sometimes, as in the happy endings of comedies, or in the ideal world of romances, we seem to be looking at a pleasanter world than we ordinarily know. Sometimes, as in tragedy and satire, we seem to be looking at a world more devoted to suffering or absurdity than we ordinarily know. In literature we always seem to be looking either up or down. It's the vertical perspective that's important, not the horizontal one that looks out to life. Of course, in the greatest works of literature we get both the up and down views, often at the same time as different aspects of one event.

There are two halves to literary experience, then. Imagination gives us both a better and a worse world than the one we usually live with, and demands that we keep looking steadily at them both. The arts follow the path of the emotions, and of the tendency of the emotions to separate the world into a half that we like and a half that we don't like. Literature is not a world of dreams, but it would be if we had only one half without the other. If we had nothing but romances and comedies with happy endings, literature would express only a wish-fulfilment dream. Some people ask why poets want to write tragedies when the world's so full of them anyway, and suggest that enjoying such things has something morbid or gloating about it. It doesn't, but it might if there were nothing else in literature.

This point is worth spending another minute on. You recall that terrible scene in *King Lear* where Gloucester's eyes are put out on the stage. That's part of a play, and a play is supposed to be entertaining. Now in what sense can a scene like that be entertaining? The fact that it's not really happening is certainly important. It would be degrading to watch a real blinding scene, and far more so to get any pleasure out of watching it. Consequently, the entertainment doesn't consist in its reminding us of a real blinding scene. If it did, one of the great scenes of drama would turn into a piece of repulsive pornography. We couldn't stop anyone from reacting in this way, and it certainly wouldn't cure him, much less help the public, to start blaming or censoring Shakespeare for putting sadistic ideas in his head. But a reaction of that kind has nothing to do with drama. In a dramatic scene of cruelty and hatred we're seeing cruelty and hatred, which we know are permanently real things in human life, from the point of view of the imagination. What the imagination suggests is horror, not the paralyzing sickening horror of a real blinding scene, but an exuberant horror, full of the energy of repudiation. This is as powerful a rendering as we can ever get of life as we don't want it.

So we see that there are moral standards in literature after all, even though they have nothing to do with calling the police when we see a word in a book that's more familiar in sound that in print. One of the things Gloucester says in that scene is: "I am tied to the stake, and I must stand the course." In Shakespeare's day it was a favorite sport to tie a bear to a stake and set dogs on it until they killed it. The Puritans suppressed this sport, according to Macaulay, not because it gave pain to the bear but because it gave pleasure to the spectators. Macaulay may have intended his remark to be a sneer at the Puritans, but surely if the Puritans did feel this way they were one hundred per cent right. What other reason is there for abolishing public hangings? Whatever their motives, the Puritans and Shakespeare were operating in the same direction. Literature keeps presenting the most vicious things to us as entertainment, but what is appeals to is not any pleasure in these things, but the exhilaration of standing apart from them and being able to see them for what they are because they aren't really happening. The more exposed we are to this, the less likely we are to find an unthinking pleasure in cruel or evil things. As the eighteenth century said in a fine mouth-filling phrase, literature refines our sensibilities.

The top half of literature is the world expressed by such words as sublime, inspiring, and the like, where what we feel is not detachment but absorption. This is the world of heroes and gods and titans and Rabelaisian giants, a world of powers and passions and moments of ecstasy far greater than anything we meet outside the imagination. Such forces would not only absorb but annihilate us if they entered ordinary life, but luckily the protecting wall of the imagination is here too. As the German poet Rilke says, we adore them because they disdain to destroy us. We seem to have got quite a long way from our emotions with their division of things into "I like this" and "I don't like this." Literature gives us an experience that stretches us vertically to the heights and depths of what the human mind can conceive, to what corresponds to the conceptions of heaven and hell in religion. In this perspective what I like or don't like disappears, because there's nothing left of me as a separate person: as a reader of literature I exist only as a representative of humanity as a whole.

No matter how much experience we may gather in life, we can

never in life get the dimension of experience that the imagination gives us. Only the arts and sciences can do that, and of these, only literature gives us the whole sweep and range of human imagination as it sees itself. It seems to be very difficult for many people to understand the reality and intensity of literary experience. To give an example that you may think a bit irrelevant: why have so many people managed to convince themselves that Shakespeare did not write Shakespeare's plays, when there is not an atom of evidence that anybody else did? Apparently because they feel that poetry must be written out of personal experience, and that Shakespeare didn't have enough experience of the right kind. But Shakespeare's plays weren't produced by his experience: they were produced by his imagination, and the way to develop the imagination is to read a good book or two. As for us, we can't speak or think or comprehend even our own experience except within the limits of our own power over words, and those limits have been established for us by our great writers.

Literature, then, is not a dream-world: it's two dreams, a wish-fulfillment dream and an anxiety dream, that are focused together, like a pair of glasses, and become a fully conscious vision. Art, according to Plato, is a dream for awakened minds, a work of imagination withdrawn from ordinary life, dominated by the same forces that dominate the dream, and yet giving us a perspective and dimension on reality that we don't get from any other approach to reality. So the poet and the dreamer are distinct, as Keats says. Ordinary life forms a community, and literature is among other things an art of communication, so it forms a community too. In ordinary life we fall into a private and separate subconscious every night, where we reshape the world according to a private and separate imagination. Underneath literature there's another kind of subconscious, which is social and not private, a need for forming a community around certain symbols, like the Queen and the flag, or around certain gods that represent order and stability, or becoming and change, or death and rebirth to a new life. This is the myth-making power of the human mind, which throws up and dissolves one civilization after another.

I've taken my title, "The Keys to Dreamland," from what is possibly the greatest single effort of the literary imagination in the twentieth century, Joyce's *Finnegans Wake*. In this book a man goes to sleep and falls, not into the Freudian separate or private subconscious, but into the deeper dream of man that creates and destroys his own societies. The entire book is written in the language of this dream. It's a subconscious language, mainly English, but connected by associations and puns with the eighteen or so other languages that Joyce knew. *Finnegans Wake* is not a book to read, but a book to decipher: as Joyce says, it's about a dreamer, but it's addressed to an ideal reader suffering from an ideal insomnia. The reader or critic, then, has a role complementing the poet's role. We need two powers in literature, a power to create and a power to understand.

In all our literary experience there are two kinds of response. There is the direct experience of the work itself, while we're reading a book or seeing a play, especially for the first time. This experience is uncritical, or rather pre-critical, so it's not infallible. If our experience is limited, we can be roused to enthusiasm or carried away by something that we can later see to have been second-rate or even phony. Then there is the conscious, critical response we make after we've finished reading or left the theatre, where we compare what we've experienced with other things of the same kind, and form a judgment of value and proportion on it. This critical response, with practice, gradually makes our pre-critical responses more sensitive and accurate, or improves our taste, as we say. But behind our responses to individual works, there's a bigger response to our literary experience as a whole, as a total possession.

The critic has always been called a judge of literature, which means, not that he's in a superior position to the poet, but that he ought to know something about literature, just as a judge's right to be on a bench depends on his knowledge of law. If he's up against something the size of Shakespeare, he's the one being judged. The critic's function is to interpret every work of literature in the light of all the literature he knows, to keep constantly struggling to understand what literature as a whole is about. Literature as a whole is not an aggregate of exhibits with red and blue ribbons attached to them, like a cat show, but the range of articulate human imagination as it extends from the height of imaginative heaven to the depth of imaginative hell. Literature is a human apocalypse, man's revelation to man, and criticism is not a body of adjudications, but the awareness of that revelation, the last judgment of mankind.

QUESTIONS

1. Frye uses the word "conventions" a number of times; what meanings does he appear to give the word? Why does he seek to show that life has conventions as does literature? Are they the same sort of conventions?
2. Early in his essay Frye makes some amusing remarks about poets and their ways. Is he making fun of them? If so, why? Does he suggest that poets are contemptible? If not, what is he trying to do?
3. Toward what sort of audience is Frye addressing his remarks?

What can you tell about the audience he has in view from the language he chooses, and from the line of development his essay takes? What conception of the relationship between life and literature does Frye assume his audience might have at the outset? Does Frye seek to persuade his audience to adopt a certain view of literature, perhaps to change a previous view? What devices in his writing (as of tone, diction, figures of speech) are directed toward persuasion?

4. What ideas about literature and its relationship to life does Frye examine and reject? Why does he reject them? What are the main features of his own position? Does he set forth that position in a single thesis sentence anywhere in the essay?

5. What is Frye's view of the moral effect of art and literature?

ROBERT FROST

Education by Poetry: A Meditative Monologue[1]

I am going to urge nothing in my talk. I am not an advocate. I am going to consider a matter, and commit a description. And I am going to describe other colleges than Amherst. Or, rather say all that is good can be taken as about Amherst; all that is bad will be about other colleges.

I know whole colleges where all American poetry is barred—whole colleges. I know whole colleges where all contemporary poetry is barred.

I once heard of a minister who turned his daughter—his poetry-writing daughter—out on the street to earn a living, because he said there should be no more books written; God wrote one book, and that was enough. (My friend George Russell, "Æ", has read no literature, he protests, since just before Chaucer.)

That all seems sufficiently safe, and you can say one thing for it. It takes the onus off the poetry of having to be used to teach children anything. It comes pretty hard on poetry, I sometimes think, what it has to bear in the teaching process.

Then I know whole colleges where, though they let in older poetry, they manage to bar all that is poetical in it by treating it as something other than poetry. It is not so hard to do that. Their reason I have often hunted for. It may be that these people act from a kind of modesty. Who are professors that they should attempt to deal with a thing as high and as fine as poetry? Who are *they*? There is a certain manly modesty in that.

1. An address given at Amherst College in 1930.

That is the best general way of settling the problem; treat all poetry as if it were something else than poetry, as if it were syntax, language, science. Then you can even come down into the American and into the contemporary without any special risk.

There is another reason they have, and that is that they are, first and foremost in life, markers. They have the marking problem to consider. Now, I stand here a teacher of many years' experience and I have never complained of having had to mark. I had rather mark anyone for anything—for his looks, carriage, his ideas, his correctness, his exactness, anything you please—I would rather give him a mark in terms of letters, A, B, C, D, than have to use adjectives on him. We are all being marked by each other all the time, classified, ranked, put in our place, and I see no escape from that. I am no sentimentalist. You have got to mark, and you have got to mark, first of all, for accuracy, for correctness. But if I am going to give a mark, that is the least part of my marking. The hard part is the part beyond that, the part where the adventure begins.

One other way to rid the curriculum of the poetry nuisance has been considered. More merciful than the others it would neither abolish nor denature the poetry, but only turn it out to disport itself, with the plays and games—in no wise discredited, though given no credit for. Any one who liked to teach poetically could take his subject, whether English, Latin, Greek or French, out into the nowhere along with the poetry. One side of a sharp line would be left to the rigorous and righteous; the other side would be assigned to the flowery where they would know what could be expected of them. Grade marks where more easily given, of course, in the courses concentrating on correctness and exactness as the only forms of honesty recognized by plain people; a general indefinite mark of X in the courses that scatter brains over taste and opinion. On inquiry I have found no teacher willing to take position on either side of the line, either among the rigors or among the flowers. No one is willing to admit that his discipline is not partly in exactness. No one is willing to admit that his discipline is not partly in taste and enthusiasm.

How shall a man go through college without having been marked for taste and judgment? What will become of him? What will his end be? He will have to take continuation courses for college graduates. He will have to go to night schools. They are having night schools now, you know, for college graduates. Why? Because they have not been educated enough to find their way around in contemporary literature. They don't know what they may safely like in the libraries and galleries. They don't know how to judge an editorial when they see one. They don't know how to judge a political campaign. They don't know when they are being fooled by a metaphor, an analogy, a parable. And metaphor is, of course, what we are talking about. Education by poetry is education by metaphor.

Suppose we stop short of imagination, initiative, enthusiasm, inspiration and originality—dread words. Suppose we don't mark in such things at all. There are still two minimal things, that we have got to take care of, taste and judgment. Americans are supposed to have more judgment than taste, but taste is there to be dealt with. That is what poetry, the only art in the colleges of arts, is there for. I for my part would not be afraid to go in for enthusiasm. There is the enthusiasm like a blinding light, or the enthusiasm of the deafening shout, the crude enthusiasm that you get uneducated by poetry, outside of poetry. It is exemplified in what I might call "sunset raving." You look westward toward the sunset, or if you get up early enough, eastward toward the sunrise, and you rave. It is oh's and ah's with you and no more.

But the enthusiasm I mean is taken through the prism of the intellect and spread on the screen in a color, all the way from hyperbole at one end—or overstatement, at one end—to understatement at the other end. It is a long strip of dark lines and many colors. Such enthusiasm is one object of all teaching in poetry. I heard wonderful things said about Virgil yesterday, and many of them seemed to me crude enthusiasm, more like a deafening shout, many of them. But one speech had range, something of overstatement, something of statement, and something of understatement. It had all the colors of an enthusiasm passed through an idea.

I would be willing to throw away everything else but that: enthusiasm tamed by metaphor. Let me rest the case there. Enthusiasm tamed to metaphor, tamed to that much of it. I do not think anybody ever knows the discreet use of metaphor, his own and other people's, the discreet handling of metaphor, unless he has been properly educated in poetry.

Poetry begins in trivial metaphors, petty metaphors, "grace" metaphors, and goes on to the profoundest thinking that we have. Poetry provides the one permissible way of saying one thing and meaning another. People say, "Why don't you say what you mean?" We never do that, do we, being all of us too much poets. We like to talk in parables and in hints and in indirections—whether from diffidence or some other instinct.

I have wanted in late years to go further and further in making metaphor the whole of thinking. I find some one now and then to agree with me that all thinking, except mathematical thinking, is metaphorical, or all thinking except scientific thinking. The mathematical might be difficult for me to bring in, but the scientific is easy enough.

Once on a time all the Greeks were busy telling each other what the All was—or was like unto. All was three elements, air, earth, and water (we once thought it was ninety elements; now we think it is

only one). All was substance, said another. All was change, said a
third. But best and most fruitful was Pythagoras' comparison of the
universe with number. Number of what? Number of feet, pounds,
and seconds was the answer, and we had science and all that has
followed in science. The metaphor has held and held, breaking down
only when it came to the spiritual and psychological or the out of the
way places of the physical.

The other day we had a visitor here, a noted scientist, whose latest
word to the world has been that the more accurately you know where
a thing is, the less accurately you are able to state how fast it is
moving. You can see why that would be so, without going back to
Zeno's problem of the arrow's flight. In carrying numbers into the
realm of space and at the same time into the realm of time you are
mixing metaphors, that is all, and you are in trouble. They won't
mix. The two don't go together.

Let's take two or three more of the metaphors now in use to live
by. I have just spoken of one of the new ones, a charming mixed
metaphor right in the realm of higher mathematics and higher
physics: that the more accurately you state where a thing is, the less
accurately you will be able to tell how fast it is moving. And, of course
everything is moving. Everything is an event now. Another metaphor. A thing, they say, is an event. Do you believe it is? Not quite. I
believe it is almost an event. But I like the comparison of a thing
with an event.

I notice another from the same quarter. "In the neighborhood of
matter space is something like curved." Isn't that a good one! It seems
to me that that is simply and utterly charming—to say that space is
something like curved in the neighborhood of matter. "Something
like."

Another amusing one is from—what is the book?—I can't say it
now; but here is the metaphor. Its aim is to restore you to your ideas
of free will. It wants to give you back your freedom of will. All right,
here it is on a platter. You know that you can't tell by name what
persons in a certain class will be dead ten years after graduation, but
you can tell actuarially how many will be dead. Now, just so this
scientist says of the particles of matter flying at a screen, striking a
screen; you can't tell what individual particles will come, but you
can say in general that a certain number will strike in a given time.
It shows, you see, that the individual particle can come freely. I asked
Bohr about that particularly, and he said, "Yes, it is so. It can come
when it wills and as it wills; and the action of the individual particle
is unpredictable. But it is not so of the action of the mass. There
you can predict." He says, "That gives the individual atom its freedom, but the mass its necessity."

Another metaphor that has interested us in our time and has done all our thinking for us is the metaphor of evolution. Never mind going into the Latin word. The metaphor is simply the metaphor of the growing plant or of the growing thing. And somebody very brilliantly, quite a while ago, said that the whole universe, the whole of everything, was like unto a growing thing. That is all. I know the metaphor will break down at some point, but it has not failed everywhere. It is a very brilliant metaphor, I acknowledge, though I myself get too tired of the kind of essay that talks about the evolution of candy, we will say, or the evolution of elevators—the evolution of this, that, and the other. Everything is evolution. I emancipate myself by simply saying that I didn't get up the metaphor and so am not much interested in it.

What I am pointing out is that unless you are at home in the metaphor, unless you have had your proper poetical education in the metaphor, you are not safe anywhere. Because you are not at ease with figurative values: you don't know the metaphor in its strength and its weakness. You don't know how far you may expect to ride it and when it may break down with you. You are not safe in science; you are not safe in history. In history, for instance—to show that is the same in history as elsewhere—I heard somebody say yesterday that Aeneas was to be likened unto (those words, "likened unto"!) George Washington. He was that type of national hero, the middle-class man, not thinking of being a hero at all, bent on building the future, bent on his children, his descendants. A good metaphor, as far as it goes, and you must know how far. And then he added that Odysseus should be likened unto Theodore Roosevelt. I don't think that is so good. Someone visiting Gibbon at the point of death, said he was the same Gibbon as of old; still at his parallels.

Take the way we have been led into our present position morally, the world over. It is by a sort of metaphorical gradient. There is a kind of thinking—to speak metaphorically—there is a kind of thinking you might say was endemic in the brothel. It is always there. And every now and then in some mysterious way it becomes epidemic in the world. And how does it do so? By using all the good words that virtue has invented to maintain virtue. It uses honesty, first—frankness, sincerity—those words; picks them up, uses them. "In the name of honesty, let us see what we are." You know. And then it picks up the word joy. "Let us in the name of joy, which is the enemy of our ancestors, the Puritans . . . Let us in the name of joy, which is the enemy of the kill-joy Puritan . . . " You see. "Let us," and so on. And then, "In the name of health . . . " Health is another good word. And that is the metaphor Freudianism trades on, mental health. And the first thing we know, it has us all in up to the top knot. I suppose we may blame the artists a good deal, because they are great people to spread by metaphor. The stage too—the stage is always a good intermediary between the two worlds, the under and the upper, if I may say so without personal prejudice to the stage.

In all this, I have only been saying that the devil can quote Scripture, which simply means that the good words you have lying around the devil can use for his purposes as well as anybody else. Never mind about my morality. I am not here to urge anything. I don't care whether the world is good or bad—not on any particular day.

Let me ask you to watch a metaphor breaking down here before you.

Somebody said to me a little while ago, "It is easy enough for me to think of the universe as a machine, as a mechanism."

I said, "You mean the universe is like a machine?"

He said, "No. I think it is one . . .Well, it is like . . ."

"I think you mean the universe is like a machine."

"All right. Let it go at that."

I asked him, "Did you ever see a machine without a pedal for the foot, or a lever for the hand, or a button for the finger?"

He said "No—no."

I said, "All right. Is the universe like that?"

And he said, "No. I mean it is like a machine, only . . ."

". . . it is different from a machine," I said.

He wanted to go just that far with that metaphor and no further. And so do we all. All metaphor breaks down somewhere. That is the beauty of it. It is touch and go with the metaphor, and until you have lived with it long enough you don't know when it is going. You don't know how much you can get out of it and when it will cease to yield. It is a very living thing. It is as life itself.

I have heard this ever since I can remember, and ever since I have taught: the teacher must teach the pupil to think. I saw a teacher once going around in a great school and snapping pupils' heads with thumb and finger and saying, "Think." That was when thinking was becoming the fashion. The fashion hasn't yet quite gone out.

We still ask boys in college to think, as in the nineties, but we seldom tell them what thinking means; we seldom tell them it is just putting this and that together; it is saying one thing in terms of another. To tell them is to set their feet on the first rung of a ladder the top of which sticks through the sky.

Greatest of all attempts to say one thing in terms of another is the philosophical attempt to say matter in terms of spirit, or spirit in terms of matter, to make the final unity. That is the greatest attempt that ever failed. We stop just short there. But it is the height of poetry, the height of all thinking, the height of all poetic thinking, that attempt to say matter in terms of spirit and spirit in terms of matter. It is wrong to call anybody a materialist simply because he tries to say spirit in terms of matter, as if that were a sin. Materialism is not the attempt to say all in terms of matter. The only materialist —be he poet, teacher, scientist, politician, or statesman—is the man who gets lost in his material without a gathering metaphor to throw it into shape and order. He is the lost soul.

We ask people to think, and we don't show them what thinking is. Somebody says we don't need to show them how to think; bye and bye they will think. We will give them the forms of sentences and, if they have any ideas, then they will know how to write them. But that is preposterous. All there is to writing is having ideas. To learn to write is to learn to have ideas.

The first little metaphor . . . Take some of the trivial ones. I would rather have trivial ones of my own to live by than the big ones of other people.

I remember a boy saying, "He is the kind of person that wounds with his shield." That may be a slender one, of course. It goes a good way in character description. It has poetic grace. "He is the kind that wounds with his shield."

The shield reminds me—just to linger a minute—the shield reminds me of the inverted shield spoken of in one of the books of the *Odyssey*, the book that tells about the longest swim on record. I forget how long it lasted—several days, was it?—but at last as Odysseus came near the coast of Phoenicia, he saw it on the horizon "like an inverted shield."

There is a better metaphor in the same book. In the end Odysseus comes ashore and crawls up the beach to spend the night under a double olive tree, and it says, as in a lonely farmhouse where it is hard to get fire—I am not quoting exactly—where it is hard to start the fire again if it goes out, they cover the seeds of fire with ashes to preserve it for the night, so Odysseus covered himself with the leaves around him and went to sleep. There you have something that gives you character, something of Odysseus himself. "Seeds of fire." So Odysseus covered the seeds of fire in himself. You get the greatness of his nature.

But these are slighter metaphors than the ones we live by. They have their charm, their passing charm. They are as it were the first steps toward the great thoughts, grave thoughts, thoughts lasting to the end.

The metaphor whose manage we are best taught in poetry—that is all there is of thinking. It may not seem far for the mind to go but it is the mind's furthest. The richest accumulation of the ages is the noble metaphors we have rolled up.

I want to add one thing more that the experience of poetry is to anyone who comes close to poetry. There are two ways of coming close to poetry. One is by writing poetry. And some people think I want people to write poetry, but I don't; that is, I don't necessarily. I only want people to write poetry if they want to write poetry. I have never encouraged anybody to write poetry that did not want to write it, and I have not always encouraged those who did want to write it. That ought to be one's own funeral. It is a hard, hard life, as they say.

(I have just been to a city in the West, a city full of poets, a city they have made safe for poets. The whole city is so lovely that you do not have to write it up to make it poetry; it is ready-made for you. But, I don't know—the poetry written in that city might not seem like poetry if read outside of the city. It would be like the jokes made when you were drunk; you have to get drunk again to appreciate them.)

But as I say, there is another way to come close to poetry, fortunately, and that is in the reading of it, not as linguistics, not as history, not as anything but poetry. It is one of the hard things for a teacher to know how close a man has come in reading poetry. How do I know whether a man has come close to Keats in reading Keats? It is hard for me to know. I have lived with some boys a whole year over some of the poets and I have not felt sure whether they have come near what it was all about. One remark sometimes told me. One remark was their mark for the year; had to be—it was all I got that told me what I wanted to know. And that is enough, if it was the right remark, if it came close enough. I think a man might make twenty fool remarks if he made one good one some time in the year. His mark would depend on that good remark.

The closeness—everything depends on the closeness with which you come, and you ought to be marked for the closeness, for nothing else. And that will have to be estimated by chance remarks, not by question and answer. It is only by accident that you know some day how near a person has come.

The person who gets close enough to poetry, he is going to know more about the word *belief* than anybody else knows, even in religion nowadays. There are two or three places where we know belief outside of religion. One of them is at the age of fifteen to twenty, in our self-belief. A young man knows more about himself than he is able to prove to anybody. He has no knowledge that anybody else will accept as knowledge. In his foreknowledge he has something that is going to believe itself into fulfilment, into acceptance.

There is another belief like that, the belief in someone else, a relationship of two that is going to be believed into fulfilment. That is what we are talking about in our novels, the belief of love. And disillusionment that the novels are full of is simply the disillusionment from disappointment in that belief. That belief can fail, of course.

Then there is a literary belief. Every time a poem is written, every

198 · *Robert Frost*

time a short story is written, it is written not by cunning, but by belief. The beauty, the something, the little charm of the thing to be, is more felt than known. There is a common jest, one that always annoys me, on the writers, that they write the last end first, and then work up to it; that they lay a train toward one sentence that they think is pretty nice and have all fixed up to set like a trap to close with. No, it should not be that way at all. No one who has ever come close to the arts has failed to see the difference between things written that way, with cunning and device, and the kind that are believed into existence, that begin in something more felt than known. This you can realize quite as well—not quite as well, perhaps, but nearly as well—in reading as you can in writing. I would undertake to separate short stories on that principle; stories that have been believed into existence and stories that have been cunningly devised. And I could separate the poems still more easily.

Now I think—I happen to think—that those three beliefs that I speak of, the self-belief, the love-belief, and the art-belief, are all closely related to the God-belief, that the belief in God is a relationship you enter into with Him to bring about the future.

There is a national belief like that, too. One feels it. I have been where I came near getting up and walking out on the people who thought that they had to talk against nations, against nationalism, in order to curry favor with internationalism. Their metaphors are all mixed up. They think that because a Frenchman and an American and an Englishman can all sit down on the same platform and receive honors together, it must be that there is no such thing as nations. That kind of bad thinking springs from a source we all know. I should want to say to anyone like that: "Look! First I want to be a person. And I want you to be a person, and then we can be as interpersonal as you please. We can pull each other's noses—do all sorts of things. But, first of all, you have got to have the personality. First of all, you have got to have the nations and then they can be as international as they please with each other."

I should like to use another metaphor on them. I want my palette, if I am a painter, I want my palette on my thumb or on my chair, all clean, pure, separate colors. Then I will do the mixing on the canvas. The canvas is where the work of art is, where we make the conquest. But we want the nations all separate, pure, distinct, things as separate as we can make them; and then in our thoughts, in our arts, and so on, we can do what we please about it.

But I go back. There are four beliefs that I know more about from having lived with poetry. One is the personal belief, which is a knowledge that you don't want to tell other people about because you cannot prove that you know. You are saying nothing about it till you see. The love belief, just the same, has that same shyness. It knows it cannot tell; only the outcome can tell. And the national belief we enter into socially with each other, all together, party of the first part, party of the second part, we enter into that to bring the future of the country. We cannot tell some people what it is we believe, partly, because they are too stupid to understand and partly because we are too proudly vague to explain. And anyway it has got to be fulfilled, and we are not talking until we know more, until we have something to show. And then the literary one in every work of art, not of cunning and craft, mind you, but of real art; that believing the thing into existence, saying as you go more than you even hoped you were going to be able to say, and coming with surprise to an end that you foreknew only with some sort of emotion. And then finally the relationship we enter into with God to believe the future in—to believe the hereafter in.

QUESTIONS

1. In what way does the subtitle describe this essay? Is it rambling? Is it unified?
2. How can the "poetry nuisance" be gotten out of the curriculum? Does Frost think it ought to stay in? Why?
3. What is meant by "enthusiasm passed through an idea" and "enthusiasm tamed to metaphor" (p. 192)? What sort of metaphors does Frost use in those phrases, and what do they imply?
4. What does Frost mean when he says "unless you have had your proper poetical education in the metaphor, you are not safe anywhere" (p. 194)? Indicate some of the metaphors Frost examines in this essay. From what fields are they drawn? What does he say about each? Nominate some further metaphors—from politics, science, sociology, or anything else—and analyze them. To what extent are they useful? Do they have a breaking point? How might they mislead beyond the breaking point?
5. Frost admires a speech that has "range, something of overstatement, something of statement, and something of understatement." Is this spectrum visible in Frost's own speech? Show where and how.

AN ALBUM OF STYLES

I

Revenge is a kind of wild justice; which the more man's nature runs to, the more ought law to weed it out. For as for the first wrong, it doth but offend the law; but the revenge of that wrong putteth the law out of office. Certainly, in taking revenge, a man is but even with his enemy; but in passing it over, he is superior; for it is a prince's part to pardon. And Salomon, I am sure, saith, *It is the glory of a man to pass by an offence.* That which is past is gone, and irrevocable; and wise men have enough to do with things present and to come: therefore they do but trifle with themselves, that labour in past matters. There is no man doth a wrong for the wrong's sake; but thereby to purchase himself profit, or pleasure, or honour, or the like. Therefore why should I be angry with a man for loving himself better than me? And if any man should do wrong merely out of ill nature, why, yet it is but like the thorn or briar, which prick and scratch, because they can do no other. The most tolerable sort of revenge is for those wrongs which there is no law to remedy; but then let a man take heed the revenge be such as there is no law to punish; else a man's enemy is still beforehand, and it is two for one. Some, when they take revenge, are desirous the party should know whence it cometh: this is the more generous. For the delight seemeth to be not so much in doing the hurt as in making the party repent: but base and crafty cowards are like the arrow that flieth in the dark. Cosmus, duke of Florence, had a desperate saying against perfidious or neglecting friends, as if those wrongs were unpardonable: *You shall read* (saith he) *that we are commanded to forgive our enemies; but you never read that we are commanded to forgive our friends.* But yet the spirit of Job was in a better tune: *Shall we* (saith he) *take good at God's hands, and not be content to take evil also?* And so of friends in a proportion. This is certain, that a man that studieth revenge keeps his own wounds green, which otherwise would heal and do well. Public revenges are for the most part fortunate; as that for the death of Caesar; for the death of Pertinax;[1] for the death of Henry the third of France;[2] and many more. But in private revenges it is not so. Nay rather, vindictive persons live the life of witches; who as they are mischievous, so end they infortunate.

—Francis Bacon, *Of Revenge*, 1625.

1. Publius Helvius Pertinax became Emperor of Rome in 193 and was assassinated three months after his accession to the throne by a soldier in his Prae-torian Guard.
2. King of France 1574–1589; assassinated during the Siege of Paris.

II

Of the wall [of China] it is very easy to assign the motives. It secured a wealthy and timorous nation from the incursions of Barbarians, whose unskillfulness in arts made it easier for them to supply their wants by rapine than by industry, and who from time to time poured in upon the habitations of peaceful commerce, as vultures descend upon domestic fowl. Their celerity and fierceness made the wall necessary, and their ignorance made it efficacious.

But for the pyramids no reason has ever been given adequate to the cost and labor of the work. The narrowness of the chambers proves that it could afford no retreat from enemies, and treasures might have been reposited at far less expense with equal security. It seems to have been erected only in compliance with that hunger of imagination which preys incessantly upon life, and must be always appeased by some employment. Those who have already all that they can enjoy, must enlarge their desires. He that has built for use, till use is supplied must begin to build for vanity, and extend his plan to the utmost power of human performance, that he may not be soon reduced to form another wish.

I consider this mighty structure as a monument of the insufficiency of human enjoyments. A king, whose power is unlimited, and whose treasures surmount all real and imaginary wants, is compelled to solace, by the erection of a pyramid, the satiety of dominion and tastelessness of pleasures, and to amuse the tediousness of declining life, by seeing thousands laboring without end, and one stone, for no purpose, laid upon another. Whoever thou art, that, not content with a moderate condition, imaginest happiness in royal magnificence, and dreamest that command or riches can feed the appetite of novelty with perpetual gratifications, survey the pyramids, and confess thy folly!

—Samuel Johnson, from *Rasselas*, 1759.

III

The human species, according to the best theory I can form of it, is composed of two distinct races, *the men who borrow*, and *the men who lend*. To these two original diversities may be reduced all those impertinent classifications of Gothic and Celtic tribes, white men, black men, red men. All the dwellers upon earth, "Parthians, and Medes, and Elamites," flock hither, and do naturally fall in with one or other of these primary distinctions. The infinite superiority of the former, which I choose to designate as the *great race*, is discernible in their figure, port, and a certain instinctive sovereignty. The latter are born degraded. "He shall serve his brethren." There is something in the air of one of this cast, lean and suspicious; contrasting with the open, trusting, generous manners of the other.

Observe who have been the greatest borrowers of all ages—Alcibiades—Falstaff—Sir Richard Steele—our late incomparable Brinsley—what a family likeness in all four!

What a careless, even deportment hath your borrower! what rosy gills! what a beautiful reliance on Providence doth he manifest—taking no more thought than lilies! What contempt for money—accounting it (yours and mine especially) no better than dross. What a liberal confounding of those pedantic distinctions of *meum* and *tuum!* or rather, what a noble simplification of language (beyond Tooke), resolving these supposed opposites into one clear, intelligible pronoun adjective! What near approaches doth he make to the primitive *community*—to the extent of one half of the principle at least!

—Charles Lamb, from "The Two Races of Men," 1820.

IV

Knowledge is one thing, virtue is another; good sense is not conscience, refinement is not humility, nor is largeness and justness of view faith. Philosophy, however enlightened, however profound, gives no command over the passions, no influential motives, no vivifying principles. Liberal Education makes not the Christian, not the Catholic, but the gentleman. It is well to be a gentleman, it is well to have a cultivated intellect, a delicate taste, a candid, equitable, dispassionate mind, a noble and courteous bearing in the conduct of life—these are the connatural qualities of a large knowledge; they are the objects of a University; I am advocating, I shall illustrate and insist upon them; but still, I repeat, they are no guarantee for sanctity or even for conscientiousness, they may attach to the man of the world, to the profligate, to the heartless, pleasant, alas, and attractive as he shows when decked out in them. Taken by themselves, they do but seem to be what they are not; they look like virtue at a distance, but they are detected by close observers, and on the long run; and hence it is that they are popularly accused of pretense and hypocrisy, not, I repeat, from their own fault, but because their professors and their admirers persist in taking them for what they are not, and are officious in arrogating for them a praise to which they have no claim. Quarry the granite rock with razors, or moor the vessel with a thread of silk; then may you hope with such keen and delicate instruments as human knowledge and human reason to contend against those giants, the passion and the pride of man.

—John Henry Newman, from *The Idea of a University*, 1852.

V

It is simple enough to say that since books have classes—fiction, biography, poetry—we should separate them and take from each what it is right that each should give us. Yet few people ask from books what books can give us. Most commonly we come to books with blurred and divided minds, asking of fiction that it shall be true, of poetry that it shall be false, of biography that it shall be flattering, of history that it shall enforce our own prejudices. If we could banish all such preconceptions when we read, that would be an admirable beginning. Do not dictate to your author; try to become him. Be his fellow-worker and accomplice. If you hang back, and reserve and criticise at first, you are preventing yourself from getting the fullest possible value from what you read. But if you open your mind as widely as possible, then signs and hints of almost imperceptible fineness, from the twist and turn of the first sentences, will bring you into the presence of a human being unlike any other. Steep yourself in this, acquaint yourself with this, and soon you will find that your author is giving you, or attempting to give you, something far more definite. The thirty-two chapters of a novel—if we consider how to read a novel first—are an attempt to make something as formed and controlled as a building: but words are more impalpable than bricks; reading is a longer and more complicated process than seeing. Perhaps the quickest way to understand the elements of what a novelist is doing is not to read, but to write; to make your own experiment with the dangers and difficulties of words. Recall, then, some event that has left a distinct impression on you—how at the corner of the street, perhaps, you passed two people talking. A tree shook; an electric light danced; the tone of the talk was comic, but also tragic; a whole vision, an entire conception, seemed contained in that moment.

But when you attempt to reconstruct it in words, you will find that it breaks into a thousand conflicting impressions. Some must be subdued; others emphasised; in the process you will lose, probably, all grasp upon the emotion itself. Then turn from your blurred and littered pages to the opening pages of some great novelist—Defoe, Jane Austen, Hardy. Now you will be better able to appreciate their mastery. It is not merely that we are in the presence of a different person—Defoe, Jane Austen, or Thomas Hardy —but that we are living in a different world. Here, in *Robinson Crusoe*, we are trudging a plain high road; one thing happens after another; the fact and the order of the fact is enough. But if the open air and adventure mean everything to Defoe they mean nothing to Jane Austen. Hers is the drawing-room, and people talking, and by the many mirrors of their talk revealing their characters. And if, when we have accustomed ourselves to the drawing-room and its reflections, we turn to Hardy, we are once more spun around. The moors are round us and the stars are above our heads. The other side of the mind is now exposed—the dark side that comes uppermost in solitude, not the light side that shows in company. Our relations are not towards people, but towards Nature and destiny. Yet different as these worlds are, each is consistent with itself. The maker of each is careful to observe the laws of his own perspective, and however great a strain they may put upon us they will never confuse us, as lesser writers so frequently do, by introducing two different kinds of reality into the same book. Thus to go from one great novelist to another—from Jane Austen to Hardy, from Peacock to Trollope, from Scott to Meredith—is to be wrenched and uprooted; to be thrown this way and then that: To read a novel is a difficult and complex art. You must be capable not only of great finesse of perception, but of great boldness of imagination if you are going to make use of all that the novelist—the great artist—gives you.

> —Virginia Woolf, "How Should One Read a Book?"
> in *The Second Common Reader*, 1932.

VI

Three merry gargoyles. Three merry harridans. Amused by a long-ago time of ignorance. They did not belong to those generations of prostitutes created in novels, with great and generous hearts, dedicated, because of the horror of circumstance, to ameliorating the luckless, barren life of men, taking money incidentally and humbly for their "understanding." Nor were they from that sensitive breed of young girl, gone wrong at the hands of fate, forced to cultivate an outward brittleness in order to protect her springtime from further shock, but knowing full well she was cut out for better things, and could make the right man happy. Neither were they the sloppy, inadequate whores who, unable to make a living at it alone, turn to drug consumption and traffic or pimps to help complete their scheme of self-destruction, avoiding suicide only to punish the memory of some absent father or to sustain the misery of some silent mother. Except for Marie's fabled love for Dewey Prince, these women hated men, all men, without shame, apology, or discrimination. They abused their visitors with a scorn grown mechanical from use. Black men, white men, Puerto Ricans, Mexicans, Jews, Poles, whatever—all were inadequate and weak, all came under their jaundiced eyes and were the recipients of their disinterested wrath. They took delight in cheating them. On one occasion the town well knew, they lured a Jew up the stairs, pounced on him, all three, held him up by the heels, shook everything out of his pants pockets, and threw him out of the window.

Neither did they have respect for women, who, although not their colleagues, so to speak, nevertheless deceived their husbands —regularly or irregularly, it made no difference. "Sugar-coated whores," they called them, and did not yearn to be in their shoes. Their only respect was for what they would have described as "good Christian colored women." The woman whose reputation was spot less, and who tended to her family, who didn't drink or smoke or run around. These women had their undying, if covert, affection. They would sleep with their husbands, and take their money, but always with a vengeance.

Nor were they protective and solicitous of youthful innocence. They looked back on their own youth as a period of ignorance, and regretted that they had not made more of it. They were not young girls in whores' clothing, or whores regretting their loss of innocence. They were whores in whores' clothing, whores who had never been young and had no word for innocence. With Pecola they were as free as they were with each other. Marie concocted stories for her because she was a child, but the stories were breezy and rough. If Pecola had announced her intention to live the life they did, they would not have tried to dissuade her or voiced any alarm.

—Toni Morrison, from *The Bluest Eye*, 1970.

VII

A very large number of people cease when quite young to add anything to a limited stock of judgments. After a certain age, say 25, they consider that their education is finished.

It is perhaps natural that having passed through that painful and boring process, called expressly education, they should suppose it over, and that they are equipped for life to label every event as it occurs and drop it into its given pigeonhole. But one who has a label ready for everything does not bother to observe any more, even such ordinary happenings as he has observed for himself, with attention, before he went to school. He merely acts and reacts.

For people who have stopped noticing, the only possible new or renewed experience, and, therefore, new knowledge, is from a work of art. Because that is the only kind of experience which they are prepared to receive on its own terms, they will come out from their shells and expose themselves to music, to a play, to a book, because it is the accepted method of enjoying such things. True, even to plays and books they may bring artistic prejudices which prevent them from seeing *that* play or comprehending *that* book. Their artistic sensibilities may be as crusted over as their minds.

But it is part of an artist's job to break crusts, or let us say rather that artists who work for the public and not merely for themselves are interested in breaking crusts because they want to communicate their intuitions.

—Joyce Cary, "On the Function of the Novelist," 1949.

VIII

This seems to be an era of gratuitous inventions and negative improvements. Consider the beer can. It was beautiful—as beautiful as the clothespin, as inevitable as the wine bottle, as dignified and reassuring as the fire hydrant. A tranquil cylinder of delightfully resonant metal, it could be opened in an instant, requiring only the application of a handy gadget freely dispensed by every grocer. Who can forget the small, symmetrical thrill of those two triangular punctures, the dainty *pffff*, the little crest of suds that foamed eagerly in the exultation of release? Now we are given, instead, a top beetling with an ugly, shmoo-shaped "tab," which, after fiercely resisting the tugging, bleeding fingers of the thirsty man, threatens his lips with a dangerous and hideous hole. However, we have discovered a way to thwart Progress, usually so unthwartable. *Turn the beer can upside down and open the bottom.* The bottom is still the way the top used to be. True, this operation gives the beer an unsettling jolt, and the sight of a consistently inverted beer can might make people edgy, not to say queasy. But the latter difficulty could be eliminated if manufacturers would design cans that looked the same whichever end was up, like playing cards. What we need is Progress with an escape hatch.

—John Updike, "Beer Can," in *Assorted Prose*, 1965.

IX

The legend of Junior Johnson! In this legend, here is a country boy, Junior Johnson, who learns to drive by running whiskey for his father, Johnson, Senior, one of the biggest copper-still operators of all time, up in Ingle Hollow, near North Wilkesboro, in northwestern North Carolina, and grows up to be a famous stock car racing driver, rich, grossing $100,000 in 1963, for example, respected, solid, idolized in his hometown and throughout the rural South. There is all this about how good old boys would wake up in the middle of the night in the apple shacks and hear a supercharged Oldsmobile engine roaring over Brushy Mountain and say, "Listen at him—there he goes!" although that part is doubtful, since some nights there were so many good old boys taking off down the road in supercharged automobiles out of Wilkes County, and running loads to Charlotte, Salisbury, Greensboro, Winston-Salem, High Point, or wherever, it would be pretty hard to pick out one. It was Junior Johnson, specifically, however, who was famous for the "bootleg turn" or "about-face," in which, if the Alcohol Tax agents had a roadblock up for you or were too close behind, you threw the car up into second gear, cocked the wheel, stepped on the accelerator and made the car's rear end skid around in a complete 180-degree arc, a complete about-face, and tore on back up the road exactly the way you came from. God! The Alcohol Tax agents used to burn over Junior Johnson. Practically every good old boy in town in Wilkesboro, the county seat, got to know the agents by sight in a very short time. They would rag them practically to their faces on the subject of Junior Johnson, so that it got to be an obsession. Finally, one night they had Junior trapped on the road up toward the bridge around Millersville, there's no way out of there, they had the barricades up and they could hear this souped-up car roaring around the bend, and here it comes—but suddenly they can hear a siren and see a red light flashing in the grille, so they think it's another agent, and boy, they run out like ants and pull those barrels and boards and sawhorses out of the way, and then—Ggghhzzzzzzzzhhhhhh-gggggggzzzzzzzeeeeeong!—gawdam! there he goes again, it was him, Junior Johnson! with a gawdam agent's sireen and a red light in his grille!

—Tom Wolfe, from *The Kandy Kolored Tangerine-Flake Streamline Baby*, 1966.

RALPH ELLISON
Living with Music

In those days it was either live with music or die with noise, and we chose rather desperately to live. In the process our apartment—what with its booby-trappings of audio equipment, wires, discs and tapes—came to resemble the Collier mansion,[1] but that was later. First there was the neighborhood, assorted drunks and a singer.

We were living at the time in a tiny ground-floor-rear apartment in which I was also trying to write. I say "trying" advisedly. To our right, separated by a thin wall, was a small restaurant with a juke box the size of the Roxy.[2] To our left, a night-employed swing enthusiast who took his lullaby music so loud that every morning promptly at nine Basie's[3] brasses started blasting my typewriter off

1. The home of two wealthy recluse brothers, packed with newspapers and junk.
2. A New York theater and music hall.
3. William ("Count") Basie, composer and pianist.

its stand. Our living room looked out across a small back yard to a rough stone wall to an apartment building which, towering above, caught every passing thoroughfare sound and rifled it straight down to me. There were also howling cats and barking dogs, none capable of music worth living with, so we'll pass them by.

But the court behind the wall, which on the far side came knee-high to a short Iroquois, was a forum for various singing and/or preaching drunks who wandered back from the corner bar. From these you sometimes heard a fair barbershop style "Bill Bailey," free-wheeling versions of "The Bastard King of England," the saga of Uncle Bud, or a deeply felt rendition of Leroy Carr's "How Long Blues." The preaching drunks took on any topic that came to mind: current events, the fate of the long-sunk *Titanic* or the relative merits of the Giants and the Dodgers. Naturally there was great argument and occasional fighting—none of it fatal but all of it loud.

I shouldn't complain, however, for these were rather entertaining drunks, who like the birds appeared in the spring and left with the first fall cold. A more dedicated fellow was there all the time, day and night, come rain, come shine. Up on the corner lived a drunk of legend, a true phenomenon, who could surely have qualified as the king of all the world's winos—not excluding the French. He was neither poetic like the others nor ambitious like the singer (to whom we'll presently come) but his drinking bouts were truly awe-inspiring and he was not without his sensitivity. In the throes of his passion he would shout to the whole wide world one concise command, "Shut up!" Which was disconcerting enough to all who heard (except, perhaps, the singer), but such were the labyrinthine acoustics of courtyards and areaways that he seemed to direct his command at me. The writer's block which this produced is indescribable. On one heroic occasion he yelled his obsessive command without one interruption longer than necessary to take another drink (and with no appreciable loss of volume, penetration or authority) for three long summer days and nights, and shortly afterwards he died. Just how many lines of agitated prose he cost me I'll never know, but in all that chaos of sound I sympathized with his obsession, for I, too, hungered and thirsted for quiet. Nor did he inspire me to a painful identification, and for that I was thankful. Identification, after all, involves feelings of guilt and responsibility, and since I could hardly hear my own typewriter keys I felt in no way accountable for his condition. We were simply fellow victims of the madding crowd. May he rest in peace.

No, these more involved feelings were aroused by a more intimate source of noise, one that got beneath the skin and worked into the very structure of one's consciousness—like the "fate" motif in Beethoven's Fifth or the knocking-at-the-gates scene in *Macbeth*.

For at the top of our pyramid of noise there was a singer who lived directly above us; you might say we had a singer on our ceiling.

Now, I had learned from the jazz musicians I had known as a boy in Oklahoma City something of the discipline and devotion to his art required of the artist. Hence I knew something of what the singer faced. These jazzmen, many of them now world-famous, lived for and with music intensely. Their driving motivation was neither money nor fame, but the will to achieve the most eloquent expression of idea-emotions through the technical mastery of their instruments (which, incidentally, some of them wore as a priest wears the cross) and the give and take, the subtle rhythmical shaping and blending of idea, tone and imagination demanded of group improvisation. The delicate balance struck between strong individual personality and the group during those early jam sessions was a marvel of social organization. I had learned too that the end of all this discipline and technical mastery was the desire to express an affirmative way of life through its musical tradition and that this tradition insisted that each artist achieve his creativity within its frame. He must learn the best of the past, and add to it his personal vision. Life could be harsh, loud and wrong if it wished, but they lived it fully, and when they expressed their attitude toward the world it was with a fluid style that reduced the chaos of living to form.

The objectives of these jazzmen were not at all those of the singer on our ceiling, but though a purist committed to the mastery of the *bel canto* style, German *lieder*, modern French art songs and a few American slave songs sung as if *bel canto*, she was intensely devoted to her art. From morning to night she vocalized, regardless of the condition of her voice, the weather or my screaming nerves. There were times when her notes, sifting through her floor and my ceiling, bouncing down the walls and ricocheting off the building in the rear, whistled like tenpenny nails, buzzed like a saw, wheezed like the asthma of a Hercules, trumpeted like an enraged African elephant—and the squeaky pedal of her piano rested plumb center above my typing chair. After a year of non-co-operation from the neighbor on my left I became desperate enough to cool down the hot blast of his phonograph by calling the cops, but the singer presented a serious ethical problem: Could I, an aspiring artist, complain against the hard work and devotion to craft of another aspiring artist?

Then there was my sense of guilt. Each time I prepared to shatter the ceiling in protest I was restrained by the knowledge that I, too, during my boyhood, had tried to master a musical instrument and to the great distress of my neighbors—perhaps even greater than that which I now suffered. For while our singer was concerned basically with a single tradition and style, I had been caught actively between two: that of the Negro folk music, both sacred and profane, slave song and jazz, and that of Western classical music. It was most confusing; the folk tradition demanded that I play what I heard and felt around me, while those who were seeking to teach the classical tradition in the schools insisted that I play strictly according to the book and express that which I was *supposed* to feel. This sometimes led to heated clashes of wills. Once during a third-grade music appreciation class a friend of mine insisted that it was a large green snake he saw swimming down a quiet brook instead of the snowy bird the teacher felt that Saint-Saëns' *Carnival of the Animals* should evoke. The rest of us sat there and lied like little black, brown and yellow Trojans about that swan, but our stalwart classmate held firm to his snake. In the end he got himself spanked and reduced the teacher to tears, but truth, reality and our environment were redeemed. For we were all familiar with snakes, while a swan was simply something the Ugly Duckling of the story grew up to be. Fortunately some of us grew up with a genuine appreciation of classical music *despite* such teaching methods. But as an aspiring trumpeter I was to wallow in sin for years before being awakened to guilt by our singer.

Caught mid-range between my two traditions, where one attitude often clashed with the other and one technique of playing was by the other opposed, I caused whole blocks of people to suffer.

Indeed, I terrorized a good part of an entire city section. During summer vacation I blew sustained tones out of the window for hours, usually starting—especially on Sunday mornings—before breakfast. I sputtered whole days through M. Arban's (he's the great authority on the instrument) double- and triple-tonguing exercises—with an effect like that of a jackass hiccupping off a big meal of briars. During school-term mornings I practiced a truly exhibitionist "Reveille" before leaving for school, and in the evening I generously gave the ever-listening world a long, slow version of "Taps," ineptly played but throbbing with what I in my adolescent vagueness felt was a romantic sadness. For it was farewell to day and a love song to life and a peace-be-with-you to all the dead and dying.

On hot summer afternoons I tormented the ears of all not blessedly deaf with imitations of the latest hot solos of Hot Lips Paige (then a local hero), the leaping right hand of Earl "Fatha" Hines, or the rowdy poetic flights of Louis Armstrong. Naturally I rehearsed also such school-band standbys as the *Light Cavalry* Overture, Sousa's "Stars and Stripes Forever," the *William Tell* Overture, and "Tiger Rag." (Not even an after-school job as office boy to a dentist could stop my efforts. Frequently, by way of encouraging my development in the proper cultural direction, the dentist

asked me proudly to render Schubert's *Serenade* for some poor devil
with his jaw propped open in the dental chair. When the drill got
going, or the forceps bit deep, I blew real strong.)

Sometimes, inspired by the even then considerable virtuosity of
the late Charlie Christian (who during our school days played marvelous riffs on a cigar box banjo), I'd give whole summer afternoons
and the evening hours after heavy suppers of black-eyed peas and
turnip greens, cracklin' bread and buttermilk, lemonade and sweet
potato cobbler, to practicing hard-driving blues. Such food oversup-
plied me with bursting energy, and from listening to Ma Raincy,
Ida Cox and Clara Smith, who made regular appearances in our
town, I knew exactly how I wanted my horn to sound. But in the
effort to make it do so (I was no embryo Joe Smith or Tricky Sam
Nanton) I sustained the curses of both Christian and infidel—a-
long with the encouragement of those more sympathetic citizens
who understood the profound satisfaction to be found in expressing
oneself in the blues.

Despite those who complained and cried to heaven for Gabriel to
blow a chorus so heavenly sweet and so hellishly hot that I'd forever
put down my horn, there were more tolerant ones who were willing
to pay in present pain for future pride.

For who knew what skinny kid with his chops wrapped around a
trumpet mouthpiece and a faraway look in his eyes might become
the next Armstrong? Yes, and send you, at some big dance a few
years hence, into an ecstasy of rhythm and memory and brassy
affirmation of the goodness of being alive and part of the community? Someone had to: for it was part of the group tradition—
though that was not how they said it.

"Let that boy blow," they'd say to the protesting ones. "He's got
to talk baby talk on that thing before he can preach on it. Next
thing you know he's liable to be up there with Duke Ellington.
Sure, plenty Oklahoma boys are up there with big bands. Son, let's
hear you try those 'Trouble in Mind Blues.' Now try and make it
sound like ole Ida Cox sings it."

And I'd draw in my breath and do Miss Cox great violence.

Thus the crimes and aspirations of my youth. It had been years
since I had played the trumpet or irritated a single ear with other
than the spoken or written word, but as far as my singing neighbor
was concerned I had to hold my peace. I was forced to listen, and
in listening I soon became involved to the point of identification. If
she sang badly I'd hear my own futility in the windy sound; if well,
I'd stare at my typewriter and despair that I should ever make my
prose so sing. She left me neither night nor day, this singer on our
ceiling, and as my writing languished I became more and more
upset. Thus one desperate morning I decided that since I seemed

doomed to live within a shrieking chaos I might as well contribute my share; perhaps if I fought noise with noise I'd attain some small peace. Then a miracle: I turned on my radio (an old Philco AM set connected to a small Pilot FM tuner) and I heard the words

Art thou troubled?
Music will calm thee ...

I stopped as though struck by the voice of an angel. It was Kathleen Ferrier, that loveliest of singers, giving voice to the aria from Handel's *Rodelinda*. The voice was so completely expressive of words and music that I accepted it without question—what lover of the vocal art could resist her?

Yet it was ironic, for after giving up my trumpet for the typewriter I had avoided too close a contact with the very art which she recommended as balm. For I had started music early and lived with it daily, and when I broke I tried to break clean. Now in this magical moment all the old love, the old fascination with music superbly rendered, flooded back. When she finished I realized that with such music in my own apartment, the chaotic sounds from without and above had sunk, if not into silence, then well below the level where they mattered. Here was a way out. If I was to live and write in that apartment, it would be only through the grace of music. I had tuned in a Ferrier recital, and when it ended I rushed out for several of her records, certain that now deliverance was mine.

But not yet. Between the hi-fi record and the ear, I learned, there was a new electronic world. In that realization our apartment was well on its way toward becoming an audio booby trap. It was 1949 and I rushed to the the Audio Fair. I have, I confess, as much gadget-resistance as the next American of my age, weight and slight income; but little did I dream of the test to which it would be put. I had hardly entered the fair before I heard David Sarser's and Mel Sprinkle's Musician's Amplifier, took a look at its schematic and, recalling a boyhood acquaintance with such matters, decided that I could build one. I did, several times before it measured within specifications. And still our system was lacking. Fortunately my wife shared my passion for music, so we went on to buy, piece by piece, a fine speaker system, a first-rate AM-FM tuner, a transcription turntable and a speaker cabinet. I built half a dozen or more preamplifiers and record compensators before finding a commercial one that satisfied my ear, and, finally, we acquired an arm, a magnetic cartridge and—glory of the house—a tape recorder. All this plunge into electronics, mind you, had as its simple end the enjoyment of recorded music as it was intended to be heard. I was obsessed with the idea of reproducing sound with such fidelity that even when using music as a defense behind which I could write, it would reach the unconscious levels of the mind with the least distortion.

And it didn't come easily. There were wires and pieces of equipment all over the tiny apartment (I became a compulsive experimenter) and it was worth your life to move about without first taking careful bearings. Once we were almost crushed in our sleep by the tape machine, for which there was space only on a shelf at the head of our bed. But it was worth it.

For now when we played a recording on our system even the drunks on the wall could recognize its quality. I'm ashamed to admit, however, that I did not always restrict its use to the demands of pleasure or defense. Indeed, with such marvels of science at my control I lost my humility. My ethical consideration for the singer up above shriveled like a plant in too much sunlight. For instead of soothing, music seemed to release the beast in me. Now when jarred from my writer's reveries by some especially enthusiastic flourish of our singer, I'd rush to my music system with blood in my eyes and burst a few decibels in her direction. If she defied me with a few more pounds of pressure against her diaphragm, then a war of decibels was declared.

If, let us say, she were singing *"Depuis le Jour"* from *Louise*, I'd put on a tape of Bidu Sayão performing the same aria, and let the rafters ring. If it was some song by Mahler, I'd match her spitefully with Marian Anderson or Kathleen Ferrier; if she offended with something from *Der Rosenkavalier*, I'd attack her flank with Lotte Lehmann. If she brought me up from my desk with art songs by Ravel or Rachmaninoff, I'd defend myself with Maggie Teyte or Jennie Tourel. If she polished a spiritual to a meaningless artiness I'd play Bessie Smith to remind her of the earth out of which we came. Once in a while I'd forget completely that I was supposed to be a gentleman and blast her with Strauss' *Zarathustra*, Bartók's *Concerto for Orchestra*, Ellington's "Flaming Sword," the famous crescendo from *The Pines of Rome*, or Satchmo scatting, "I'll be Glad When You're Dead" (you rascal you!). Oh, I was living with music with a sweet vengeance.

One might think that all this would have made me her most hated enemy, but not at all. When I met her on the stoop a few weeks after my rebellion, expecting her fully to slap my face, she astonished me by complimenting our music system. She even questioned me concerning the artist I had used against her. After that, on days when the acoustics were right, she'd stop singing until the piece was finished and then applaud—not always, I guessed, without a justifiable touch of sarcasm. And although I was now getting on with my writing, the unfairness of this business bore in upon me. Aware that I could not have withstood a similar comparison with literary artists of like caliber, I grew remorseful. I also came to admire the singer's courage and control, for she was neither intimidated into silence nor goaded into undisciplined screaming; she persevered, she marked the phrasing of the great singers I sent her way, she improved her style.

Better still, she vocalized more softly, and I, in turn, used music less and less as a weapon and more for its magic with mood and memory. After a while a simple twirl of the volume control up a few decibels and down again would bring a live-and-let-live reduction of her volume. We have long since moved from that apartment and that most interesting neighborhood and now the floors and walls of our present apartment are adequately thick and there is even a closet large enough to house the audio system; the only wire visible is that leading from the closet to the corner speaker system. Still we are indebted to the singer and the old environment for forcing us to discover one of the most deeply satisfying aspects of our living. Perhaps the enjoyment of music is always suffused with past experience; for me, at least, this is true.

It seems a long way and a long time from the glorious days of Oklahoma jazz dances, the jam sessions at Halley Richardson's place on Deep Second, from the phonographs shouting the blues in the back alleys I knew as a delivery boy, and from the days when watermelon men with voices like mellow bugles shouted their wares in time with the rhythm of their horses' hoofs and farther still from the washerwomen singing slave songs as they stirred sooty tubs in sunny yards; and a long time, too, from those intense, conflicting days when the school music program of Oklahoma City was tuning our earthy young ears to classical accents—with music appreciation classes and free musical instruments and basic instruction for any child who cared to learn and uniforms for all who made the band. There was a mistaken notion on the part of some of the teachers that classical music had nothing to do with the rhythms, relaxed or hectic, of daily living, and that one should crook the little finger when listening to such refined strains. And the blues and the spirituals—jazz—? they would have destroyed them and scattered the pieces. Nevertheless, we learned some of it, for in the United States when traditions are juxtaposed they tend, regardless of what we do to prevent it, irresistibly to merge. Thus musically at least each child in our town was an heir of all the ages. One learns by moving from the familiar to the unfamiliar, and while it might sound incongruous at first, the step from the spirituality of the spirituals to that of the Beethoven of the symphonies or the Bach of the chorales is not as vast as it seems. Nor is the romanticism of a Brahms or Chopin completely unrelated to that of Louis Armstrong. Those who know their native culture and love it unchauvinistically are never lost when encountering the unfamiliar.

Living with music today we find Mozart and Ellington, Kirsten Flagstad and Chippie Hill, William L. Dawson and Carl Orff all forming part of our regular fare. For all exalt life in rhythm and melody; all add to its significance. Perhaps in the swift change of American society in which the meanings of one's origin are so quickly lost, one of the chief values of living with music lies in its power to give us an orientation in time. In doing so, it gives significance to all those indefinable aspects of experience which nevertheless help to make us what we are. In the swift whirl of time music is a constant, reminding us of what we were and of that toward which we aspired. Art thou troubled? Music will not only calm, it will ennoble thee.

KENNETH CLARK
The Blot and the Diagram

I have been told to "look down from a high place over the whole extensive landscape of modern art." We all know how tempting high places can be, and how dangerous. I usually avoid them myself. But if I must do as I am told, I shall try to find out why modern art has taken its peculiar form, and to guess how long that form will continue.

I shall begin with Leonardo da Vinci, because although all processes are gradual, he does represent one clearly marked turning point in the history of art. Before that time, the painters intentions were quite simple; they were first of all to tell a story, secondly to make the invisible visible, and thirdly to turn a plain surface into a decorated surface. Those are all very ancient aims, going back to the earliest civilizations, or beyond; and for three hundred years painters had been instructed how to carry them out by means of a workshop tradition. Of course, there had been breaks in that tradition—in the fourth century, maybe, and towards the end of the seventh century; but broadly speaking, the artist learnt what he could about the technique of art from his master in his workshop, and then set up shop on his own and tried to do better.

As is well known, Leonardo had a different view of art. He thought that it involved both science and the pursuit of some peculiar attribute called beauty or grace. He was, by inclination, a scientist: he wanted to find out how things worked, and he believed that this knowledge could be stated mathematically. He said "Let no one who is not a mathematician read my works," and he tried to relate this belief in measurement to his belief in beauty. This involved him in two rather different lines of thought, one concerned with magic—the magic of numbers—the other with science. Ever since Pythagoras had discovered that the musical scale could be stated mathematically, by means of the length of the strings, etc., and so had thrown a bridge between intellectual analysis and sensory perception, thinkers on art had felt that it should be possible to do the same for painting. I must say that their effort had not been very rewarding; the modulus, or golden section, and the logarithmic spiral of shells are practically the only undisputed results. But Leonardo lived at a time when it was still possible to hope great things from perspective, which should not only define space, but order it harmoniously; and he also inherited a belief that ideal mathematical combinations could be derived from the proportions of the human body. This line of thought may be called the *mystique* of measurement. The other line may be called *the use* of measurement. Leonardo wished to state mathematically various facts related to the act of seeing. How do we see light passing over a sphere? What happens when objects make themselves perceptible on our retina? Both these lines of thought involved him in drawing diagrams and taking measurements, and for this reason were closely related in his mind. No painter except perhaps Piero della Francesca has tried more strenuously to find a mathematical statement of art, nor has had a greater equipment for doing so.

But Leonardo was also a man of powerful and disturbing imagination. In his notebooks, side by side with his attempts to achieve *order* by mathematics, are drawings and descriptions of the most violent scenes of *disorder* which the human mind can conceive—battles, deluges, eruptions. And he included in his treatise on painting advice on how to develop this side of the artistic faculty also. The passages in which he does so have often been quoted, but they are so incredibly foreign to the whole Renaissance idea of art, although related to a remark in Pliny,[1] that each time I read them, they give me a fresh surprise. I will, therefore, quote them again.

I shall not refrain from including among these precepts a new and speculative idea, which although it may seem trivial and almost laughable, is none the less of great value in quickening the spirit of invention. It is this: that you should look at certain walls stained with damp or at stones of uneven color. If you have to invent some setting you will be able to see in these the likeness of divine landscapes, adorned with mountains, ruins, rocks, woods, great plains, hills and valleys in great variety; and then again you will see there battles and strange figures in violent action, expressions of faces and clothes and an infinity of things which you will be able to reduce to their complete and proper forms. In such walls the same thing happens as in the sound of bells, in whose strokes you may find every named word which you can imagine.

Later he repeats this suggestion in slightly different form, advising the painter to study not only marks on walls, but also "the embers of the fire, or clouds or mud, or other similar objects from which you will find most admirable ideas . . . because from a confusion of shapes the spirit is quickened to new inventions."

I hardly need to insist on how relevant these passages are to modern painting. Almost every morning I receive cards inviting me

1. Roman naturalist, first century A.D.

to current exhibitions, and on the cards are photographs of the works exhibited. Some of them consist of blots, some of scrawls, some look like clouds, some like embers of the fire, some are like mud—some of them are mud; a great many look like stains on walls, and one of them, I remember, consisted of actual stains on walls, photographed and framed. Leonardo's famous passage has been illustrated in every particular. And yet I doubt if he would have been satisfied with the results, because he believed that we must somehow unite the two opposite poles of our faculties. Art itself was the connection between the diagram and the blot.

Now in order to prevent the impression that I am taking advantage of a metaphor, as writers on art are often bound to do, I should explain how I am going to use these words. By "diagram" I mean a rational statement in a visible form, involving measurements, and usually done with an ulterior motive. The theorem of Pythagoras is proved by a diagram. Leonardo's drawings of light striking a sphere are diagrams; but the works of Mondrian, although made up of straight lines, are not diagrams, because they are not done in order to prove or measure some experience, but to please the eye. That they look like diagrams is due to influences which I will examine later. But diagrams can exist with no motive other than their own perfection, just as mathematical propositions can.

By "blots" I mean marks or areas which are not intended to convey information, but which, for some reason, seem pleasant and memorable to the maker, and can be accepted in the same sense by the spectator. I said that these blots were not intended to convey information, but of course they do, and that of two kinds. First, they tell us through association, about things we had forgotten; that was the function of Leonardo's stains on walls, which as he said, quickened the spirit of invention, and it can be the function of man-made blots as well; and secondly a man-made blot will tell us about the artist. Unless it is made entirely accidentally, as by spilling an inkpot, it will be a commitment. It is quite difficult to make a non-committal blot. Although the two are connected, I think we can distinguish between analogy blots and gesture blots.

Now let me try to apply this to modern art. Modern art is not a subject on which one can hope for a large measure of agreement, but I hope I may be allowed two assumptions. The first is that the kind of painting and architecture which we call, with varying inflections of the voice, "modern," is a true and vital expression of our own day; and the second assumption is that it differs radically from any art which has preceded it. Both these assumptions have been questioned. It has been said that modern art is "a racket" engineered by art dealers, who have exploited the incompetence of artists and the gullibility of patrons, that the whole thing is a kind of vast and very expensive practical joke. Well, fifty years is a long time to keep up a hoax of this kind, and during these years modern art has spread all over the free world and created a complete international style. I don't think that any honest-minded historian, whether he liked it or not, could pretend that modern art was the result of an accident or a conspiracy. The only doubt he could have would be whether it is, so to say, a long-term or a short-term movement. In the history of art there are stylistic changes which appear to develop from purely internal causes, and seem almost accidental in relation to the other circumstances of life and society. Such, for example, was the state of art in Italy (outside Venice) from about 1530 to 1600. When all is said about the religious disturbances of the time, the real cause of the Mannerist style was the domination of Michelangelo, who had both created an irresistible style and exhausted its possibilities. It needed the almost equally powerful pictorial imagination of Caravaggio to produce a counter-infection, which could spread from Rome to Spain and the Netherlands and prepare the way for Rembrandt. I can see nothing in the history of man's spirit to account for this episode. It seems to me to be due to an internal and specifically artistic chain of events which are easily related to one another, and comprehensible within the general framework of European art. On the other hand, there are events in the history of art which go far beyond the interaction of styles and which evidently reflect a change in the whole condition of the human spirit. Such an event took place towards the end of the fifth century, when the Hellenistic-Roman style gradually became what we call Byzantine; and again in the early thirteenth century, when the Gothic cathedrals shot up out of the ground. In each case the historian could produce a series of examples to prove that the change was inevitable. But actually, it was nothing of the sort; it was wholly unpredictable; and was part of a complete spiritual revolution.

Whether we think that modern art represents a transformation of style or a change of spirit depends to some extent on my second assumption, that it differs radically from anything which has preceded it. This too has been questioned; it has been said that Léger is only a logical development of Poussin, or Mondrian of Vermeer.[2] And it is true that the element of design in each has something in common. If we pare a Poussin down to its bare bones, there are combinations of curves and cubes which are the foundations of much classical painting, and Léger had the good sense to make use of them. Similarly, in Vermeer there is a use of rectangles, large areas contrasted with very narrow ones, and a feeling for shallow recessions, which became the preferred theme of Mondrian. But such analogies are trifling compared with the differences. Poussin was a very intelligent man who thought deeply about his art, and if anyone

2. Léger and Mondrian: French and Dutch modern painters, respectively. Poussin, French, and Vermeer, Dutch, were both seventeenth-century painters.

had suggested to him that his pictures were praiseworthy solely on account of their construction, he would have been incredulous and affronted.

So let us agree that the kind of painting and architecture which we find most representative of our times—say, the painting of Jackson Pollock and the architecture of the Lever building—is deeply different from the painting and architecture of the past; and is not a mere whim of fashion, but the result of a great change in our ways of thinking and feeling.

How did this great change take place and what does it mean? To begin with, I think it is related to the development upon which all industrial civilization depends, the differentiation of function. Leonardo was exceptional, almost unique in his integration of functions —the scientific and the imaginative. Yet he foreshadowed more than any other artist their disintegration, by noting and treating in isolation the diagrammatic faculty and the blot-making faculty. The average artist took the unity of these faculties for granted. They were united in Leonardo, and in lesser artists, by *interest or pleasure in the thing seen*. The external object was like a magnetic pole which drew the two faculties together. At some point the external object became a negative rather than a positive charge. Instead of drawing together the two faculties, it completely dissociated them; architecture went off in one direction with the diagram, painting went in the other direction with the blot.

This disintegration was related to a radical change in the philosophy of art. We all know that such changes, however harmless they sound when first enunciated, can have drastic consequences in the world of action. Rulers who wish to maintain the *status quo* are well advised to chop off the heads of all philosophers. What Hilaire Belloc called the "remote and ineffectual don" is more dangerous than the busy columnist with his eye on the day's news. The revolution in our ideas about the nature of painting seems to have been hatched by a don who was considered remote and ineffectual even by Oxford standards—Walter Pater. It was he (inspired, I believe, by Schopenhauer) who first propounded the idea of the aesthetic sensation, intuitively perceived.

In its primary aspect [Pater said] a great picture has no more difficult message for us than an accidental play of sunlight and shadow for a few moments on the wall or floor; in itself, in truth, a space of such fallen light, caught, as in the colors of an Eastern carpet, but refined upon and dealt with more subtly and exquisitely than by nature itself.

It is true that his comparison with an Eastern carpet admits the possibility of "pleasant sensations" being arranged or organized; and Pater confirms this need for organization a few lines later, when he sets down his famous dictum that "all art constantly aspires towards the condition of music." He does not believe in blots uncontrolled by the conscious mind. But he is very far from the information-giving diagram.

This belief that art has its origin in our intuitive rather than our rational faculties, picturesquely asserted by Pater, was worked out historically and philosophically, in the somewhat wearisome volumes of Benedetto Croce, and owing to his authoritative tone, he is usually considered the originator of a new theory of aesthetics. It was, in fact, the reversion to a very old idea. Long before the Romantics had stressed the importance of intuition and self-expression, men had admitted the Dionysiac nature of art. But philosophers had always assumed that the frenzy of inspiration must be controlled by law and by the intellectual power of putting things into harmonious order. And this general philosophic concept of art as a combination of intuition and intellect had been supported by technical necessities. It was necessary to master certain laws and to use the intellect in order to build the Gothic cathedrals, or set up the stained glass windows of Chartres or cast the bronze doors of the Florence Baptistry. When this bracing element of craftsmanship ceased to dominate the artist's outlook, as happened soon after the time of Leonardo, new scientific disciples had to be invented to maintain the intellectual element in art. Such were perspective and anatomy. From a purely artistic point of view, they were unneccessary. The Chinese produced some of the finest landscapes ever painted, without any systematic knowledge of perspective. Greek figure sculpture reached its highest point before the study of anatomy had been systematized. But from the Renaissance onwards, painters felt that these two sciences made their art intellectually respectable. They were two ways of connecting the diagram and the blot.

In the nineteenth century, belief in art as a scientific activity declined, for a quantity of reasons. Science and technology withdrew into specialization. Voltaire's efforts to investigate the nature of heat seem to us ludicrous; Goethe's studies of botany and physics a waste of a great poet's time. In spite of their belief in inspiration, the great Romantics were aware of the impoverishment of the imagination which would take place when science had drifted out of reach, and both Shelley and Coleridge spent much time in chemical experiments. Even Turner, whose letters reveal a singular lack of analytic faculty, annotated Goethe's theories of color, and painted two pictures to demonstrate them. No good. The laws which govern the movement of the human spirit are inexorable. The enveloping assumption, within which the artist has to function, was that science was no longer approachable by any but the specialist. And gradually there grew up the idea that all intellectual activities were hostile to art.

I have mentioned the philosophic development of this view of Croce. Let me give one example of its quiet acceptance by the official mind. The British Council sends all over the world, even to Florence and Rome, exhibitions of children's art—the point of these children's pictures being that they have no instruction of any kind, and do not attempt the troublesome task of painting what they see. Well, why not, after all? The results are quite agreeable—sometimes strangely beautiful; and the therapeutic effect on the children is said to be excellent. It is like one of those small harmless heresies which we are shocked to find were the object of persecution by the Mediaeval Church. When, however, we hear admired modern painters saying that they draw their inspiration from the drawings of children and lunatics, as well as from stains on walls, we recognize that we have accomplices in a revolution.

The lawless and intuitive character of modern art is a familiar theme and certain historians have said that it is symptomatic of a decline in Western civilization. This is journalism—one of those statements that sound well to-day and nonsense to-morrow. It is obvious that the development of physical science in the last hundred years has been one of the most colossal efforts the human intellect has ever made. But I think it is also true that human beings can produce, in a given epoch, only a certain amount of creative energy, and that this is directed to different ends and different times —music in the eighteenth century is the obvious example; and I believe that the dazzling achievements of science during the last seventy years have deflected far more of those skills and endowments which go to the making of a work of art than is usually realized. To begin with, there is the sheer energy. In every molding of a Renaissance palace we are conscious of an immense intellectual energy, and it is the absence of this energy in the nineteenth-century copies of Renaissance buildings which makes them seem so dead. To find a form with the same vitality as a window molding of the Palazzo Farnese I must wait till I get back into an aeroplane, and look at the relation of the engine to the wing. That form is alive, not (as used to be said) because it is functional—many functional shapes are entirely uninteresting—but because it is animated by the breath of modern science.

The deflections from art to science are the more serious because these are not, as used to be supposed, two contrary activities, but in fact draw on many of the same capacities of the human mind. In the last resort each depends on the imagination. Artist and scientist alike are both trying to give concrete form to dimly apprehended ideas. Dr. Bronowski has put it very well: "All science is the search for unity in hidden likenesses, and the starting point is an image, because then the unity is·before our mind's eye." Even if we no longer have to pretend that a group of stars looks like a plough or a bear, our scientists still depend on humanly comprehensible images, and it is striking that the valid symbols of our time, invented to embody some scientific truth, have taken root in the popular imagination. Do those red and blue balls connected by rods really resemble a type of atomic structure? I am too ignorant to say. I accept the symbol just as an early Christian accepted the Fish or the Lamb, and I find it echoed or even (it would seem) anticipated in the work of modern artists like Kandinsky and Miró.

Finally, there is the question of popular interest and approval. We have grown accustomed to the idea that artists can work in solitude and incomprehension; but that was not the way things happened in the Renaissance or the seventeenth century, still less in ancient Greece. The pictures carried through the streets by cheering crowds, the *Te Deum* sung on completion of a public building—all this indicates a state of opinion in which men could undertake great works of art with a confidence quite impossible to-day. The research scientist, on the other hand, not only has millions of pounds worth of plant and equipment for the asking, he has principalities and powers waiting for his conclusions. He goes to work, as Titian once did, confident that he will succeed because the strong tide of popular admiration is flowing with him.

But although science has absorbed so many of the functions of art and deflected (I believe) so many potential artists, it obviously cannot be a *substitute* for art. Its mental process may be similar, but its ends are different. There have been three views about the purpose of art. First that it aims simply at imitation; secondly that it should influence human conduct; and thirdly that it should produce a kind of exalted happiness. The first view, which was developed in ancient Greece, must be reckoned one of the outstanding failures of Greek thought. It is simply contrary to experience, because if the visual arts aimed solely at imitating things they would be of very little importance; whereas the Greeks above all people knew that they were important, and treated them as such. Yet such was the prestige of Greek thought that this theory of art was revived in the Renaissance, in an uncomfortable sort of way, and had a remarkable recrudescence in the nineteenth century. The second view, that art should influence conduct and opinions, is more respectable, and held the field throughout the Middle Ages; indeed the more we learn about the art of the past and motives of those who commissioned it, the more important this particular aim appears to be; it still dominated art theory in the time of Diderot. The third view, that art should produce a kind of exalted happiness, was invented by the Romantics at the beginning of the nineteenth century (well, perhaps *invented* by Plotinus, but given currency by the Romantics), and gradually gained ground until by the end of the century it was believed in by almost all educated people. It has held the field in Western Europe till the present day. Leaving aside the question which of these theories is correct, let me ask which of them is most likely to be a helpful background to art (for that is all that a theory of aesthetics can be) in an age when science has such an overwhelming domination over the human mind. The first aim must be reckoned *by itself* to be pointless, since science has now discovered so many ways of imitating appearances, which are incomparably more accurate and convincing than even the most realistic picture. Painting might defend itself against the daguerreotype, but not against Cinerama.

The popular application of science has also, it seems to me, invalidated the second aim of art, because it is quite obvious that no picture can influence human conduct as effectively as a television advertisement. It is quite true that in totalitarian countries artists are still instructed to influence conduct. But that is either due to technical deficiencies, as in China, where in default of T.V., broadsheets and posters are an important way of communicating with an illiterate population; or, in Russia, to a philosophic time-lag. The fact is that very few countries have had the courage to take Plato's advice and exclude works of art altogether. They have, therefore, had to invent some excuse for keeping them on, and the Russians are still using the pretext that paintings and sculpture can influence people in favor of socialist and national policies, although it must have dawned on them that these results can be obtained far more effectively by the cinema and television.

So it seems to me that of these three possible purposes of art—imitation, persuasion, or exalted pleasure—only the third still holds good in an age of science; and it must be justified very largely by the fact that it is a feeling which is absent from scientific achievements—although mathematicians have told us that it is similar to the feeling aroused by their finest calculations. We might say that in the modern world the art of painting is defensible only in so far as it is complementary to science.

We are propelled in the same direction by another achievement of modern science, the study of psychology. That peeling away of the psyche, which was formerly confined to spiritual instructors, or the great novelists, has become a commonplace of conversation. When a good, solid, external word like Duty is turned into a vague, uneasy, internal word like Guilt, one cannot expect artists to take much interest in good, solid, external objects. The artist has always been involved in the painful process of turning himself inside out, but in the past his inner convictions have been of such a kind that they can, so to say, re-form themselves round an object. But, as we have seen, even in Leonardo's time, there were certain obscure needs and patterns of the spirit, which could discover themselves only through less precise analogies—the analogies provided by stains on walls or the embers of a fire. Now, I think that in this inward-looking age, when we have become so much more aware of the vagaries of the spirit, and so respectful of the working of the unconscious, the artist is more likely to find his point of departure in analogies of this kind. They are more exciting because they, so to say, take us by surprise, like forgotten smells; and they seem to be more profound because the memories they awaken have been deeply buried in our minds. Whether Jung is right in believing that this free, undirected, illogical form of mental activity will allow us to pick up, like a magic radio station, some deep memories of our race which can be of universal interest, I do not know. The satisfaction we derive from certain combinations of shape and color does seem to be inexplicable even by the remotest analogies, and may perhaps involve inherited memories. It is not yet time for the art-historian to venture in to that mysterious jungle. I must, however, observe that our respect for the unconscious mind not only gives us an interest in analogy blots, but in what I called "gesture blots" as well. We recognize how free and forceful such a communication can be, and this aspect of art has become more important in the last ten years. An apologist of modern art has said: "What we want to know is not what the world looks like, but what we mean to each other." So the gesture blot becomes a sort of ideogram, like primitive Chinese writing. Students of Zen assure us it is a means of communication more direct and complete than anything which our analytic system can achieve. Almost 2,000 years before Leonardo looked for images in blots, Lao-tzu had written:

> The Tao is something blurred and indistinct.
> How indistinct! How blurred!
> Yet within are images,
> How blurred! How indistinct!
> Yet within are things.

I said that when the split took place between our faculties of measurement and intuition, *architecture* went off with the diagram. Of course architecture had always been involved with measurement and calculation, but we tend to forget how greatly it was also involved with the imitation of external objects. "The question to be determined," said Ruskin, "is whether architecture is a frame for the sculpture, or the sculpture an ornament of the architecture." And he came down on the first alternative. He thought that a building became architecture only in so far as it was a frame for figurative sculpture. I wonder if there is a single person alive who would agree with him. And yet Ruskin had the most sensitive eye and the keenest analytic faculty that has ever been applied to architecture. Many people disagreed with him in his own day; they thought that sculpture should be subordinate to the total design of the building. But that anything claiming to be architecture could dispense with ornament altogether never entered anyone's head till a relatively short time ago.

A purely diagrammatic architecture is only about thirty years older than a purely blottesque painting; yet it has changed the face of the world and produced in every big city a growing uniformity. Perhaps because it is a little older, perhaps because it seems to have a material justification, we have come to accept it without question. People who are still puzzled or affronted by action painting are proud of the great steel and glass boxes which have arisen so miraculously in the last ten years. And yet these two are manifestations of the same state of mind. The same difficulties of function, the same deflection from the external object, and the same triumph of science. Abstract painting and glass box architecture are related in two different ways. There is the direct relationship of style—the kind of relationship which painting and architecture had with one another in the great consistent ages of art like the 13th and 17th centuries. For modern architecture is not simply functional; at its best it has a style which is almost as definite and as arbitrary as Gothic. And this leads me back to my earlier point: that diagrams can be drawn in order to achieve some imagined perfection, similar to that of certain mathematical propositions. Thirty years after Pater's famous dictum, painters in Russia, Holland, and France began to put into practice the theory that "all art constantly aspires to the condition of music"; and curiously enough this Pythagorean mystique of measurements produced a style—the style which reached its purest expression in the Dutch painter, Mondrian. And through the influence of the Bauhaus, this became the leading style of modern architecture.

The other relationship between contemporary architecture and painting appears to be indirect and even accidental. I am thinking of the visual impact when the whole upper part of a tall glass building mirrors the clouds or the dying embers of a sunset, and so becomes a frame for a marvelous, moving Tachiste[3] picture. I do not think that future historians of art will find this accidental at all, but will see it as the culmination of a long process beginning in the Romantic period, in which, from Wordsworth and De Quincey onwards, poets and philosophers recognized the movement of clouds as the symbol of a newly discovered mental faculty.

Such, then, would be my diagnosis of the present condition of art. I must now, by special request, say what I think will happen to art in the future. I think that the state of affairs which I have called the blot and the diagram will last for a long time. Architecture will continue to be made up of glass boxes and steel grids, without ornament of any kind. Painting will continue to be subjective and arcane, an art of accident rather than rule, of stains on walls rather than of calculation, of inscape rather than of external reality.

3. A method of nonrepresentational contemporary painting which exploits the quality of freely flowing oil paint for its own sake.

This conclusion is rejected by those who believe in a social theory of art. They maintain that a living art must depend on the popular will, and that neither the blot nor the diagram is popular; and, since those who hold a social theory of art are usually Marxists, they point to Soviet Russia as a country where all my conditions obtain—differentiation of function, the domination of science and so forth—and yet what we call modern art has gained no hold. This argument does not impress me. There is of course, nothing at all in the idea that Communist doctrines inevitably produce social realism. Painting in Yugoslavia, in Poland and Hungary is in the same modern idiom as painting in the United States, and shows remarkable vitality. Whereas the official social realism of the U.S.S.R., except for a few illustrators, lacks life or conviction, and shows no evidence of representing the popular will. In fact Russian architecture has already dropped the grandiose official style, and I am told that this is now taking place in painting also. In spite of disapproval amounting to persecution, experimental painters exist and find buyers.

I doubt if the Marxists are even correct in saying that the blot and the diagram are not popular. The power, size, and splendor of, say, the Seagram building in New York makes it as much the object of pride and wonder as great architecture was in the past. And one of the remarkable things about Tachisme is the speed with which it has spread throughout the world, not only in sophisticated centers, but in small local art societies. It has become as much an international style as Gothic in the 14th and Baroque in the 17th centuries. I recently visited the exhibition of a provincial academy in the north of England, a very respectable body then celebrating its hundred and fiftieth anniversary. A few years ago it had been full of Welsh mountain landscapes, and scenes of streets and harbors, carefully delineated. Now practically every picture was in the Tachiste style, and I found that many of them were painted by the same artists, often quite elderly people, who had previously painted the mountains and streets. As works of art, they seemed to me neither better nor worse. But I could not help thinking that they must have been less trouble to do, and I reflected that the painters must have had a happy time releasing the Dionysiac elements in their natures. However, we must not be too cynical about this. I do not believe that the spread of action painting is due solely to the fact that it is easy to do. Cubism, especially synthetic Cubism, also looks easy to do, and never had this immense diffusion. It remained the style of a small élite of professional painters and specialized art lovers; whereas Tachisme has spread to fabrics, to the decoration of public buildings, to the backgrounds of television programs, to advertising of all kinds. Indeed the closest analogy to action painting is the most popular art of all—the art of jazz. The trumpeter who rises

from his seat as one possessed, and squirts out his melody like a
scarlet scrawl against a background of plangent dashes and dots, is
not as a rule performing for a small body of intellectuals.

Nevertheless, I do not think that the style of the blot and the
diagram will last forever. For one thing, I believe that the imitation
of external reality is a fundamental human instinct which is bound
to reassert itself. In his admirable book on sculpture called *Aratra
Pentelici*, Ruskin describes an experience which many of us could
confirm. "Having been always desirous," he says,

> that the education of women should begin in learning how to cook, I got
> leave, one day, for a little girl of eleven years old to exchange, much to her
> satisfaction, her schoolroom for the kitchen. But as ill fortune would have
> it, there was some pastry toward, and she was left unadvisedly in command
> of some delicately rolled paste; whereof she made no pies, but an unlimited
> quantity of cats and mice....
>
> Now [he continues] you may read the works of the gravest critics of
> art from end to end; but you will find, at last, they can give you no other
> true account of the spirit of sculpture than that it is an irresistible human
> instinct for the making of cats and mice, and other imitable living crea-
> tures, in such permanent form that one may play with the images at leisure.

I cannot help feeling that he was right. I am fond of works of art,
and I collect them. But I do not want to hang them on the wall
simply in order to get an electric shock every time that I pass them.
I want to hold them, and turn them round and re-hang them—in
short, to play with the images at leisure. And, putting aside what
may be no more than a personal prejudice, I rather doubt if an art
which depends solely on the first impact on our emotions is
permanently valid. When the shock is exhausted, we have nothing
to occupy our minds. And this is particularly troublesome with an
art which depends so much on the unconscious, because, as we
know from the analysis of dreams, the furniture of our unconscious
minds is even more limited, repetitive, and commonplace than that
of our conscious minds. The blots and stains of modern painting
depend ultimately on the memories of things seen, memories sunk
deep in the unconscious, overlaid, transformed, assimilated to a
physical condition, but memories none the less. *Ex nihilo nihil fit.*
It is not possible for a painter to lose contact with the visible world.

At this point the apes have provided valuable evidence. There is
no doubt that they are Tachiste painters of considerable accomplishment. I do not myself care for the work of Congo the chimp, but
Sophie, the Rotterdam gorilla, is a charming artist, whose delicate
traceries remind me of early Paul Klee. As you know, apes take
their painting seriously. The patterns they produce are not the
result of mere accident, but of intense, if short-lived, concentration,
and a lively sense of balance and space-filling. If you compare the
painting of a young ape with that of a human child of relatively the
same age, you will find that in the first, expressive, pattern-making

stage, the ape is superior. Then, automatically and inexorably the child begins to draw *things*—man, house, truck, etc. This the ape never does. Of course his Tachiste paintings are far more attractive than the child's crude conceptual outlines. But they cannot develop. They are monotonous and ultimately rather depressing.

The difference between the child and the ape does not show itself in aesthetic perception, or in physical perception of any kind, but in the child's power to form a concept. Later, as we know, he will spend his time trying to adapt his concept to the evidence of physical sensation; in that struggle lies the whole of style. But the concept —the need to draw a line round his thought—comes first. Now it is a truism that the power to form concepts is what distinguishes man from the animals; although the prophets of modern society, Freud, Jung, D. H. Lawrence, have rightly insisted on the importance of animal perceptions in balanced human personality, the concept-forming faculty has not declined in modern man. On the contrary, it is the basis of that vast scientific achievement which, as I said earlier, seems almost to have put art out of business.

Now, if the desire to represent external reality depended solely on an interest in visual sensation, I would agree that it might disappear from art and never return. But if, as the evidence of children and monkeys indicates, it depends primarily on the formation of concepts, which are then modified by visual sensation, I think it is bound to return. For I consider the human faculty of forming concepts at least as "inalienable" as "life, liberty, and the pursuit of happiness. . . ."

I am not, of course, suggesting that the imitation of external reality will ever again become what it was in European art from the mid-17th to the late 19th centuries. Such a subordination of the concept to the visual sensation was altogether exceptional in the history of art. Much of the territory won by modern painting will, I believe, be held. For example, freedom of association, the immediate passage from one association to another—which is so much a part of Picasso's painting and Henry Moore's sculpture, is something which has existed in music since Wagner and in poetry since Rimbaud and Mallarmé. (I mean existed consciously; of course it underlies all great poetry and music.) It need not be sacrificed in a return to external reality. Nor need the direct communication of intuition, through touch and an instinctive sense of materials. This I consider pure gain. In the words of my original metaphor, both the association blot and the gesture blot can remain. But they must be given more nourishment: they must be related to a fuller knowledge of the forms and structures which impress us most powerfully, and so become part of our concept of natural order. At the end of the passage in which Leonardo tells the painter that he can look for battles, landscapes, and animals in the stains on walls, he adds this caution, "But first be sure that you know all the members of all things you wish to depict, both the members of the animals and the members of landscapes, that is to say of rocks, plants, and so forth." It is because one feels in Henry Moore's sculpture this knowledge of the members of animals and plants, that his work, even at its most abstract, makes an impression on us different from that of his imitators. His figures are not merely pleasing examples of design, but seem to be a part of nature, "rolled round in Earth's diurnal course with rocks and stones and trees."

Those lines of Wordsworth lead me to the last reason why I feel that the intuitive blot and scribble may not dominate painting forever. Our belief in the whole purpose of art may change. I said earlier that we now believe it should aim at producing a kind of exalted happiness: this really means that art becomes an end in itself. Now it is an incontrovertible fact of history that the greatest art has always been *about* something, a means of communicating some truth which is assumed to be more important than the art itself. The truths which art has been able to communicate have been of a kind which could not be put in any other way. They have been ultimate truths, stated symbolically. Science has achieved its triumph precisely by disregarding such truths, by not asking unanswerable questions, but sticking to the question "how." I confess it looks to me as if we shall have to wait a long time before there is some new belief which requires expression through art rather than through statistics or equations. And until this happens, the visual arts will fall short of the greatest epochs, the ages of the Parthenon, the Sistine Ceiling, and Chartres Cathedral.

I am afraid there is nothing we can do about it. No amount of goodwill and no expenditure of money can affect that sort of change. We cannot even dimly foresee when it will happen or what form it will take. We can only be thankful for what we have got—a vigorous, popular, decorative art, complementary to our architecture and our science, somewhat monotonous, somewhat prone to charlatanism, but genuinely expressive of our time.

QUESTIONS

1. What definition does Clark give of his central metaphor, "the blot and the diagram"? Are "blot" and "diagram" the equivalents of "art" and "science"? Explain.
2. What distinction does Clark make between "analogy (or association) blot" and "gesture blot"? What importance does the distinction have for his discussion of modern painting?
3. In what ways, according to Clark, is the place of science in the modern world similar to the place occupied by science in the past? What past functions of art has science assumed? To what extent does Clark consider the situation satisfactory? What defects does he mention?

4. How does Clark show "blot" painting and "diagram" architecture to be related? Is architecture today an art or a science? How scientific is painting?
5. Clark points out that "the closest analogy to action painting is the most popular art of all—the art of jazz" (p. 226). Is there any jazz analogous to "diagram"? Explain.
6. Study closely some examples of advertising layout. To what extent do they appear influenced by "blot"? Is there influence of "diagram" in any? Are any exemplary of "blot" and "diagram" in harmony?
7. What extensions into other disciplines can be made of Clark's blot-diagram antithesis? Does it apply in literature? In psychology?
8. Why, according to Clark, will man's concept-forming nature eventually bring about a change of style in art?

CHRISTOPHER FRY

Laughter

A friend once told me that when he was under the influence of ether, he dreamed he was turning over the pages of a great book, in which he knew he would find, on the last page, the meaning of life. The pages of the book were alternately tragic and comic, and he turned page after page, his excitement growing, not only because he was approaching the answer but because he couldn't know, until he arrived, on which side of the book the final page would be. At last it came: the universe opened up to him in a hundred words: and they were uproariously funny. He came back to consciousness crying with laughter, remembering everything. He opened his lips to speak. It was then that the great and comic answer plunged back out of his reach.

If I had to draw a picture of the person of Comedy, it is so I should like to draw it: the tears of laughter running down the face, one hand still lying on the tragic page which so nearly contained the answer, the lips about to frame the great revelation, only to find it had gone as disconcertingly as a chair twitched away when we want to sit down. Comedy is an escape, not from truth but from despair: a narrow escape into faith. It believes in a universal cause for delight, even though knowledge of the cause is always twitched away from under us, which leaves us to rest on our own buoyancy. In tragedy every moment is eternity; in comedy eternity is a moment. In tragedy we suffer pain; in comedy pain is a fool, suffered gladly.

Charles Williams once said to me, indeed it was the last thing he said to me (he died not long after), and it was shouted from the

tailboard of a moving bus, over the heads of pedestrians and bicycl-
ists outside the Midland Station, Oxford: "When we're dead we
shall have the sensation of having enjoyed life altogether, whatever
has happened to us." The distance between us widened, and he
leaned out into the space so that his voice should reach me: "Even
if we've been murdered, what a pleasure to have been capable of
it!"; and, having spoken the words for comedy, away he went like
that revelation which almost came out of the ether.

He was not at all saying that everything is for the best in the best
of all possible worlds. He was saying—or so it seems to me—that
there is an angle of experience where the dark is distilled into light:
either here or hereafter, in or out of time: where our tragic fate
finds itself with perfect pitch, and goes straight to the key which
creation was composed in. And comedy senses and reaches out to
this experience. It says, in effect, that, groaning as we may be, we
move in the figure of a dance, and, so moving, we trace the outline
of the mystery. Laughter did not come by chance, but how or why
it came is beyond comprehension, unless we think of it as a kind of
perception. The human animal, beginning to feel his spiritual
inches, broke in onto an unfamiliar tension of life, where laughter
became inevitable. But how? Could he, in his first unlaughing condition, have contrived a comic view of life and then developed the
strange rib-shaking response?

Or is it not more likely that when he was able to grasp the tragic
nature of time he was of a stature to sense its comic nature also;
and, by the experience of tragedy and the intuition of comedy, to
make his difficult way? The difference between tragedy and comedy
is the difference between experience and intuition. In the experience we strive against every condition of our animal life: against
death, against the frustration of ambition, against the instability of
human love. In the intuition we trust the arduous eccentricities
we're born to, and see the oddness of a creature who has never got
acclimatized to being created. Laughter inclines me to know that
man is essential spirit; his body, with its functions and accidents
and frustrations, is endlessly quaint and remarkable to him; and
though comedy accepts our position in time, it barely accepts our
posture in space.

The bridge by which we cross from tragedy to comedy and back
again is precarious and narrow. We find ourselves in one or the
other by the turn of a thought; a turn such as we make when we
turn from speaking to listening. I know that when I set about writing a comedy the idea presents itself to me first of all as tragedy.
The characters press on to the theme with all their divisions and
perplexities heavy about them; they are already entered for the race
to doom, and good and evil are an infernal tangle skinning the
fingers that try to unravel them. If the characters were not qualified

for tragedy there would be no comedy, and to some extent I have to cross the one before I can light on the other. In a century less flayed and quivering we might reach it more directly; but not now, unless every word we write is going to mock us. A bridge has to be crossed, a thought has to be turned. Somehow the characters have to unmortify themselves: to affirm life and assimilate death and persevere in joy. Their hearts must be as determined as the phoenix; what burns must also light and renew: not by a vulnerable optimism but by a hard-won maturity of delight, by the intuition of comedy, an active patience declaring the solvency of good. The Book of Job is the great reservoir of comedy. "But there is a spirit in man. . . . Fair weather cometh out of the north. . . . The blessing of him that was ready to perish came upon me: and I caused the widow's heart to sing for joy."

I have come, you may think, to the verge of saying that comedy is greater than tragedy. On the verge I stand and go no further. Tragedy's experience hammers against the mystery to make a breach which would admit the whole triumphant answer. Intuition has no such potential. But there are times in the state of man when comedy has a special worth, and the present is one of them: a time when the loudest faith has been faith in a trampling materialism, when literature has been thought unrealistic which did not mark and remark our poverty and doom. Joy (of a kind) has been all on the devil's side, and one of the necessities of our time is to redeem it. If not, we are in poor sort to meet the circumstances, the circumstances being the contention of death with life, which is to say evil with good, which is to say desolation with delight. Laughter may only seem to be like an exhalation of air, but out of that air we came; in the beginning we inhaled it; it is a truth, not a fantasy, a truth voluble of good which comedy stoutly maintains.

On Politics
and Government

GEORGE ORWELL
Politics and the English Language

Most people who bother with the matter at all would admit that the English language is in a bad way, but it is generally assumed that we cannot by conscious action do anything about it. Our civilization is decadent and our language—so the argument runs—must inevitably share in the general collapse. It follows that any struggle against the abuse of language is a sentimental archaism, like preferring candles to electric light or hansom cabs to aeroplanes. Underneath this lies the half-conscious belief that language is a natural growth and not an instrument which we shape for our own purposes.

Now, it is clear that the decline of a language must ultimately have political and economic causes: it is not due simply to the bad influence of this or that individual writer. But an effect can become a cause, reinforcing the original cause and producing the same effect in an intensified form, and so on indefinitely. A man may take to drink because he feels himself to be a failure, and then fail all the more completely because he drinks. It is rather the same thing that is happening to the English language. It becomes ugly and inaccurate because our thoughts are foolish, but the slovenliness of our language makes it easier for us to have foolish thoughts. The point is that the process is reversible. Modern English, especially written English, is full of bad habits which spread by imitation and which can be avoided if one is willing to take the necessary trouble. If one gets rid of these habits one can think more clearly, and to think clearly is a necessary first step towards political regeneration: so that the fight against bad English is not frivolous and is not the exclusive concern of professional writers. I will come back to this presently, and I hope that by that time the meaning of what I have said here will have become clearer. Meanwhile, here are five specimens of the English language as it is now habitually written.

These five passages have not been picked out because they are especially bad—I could have quoted far worse if I had chosen—but because they illustrate various of the mental vices from which we now suffer. They are a little below the average, but are fairly representative samples. I number them so that I can refer back to them when necessary:

"(1) I am not, indeed, sure whether it is not true to say that the Milton who once seemed not unlike a seventeenth-century Shelley had not become, out of an experience ever more bitter in each year, more alien [*sic*] to the founder of that Jesuit sect which nothing could induce him to tolerate."

Professor Harold Laski (Essay in *Freedom of Expression*).

"(2) Above all, we cannot play ducks and drakes with a native battery of idioms which prescribes such egregious collocations of vocables as the Basic *put up with* for *tolerate* or *put at a loss* for *bewilder*."

Professor Lancelot Hogben (*Interglossa*).

"(3) On the one side we have the free personality: by definition it is not neurotic, for it has neither conflict nor dream. Its desires, such as they are, are transparent, for they are just what institutional approval keeps in the forefront of consciousness; another institutional pattern would alter their number and intensity; there is little in them that is natural, irreducible, or culturally dangerous. But *on the other side*, the social bond itself is nothing but the mutual reflection of these self-secure integrities. Recall the definition of love. Is not this the very picture of a small academic? Where is there a place in this hall of mirrors for either personality or fraternity?"

Essay on psychology in *Politics* (New York).

"(4) All the 'best people' from the gentlemen's clubs, and all the frantic fascist captains, united in common hatred of Socialism and bestial horror of the rising tide of the mass revolutionary movement, have turned to acts of provocation, to foul incendiarism, to medieval legends of poisoned wells, to legalize their own destruction of proletarian organizations, and rouse the agitated petty-bourgeoisie to chauvinistic fervour on behalf of the fight against the revolutionary way out of the crisis."

Communist pamphlet.

"(5) If a new spirit *is* to be infused into this old country, there is one thorny and contentious reform which must be tackled, and that is the humanization and galvanization of the B.B.C. Timidity here will bespeak cancer and atrophy of the soul. The heart of Britain may be sound and of strong beat, for instance, but the British lion's roar at present is like that of Bottom in Shakespeare's *Midsummer Night's Dream*—as gentle as any sucking dove. A virile new Britain cannot continue indefinitely to be traduced in the eyes or rather ears, of the world by the effete languors of Langham Place, brazenly masquerading as 'standard English'. When the Voice of Britain is heard at nine o'clock, better far and infinitely less ludicrous to hear aitches honestly dropped than the present priggish, inflated, inhibited, school-ma'amish arch braying of blameless bashful mewing maidens!"

Letter in *Tribune*.

Each of these passages has faults of its own, but, quite apart from avoidable ugliness, two qualities are common to all of them. The first is staleness of imagery: the other is lack of precision. The writer either has a meaning and cannot express it, or he inadvertently says something else, or he is almost indifferent as to whether his words mean anything or not. This mixture of vagueness and sheer incompetence is the most marked characteristic of modern English prose, and especially of any kind of political writing. As soon as certain topics are raised, the concrete melts into the abstract and no one seems able to think of turns of speech that are not hackneyed: prose consists less and less of *words* chosen for the sake of their meaning, and more and more of *phrases* tacked together like the sections of a prefabricated hen-house. I list below, with notes and examples, various of the tricks by means of which the work of prose-construction is habitually dodged:

Dying Metaphors

A newly invented metaphor assists thought by evoking a visual image, while on the other hand a metaphor which is technically "dead" (e.g. *iron resolution*) has in effect reverted to being an ordinary word and can generally be used without loss of vividness. But in between these two classes there is a huge dump of worn-out metaphors which have lost all evocative power and are merely used because they save people the trouble of inventing phrases for themselves. Examples are: *Ring the changes on, take up the cudgels for, toe the line, ride roughshod over, stand shoulder to shoulder with, play into the hands of, no axe to grind, grist to the mill, fishing in troubled waters, on the order of the day, Achilles' heel, swan song, hotbed.* Many of these are used without knowledge of their meaning (what is a "rift", for instance?), and incompatible metaphors are frequently mixed, a sure sign that the writer is not interested in what he is saying. Some metaphors now current have been twisted out of their original meaning without those who use them even being aware of the fact. For example, *toe the line* is sometimes written *tow the line*. Another example is *the hammer and the anvil*, now always used with the implication that the anvil gets the worst of it. In real life it is always the anvil that breaks the hammer, never the other way about: a writer who stopped to think what he was saying would be aware of this, and would avoid perverting the original phrase.

Operators or Verbal False Limbs

These save the trouble of picking out appropriate verbs and nouns, and at the same time pad each sentence with extra syllables which give it an appearance of symmetry. Characteristic phrases are: *render inoperative, militate against, make contact with, be subjected to, give rise to, give grounds for, have the effect of, play a leading part (role) in, make itself felt, take effect, exhibit a tendency to, serve the purpose of,* etc., etc. The keynote is the elimination of simple verbs. Instead of being a single word, such as *break, stop, spoil, mend, kill,* a verb becomes a *phrase,* made up of a noun or adjective tacked on to some general-purposes verb such as *prove, serve, form, play, render.* In addition, the passive voice is wherever possible used in preference to the active, and noun constructions are used instead of gerunds (*by examination of* instead of *by examining*). The range of verbs is further cut down by means of the *-ize* and *de-* formation, and the banal statements are given an appearance of profundity by means of the *not un-* formation. Simple conjunctions and prepositions are replaced by such phrases as *with respect to, having regard to, the fact that, by dint of, in view of, in the interests of, on the hypothesis that;* and the ends of sentences are saved from anticlimax by such resounding commonplaces as *greatly to be desired, cannot be left out of account, a development to be expected in the near future, deserving of serious consideration, brought to a satisfactory conclusion,* and so on and so forth.

Pretentious Diction

Words like *phenomenon, element, individual* (as noun), *objective, categorical, effective, virtual, basic, primary, promote, constitute, exhibit, exploit, utilize, eliminate, liquidate,* are used to dress up simple statements and give an air of scientific impartiality to biased judgments. Adjectives like *epoch-making, epic, historic, unforgettable, triumphant, age-old, inevitable, inexorable, veritable,* are used to dignify the sordid processes of international politics, while writing that aims at glorifying war usually takes on an archaic colour, its characteristic words being: *realm, throne, chariot, mailed fist, trident, sword, shield, buckler, banner, jackboot, clarion.* Foreign words and expressions such as *cul de sac, ancien régime, deus ex machina, mutatis mutandis, status quo, gleichschaltung, weltanschauung,* are used to give an air of culture and elegance. Except for the useful abbreviations *i.e., e.g.,* and *etc.,* there is no real need for any of the hundreds of foreign phrases now current in English. Bad writers, and especially scientific, political and sociological writers, are nearly always haunted by the notion that Latin or Greek words are grander than Saxon ones, and unnecessary words like *expedite, ameliorate, predict, extraneous, deracinated, clandestine, subaqueous* and hundreds of others constantly gain ground from their Anglo-Saxon opposite numbers.[1] The jargon peculiar to Marxist

1. An interesting illustration of this is the way in which the English flower names which were in use till very recently are being ousted by Greek ones, *snapdragon* becoming *antirrhinum, forget-me-not* becoming *myosotis,* etc. It is hard to see any practical reason for this change of fashion: it is probably due to an instinctive turning-away from the more homely word and a vague feeling that the Greek word is scientific.

writing (*hyena, hangman, cannibal, petty bourgeois, these gentry, lacquey, flunkey, mad dog, White Guard,* etc.) consists largely of words and phrases translated from Russian, German or French; but the normal way of coining a new word is to use a Latin or Greek root with the appropriate affix and, where necessary, the *-ize* formation. It is often easier to make up words of this kind (*deregionalize, impermissible, extramarital, nonfragmentatory* and so forth) than to think up the English words that will cover one's meaning. The result, in general, is an increase in slovenliness and vagueness.

Meaningless Words

In certain kinds of writing, particularly in art criticism and literary criticism, it is normal to come across long passages which are almost completely lacking in meaning.[2] Words like *romantic, plastic, values, human, dead, sentimental, natural, vitality,* as used in art criticism, are strictly meaningless in the sense that they not only do not point to any discoverable object, but are hardly ever expected to do so by the reader. When one critic writes, "The outstanding feature of Mr. X's work is its living quality", while another writes, "The immediately striking thing about Mr. X's work is its peculiar deadness", the reader accepts this as a simple difference of opinion. If words like *black* and *white* were involved, instead of the jargon words *dead* and *living,* he would see at once that language was being used in an improper way. Many political words are similarly abused. The word *Fascism* has now no meaning except in so far as it signifies "something not desirable". The words *democracy, socialism, freedom, patriotic, realistic, justice,* have each of them several different meanings which cannot be reconciled with one another. In the case of a word like *democracy,* not only is there no agreed definition, but the attempt to make one is resisted from all sides. It is almost universally felt that when we call a country democratic we are praising it: consequently the defenders of every kind of régime claim that it is a democracy, and fear that they might have to stop using the word if it were tied down to any one meaning. Words of this kind are often used in a consciously dishonest way. That is, the person who uses them has his own private definition, but allows his hearer to think he means something quite different. Statements like *Marshal Pétain was a true patriot, The Soviet Press is the freest in the world, The Catholic Church is opposed to persecution,* are almost always made with intent to deceive. Other words used in var-

---

2. Example: "Comfort's catholicity of perception and image, strangely Whitmanesque in range, almost the exact opposite in aesthetic compulsion, continues to evoke that trembling atmospheric accumulative hinting at a cruel, an inexorably serene timelessness ... Wrey Gardiner scores by aiming at simple bull's-eyes with precision. Only they are not so simple, and through this contented sadness runs more than the surface bittersweet of resignation." (*Poetry Quarterly.*)

iable meanings, in most cases more or less dishonestly, are: *class, totalitarian, science, progressive, reactionary, bourgeois, equality*.

Now that I have made this catalogue of swindles and perversions, let me give another example of the kind of writing that they lead to. This time it must of its nature be an imaginary one. I am going to translate a passage of good English into modern English of the worst sort. Here is a well-known verse from *Ecclesiastes*:

"I returned and saw under the sun, that the race is not to the swift, nor the battle to the strong, neither yet bread to the wise, nor yet riches to men of understanding, nor yet favour to men of skill; but time and chance happeneth to them all."

Here it is in modern English:

"Objective consideration of contemporary phenomena compels the conclusion that success or failure in competitive activities exhibits no tendency to be commensurate with innate capacity, but that a considerable element of the unpredictable must invariably be taken into account."

This is a parody, but not a very gross one. Exhibit (3), above, for instance, contains several patches of the same kind of English. It will be seen that I have not made a full translation. The beginning and ending of the sentence follow the original meaning fairly closely, but in the middle the concrete illustrations—race, battle, bread—dissolve into the vague phrase "success or failure in competitive activities". This had to be so, because no modern writer of the kind I am discussing—no one capable of using phrases like "objective consideration of contemporary phenomena"—would ever tabulate his thoughts in that precise and detailed way. The whole tendency of modern prose is away from concreteness. Now analyse these two sentences a little more closely. The first contains forty-nine words but only sixty syllables, and all its words are those of everyday life. The second contains thirty-eight words of ninety syllables: eighteen of its words are from Latin roots, and one from Greek. The first sentence contains six vivid images, and only one phrase ("time and chance") that could be called vague. The second contains not a single fresh, arresting phrase, and in spite of its ninety syllables it gives only a shortened version of the meaning contained in the first. Yet without a doubt it is the second kind of sentence that is gaining ground in modern English. I do not want to exaggerate. This kind of writing is not yet universal, and outcrops of simplicity will occur here and there in the worst-written page. Still, if you or I were told to write a few lines on the uncertainty of human fortunes, we should probably come much nearer to my imaginary sentence than to the one from *Ecclesiastes*.

As I have tried to show, modern writing at its worst does not consist in picking out words for the sake of their meaning and inventing images in order to make the meaning clearer. It consists in gumming together long strips of words which have already been set in order by someone else, and making the results presentable by sheer humbug. The attraction of this way of writing is that it is easy. It is easier—even quicker, once you have the habit—to say *In my opinion it is a not unjustifiable assumption that* than to say *I think.* If you use ready-made phrases, you not only don't have to hunt about for words; you also don't have to bother with the rhythms of your sentences, since these phrases are generally so arranged as to be more or less euphonious. When you are composing in a hurry— when you are dictating to a stenographer, for instance, or making a public speech—it is natural to fall into a pretentious, Latinized style. Tags like *a consideration which we should do well to·bear in mind* or *a conclusion to which all of us would readily assent* will save many a sentence from coming down with a bump. By using stale metaphors, similes and idioms, you save much mental effort, at the cost of leaving your meaning vague, not only for your reader but for yourself. This is the significance of mixed metaphors. The sole aim of a metaphor is to call up a visual image. When these images clash—as in *The Fascist octopus has sung its swan song, the jackboot is thrown into the melting pot*—it can be taken as certain that the writer is not seeing a mental image of the objects he is naming; in other words he is not really thinking. Look again at the examples I gave at the beginning of this essay. Professor Laski (1) uses five negatives in fifty-three words. One of these is superfluous, making nonsense of the whole passage, and in addition there is the slip *alien* for akin, making further nonsense, and several avoidable pieces of clumsiness which increase the general vagueness. Professor Hogben (2) plays ducks and drakes with a battery which is able to write prescriptions, and, while disapproving of the everyday phrase *put up with,* is unwilling to look *egregious* up in the dictionary and see what it means. (3), if one takes an uncharitable attitude towards it, is simply meaningless: probably one could work out its intended meaning by reading the whole of the article in which it occurs. In (4), the writer knows more or less what he wants to say, but an accumulation of stale phrases chokes him like tea leaves blocking a sink. In (5), words and meaning have almost parted company. People who write in this manner usually have a general emotional meaning—they dislike one thing and want to express solidarity with another—but they are not interested in the detail of what they are saying. A scrupulous writer, in every sentence that he writes, will ask himself at least four questions, thus: What am I trying to say? What words will express it? What image or idiom will make it clearer? Is this image fresh enough to have an effect? And he will probably ask himself two more: Could I put it more shortly? Have I said anything that is avoidably ugly? But you are not obliged to go to all this trouble. You can shirk it by simply throwing your mind open and letting the ready-made phrases come crowding in. They will construct your sentences for you—even think your thoughts for you, to a certain extent—and at need they will perform the important service of partially concealing your meaning even from yourself. It is at this point that the special connection between politics and the debasement of language becomes clear.

In our time it is broadly true that political writing is bad writing. Where it is not true, it will generally be found that the writer is some kind of rebel, expressing his private opinions and not a "party line". Orthodoxy, of whatever colour, seems to demand a lifeless, imitative style. The political dialects to be found in pamphlets, leading articles, manifestos, White Papers and the speeches of under-secretaries do, of course, vary from party to party, but they are all alike in that one almost never finds in them a fresh, vivid, home-made turn of speech. When one watches some tired hack on the platform mechanically repeating the familiar phrases—*bestial atrocities, iron heel, bloodstained tyranny, free peoples of the world, stand shoulder to shoulder*—one often has a curious feeling that one is not watching a live human being but some kind of dummy: a feeling which suddenly becomes stronger at moments when the light catches the speaker's spectacles and turns them into blank discs which seem to have no eyes behind them. And this is not alto-gether fanciful. A speaker who uses that kind of phraseology has gone some distance towards turning himself into a machine. The appropriate noises are coming out of his larynx, but his brain is not involved as it would be if he were choosing his words for himself. If the speech he is making is one that he is accustomed to make over and over again, he may be almost unconscious of what he is saying, as one is when one utters the responses in church. And this reduced state of consciousness, if not indispensable, is at any rate favourable to political conformity.

In our time, political speech and writing are largely the defence of the indefensible. Things like the continuance of British rule in India, the Russian purges and deportations, the dropping of the atom bombs on Japan, can indeed be defended, but only by argu-ments which are too brutal for most people to face, and which do not square with the professed aims of political parties. Thus politi-cal language has to consist largely of euphemism, question-begging and sheer cloudy vagueness. Defenceless villages are bombarded from the air, the inhabitants driven out into the countryside, the cattle machine-gunned, the huts set on fire with incendiary bullets: this is called *pacification*. Millions of peasants are robbed of their farms and sent trudging along the roads with no more than they can carry: this is called *transfer of population* or *rectification of fron-tiers*. People are imprisoned for years without trial, or shot in the back of the neck or sent to die of scurvy in Arctic lumber camps: this is called *elimination of unreliable elements*. Such phraseology is needed if one wants to name things without calling up mental pictures of them. Consider for instance some comfortable English professor defending Russian totalitarianism. He cannot say outright, "I believe in killing off your opponents when you can get good results by doing so". Probably, therefore, he will say something like this:

"While freely conceding that the Soviet régime exhibits certain features which the humanitarian may be inclined to deplore, we must, I think, agree that a certain curtailment of the right to political opposition is an unavoidable concomitant of transitional periods, and that the rigours which the Russian people have been called upon to undergo have been amply justified in the sphere of concrete achievement."

The inflated style is itself a kind of euphemism. A mass of Latin words falls upon the facts like soft snow, blurring the outlines and covering up all the details. The great enemy of clear language is insincerity. When there is a gap between one's real and one's declared aims, one turns as it were instinctively to long words and exhausted idioms, like a cuttlefish squirting out ink. In our age there is no such thing as "keeping out of politics". All issues are political issues, and politics itself is a mass of lies, evasions, folly, hatred and schizophrenia. When the general atmosphere is bad, language must suffer. I should expect to find—this is a guess which I have not sufficient knowledge to verify—that the German, Russian and Italian languages have all deteriorated in the last ten or fifteen years, as a result of dictatorship.

But if thought corrupts language, language can also corrupt thought. A bad usage can spread by tradition and imitation, even among people who should and do know better. The debased language that I have been discussing is in some ways very convenient. Phrases like *a not unjustifiable assumption, leaves much to be desired, would serve no good purpose, a consideration which we should do well to bear in mind*, are a continuous temptation, a packet of aspirins always at one's elbow. Look back through this essay, and for certain you will find that I have again and again committed the very faults I am protesting against. By this morning's post I have received a pamphlet dealing with conditions in Germany. The author tells me that he "felt impelled" to write it. I open it at random, and here is almost the first sentence that I see: "(The Allies) have an opportunity not only of achieving a radical transformation of Germany's social and political structure in such a way as to avoid a nationalistic reaction in Germany itself, but at the same time of laying the foundations of a co-operative and unified Europe." You see, he "feels impelled" to write—feels, presumably, that he has something new to say—and yet his words, like cavalry horses answering the bugle, group themselves automatically into the familiar dreary pattern. This invasion of one's mind by ready-made phrases (*lay the foundations, achieve a radical transformation*) can only be prevented if one is constantly on guard against them, and every such phrase anaesthetizes a portion of one's brain.

I said earlier that the decadence of our language is probably curable. Those who deny this would argue, if they produced an argument at all, that language merely reflects existing social conditions, and that we cannot influence its development by any direct tinkering with words and constructions. So far as the general tone or spirit of a language goes, this may be true, but it is not true in detail. Silly words and expressions have often disappeared, not through any evolutionary process but owing to the conscious action of a minority. Two recent examples were *explore every avenue* and *leave no stone unturned*, which were killed by the jeers of a few journalists. There is a long list of flyblown metaphors which could similarly be got rid of if enough people would interest themselves in the job; and it should also be possible to laugh the *not un-* formation out of existence,[3] to reduce the amount of Latin and Greek in the average sentence, to drive out foreign phrases and strayed scientific words, and, in general, to make pretentiousness unfashionable. But all these are minor points. The defence of the English language implies more than this, and perhaps it is best to start by saying what it does *not* imply.

To begin with it has nothing to do with archaism, with the salvaging of obsolete words and turns of speech, or with the setting up of a "standard English" which must never be departed from. On the contrary, it is especially concerned with the scrapping of every word or idiom which has outworn its usefulness. It has nothing to do with correct grammar and syntax, which are of no importance so long as one makes one's meaning clear, or with the avoidance of Americanisms, or with having what is called a "good prose style". On the other hand it is not concerned with fake simplicity and the attempt to make written English colloquial. Nor does it even imply in every case preferring the Saxon word to the Latin one, though it does imply using the fewest and shortest words that will cover one's meaning. What is above all needed is to let the meaning choose the word, and not the other way about. In prose, the worst thing one can do with words is to surrender to them. When you think of a concrete object, you think wordlessly, and then, if you want to describe the thing you have been visualizing you probably hunt about till you find the exact words that seem to fit. When you

3. One can cure oneself of the *not un-* formation by memorizing this sentence: *A not unblack dog was chasing a not unsmall rabbit across a not ungreen field.*

think of something abstract you are more inclined to use words from the start, and unless you make a conscious effort to prevent it, the existing dialect will come rushing in and do the job for you, at the expense of blurring or even changing your meaning. Probably it is better to put off using words as long as possible and get one's meaning as clear as one can through pictures or sensations. Afterwards one can choose—not simply *accept*—the phrases that will best cover the meaning, and then switch round and decide what impression one's words are likely to make on another person. This last effort of the mind cuts out all stale or mixed images, all prefabricated phrases, needless repetitions, and humbug and vagueness generally. But one can often be in doubt about the effect of a word or a phrase, and one needs rules that one can rely on when instinct fails. I think the following rules will cover most cases:

(i) Never use a metaphor, simile or other figure of speech which you are used to seeing in print.
(ii) Never use a long word where a short one will do.
(iii) If it is possible to cut a word out, always cut it out.
(iv) Never use the passive where you can use the active.
(v) Never use a foreign phrase, a scientific word or a jargon word if you can think of an everyday English equivalent.
(vi) Break any of these rules sooner than say anything outright barbarous.

These rules sound elementary, and so they are, but they demand a deep change of attitude in anyone who has grown used to writing in the style now fashionable. One could keep all of them and still write bad English, but one could not write the kind of stuff that I quoted in those five specimens at the beginning of this article.

I have not here been considering the literary use of language, but merely language as an instrument for expressing and not for concealing or preventing thought. Stuart Chase and others have come near to claiming that all abstract words are meaningless, and have used this as a pretext for advocating a kind of political quietism. Since you don't know what Fascism is, how can you struggle against Fascism? One need not swallow such absurdities as this, but one ought to recognize that the present political chaos is connected with the decay of language, and that one can probably bring about some improvement by starting at the verbal end. If you simplify your English, you are freed from the worst follies of orthodoxy. You cannot speak any of the necessary dialects, and when you make a stupid remark its stupidity will be obvious, even to yourself. Political language—and with variations this is true of all political parties, from Conservatives to Anarchists—is designed to make lies sound truthful and murder respectable, and to give an appearance of solidity to pure wind. One cannot change this all in a moment, but one can at least change one's own habits, and from time to time one can even, if one jeers loudly enough, send some worn-out and useless phrase—some *jackboot, Achilles' heel, hotbed, melting pot, acid test, veritable inferno* or other lump of verbal refuse—into the dustbin where it belongs.

QUESTIONS

1. What is Orwell's pivotal point? Where is it best stated?
2. In his aversion to foreign words Orwell anticipates De Gaulle's repudiation of "Franglais" (French adoption of English words). Does Orwell operate on a xenophobic assumption? Look at the foreign words he gives as examples. Are some of them useful additions to English because they cover a situation not covered by any English word, or would you agree with Orwell's assertion that "there is no real need for any of the hundreds of foreign phrases now current in English"?
3. Orwell's essay was written at the time of World War II. How far has that historical context influenced him in his choice of examples? Can his catalogue of swindles be brought up to date with more recent examples?
4. Discuss Orwell's assertion that "the decline of a language must ultimately have political and economic causes." Is this "clear," as he claims?
5. How can you be sure that a metaphor is dying, rather than alive or dead? Is Orwell's test of seeing it often in print a sufficient one? Can you defend any of his examples of dying metaphors as necessary or useful additions to our vocabularies?
6. Orwell gives a list of questions for the writer to ask himself (p. 239) and later a list of rules for the writer to follow (p. 243). Why does he consider it necessary to give both kinds of advice? How much do the two overlap? Are both consistent with Orwell's major ideas expressed elsewhere in the essay? Does his injunction to "break any of these rules sooner than say anything outright barbarous" beg the question?
7. Orwell suggests that if you look back through his essay you will find that he has "again and again committed the very faults" he is protesting against. Is this true? If it is, does it affect the validity of his major points?
8. Words create a personality or confer a character. Describe the personality that would be created by following Orwell's six rules; show that character in action.

W. E. B. DU BOIS
Jacob and Esau[1]

I remember very vividly the Sunday-school room where I spent the Sabbaths of my early years. It had been newly built after a disastrous fire; the room was large and full of sunlight; nice new chairs were grouped around where the classes met. My class was in the center, so that I could look out upon the elms of Main Street and see the passersby. But I was interested usually in the lessons and in my fellow students and the frail rather nervous teacher, who tried to make the Bible and its ethics clear to us. We were a trial to her, full of mischief, restless and even noisy; but perhaps more especially when we asked questions. And on the story of Jacob and Esau we did ask questions. My judgment then and my judgment now is very unfavorable to Jacob. I thought that he was a cad and a liar and I did not see how possibly he could be made the hero of a Sunday-school lesson.

Many days have passed since then and the world has gone through astonishing changes. But basically, my judgment of Jacob has not greatly changed and I have often promised myself the pleasure of talking about him publicly, and especially to young people. This is the first time that I have had the opportunity.

My subject then is "Jacob and Esau," and I want to examine these two men and the ideas which they represent; and the way in which those ideas have come to our day. Of course, our whole interpretation of this age-old story of Jewish mythology has greatly changed. We look upon these Old Testament stories today not as untrue and yet not as literally true. They are simple, they have their truths, and yet they are not by any means the expression of eternal verity. Here were brought forward for the education of Jewish children and for the interpretation of Jewish life to the world, two men: one small, lithe and quick-witted; the other tall, clumsy and impetuous; a hungry, hard-bitten man.

Historically, we know how these two types came to be set forth by the Bards of Israel. When the Jews marched north after escaping from slavery in Egypt, they penetrated and passed through the land of Edom; the land that lay between the Dead Sea and Egypt. It was an old center of hunters and nomads and the Israelites, while they admired the strength and organization of the Edomites, looked down upon them as lesser men; as men who did not have the Great Plan. Now the Great Plan of the Israelites was the building of a strong, concentered state under its own God, Jehovah, devoted to

1. Commencement address at Talladega College, June 5, 1944.

agriculture and household manufacture and trade. It raised its own food by careful planning. It did not wander and depend upon chance wild beasts. It depended upon organization, strict ethics, absolute devotion to the nation through strongly integrated planned life. It looked upon all its neighbors, not simply with suspicion, but with the exclusiveness of a chosen people, who were going to be the leaders of earth.

This called for sacrifice, for obedience, for continued planning. The man whom we call Esau was from the land of Edom, or inter-married with it, for the legend has it that he was twin of Jacob the Jew but the chief fact is that, no matter what his blood relations were, his cultural allegiance lay among the Edomites. He was trained in the free out-of-doors; he chased and faced the wild beasts; he knew vast and imperative appetite after long self-denial, and even pain and suffering; he gloried in food, he traveled afar; he gathered wives and concubines and he represented continuous prim-itive strife.

The legacy of Esau has come down the ages to us. It has not been dominant, but it has always and continually expressed and re-expressed itself; the joy of human appetites, the quick resentment that leads to fighting, the belief in force, which is war.

As I look back upon my own conception of Esau, he is not nearly as clear and definite a personality as Jacob. There is something rather shadowy about him; and yet he is curiously human and easily conceived. One understands his contemptuous surrender of his birthright; he was hungry after long days of hunting; he wanted rest and food, the stew of meat and vegetables which Jacob had in his possession, and determined to keep unless Esau bargained. "And Esau said, Behold, I am at the point to die: and what profit shall this birthright be to me? And Jacob said, Swear to me this day; and he swore unto him: and he sold his birthright unto Jacob."

On the other hand, the legacy of Jacob which has come down through the years, not simply as a Jewish idea, but more especially as typical of modern Europe, is more complicated and expresses itself something like this: life must be planned for the Other Self, for that personification of the group, the nation, the empire, which has eternal life as contrasted with the ephemeral life of individuals. For this we must plan, and for this there must be timeless and unceasing work. Out of this, the Jews as chosen children of Jehovah would triumph over themselves, over all Edom and in time over the world.

Now it happens that so far as actual history is concerned, this dream and plan failed. The poor little Jewish nation was dispersed to the ends of the earth by the overwhelming power of the great nations that arose East, North, and South and eventually became united in the vast empire of Rome. This was the diaspora, the dispersion of the Jews. But the idea of the Plan with a personality of its own took hold of Europe with relentless grasp and this was the real legacy of Jacob, and of other men of other peoples, whom Jacob represents.

There came the attempt to weld the world into a great unity, first under the Roman Empire, then under the Catholic Church. When this attempt failed, and the empire fell apart, there arose the individual states of Europe and of some other parts of the world; and these states adapted the idea of individual effort to make each of them dominant. The state was *all*, the individual subordinate, but right here came the poison of the Jacobean idea. How could the state get this power? Who was to wield the power within the state? So long as power was achieved, what difference did it make how it was gotten? Here then was war—but not Esau's war of passion, hunger and revenge, but Jacob's war of cold acquisition and power.

Granting to Jacob, as we must, the great idea of the family, the clan, and the state as dominant and superior in its claims, nevertheless, there is the bitter danger in trying to seek these ends without reference to the great standards of right and wrong. When men begin to lie and steal, in order to make the nation to which they belong great, then comes not only disaster, but rational contradiction which in many respects is worse than disaster, because it ruins the leadership of the divine machine, the human reason, by which we chart and guide our actions.

It was thus in the middle age and increasingly in the seventeenth and eighteenth and more especially in the nineteenth century, there arose the astonishing contradiction: that is, the action of men like Jacob who were perfectly willing and eager to lie and steal so long as their action brought profit to themselves and power to their state. And soon identifying themselves and their class with the state they identified their own wealth and power as that of the state. They did not listen to any arguments of right or wrong; might was right; they came to despise and deplore the natural appetites of human beings and their very lives, so long as by their suppression, they themselves got rich and powerful. There arose a great, rich Italy; a fabulously wealthy Spain; a strong and cultured France and, eventually, a British Empire which came near to dominating the world. The Esaus of those centuries were curiously represented by various groups of people: by the slum-dwellers and the criminals who, giving up all hope of profiting by the organized state, sold their birthrights for miserable messes of pottage. But more than that, the great majority of mankind, the peoples who lived in Asia, Africa and America and the islands of the sea, became subordinate tools for the profit-making of the crafty planners of great things, who worked regardless of religion or ethics.

It is almost unbelievable to think what happened in those centuries, when it is put in cold narrative; from whole volumes of tales, let me select only a few examples. The peoples of whole islands and countries were murdered in cold blood for their gold and jewels. The mass of the laboring people of the world were put to work for wages which led them into starvation, ignorance and disease. The right of the majority of mankind to speak and to act; to play and to dance was denied, if it interfered with profit-making work for others, or was ridiculed if it could not be capitalized. Karl Marx writes of Scotland: "As an example of the method of obtaining wealth and power in nineteenh century; the story of the Duchess of Sutherland will suffice here. This Scottish noblewoman resolved, on entering upon the government of her clan of white Scottish people, to turn the whole country, whose population had already been, by earlier processes, reduced to 15,000, into a sheep pasture. From 1814 to 1820 these 15,000 inhabitants were systematically hunted and rooted out. All their villages were destroyed and burnt, all their fields turned into pasture. Thus this lady appropriated 794,000 acres of land that had from time immemorial been the property of the people. She assigned to the expelled inhabitants about 6,000 acres on the seashore. The 6,000 acres had until this time lain waste, and brought in no income to their owners. The Duchess, in the nobility of her heart, actually went so far as to let these at an average rent of 50 cents per acre to the clansmen, who for centuries had shed their blood for her family. The whole of the stolen clan-land she divided into 29 great sheep farms, each inhabited by a single imported English family. In the year 1835 the 15,-000 Scotsmen were already replaced by 131,000 sheep."[1]

The discovery of gold and silver in America, the extirpation, enslavement and entombment in mines of the Indian population, the beginning of the conquest and looting of the East Indies, the turning of Africa into a warren for the commercial hunting of black-skins, signalized the rosy dawn of power of those spiritual children of Jacob, who owned the birthright of the masses by fraud and murder. These idyllic proceedings are the chief momenta of primary accumulation of capital in private hands. On their heels tread the commercial wars of the European nations, with the globe for a theater. It begins with the revolt of the Netherlands from Spain, assumes giant dimensions in England's anti-jacobin war, and continues in the opium wars against China.

Of the Christian colonial system, Howitt says: "The barbarities

1. This is a quotation from Karl Marx's *Capital*. However, Du Bois in places has paraphrased Marx and interpolated his own words for those of the English translation of the work. The essential meaning, however, is not distorted. Since it is likely Du Bois used the translation of *Capital* by Samuel Moore and Edward Aveling (published by Charles H. Kerr and Co., Chicago, 1906) the reader can compare Du Bois's rendition with the original by consulting pp. 801–802, vol. I, of the Kerr edition of *Capital*. [This and subsequent notes are those of Du Bois's editor, Philip S. Foner.]

and desperate outrages of the so-called Christians, throughout every region of the world, and upon people they have been able to subdue, are not to be paralleled by those of any other race, in any age of the earth." This history of the colonial administration of Holland—and Holland was the head capitalistic nation of the seventeenth century—is one of the most extraordinary relations of treachery, bribery, massacre, and meanness.

Nothing was more characteristic than the Dutch system of stealing men, to get slaves for Java. The men-stealers were trained for this purpose. The thief, the interpreter, and the seller were the chief agents in this trade; the native princes, the chief sellers. The young people stolen, were thrown into the secret dungeons of Celebes, until they were ready for sending to the slave ships. . . .

The English East India Company, in the seventeenth and eighteenth centuries, obtained, besides the political rule in India, the exclusive monopoly of the tea trade, as well as of the Chinese trade in general, and of the transport of goods to and from Europe. But the coasting trade of India was the monopoly of the higher employees of the company. The monopolies of salt, opium, betel nuts and other commodities, were inexhaustible mines of wealth. The employees themselves fixed the price and plundered at will the unhappy Hindus. The Governor General took part in this private traffic. His favorites received contracts under conditions whereby they, cleverer than the alchemists, made gold out of nothing. Great English fortunes sprang up like mushrooms in a day; investment profits went on without the advance of a shilling. The trial of Warren Hastings swarms with such cases. Here is an instance: a contract for opium was given to a certain Sullivan at the moment of his departure on an official mission. Sullivan sold his contract to one Binn for $200,000; Binn sold it the same day for $300,000 and the ultimate purchaser who carried out the contract declared that after all he realized an enormous gain. According to one of the lists laid before Parliament, the East India Company and its employees from 1757 to 1766 got $30,000,000 from the Indians as gifts alone.

The treatment of the aborigines was, naturally, most frightful in plantation colonies destined for export trade only, such as the West Indies, and in rich and well-populated countries, such as Mexico and India, that were given over to plunder. But even in the colonies properly so called, the followers of Jacob outdid him. These sober Protestants, the Puritans of New England, in 1703, by decrees of their assembly set a premium of $200 on every Indian scalp and every captured redskin: in 1720 a premium of $500 on every scalp; in 1744, after Massachusetts Bay had proclaimed a certain tribe as rebels, the following prices prevailed: for a male scalp of 12 years upward, $500 (new currency); for a male prisoner, $525; for women and children prisoners, $250; for scalps of women and children, $250. Some decades later, the colonial system took its revenge on the descendants of the pious pilgrim fathers, who had grown seditious in the meantime. At English instigation and for English pay they were tomahawked by redskins. The British Parliament proclaimed bloodhounds and scalping as "means that God and Nature had given into its hands."[2]

With the development of national industry during the eighteenth century, the public opinion of Europe had lost the last remnant of shame and conscience. The nations bragged cynically of every infamy that served them as a means to accumulating private wealth. Read, e.g., the naive *Annals of Commerce* of Anderson. Here it is trumpeted forth as a triumph of English statecraft that at the Peace of Utrecht, England extorted from the Spaniards by the Asiento Treaty the privilege of being allowed to ply the slave trade, between Africa and Spanish America. England thereby acquired the right of supplying Spanish America until 1743 with 4,800 Negroes yearly. This threw, at the same time, an official cloak over British smuggling. Liverpool waxed fat on the slave trade. . . . ·Aikin (1795) quotes that spirit of bold adventure which has characterized the trade of Liverpool and rapidly carried it to its present state of prosperity; has occasioned vast employment for shipping and sailors, and greatly augmented the demand for the manufactures of the country; Liverpool employed in the slave trade, in 1730, 15 ships; in 1760, 74; in 1770, 96; and in 1792, 132.[3]

Henry George wrote of *Progress and Poverty* in the 1890s. He says: "At the beginning of this marvelous era it was natural to expect, and it was expected, that labor-saving inventions would lighten the toil and improve the condition of the laborer; that the enormous increase in the power of producing wealth would make real poverty a thing of the past. Could a man of the last century [the eighteenth]—a Franklin or a Priestley—have seen, in a vision of the future, the steamship taking the place of the sailing vessel; the railroad train, of the wagon; the reaping machine, of the scythe; the threshing machine, of the flail; could he have heard the throb of the engines that in obedience to human will, and for the satisfaction of the human desire, exert a power greater than that of all the men and all the beasts of burden of the earth combined; could he have seen the forest tree transformed into finished lumber—into doors, sashes, blinds, boxes or barrels, with hardly the touch of a human hand; the great workshops where boots and shoes are turned out by the case with less labor than the old-fashioned cobbler could have put on a sole; the factories where, under the eye of one girl, cotton becomes cloth faster than hundreds of stalwart weavers could have turned it out with their hand-looms; could he have seen steam

2. *Ibid.*, pp. 823–826.   3. *Ibid.*, pp. 832–833.

hammers shaping mammoth shafts and mighty anchors, and delicate machinery making tiny watches; the diamond drill cutting
through the heart of the rocks, and coal oil sparing the whale; could
he have realized the enormous saving of labor resulting from
improved facilities of exchange and communication—sheep killed in
Australia eaten fresh in England, and the order given by the
London banker in the afternoon executed in San Francisco in the
morning of the same day; could he have conceived of the hundred
thousand improvements which these only suggest, what would he
have inferred as to the social condition of mankind?

"It would not have seemed like an inference; further than the
vision went it would have seemed as though he saw; and his heart
would have leaped and his nerves would have thrilled, as one who
from a height beholds just ahead of the thirst-stricken caravan the
living gleam of rustling woods and the glint of laughing waters.
Plainly, in the sight of the imagination, he would have beheld these
new forces elevating society from its very foundations, lifting the
very poorest above the possibility of want, exempting the very
lowest from anxiety for the material needs of life; he would have
seen these slaves of the lamp of knowledge taking on themselves the
traditional curse, these muscles of iron and sinews of steel making
the poorest laborer's life a holiday, in which every high quality and
noble impulse could have scope to grow."[4]

This was the promise of Jacob's life. This would establish the
birthright which Esau despised. But, says George, "Now, however,
we are coming into collision with facts which there can be no mis-
taking. From all parts of the civilized world," he says speaking fifty
years ago, "come complaints of industrial depression; of labor
condemned to involuntary idleness; of capital massed and wasting;
of pecuniary distress among businessmen; of want and suffering and
anxiety among the working classes. All the full, deadening pain, all
the keen, maddening anguish, that to great masses of men are involved in the words 'hard times,' afflict the world today."[5] What
would Henry George have said in 1933 after airplane and radio and
mass production, turbine and electricity had come?

Science and art grew and expanded despite all this, but it was
warped by the poverty of the artist and the continuous attempt to
make science subservient to industry. The latter effort finally succeeded so widely that modern civilization became typified as
industrial technique. Education became learning a trade. Men
thought of civilization as primarily mechanical and the mechanical
means by which they reduced wool and cotton to their purposes,

4. Henry George, *Progress and Poverty*, New York, Robert Schalkenbach
Foundation, 1939, pp. 3–4. This work,
originally published in 1879, argued that
the land belonged to society, which created its value and should properly tax
that value, not improvements on the land.
George's proposal for such a "Single
Tax" gained many adherents.
5. *Ibid.*, pp. 5–6.

also reduced and bent humankind to their will. Individual initiative remained but it was cramped and distorted and there spread the idea of patriotism to one's country as the highest virtue, by which it became established, that just as in the case of Jacob, a man not only could lie, steal, cheat and murder for his native land, but by doing so, he became a hero whether his cause was just or unjust.

One remembers that old scene between Esau who had thoughtlessly surrendered his birthright and the father who had blessed his lying son: "Jacob came unto his father, and said, My Father: and he said, Here am I; who art thou? And Jacob said unto his father, I am Esau thy firstborn; I have done according as thou badest me: arise, I pray thee, sit and eat of my venison, that thy soul may bless me." In vain did clumsy, careless Esau beg for a blessing—some little blessing. It was denied and Esau hated Jacob because of the blessing: and Esau said in his heart, "The days of mourning for my father are at hand; then I will slay my brother Jacob." So revolution entered—so revolt darkened a dark world.

The same motif was repeated in modern Europe and America in the nineteenth and twentieth centuries, when there grew the superstate called the Empire. The Plan had now regimented the organization of men covering vast territories, dominating immense force and immeasurable wealth and determined to reduce to subserviency as large a part as possible, not only of Europe's own internal world, but of the world at large. Colonial imperialism swept over the earth and initiated the First World War, in envious scramble for division of power and profit.

Hardly a moment of time passed after that war, a moment in the eyes of the eternal forces looking down upon us when again the world, using all of that planning and all of that technical superiority for which its civilization was noted; and all of the accumulated and accumulating wealth which was available, proceeded to commit suicide on so vast a scale that it is almost impossible for us to realize the meaning of the catastrophe. Of course, this sweeps us far beyond anything that the peasant lad Jacob, with his petty lying and thievery had in mind. Whatever was begun there of ethical wrong among the Jews was surpassed in every particular by the white world of Europe and America and carried to such length of universal cheating, lying and killing that no comparisons remain.

We come therefore to the vast impasse of today: to the great question, what was the initial right and wrong of the original Jacobs and Esaus and of their spiritual descendants the world over? We stand convinced today, at least those who remain sane, that lying and cheating and killing will build no world organization worth the building. We have got to stop making income by unholy methods; out of stealing the pittances of the poor and calling it insurance; out of seizing and monopolizing the natural resources of the world and then making the world's poor pay exorbitant prices for alumi-num, copper and oil, iron and coal. Not only have we got to stop these practices, but we have got to stop lying about them and seek-ing to convince human beings that a civilization based upon the enslavement of the majority of men for the income of the smart minority is the highest aim of man.

But as is so usual in these cases, these transgressions of Jacob do not mean that the attitude of Esau was flawless. The conscienceless greed of capital does not excuse the careless sloth of labor. Life cannot be all aimless wandering and indulgence if we are going to constrain human beings to take advantage of their brain and make successive generations stronger and wiser than the previous. There must be reverence for the *birthright* of inherited *culture* and that birthright cannot be sold for a dinner course, a dress suit or a winter in Florida. It must be valued and conserved.

The method of conservation is work, endless and tireless and planned work and this is the legacy which the Esaus of today who condemn the Jacobs of yesterday have got to substitute as their path of life, not vengeful revolution, but building and rebuilding. Curiously enough, it will not be difficult to do this, because the great majority of men, the poverty-stricken and diseased are the *real workers* of the world. They are the ones who have made and are making the *wealth* of this universe, and their future path is clear. It is to accumulate such knowledge and balance of judgment that they can reform the world, so that the workers of the world receive just share of the wealth which they make and that all human beings who are capable of work shall work. Not national glory and empire for the few, but food, shelter and happiness for the many. With the disappearance of systematic lying and killing, we may come into that birthright which so long we have called Freedom: that is, the right to act in a manner that seems to be beautiful; which makes life worth living and joy the only possible end of life. This is the experience which is Art and planning for this is the highest satisfac-tion of civilized needs. So that looking back upon the allegory and the history, tragedy and promise, we may change our subject and speak in closing of Esau and Jacob, realizing that neither was per-fect, but that of the two, Esau had the elements which lead more naturally and directly to the salvation of man; while Jacob with all his crafty planning and cold sacrifice, held in his soul the things that are about to ruin mankind: exaggerated national patriotism, individual profit, the despising of men who are not the darlings of our particular God and the consequent lying and stealing and kill-ing to monopolize power.

May we not hope that in the world after this catastrophe of blood, sweat and fire, we may have a new Esau and Jacob; a new allegory of men who enjoy life for life's sake; who have the Freedom of Art and wish for all men of all sorts the same freedom and enjoyment that they seek themselves and who work for all this and work hard.

Gentlemen and ladies of the class of 1944: in the days of the years of my pilgrimage, I have greeted many thousands of young men and women at the commencement of their careers as citizens of the select commonwealth of culture. In no case have I welcomed them to such a world of darkness and distractions as that into which I usher you. I take joy only in the thought that if work to be done is measure of man's opportunity you inherit a mighty fortune. You have only to remember that the birthright which is today in symbol draped over your shoulders is a heritage which has been preserved all too often by the lying, stealing and murdering of the Jacobs of the world, and if these are the only means by which this birthright can be preserved in the future, it is not worth the price. I do not believe this, and I lay it upon your hearts to prove that this not only need not be true, but is eternally and forever false.

GEORGE L. JACKSON
Letter from Soledad Prison

DEAR FAY,

For very obvious reasons it pains me to dwell on the past. As an individual, and as the male of our order I have only the proud flesh[1] of very recent years to hold up as proof that I did not die in the sickbed in which I lay for so long. I've taken my lesson from the past and attempted to close it off.

I've drunk deeply from the cisterns of gall, swam against the current in Blood Alley, Urban Fascist Amerika, experienced the nose rub in shit, armed myself with a monumental hatred and tried to forget and pretend. A standard black male defense mechanism.

It hasn't worked. It may just be me, but I suspect that it's part of the pitiful black condition that the really bad moments record themselves so clearly and permanently in the mind, while the few brief flashes of gratification are lost immediately, nightmare overhanging darkly.

My recall is nearly perfect, time has faded nothing. I recall the very first kidnap. I've lived through the passage, died on the passage, lain in the unmarked, shallow graves of the millions who fertilized the Amerikan soil with their corpses; cotton and corn growing out of my chest, "unto the third and fourth generation," the tenth, the hundredth. My mind ranges back and forth through the

1. Proud flesh is a medical term for the abnormal growth of flesh that some- times forms round a healing wound.

uncounted generations, and I feel all that they ever felt, but double. I can't help it; there are too many things to remind me of the 23½ hours that I'm in this cell. Not ten minutes pass without a reminder. In between, I'm left to speculate on what form the reminder will take.

Down here we hear relaxed, matter-of-fact conversations center-ing around how best to kill all the nation's niggers and in what order. It's not the fact that they consider killing me that upsets. They've been "killing all the niggers" for nearly half a millennium now, but I am still alive. I might be the most resilient dead man in the universe. The upsetting thing is that they never take into con-sideration the fact that I am going to resist. No they honestly believe that shit. They do! That's what they think of us. That they have beaten and conditioned all the defense and attack reflexes from us. That the region of the mind that stores the principles upon which men base their rationale to resist is missing in us. Don't they talk of concentration camps? Don't they state that it couldn't happen in the U.S. because the fascists here are nice fascists? Not because it's impossible to incarcerate 30 million resisters, but because they are humane imperialists, enlightened fascists.

Well, they've made a terrible mistake. I recall the day I was born, the first day of my generation. It was during the second (and most destructive) capitalist world war for colonial privilege, early on a rainy Wednesday morning, late September, Chicago. It happened to me in a little fold-into-the-wall bed, in a little half-flat on Racine and Lake. Dr. Rogers attended. The el train that rattled by within fifteen feet of our front windows (the only two windows) screamed in at me like the banshee, portentous of pain, death, threatening and imminent. The first motion that my eyes focused on was this pink hand swinging in a wide arc in the general direction of my black ass. I stopped that hand, the left downward block, and countered the right needle finger to the eye. I was born with my defence reflexes well developed.

It's going to be "Kill me if you can," fool, not "Kill me if you please."

But let them make their plans on the supposition, "like slave, like son." I'm not going for it, though, and they've made my defence easier. A cop gives the keys to a group of right-wing cons. They're going to open our cells—one at a time—all over the building. They don't want to escape, or deal with the men who hold them here. They can solve their problems only if they kill all of us—think about that—these guys live a few cells from me. None of them have ever lived, most are state-raised in institutions like this one. They have nothing coming, nothing at all, they have nothing at stake in this order of things. In defending right-wing ideals and the status quo they're saying in effect that ninety-nine years and a dark day in prison is their idea of fun. Most are in and out, and mostly in, all of their life. The periods that they pass on the outside are considered runs. Simply stated, they consider the periods spent in the joint more natural, more in keeping with their tastes. Well, I understand their condition, and I know how they got that way. I could honestly sympathize with them if they were not so wrong, so stupid as to let the pigs use them. Sounds like Germany of the thirties and forties to me. It's the same on the outside there. I'll venture to say that there's not one piece of stock, not one bond owned by anyone in any of the families of the pigs who murdered Fred Hampton.[2] They organize marches around the country, marches and demonstrations in support of total immediate destruction of Vietnam, and afterwards no one is able to pick up the tab. The fascists, it seems, have a standard M.O. for dealing with the lower classes. Actually oppressive power throughout history has used it. They turn a man against himself—think of all the innocent things that make us feel good, but that make some of us also feel guilty. Think of how the people of the lower classes weigh themselves against the men who rule. Consider the con going through the courts on a capital offence who supports capital punishment. I swear I heard something just like that today. Look how long Hershey ran Selective Service. Blacks embrace capitalism, the most unnatural and outstanding example of man against himself that history can offer. After the Civil War, the form of slavery changed from chattel to economic slavery, and we were thrown on to the labor market to compete at a disadvantage with poor whites. Ever since that time, our principal enemy must be isolated and identifed as capitalism. The slaver was and is the factory owner, the businessman of capitalist Amerika, the man responsible for employment, wages, prices, control of the nation's institutions and culture. It was the capitalist infrastructure of Europe and the U.S. which was responsible for the rape of Africa and Asia. Capitalism murdered those 30 million in the Congo. Believe me, the European and Anglo-Amerikan capitalist would never have wasted the ball and powder were it not for the profit principle. The men, all the men who went into Africa and Asia, the fleas who climbed on that elephant's back with rape on their minds, richly deserve all that they are called. Every one of them deserved to die for their crimes. So do the ones who are still in Vietnam, Angola, Union of South Africa (U.S.A.!!). But we must not allow the emotional aspects of these issues, the scum at the surface, to obstruct our view of the big picture, the whole rotten hunk. It was capitalism that armed the ships, free enterprise that launched them, private ownership of property that fed the troops. Imperialism took up where the slave trade left off. It wasn't until after the slave trade

2. Black Panther leader, killed by a Chicago policeman in December 1970.

ended that Amerika, England, France, and the Netherlands invaded and settled in on Afro-Asian soil in earnest. As the European industrial revolution took hold, new economic attractions replaced the older ones; chattel slavery was replaced by neoslavery. Capitalism, "free" enterprise, private ownership of public property armed and launched the ships and fed the troops; it should be clear that it was the profit motive that kept them there.

It was the profit motive that built the tenement house and the city project. Profit and loss prevents repairs and maintenance. Free enterprise brought the monopolistic chain store into the neighbourhood. The concept of private ownership of facilities that the people need to exist brought the legions of hip-shooting, brainless pigs down upon our heads, our homes, our streets. They're there to protect the entrepreneur!! His chain store, and his property that you' are renting, his bank.

If the entrepreneur decides that he no longer wants to sell you food, let's say, because the Yankee dollar that we value so dearly has suddenly lost its last thirty cents of purchasing power, private ownership means that the only way many of the people will eat is to break the law. Fat Rat Daley has ordered all looters shot.[3]

Black capitalism, black against itself. The silliest contradiction in a long train of spineless, mindless contradictions. Another painless, ultimate remedy: be a better fascist than the fascist. Bill Cosby, acting out the establishment agent—what message was this soul brother conveying to our children? *I Spy* was certainly programmed to a child's mentality. This running dog in the company of a fascist with a cause, a flunky's flunky, was transmitting the credo of the slave to our youth, the mod version of the old house nigger. We can never learn to trust as long as we have them. They are as much a part of the repression, more even than the real live, rat-informer-pig. Aren't they telling our kids that it is romantic to be a running dog? The kids are so hungry to see the black male do some shooting and throw some hands that they can't help themselves from identifying with the quislings. So first they turn us against ourselves, precluding all possibility of trust, then fascism takes any latent divisible forces and develops them into divisions in fact: racism, nationalism, religions.

You have Spic, Dago, Jew, Jap, Chink, Gook, Pineapple, and the omnibus nigger to represent the nations of Africa. The point being that it is easier to persuade that little man who joined the army to see the world and who has never murdered before to murder a Gook. Well, it's not quite like murdering a man. Polack, Frog, Kraut, etc.

The wheels just fell off altogether in the thirties. People in cer-

3. During race riots in Chicago Mayor all looters on sight.
Richard Daley ordered police to shoot

tain circles like to forget it, and any reference to the period draws
from these circles such defensive epithets as "old-fashioned," "simple
old-style socialism," and "out of date." But fashion doesn't concern
me, I'm after the facts. The facts are that no one, absolutely no one
in the Western world, and very few anywhere else (this includes
even those who may have been born yesterday), is unaffected by
those years when capitalism's roulette wheel locked in depression. It
affected every nation-state on earth. Of course Russia had no stock
market and consequently no business cycle, but it was affected by
the war that grew out of the efforts to restart the machines and by
the effect it had on other nations with which Russia has had to
deal. Relativism enters. Since international capitalism was at the
time in its outward peak of expansion, there were no African, Asian,
or Latin lands organized along nation-state lines that were not
adversely affected. Every society in the world that lived by a money
economy was part of the depression. Although Russia had abandoned the forms and vacillations of capitalism, it too was damaged
due to the principles of relativism.

If there is any question whether those years have any effect on, or
relevance to now, just consider the effect on today's mentality. Had
the world's people been struck with hereditary cretinism all at once,
instead of Adam Smith's "invisible hand,"[4] the analogy couldn't be
more perfect. I mean cretinism in its literal, medical sense: a congenital deficiency in the secretions of the thyroid gland resulting in
deformity and idiocy. Causation links that depression with World
War II. The rise of power to Europe's Nazis can be attributed to
the depression. The WASP fascists of Amerika secretly desired a
war with Japan to stimulate demand and control unemployment.
The syllogism is perfect.

So question and analyze the state of being of Europe's Jews who
survive. Do the same with the people of Hiroshima and Nagasaki.
But we don't have to isolate groups. Causation and relativism link
everyone inescapably with the past. None of the righteous people
would even be alive had their parents died of the underconsump-
tion of that period or the desperate fascist chicanery aimed at
diverting the lower classes from the economic reality of class struggle. The Nazis actually succeeded in foisting upon the lower-class
Germans and some of the other European national groups the
notion that their economic plight was due not to bad economic
principles but caused by the existence of Jews within the system
and the shortage of markets (colonies). The obvious intent being to
pit lower-class, depressed German against lower-class Jew, instead of
exploited lower-class German against privileged upper-class German.

4. Term used by Smith in his *Wealth of Nations* to describe the individual's self-interest as a self-regulating market mechanism.

The Amerikan fascist used a thousand similar devices, delaying maneuvers, to prevent the people from questioning the validity of the principles upon which capitalism is founded, to turn the people against themselves, people against people, people against other groups of people. Always they will promote competition (while they cooperate), division, mistrust, a sense of isolation. The antipodes of love. The M.O. of the fascist arrangement is always to protect the capitalist class by destroying the consciousness, the trust, the unity of the lower classes. My father is in his forties today; thirty-five years ago he was living through his most formative years. He was a child of the Great Depression. I want you to notice for later reference that I emphasize and differentiate *Great* Depression. There were many more international, national, and regional depressions during the period in history relevant to this comment.

There are millions of blacks of my father's generation now living. they are all products of a totally depressed environment. All of the males have lived all of their lives in a terrible quandary; none were able to grasp that a morbid economic deprivation, an outrageous and enormous abrasion, formed the basis of their character.

My father developed his character, convention, convictions, his traits, his life style, out of a situation that began with his mother running out. She left him and his oldest brother on the corner of one of the canyons in East St. Louis. They raised themselves, in the streets, then on a farm somewhere in Louisiana, then in C.C.C. camps. This brother, my father, had no formal education at all. He taught himself the essentials later on. Alone, in the most hostile jungle on earth, ruled over by the king of beasts in the first throes of a bloody and protracted death. Alone, in the most savage moment of history, without arms, and burdened by a black face that he's been hiding ever since.

I love this brother, my father, and when I use the word "love" I am not making an attempt at rhetoric. I am attempting to express a refulgent, unrestrained emanation from the deepest, most durable region of my soul, an unshakeable thing that I have never questioned. But no one can come through his ordeal without suffering the penalty of psychosis. It was the price of survival. I would venture that there are no healthy brothers of his generation, *none at all*.

The brother has reached the prime of his life without ever showing in my presence or anywhere, to my knowledge, an overt manifestation of *real* sensitivity, affection, or sentiment. He has lived his entire life in a state of shock. Nothing can touch him now, his calm is complete, his immunity to pain is total. When I can fix his eyes, which is not often since when they aren't closed they are shaded, I see staring back at me the expressionless mask of the zombie.

But he must have loved us, of this I am certain. Part of the credo of the neoslave, the latter-day slave, who is free to move from place to place if he can come by the means, is to shuffle away from any situation that becomes too difficult. He stayed with us, worked sixteen hours a day, after which he would eat, bathe and sleep—period. He never owned more than two pairs of shoes in his life and in the time I was living with him never more than one suit, never took a drink, never went to a nightclub, expressed no feelings about such things, and never once reminded any one of us, or so it seemed, never expected any notice of the fact that he was giving to us all of the life force and activity that the monster-machine had left to him. The part that the machine seized, that death of the spirit visited upon him by a world that he never influenced, was mourned by us, and most certainly by me, but no one ever made a real effort to give him solace. How do you console a man who is unapproachable?

He came to visit me when I was in San Quentin. He was in his forties then too, an age in men when they have grown full. I had decided to reach for my father, to force him with my revolutionary dialectic to question some of the mental barricades he'd thrown up to protect his body from what to him was an undefinable and omnipresent enemy. An enemy that would starve his body, expose it to the elements, chain his body, jail it, club it, rip it, hang it, electrify it, and poison-gas it. I would have him understand that although he had saved his body he had done so at a terrible cost to his mind. I felt that if I could superimpose the explosive doctrine of self-determination through people's government and revolutionary culture upon what remained of his mind, draw him out into the real world, isolate and identify his real enemies, if I could hurl him through Fanon's[5] revolutionary catharsis, I would be serving him, the people, the historical obligation.

San Quentin was in the riot season. It was early January 1967. The pigs had for the last three months been on a search-and-destroy foray into our cells. All times of the day or night our cells were being invaded by the goon squad: you wake up, take your licks, get skin-searched, and wait on the tier naked while they mangled your few personal effects. This treatment, fear therapy, was not accorded to all however. Some Chicanos behind dope, some whites behind extortionate activities were exempted. Mostly, it came down on us. Rehabilitational terror. Each new pig must go through a period of in-service training where he learns the Gestapo arts, the full range of anti-body tactics that he will be expected to use on the job. Part of this in-service training is a crash course in close-order combat where the pigs are taught how to use club and sap, and how to

5. Frantz Fanon, African revolutionary and philosopher who was devoted to the overthrow of colonialism.

form and use the simpler karate hands, where to hit a man with these hands for the best (or worst) effect.

The new pigs usually have to serve a period on the goon squad before they fall into their regular role on the animal farm. They are always anxious to try their new skills—"to see if it really works"— we were always forced to do something to slow them down, to demonstrate that violence was a two-edged sword. This must be done at least once every year, or we would all be as punchy and fractured as a Thai Boxer before our time was up. The brothers wanted to protest. The usual protest was a strike, a work stoppage, closing the sweatshops where industrial products are worked up for two cents an hour. (Some people get four cents after they've been on the job for six months.) The outside interests who made the profits didn't dig strikes. That meant the captain didn't like them either since it meant pressure on him from these free-enterprising political connections.

January in San Quentin is the worst way to be. It's cold when you don't have proper clothing, it's wet, dreary. The drab green, barred, buttressed walls that close in the upper yard are sixty to seventy feet high. They make you feel that your condition may be permanent.

On the occasion I wish to relate, my father had driven all night from Los Angeles alone; he had not slept more than a couple of hours in the last forty-eight.

We shook hands and the dialectic began. He listened while I scorned the diabolical dog—capitalism. Didn't it raise pigs and murder Vietnamese? Didn't it glut some and starve most of us? Didn't it build housing projects that resemble prisons and luxury hotels and apartments that resemble the Hanging Gardens on the same street? Didn't it build a hospital and then a bomb? Didn't it erect a school and then open a whorehouse? Build an airplane to sell a tranquilizer tablet? For every church didn't it construct a prison? For each new medical discovery didn't it produce as a by-product ten new biological warfare agents? Didn't it aggrandize men like Hunt and Hughes[6] and dwarf him?

He said, "Yes, but what can we do? There's too many of the bastards." His eyes shaded over and his mind went into a total regression, a relapse back through time, space, pain, neglect, a thousand dreams deferred, broken promises, forgotten ambitions, back through the hundreds of renewed hopes shattered to a time when he was young, roaming the Louisiana countryside for something to eat. He talked for ten minutes of things that were not in the present, people that I didn't know. "We'll have to take something

6. H. L. **Hunt** and Howard **Hughes**, multimillionaires.

back to Aunt Bell." He talked of places that we had never seen together. He called me by his brother's name twice. I was so shocked I could only sit and blink. This was the guy who took nothing seriously, the level-headed, practical Negro, the work-a-day, never-complain, cool, smooth, colored gentleman. They have driven him to the abyss of madness; just behind the white veneer waits the awesome, vindictive black madness. There are a lot of blacks living in his generation, the one of the Great Depression, when it was no longer possible to maintain the black self by serving. Even that had dried up. Blacks were beaten and killed for jobs like porter, bellboy, stoker, pearl diver, and bootblack. My clenched fist goes up for them; I forgive them, I understand, and if they will stop their collaboration with the fascist enemy, stop it now, and support our revolution with just a nod, we'll forget and forgive them for casting us naked into a grim and deleterious world.

The black colonies of Amerika have been locked in depression since the close of the Civil War. We have lived under regional depression since the end of chattel slavery. The beginning of the new slavery was marked by massive unemployment and underemployment. That remains with us still. The Civil War destroyed the *landed* aristocracy. The dictatorship of the agrarian class was displaced by the dictatorship of the manufacturing-capitalist class. The neoslaver destroyed the uneconomic plantation, and built upon its ruins a factory and a thousand subsidiaries to serve the factory setup. Since we had no skills, outside of the farming techniques that had proved uneconomic, the subsidiary service trades and menial occupations fell to us. It is still so today. We are a subsidiary subculture, a depressed area within the parent monstrosity. The other four stages of the capitalist business cycle are: recovery, expansion, inflation, and recession. Have we ever gone through a recovery or expansion stage? We are affected adversely by inflationary trends within the larger economy. Who suffers most when the prices of basic, necessary commodities go up? When the parent economy dips into inflation and recession we dip into subdepression. When it goes into depression, we go into total desperation. The difference between what my father's generation went through during the *Great* Depression and what we are going through now is simply a matter of degree. We can sometimes find a service to perform across the tracks. They couldn't. We can go home to Mama for a meal when things get really tight. They couldn't. There's welfare and housework for Mama now. Then there was no such thing as welfare.

Depression is an economic condition. It is a part of the capitalist business cycle, a necessary concomitant of capitalism. Its colonies—secondary markets—will always be depressed areas, because the steadily decreasing labour force, decreasing and growing more skilled under the advances of automation, casts the unskilled colonial subject into economic roles that preclude economic mobility. Learning the new skills even if we were allowed wouldn't help. It wouldn't help the masses even if they learned them. It wouldn't help because there is a fixed ceiling on the labor force. This ceiling gets lower with every advance in the arts of production. Learning the newer skills would merely put us into a competition with established labor that we could not win. One that we don't want. There are absolutely no vacuums for us to fill in the business world. We don't want to capitalize on people anyway. Capitalism is the enemy. It must be destroyed. There is no other recourse. The System is not workable in view of the modern industrial city-based society. Men are born disenfranchised. The contract between ruler and ruled perpetuates this disenfranchisement.

Men in positions of trust owe an equitable distribution of wealth and privilege to the men who have trusted them. Each individual born in these Amerikan cities should be born with those things that are necessary to survival. Meaningful social roles, education, medical care, food, shelter, and understanding should be guaranteed at birth. They have been part of all civilized human societies—until this one. Why else do men allow other men to govern? To what purpose is a Department of Health, Education, and Welfare, or of Housing and Urban Development, etc.? Why do we give these men power over us? Why do we give them taxes? For nothing? So they can say that the world owes our children nothing? This world owes each of us a living the very day we are born. If not we can make no claims to civilization and we can stop recognizing the power of any administrator. Evolution of the huge modern city-based society has made our dependence upon government complete. Individually, we cannot feed ourselves and our children. We cannot, by ourselves, train and educate them at home. We cannot organize our own work inside the city structure by ourselves. Consequently, we must allow men to specialize in coordinating these activities. We pay them, honor them, and surrender control of certain aspects of our lives to them so that they will in return take each new, helpless entry into the social group and work on him until he is no longer helpless, until he can start to support himself and make his contribution to the continuity of the society.

If a man is born into Amerikan society with nothing coming, if the capitalist creed that runs "The world doesn't owe you a living" is true, then the thing that my father's mother did is not outrageous at all. If it is true that government shouldn't organize then the fact that my father had no place to seek help until he could help himself has little consequence. But it would also mean that we are all in the grip of some monstrous contradiction. And that we have no more claim to civilization than a pack of baboons.

What is it then that *really* destroyed my father's comfort, that doomed his entire generation to a life without content? What is it that has been working against my generation from the day we were born through every day to this one?

Capitalism and capitalist man, wrecker of worlds, scourge of the people. It cannot address itself to our needs, it cannot and will not change itself to adapt to natural changes within the social structure.

To the black male the losses were most tragic of all. It will do us no good to linger over the fatalities, they're numberless and beyond our reach. But we who have survived must eventually look at ourselves and wonder why. The competition at the bottom of the social spectrum is for symbols, honors, and objects; black against itself, black against lower-class whites and browns, virulent, cut-throat, back-stabbing competition, the Amerikan way of life. But the fascists cooperate. The four estates of power form a morbid lone quadrangle. The competition has destroyed trust. Among the black males a premium has been placed on distrust. Every other black male is viewed as the competition; the wise and practical black is the one who cares nothing for any living ass, the cynic who has got over any principles he may have picked up by mistake. We can't express love on the supposition that the recipient will automatically use it against us as a weapon. We're going to have to start all over again. This next time around we'll let it all hang out, we'll stop betraying ourselves, and we'll add some trust and love.

I do not include those who support capitalism in any appreciable degree or who feel they have something to lose with its destruction. They are our irreconcilable enemy. We can never again trust people like Cosby, Gloves Davis,[7] or the old Negro bus driver who testified in the Huey Newton[8] trial. Any man who stands up to speak in defense of capitalism must be slapped down.

Right now our disease must be identified as capitalist man and his monstrous machine, a machine with the senseless and calloused ability to inflict these wounds programmed into its every cycle.

I was born with terminal cancer, a suppurating, malignant sore that attacked me in the region just behind the eyes and moves outward to destroy my peace.

It has robbed me of these twenty-eight years. It has robbed us all for nearly half a millennium. The greatest bandit of all time, we'll stop him now.

7. The black Chicago policeman who was reported to have shot Fred Hampton.
8. Newton, minister of defense of the Black Panther Party, was convicted of voluntary manslaughter in the killing of an Oakland, California, policeman in 1968; the conviction was overturned in 1970.

Recall the stories you've read about the other herd animals, the great Amerikan bison, the caribou or Amerikan reindeer.

The great Amerikan bison or buffalo—he's a herd animal, or social animal if you prefer, just like us in that. We're social animals, we need others of our general kind about us to feel secure. Few men would enjoy total isolation. To be alone constantly is torture to normal men. The buffalo, cattle, caribou, and some others are like folks in that they need company most of the time. They need to butt shoulders and butt butts. They like to rub noses. We shake hands, slap backs, and rub lips. Of all the world's people we blacks love the company of others most, we are the most socialistic. Social animals eat, sleep, and travel in company, they need this company to feel secure. This fact means that socialistic animals also need leaders. It follows logically that if the buffalo is going to eat, sleep, and travel in groups some coordinating factor is needed or some will be sleeping when others are traveling. Without the leadership-follower complex, in a crisis the company would roar off in a hundred different directions. But the buffalo did evolve the leader-follower complex as did the other social animals; if the leader of a herd of caribou loses his footing and slips to his death from some high place, it is very likely that the whole herd will die behind. The leader-follower complex. The hunter understood this. Predatory man learned of the natural occurrence of leadership in all of the social animals; that each group will by nature produce a leader, and to these natural leaders fall the responsibility for coordination of the group's activity, organizing them for survival. The buffalo hunter knew that if he could isolate and identify the leader of the herd and kill him first, the rest of the herd would be helpless, at his mercy, to be killed off as he saw fit.

We blacks have the same problem the buffalo had; we have the same weakness also, and predatory man understands this weakness well.

Huey Newton, Ahmed Evans, Bobby Seale,[9] and the hundreds of others will be murdered according to the fascist scheme.

A sort of schematic natural selection in reverse: Medgar Evers, Malcolm X, Bobby Hutton, Brother Booker, W. L. Noland, M. L. King, Featherstone, Mark Clark, and Fred Hampton[1]—just a few who have already gone the way of the buffalo.

The effect these moves from the right have had on us is a classic textbook exercise in fascist political economy. At the instant a black head rises out of our crisis existence, it's lopped off and hung from the highest courthouse or newspaper firm. Our predetermined

9. Prominent members of the Black Panther Party.

1. Black leaders, all of whom have been killed beginning in 1963.

response is a schizophrenic indifference, withdrawal, and an appreciation of things that do not exist. "Oh happy days. Oh happy days. Oh happy days." Self-hypnotically induced hallucinations.

The potential black leadership looks at the pitiable condition of the black herd: the corruption, the preoccupation with irrelevance, the apparent ineptitude concerning matters of survival. He knows that were he to give the average brother an M-16, this brother wouldn't have anything but a club for a week. He weighs this thing that he sees in the herd against the possible risks he'll be taking at the hands of the fascist monster and he naturally decides to go for himself, feeling that he can't help us because we are beyond help, that he may as well get something out of existence. These are the 'successful Negroes,' the opposite of the 'failures'. You find them on the ball courts and fields, the stage, pretending and playing children's games. And looking for all the world just as pitiable as the so-called failures.

We were colonized by the white predatory fascist economy. It was from them that we evolved our freak subculture, and the attitudes that perpetuate our conditions. These attitudes cause us to give each other up to the Klan pigs. We even on occasion work gun in hand right with them. A black killed Fred Hampton; blacks working with the C.I.A. killed Malcolm X; blacks are plentiful on the payroll of the many police forces that fascism must employ to protect itself from the people. These fascist subcultural attitudes have sent us to Europe, Asia (one-fourth of the fatalities in Vietnam are black fatalities), and even Africa (the Congo during the Simba attempt to establish people's government) to die for nothing. In the recent cases of Africa and Asia we have allowed the neoslaver to use us to help enslave people we love. We are so confused, so foolishly simple that we not only fail to distinguish what is generally right and what is wrong, but we also fail to appreciate what is good and not good for us in very personal matters concerning the black colony and its liberation. The ominous government economic agency whose only clear motive is to further enslave, number, and spy on us, the black agency subsidized by the government to infiltrate us and retard liberation, is accepted, and by some, even invited and welcomed, while the Black Panther is avoided and hard-pressed to find protection among the people. The Black Panther is our brother and son, the one who wasn't afraid. He wasn't so lazy as the rest, or so narrow and restricted in his vision. If we allow the fascist machine to destroy these brothers, our dream of eventual self-determination and control over the factors surrounding our survival is going to die with them, and the generations to come will curse and condemn us for irresponsible cowardice. I have a young courageous brother whom I love more than I love myself, but I have given him up to the revolution. I accept the possibility of his eventual death as I accept the possibility of my own. Some moment of weakness, a slip, a mistake, since we are the men who can make none, will bring the blow that kills. I accept this as a necessary part of our life. I don't want to raise any more black slaves. We have a determined enemy who will accept us only on a master-slave basis. When I revolt, slavery dies with me. I refuse to pass it down again. The terms of my existence are founded on that.

Black Mama, you're going to have to stop making cowards: "Be a good *boy;*" "You're going to worry me to death, *boy;*" "Don't trust those niggers;" "Stop letting those bad niggers lead you around, *boy;*" "Make you a dollar, *boy.*" Black Mama, your overriding concern with the survival of our sons is mistaken if it is survival at the cost of their manhood.

The young Panther party member, our vanguard, must be embraced, protected, allowed to develop. We must learn from him and teach him; he'll be full grown soon, a son and brother of whom we can be proud. If he sags we'll brace him up, when he takes a step we'll step with him, our dialectic, our communion in perfect harmony, and there'll never, never be another Fred Hampton affair.

Power to the people.

GEORGE

QUESTIONS

1. Jackson speaks of revolutionary dialectic; where in his discussion do you see the clearest example of its workings? What is its relation to revolutionary rhetoric?
2. Analyze the transitions within the paragraph on p. 259 beginning, "The Amerikan fascist. . . ."
3. What was Jackson's motive for deciding "to reach" for his father, "to force" him to question his defences?
4. Jackson disclaims any attempt at rhetoric when he speaks of his love for his father and then defines his love (p. 259). What is the source of the impact of his definition?

JONATHAN SWIFT
A Modest Proposal

For Preventing the Children of Poor People in Ireland from Being a Burden to Their Parents or Country, and for Making Them Beneficial to the Public

It is a melancholy object to those who walk through this great town or travel in the country, when they see the streets, the roads, and cabin doors, crowded with beggars of the female-sex, followed by three, four, or six children, all in rags and importuning every passenger for an alms. These mothers, instead of being able to work for their honest livelihood, are forced to employ all their time in strolling to beg sustenance for their helpless infants, who, as they grow up, either turn thieves for want of work, or leave their dear native country to fight for the Pretender in Spain, or sell themselves to the Barbadoes.[1]

I think it is agreed by all parties that this prodigious number of children in the arms, or on the backs, or at the heels of their mothers, and frequently of their fathers, is in the present deplorable state of the kingdom a very great additional grievance; and therefore whoever could find out a fair, cheap, and easy method of making these children sound, useful members of the commonwealth would deserve so well of the public as to have his statue set up for a preserver of the nation.

But my intention is very far from being confined to provide only for the children of professed beggars; it is of a much greater extent, and shall take in the whole number of infants at a certain age who are born of parents in effect as little able to support them as those who demand our charity in the streets.

As to my own part, having turned my thoughts for many years upon this important subject, and maturely weighed the several schemes of other projectors, I have always found them grossly mistaken in their computation. It is true, a child just dropped from its dam may be supported by her milk for a solar year, with little other nourishment; at most not above the value of two shillings, which the mother may certainly get, or the value in scraps, by her lawful occupation of begging; and it is exactly at one year old that I propose to provide for them in such a manner as instead of being a charge upon their parents or the parish, or wanting food and raiment for the rest of their lives, they shall on the contrary contribute to the feeding, and partly to the clothing, of many thousands.

There is likewise another great advantage in my scheme, that it

1. That is, bind themselves to work for a period of years, in order to pay for their transportation to a colony.

will prevent those voluntary abortions, and that horrid practice of women murdering their bastard children, alas, too frequent among us, sacrificing the poor innocent babes, I doubt, more to avoid the expense than the shame, which would move tears and pity in the most savage and inhuman breast.

The number of souls in this kingdom being usually reckoned one million and a half, of these I calculate there may be about two hundred thousand couple whose wives are breeders; from which number I subtract thirty thousand couples who are able to maintain their own children, although I apprehend there cannot be so many under the present distresses of the kingdom; but this being granted, there will remain an hundred and seventy thousand breeders. I again subtract fifty thousand for those women who miscarry, or whose children die by accident or disease within the year. There only remain an hundred and twenty thousand children of poor parents annually born. The question therefore is, how this number shall be reared and provided for, which, as I have already said, under the present situation of affairs, is utterly impossible by all the methods hitherto proposed. For we can neither employ them in handicraft or agriculture; we neither build houses (I mean in the country) nor cultivate land. They can very seldom pick up a livelihood by stealing till they arrive at six years old, except where they are of towardly parts; although I confess they learn the rudiments much earlier, during which time they can however be looked upon only as probationers, as I have been informed by a principal gentleman in the county of Cavan, who protested to me that he never knew above one or two instances under the age of six, even in a part of the kingdom so renowned for the quickest proficiency in that art.

I am assured by our merchants that a boy or a girl before twelve years old is no salable commodity; and even when they come to this age they will not yield above three pounds, or three pounds and half a crown at most on the Exchange; which cannot turn to account either to the parents or the kingdom, the charge of nutriment and rags having been at least four times that value.

I shall now therefore humbly propose my own thoughts, which I hope will not be liable to the least objection.

I have been assured by a very knowing American of my acquaintance in London, that a young healthy child well nursed is at a year old a most delicious, nourishing, and wholesome food, whether stewed, roasted, baked, or boiled; and I make no doubt that it will equally serve in a fricassee or a ragout.

I do therefore humbly offer it to public consideration that of the hundred and twenty thousand children, already computed, twenty thousand may be reserved for breed, whereof only one fourth part to be males, which is more than we allow to sheep, black cattle, or swine; and my reason is that these children are seldom the fruits of marriage, a circumstance not much regarded by our savages, therefore one male will be sufficient to serve four females. That the remaining hundred thousand may at a year old be offered in sale to the persons of quality and fortune through the kingdom, always advising the mother to let them suck plentifully in the last month, so as to render them plump and fat for a good table. A child will make two dishes at an entertainment for friends; and when the family dines alone, the fore or hind quarter will make a reasonable dish, and seasoned with a little pepper or salt will be very good boiled on the fourth day, especially in winter.

I have reckoned upon a medium that a child just born will weigh twelve pounds, and in a solar year if tolerably nursed increaseth to twenty-eight pounds.

I grant this food will be somewhat dear, and therefore very proper for landlords, who, as they have already devoured most of the parents, seem to have the best title to the children.

Infant's flesh will be in season throughout the year, but more plentiful in March, and a little before and after. For we are told by a grave author, an eminent French physician,[2] that fish being a prolific diet, there are more children born in Roman Catholic countries about nine months after Lent than at any other season; therefore, reckoning a year after Lent, the markets will be more glutted than usual, because the number of popish infants is at least three to one in this kingdom; and therefore it will have one other collateral advantage, by lessening the number of Papists among us.

I have already computed the charge of nursing a beggar's child (in which list I reckon all cottagers, laborers, and four fifths of the farmers) to be about two shillings per annum, rags included; and I believe no gentleman would repine to give ten shillings for the carcass of a good fat child, which, as I have said, will make four dishes of excellent nutritive meat, when he hath only some particular friend or his own family to dine with him. Thus the squire will learn to be a good landlord, and grow popular among the tenants; the mother will have eight shillings net profit, and be fit for work till she produces another child.

Those who are more thrifty (as I must confess the times require) may flay the carcass; the skin of which artificially dressed will make admirable gloves for ladies, and summer boots for fine gentlemen.

As to our city of Dublin, shambles may be appointed for this purpose in the most convenient parts of it, and butchers we may be assured will not be wanting; although I rather recommend buying the children alive, and dressing them hot from the knife as we do roasting pigs.

A very worthy person, a true lover of his country, and whose

2. Rabelais.

virtues I highly esteem, was lately pleased in discoursing on this matter to offer a refinement upon my scheme. He said that many gentlemen of this kingdom, having of late destroyed their deer, he conceived that the want of venison might be well supplied by the bodies of young lads and maidens, not exceeding fourteen years of age nor under twelve, so great a number of both sexes in every county being now ready to starve for want of work and service; and these to be disposed of by their parents, if alive, or otherwise by their nearest relations. But with due deference to so excellent a friend and so deserving a patriot, I cannot be altogether in his sentiments; for as to the males, my American acquaintance assured me from frequent experience that their flesh was generally tough and lean, like that of our schoolboys, by continual exercise, and their taste disagreeable; and to fatten them would not answer the charge. Then as to the females, it would, I think with humble submission, be a loss to the public, because they soon would become breeders themselves: and besides, it is not improbable that some scrupulous people might be apt to censure such a practice (although indeed very unjustly) as a little bordering upon cruelty; which, I confess, hath always been with me the strongest objection against any project, how well soever intended.

But in order to justify my friend, he confessed that this expedient was put into his head by the famous Psalmanazar, a native of the island Formosa, who came from thence to London above twenty years ago, and in conversation told my friend that in his country when any young person happened to be put to death, the executioner sold the carcass to persons of quality as a prime dainty; and that in his time the body of a plump girl of fifteen, who was crucified for an attempt to poison the emperor, was sold to his Imperial Majesty's prime minister of state, and other great mandarins of the court, in joints from the gibbet, at four hundred crowns. Neither indeed can I deny that if the same use were made of several plump young girls in this town, who without one single groat to their fortunes cannot stir abroad without a chair, and appear at the playhouse and assemblies in foreign fineries which they never will pay for, the kingdom would not be the worse.

Some persons of a desponding spirit are in great concern about that vast number of poor people who are aged, diseased, or maimed, and I have been desired to employ my thoughts what course may be taken to ease the nation of so grievous an encumbrance. But I am not in the least pain upon that matter, because it is very well known that they are every day dying and rotting by cold and famine, and filth and vermin, as fast as can be reasonably expected. And as to the younger laborers, they are now in almost as hopeful a condition. They cannot get work, and consequently pine away for want of nourishment to a degree that if at any time they are accidentally hired to common labor, they have not strength to perform it; and thus the country and themselves are happily delivered from the evils to come.

I have too long digressed, and therefore shall return to my subject. I think the advantages by the proposal which I have made are obvious and many, as well as of the highest importance.

For first, as I have already observed, it would greatly lessen the number of Papists, with whom we are yearly overrun, being the principal breeders of the nation as well as our most dangerous enemies; and who stay at home on purpose to deliver the kingdom to the Pretender, hoping to take their advantage by the absence of so many good Protestants, who have chosen rather to leave their country than to stay at home and pay tithes against their conscience to an Episcopal curate.

Secondly, the poorer tenants will have something valuable of their own, which by law may be made liable to distress, and help to pay their landlord's rent, their corn and cattle being already seized and money a thing unknown.

Thirdly, whereas the maintenance of an hundred thousand children, from two years old and upwards, cannot be computed at less than ten shillings a piece per annum, the nation's stock will be thereby increased fifty thousand pounds per annum, besides the profit of a new dish introduced to the tables of all gentlemen of fortune in the kingdom who have any refinement in taste. And the money will circulate among ourselves, the goods being entirely of our own growth and manufacture.

Fourthly, the constant breeders, besides the gain of eight shillings sterling per annum by the sale of their children, will be rid of the charge of maintaining them after the first year.

Fifthly, this food would likewise bring great custom to taverns, where the vintners will certainly be so prudent as to procure the best receipts for dressing it to perfection, and consequently have their houses frequented by all the fine gentlemen, who justly value themselves upon their knowledge in good eating; and a skillful cook, who understands how to oblige his guests, will contrive to make it as expensive as they please.

Sixthly, this would be a great inducement to marriage, which all wise nations have either encouraged by rewards or enforced by laws and penalties. It would increase the care and tenderness of mothers toward their children, when they were sure of a settlement for life to the poor babes, provided in some sort by the public, to their annual profit instead of expense. We should see an honest emulation among the married women, which of them could bring the fattest child to the market. Men would become as fond of their wives during the time of their pregnancy as they are now of their mares in foal, their cows in calf, or sows when they are ready to farrow;

nor offer to beat or kick them (as is too frequent a practice) for fear of a miscarriage.

Many other advantages might be enumerated. For instance, the addition of some thousand carcasses in our exportation of barreled beef, the propagation of swine's flesh, and improvement in the art of making good bacon, so much wanted among us by the great destruction of pigs, too frequent at our tables, which are no way comparable in taste or magnificence to a well-grown, fat, yearling child, which roasted whole will make a considerable figure at a lord mayor's feast or any other public entertainment. But this and many others I omit, being studious of brevity.

Supposing that one thousand families in this city would be constant customers for infants' flesh, besides others who might have it at merry meetings, particularly weddings and christenings, I compute that Dublin would take off annually about twenty thousand carcasses, and the rest of the kingdom (where probably they will be sold somewhat cheaper) the remaining eighty thousand.

I can think of no one objection that will possibly be raised against this proposal, unless it should be urged that the number of people will be thereby much lessened in the kingdom. This I freely own, and it was indeed one principal design in offering it to the world. I desire the reader will observe, that I calculate my remedy for this one individual kingdom of Ireland and for no other that ever was, is, or I think ever can be upon earth. Therefore let no man talk to me of other expedients: of taxing our absentees at five shillings a pound: of using neither clothes nor household furniture except what is of our own growth and manufacture: of utterly rejecting the materials and instruments that promote foreign luxury: of curing the expensiveness of pride, vanity, idleness, and gaming in our women: of introducing a vein of parsimony, prudence, and temperance: of learning to love our country, in the want of which we differ even from Laplanders and the inhabitants of Topinamboo[3]: of quitting our animosities and factions, nor acting any longer like the Jews, who were murdering one another at the very moment their city was taken: of being a little cautious not to sell our country and conscience for nothing: of teaching landlords to have at least one degree of mercy toward their tenants: lastly, of putting a spirit of honesty, industry, and skill into our shopkeepers; who, if a resolution could now be taken to buy only our native goods, would immediately unite to cheat and exact upon us in the price, the measure, and the goodness, nor could ever yet be brought to make one fair proposal of just dealing, though often and earnestly invited to it.[4]

Therefore I repeat, let no man talk to me of these and the like

3. A district in Brazil.
4. Swift himself has made these various proposals in previous works.

expedients, till he hath at least some glimpse of hope that there will ever be some hearty and sincere attempt to put them in practice.

But as to myself, having been wearied out for many years with offering vain, idle, visionary thoughts, and at length utterly despairing of success, I fortunately fell upon this proposal, which, as it is wholly new, so it hath something solid and real, of no expense and little trouble, full in our own power, and whereby we can incur no danger in disobliging England. For this kind of commodity will not bear exportation, the flesh being of too tender a consistence to admit a long continuance in salt, although perhaps I could name a country which would be glad to eat up our whole nation without it.

After all, I am not so violently bent upon my own opinion as to reject any offer proposed by wise men, which shall be found equally innocent, cheap, easy, and effectual. But before something of that kind shall be advanced in contradiction to my scheme, and offering a better, I desire the author or authors will be pleased maturely to consider two points. First, as things now stand, how they will be able to find food and raiment for an hundred thousand useless mouths and backs. And secondly, there being a round million of creatures in human figure throughout this kingdom, whose sole subsistence put into a common stock would leave them in debt two millions of pounds sterling, adding those who are beggars by profession to the bulk of farmers, cottagers, and laborers, with their wives and children who are beggars in effect; I desire those politicians who dislike my overture, and may perhaps be so bold to attempt an answer, that they will first ask the parents of these mortals whether they would not at this day think it a great happiness to have been sold for food at a year old in the manner I prescribe, and thereby have avoided such a perpetual scene of misfortunes as they have since gone through by the oppression of landlords, the impossibility of paying rent without money or trade, the want of common sustenance, with neither house nor clothes to cover them from the inclemencies of the weather, and the most inevitable prospect of entailing the like or greater miseries upon their breed forever.

I profess, in the sincerity of my heart, that I have not the least personal interest in endeavoring to promote this necessary work, having no other motive than the public good of my country, by advancing our trade, providing for infants, relieving the poor, and giving some pleasure to the rich. I have no children by which I can propose to get a single penny; the youngest being nine years old, and my wife past childbearing.

QUESTIONS

1. This essay has been called one of the best examples of sustained irony in the English language. Irony is difficult to handle because

there is always the danger that the reader will miss the irony and take what is said literally. What does Swift do to try to prevent this? In answering this question, consider such matters as these: Is the first sentence of the essay ironic? At what point do you begin to suspect that Swift is using irony? What further evidence accumulates to make you certain that Swift is being ironic?

2. What is the speaker like? How are his views and character different from Swift's? Is the character of the speaker consistent? What is the purpose of the essay's final sentence?

3. Why does Swift use such phrases as "just dropt from its dam," "whose wives are breeders," "one fourth part to be males"?

4. Does the essay shock you? Was it Swift's purpose to shock you?

5. What is the main target of Swift's attack? What subsidiary targets are there? Does Swift offer any serious solutions for the problems and conditions he is describing?

6. What devices of argument, apart from the use of irony, does Swift use that could be successfully applied to other subjects?

7. Compare Swift's methods of drawing in or engaging his audience to Coffin's ("What Crucified Christ?" pp. 450–465).

JAMES THURBER
The Rabbits Who Caused All the Trouble

Within the memory of the youngest child there was a family of rabbits who lived near a pack of wolves. The wolves announced that they did not like the way the rabbits were living. (The wolves were crazy about the way they themselves were living, because it was the only way to live.) One night several wolves were killed in an earthquake and this was blamed on the rabbits, for it is well known that rabbits pound on the ground with their hind legs and cause earthquakes. On another night one of the wolves was killed by a bolt of lightning and this was also blamed on the rabbits, for it is well known that lettuce-eaters cause lightning. The wolves threatened to civilize the rabbits if they didn't behave, and the rabbits decided to run away to a desert island. But the other animals, who lived at a great distance, shamed them, saying, "You must stay where you are and be brave. This is no world for escapists. If the wolves attack you, we will come to your aid, in all probability." So the rabbits continued to live near the wolves and one day there was a terrible flood which drowned a great many wolves. This was blamed on the rabbits, for it is well known that carrot-nibblers with long ears cause floods. The wolves descended on the rabbits, for their own good, and imprisoned them in a dark cave, for their own protection.

When nothing was heard about the rabbits for some weeks, the other animals demanded to know what had happened to them. The wolves replied that the rabbits had been eaten and since they had been eaten the affair was a purely internal matter. But the other animals warned that they might possibly unite against the wolves unless some reason was given for the destruction of the rabbits. So the wolves gave them one. "They were trying to escape," said the wolves, "and, as you know, this is no world for escapists." *Moral: Run, don't walk, to the nearest desert island.*

NICCOLÒ MACHIAVELLI
The Morals of the Prince[1]

On Things for Which Men, and Particularly Princes, Are Praised or Blamed

We now have left to consider what should be the manners and attitudes of a prince toward his subjects and his friends. As I know that many have written on this subject I feel that I may be held presumptuous in what I have to say, if in my comments I do not follow the lines laid down by others. Since, however, it has been my intention to write something which may be of use to the understanding reader, it has seemed wiser to me to follow the real truth of the matter rather than what we imagine it to be. For imagination has created many principalities and republics that have never been seen or known to have any real existence, for how we live is so different from how we ought to live that he who studies what ought to be done rather than what is done will learn the way to his downfall rather than to his preservation. A man striving in every way to be good will meet his ruin among the great number who are not good. Hence it is necessary for a prince, if he wishes to remain in power, to learn how not to be good and to use his knowledge or refrain from using it as he may need.

Putting aside then the things imagined as pertaining to a prince and considering those that really do, I will say that all men, and particularly princes because of their prominence, when comment is made of them, are noted as having some characteristics deserving either praise or blame. One is accounted liberal, another stingy, to use a Tuscan term—for in our speech avaricious (*avaro*) is applied to such as are desirous of acquiring by rapine whereas stingy (*misero*) is the term used for those who are reluctant to part with their own—one is considered bountiful, another rapacious; one cruel, another tender-hearted; one false to his word, another trustworthy; one effeminate and pusillanimous, another wild and spirited; one humane, another haughty; one lascivious, another chaste; one a man of integrity and another sly; one tough and another pliant; one serious and another frivolous; one religious and another skeptical, and so on. Everyone will agree, I know, that it would be a most praiseworthy thing if all the qualities accounted as good

1. Chapters 15-18 of *The Prince*.

in the above enumeration were found in a Prince. But since they cannot be so possessed nor observed because of human conditions which do not allow of it, what is necessary for the prince is to be prudent enough to escape the infamy of such vices as would result in the loss of his state; as for the others which would not have that effect, he must guard himself from them as far as possible but if he cannot, he may overlook them as being of less importance. Further, he should have no concern about incurring the infamy of such vices without which the preservation of his state would be difficult. For, if the matter be well considered, it will be seen that some habits which appear virtuous, if adopted would signify ruin, and others that seem vices lead to security and the well-being of a prince.

Generosity and Meanness

To begin then with the first characteristic set forth above, I will say that it would be well always to be considered generous, yet generosity used in such a way as not to bring you honor does you harm, for if it is practiced virtuously and as it is meant to be practiced it will not be publicly known and you will not lose the name of being just the opposite of generous. Hence to preserve the reputation of being generous among your friends you must not neglect any kind of lavish display, yet a prince of this sort will consume all his property in such gestures and, if he wishes to preserve his reputation for generosity, he will be forced to levy heavy taxes on his subjects and turn to fiscal measures and do everything possible to get money. Thus he will begin to be regarded with hatred by his subjects and should he become poor he will be held in scant esteem; having by his prodigality given offense to many and rewarded only a few, he will suffer at the first hint of adversity, and the first danger will be critical for him. Yet when he realizes this and tries to reform he will immediately get the name of being a miser. So a prince, as he is unable to adopt the virtue of generosity without danger to himself, must, if he is a wise man, accept with indifference the name of miser. For with the passage of time he will be regarded as increasingly generous when it is seen that, by virtue of his parsimony, his income suffices for him to defend himself in wartime and undertake his enterprises without heavily taxing his people. For in that way he practices generosity towards all from whom he refrains from taking money, who are many, and stinginess only toward those from whom he withholds gifts, who are few.

In our times we have seen great things accomplished only by such as have had the name of misers; all others have come to naught. Pope Julius made use of his reputation for generosity to make himself Pope but later, in order to carry on his war against the King of France, he made no effort to maintain it; and he has waged a great number of wars without having had recourse to heavy taxation because his persistent parsimony has made up for the extra expenses. The present King of Spain, had he had any reputation for generosity, would never have carried through to victory so many enterprises.

A prince then, if he wishes not to rob his subjects but to be able to defend himself and not to become poor and despised nor to be obliged to become rapacious, must consider it a matter of small importance to incur the name of miser, for this is one of the vices which keep him on his throne. Some may say Caesar through generosity won his way to the purple, and others either through being generous or being accounted so have risen to the highest ranks. But I will answer by pointing out that either you are already a prince or you are on the way to becoming one and in the first case generosity is harmful while in the second it is very necessary to be considered open-handed. Caesar was seeking to arrive at the domination of Rome but if he had survived after reaching his goal and had not moderated his lavishness he would certainly have destroyed the empire.

It might also be objected that there have been many princes, accomplishing great things with their armies, who have been acclaimed for their generosity. To which I would answer that the prince either spends his own (or his subjects') money or that of others; in the first case he must be very sparing but in the second he should overlook no aspect of open-handedness. So the prince who leads his armies and lives on looting and extortion and booty, thus handling the wealth of others, must indeed have this quality of generosity for otherwise his soldiers will not follow him. You can be very free with wealth not belonging to yourself or your subjects, in the fashion of Cyrus, Caesar, or Alexander, for spending what belongs to others rather enhances your reputation than detracts from it; it is only spending your own wealth that is dangerous. There is nothing that consumes itself as does prodigality; even as you practice it you lose the faculty of practicing it and either you become poor and despicable or, in order to escape poverty, rapacious and unpopular. And among the things a prince must guard against is precisely the danger of becoming an object either of contempt or of hatred. Generosity leads you to both these evils, wherefore it is wiser to accept the name of miserly, since the reproach it brings is without hatred, than to seek a reputation for generosity and thus perforce acquire the name of rapacious, which breeds hatred as well as infamy.

Cruelty and Clemency and Whether It Is Better to Be Loved or Feared

Now to continue with the list of characteristics. It should be the desire of every prince to be considered merciful and not cruel, yet he should take care not to make poor use of his clemency. Cesare Borgia was regarded as cruel, yet his cruelty reorganized Romagna and united it in peace and loyalty. Indeed, if we reflect, we shall see that this man was more merciful than the Florentines who, to avoid the charge of cruelty, allowed Pistoia to be destroyed.[2] A prince should care nothing for the accusation of cruelty so long as he keeps his subjects united and loyal; by making a very few examples he can be more truly merciful than those who through too much tender-heartedness allow disorders to arise whence come killings and rapine. For these offend an entire community, while the few executions ordered by the prince affect only a few individuals. For a new prince above all it is impossible not to earn a reputation for cruelty since new states are full of dangers. Virgil indeed has Dido apologize for the inhumanity of her rule because it is new, in the words:

> *Res dura et regni novitas me talia cogunt*
> *Moliri et late fines custode tueri.*[3]

Nevertheless a prince should not be too ready to listen to tale-bearers nor to act on suspicion, nor should he allow himself to be easily frightened. He should proceed with a mixture of prudence and humanity in such a way as not to be made incautious by over-confidence nor yet intolerable by excessive mistrust.

Here the question arises; whether it is better to be loved than feared or feared than loved. The answer is that it would be desirable to be both but, since that is difficult, it is much safer to be feared than to be loved, if one must choose. For on men in general this observation may be made: they are ungrateful, fickle, and deceitful, eager to avoid dangers, and avid for gain, and while you are useful to them they are all with you, offering you their blood, their property, their lives, and their sons so long as danger is remote, as we noted above, but when it approaches they turn on you. Any prince, trusting only in their words and having no other preparations made, will fall to his ruin, for friendships that are bought at a price and not by greatness and nobility of soul are paid for indeed, but they are not owned and cannot be called upon in time of need. Men have less hesitation in offending a man who is loved than one who is feared, for love is held by a bond of obligation which, as men are wicked, is broken whenever personal advantage suggests it, but fear is accompanied by the dread of punishment which never relaxes.

Yet a prince should make himself feared in such a way that, if he does not thereby merit love, at least he may escape odium, for being feared and not hated may well go together. And indeed the prince may attain this end if he but respect the property and the

2. By unchecked rioting between opposing factions (1502).
3. ". . . my cruel fate / And doubts attending an unsettled state / Force me to guard my coast from foreign foes"— DRYDEN.

women of his subjects and citizens. And if it should become necessary to seek the death of someone, he should find a proper justification and a public cause, and above all he should keep his hands off another's property, for men forget more readily the death of their father than the loss of their patrimony. Besides, pretexts for seizing property are never lacking, and when a prince begins to live by means of rapine he will always find some excuse for plundering others, and conversely pretexts for execution are rarer and are more quickly exhausted.

A prince at the head of his armies and with a vast number of soldiers under his command should give not the slightest heed if he is esteemed cruel, for without such a reputation he will not be able to keep his army united and ready for action. Among the marvelous things told of Hannibal is that, having a vast army under his command made up of all kinds and races of men and waging war far from his own country, he never allowed any dissension to arise either as between the troops and their leaders or among the troops themselves, and this both in times of good fortune and bad. This could only have come about through his most inhuman cruelty which, taken in conjunction with his great valor, kept him always an object of respect and terror in the eyes of his soldiers. And without the cruelty his other characteristics would not have achieved this effect. Thoughtless writers have admired his actions and at the same time deplored the cruelty which was the basis of them. As evidence of the truth of our statement that his other virtues would have been insufficient let us examine the case of Scipio, an extraordinary leader not only in his own day but for all recorded history. His army in Spain revolted and for no other reason than because of his kind-heartedness, which had allowed more license to his soldiery than military discipline properly permits. His policy was attacked in the Senate by Fabius Maximus, who called him a corrupter of the Roman arms. When the Locrians had been mishandled by one of his lieutenants, his easy-going nature prevented him from avenging them or disciplining his officer, and it was apropos of this incident that one of the senators remarked, wishing to find an excuse for him, that there were many men who knew better how to avoid error themselves than to correct it in others. This characteristic of Scipio would have clouded his fame and glory had he continued in authority, but as he lived under the government of the Senate, its harmful aspect was hidden and it reflected credit on him.

Hence, on the subject of being loved or feared I will conclude that since love depends on the subjects, but the prince has it in his own hands to create fear, a wise prince will rely on what is his own, remembering at the same time that he must avoid arousing hatred, as we have said.

In What Manner Princes Should Keep Their Word

How laudable it is for a prince to keep his word and govern his actions by integrity rather than trickery will be understood by all. Nonetheless we have in our times seen great things accomplished by many princes who have thought little of keeping their promises and have known the art of mystifying the minds of men. Such princes have won out over those whose actions were based on fidelity to their word.

It must be understood that there are two ways of fighting, one with laws and the other with arms. The first is the way of men, the second is the style of beasts, but since very often the first does not suffice it is necessary to turn to the second. Therefore a prince must know how to play the beast as well as the man. This lesson was taught allegorically by the ancient writers who related that Achilles and many other princes were brought up by Chiron the Centaur, who took them under his discipline. The clear significance of this half-man and half-beast preceptorship is that a prince must know how to use either of these two natures and that one without the other has no enduring strength. Now since the prince must make use of the characteristics of beasts he should choose those of the fox and the lion, though the lion cannot defend himself against snares and the fox is helpless against wolves. One must be a fox in avoiding traps and a lion in frightening wolves. Such as choose simply the rôle of a lion do not rightly understand the matter. Hence a wise leader cannot and should not keep his word when keeping it is not to his advantage or when the reasons that made him give it are no longer valid. If men were good, this would not be a good precept, but since they are wicked and will not keep faith with you, you are not bound to keep faith with them.

A prince has never lacked legitimate reasons to justify his breach of faith. We could give countless recent examples and show how any number of peace treaties or promises have been broken and rendered meaningless by the faithlessness of princes, and how success has fallen to the one who best knows how to counterfeit the fox. But it is necessary to know how to disguise this nature well and how to pretend and dissemble. Men are so simple and so ready to follow the needs of the moment that the deceiver will always find some one to deceive. Of recent examples I shall mention one. Alexander VI did nothing but deceive and never thought of anything else and always found some occasion for it. Never was there a man more convincing in his asseverations nor more willing to offer the most solemn oaths nor less likely to observe them. Yet his deceptions were always successful for he was an expert in this field.

So a prince need not have all the aforementioned good qualities, but it is most essential that he appear to have them. Indeed, I should go so far as to say that having them and always practising them is harmful, while seeming to have them is useful. It is good to appear clement, trustworthy, humane, religious, and honest, and also to be so, but always with the mind so disposed that, when the occasion arises not to be so, you can become the opposite. It must be understood that a prince and particularly a new prince cannot practise all the virtues for which men are accounted good, for the necessity of preserving the state often compels him to take actions which are opposed to loyalty, charity, humanity, and religion. Hence he must have a spirit ready to adapt itself as the varying winds of fortune command him. As I have said, so far as he is able, a prince should stick to the path of good but, if the necessity arises, he should know how to follow evil.

A prince must take great care that no word ever passes his lips that is not full of the above mentioned five good qualities, and he must seem to all who see and hear him a model of piety, loyalty, integrity, humanity, and religion. Nothing is more necessary than to seem to possess this last quality, for men in general judge more by the eye than the hand, as all can see but few can feel. Everyone sees what you seem to be, few experience what you really are and these few do not dare to set themselves up against the opinion of the majority supported by the majesty of the state. In the actions of all men and especially princes, where there is no court of appeal, the end is all that counts. Let a prince then concern himself with the acquisition or the maintenance of a state; the means employed will always be considered honorable and praised by all, for the mass of mankind is always swayed by appearances and by the outcome of an enterprise. And in the world there is only the mass, for the few find their place only when the majority has no base of support.

GARRETT HARDIN
The Tragedy of the Commons

At the end of a thoughtful article on the future of nuclear war, Wiesner and York[1] concluded that: "Both sides in the arms race are . . . confronted by the dilemma of steadily increasing military power and steadily decreasing national security. *It is our considered professional judgment that this dilemma has no technical solution.* If the great powers continue to look for solutions in the area of science and technology only, the result will be to worsen the situation."

I would like to focus your attention not on the subject of the article (national security in a nuclear world) but on the kind of

1. J. B. Wiesner and H. F. York, *Sci.* *Amer.* 211 (No. 4), 27 (1964) [Hardin's note].

conclusion they reached, namely that there is no technical solution to the problem. An implicit and almost universal assumption of discussions published in professional and semipopular scientific journals is that the problem under discussion has a technical solution. A technical solution may be defined as one that requires a change only in the techniques of the natural sciences, demanding little or nothing in the way of change in human values or ideas of morality.

In our day (though not in earlier times) technical solutions are always welcome. Because of previous failures in prophecy, it takes courage to assert that a desired technical solution is not possible. Wiesner and York exhibited this courage; publishing in a science journal, they insisted that the solution to the problem was not to be found in the natural sciences. They cautiously qualified their statement with the phrase, "It is our considered professional judgment. . . ." Whether they were right or not is not the concern of the present article. Rather, the concern here is with the important concept of a class of human problems which can be called "no technical solution problems," and, more specifically, with the identification and discussion of one of these.

It is easy to show that the class is not a null class. Recall the game of tick-tack-toe. Consider the problem, "How can I win the game of tick-tack-toe?" It is well known that I cannot, if I assume (in keeping with the conventions of game theory) that my opponent understands the game perfectly. Put another way, there is no "technical solution" to the problem. I can win only by giving a radical meaning to the word "win." I can hit my opponent over the head; or I can drug him; or I can falsify the records. Every way in which I "win" involves, in some sense, an abandonment of the game, as we intuitively understand it. (I can also, of course, openly abandon the game—refuse to play it. This is what most adults do.)

The class of "no technical solution problems" has members. My thesis is that the "population problem," as conventionally conceived, is a member of this class. How it is conventionally conceived needs some comment. It is fair to say that most people who anguish over the population problem are trying to find a way to avoid the evils of overpopulation without relinquishing any of the privileges they now enjoy. They think that farming the seas or developing new strains of wheat will solve the problem—technologically. I try to show here that the solution they seek cannot be found. The population problem cannot be solved in a technical way, any more than can the problem of winning the game of tick-tack-toe.

What Shall We Maximize?

Population, as Malthus said, naturally tends to grow "geometrically," or, as we would now say, exponentially. In a finite world this means that the per capita share of the world's goods must steadily decrease. Is ours a finite world?

A fair defense can be put forward for the view that the world is infinite; or that we do not know that it is not. But, in terms of the practical problems that we must face in the next few generations with the foreseeable technology, it is clear that we will greatly increase human misery if we do not, during the immediate future, assume that the world available to the terrestrial human population is finite. "Space" is no escape.[2]

A finite world can support only a finite population; therefore, population growth must eventually equal zero. (The case of perpetual wide fluctuations above and below zero is a trivial variant that need not be discussed.) When this condition is met, what will be the situation of mankind? Specifically, can Bentham's goal of "the greatest good for the greatest number" be realized?

No—for two reasons, each sufficient by itself. The first is a theoretical one. It is not mathematically possible to maximize for two (or more) variables at the same time. This was clearly stated by von Neumann and Morgenstern,[3] but the principle is implicit in the theory of partial differential equations, dating back at least to D'Alembert (1717–1783).

The second reason springs directly from biological facts. To live, any organism must have a source of energy (for example, food). This energy is utilized for two purposes: mere maintenance and work. For man, maintenance of life requires about 1600 kilo-calories a day ("maintenance calories"). Anything that he does over and above merely staying alive will be defined as work, and is supported by "work calories" which he takes in. Work calories are used not only for what we call work in common speech; they are also required for all forms of enjoyment, from swimming and automobile racing to playing music and writing poetry. If our goal is to maximize population it is obvious what we must do: We must make the work calories per person approach as close to zero as possible. No gourmet meals, no vacations, no sports, no music, no literature, no art. . . . I think that everyone will grant, without argument or proof, that maximizing population does not maximize goods. Bentham's goal is impossible.

In reaching this conclusion I have made the usual assumption that it is the acquisition of energy that is the problem. The appearance of atomic energy has led some to question this assumption. However, given an infinite source of energy, population growth still produces an inescapable problem. The problem of the acquisition of

2. G. Hardin, *J. Hered.* 50, 68 (1959); S. von Hoerner, *Science,* 137, 18 (1962) [Hardin's note].
3. J. von Neumann and O. Morgen-stern, *Theory of Games and Economic Behavior* (Princeton Univ. Press, Princeton, N.J., 1947), p. 11 [Hardin's note].

energy is replaced by the problem of its dissipation, as J. H. Fremlin has so wittily shown.[4] The arithmetic signs in the analysis are, as it were, reversed; but Bentham's goal is still unobtainable.

The optimum population is, then, less than the maximum. The difficulty of defining the optimum is enormous; so far as I know, no one has seriously tackled this problem. Reaching an acceptable and stable solution will surely require more than one generation of hard analytical work—and much persuasion.

We want the maximum good per person; but what is good? To one person it is wilderness, to another it is ski lodges for thousands. To one it is estuaries to nourish ducks for hunters to shoot; to another it is factory land. Comparing one good with another is, we usually say, impossible because goods are incommensurable. Incommensurables cannot be compared.

Theoretically this may be true; but in real life incommensurables *are* commensurable. Only a criterion of judgment and a system of weighting are needed. In nature the criterion is survival. Is it better for a species to be small and hideable, or large and powerful? Natural selection commensurates the incommensurables. The compromise achieved depends on a natural weighting of the values of the variables.

Man must imitate this process. There is no doubt that in fact he already does, but unconsciously. It is when the hidden decisions are made explicit that the arguments begin. The problem for the years ahead is to work out an acceptable theory of weighting. Synergistic effects, nonlinear variation, and difficulties in discounting the future make the intellectual problem difficult, but not (in principle) insoluble.

Has any cultural group solved this practical problem at the present time, even on an intuitive level? One simple fact proves that none has: there is no prosperous population in the world today that has, and has had for some time, a growth rate of zero. Any people that has intuitively identified its optimum point will soon reach it, after which its growth rate becomes and remains zero.

Of course, a positive growth rate might be taken as evidence that a population is below its optimum. However, by any reasonable standards, the most rapidly growing populations on earth today are (in general) the most miserable. This association (which need not be invariable) casts doubt on the optimistic assumption that the positive growth rate of a population is evidence that it has yet to reach its optimum.

We can make little progress in working toward optimum population size until we explicitly exorcize the spirit of Adam Smith in the field of practical demography. In economic affairs, *The Wealth of*

4. J. H. Fremlin, *New Sci.*, No. 415 (1964), p. 285 [Hardin's note].

Nations (1776) popularized the "invisible hand," the idea that an individual who "intends only his own gain," is, as it were, "led by an invisible hand to promote . . . the public interest."[5] Adam Smith did not assert that this was invariably true, and perhaps neither did any of his followers. But he contributed to a dominant tendency of thought that has ever since interfered with positive action based on rational analysis, namely, the tendency to assume that decisions reached individually will, in fact, be the best decisions for an entire society. If this assumption is correct it justifies the continuance of our present policy of laissez-faire in reproduction. If it is correct we can assume that men will control their individual fecundity so as to produce the optimum population. If the assumption is not correct, we need to reexamine our individual freedoms to see which ones are defensible.

Tragedy of Freedom in a Commons

The rebuttal to the invisible hand in population control is to be found in a scenario first sketched in a little-known pamphlet[6] in 1833 by a mathematical amateur named William Forster Lloyd (1794–1852). We may well call it "the tragedy of the commons," using the word "tragedy" as the philosopher Whitehead used it:[7] "The essence of dramatic tragedy is not unhappiness. It resides in the solemnity of the remorseless working of things." He then goes on to say, "This inevitableness of destiny can only be illustrated in terms of human life by incidents which in fact involve unhappiness. For it is only by them that the futility of escape can be made evident in the drama."

The tragedy of the commons develops in this way. Picture a pasture open to all. It is to be expected that each herdsman will try to keep as many cattle as possible on the commons. Such an arrangement may work reasonably satisfactorily for centuries because tribal wars, poaching, and disease keep the numbers of both man and beast well below the carrying capacity of the land. Finally, however, comes the day of reckoning, that is, the day when the long-desired goal of social stability becomes a reality. At this point, the inherent logic of the commons remorselessly generates tragedy.

As a rational being, each herdsman seeks to maximize his gain. Explicitly or implicitly, more or less consciously, he asks, "What is the utility *to me* of adding one more animal to my herd?" This utility has one negative and one positive component.

5. A. Smith, *The Wealth of Nations* (Modern Library, New York, 1937), p. 423 [Hardin's note].

6. W. F. Lloyd, *Two Lectures on the Checks to Population* (Oxford Univ. Press, Oxford, England, 1833), reprinted (in part) in *Population, Evolution, and Birth Control*, G. Hardin, ed. (Freeman, San Francisco, 1964), p. 37 [Hardin's note].

7. A. N. Whitehead, *Science and the Modern World* (Mentor, New York, 1948), p. 17 [Hardin's note].

1. The positive component is a function of the increment of one animal. Since the herdsman receives all the proceeds from the sale of the additional animal, the positive utility is nearly $+1$.

2. The negative component is a function of the additional overgrazing created by one more animal. Since, however, the effects of overgrazing are shared by all the herdsmen, the negative utility for any particular decision-making herdsman is only a fraction of -1.

Adding together the component partial utilities, the rational herdsman concludes that the only sensible course for him to pursue is to add another animal to his herd. And another; and another. . . . But this is the conclusion reached by each and every rational herdsman sharing a commons. Therein is the tragedy. Each man is locked into a system that compels him to increase his herd without limit—in a world that is limited. Ruin is the destination toward which all men rush, each pursuing his own best interest in a society that believes in the freedom of the commons. Freedom in a commons brings ruin to all.

Some would say that this is a platitude. Would that it were! In a sense, it was learned thousands of years ago, but natural selection favors the forces of psychological denial.[8] The individual benefits as an individual from his ability to deny the truth even though society as a whole, of which he is a part, suffers. Education can counteract the natural tendency to do the wrong thing, but the inexorable succession of generations requires that the basis for this knowledge be constantly refreshed.

A simple incident that occured a few years ago in Leominister, Massachusetts, shows how perishable the knowledge is. During the Christmas shopping season the parking meters downtown were covered with plastic bags that bore tags reading: "Do not open until after Christmas. Free parking courtesy of the mayor and city council." In other words, facing the prospect of an increased demand for already scarce space, the city fathers reinstituted the system of the commons. Cynically, we suspect that they gained more votes than they lost by this retrogressive act.)

In an approximate way, the logic of the commons has been understood for a long time, perhaps since the discovery of agriculture or the invention of private property in real estate. But it is understood mostly only in special cases which are not sufficiently generalized. Even at this late date, cattlemen leasing national land on the western ranges demonstrate no more than an ambivalent understanding, in constantly pressuring federal authorities to increase the head count to the point where overgrazing produces erosion and weed-dominance. Likewise, the oceans of the world continue to suffer

---

8. G. Hardin, Ed. *Population, Evolution, and Birth Conrtol* (Freeman, San Francisco, 1964), 56 [Hardin's note].

from the survival of the philosophy of the commons. Maritime nations still respond automatically to the shibboleth of the "freedom of the seas." Professing to believe in the "inexhaustible resources of the oceans," they bring species after species of fish and whales closer to extinction.[9]

The national parks present another instance of the working out of the tragedy of the commons. At present, they are open to all, without limit. The parks themselves are limited in extent—there is only one Yosemite Valley—whereas population seeems to grow without limit. The values that visitors seek in the parks are steadily eroded. Plainly, we must soon cease to treat the parks as commons or they will be of no value to anyone.

What shall we do? We have several options. We might sell them off as private property. We might keep them as public property, but allocate the right to enter them. The allocation might be on the basis of wealth, by the use of an auction system. It might be on the basis of merit, as defined by some agreed-upon standards. It might be by lottery. Or it might be on a first-come, first-served basis, administered to long queues. These, I think, are all the reasonable possibilities. They are all objectionable. But we must choose —or acquiesce in the destruction of the commons that we call our national parks.

Pollution

In a reverse way, the tragedy of the commons reappears in problems of pollution. Here it is not a question of taking something out of the commons, but of putting something in—sewage, or chemical, radioactive, and heat wastes into water; noxious and dangerous fumes into the air; and distracting and unpleasant advertising signs into the line of sight. The calculations of utility are much the same as before. The rational man finds that his share of the cost of the wastes he discharges into the commons is less than the cost of purifying his wastes before releasing them. Since this is true for everyone, we are locked into a system of "fouling our own nest," so long as we behave only as independent, rational, free-enterprisers.

The tragedy of the commons as a food basket is averted by private property, or something formally like it. But the air and waters surrounding us cannot readily be fenced, and so the tragedy of the commons as a cesspool must be prevented by different means, by coercive laws or taxing devices that make it cheaper for the polluter to treat his pollutants than to discharge them untreated. We have not progressed as far with the solution of this problem as we have with the first. Indeed, our particular concept of private property, which deters us from exhausting the positive resources of the earth,

9. S. McVay, *Sci. Amer.* 216 (No. 8), 13 (1966) [Hardin's note].

favors pollution. The owner of a factory on the bank of a stream—whose property extends to the middle of the stream—often has difficulty seeing why it is not his natural right to muddy the waters flowing past his door. The law, always behind the times, requires elaborate stitching and fitting to adapt it to this newly perceived aspect of the commons.

The pollution problem is a consequence of population. It did not much matter how a lonely American frontiersman disposed of his waste. "Flowing water purifies itself every ten miles," my grandfather used to say, and the myth was near enough to the truth when he was a boy, for there were not too many people. But as population became denser, the natural chemical and biological recycling processes became overloaded, calling for a redefinition of property rights.

How to Legislate Temperance?

Analysis of the pollution problem as a function of population density uncovers a not generally recognized principle of morality, namely: *the morality of an act is a function of the state of the system at the time it is performed.*[1] Using the commons as a cesspool does not harm the general public under frontier conditions, because there is no public; the same behavior in a metropolis is unbearable. A hundred and fifty years ago a plainsman could kill an American bison, cut out only the tongue for his dinner, and discard the rest of the animal. He was not in any important sense being wasteful. Today, with only a few thousand bison left, we would be appalled at such behavior.

In passing, it is worth noting that the morality of an act cannot be determined from a photograph. One does not know whether a man killing an elephant or setting fire to the grassland is harming others until one knows the total system in which his act appears. "One picture is worth a thousand words," said an ancient Chinese; but it may take 10,000 words to validate it. It is as tempting to ecologists as it is to reformers in general to try to persuade others by way of the photographic shortcut. But the essence of an argument cannot be photographed: it must be presented rationally—in words.

That morality is system-sensitive escaped the attention of most codifiers of ethics in the past. "Thou shalt not . . ." is the form of traditional ethical directives which make no allowance for particular circumstances. The laws of our society follow the pattern of ancient ethics, and therefore are poorly suited to governing a complex, crowded, changeable world. Our epicyclic solution is to augment statutory law with administrative law. Since it is practically impossible to spell out all the conditions under which it is safe to burn

1. J. Fletcher, *Situation Ethics* (Westminster, Philadelphia, 1966) [Hardin's note].

290 · Garrett Hardin

trash in the back yard or to run an automobile without smog-control, by law we delegate the details to bureaus. The result is administrative law, which is rightly feared for an ancient reason—*Quis custodiet ipsos custodes?*—"Who shall watch the watchers themselves?" John Adams said that we must have "a government of laws and not men." Bureau administrators, trying to evaluate the morality of acts in the total system, are singularly liable to corruption, producing a government by men, not laws.

Prohibition is easy to legislate (though not necessarily to enforce); but how do we legislate temperance? Experience indicates that it can be accomplished best through the mediation of administrative law. We limit possibilities unnecessarily if we suppose that the sentiment of *Quis custodiet* denies us the use of administrative law. We should rather retain the phrase as a perpetual reminder of fearful dangers we cannot avoid. The great challenge facing us now is to invent the corrective feedbacks that are needed to keep custodians honest. We must find ways to legitimate the needed authority of both the custodians and the corrective feedbacks.

Freedom to Breed Is Intolerable

The tragedy of the commons is involved in population problems in another way. In a world governed solely by the principle of "dog eat dog"—if indeed there ever was such a world—how many children a family had would not be a matter of public concern. Parents who bred too exuberantly would leave fewer descendants, not more, because they would be unable to care adequately for their children. David Lack and others have found that such a negative feedback demonstrably controls the fecundity of birds.[2] But men are not birds, and have not acted like them for millenniums, at least.

If each human family were dependent only on its own resources; if the children of improvident parents starved to death; if, thus, overbreeding brought its own "punishment" to the germ line—*then* there would be no public interest in controlling the breeding of families. But our society is deeply committed to the welfare state,[3] and hence is confronted with another aspect of the tragedy of the commons.

In a welfare state, how shall we deal with the family, the religion, the race, or the class (or indeed any distinguishable and cohesive group) that adopts overbreeding as a policy to secure its own aggrandizement?[4] To couple the concept of freedom to breed with the belief that everyone born has an equal right to the commons is to lock the world into a tragic course of action.

2. D. Lack, *The Natural Regulation of Animal Numbers* (Clarendon Press, Oxford, 1954 [Hardin's note].
3. H. Girvetz, *From Wealth to Welfare* (Stanford Univ. Press, Stanford, Calif., 1950) [Hardin's note].
4. G. Hardin, *Perspec. Biol. Med.* 6, 366 (1963) [Hardin's note].

Unfortunately this is just the course of action that is being pursued by the United Nations. In late 1967, some thirty nations agreed to the following:[5]

The Universal Declaration of Human Rights describes the family as the natural and fundamental unit of society. It follows that any choice and decision with regard to the size of the family must irrevocably rest with the family itself, and cannot be made by anyone else.

It is painful to have to deny categorically the validity of this right; denying it, one feels as uncomfortable as a resident of Salem, Massachusetts, who denied the reality of witches in the seventeenth century. At the present time, in liberal quarters, something like a taboo acts to inhibit criticism of the United Nations. There is a feeling that the United Nations is "our last and best hope," that we shouldn't find fault with it; we shouldn't play into the hands of the archconservatives. However, let us not forget what Robert Louis Stevenson said: "The truth that is suppressed by friends is the readiest weapon of the enemy." If we love the truth we must openly deny the validity of the Universal Declaration of Human Rights, even though it is promoted by the United Nations. We should also join with Kingsley Davis[6] in attempting to get Planned Parenthood-World Population to see the error of its ways in embracing the same tragic ideal.

Conscience Is Self-Eliminating

It is a mistake to think that we can control the breeding of mankind in the long run by an appeal to conscience. Charles Galton Darwin made this point when he spoke on the centennial of the publication of his grandfather's great book. The argument is straightforward and Darwinian.

People vary. Confronted with appeals to limit breeding, some people will undoubtedly respond to the plea more than others. Those who have more children will produce a larger fraction of the next generation than those with more susceptible consciences. The difference will be accentuated, generation by generation.

In C. G. Darwin's words: "It may well be that it would take hundreds of generations for the progenitive instinct to develop in this way, but if it should do so, nature would have taken her revenge, and the variety *Homo contracipiens*[7] would become extinct and would be replaced by the variety *Homo progenitivus*."[8]

The argument assumes that conscience or the desire for children

5. U. Thant, *Int. Planned Parenthood News*, No. 168 (February, 1968), p. 3 [Hardin's note].

6. K. Davis, *Science* 158, 730 (1967) [Hardin's note].

7. *Homo contracipiens* means "non-reproductive man," *homo progenitivus* "reproductive man."

8. S. Tax, ed., *Evolution after Darwin* (Univ. of Chicago Press, Chicago, 1960), vol. 2, p. 469 [Hardin's note].

(no matter which) is hereditary—but hereditary only in the most general formal sense. The result will be the same whether the attitude is transmitted through germ cells, or exosomatically, to use A. J. Lotka's term. (If one denies the latter possibility as well as the former, then what's the point of education?) The argument has here been stated in the context of the population problem, but it applies equally well to any instance in which society appeals to an individual exploiting a commons to restrain himself for the general good—by means of his conscience. To make such an appeal is to set up a selective system that works toward the elimination of conscience from the race.

Pathogenic Effects of Conscience

The long-term disadvantage of an appeal to conscience should be enough to condemn it; but it has serious short-term disadvantages as well. If we ask a man who is exploiting a commons to desist "in the name of conscience," what are we saying to him? What does he hear?—not only at the moment but also in the wee small hours of the night when, half asleep, he remembers not merely the words we used but also the nonverbal communications cues we gave him unawares? Sooner or later, consciously or subconsciously, he senses that he has received two communications, and that they are contradictory: (i) (intended communication) "If you don't do as we ask, we will openly condemn you for not acting like a responsible citizen"; (ii) (the unintended communication) "If you *do* behave as we ask, we will secretly condemn you for a simpleton who can be shamed into standing aside while the rest of us exploit the commons."

Every man then is caught in what Bateson has called a "double bind." Bateson and his coworkers have made a plausible case for viewing the double bind as an important causative factor in the genesis of schizophrenia.[9] The double bind may not always be so damaging, but it always endangers the mental health of anyone to whom it is applied. "A bad conscience," said Nietzsche, "is a kind of illness."

To conjure up a conscience in others is tempting to anyone who wishes to extend his control beyond the legal limits. Leaders at the highest level succumb to this temptation. Has any president during the past generation failed to call on labor unions to moderate voluntarily their demands for higher wages, or to steel companies to honor voluntary guidelines on prices? I can recall none. The rhetoric used on such occasions is designed to produce feelings of guilt in noncooperators.

For centuries it was assumed without proof that guilt was a valua-

9. G. Bateson, D. D. Jackson, J.   (1956) [Hardin's note].
Haley, J. Weakland, *Behav. Sci.* 1, 251

ble, perhaps even an indispensable, ingredient of the civilized life. Now, in this post-Freudian world, we doubt it.

Paul Goodman speaks from the modern point of view when he says: "No good has ever come from feeling guilty, neither intelligence, policy, nor compassion. The guilty do not pay attention to the object but only to themselves, and not even to their own interests, which might make sense, but to their anxieties."[1]

One does not have to be a professional psychiatrist to see the consequences of anxiety. We in the Western world are just emerging from a dreadful two-centuries-long Dark Ages of Eros that was sustained partly by prohibition laws, but perhaps more effectively by the anxiety-generating mechanisms of education. Alex Comfort has told the story well in *The Anxiety Makers;*[2] it is not a pretty one.

Since proof is difficult, we may even concede that the results of anxiety may sometimes, from certain points of view, be desirable. The larger question we should ask is whether, as a matter of policy, we should ever encourage the use of a technique the tendency (if not the intention) of which is psychologically pathogenic. We hear much talk these days of responsible parenthood; the coupled words are incorporated into the titles of some organizations devoted to birth control. Some people have proposed massive propaganda campaigns to instill responsibility into the nation's (or the world's) breeders, But what is the meaning of the word responsibility in this context? Is it not merely a synonym for the word conscience? When we use the word responsibility in the absence of substantial sanctions are we not trying to browbeat a free man in a commons into acting against his own interest? Responsibility is a verbal counterfeit for a substantial *quid pro quo.* It is an attempt to get something for nothing.

If the word responsibility is to be used at all, I suggest that it be in the sense Charles Frankel uses it.[3] "Responsibility," says this philosopher, "is the product of definite social arrangements." Notice that Frankel calls for social arrangements—not propaganda.

Mutual Coercion Mutually Agreed Upon

The social arrangements that produce responsibility are arrangements that create coercion, of some sort. Consider bank-robbing. The man who takes money from a bank acts as if the bank were a commons. How do we prevent such action? Certainly not by trying to control his behavior solely by a verbal appeal to his sense of responsibility. Rather than rely on propaganda we follow Frankel's lead and insist that a bank is not a commons; we seek the definite social

1. P. Goodman, *New York Rev. Books* 10 (18), 22 (23 May 1968) [Hardin's note].

2. A. Comfort, *The Anxiety Makers* (Nelson, London, 1967) [Hardin's note].

3. C. Frankel, *The Case for Modern Man* (Harper, New York, 1955), p. 203 [Hardin's note].

arrangements that will keep it from becoming a commons. That we thereby infringe on the freedom of would-be robbers we neither deny nor regret.

The morality of bank-robbing is particularly easy to understand because we accept complete prohibition of this activity. We are willing to say "Thou shalt not rob banks," without providing for exceptions. But temperance also can be created by coercion. Taxing is a good coercive device. To keep downtown shoppers temperate in their use of parking space we introduce parking meters for short periods, and traffic fines for longer ones. We need not actually forbid a citizen to park as long as he wants to; we need merely make it increasingly expensive for him to do so. Not prohibition, but carefully biased options are what we offer him. A Madison Avenue man might call this persuasion; I prefer the greater candor of the word coercion.

Coercion is a dirty word to most liberals now, but it need not forever be so. As with the four-letter words, its dirtiness can be cleansed away by exposure to the light, by saying it over and over without apology or embarrassment. To many, the word coercion implies arbitrary decisions of distant and irresponsible bureaucrats; but this is not a necessary part of its meaning. The only kind of coercion I recommend is mutual coercion, mutually agreed upon by the majority of the people affected.

To say that we mutually agree to coercion is not to say that we are required to enjoy it, or even to pretend we enjoy it. Who enjoys taxes? We all grumble about them. But we accept compulsory taxes because we recognize that voluntary taxes would favor the conscienceless. We institute and (grumblingly) support taxes and other coercive devices to escape the horror of the commons.

An alternative to the commons need not be perfectly just to be preferable. With real estate and other material goods, the alternative we have chosen is the institution of private property coupled with legal inheritance. Is this system perfectly just? As a genetically trained biologist I deny that it is. It seems to me that, if there are to be differences in individual inheritance, legal possession should be perfectly correlated with biological inheritance—that those who are biologically more fit to be the custodians of property and power should legally inherit more. But genetic recombination continually makes a mockery of the doctrine of "like father, like son" implicit in our laws of legal inheritance. An idiot can inherit millions, and a trust fund can keep his estate intact. We must admit that our legal system of private property plus inheritance is unjust—but we put up with it because we are not convinced, at the moment, that anyone has invented a better system. The alternative of the commons is too horrifying to contemplate. Injustice is preferable to total ruin.

It is one of the peculiarities of the warfare between reform and the status quo that it is thoughtlessly governed by a double standard. Whenever a reform measure is proposed it is often defeated when its opponents triumphantly discover a flaw in it. As Kingsley Davis has pointed out,[4] worshippers of the status quo sometimes imply that no reform is possible without unanimous agreement, an implication contrary to historical fact. As nearly as I can make out, automatic rejection of proposed reforms is based on one of two unconscious assumptions: (i) that the status quo is perfect; or (ii) that the choice we face is between reform and no action; if the proposed reform is imperfect, we presumably should take no action at all, while we wait for a perfect proposal.

But we can never do nothing. That which we have done for thousands of years is also action. It also produces evils. Once we are aware that the status quo is action, we can then compare its discoverable advantages and disadvantages with the predicted advantages and disadvantages of the proposed reform, discounting as best we can for our lack of experience. On the basis of such a comparison, we can make a rational decision which will not involve the unworkable assumption that only perfect systems are tolerable.

Recognition of Necessity

Perhaps the simplest summary of this analysis of man's population problems is this: the commons, if justifiable at all, is justifiable only under conditions of low-population density. As the human population has increased, the commons has had to be abandoned in one aspect after another.

First we abandoned the commons in food gathering, enclosing farm land and restricting pastures and hunting and fishing areas. These restrictions are still not complete throughout the world.

Somewhat later we saw that the commons as a place for waste disposal would also have to be abandoned. Restrictions on the disposals of domestic sewage are widely accepted in the Western world; we are still struggling to close the commons to pollution by automobiles, factories, insecticide sprayers, fertilizing operations, and atomic energy installations.

In a still more embryonic state is our recognition of the evils of the commons in matters of pleasure. There is almost no restriction on the propagation of sound waves in the public medium. The shopping public is assaulted with mindless music, without its consent. Our government is paying out billions of dollars to create supersonic transport which will disturb 50,000 people for every one person who is whisked from coast to coast three hours faster. Adver-

---

4. J. D. Roslansky, *Genetics and the Future of Man* (Appleton-Century-Crofts, New York, 1966), p. 177 [Hardin's note].

tisers muddy the airwaves of radio and television and pollute the view of travelers. We are a long way from outlawing the commons in matters of pleasure. Is this because our Puritan inheritance makes us view pleasure as something of a sin, and pain (that is, the pollution of advertising) as the sign of virtue?

Every new enclosure of the commons involves the infringement of somebody's personal liberty. Infringements made in the distant past are accepted because no contemporary complains of a loss. It is the newly proposed infringements that we vigorously oppose; cries of "rights" and "freedom" fill the air. But what does "freedom" mean? When men mutually agreed to pass laws against robbing, mankind became more free, not less so. Individuals locked into the logic of the commons are free only to bring on universal ruin; once they see the necessity of mutual coercion, they become free to pursue other goals. I believe it was Hegel who said, "Freedom is the recognition of necessity."

The most important aspect of necessity that we must now recognize, is the necessity of abandoning the commons in breeding. No technical solution can rescue us from the misery of overpopulation. Freedom to breed will bring ruin to all. At the moment, to avoid hard deeisions many of us are tempted to propagandize for conscience and responsible parenthood. The temptation must be resisted, because an appeal to independently acting consciences selects for the the disappearance of all conscience in the long run, and an increase in anxiety in the short.

The only way we can preserve and nurture other and more precious freedoms is by relinquishing the freedom to breed, and that very soon. "Freedom is the recognition of necessity"—and it is the role of education to reveal to all the necessity of abandoning the freedom to breed. Only so, can we put an end to this aspect of the tragedy of the commons.

E. B. WHITE

Democracy

July 3, 1943

We received a letter from the Writers' War Board the other day asking for a statement on "The Meaning of Democracy." It presumably is our duty to comply with such a request, and it is certainly our pleasure.

Surely the Board knows what democracy is. It is the line that forms on the right. It is the don't in don't shove. It is the hole in the stuffed shirt through which the sawdust slowly trickles; it is the dent in the high hat. Democracy is the recurrent suspicion that more than half of the people are right more than half of the time. It is the feeling of privacy in the voting booths, the feeling of communion in the libraries, the feeling of vitality everywhere. Democracy is a letter to the editor. Democracy is the score at the beginning of the ninth. It is an idea which hasn't been disproved yet, a song the words of which have not gone bad. It's the mustard on the hot dog and the cream in the rationed coffee. Democracy is a request from a War Board, in the middle of a morning in the middle of a war, wanting to know what democracy is.

QUESTIONS

1. White's piece is dated July 3, 1943, the middle of World War II. How did the occasion shape what White says about democracy?
2. Look up "democracy" in a standard desk dictionary. Of the several meanings given, which one best applies to White's definition (below)? Does more than one apply?
3. Translate White's definition into non-metaphorical language. (For example, "It is the line that forms on the right" might be translated by "It has no special privileges.") Determine what is lost in the translation, or, in other words, what White has gained by using figurative language.

CARL BECKER

Democracy[1]

Democracy, like liberty or science or progress, is a word with which we are all so familiar that we rarely take the trouble to ask what we mean by it. It is a term, as the devotees of semantics say, which has no "referent"—there is no precise or palpable thing or object which we all think of when the word is pronounced. On the contrary, it is a word which connotes different things to different people, a kind of conceptual Gladstone bag which, with a little manipulation, can be made to accommodate almost any collection of social facts we may wish to carry about in it. In it we can as easily pack a dictatorship as any other form of government. We have only to stretch the concept to include any form of government supported by a majority of the people, for whatever reasons and by whatever means of expressing assent, and before we know it the empire of Napoleon, the Soviet regime of Stalin, and the Fascist systems of Mussolini and Hitler are all safely in the bag. But if this is what we mean by democracy, then virtually all forms of government are democratic, since virtually all governments, except

1. From Lecture I, "The Ideal," in *Modern Democracy*, 1941.

in times of revolution, rest upon the explicit or implicit consent of the people. In order to discuss democracy intelligently it will be necessary, therefore, to define it, to attach to the word a sufficiently precise meaning to avoid the confusion which is not infrequently the chief result of such discussions.

All human institutions, we are told, have their ideal forms laid away in heaven, and we do not need to be told that the actual institutions conform but indifferently to these ideal counterparts. It would be possible then to define democracy either in terms of the ideal or in terms of the real form—to define it as government of the people, by the people, for the people; or to define it as government of the people, by the politicians, for whatever pressure groups can get their interests taken care of. But as a historian I am naturally disposed to be satisfied with the meaning which, in the history of politics, men have commonly attributed to the word—a meaning, needless to say, which derives partly from the experience and partly from the aspirations of mankind. So regarded, the term democracy refers primarily to a form of government, and it has always meant government by the many as opposed to government by the one—government by the people as opposed to government by a tyrant, a dictator, or an absolute monarch. This is the most general meaning of the word as men have commonly understood it.

In this antithesis there are, however, certain implications, always tacitly understood, which give a more precise meaning to the term. Peisistratus, for example, was supported by a majority of the people, but his government was never regarded as a democracy for all that. Caesar's power derived from a popular mandate, conveyed through established republican forms, but that did not make his government any the less a dictatorship. Napoleon called his government a democratic empire, but no one, least of all Napoleon himself, doubted that he had destroyed the last vestiges of the democratic republic. Since the Greeks first used the term, the essential test of democratic government has always been this: the source of political authority must be and remain in the people and not in the ruler. A democratic government has always meant one in which the citizens, or a sufficient number of them to represent more or less effectively the common will, freely act from time to time, and according to established forms, to appoint or recall the magistrates and to enact or revoke the laws by which the community is governed. This I take to be the meaning which history has impressed upon the term democracy as a form of government.

On History

HENRY DAVID THOREAU
The Battle of the Ants[1]

One day when I went out to my wood-pile, or rather my pile of stumps, I observed two large ants, the one red, the other much larger, nearly half an inch long, and black, fiercely contending with one another. Having once got hold they never let go, but struggled and wrestled and rolled on the chips incessantly. Looking farther, I was surprised to find that the chips were covered with such combatants, that it was not a *duellum*, but a *bellum*, a war between two races of ants, the red always pitted against the black, and frequently two red ones to one black. The legions of these Myrmidons covered all the hills and vales in my wood-yard, and the ground was already strewn with the dead and dying, both red and black. It was the only battle which I have ever witnessed, the only battle-field I ever trod while the battle was raging; internecine war; the red republicans on the one hand, and the black imperialists on the other. On every side they were engaged in deadly combat, yet without any noise that I could hear, and human soldiers never fought so resolutely. I watched a couple that were fast locked in each other's embraces, in a little sunny valley amid the chips, now at noonday prepared to fight till the sun went down, or life went out. The smaller red champion had fastened himself like a vice to his adversary's front, and through all the tumblings on that field never for an instant ceased to gnaw at one of his feelers near the root, having already caused the other to go by the board; while the stronger black one dashed him from side to side, and, as I saw on looking nearer, had already divested him of several of his members. They fought with more pertinacity than bulldogs. Neither manifested the least disposi-

1. From "Brute Neighbors," Chapter XII of *Walden*.

299

tion to retreat. It was evident that their battle-cry was "Conquer or die." In the meanwhile there came along a single red ant on the hillside of this valley, evidently full of excitement, who either had despatched his foe, or had not yet taken part in the battle; probably the latter, for he had lost none of his limbs; whose mother had charged him to return with his shield or upon it. Or perchance he was some Achilles, who had nourished his wrath apart, and had now come to avenge or rescue his Patroclus.[2] He saw this unequal combat from afar—for the blacks were nearly twice the size of the red—he drew near with rapid pace till he stood on his guard within half an inch of the combatants; then, watching his opportunity, he sprang upon the black warrior, and commenced his operations near the root of his right fore leg, leaving the foe to select among his own members; and so there were three united for life, as if a new kind of attraction had been invented which put all other locks and cements to shame. I should not have wondered by this time to find that they had their respective musical bands stationed on some eminent chip, and playing their national airs the while, to excite the slow and cheer the dying combatants. I was myself excited somewhat even as if they had been men. The more you think of it, the less the difference. And certainly there is not the fight recorded in Concord history, at least, if in the history of America, that will bear a moment's comparison with this, whether for the numbers engaged in it, or for the patriotism and heroism displayed. For numbers and for carnage it was an Austerlitz or Dresden.[3] Concord Fight! Two killed on the patriots' side, and Luther Blanchard wounded! Why here every ant was a Buttrick—"Fire! for God's sake fire!"—and thousands shared the fate of Davis and Hosmer. There was not one hireling there. I have no doubt that it was a principle they fought for, as much as our ancestors, and not to avoid a three-penny tax on their tea; and the results of this battle will be as important and memorable to those whom it concerns as those of the battle of Bunker Hill, at least.

I took up the chip on which the three I have particularly described were struggling, carried into my house, and placed it under a tumbler on my window-sill, in order to see the issue. Holding a microscope to the first-mentioned red ant, I saw that, though he was assiduously gnawing at the near fore leg of his enemy, having severed his remaining feeler, his own breast was all torn away, exposing what vitals he had there to the jaws of the black warrior, whose breastplate was apparently too thick for him to pierce; and the dark carbuncles of the sufferer's eyes shone with ferocity such as war only could excite. They struggled half an hour longer under the tumbler, and when I looked again the black soldier had severed the heads of his foes from their bodies, and the still living heads were hanging on

2. A Greek warrior in the *Iliad*, whose death Achilles avenges.
3. Bloody Napoleonic victories.

either side of him like ghastly trophies at his saddle-bow, still apparently as firmly fastened as ever, and he was endeavoring with feeble struggles, being without feelers, and with only the remnant of a leg, and I know not how many other wounds, to divest himself of them; which at length, after half an hour more, he accomplished. I raised the glass, and he went off over the window-sill in that crippled state. Whether he finally survived that combat, and spent the remainder of his days in some Hôtel des Invalides, I do not know; but I thought that his industry would not be worth much thereafter. I never learned which party was victorious, nor the cause of the war, but I felt for the rest of that day as if I had my feelings excited and harrowed by witnessing the struggle, the ferocity and carnage, of a human battle before my door.

Kirby and Spence tell us that the battles of ants have long been celebrated and the date of them recorded, though they say that Huber[4] is the only modern author who appears to have witnessed them. "Aeneas Sylvius," say they, "after giving a very circumstantial account of one contested with great obstinacy by a great and small species on the trunk of a pear tree," adds that " 'this action was fought in the pontificate of Eugenius the Fourth, in the presence of Nicholas Pistoriensis, an eminent lawyer, who related the whole history of the battle with the greatest fidelity.' A similar engagement between great and small ants is recorded by Olaus Magnus, in which the small ones, being victorious, are said to have buried the bodies of their own soldiers, but left those of their giant enemies a prey to the birds. This event happened previous to the expulsion of the tyrant Christiern the Second from Sweden." The battle which I witnessed took place in the Presidency of Polk, five years before the passage of Webster's Fugitive-Slave Bill.

4. Kirby and Spence were nineteenth-century American entomologists; Huber was a great Swiss entomologist.

QUESTIONS

1. Thoreau uses the Latin word *bellum* to describe the struggle of the ants and he quickly follows this with a reference to the Myrmidons of Achilles. What comparison is implicit here? Find further examples of it. This passage comes from a chapter entitled *"Brute Neighbors"*; how does this comparison amplify the meaning of that title?
2. Describe the life, or part of the life, of an animal so that, while remaining faithful to the facts as you understand them, your description opens outward, as does that of Thoreau.

DEE BROWN
The War for the Black Hills[1]

Not long after Red Cloud and Spotted Tail and their Teton peoples settled down on their reservations in northwestern Nebraska,
rumors began to fly among the white settlements that immense
amounts of gold were hidden in the Black Hills. *Paha Sapa*, the
Black Hills, was the center of the world, the place of gods and holy
mountains, where warriors went to speak with the Great Spirit and
await visions. In 1868 the Great Father considered the hills worthless and gave them to the Indians forever by treaty. Four years
later white miners were violating the treaty. They invaded *Paha
Sapa*, searching the rocky passes and clear-running streams for the
yellow metal which drove white men crazy. When Indians found
these crazy white men in their sacred hills, they killed them or
chased them out. By 1874 there was such a mad clamor from gold-
hungry Americans that the Army was ordered to make a reconnaissance into the Black Hills. The United States government did
not bother to obtain consent from the Indians before starting on
this armed invasion, although the treaty of 1868 prohibited entry
of white men without the Indians' permission.

During the Moon of Red Cherries, more than a thousand pony
soldiers marched across the Plains from Fort Abraham Lincoln to
the Black Hills. They were the Seventh Cavalry, and at their head
rode General George Armstrong Custer, the same Star Chief who in
1868 had slaughtered Black Kettle's Southern Cheyennes on the
Washita. The Sioux called him Pahuska, the Long Hair, and because
they had no warning of his coming, they could only watch from
afar as the long columns of blue-uniformed cavalrymen and canvas-
covered supply wagons invaded their sacred country.

When Red Cloud heard about the Long Hair's expedition, he
protested: "I do not like General Custer and all his soldiers going
into the Black Hills, as that is the country of the Oglala Sioux." It
was also the country of the Cheyennes, Arapahos, and other Sioux
tribes. The anger of the Indians was strong enough that the Great
Father, Ulysses Grant, announced his determination "to prevent all
invasion of this country by intruders so long as by law and treaty it
is secured to the Indians."[2]

But when Custer reported that the hills were filled with gold
"from the grass roots down," parties of white men began forming
like summer locusts, crazy to begin panning and digging. The trail

1. From *Bury My Heart at Wounded*   2. New York *Herald*, August 27 and
Knee, 1971. (All footnotes are Brown's.)   September 25, 1874.

that Custer's supply wagons had cut into the heart of *Paha Sapa* soon became the Thieves' Road.

Red Cloud was having trouble that summer with his reservation agent, J. J. Saville, over the poor quality of rations and supplies being issued to the Oglalas. Preoccupied as he was, Red Cloud failed to assess the full impact upon the Sioux of Custer's intrusion into the Black Hills, especially upon those who left the reservations every spring to hunt and camp near the hills. Like many other aging leaders, Red Cloud was too much involved with petty details, and he was losing touch with the younger tribesmen.

In the autumn following Custer's expedition, the Sioux who had been hunting in the north began returning to the Red Cloud agency. They were angry as hornets over the invasion of *Paha Sapa*, and some talked of forming a war party to go back after the miners who were pouring into the hills. Red Cloud listened to the talk, but advised the young men to be patient; he was sure the Great Father would keep his promise and send soldiers to drive out the miners. In the Moon of Falling Leaves, however, something happened that made Red Cloud realize just how angry his young men were at the Long Hair's soldiers. On October 22 agent Saville sent some of his white workmen to cut a tall pine and bring the trunk back to the stockade. When the Indians saw the pine pole lying on the ground they asked Saville what it was to be used for. A flagpole, the agent told them; he was going to fly a flag over the stockade. The Indians protested. Long Hair Custer had flown flags in his camps across the Black Hills; they wanted no flags or anything else in their agency to remind them of soldiers.

Saville paid no attention to the protests, and next morning he put his men to work digging a hole for the flagpole. In a few minutes a band of young warriors came with axes and began chopping the pole to pieces. Saville ordered them to stop, but they paid no attention to him, and the agent strode across to Red Cloud's office and begged him to stop the warriors. Red Cloud refused; he knew the warriors were only expressing their rancor over the Long Hair's invasion of the Black Hills.

Infuriated, Saville now ordered one of his workmen to ride to the Soldiers' Town (Fort Robinson) and request a company of cavalrymen to come to his aid. When the demonstrating warriors saw the man riding toward the fort, they guessed his mission. They rushed for their tepee camps, armed and painted themselves for battle, and went to intercept the cavalrymen. There were only twenty-six Bluecoats led by a lieutenant; the warriors encircled them, fired their guns into the air, and yelled a few war cries. The lieutenant (Emmet Crawford) betrayed no fear. Through the great cloud of dust thrown up by the milling warriors, he kept his men moving steadily toward the agency. Some of the younger warriors began riding in close, colliding their ponies with the troopers' mounts, determined to precipitate a fight.

This time it was not another troop of cavalry which came galloping to Lieutenant Crawford's rescue, but a band of agency Sioux led by Young-Man-Afraid-of-His-Horses, son of Old-Man-Afraid. The agency Indians broke through the ring of warriors, formed a protective wall around the Bluecoats, and escorted them on to the stockade. The belligerent warriors were still so angry, however, that they tried to burn down the stockade, and only the persuasive oratory of Red Dog and Old-Man-Afraid-of-His-Horses stopped the demonstration.

Again Red Cloud refused to interfere. He was not surprised when many of the protesters packed up, dismantled their tepees, and started back north to spend the winter off the reservation. They had proved to him that there were still Sioux warriors who would never take lightly any invasion of *Paha Sapa*, yet apparently Red Cloud did not realize that he was losing these young men forever. They had rejected his leadership for that of Sitting Bull and Crazy Horse, neither of whom had ever lived on a reservation or taken the white man's handouts.

By the spring of 1875, tales of Black Hills gold had brought hundreds of miners up the Missouri River and out upon the Thieves' Road. The Army sent soldiers to stop the flow of prospectors. A few were removed from the hills, but no legal action was taken against them, and they soon returned to prospect their claims. General Crook (the Plains Indians called him Three Stars instead of Gray Wolf) made a reconnaissance of the Black Hills, and found more than a thousand miners in the area. Three Stars politely informed them that they were violating the law and ordered them to leave, but he made no effort to enforce his orders.

Alarmed by the white men's gold craze and the Army's failure to protect their territory, Red Cloud and Spotted Tail made strong protests to Washington officials. The Great Father's response was to send out a commission "to treat with the Sioux Indians for the relinquishment of the Black Hills." In other words, the time had come to take away one more piece of territory that had been assigned to the Indians in perpetuity. As usual, the commission was made up of politicians, missionaries, traders, and military officers. Senator William B. Allison of Iowa was the chairman. Reverend Samuel D. Hinman, who had long endeavored to replace the Santees' religion and culture with Christianity, was the principal missionary. General Alfred Terry represented the military. John Collins, post trader at Fort Laramie, represented the commercial interests.

To ensure representation of nonagency as well as agency Indians, runners were sent to invite Sitting Bull, Crazy Horse, and other "wild" chiefs to the council. Half-breed Louis Richard took the government letter to Sitting Bull and read it to him. "I want you to go and tell the Great Father," Sitting Bull responded, "that I do not want to sell any land to the government." He picked up a pinch of dust and added: "Not even as much as this."[3] Crazy Horse was also opposed to the selling of Sioux land, especially the Black Hills. He refused to attend the council, but Little Big Man would go as an observer for the free Oglalas.

If the commissioners expected to meet quietly with a few compliant chiefs and arrange an inexpensive trade, they were in for a rude surprise. When they arrived at the meeting place—on White River between the Red Cloud and Spotted Tail agencies—the Plains for miles around were covered with Sioux camps and immense herds of grazing ponies. From the Missouri River on the east to the Bighorn country on the west, all the nations of the Sioux and many of their Cheyenne and Arapaho friends had gathered there—more than twenty thousand Indians.

Few of them had ever seen a copy of the treaty of 1868, but a goodly number knew the meaning of a certain clause in that sacred document: "No treaty for the cession of any part of the reservation herein described . . . shall be of any validity or force . . . unless executed and signed by at least *three-fourths of all the adult male Indians,* occupying or interested in the same."[4] Even if the commissioners had been able to intimidate or buy off every chief present, they could not have obtained more than a few dozen signatures from those thousands of angry, well-armed warriors who were determined to keep every pinch of dust and blade of grass within their territory. On September 20, 1875, the commission assembled under the shade of a large tarpaulin which had been strung beside a lone cottonwood on the rolling plain. The commissioners seated themselves on chairs facing the thousands of Indians who were moving restlessly about in the distance. A troop of 120 cavalrymen on white horses filed in from Fort Robinson and drew up in a line behind the canvas shelter. Spotted Tail arrived in a wagon from his agency, but Red Cloud had announced that he would not be there. A few other chiefs drifted in, and then suddenly a cloud of dust boiled up from the crest of a distant rise. A band of Indians came galloping down upon the council shelter. The warriors were dressed for battle, and as they came nearer they swerved to encircle the commissioners, fired their rifles skyward, and gave out a few whoops before trotting off to form a line immediately in the rear of the cavalrymen. By this time a second band of Indians was approaching, and thus tribe by tribe the Sioux warriors came in, making their demonstrations of power, until a great circle of several thousand Indians enclosed the

3. Gilbert, Hila. *"Big Bat" Pourier.* Sheridan, Wyoming, Mills Company, 1968, p. 43.

4. Kappler, Charles J. *Indian Affairs, Laws and Treaties.* Vol. 2, p. 1002.

council. Now the chiefs came forward, well satisfied that they had given the commissioners something strong to think about. They sat in a semicircle facing the nervous white men, eager to hear what they would have to say about the Black Hills.

During the few days that the commissioners had been at Fort Robinson observing the mood of the Indians, they recognized the futility of trying to buy the hills and had decided instead to negotiate for the mineral rights. "We have now to ask you if you are willing to give our people the right to mine in the Black Hills," Senator Allison began, "as long as gold or other valuable minerals are found, for a fair and just sum. If you are so willing, we will make a bargain with you for this right. When the gold or other valuable minerals are taken away, the country will again be yours to dispose of in any manner you may wish."

Spotted Tail took this proposal as a ludicrous joke. Was the commissioner asking the Indians to *lend* the Black Hills to the white men for a while? His rejoinder was to ask Senator Allison if he would lend him a team of mules on such terms.

"It will be hard for our government to keep the whites out of the hills," Allison continued. "To try to do so will give you and our government great trouble, because the whites that may wish to go there are very numerous." The senator's ignorance of the Plains Indians' feeling for the Powder River country was displayed in his next proposal: "There is another country lying far toward the setting sun, over which you roam and hunt, and which territory is yet unceded, extending to the summit of the Bighorn Mountains. . . . It does not seem to be of very great value or use to you, and our people think they would like to have the portion of it I have described."[5]

While Senator Allison's incredible demands were being translated, Red Dog rode up on a pony and announced that he had a message from Red Cloud. The absent Oglala chief, probably anticipating the greed of the commissioners, requested a week's recess to give the tribes time to hold councils of their own in which to consider all proposals concerning their lands. The commissioners considered the matter and agreed to give the Indians three days for holding tribal councils. On September 23 they would expect definite replies from the chiefs.

The idea of giving up their last great hunting ground was so preposterous that none of the chiefs even discussed it during their councils. They did debate very earnestly the question of the Black Hills. Some reasoned that if the United States government had no intention of enforcing the treaty and keeping the white miners out, then perhaps the Indians should demand payment—a great deal of mon-

ey—for the yellow metal taken from the hills. Others were determined not to sell at any price. The Black Hills belonged to the
Indians, they argued; if the Bluecoat soldiers would not drive out
the miners, then the warriors must.

On September 23 the commissioners, riding in Army ambulances
from Fort Robinson and escorted by a somewhat enlarged cavalry
troop, again arrived at the council shelter. Red Cloud was there
early, and he protested vigorously about the large number of soldiers. Just as he was preparing to give his preliminary speech to the
commissioners, a sudden commotion broke out among the warriors
far in the distance. About three hundred Oglalas who had come in
from the Powder River country trotted their ponies down a slope,
occasionally firing off rifles. Some were chanting a song in Sioux:

> The Black Hills is my land and I love it
> And whoever interferes
> Will hear this gun.[6]

An Indian mounted on a gray horse forced his way through the
ranks of warriors gathered around the canvas shelter. He was Crazy
Horse's envoy, Little Big Man, stripped for battle and wearing two
revolvers belted to his waist. "I will kill the first chief who speaks
for selling the Black Hills!" he shouted. He danced his horse across
the open space between the commissioners and the chiefs.[7]

Young-Man-Afraid-of-His-Horses and a group of unofficial Sioux
policemen immediately swarmed around Little Big Man and moved
him away. The chiefs and the commissioners, however, must have
guessed that Little Big Man voiced the feelings of most of the warriors present. General Terry suggested to his fellow commissioners
that they board the Army ambulances and return to the safety of
Fort Robinson.

After giving the Indians a few days to calm down, the commissioners quietly arranged a meeting with twenty chiefs in the headquarters building of the Red Cloud agency. During three days of
speech making, the chiefs made it quite clear to the Great Father's
representatives that the Black Hills could not be bought cheaply, if
at any price. Spotted Tail finally grew impatient with the commissioners and asked them to submit a definite proposal in writing.

The offer was four hundred thousand dollars a year for the mineral rights; or if the Sioux wished to sell the hills outright the price
would be six million dollars payable in fifteen annual installments.
(This was a markdown price indeed, considering that one Black
Hills mine alone yielded more than five hundred million dollars in
gold.)

Red Cloud did not even appear for the final meeting, letting

6. Gilbert, p. 43.   D.C., 1918, p. 168.
7. Mills, Anson, *My Story*, Washington,

Spotted Tail speak for all the Sioux. Spotted Tail rejected both offers, firmly. The Black Hills were not for lease or for sale.

The commissioners packed up, returned to Washington, reported their failure to persuade the Sioux to relinquish the Black Hills, and recommended that Congress disregard the wishes of the Indians and appropriate a sum fixed "as a fair equivalent of the value of the hills." This forced purchase of the Black Hills should be "presented to the Indians as a finality," they said.[8]

Thus was set in motion a chain of actions which would bring the greatest defeat ever suffered by the United States Army in its wars with the Indians, and ultimately would destroy forever the freedom of the northern Plains Indians:

November 9, 1875: E. T. Watkins, special inspector for the Indian Bureau, reported to the Commissioner of Indian Affairs that Plains Indians living outside reservations were fed and well armed, were lofty and independent in their attitudes, and were therefore a threat to the reservation system. Inspector Watkins recommended that troops be sent against these uncivilized Indians "in the winter, the sooner the better, and *whip* them into subjection."[9]

November 22, 1875: Secretary of War W. W. Belknap warned of trouble in the Black Hills "unless something is done to obtain possession of that section for the white miners who have been strongly attracted there by reports of rich deposits of the precious metal."[9a]

December 3, 1875: Commissioner of Indian Affairs Edward P. Smith ordered Sioux and Cheyenne agents to notify all Indians off reservations to come in and report to their agencies by January 31, 1876, or a "military force would be sent to compel them."

February 1, 1876: The Secretary of the Interior notified the Secretary of War that the time given the "hostile Indians" to come in to their reservations had expired, and that he was turning them over to the military authorities for such action as the Army might deem proper under the circumstances.[1]

February 7, 1876: The War Department authorized General Sheridan, commanding the Military Division of the Missouri, to commence operations against the "hostile Sioux," including the bands under Sitting Bull and Crazy Horse.

February 8, 1876: General Sheridan ordered generals Crook and Terry to begin preparations for military operations in the direction of the headwaters of the Powder, Tongue, Rosebud, and Bighorn rivers, "where Crazy Horse and his allies frequented."[2]

8. U.S. Commissioner of Indian Affairs. Report, 1875, p. 199.
9. U.S. Congress. 44th. 1st session. House Executive Document 184, pp. 8–9.
9a. U.S. Secretary of War. Report, 1875, p. 21.
1. U.S. Congress. 44th. 1st session. House Executive Document 184, pp. 10, 17–18.
2. U.S. Secretary of War. Report, 1876, p. 441.

Once this machinery of government began moving, it became an inexorable force, mindless and uncontrollable. When runners went out from the agencies late in December to warn the non-agency chiefs to come in, heavy snows blanketed the northern Plains. Blizzards and severe cold made it impossible for some couriers to return until weeks after the January 31 deadline; it would have been impossible to move women and children by ponies and travois. Had a few thousand "hostiles" somehow managed to reach the agencies, they would have starved there. On the reservations during the late winter, food supplies were so short that hundreds of Indians left in March to go north in search of game to supplement their meager government rations.

In January a courier found Sitting Bull camped near the mouth of the Powder. The Hunkpapa chief sent the messenger back to the agent, informing him that he would consider the order to come in, but could not do so until the Moon When the Green Grass Is Up.

Crazy Horse's Oglalas were in winter camp near Bear Butte, where the Thieves' Road came into the Black Hills from the north. During the spring it would be a good place to make up raiding parties to go against the miners violating *Paha Sapa*. When agency couriers made their way through the snow to Crazy Horse, he told them politely that he could not come until the cold went away. "It was very cold," a young Oglala remembered afterward, "and many of our people and ponies would have died in the snow. Also, we were in our own country and were doing no harm."[3]

The January 31 ultimatum was little short of a declaration of war against the independent Indians, and many of them accepted it as that. But they did not expect the Bluecoats to strike so soon. In the Moon of the Snowblind, Three Stars Crook came marching north from Fort Fetterman along the old Bozeman Road, where ten years before Red Cloud had begun his stubborn fight to keep the Powder River country inviolate.

About this same time, a mixed band of Northern Cheyennes and Oglala Sioux left Red Cloud agency to go to the Powder River country, where they hoped to find a few buffalo and antelope. About the middle of March they joined some nonagency Indians camped a few miles from where the Little Powder runs into the Powder. Two Moon, Little Wolf, Old Bear, Maple Tree, and White Bull were the Cheyenne leaders. Low Dog was the Oglala chief, and some of the warriors with him were from Crazy Horse's village farther north.

Without warning, at dawn on March 17, Crook's advance column under Colonel Joseph J. Reynolds attacked this peaceful camp. Fearing nothing in their own country, the Indians were

3. Neihardt, John G. *Black Elk Speaks*. Lincoln, University of Nebraska Press, 1961, p. 90.

asleep when Captain James Egan's white-horse troop, formed in a company front, dashed into the tepee village, firing pistols and carbines. At the same time, a second troop of cavalry came in on the left flank, and a third swept away the Indians' horse herd.

The first reaction from the warriors was to get as many women and children as possible out of the way of the soldiers, who were firing recklessly in all directions. "Old people tottered and hobbled away to get out of reach of the bullets singing among the lodges," Wooden Leg said afterward. "Braves seized whatever weapons they had and tried to meet the attack." As soon as the noncombatants were started up a rugged mountain slope, the warriors took positions on ledges or behind huge rocks. From these places they held the soldiers at bay until the women and children could escape across the Powder.

"From a distance we saw the destruction of our village," Wooden Leg said. "Our tepees were burned with everything in them. . . . I had nothing left but the clothing I had on." The Bluecoats destroyed all the pemmican and saddles in the camp, and drove away almost every pony the Indians owned, "between twelve and fifteen hundred head."[4] As soon as darkness fell, the warriors went back to where the Bluecoats were camped, determined to recover their stolen horses. Two Moon succinctly described what happened: "That night the soldiers slept, leaving the horses to one side; so we crept up and stole them back again, and then we went away."[5]

Three Stars Crook was so angry at Colonel Reynolds for allowing the Indians to escape from their village and recover their horses that he ordered him court-martialed. The Army reported this foray as "the attack on Crazy Horse's village," but Crazy Horse was camped miles away to the northeast. That was where Two Moon and the other chiefs led their homeless people in hopes of finding food and shelter. They were more than three days making the journey; the temperature was below zero at night; only a few had buffalo robes; and there was very little food.

Crazy Horse received the fugitives hospitably, gave them food and robes, and found room for them in the Oglala tepees. "I'm glad you are come," he said to Two Moon after listening to accounts of the Bluecoats plundering the village. "We are going to fight the white man again."

"All right," Two Moon replied. "I am ready to fight. I have fought already. My people have been killed, my horses stolen; I am satisfied to fight."[6]

4. Marquis, Thomas B. *Wooden Leg, a Warrior Who Fought Custer.* Lincoln, University of Nebraska Press, 1957, pp. 165, 168. De Barthe, Joe. *Life and Adventures of Frank Grouard.* Norman, University of Oklahoma Press, 1958, p. 98.

5. Garland, Hamlin. "General Custer's Last Fight as Seen by Two Moon." *McClure's Magazine,* Vol. 11, 1898, p. 444.

6. *Ibid.,* p. 445.

In the Geese Laying Moon, when the grass was tall and the horses strong, Crazy Horse broke camp and led the Oglalas and Cheyennes north to the mouth of Tongue River, where Sitting Bull and the Hunkpapas had been living through the winter. Not long after that, Lame Deer arrived with a band of Minneconjous and asked permission to camp nearby. They had heard about all the Bluecoats marching through the Sioux hunting grounds and wanted to be near Sitting Bull's powerful band of Hunkpapas should there be any trouble.

As the weather warmed, the tribes began moving northward in search of wild game and fresh grass. Along the way they were joined by bands of Brulés, Sans Arcs, Blackfoot Sioux, and additional Cheyennes. Most of these Indians had left their reservations in accordance with their treaty rights as hunters, and those who had heard of the January 31 ultimatum either considered it as only another idle threat of the Great Father's agents or did not believe it applied to peaceful Indians. "Many young men were anxious to go for fighting the soldiers," said the Cheyenne warrior Wooden Leg. "But the chiefs and old men all urged us to keep away from the white men."[7]

While these several thousand Indians were camped on the Rosebud, many young warriors joined them from the reservations. They brought rumors of great forces of Bluecoats marching from three directions. Three Stars Crook was coming from the south. The One Who Limps (Colonel John Gibbon) was coming from the west. One Star Terry and Long Hair Custer were coming from the east.

Early in the Moon of Making Fat, the Hunkpapas had their annual sun dance. For three days Sitting Bull danced, bled himself, and stared at the sun until he fell into a trance. When he rose again, he spoke to his people. In his vision he had heard a voice crying: "I give you these because they have no ears." When he looked into the sky he saw soldiers falling like grasshoppers, with their heads down and their hats falling off. They were falling right into the Indian camp. Because the white men had no ears and would not listen, Wakantanka the Great Spirit was giving these soldiers to the Indians to be killed.[8]

A few days later a hunting party of Cheyennes sighted a column of Bluecoats camped for the night in the valley of the Rosebud. The hunters rode back to camp, sounding the wolf howl of danger. Three Stars was coming, and he had employed mercenary Crows and Shoshones to scout ahead of his troops.

The different chiefs sent criers through their villages and then held hasty councils. It was decided to leave about half the warriors to protect the villages while the others would travel through the

7. Marquis, p. 185.
8. Vestal, Stanley. *Sitting Bull, Cham-*   *pion of the Sioux.* Norman, University of Oklahoma Press, 1957, pp. 150–51.

night and attack Three Stars's soldiers the next morning. About a
thousand Sioux and Cheyennes formed the party. A few women
went along to help with the spare horses. Sitting Bull, Crazy Horse,
and Two Moon were among the leaders. Just before daylight they
unsaddled and rested for a while; then they turned away from the
river and rode across the hills.

Three Stars's Crow scouts had told him of a great Sioux village
down the Rosebud, and the general started these mercenaries out
early that morning. As the Crows rode over the crest of a hill and
started down, they ran into the Sioux and Cheyenne warriors. At
first the Sioux and Cheyennes chased the Crows in all directions,
but Bluecoats began coming up fast, and the warriors pulled back.

For a long time Crazy Horse had been waiting for a chance to
test himself in battle with the Bluecoats. In all the years since the
Fetterman fight at Fort Phil Kearny, he had studied the soldiers
and their ways of fighting. Each time he went into the Black Hills
to seek visions, he had asked Wakantanka to give him secret powers
so that he would know how to lead the Oglalas to victory if the
white men ever came again to make war upon his people. Since the
time of his youth, Crazy Horse had known that the world men
lived in was only a shadow of the real world. To get into the real
world, he had to dream, and when he was in the real world everything seemed to float or dance. In this real world his horse danced
as if it were wild or crazy, and this was why he called himself Crazy
Horse. He had learned that if he dreamed himself into the real
world before going into a fight, he could endure anything.

On this day, June 17, 1876, Crazy Horse dreamed himself into
the real world, and he showed the Sioux how to do many things
they had never done before while fighting the white man's soldiers.
When Crook sent his pony soldiers in mounted charges, instead of
rushing forward into the fire of their carbines, the Sioux faded off to
their flanks and struck weak places in their lines. Crazy Horse kept
his warriors mounted and always moving from one place to another.
By the time the sun was in the top of the sky he had the soldiers all
mixed up in three separate fights. The Bluecoats were accustomed
to forming skirmish lines and strong fronts, and when Crazy Horse
prevented them from fighting like that they were thrown into confusion. By making many darting charges on their swift ponies, the
Sioux kept the soldiers apart and always on the defensive. When
the Bluecoats' fire grew too hot, the Sioux would draw away, tanta-
lize a few soldiers into pursuit, and then turn on them with a fury.

The Cheyennes also distinguished themselves that day, especially
in the dangerous charges. Chief-Comes-in-Sight was the bravest of
all, but as he was swinging his horse about after a charge into the
soldiers' flank the animal was shot down in front of a Bluecoat
infantry line. Suddenly another horse and rider galloped out from

the Cheyennes' position and swerved to shield Chief-Comes-in-Sight from the soldiers' fire. In a moment Chief-Comes-in-Sight was up behind the rider. The rescuer was his sister Buffalo-Calf-Road-Woman, who had come along to help with the horse herds. That was why the Cheyennes always remembered this fight as the Battle Where the Girl Saved Her Brother. The white men called it the Battle of the Rosebud.

When the sun went down, the fighting ended. The Indians knew they had given Three Stars a good fight, but they did not know until the next morning that they had whipped him. At first daylight, Sioux and Cheyenne scouts went out along the ridges, and they could see the Bluecoat column retreating far away to the south. General Crook was returning to his base camp on Goose Creek to await reinforcements or a message from Gibbon, Terry, or Custer. The Indians on the Rosebud were too strong for one column of soldiers.

After the fight on the Rosebud, the chiefs decided to move west to the valley of the Greasy Grass (Little Bighorn). Scouts had come in with reports of great herds of antelope west of there, and they said grass for the horses was plentiful on the nearby benchlands. Soon the camp circles were spread along the west bank of the twisting Greasy Grass for almost three miles. No one knew for certain how many Indians were there, but the number could not have been smaller than ten thousand people, including three or four thousand warriors. "It was a very big village and you could hardly count the tepees," Black Elk said.[9]

Farthest upstream toward the south was the Hunkpapa camp, with the Blackfoot Sioux nearby. The Hunkpapas always camped at the entrance, or at the head end of the circle, which was the meaning of their name. Below them were the Sans Arcs, Minneconjous, Oglalas, and Brulés. At the north end were the Cheyennes.

The time was early in the Moon When the Chokecherries Are Ripe, with days hot enough for boys to swim in the melted snow water of the Greasy Grass. Hunting parties were coming and going in the direction of the Bighorns, where they had found a few buffalo as well as antelope. The women were digging wild turnips out on the prairies. Every night one or more of the tribal circles held dances, and some nights the chiefs met in councils. "The chiefs of the different tribes met together as equals," Wooden Leg said. "There was only one who was considered as being above all the others. This was Sitting Bull. He was recognized as the one old man chief of all the camps combined."[1]

Sitting Bull did not believe the victory on the Rosebud had fulfilled his prophecy of soldiers falling into the Indian camp. Since the retreat of Three Stars, however, no hunting parties had sighted any Bluecoats between the Powder and the Bighorn.

They did not know until the morning of June 24 that Long Hair Custer was prowling along the Rosebud. Next morning scouts reported that the soldiers had crossed the last high ridge between the Rosebud and the Indian camp and were marching toward the Little Bighorn.

The news of Custer's approach came to the Indians in various ways:

"I and four women were a short distance from the camp digging wild turnips," said Red Horse, one of the Sioux council chiefs. "Suddenly one of the women attracted my attention to a cloud of dust rising a short distance from camp. I soon saw that the soldiers were charging the camp. To the camp I and the women ran. When I arrived a person told me to hurry to the council lodge. The soldiers charged so quickly that we could not talk. We came out of the council lodge and talked in all directions. The Sioux mount horses, take guns, and go fight the soldiers. Women and children mount horses and go, meaning to get out of the way."[2]

Pte-San-Waste-Win, a cousin of Sitting Bull, was one of the young women digging turnips that morning. She said the soldiers were six to eight miles distant when first sighted. "We could see the flashing of their sabers and saw that there were very many soldiers in the party." The soldiers first seen by Pte-San-Waste-Win and other Indians in the middle of the camp were those in Custer's battalion. These Indians were not aware of Major Marcus Reno's surprise attack against the south end of camp until they heard rifle fire from the direction of the Blackfoot Sioux lodges. "Like that the soldiers were upon us. Through the tepee poles their bullets rattled. ... The women and children cried, fearing they would be killed, but the men, the Hunkpapa and Blackfeet, the Oglala and Minneconjou, mounted their horses and raced to the Blackfoot tepees. We could still see the soldiers of Long Hair marching along in the distance, and our men, taken by surprise, and from a point whence they had not expected to be attacked, went singing the song of battle into the fight behind the Blackfoot village."[3]

Black Elk, a thirteen-year-old Oglala boy, was swimming with his companions in the Little Bighorn. The Sun was straight above and was getting very hot when he heard a crier shouting in the Hunkpapa camp: "The chargers are coming! They are charging! The chargers are coming!" The warning was repeated by an Oglala crier, and Black Elk could hear the cry going from camp to camp northward to the Cheyennes.[4]

2. U.S. Bureau of American Ethnology. Annual Report, 19th, 1888–89, p. 564.
3. McLaughlin, James. *My Friend the* *Indian.* Boston, Houghton Mifflin Co.. 1910, pp.168–69.
4. Neihardt, pp. 108–09.

Low Dog, an Oglala chief, heard this same warning cry. "I did not believe it. I thought it was a false alarm. I did not think it possible that any white man would attack us, so strong as we were. . . . Although I did not believe it was a true alarm, I lost no time getting ready. When I got my gun and came out of my lodge the attack had begun at the end of the camp where Sitting ·Bull and the Hunkpapas were."

Iron Thunder was in the Minneconjou camp. "I did not know anything about Reno's attack until his men were so close that the bullets went through the camp, and everything was in confusion. The horses were so frightened we could not catch them."

Crow King, who was in the Hunkpapa camp, said that Reno's pony soldiers commenced firing at about four hundred yards' distance. The Hunkpapas and Blackfoot Sioux retreated slowly on foot to give the women and children time to go to a place of safety. "Other Indians got our horses. By that time we had warriors enough to turn upon the ̇whites."[5]

Near the Cheyenne camp, three miles to the north, Two Moon was watering his horses. "I washed them off with cool water, then took a swim myself. I came back to the camp afoot. When I got near my lodge, I looked up the Little Bighorn toward Sitting Bull's camp. I saw a great dust rising. It looked like a whirlwind. Soon a Sioux horseman came rushing into camp shouting: 'Soldiers come! Plenty white soldiers!' "

Two Moon ordered the Cheyenne warriors to get their horses, and then told the women to take cover away from the tepee village. "I rode swiftly toward Sitting Bull's camp. Then I saw the white soldiers fighting in a line [Reno's men]. Indians covered the flat. They began to drive the soldiers all mixed up—Sioux, then soldiers, then more Sioux, and all shooting. The air was full of smoke and dust. I saw the soldiers fall back and drop into the riverbed like buffalo fleeing."[6]

The war chief who rallied the Indians and turned back Reno's attack was a muscular, full-chested, thirty-six-year-old Hunkpapa named Pizi, or Gall. Gall had grown up in the tribe as an orphan. While still a young man he distinguished himself as a hunter and warrior, and Sitting Bull adopted him as a younger brother. Some years before, while the commissioners were attempting to persuade the Sioux to take up farming as a part of the treaty of 1868, Gall went to Fort Rice to speak for the Hunkpapas. "We were born naked," he said, "and have been taught to hunt and live on the game. You tell us that we must learn to farm, live in one house, and take on your ways. Suppose the people living beyond the great

5. *Leavenworth* (Kansas) *Weekly Times*, August 18, 1881.

6. Garland, p. 446.

sea should come and tell you that you must stop farming and kill your cattle, and take your houses and lands, what would you do? Would you not fight them?"[7] In the decade following that speech, nothing changed Gall's opinion of the white man's self-righteous arrogance, and by the summer of 1876 he was generally accepted by the Hunkpapas as Sitting Bull's lieutenant, the war chief of the tribe.

Reno's first onrush caught several women and children in the open, and the cavalry's flying bullets virtually wiped out Gall's family. "It made my heart bad," he told a newspaperman some years later. "After that I killed all my enemies with the hatchet." His description of the tactics used to block Reno was equally terse: "Sitting Bull and I were at the point where Reno attacked. Sitting Bull was big medicine. The women and children were hastily moved downstream. . . . The women and children caught the horses for the bucks to mount them; the bucks mounted and charged back Reno and checked him, and drove him into the timber."[8]

In military terms, Gall turned Reno's flank and forced him into the woods. He then frightened Reno into making a hasty retreat which the Indians quickly turned into a rout. The result made it possible for Gall to divert hundreds of warriors for a frontal attack against Custer's column, while Crazy Horse and Two Moon struck the flank and rear.

Meanwhile Pte-San-Waste-Win and the other women had been anxiously watching the Long Hair's soldiers across the river. "I could hear the music of the bugle and could see the column of soldiers turn to the left to march down to the river where the attack was to be made. . . . Soon I saw a number of Cheyennes ride into the river, then some young men of my band, then others, until there were hundreds of warriors in the river and running up into the ravine. When some hundreds had passed the river and gone into the ravine, the others who were left, still a very great number, moved back from the river and waited for the attack. And I knew that the fighting men of the Sioux, many hundreds in number, were hidden in the ravine behind the hill upon which Long Hair was marching, and he would be attacked from both sides."[9]

Kill Eagle, a Blackfoot Sioux chief, later said that the movement of Indians toward Custer's column was "like a hurricane . . . like bees swarming out of a hive." Hump, the Minneconjou comrade of Gall and Crazy Horse during the old Powder River days, said the first massive charge by the Indians caused the long-haired chief and his men to become confused. "The first dash the Indians made my horse was shot from under me and I was wounded—shot above the

7. Robinson, D. W. "Editorial Notes on Historical Sketch of North and South Dakota." *South Dakota Historical Collections,* Vol. I, 1902, p. 151.

8. *St. Paul* (Minnesota) *Pioneer Press,* July 18, 1886.
9. McLaughlin, pp. 172-73.

knee, and the ball came out at the hip, and I fell and lay right there." Crow King, who was with the Hunkpapas, said: "The greater portion of our warriors came together in their front and we rushed our horses on them. At the same time warriors rode out on each side of them and circled around them until they were surrounded."[1] Thirteen-year-old Black Elk, watching from across the river, could see a big dust whirling on the hill, and then horses began coming out of it with empty saddles.

"The smoke of the shooting and the dust of the horses shut out the hill," Pte-San-Waste-Win said, "and the soldiers fired many shots, but the Sioux shot straight and the soldiers fell dead. The women crossed the river after the men of our village, and when we came to the hill there were no soldiers living and Long Hair lay dead among the rest. . . . The blood of the people was hot and their hearts bad, and they took no prisoners that day."[2]

Crow King said that all the soldiers dismounted when the Indians surrounded them. "They tried to hold on to their horses, but as we pressed closer they let go their horses. We crowded them toward our main camp and killed them all. They kept in order and fought like brave warriors as long as they had a man left."[3]

According to Red Horse, toward the end of the fighting with Custer, "these soldiers became foolish, many throwing away their guns and raising their hands, saying, 'Sioux, pity us; take us prisoners.' The Sioux did not take a single soldier prisoner, but killed all of them; none were alive for even a few minutes."[4]

Long after the battle, White Bull of the Minneconjous drew four pictographs showing himself grappling with and killing a soldier identified as Custer. Among others who claimed to have killed Custer were Rain-in-the-Face, Flat Hip, and Brave Bear. Red Horse said that an unidentified Santee warrior killed Custer. Most Indians who told of the battle said they never saw Custer and did not know who killed him. "We did not know till the fight was over that he was the white chief," Low Dog said.[5]

In an interview given in Canada a year after the battle, Sitting Bull said that he never saw Custer, but that other Indians had seen and recognized him just before he was killed. "He did not wear his long hair as he used to wear it," Sitting Bull said. "It was short, but it was the color of the grass when the frost comes. . . . Where the last stand was made, the Long Hair stood like a sheaf of corn with all the ears fallen around him."[6] But Sitting Bull did not say who killed Custer.

1. New York *Herald*, September 24, 1876. Easterwood, T. J. *Memories of Seventy-Six*. Dundee, Oregon, 1880, p. 15.

2. McLaughlin, p. 175.

3. *Leavenworth* (Kansas) *Weekly Times*, August 18, 1881.

4. U.S. Bureau of American Ethnology. Annual Report, 10th, 1888–89, p. 565.

5. *Leavenworth* (Kansas) *Weekly Times*, August 18, 1881.

6. New York *Herald*, November 16, 1877.

An Arapaho warrior who was riding with the Cheyennes said that
Custer was killed by several Indians. "He was dressed in buckskin,
coat and pants, and was on his hands and knees. He had been shot
through the side, and there was blood coming from his mouth. He
seemed to be watching the Indians moving around him. Four soldiers were sitting up around him, but they were all badly wounded.
All the other soldiers were down. Then the Indians closed in
around him, and I did not see any more."[7]

Regardless of who had killed him, the Long Hair who made the
Thieves' Road into the Black Hills was dead with all his men.
Reno's soldiers, however, reinforced by those of Major Frederick
Benteen, were dug in on a hill farther down the river. The Indians
surrounded the hill completely and watched the soldiers through
the night, and next morning started fighting them again. During
the days, scouts sent out by the chiefs came back with warnings of
many more soldiers marching in the direction of the Little Bighorn.

After a council it was decided to break camp. The warriors had
expended most of their ammunition, and they knew it would be
foolish to try to fight so many soldiers with bows and arrows. The
women were told to begin packing, and before sunset they started
up the valley toward the Bighorn Mountains, the tribes separating
along the way and taking different directions.

When the white men in the East heard of the Long Hair's
defeat, they called it a massacre and went crazy with anger. They
wanted to punish all the Indians in the West. Because they could
not punish Sitting Bull and the war chiefs, the Great Council in
Washington decided to punish the Indians they could find—those
who remained on the reservations and had taken no part in the
fighting.

On July 22 the Great Warrior Sherman received authority to
assume military control of all reservations in the Sioux country and
to treat the Indians there as prisoners of war. On August 15 the
Great Council made a new law requiring the Indians to give up all
rights to the Powder River country and the Black Hills. They did
this without regard to the treaty of 1868, maintaining that the Indians had violated the treaty by going to war with the United States.
This was difficult for the reservation Indians to understand, because
they had not attacked United States soldiers, nor had Sitting Bull's
followers attacked them until Custer sent Reno charging through
the Sioux villages.

To keep the reservation Indians peaceful, the Great Father sent
out a new commission in September to cajole and threaten the
chiefs and secure their signatures to legal documents transferring

7. Graham, W. A. *The Custer Myth.*   110.
Harrisburg, Pa., Stackpole Co., 1953, p.

The War for the Black Hills · 319

the immeasurable wealth of the Black Hills to white ownership. Several members of this commission were old hands at stealing Indian lands, notably Newton Edmunds, Bishop Henry Whipple, and the Reverend Samuel D. Hinman. At the Red Cloud agency, Bishop Whipple opened the proceedings with a prayer, and then Chairman George Manypenny read the conditions laid down by Congress. Because these conditions were stated in the usual obfuscated language of lawmakers, Bishop Whipple attempted to explain them in phrases which could be used by the interpreters.

"My heart has for many years been very warm toward the red man. We came here to bring a message to you from your Great Father, and there are certain things we have given to you in his exact words. We cannot alter them even to the scratch of a pen. . . . When the Great Council made the appropriation this year to continue your supplies they made certain provisions, three in number, and unless they were complied with no more appropriations would be made by Congress. Those three provisions are: First, that you shall give up the Black Hills country and the country to the north; second, that you shall receive your rations on the Missouri River; and third, that the Great Father shall be permitted to locate three roads from the Missouri River across the reservation to that new country where the Black Hills are. . . . The Great Father said that his heart was full of tenderness for his red children, and he selected this commission of friends of the Indians that they might devise a plan, as he directed them, in order that the Indian nations might be saved, and that instead of growing smaller and smaller until the last Indian looks upon his own grave, they might become as the white man has become, a great and powerful people."[8]

To Bishop Whipple's listeners, this seemed a strange way indeed to save the Indian nations, taking away their Black Hills and hunting grounds, and moving them far away to the Missouri River. Most of the chiefs knew that it was already too late to save the Black Hills, but they protested strongly against having their reservations moved to the Missouri. "I think if my people should move there," Red Cloud said, "they would all be destroyed. There are a great many bad men there and bad whiskey; therefore I don't want to go there."[9]

No Heart said that white men had already ruined the Missouri River country so that Indians could not live there. "You travel up and down the Missouri River and you do not see any timber," he declared. "You have probably seen where lots of it has been, and the Great Father's people have destroyed it."

"It is only six years since we came to live on this stream where we are living now," Red Dog said, "and nothing that has been

8. U.S. Congress. 44th. 2nd session. Senate Executive Document 9, pp. 5, 31.   9. New York *Herald* 33, September 23, 1876.

promised us has been done." Another chief remembered that since the Great Father promised them that they would never be moved they had been moved five times. "I think you had better put the Indians on wheels," he said sardonically, "and you can run them about whenever you wish."

Spotted Tail accused the government and the commissioners of betraying the Indians, of broken promises and false words. "This war did not spring up here in our land; this was was brought upon us by the children of the Great Father who came to take our land from us without price, and who, in our land, do a great many evil things. . . . This war has come from robbery—from the stealing of our land."[1] As for moving to the Missouri, Spotted Tail was utterly opposed, and he told the commissioners he would not sign away the Black Hills until he could go to Washington and talk to the Great Father.

The commissioners gave the Indians a week to discuss the terms among themselves, and it soon became evident that they were not going to sign anything. The chiefs pointed out that the treaty of 1868 required the signatures of three-fourth of the male adults of the Sioux tribes to change anything in it, and more than half of the warriors were in the north with Sitting Bull and Crazy Horse. In reply to this the commissioners explained that the Indians off the reservations were hostiles; only friendly Indians were covered by the treaty. Most of the chiefs did not accept this. To break down their opposition, the commissioners dropped strong hints that unless they signed, the Great Council in its anger would cut off all rations immediately, would remove them to the Indian Territory in the south, and the Army would take all their guns and horses.

There was no way out. The Black Hills were stolen; the Powder River country and its herds of wild game were gone. Without wild game or rations, the people would starve. The thought of moving far away to a strange country in the south was unbearable, and if the Army took their guns and ponies they would no longer be men.

Red Cloud and his subchiefs signed first, and then Spotted Tail and his people signed. After that the commissioners went to agencies at Standing Rock, Cheyenne River, Crow Creek, Lower Brulé, and Santee, and badgered the other Sioux tribes into signing. Thus did *Paha Sapa*, its spirits and its mysteries, its vast pine forests, and its billion dollars in gold pass forever from the hands of the Indians into the domain of the United States.

1. U.S. Congress. 44th. 2nd session.   38–40, 66.
Senate Executive Document 9, pp. 8,

CHIEF SEATTLE

Address[1]

The Governor made a fine speech, but he was outranged and out-classed that day. Chief Seattle, who answered on behalf of the Indians, towered a foot above the Governor. He wore his blanket like the toga of a Roman senator, and he did not have to strain his famous voice, which everyone agreed was audible and distinct at a distance of half a mile.

Seattle's oration was in Duwamish. Doctor Smith, who had learned the language, wrote it down; under the flowery garlands of his translation the speech rolls like an articulate iron engine, grim with meanings that outlasted his generation and may outlast all the generations of men. As the amiable follies of the white race become less amiable, the iron rumble of old Seattle's speech sounds louder and more ominous.

Standing in front of Doctor Maynard's office in the stumpy clearing, with his hand on the little Governor's head, the white invaders about him and his people before him, Chief Seattle said:

"Yonder sky that has wept tears of compassion upon my people for centuries untold, and which to us appears changeless and eternal, may change. Today is fair. Tomorrow may be overcast with clouds. My words are like the stars that never change. Whatever Seattle says the great chief at Washington can rely upon with as much certainty as he can upon the return of the sun or the seasons. The White Chief says that Big Chief at Washington sends us greetings of friendship and goodwill. That is kind of him for we know he has little need of our friendship in return. His people are many. They are like the grass that covers vast prairies. My people are few. They resemble the scattering trees of a storm-swept plain. The great, and—I presume—good, White Chief sends us word that he wishes to buy our lands but is willing to allow us enough to live comfortably. This indeed appears just, even generous, for the Red Man no longer has rights that he need respect, and the offer may be wise also, as we are no longer in need of an extensive country. . . . I will not dwell on, nor mourn over, our untimely decay, nor reproach our paleface brothers with hastening it, as we too may have been somewhat to blame.

"Youth is impulsive. When our young men grow angry at some real or imaginary wrong, and disfigure their faces with black paint,

1. In 1854, Governor Isaac Stevens, Commissioner of Indian Affairs for the Washington Territory, proffered a treaty to the Indians providing for the sale of two million acres of their land to the federal government. This address is the reply of Chief Seattle of the Duwampo tribe. The translator was Henry A. Smith.

it denotes that their hearts are black, and then they are often cruel and relentless, and our old men and old women are unable to restrain them. Thus it has ever been. Thus it was when the white men first began to push our forefathers further westward. But let us hope that the hostilities between us may never return. We would have everything to lose and nothing to gain. Revenge by young men is considered gain, even at the cost of their own lives, but old men who stay at home in times of war, and mothers who have sons to lose, know better.

"Our good father at Washington—for I presume he is now our father as well as yours, since King George has moved his boundaries further north—our great good father, I say, sends us word that if we do as he desires he will protect us. His brave warriors will be to us a bristling wall of strength, and his wonderful ships of war will fill our harbors so that our ancient enemies far to the northward—the Hydas and Tsimpsians—will cease to frighten our women, children, and old men. Then in reality will he be our father and we his children. But can that ever be? Your God is not our God! Your God loves your people and hates mine. He folds his strong and protecting arms lovingly about the paleface and leads him by the hand as a father leads his infant son—but He has forsaken His red children —if they really are his. Our God, the Great Spirit, seems also to have forsaken us. Your God makes your people wax strong every day. Soon they will fill the land. Our people are ebbing away like a rapidly receding tide that will never return. The white man's God cannot love our people or He would protect them. They seem to be orphans who can look nowhere for help. How then can we be brothers? How can your God become our God and renew our prosperity and awaken in us dreams of returning greatness? If we have a common heavenly father He must be partial—for He came to his paleface children. We never saw Him. He gave you laws but He had no word for His red children whose teeming multitudes once filled this vast continent as stars fill the firmament. No; we are two distinct races with separate origins and separate destinies. There is little in common between us.

"To us the ashes of our ancestors are sacred and their resting place is hallowed ground. You wander far from the graves of your ancestors and seemingly without regret. Your religion was written upon tables of stone by the iron finger of your God so that you could not forget. The Red Man could never comprehend nor remember it. Our religion is the traditions of our ancestors—the dreams of our old men, given them in solemn hours of night by the Great Spirit; and the visions of our sachems; and it is written in the hearts of our people.

"Your dead cease to love you and the land of their nativity as soon as they pass the portals of the tomb and wander way beyond the stars. They are soon forgotten and never return. Our dead never forget the beautiful world that gave them being.

"Day and night cannot dwell together. The Red Man has ever fled the approach of the White Man, as the morning mist flees before the morning sun. However, your proposition seems fair and I think that my people will accept it and will retire to the reservation you offer them. Then we will dwell apart in peace, for the words of the Great White Chief seem to be the words of nature speaking to my people out of dense darkness.

"It matters little where we pass the remnant of our days. They will not be many. A few more moons; a few more winters—and not one of the descendants of the mighty hosts that once moved over this broad land or lived in happy homes, protected by the Great Spirit, will remain to mourn over the graves of a people once more powerful and hopeful than yours. But why should I mourn at the untimely fate of my people? Tribe follows tribe, and nation follows nation, like the waves of the sea. It is the order of nature, and regret is useless. Your time of decay may be distant, but it will surely come, for even the White Man whose God walked and talked with him as friend with friend, cannot be exempt from the common destiny. We may be brothers after all. We will see.

"We will ponder your proposition, and when we decide we will let you know. But should we accept it, I here and now make this condition that we will not be denied the privilege without molestation of visiting at any time the tombs of our ancestors, friends and children. Every part of this soil is sacred in the estimation of my people. Every hillside, every valley, every plain and grove, has been hallowed by some sad or happy event in days long vanished. . . . The very dust upon which you now stand responds more lovingly to their footsteps than to yours, because it is rich with the blood of our ancestors and our bare feet are conscious of the sympathetic touch. . . . Even the little children who lived here and rejoiced here for a brief season will love these somber solitudes and at eventide they greet shadowy returning spirits. And when the last Red Man shall have perished, and the memory of my tribe shall have become a myth among the White Men, these shores will swarm with the invisible dead of my tribe, and when your children's children think themselves alone in the field, the store, the shop, upon the highway, or in the silence of the pathless woods, they will not be alone. . . . At night when the streets of your cities and villages are silent and you think them deserted, they will throng with the returning hosts that once filled and still love this beautiful land. The White Man will never be alone.

"Let him be just and deal kindly with my people, for the dead are not powerless. Dead, did I say? There is no death, only a change of worlds."

ERIC HOFFER
The Role of the Undesirables

In the winter of 1934, I spent several weeks in a federal transient camp in California. These camps were originally established by Governor Rolph in the early days of the Depression to care for the single homeless unemployed of the state. In 1934 the federal government took charge of the camps for a time, and it was then that I first heard of them.

How I happened to get into one of the camps is soon told. Like thousands of migrant agricultural workers in California I then followed the crops from one part of the state to the other. Early in 1934 I arrived in the town of El Centro, in the Imperial Valley. I had been given a free ride on a truck from San Diego, and it was midnight when the truck driver dropped me on the outskirts of El Centro. I spread my bedroll by the side of the road and went to sleep. I had hardly dozed off when the rattle of a motorcycle drilled itself into my head and a policeman was bending over me saying, "Roll up, Mister." It looked as though I was in for something; it happened now and then that the police got overzealous and rounded up the freight trains. But this time the cop had no such thought. He said, "Better go over to the federal shelter and get yourself a bed and maybe some breakfast." He directed me to the place.

I found a large hall, obviously a former garage, dimly lit, and packed with cots. A concert of heavy breathing shook the thick air. In a small office near the door, I was registered by a middle-aged clerk. He informed me that this was the "receiving shelter" where I would get one night's lodging and breakfast. The meal was served in the camp nearby. Those who wished to stay on, he said, had to enroll in the camp. He then gave me three blankets and excused himself for not having a vacant cot. I spread the blankets on the cement floor and went to sleep.

I awoke with dawn amid a chorus of coughing, throat-clearing, the sound of running water, and the intermittent flushing of toilets in the back of the hall. There were about fifty of us, all colors and ages, all of us more or less ragged and soiled. The clerk handed out tickets for breakfast, and we filed out to the camp located several blocks away, near the railroad tracks.

From the outside the camp looked like a cross between a factory and a prison. A high fence of wire enclosed it, and inside were three large sheds and a huge boiler topped by a pillar of black smoke. Men in blue shirts and dungarees were strolling across the sandy yard. A ship's bell in front of one of the buildings announced breakfast. The regular camp members—there was a long line of them—ate first. Then we filed in through the gate, handing our tickets to the guard.

It was a good, plentiful meal. After breakfast our crowd dispersed. I heard some say that the camps in the northern part of the state were better, that they were going to catch a northbound freight. I decided to try this camp in El Centro.

My motives in enrolling were not crystal clear. I wanted to clean up. There were shower baths in the camp and wash tubs and plenty of soap. Of course I could have bathed and washed my clothes in one of the irrigation ditches, but here in the camp I had a chance to rest, get the wrinkles out of my belly, and clean up at leisure. In short, it was the easiest way out.

A brief interview at the camp office and a physical examination were all the formalities for enrollment.

There were some two hundred men in the camp. They were the kind I had worked and traveled with for years. I even saw familiar faces—men I had worked with in orchards and fields. Yet my predominant feeling was one of strangeness. It was my first experience of life in intimate contact with a crowd. For it is one thing to work and travel with a gang, and quite another thing to eat, sleep, and spend the greater part of the day cheek by jowl with two hundred men.

I found myself speculating on a variety of subjects: the reasons for their chronic bellyaching and beefing—it was more a ritual than the expression of a grievance; the amazing orderliness of the men; the comic seriousness with which they took their games of cards, checkers, and dominoes; the weird manner of reasoning one overheard now and then. Why, I kept wondering, were these men within the enclosure of a federal transient camp? Were they people temporarily hard up? Would jobs solve all their difficulties? Were we indeed like the people outside?

Up to then I was not aware of being one of a specific species of humanity. I had considered myself simply a human being—not particularly good or bad, and on the whole harmless. The people I worked and traveled with I knew as Americans and Mexicans, whites and Negroes, Northerners and Southerners, etc. It did not occur to me that we were a group possessed of peculiar traits, and that there was something—innate or acquired—in our makeup which made us adopt a particular mode of existence.

It was a slight thing that started me on a new track.

I got to talking to a mild-looking, elderly fellow. I liked his soft speech and pleasant manner. We swapped trivial experiences. Then he suggested a game of checkers. As we started to arrange the pieces on the board, I was startled by the sight of his crippled right hand. I had not noticed it before. Half of it was chopped off lengthwise, so that the horny stump with its three fingers looked like a hen's leg. I was mortified that I had not noticed the hand until he dangled it, so to speak, before my eyes. It was, perhaps, to bolster my shaken confidence in my powers of observation that I now began paying close attention to the hands of the people around me. The result was astounding. It seemed that every other man had had his hand mangled. There was a man with one arm. Some men limped. One young, good-looking fellow had a wooden leg. It was as though the majority of the men had escaped the snapping teeth of a machine and left part of themselves behind.

It was, I knew, an exaggerated impression. But I began counting the cripples as the men lined up in the yard at mealtime. I found thirty (out of two hundred) crippled either in arms or legs. I immediately sensed where the counting would land me. The simile preceded the statistical deduction: we in the camp were a human junk pile.

I began evaluating my fellow tramps as human material, and for the first time in my life I became face-conscious. There were some good faces, particularly among the young. Several of the middle-aged and the old looked healthy and well preserved. But the damaged and decayed faces were in the majority. I saw faces that were wrinkled, or bloated, or raw as the surface of a peeled plum. Some of the noses were purple and swollen, some broken, some pitted with enlarged pores. There were many toothless mouths (I counted seventy-eight). I noticed eyes that were blurred, faded, opaque, or bloodshot. I was struck by the fact that the old men, even the very old, showed their age mainly in the face. Their bodies were still slender and erect. One little man over sixty years of age looked a mere boy when seen from behind. The shriveled face joined to a boyish body made a startling sight.

My diffidence had now vanished. I was getting to know everybody in the camp. They were a friendly and talkative lot. Before many weeks I knew some essential fact about practically everyone.

And I was continually counting. Of the two hundred men in the camp there were approximately as follows:

Cripples	30
Confirmed drunkards	60
Old men (55 and over)	50
Youths under twenty	10
Men with chronic diseases, heart, asthma, TB	12
Mildly insane	4
Constitutionally lazy	6
Fugitives from justice	4
Apparently normal	70

(The numbers do not tally up to two hundred since some of the men were counted twice or even thrice—as cripples and old, or as old and confirmed drunks, etc.)

In other words: less than half the camp inmates (seventy normal, plus ten youths) were unemployed workers whose difficulties would be at an end once jobs were available. The rest (60 per cent) had handicaps in addition to unemployment.

I also counted fifty war veterans, and eighty skilled workers representing sixteen trades. All the men (including those with chronic diseases) were able to work. The one-armed man was a wizard with the shovel.

I did not attempt any definite measurement of character and intelligence. But it seemed to me that the intelligence of the men in the camp was certainly not below the average. And as to character, I found much forbearance and genuine good humor. I never came across one instance of real viciousness. Yet, on the whole, one would hardly say that these men were possessed of strong characters. Resistance, whether to one's appetites or to the ways of the world, is a chief factor in the shaping of character; and the average tramp is, more or less, a slave of his few appetites. He generally takes the easiest way out.

The connection between our makeup and our mode of existence as migrant workers presented itself now with some clarity.

The majority of us were incapable of holding onto a steady job. We lacked self-discipline and the ability to endure monotonous, leaden hours. We were probably misfits from the very beginning. Our contact with a steady job was not unlike a collision. Some of us were maimed, some got frightened and ran away, and some took to drink. We inevitably drifted in the direction of least resistance—the open road. The life of a migrant worker is varied and demands only a minimum of self-discipline. We were now in one of the drainage ditches of ordered society. We could not keep a footing in the ranks of respectability and were washed into the slough of our present existence.

Yet, I mused, there must be in this world a task with an appeal so strong that were we to have a taste of it we would hold on and be rid for good of our restlessness.

My stay in the camp lasted about four weeks. Then I found a haying job not far from town, and finally, in April, when the hot winds began blowing, I shouldered my bedroll and took the highway to San Bernardino.

It was the next morning, after I had got a lift to Indio by truck, that a new idea began to take hold of me. The highway out of Indio leads through waving date groves, fragrant grapefruit orchards, and lush alfalfa fields; then, abruptly, passes into a desert of white sand. The sharp line between garden and desert is very striking. The turning of white sand into garden seemed to me an act of magic. This, I thought, was a job one would jump at—even the men in the transient camps. They had the skill and ability of the average American. But their energies, I felt, could be quickened only by a task that was spectacular, that had in it something of the miraculous. The pioneer task of making the desert flower would certainly fill the bill.

Tramps as pioneers? It seemed absurd. Every man and child in California knows that the pioneers had been giants, men of boundless courage and indomitable spirit. However, as I strode on across the white sand, I kept mulling the idea over.

Who were the pioneers? Who were the men who left their homes and went into the wilderness? A man rarely leaves a soft spot and goes deliberately in search of hardship and privation. People become attached to the places they live in; they drive roots. A change of habitat is a painful act of uprooting. A man who has made good and has a standing in his community stays put. The successful businessmen, farmers, and workers usually stayed where they were. Who then left for the wilderness and the unknown? Obviously those who had not made good: men who went broke or never amounted to much; men who though possessed of abilities were too impulsive to stand the daily grind; men who were slaves of their appetites—drunkards, gamblers, and woman-chasers; outcasts—fugitives from justice and ex-jailbirds. There were no doubt some who went in search of health—men suffering with TB, asthma, heart trouble. Finally there was a sprinkling of young and middle-aged in search of adventure.

All these people craved change, some probably actuated by the naïve belief that a change in place brings with it a change in luck. Many wanted to go to a place where they were not known and there make a new beginning. Certainly they did not go out deliberately in search of hard work and suffering. If in the end they shouldered enormous tasks, endured unspeakable hardships, and accomplished the impossible, it was because they had to. They became men of action on the run. They acquired strength and skill in the inescapable struggle for existence. It was a question of do or die. And once they tasted the joy of achievement, they craved for more.

Clearly the same types of people which now swelled the ranks of migratory workers and tramps had probably in former times made up the bulk of the pioneers. As a group the pioneers were probably as unlike the present-day "native sons"—their descendants—as one could well imagine. Indeed, were there to be today a new influx of typical pioneers, twin brothers of the forty-niners only in a modern garb, the citizens of California would consider it a menace to health, wealth, and morals.

With few exceptions, this seems to be the case in the settlement of all new countries. Ex-convicts were the vanguard in the settling of Australia. Exiles and convicts settled Siberia. In this country, a large portion of our earlier and later settlers were failures, fugitives, and felons. The exceptions seemed to be those who were motivated by religious fervor, such as the Pilgrim Fathers and the Mormons.

Although quite logical, this train of thought seemed to me then a wonderful joke. In my exhilaration I was eating up the road in long strides, and I reached the oasis of Elim in what seemed almost no time. A passing empty truck picked me up just then and we thundered through Banning and Beaumont, all the way to Riverside. From there I walked the seven miles to San Bernardino.

Somehow, this discovery of a family likeness between tramps and pioneers took a firm hold on my mind. For years afterward it kept intertwining itself with a mass of observations which on the face of them had no relation to either tramps or pioneers. And it moved me to speculate on subjects in which, up to then, I had no real interest, and of which I knew very little.

I talked with several old-timers—one of them over eighty and a native son—in Sacramento, Placerville, Auburn, and Fresno. It was not easy, at first, to obtain the information I was after. I could not make my questions specific enough. "What kind of people were the early settlers and miners?" I asked. They were a hard-working, tough lot, I was told. They drank, fought, gambled, and wenched. They were big-hearted, grasping, profane, and God-fearing. They wallowed in luxury, or lived on next to nothing with equal ease. They were the salt of the earth.

Still it was not clear what manner of people they were.

If I asked what they looked like, I was told of whiskers, broad-brimmed hats, high boots, shirts of many colors, sun-tanned faces, horny hands. Finally I asked: "What group of people in present-day California most closely resembles the pioneers?" The answer, usually after some hesitation, was invariably the same: "The Okies and the fruit tramps."

I tried also to evaluate the tramps as potential pioneers by watching them in action. I saw them fell timber, clear firebreaks, build rock walls, put up barracks, build dams and roads, handle steam shovels, bulldozers, tractors, and concrete mixers. I saw them put in a hard day's work after a night of steady drinking. They sweated and growled, but they did the work. I saw the tramps elevated to positions of authority as foremen and superintendents. Then I could notice a remarkable physical transformation: a seamed face gradually smoothed out and the skin showed a healthy hue: an indifferent mouth became firm and expressive; dull eyes cleared and brightened; voices actually changed; there was even an apparent increase in stature. In almost no time these promoted tramps looked as if they had been on top all their lives. Yet sooner or later

I would meet up with them again in a railroad yard, on some skid row, or in the fields—tramps again. It was usually the same story: they got drunk or lost their temper and were fired, or they got fed up with the steady job and quit. Usually, when a tramp becomes a foreman, he is careful in his treatment of the tramps under him; he knows the day of reckoning is never far off.

In short, it was not difficult to visualize the tramps as pioneers. I reflected that if they were to find themselves in a singlehanded life-and-death struggle with nature, they would undoubtedly display persistence. For the pressure of responsibility and the heat of battle steel a character. The inadaptable would perish, and those who survived would be the equal of the successful pioneers.

I also considered the few instances of pioneering engineered from above—that is to say, by settlers possessed of lavish means, who were classed with the best where they came from. In these instances, it seemed to me, the resulting social structure was inevitably precarious. For pioneering deluxe usually results in a plantation society, made up of large landowners and peon labor, either native or imported. Very often there is a racial cleavage between the two. The colonizing activities of the Teutonic barons in the Baltic, the Hungarian nobles in Transylvania, the English in Ireland, the planters in our South, and the present-day plantation societies in Kenya and other British and Dutch colonies are cases in point. Whatever their merits, they are characterized by poor adaptability. They are likely eventually to be broken up either by a peon revolution or by an influx of typical pioneers—who are usually of the same race or nation as the landowners. The adjustment is not necessarily implemented by war. Even our old South, had it not been for the complication of secession, might eventually have attained stability without war: namely, by the activity of its own poor whites or by an influx of the indigent from other states.

There is in us a tendency to judge a race, a nation, or an organization by its least worthy members. The tendency is manifestly perverse and unfair; yet it has some justification. For the quality and destiny of a nation is determined to a considerable extent by the nature and potentialities of its inferior elements. The inert mass of a nation is in its middle section. The industrious, decent, well-to-do, and satisfied middle classes—whether in cities or on the land—are worked upon and shaped by minorities at both extremes: the best and the worst.

The superior individual, whether in politics, business, industry, science, literature, or religion, undoubtedly plays a major role in the shaping of a nation. But so do the individuals at the other extreme: the poor, the outcasts, the misfits, and those who are in the grip of some overpowering passion. The importance of these inferior elements as formative factors lies in the readiness with which they are swayed in any direction. This peculiarity is due to their inclination to take risks ("not giving a damn") and their propensity for united action. They crave to merge their drab, wasted lives into something grand and complete. Thus they are the first and most fervent adherents of new religions, political upheavals, patriotic hysteria, gangs, and mass rushes to new lands.

And the quality of a nation—its innermost worth—is made manifest by its dregs as they rise to the top: by how brave they are, how humane, how orderly, how skilled, how generous, how independent or servile; by the bounds they will not transgress in their dealings with man's soul, with truth, and with honor.

The average American of today bristles with indignation when he is told that his country was built, largely, by hordes of undesirables from Europe. Yet, far from being derogatory, this statement, if true, should be a cause for rejoicing, should fortify our pride in the stock from which we have sprung.

This vast continent with its towns, farms, factories, dams, aqueducts, docks, railroads, highways, powerhouses, schools, and parks is the handiwork of common folk from the Old World, where for centuries men of their kind had been as beasts of burden, the property of their masters—kings, nobles, and priests—and with no will and no aspirations of their own. When on rare occasions one of the lowly had reached the top in Europe he had kept the pattern intact and, if anything, tightened the screws. The stuffy little corporal from Corsica harnessed the lusty forces released by the French Revolution to a gilded state coach, and could think of nothing grander than mixing his blood with that of the Hapsburg masters and establishing a new dynasty. In our day a bricklayer in Italy, a house painter in Germany, and a shoemaker's son in Russia have made themselves masters of their nations; and what they did was to re-establish and reinforce the old pattern.

Only here, in America, were the common folk of the Old World given a chance to show what they could do on their own, without a master to push and order them about. History contrived an earth-shaking joke when it lifted by the nape of the neck lowly peasants, shopkeepers, laborers, paupers, jailbirds, and drunks from the midst of Europe, dumped them on a vast, virgin continent and said: "Go to it; it is yours!"

And the lowly were not awed by the magnitude of the task. A hunger for action, pent up for centuries, found an outlet. They went to it with ax, pick, shovel, plow, and rifle; on foot, on horse, in wagons, and on flatboats. They went to it praying, howling, singing, brawling, drinking, and fighting. Make way for the people! This is how I read the statement that this country was built by hordes of undesirables from the Old World.

Small wonder that we in this country have a deeply ingrained faith in human regeneration. We believe that, given a chance, even the degraded and the apparently worthless are capable of constructive work and great deeds. It is a faith founded on experience, not on some idealistic theory. And no matter what some anthropologists, sociologists, and geneticists may tell us, we shall go on believing that man, unlike other forms of life, is not a captive of his past—of his heredity and habits—but is possessed of infinite plasticity, and his potentialities for good and for evil are never wholly exhausted.

QUESTIONS

The following poem by Carl Sandburg speaks about "undesirables"—"rabble," "vagabonds," "hungry men." What other words might Sandburg have used for the "undesirables"? What effect do the words he uses create? Compare the terms used by Sandburg and Hoffer and determine the ways in which their words suggest similar or different attitudes toward these people.

Now the stone house on the lake front is finished and the
    workmen are beginning the fence.
The palings are made of iron bars with steel points that can
    stab the life out of any man who falls on them.
As a fence, it is a masterpiece, and will shut off the
    rabble and all vagabonds and hungry men and all
    wandering children looking for a place to play.
Passing through the bars and over the steel points will go
    nothing except Death and the Rain and To-morrow.
                —Carl Sandburg, "A Fence"

IAN WATT
"The Bridge over the River Kwai" as Myth

The Kwai is a real river in Thailand, and nearly thirty years ago prisoners of the Japanese—including myself—really did build a bridge across it: actually, two. Anyone who was there knows that Boulle's novel, *The Bridge on the River Kwai,* and the movie based on it, are both completely fictitious. What is odd is how they combined to create a world-wide myth, and how that myth is largely the result of those very psychological and political delusions which the builders of the real bridges had been forced to put aside.

The Real Bridges

The origin of the myth can be traced back to two historical realities.

Early in 1942, Singapore, the Dutch East Indies, and the Philippines surrendered; and Japan was suddenly left with the task of looking after over two hundred thousand prisoners of war. The normal procedure is to separate the officers from the enlisted men and put them into different camps; but the Japanese hadn't got the staff to spare and left the job of organizing the prison-camps to the prisoners themselves; which in effect meant the usual chain of command. This was one essential basis for Boulle's story: prisoners of war, like other prisoners, don't normally command anyone; and so they don't have anything to negotiate with.

The other main reality behind the myth is the building of that particular bridge. Once their armies started driving towards India, the Japanese realized they needed a railway from Bangkok to Rangoon. In the summer of 1942 many trainloads of prisoners from Singapore were sent up to Thailand and started to hack a two-hundred-mile trace through the jungle along a river called the Khwae Noi. In Thai, *Khwae* just means "stream;" *Noi* means "small." The "small stream" rises near the Burma border, at the Three Pagodas Pass; and it joins the main tributary of the Me Nam, called the Khwae Yai, or "Big Stream," at the old city of Kamburi, some eighty miles west of Bangkok. It was there that the Japanese faced the big task of getting the railway across the river. So, early in the autumn of 1942, a large construction camp was set up at a place called Tha Makham, about three miles west of Kamburi.

Like the hundred of other Japanese prison camps, Tha Makham had a very small and incompetent staff. To the Japanese the idea of being taken prisoner of war is—or was then—deeply shameful; even looking after prisoners shared some of this humiliation. Consequently, most of the Japanese staff were men who for one reason or another were thought unfit for combat duty; too old, perhaps, in disgrace, or just drunks. What was special about Tha Makham and the other camps on the Kwai was that they were also partly controlled by Japanese military engineers who were building the railway. These engineers usually despised the Japanese troops in charge of running the camps almost as much as they despised the prisoners.

The continual friction between the Japanese prison staff and the engineers directly affected our ordinary lives as prisoners. Daily routine in the camps in November 1942, when work on the Kwai bridge began, normally went like this: up at dawn; tea and rice for breakfast; and then on parade for the day's work. We might wait anything from ten minutes to half an hour for the Korean guard to count the whole parade and split it up into work groups. Then we marched to a small bamboo shed where the picks, shovels and so on were kept. Under any circumstances it would take a long time for one guard to issue tools for thousands of men out of one small shed; the delay was made worse by the fact that the tools usually belonged to the engineers, so two organizations were involved merely in issuing and checking picks and shovels. That might take another half hour, and then we would be reassembled and counted all over again before finally marching off to work.

When we had finally got out on the line, and found the right work site, the Japanese engineer in charge might be there to explain the day's task; but more probably not. He had a very long section of embankment or bridge to look after and perhaps thirty working parties in widely separate places to supervise. He had usually given some previous instructions to the particular guard at each site; but these orders might not be clear, or, even worse, they might be clear to us, but not to the guard.

There were many organizational problems. For instance, in the early days of the railway the total amount of work each man was supposed to do—moving a cubic meter of earth or driving in so many piles—was quite reasonable under normal circumstances. But the task often fell very unequally: some groups might have to carry their earth much further than others, or drive their teak piles into much rockier ground. So, as the day wore on, someone in a group with a very difficult, or impossible, assignment would get beaten up: all the guard thought about was that he'd probably be beaten up himself if the work on the section wasn't finished: so he lashed out.

Meanwhile, many other prisoners would already have finished their task, and would be sitting around waiting, or—even worse— pretending to work. The rule was that the whole day's task had to be finished, and often inspected by the Japanese engineer, before any single work party could leave the construction site. So some more prisoners would be beaten up for lying down in the shade when they were supposed to look as though there were still work to do in the sun.

At the end of the day's work an individual prisoner might well have been on his feet under the tropical sun from 7 in the morning until 7 or 8 even 9 at night, even though he'd only done three or four hours' work. He would come back late for the evening meal; there would be no lights in the huts; and as most of the guards went off duty at 6, he probably wouldn't be allowed to go down to the river to bathe, or wash his clothes.

So our lives were poisoned, not by calculated Japanese brutality, but merely by a special form of the boredom, waste of time, and demoralization which are typical of modern industrial society. Our most pressing daily problems were really the familiar trade-union issues of long portal-to-portal hours of work, and the various tensions arising from failures of communication between the technical specialists, the personnel managers, and the on-site foremen—in our case the Japanese engineers, the higher prisoner administration, and the guards.

The people best able to see the situation as a whole were probably the officer-prisoners in charge of individual working parties. (This was before officers had been forced to do manual work.) These officers, however, normally dealt only with the particular guards on their section of the line; and back at camp headquarters neither the Japanese prison staff nor the senior British officers had much direct knowledge of conditions out on the trace. But since— mainly because of a shortage of interpreters—most of the Japanese orders were handed down through Allied officers, who were in fact virtually impotent, everything tended to increase the confusion and mistrust in our own ranks.

At first the difficulties in the Bridge Camp of Tha Makham were much like those in all the others. But soon they began to change, mainly because of the personality of its senior British officer.

Colonel Philip Toosey was tall, rather young, and with one of those special English faces like a genial but sceptical bulldog. Unlike Boulle's Colonel Nicholson, he was not a career officer but a territorial.

Toosey's previous career had been managerial. Now a cotton merchant and banker, he had earlier run a factory, where he had experienced the decline of the Lancashire cotton industry, strikes, unemployment, the Depression; he'd even gone bankrupt himself. This past training helped him to see that the problem confronting him wasn't a standard military problem at all: it had an engineering side, a labor-organization side, and above all, a very complicated morale side affecting both the prisoners and their captors.

Escaping or refusing to work on a strategic bridge were both out of the question. Trying either could only mean some men killed, and the rest punished. We had already learned that in a showdown the Japanese would always win; they had the power, and no scruples about using it. But Toosey had the imagination to see that there was a shade more room for manoeuvre than anybody else had suspected—as long as the manoeuvres were of exactly the right kind. He was a brave man, but he never forced the issue so as to make the Japanese lose face; instead he first awed them with an impressive display of military swagger; and then proceeded to charm them with his apparently immovable assumption that no serious difficulty could arise between honorable soldiers whose only thought was to do the right thing.

The right thing from our point of view, obviously, was to do everything possible to increase food and medical supplies, improve working conditions, and allocate the work more reasonably. Gradually, Toosey persuaded the Japanese that things like issuing tools or allocating the day's tasks to each working party more evenly would be better handled if we did it ourselves. He also persuaded the Japanese that output would be much improved if the duties of the guards were limited entirely to preventing the prisoners from escaping. We would be responsible for our own organization and discipline. The officers in charge of working parties would supervise the construction work; while back at camp headquarters, if the Japanese engineers would assign the next day's work to Colonel Toosey, he and his staff would see how best to carry it out.

The new organization completely transformed our conditions of life. There was much less waste of time; daily tasks were often finished early in the afternoon; weeks passed without any prisoner being beaten; and the camp became almost happy.

Looked at from outside, Toosey's remarkable success obviously involved an increase in the degree of our collaboration with the enemy. But anybody on the spot knew that the real issue was not between building or not building the bridge; it was merely how many prisoners would die, be beaten up, or break down, in the process. There was only one way to persuade the Japanese to improve rations, provide medical supplies, allow regular holidays, or reduce the brutality of the guards: to convince them that the work got done better our way.

Toosey's drive and panache soon won him the confidence of the Japanese at the camp: they got about the same amount of work out of us, and their working day was much shorter too. At the same time Toosey was never accused by his fellow prisoners—as Boulle's Colonel Nicholson certainly would have been—of being "Jap-happy." Some regarded him as a bit too regimental for their taste; but, unanswerably, he delivered the goods. Eventually, in all the dozens of camps up and down the River Kwai, Toosey became a legend: he was the man who could "handle the Nips." His general strategy of taking over as much responsibility as possible (often much more than the Japanese knew), was gradually put into practice by the most successful British, American, Australian and Dutch commanders in the other camps. Even more convincingly, in 1945, when the Japanese saw defeat ahead, and finally concentrated all their officer prisoners in one camp, the vast majority of the three thousand or so allied officers collected there agitated until various senior commanding officers were successively removed and Colonel Toosey was put in charge. He remained in command until the end of the war in August 1945, when, to general consternation, all kinds of ancient military characters precipitately emerged from the wood-work to reclaim the privileges of seniority.

The Myth Begins

But Toosey, like all the other heroes—and non-heroes—of our prisoner-of-war days, would normally have been forgotten when peace finally broke out. That he left any mark on the larger world is only because a Free-French officer, Pierre Boulle, who had never known him, had never been near the railway, and was never a prisoner of the Japanese, wrote a novel called *Le Pont de la Rivière Kwai*.

The book was not in any sense intended as history. Though he took the river's real name, Boulle placed his bridge near the Burmese frontier, two hundred miles from the only actual bridge *across* the Kwai, the one at Tha Makham. And, as Boulle recounted in his fascinating but—on this topic—not very explicit autobiographical memoir, *The Sources of the River Kwai* (1966), Colonel Nicholson was based, not on any prisoner of war but on two French colonels he had known in Indo-China. Having been Boulle's comrades in arms until the collapse of France in 1941, they then sided with Vichy, and eventually punished Boulle's activities on behalf of the Allies as treason, quite blind to the notion that it was they, and not Boulle, who had changed sides.

In his novel Boulle made Nicholson's "collaboration" much more extreme: he built a better bridge than the one the Japanese had started, and in a better place. Boulle may have got the idea from the fact that the Japanese actually built two bridges over the Kwai at Tha Makham: a temporary wooden structure, which no longer survives; and another begun at the same time and finished in May, 1943, which was a permanent iron-trestle bridge on concrete piers, and still stands. Both bridges showed up clearly on Allied aerial photographs; and Boulle may have seen these photographs when he was a Free-French Intelligence officer in Calcutta during the last year of the war.

Boulle's main aim in the novel was presumably to dramatize the ironic contradictions which he had personally experienced in Indo-China. First, Nicholson embodied the paradox of how the military —like any other institutional—mind will tend to generate its own objectives, objectives which are often quite different from, and may even be contrary to, the original purposes of the institution. Secondly, there was the political paradox—the total reversals of attitude which continually occur, almost unnoticed, in our strange world of changing ideological alliances. To drive this point home Boulle also invented the Allied commandos who were sent to blow up the bridge with exactly the same patient technological expertness as had been used by their former comrades in arms who had built it.

The book's interest for the reader comes mainly from the similar but opposite efforts of the commandos and the prisoners. Like Nicholson we forget about aims because the means are absorbing; we watch how well the two jobs are being done, and it's only at the end that we wake up and realize that all this marvellous technological expertness harnessed to admirable collective effort has been leading to nothing except death; Nicholson sabotages the saboteurs, and then dies under the fire of Warden's mortar. So, finally, we see that the novel is not really about the Kwai, but about how the vast scale and complication of the operations which are rendered possible, and are even in a sense required, by modern technology tend finally to destroy human meanings and purposes. The West is the master of its means, but not of its ends.

This basic idea was lost, of course, in the movie; but there were many other elements in Boulle's narrative which gave it a more universal appeal.

First, there was the character of Nicholson, which was very little changed in the movie: an amiable fellow in his way, but egocentric; admirable, but ridiculous; intelligent, but basically infantile. Here we come back to a very ancient French myth about the English character, a stereotype which was already fully established in a book written about an English colonel by a French liaison officer after the first world war—in André Maurois' *The Silences of Colonel Bramble*. The infantile and egocentric side of Nicholson's character is essential to the plot; the book is after all about a monomaniac who falls in love with a boy's hobby: to build a bridge, but not with an Erector set, and not for toy trains.

The audience, of course, gets caught up in the hobby too; perhaps because it fulfills the greatest human need in the modern world: being able to love one's work. Along the Kwai there had been a daily conflict between the instinct of workmanship and disgust with what one was being forced to do: people would spend hours trying to get a perfect alignment of piles, and then try to hide termites or rotten wood in an important joint. These sabotage games weren't really very significant; but they expressed a collective need to pretend we were still fighting the enemy, and to resist any tendency to see things the Japanese way. We were always on the lookout for people becoming what we called "Jap-happy"; and if anyone had started talking about "my bridge," like Nicholson, he'd have been replaced at once.

Neither the novel nor the film even hint at these conflicting impulses; and so the question arises, "How can Boulle's shrewd and experienced mind ever have imagined that Nicholson could plausibly get away with his love affair for a Japanese bridge?"

There are at least three possible reasons. First, Boulle himself was born in Avignon, site of the world's most famous ruined bridge. Secondly, he was trained as an engineer and presumably shared the mystique of his profession. These were two positive motives for loving bridges; and there was also the general intellectual and political context of the post-war world. Boulle's first collection of short stories, *Tales of the Absurd*, expressed not only a sense that history had arrived at a meaningless dead-end, but the whole Existential perspective on the human condition in general; all political causes and individual purposes were equally fictitious and ridiculous. Boulle certainly intended *The Bridge on the River Kwai* to have the same implication; as we can see from his epigraph, taken from Conrad's *Victory*: "No, it was not funny; it was, rather, pathetic; he was so representative of all the past victims of the Great Joke. But it is by folly alone that the world moves, and so it is a respectable thing on the whole. And besides, he was what one would call a good man."

The Movie

Boulle's book was published in 1952 and sold about 6,000 copies annually in France until 1958. That year sales leaped to 122,000—the movie had come out. Later, the film's success caused the book to be translated into more than twenty languages, and to sell millions of copies; it also, of course, created the myth.

Hollywood has been a great creator of myths, but they have usually been personal—myths of individual actors, such as Charlie Chaplin or Humphrey Bogart, or of character-types, such as the cowboy or the private eye. The Hungarian producer, Sam Spiegel, and the English director, David Lean, turned a little river in Thailand that is not marked in most atlases into a household word.

So great a success obviously presupposes a very complete adaptation to the tastes of the international cinema public: and this adaptive process can be seen in the differences between the book and the movie, which is even further from what really happened on the railway. Of course, one can't fairly blame the movie for not showing the real life of the prisoner-of-war camps along the Kwai, if only because that life was boring even to those who lived it. On the other hand, using the name of an actual river suggested an element of authenticity; and the movie's version of events at the bridge certainly seemed to the survivors a gross insult on their intelligence and on that of their commanders. When news of the film's being made came out, various ex-prisoner-of-war associations, led, among other people, by Colonel Toosey, protested against the movie's distortion of what had actually happened; since the name of the river was fairly well known, people were bound to think there was an element of truth in the film. But history had given Sam Spiegel a lot of free publicity, and he refused even to change the film's title. This was vital, not only for the aura of historical truth at the box-office, but for the growth of the myth; since, in the curious limbo of mythic reality, collective fantasies need to be anchored on some real name of a place or a person.

The movie's air of pseudo-reality was also inevitably enforced by its medium. No one reading Boulle could have failed to notice from his style alone that the book aimed at ironic fantasy, rather than detailed historical realism; but the camera can't help giving an air of total visual authenticity; and the effect of this technical authenticity tends to spread beyond the visual image to the substance of what is portrayed. Every moviegoer knows in some way that—whenever he can check against his own experience—life isn't really like that; but he forgets it most of the time, especially when the substance of what he sees conforms to his own psychological or political point of view.

Politically, the movie gave no inkling of the unpleasant facts about the terrible poverty and disease along the real river Kwai. Instead, the audience must have taken away some vague impression that the poor jungle villagers of South-East Asia all have perfect complexions, and fly elaborately lovely kites. They don't. Equally unrealistically, the movie suggested that beautiful Thai girls don't have any boyfriends until some handsome white man comes along. Much more dangerously, the movie incidentally promoted the political delusion—less common now than in 1958—that the people of these poor villages are merely marking time until they are given an opportunity to sacrifice their lives on behalf of the ideology of the Western powers. All these are examples of the colonialist attitudes which were also present in the central idea of the novel: although the Japanese had beaten the Allies in a campaign that, among other things, showed a remarkable command of very difficult engineering and transport problems, Boulle presented them as comically inferior to their captives as bridge builders. Both the novel and the movie, in fact, contained as a primary assumption the myth of white superiority whose results we have seen most recently in that same Vietnam that Boulle had known.

In the movie the bridge itself, of course, also had to be transformed into a symbol of Western engineering mastery. The form and color of those two giant cantilevers had a poised serenity which almost justified Nicholson's infatuation; but it was totally beyond the technical means and the military needs of the actual bridges over the Kwai; and its great beauty soon made one forget the sordid realities of the war and the prison camp. What actually happened was that the movie-makers went to Thailand, took one look at the Kwai, and saw it wouldn't do. The area wasn't particularly interesting— too flat, and not at all wild; there was already a bridge over the river —the real one; and in any case there wasn't any accommodation in the little provincial town of Kamburi to match the splendors of the Mount Lavinia Hotel in Ceylon, where most of the movie was eventually shot.

All this is a normal, perhaps inevitable, part of making movies; and one's only legitimate objection is that ultimately the pseudo-realism of Hollywood has the accidental effect of making millions of people think they are seeing what something is really like when actually they are not.

The biggest departure of the movie both from history and from the novel, was the blowing up of the bridge, which distorted reality in a rather similar direction. The movie credits read "Screenplay by Pierre Boulle, Based on His Novel." Actually, though Boulle got an Oscar for the screenplay, he took only a "modest" part in the preliminary discussions of the screenplay with Spiegel and Lean; and the real writer—who couldn't then be named—was Carl Foreman, who had been blacklisted by Hollywood during the McCarthy era. Pierre Boulle eventually approved their final version; but only after he'd objected to many of their changes, and especially to the one which contradicted his whole purpose: that in the movie the bridge was blown up. He was told that the audience would have watched the screen "for more than two hours . . . in the hope and expectation" of just that big bang; if it didn't happen "they would feel frustrated"; and anyway it was quite impossible to pass up "such a sensational bit of action." So, on March 12, 1957, a beautiful bridge that had cost a quarter of a million dollars to build was blown up with a real train crossing it.

Building a bridge just to blow it up again so that the movie public won't feel frustrated was an unbelievably apt illustration of Boulle's point about how contemporary society employs its awesome technological means in the pursuit of largely derisory ends.

Boulle's readers had been made to think about that; not so the moviegoers. Their consciences were kept quiet by a well-intentioned anti-war message—the killing of the terrified young Japanese soldier, for example—while they were having a rip-roaring time. But, as we all know, you can't have it both ways. You can't turn an exotic adventure-comedy into a true film about war just by dunking it in blood. The film only seemed to take up real problems; at the end a big explosion showed that there was no point in thinking things over—when things will work out nicely anyway, why bother?

In the movie of the *Bridge on the River Kwai*, then, historical and political and psychological reality became infinitely plastic to the desires of the audience. All over the world audiences gratefully responded; and in the end they even caused the myth to be reincarnated where it had begun.

Reincarnation on the Kwai

The decisive phase of a myth is when the story wins a special status for itself; when people begin to think of it, not exactly as history, but as something which, in some vague way, really happened; and then, later, the fiction eventually imposes itself on the world as literally true. The earliest signs of this are normally the erection of shrines, and the beginning of pilgrimages; but the process of reincarnation is only complete when whatever is left of the truth which conflicts with the myth's symbolic meaning is forgotten or transformed. All this has begun to happen to the myth of the Kwai.

After the war ended, in August 1945, and the last train had evacuated the sad remnants of the Japanese army in Burma, silence at last descended on the railway. Robbers furtively stole the telegraph wire; termites ate away the wooden sleepers of the line and the timbers of the bridges; the monsoon rains washed away parts of the embankment; and sensing that all was normal again, the wild elephants (which few prisoners had ever seen) once again emerged from the jungle, and, finding the railway trace a convenient path, leaned against whatever telegraph poles inconvenienced their passage. By the time that, in 1946, the Thai government bought the Kwai railway from the Japanese for about $4,000,000, its track was on the way to being derelict.

Eventually it was decided to keep the railway going only as far up as a place called Nam Tok, some hundred miles above the bridge over the Kwai. Nam Tok was probably chosen as terminus because there are beautiful waterfalls nearby, waterfalls that are very famous in Thai history and legend. In 1961 the whole area was scheduled as a National Park; and now three trains a day carry villagers and tourists up to see the sights.

When I visited Nam Tok in 1966 I found that, just at the end of the embankment, the local villagers had set up a little shrine. On the altar table, in front of the little gilded image of the local tutelary deity, or *Chao Tee*, there were the usual propitiatory offerings, flowers, incense-sticks, fruit, sweets, candles, paper garlands; but in the place of honor were two rusty old iron spikes—the kind we had used to fasten the rails to the wooden ties.

There are also other and much vaster shrines near the Tha Makham bridge: an Allied cemetery for 6,982 Australian, British and Dutch prisoners of war; a Roman Catholic chapel just opposite; a Chinese burial ground for a few of the Asiatic forced-laborers of whom over a hundred thousand died along the Kwai; and a Japanese Memorial to all the casualties of the railway, including their own. All these shrines are much visited, as the fresh flowers and incense sticks testify: the Japanese Ambassador regularly lays a wreath at the Japanese Memorial; and there is an annual commemoration service in the Allied cemetery.

There are also other kinds of pilgrim. In Bangkok, "Sincere Travel Service," for instance, advertises

Tour No. 11 Daily: 7:30 a.m. Whole day soft drinks and lunch provided. The Bridge over River Kwai and the notorious 'Death Railway' of World War fame is at Karnburi. The tourists will definitely have the joy of their life when cruising along the *real River Kwai* on the way to pay a visit to the Chungkai War Memorial Cemetery, then follows a delicious lunch by the Bridge Over River Kwai and see the real train rolling across it. All inclusive rate: US $20.–per person minimum 2 persons.

The world wide diffusion of Boulle's novel through the cinema, then, has left its mark on the Kwai. Outside the Karnburi cemetery there stands today a road sign which reads: "Bridge over the River Kwai 2.590 kilometers." It points to a real bridge; but it is only worth pointing to because of the bridge the whole world saw in the movie.

In a recent pictorial guide to Thailand there is an even more striking example of how the power of the myth is beginning to transform reality. The book gives a fine photograph of what is actually the Wang Pho viaduct along a gorge some fifty miles further up the line; but the caption reads "Bridge on the River Kwai." Some obscure need, disappointed by the failure of the real bridge *over* the river Kwai to live up to the beauty of the one in the movie, has relocated the home of the myth, and selected the most spectacular view along the railway as a more appropriate setting.

The Myth and the Reality

The myth, then, is established. What does it mean?

When *The Bridge on the River Kwai* was first televised it drew the largest TV audience ever recorded. Millions of people must have responded to it because—among other things—it expressed the same delusions as are responsible for much unreal political thinking. There was, as I've already said, the colonial myth—the odd notion that the ordinary people of South-East Asia instinctively love the white strangers who have come to their lands, and want to sacrifice themselves on their behalf. There was also the implication of the blowing-up of the bridge—however muddled we may be about our political aims, advanced high-explosive technology will always come out on top in the end. The Big Bang theory of war, of course, fitted in very nicely with the consoling illusion of a world of Friendly (and militarily backward) Natives.

The theory, and the illusion, have one fatal weakness: they clash with what Sartre calls *"la force des choses."*[1] What happened to the real bridge illustrates this very neatly.

In the summer of 1944 the new American long-range bombers, the B 29's, started flying over the Kwai, and bombing the bridges.

1. The force of things as they are.

To anyone who knows any military history, what happened was absolutely predictable. Quite a lot of people, mainly prisoners, were killed; but eventually the bombers got some direct hits, and two spans of the steel bridge fell into the river. While it was being repaired, the low wooden bridge was put back into use; and when that, too, was damaged, it was easily restored by the labor of the prisoners in the nearby camps. Japanese military supplies weren't delayed for a single day. If you can build a bridge, you can repair it; in the long run, bombing military targets is only significant if the target can later be captured and held.

The Allied command in Ceylon knew this very well. They bombed the Kwai railway then because their armies were advancing in Burma and preparing to attack Thailand: but this vital context is absent from the novel and the film. Actually there were also Allied commandos in the bridge area at the time: not to blow up the bridge, though, but to link up with the Thai resistance, and help liberate prison camps once the invasion started. Boulle probably knew this, since he called his commandos Force 316, whereas the real ones were Force 136. Still, Boulle's novel certainly undercuts the Big Bang theory, and one imagines that he found in its blind destructive credulity a folly that wasn't exclusively military. Since 1866, and Nobel's invention of dynamite, all kinds of individuals and social groups have attributed magical powers to dynamite; they've refused to see that the best you can expect from explosives is an explosion.

The Big Bang theory of war is rather like the colonial myth, and even the schoolboy dream of defying the adult world; all three are essentially expressions of what Freud called the childish delusion of the omnipotence of thought. The myth of the Kwai deeply reflects this delusion, and shapes it according to the particular values of contemporary culture.

Hollywood, the advertising industry, Existentialism, even the current counter-culture are alike in their acceptance or their exploitation of the delusion of the omnipotence of thought. From this come many of their other similarities: that they are ego-centered, romantic, anti-historical; that they all show a belief in rapid and absolute solutions of human problems. They are all, in the last analysis, institutional patterns based on the posture of anti-institutionalism.

These basic assumptions of the myth are perhaps most obvious in the kernel of the story, which the movie made much more recognizable as a universal fantasy, the schoolboy's perennial dream of defying the adult world. Young Nicholson cheeks the mean old headmaster, called Saito: he gets a terrible beating, but the other students kick up such a row about it that Saito just has to give in. Confrontation tactics win out; and Nicholson is carried back in triumph across the playground. In the end, of course, he becomes the best student-body president Kwai High ever had.

I don't know if anything like this—total rebellion combined with total acceptance—has ever occurred in any educational institution; but I am forced to report that nothing like it ever happened in the prison-camps along the Kwai. There, all our circumstances were hostile to individual fantasies; surviving meant accepting the intractable realities which surrounded us, and making sure that our fellow prisoners accepted them too.

No one would even guess from the novel or the film that there were any wholly intractable realities on the Kwai. Boulle proposes a simple syllogism: war is madness; war is fought by soldiers; therefore, soldiers are mad. It's a flattering notion, no doubt, to non-soldiers, but it happens not to be true; and it's really much too easy a way out to delude ourselves with the belief that wars and injustices are caused only by lunatics, by people who don't see things as we see them.

Neither the novel nor the film admits that certain rational distinctions remain important even under the most difficult or confusing circumstances. They seem instead to derive a peculiar satisfaction from asserting that in a world of madness the weakness of our collective life can find its salvation only in the strength of madmen. There is no need to insist on the authoritarian nature of this idea, but it does seem necessary to enquire why these last decades have created a myth which totally subverts the stubbornness of facts and of the human will to resist unreason.

The basic reason is presumably the widespread belief that institutions are at the same time immoral, ridiculous, and unreal, whereas individuals exist in a world whose circumstances are essentially tractable. A prisoner-of-war camp has at least one thing in common with our modern world in general: both offer a very limited range of practical choices. No wonder the public acclaimed a film where, under the most limiting circumstances imaginable, one solitary individual managed to do just what he planned to do. Of course his triumph depended on making everything else subservient to his fantasy; and if our circumstances on the Kwai had been equally pliable, there would have been no reason whatever for Toosey or anybody else to act as they did.

It's probably true that at the beginning of our captivity many of us thought that at last the moment had arrived for revolt, if not against the Japanese, at least against our own military discipline and anything else that interfered with our individual liberty. But then circumstances forced us to see that this would be suicidal. We were terribly short of food, clothes, and medicine; theft soon became a real threat to everyone; and so we had to organize our own police. At first it seemed too ridiculous, but not for long. When cholera broke out, for instance, whole camps of Asiatic laborers were wiped out, whereas in our own camps nearby, with an effective organization to make sure everyone used the latrines and ate or drank only what had been boiled, we often had no deaths, even though we had no vaccine.

In the myth, then, the actual circumstances of our experience on the Kwai were overwhelmed by the deep blindness of our culture both to the stubbornness of reality and to the continuities of history. It was surely this blindness which encouraged the public, in accepting the plausibility of Nicholson's triumph, to assert its belief in the combined wickedness, folly, and unreality of institutions— notably of those which were in conflict on the Kwai: the Japanese and their prisoners.

It isn't only on the walls of the Sorbonne that we can see the slogan "It is forbidden to forbid." It is written on all individuals at birth, in the form "It is forbidden to forbid me"; and this text has been adopted to their great profit by the movie and advertising industries: by Hollywood, in the version "You don't get rich by saying no to dreams," and by Madison Avenue in the version "Tell 'em they're suckers if they don't have everything they want."

The movie, incidentally, added one apt illustration of this slogan which had no basis whatever in Boulle or reality. No one wants to be a prisoner; you don't have to be; and so William Holden escapes, easily. On the Kwai, hundreds tried; most of them were killed; no one succeeded.

Among today's pilgrims to the present cemeteries on the Kwai, an increasing number come from the American forces in Thailand and Vietnam. When I leafed through the Visitors' Book, one entry caught my eye. A private from Apple Creek, Wisconsin, stationed at Da Nang, had been moved to write a protest that made all the other banal pieties look pale: "PEOPLE are STUPID."

Stupid, among other things, because they are mainly led by what they want to believe, not by what they know. It's easier to go along with the implication of the movie, and believe that a big bang— anywhere—will somehow end the world's confusion and our own fatigue. It would undoubtedly end it, but only in larger cemeteries for the victims of the last Great Joke.

Vietnam has been a painful lesson in the kinds of mythical thinking which *The Bridge on the River Kwai* both reflected and reinforced; we seem now to be slowly recovering from some of the political forms of the omnipotence-of-thought fantasy. Recently, I observed that the main audience reaction to the movie was ironical laughter.

If we can accept the notion that in all kinds of spheres some individual has to be responsible for the organization and continuity of human affairs, we should perhaps look again at the man without whom the myth would not have come into being. Along the Kwai, Colonel Toosey was almost universally recognized for what he was —a hero of the only kind we could afford then, and there. For he was led, not by what he wanted to believe, but by what he knew: he knew that the world would not do his bidding; that he could not beat the Japanese: that on the Kwai—even more obviously than at home—we were for the most part helpless prisoners of coercive circumstance. But he also knew that if things were as intractable as they looked, the outlook for the years ahead was hopeless: much death, and total demoralization, for the community he found himself in. The only thing worth working for was the possibility that tenacity and imagination could find a way by which the chances of decent survival could be increased. It was, no doubt, a very modest objective for so much work and restraint—two of Conrad's moral imperatives that Boulle didn't quote, incidentally; but in our circumstances then on the Kwai, the objective was quite enough to be getting on with; as it is here, now.

EDWARD HALLETT CARR

The Historian and His Facts[1]

What is history? Lest anyone think the question meaningless or superfluous, I will take as my text two passages relating respectively to the first and second incarnations of *The Cambridge Modern History*. Here is Acton in his report of October 1896 to the Syndics of the Cambridge University Press on the work which he had undertaken to edit:

It is a unique opportunity of recording, in the way most useful to the greatest number, the fullness of the knowledge which the nineteenth century is about to bequeath.... By the judicious division of labor we should be able to do it, and to bring home to every man the last document, and the ripest conclusions of international research.

Ultimate history we cannot have in this generation; but we can dispose of conventional history, and show the point we have reached on the road from one to the other, now that all information is within reach, and every problem has become capable of solution.[2]

And almost exactly sixty years later Professor Sir George Clark, in his general introduction to the second *Cambridge Modern History*, commented on this belief of Acton and his collaborators that it would one day be possible to produce "ultimate history," and went on:

Historians of a later generation do not look forward to any such prospect. They expect their work to be superseded again and again. They consider that knowledge of the past has come down through one or more human minds, has been "processed" by them, and therefore cannot consist of ele-

1. Chapter I of *What is History?*, 1961.
2. *The Cambridge Modern History: Its Origin, Authorship and Production*
(Cambridge University Press, 1907), pp. 10-12 [This and the following footnotes are Carr's].

mental and impersonal atoms which nothing can alter.... The exploration seems to be endless, and some impatient scholars take refuge in scepticism, or at least in the doctrine that, since all historical judgments involve persons and points of view, one is as good as another and there is no "objective" historical truth.[3]

Where the pundits contradict each other so flagrantly the field is open to enquiry. I hope that I am sufficiently up-to-date to recognize that anything written in the 1890's must be nonsense. But I am not yet advanced enough to be committed to the view that anything written in the 1950's necessarily makes sense. Indeed, it may already have occurred to you that this enquiry is liable to stray into something even broader than the nature of history. The clash between Acton and Sir George Clark is a reflection of the change in our total outlook on society over the interval between these two pronouncements. Acton speaks out of the positive belief, the clear-eyed self-confidence of the later Victorian age; Sir George Clark echoes the bewilderment and distracted scepticism of the beat generation. When we attempt to answer the question, What is history?, our answer, consciously or unconsciously, reflects our own position in time, and forms part of our answer to the broader question, what view we take of the society in which we live. I have no fear that my subject may, on closer inspection, seem trivial. I am afraid only that I may seem presumptuous to have broached a question so vast and so important.

The nineteenth century was a great age for facts. "What I want," said Mr. Gradgrind in *Hard Times*, "is Facts. . . . Facts alone are wanted in life." Nineteenth-century historians on the whole agreed with him. When Ranke in the 1830's, in legitimate protest against moralizing history, remarked that the task of the historian was "simply to show how it really was [*wie es eigentlich gewesen*]" this not very profound aphorism had an astonishing success. Three generations of German, British, and even French historians marched into battle intoning the magic words, "*Wie es eigentlich gewesen*" like an incantation—designed, like most incantations, to save them from the tiresome obligation to think for themselves. The Positivists, anxious to stake out their claim for history as a science, contributed the weight of their influence to this cult of facts. First ascertain the facts, said the positivists, then draw your conclusions from them. In Great Britain, this view of history fitted in perfectly with the empiricist tradition which was the dominant strain in British philosophy from Locke to Bertrand Russell. The empirical theory of knowledge presupposes a complete separation between subject and object. Facts, like sense-impressions, impinge on the observer from outside, and are independent of his consciousness. The process of reception is passive: having received the data, he then acts on them. *The Shorter Oxford English Dictionary,*

3. *The New Cambridge Modern History,* I (Cambridge University Press, 1957), pp. xxiv-xxv.

a useful but tendentious work of the empirical school, clearly marks the separateness of the two processes by defining a fact as "a datum of experience as distinct from conclusions." This is what may be called the common-sense view of history. History consists of a corpus of ascertained facts. The facts are available to the historian in documents, inscriptions, and so on, like fish on the fishmonger's slab. The historian collects them, takes them home, and cooks and serves them in whatever style appeals to him. Acton, whose culinary tastes were austere, wanted them served plain. In his letter of instructions to contributors to the first *Cambridge Modern History* he announced the requirement "that our Waterloo must be one that satisfies French and English, German and Dutch alike; that nobody can tell, without examining the list of authors where the Bishop of Oxford laid down the pen, and whether Fairbairn or Gasquet, Liebermann or Harrison took it up."[4] Even Sir George Clark, critical as he was of Acton's attitude, himself contrasted the "hard core of facts" in history with the "surrounding pulp of disputable interpretation"[5]—forgetting perhaps that the pulpy part of the fruit is more rewarding than the hard core. First get your facts straight, then plunge at your peril into the shifting sands of interpretation—that is the ultimate wisdom of the empirical, common-sense school of history. It recalls the favorite dictum of the great liberal journalist C. P. Scott: "Facts are sacred, opinion is free."

Now this clearly will not do. I shall not embark on a philosophical discussion of the nature of our knowledge of the past. Let us assume for present purposes that the fact that Caesar crossed the Rubicon and the fact that there is a table in the middle of the room are facts of the same or of a comparable order, that both these facts enter our consciousness in the same or in a comparable manner, and that both have the same objective character in relation to the person who knows them. But, even on this bold and not very plausible assumption, our argument at once runs into the difficulty that not all facts about the past are historical facts, or are treated as such by the historian. What is the criterion which distinguishes the facts of history from other facts about the past?

What is a historical fact? This is a crucial question into which we must look a little more closely. According to the common-sense view, there are certain basic facts which are the same for all historians and which form, so to speak, the backbone of history—the fact, for example, that the Battle of Hastings was fought in 1066. But this view calls for two observations. In the first place, it is not with facts like these that the historian is primarily concerned. It is no doubt important to know that the great battle was fought in 1066 and not in 1065 or 1067, and that it was fought at Hastings and not at Eastbourne or Brighton. The historian must

4. Acton: *Lectures on Modern History* (London: Macmillan & Co., 1906), p. 318.   5. Quoted in *The Listener* (June 19, 1952), p. 992.

not get these things wrong. But when points of this kind are raised, I am reminded of Housman's remark that "accuracy is a duty, not a virtue."[6] To praise a historian for his accuracy is like praising an architect for using well-seasoned timber or properly mixed concrete in his building. It is a necessary condition of his work, but not his essential function. It is precisely for matters of this kind that the historian is entitled to rely on what have been called the "auxiliary sciences" of history—archaeology, epigraphy, numismatics, chronology, and so forth. The historian is not required to have the special skills which enable the expert to determine the origin and period of a fragment of pottery or marble, or decipher an obscure inscription, or to make the elaborate astronomical calculations necessary to establish a precise date. These so-called basic facts which are the same for all historians commonly belong to the category of the raw materials of the historian rather than of history itself. The second observation is that the necessity to establish these basic facts rests not on any quality in the facts themselves, but on an *a priori* decision of the historian. In spite of C. P. Scott's motto, every journalist knows today that the most effective way to influence opinion is by the selection and arrangement of the appropriate facts. It used to be said that facts speak for themselves. This is, of course, untrue. The facts speak only when the historian calls on them: It is he who decides to which facts to give the floor, and in what order or context. It was, I think, one of Pirandello's characters who said that a fact is like a sack—it won't stand up till you've put something in it. The only reason why we are interested to know that the battle was fought at Hastings in 1066 is that historians regard it as a major historical event. It is the historian who has decided for his own reasons that Caesar's crossing of that petty stream, the Rubicon, is a fact of history, whereas the crossing of the Rubicon by millions of other people before or since interests nobody at all. The fact that you arrived in this building half an hour ago on foot, or on a bicycle, or in a car, is just as much a fact about the past as the fact that Caesar crossed the Rubicon. But it will probably be ignored by historians. Professor Talcott Parsons once called science "a selective system of cognitive orientations to reality."[7] It might perhaps have been put more simply. But history is, among other things, that. The historian is necessarily selective. The belief in a hard core of historical facts existing objectively and independently of the interpretation of the historian is a preposterous fallacy, but one which it is very hard to eradicate.

Let us take a look at the process by which a mere fact about

6. M. Manilius: *Astronomicon: Liber Primus*, 2nd ed. (Cambridge University Press, 1937), p. 87.
7. Talcott Parsons and Edward A.

Shils: *Toward a General Theory of Action*, 3rd ed. (Cambridge, Mass.: Harvard University Press, 1954), p. 167.

the past is transformed into a fact of history. At Stalybridge Wakes in 1850, a vendor of gingerbread, as the result of some petty dispute, was deliberately kicked to death by an angry mob. Is this a fact of history? A year ago I should unhesitatingly have said "no." It was recorded by an eyewitness in some little-known memoirs;[8] but I had never seen it judged worthy of mention by any historian. A year ago Dr. Kitson Clark cited it in his Ford lectures in Oxford.[9] Does this make it into a historical fact? Not, I think, yet. Its present status, I suggest, is that it has been proposed for membership of the select club of historical facts. It now awaits a seconder and sponsors. It may be that in the course of the next few years we shall see this fact appearing first in footnotes, then in the text, of articles and books about nineteenth-century England, and that in twenty or thirty years' time it may be a well established historical fact. Alternatively, nobody may take it up, in which case it will relapse into the limbo of unhistorical facts about the past from which Dr. Kitson Clark has gallantly attempted to rescue it. What will decide which of these two things will happen? It will depend, I think, on whether the thesis or interpretation in support of which Dr. Kitson Clark cited this incident is accepted by other historians as valid and significant. Its status as a historical fact will turn on a question of interpretation. This element of interpretation enters into every fact of history.

May I be allowed a personal reminiscence? When I studied ancient history in this university many years ago, I had as a special subject "Greece in the period of the Persian Wars." I collected fifteen or twenty volumes on my shelves and took it for granted that there, recorded in these volumes, I had all the facts relating to my subject. Let us assume—it was very nearly true—that those volumes contained all the facts about it that were then known, or could be known. It never occurred to me to enquire by what accident or process of attrition that minute selection of facts, out of all the myriad facts that must have once been known to somebody, had survived to become *the* facts of history. I suspect that even today one of the fascinations of ancient and mediaeval history is that it gives us the illusion of having all the facts at our disposal within a manageable compass: the nagging distinction between the facts of history and other facts about the past vanishes because the few known facts are all facts of history. As Bury, who had worked in both periods, said "the records of ancient and mediaeval history are starred with lacunae."[1] History has been called an enormous jig-saw with a lot of missing parts. But the main trouble does not consist of the lacunae. Our picture of Greece in the fifth

8. Lord George Sanger: *Seventy Years a Showman* (London: J. M. Dent & Sons, 1926), pp. 188-9.
9. These will shortly be published under the title *The Making of Victorian England.*
1. John Bagnell Bury: *Selected Essays* (Cambridge University Press, 1930, p. 52.)

century B.C. is defective not primarily because so many of the bits have been accidentally lost, but because it is, by and large, the picture formed by a tiny group of people in the city of Athens. We know a lot about what fifth-century Greece looked like to an Athenian citizen; but hardly anything about what it looked like to a Spartan, a Corinthian, or a Theban—not to mention a Persian, or a slave or other non-citizen resident in Athens. Our picture has been preselected and predetermined for us, not so much by accident as by people who were consciously or unconsciously imbued with a particular view and thought the facts which supported that view worth preserving. In the same way, when I read in a modern history of the Middle Ages that the people of the Middle Ages were deeply concerned with religion, I wonder how we know this, and whether it is true. What we know as the facts of mediaeval history have almost all been selected for us by generations of chroniclers who were professionally occupied in the theory and practice of religion, and who therefore thought it supremely important, and recorded everything relating to it, and not much else. The picture of the Russian peasant as devoutly religious was destroyed by the revolution of 1917. The picture of mediaeval man as devoutly religious, whether true or not, is indestructible, because nearly all the known facts about him were preselected for us by people who believed it, and wanted others to believe it, and a mass of other facts, in which we might possibly have found evidence to the contrary, has been lost beyond recall. The dead hand of vanished generations of historians, scribes, and chroniclers has determined beyond the possibility of appeal the pattern of the past. "The history we read," writes Professor Barraclough, himself trained as a mediaevalist, "though based on facts, is, strictly speaking, not factual at all, but a series of accepted judgments."[2]

But let us turn to the different, but equally grave, plight of the modern historian. The ancient or mediaeval historian may be grateful for the vast winnowing process which, over the years, has put at his disposal a manageable corpus of historical facts. As Lytton Strachey said in his mischievous way, "ignorance is the first requisite of the historian, ignorance which simplifies and clarifies, which selects and omits."[3] When I am tempted, as I sometimes am, to envy the extreme competence of colleagues engaged in writing ancient or mediaeval history, I find consolation in the reflection that they are so competent mainly because they are so ignorant of their subject. The modern historian enjoys none of the advantages of this built-in ignorance. He must cultivate this necessary ignorance for himself—the more so the nearer he comes to his own times. He has the dual task of discovering the few significant facts and turn-

2. Geoffrey Barraclough: *History in a Changing World* (London; Basil Blackwell & Mott, 1955), p. 14.

3. Lytton Strachey: Preface to *Eminent Victorians*.

ing them into facts of history, and of discarding the many insignificant facts as unhistorical. But this is the very converse of the nineteenth-century heresy that history consists of the compilation of a maximum number of irrefutable and objective facts. Anyone who succumbs to this heresy will either have to give up history as a bad job, and take to stamp-collecting or some other form of antiquarianism, or end in a madhouse. It is this heresy, which during the past hundred years has had such devastating effects on the modern historian, producing in Germany, in Great Britain, and in the United States a vast and growing mass of dry-as-dust factual histories, of minutely specialized monographs, of would-be historians knowing more and more about less and less, sunk without trace in an ocean of facts. It was, I suspect, this heresy—rather than the alleged conflict between liberal and Catholic loyalties—which frustrated Acton as a historian. In an early essay he said of his teacher Döllinger: "He would not write with imperfect materials, and to him the materials were always imperfect."[4] Acton was surely here pronouncing an anticipatory verdict on himself, on that strange phenomenon of a historian whom many would regard as the most distinguished occupant the Regius Chair of Modern History in this university has ever had—but who wrote no history. And Acton wrote his own epitaph in the introductory note to the first volume of the *Cambridge Modern History*, published just after his death, when he lamented that the requirements pressing on the historian "threaten to turn him from a man of letters into the compiler of an encyclopedia."[5] Something had gone wrong. What had gone wrong was the belief in this untiring and unending accumulation of hard facts as the foundation of history, the belief that facts speak for themselves and that we cannot have too many facts, a belief at that time so unquestioning that few historians then thought it necessary—and some still think it unnecessary today —to ask themselves the question: What is history?

The nineteenth-century fetishism of facts was completed and justified by a fetishism of documents. The documents were the Ark of the Covenant in the temple of facts. The reverent historian approached them with bowed head and spoke of them in awed tones. If you find it in the documents, it is so. But what, when we get down to it, do these documents—the decrees, the treaties, the rent-rolls, the blue books, the official correspondence, the private letters and diaries—tell us? No document can tell us more than what the author of the document thought—what he thought had happened, what he thought ought to happen or would happen,

4. Quoted in George P. Gooch: *History and Historians in the Nineteenth Century* (London: Longmans, Green & Company, 1952), p. 385. Later Acton said of Döllinger that "it was given him to form his philosophy of history on the largest induction ever available to man" (*History of Freedom and Other Essays* [London: Macmillan & Co., 1907], p. 435).
5. *The Cambridge Modern History*, I (1902), p. 4.

or perhaps only what he wanted others to think he thought, or even only what he himself thought he thought. None of this means anything until the historian has got to work on it and deciphered it. The facts, whether found in documents or not, have still to be processed by the historian before he can make any use of them: the use he makes of them is, if I may put it that way, the processing process.

Let me illustrate what I am trying to say by an example which I happen to know well. When Gustav Stresemann, the Foreign Minister of the Weimar Republic, died in 1929, he left behind him an enormous mass—300 boxes full—of papers, official, semi-official, and private, nearly all relating to the six years of his tenure of office as Foreign Minister. His friends and relatives naturally thought that a monument should be raised to the memory of so great a man. His faithful secretary Bernhardt got to work; and within three years there appeared three massive volumes, of some 600 pages each, of selected documents from the 300 boxes, with the impressive title *Stresemanns Vermächtnis*.[6] In the ordinary way the documents themselves would have moldered away in some cellar or attic and disappeared for ever; or perhaps in a hundred years or so some curious scholar would have come upon them and set out to compare them with Bernhardt's text. What happened was far more dramatic. In 1945 the documents fell into the hands of the British and the American governments, who photographed the lot and put the photostats at the disposal of scholars in the Public Record Office in London and in the National Archives in Washington, so that, if we have sufficient patience and curiosity, we can discover exactly what Bernhardt did. What he did was neither very unusual nor very shocking. When Stresemann died, his Western policy seemed to have been crowned with a series of brilliant successes—Locarno, the admission of Germany to the League of Nations, the Dawes and Young plans and the American loans, the withdrawal of allied occupation armies from the Rhineland. This seemed the important and rewarding part of Stresemann's foreign policy; and it was not unnatural that it should have been over-represented in Bernhardt's selection of documents. Stresemann's Eastern policy, on the other hand, his relations with the Soviet Union, seemed to have led nowhere in particular; and, since masses of documents about negotiations which yielded only trivial results were not very interesting and added nothing to Stresemann's reputation, the process of selection could be more rigorous. Stresemann in fact devoted a far more constant and anxious attention to relations with the Soviet Union, and they played a far larger part in his foreign policy as a whole, than the reader of the Bernhardt selection would surmise. But the Bernhardt volumes compare

6. *Stresemann's Legacy.*

favorably, I suspect, with many published collections of documents on which the ordinary historian implicitly relies.

This is not the end of my story. Shortly after the publication of Bernhardt's volumes, Hitler came into power. Stresemann's name was consigned to oblivion in Germany, and the volumes disappeared from circulation: many, perhaps most, of the copies must have been destroyed. Today *Stresemanns Vermächtnis* is a rather rare book. But in the West Stresemann's reputation stood high. In 1935 an English publisher brought out an abbreviated translation of Bernhardt's work—a selection from Bernhardt's selection; perhaps one third of the original was omitted. Sutton, a well-known translator from the German, did his job competently and well. The English version, he explained in the preface, was "slightly condensed, but only by the omission of a certain amount of what, it was felt, was more ephemeral matter . . . of little interest to English readers or students."[7] This again is natural enough. But the result is that Stresemann's Eastern policy, already under-represented in Bernhardt, recedes still further from view, and the Soviet Union appears in Sutton's volumes merely as an occasional and rather unwelcome intruder in Stresemann's predominantly Western foreign policy. Yet it is safe to say that, for all except a few specialists, Sutton and not Bernhardt—and still less the documents themselves—represents for the Western world the authentic voice of Stresemann. Had the documents perished in 1945 in the bombing, and had the remaining Bernhardt volumes disappeared, the authenticity and authority of Sutton would never have been questioned. Many printed collections of documents gratefully accepted by historians in default of the originals rest on no securer basis than this.

But I want to carry the story one step further. Let us forget about Bernhardt and Sutton, and be thankful that we can, if we choose, consult the authentic papers of a leading participant in some important events in recent European history. What do the papers tell us? Among other things they contain records of some hundreds of Stresemann's conversations with the Soviet ambassador in Berlin and of a score or so with Chicherin.[8] These records have one feature in common. They depict Stresemann as having the lion's share of the conversations and reveal his arguments as invariably well put and cogent, while those of his partner are for the most part scanty, confused, and unconvincing. This is a familiar characteristic of all records of diplomatic conversations. The documents do not tell us what happened, but only what Stresemann thought had happened. It was not Sutton or Bernhardt, but Stresemann himself, who started the process of selection. And, if we had, say, Chicherin's records of these same conversations, we should still learn from

7. *Gustav Stresemann: His Diaries, Letters, and Papers* (London: Macmillan & Co.; 1935), I.

8. Soviet foreign minister 1918-28 [Editor's note].

them only what Chicherin thought, and what really happened would still have to be reconstructed in the mind of the historian. Of course, facts and documents are essential to the historian. But do not make a fetish of them. They do not by themselves constitute history; they provide in themselves no ready-made answer to this tiresome question: What is history?

At this point I should like to say a few words on the question of why nineteenth-century historians were generally indifferent to the philosophy of history. The term was invented by Voltaire, and has since been used in different senses; but I shall take it to mean, if I use it at all, our answer to the question: What is history? The nineteenth century was, for the intellectuals of Western Europe, a comfortable period exuding confidence and optimism. The facts were on the whole satisfactory; and the inclination to ask and answer awkward questions about them was correspondingly weak. Ranke piously believed that divine providence would take care of the meaning of history if he took care of the facts; and Burckhardt with a more modern touch of cynicism observed that "we are not initiated into the purposes of the eternal wisdom." Professor Butterfield as late as 1931 noted with apparent satisfaction that "historians have reflected little upon the nature of things and even the nature of their own subject."[9] But my predecessor in these lectures, Dr. A. L. Rowse, more justly critical, wrote of Sir Winston Churchill's *The World Crisis*—his book about the First World War— that, while it matched Trotsky's *History of the Russian Revolution* in personality, vividness, and vitality, it was inferior in one respect: it had "no philosophy of history behind it."[1] British historians refused to be drawn, not because they believed that history had no meaning, but because they believed that its meaning was implicit and self-evident. The liberal nineteenth-century view of history had a close affinity with the economic doctrine of *laissez-faire*—also the product of a serene and self-confident outlook on the world. Let everyone get on with his particular job, and the hidden hand would take care of the universal harmony. The facts of history were themselves a demonstration of the supreme fact of a beneficent and apparently infinite progress towards higher things. This was the age of innocence, and historians walked in the Garden of Eden, without a scrap of philosophy to cover them, naked and unashamed before the god of history. Since then, we have known Sin and experienced a Fall; and those historians who today pretend to dispense with a philosophy of history are merely trying, vainly and self-consciously, like members of a nudist colony, to recreate the Garden of Eden in their garden suburb. Today the awkward question can no longer be evaded. * * *

9. Herbert Butterfield: *The Whig Interpretation of History* (London: George Bell & Sons, 1931), p. 67.

1. Alfred L. Rowse: *The End of an Epoch* (London: Macmillan & Co., 1947), pp. 282-3.

During the past fifty years a good deal of serious work has been done on the question: What is history? It was from Germany, the country which was to do so much to upset the comfortable reign of nineteenth-century liberalism, that the first challenge came in the 1880's and 1890's to the doctrine of the primacy and autonomy of facts in history. The philosophers who made the challenge are now little more than names: Dilthey is the only one of them who has recently received some belated recognition in Great Britain. Before the turn of the century, prosperity and confidence were still too great in this country for any attention to be paid to heretics who attacked the cult of facts. But early in the new century, the torch passed to Italy, where Croce began to propound a philosophy of history which obviously owed much to German masters. All history is "contemporary history," declared Croce,[2] meaning that history consists essentially in seeing the past through the eyes of the present and in the light of its problems, and that the main work of the historian is not to record, but to evaluate; for, if he does not evaluate, how can he know what is worth recording? In 1910 the American philosopher, Carl Becker, argued in deliberately provocative language that "the facts of history do not exist for any historian till he creates them."[3] These challenges were for the moment little noticed. It was only after 1920 that Croce began to have a considerable vogue in France and Great Britain. This was not perhaps because Croce was a subtler thinker or a better stylist than his German predecessors, but because, after the First World War, the facts seemed to smile on us less propitiously than in the years before 1914, and we were therefore more accessible to a philosophy which sought to diminish their prestige. Croce was an important influence on the Oxford philosopher and historian Collingwood, the only British thinker in the present century who has made a serious contribution to the philosophy of history. He did not live to write the systematic treatise he had planned; but his published and unpublished papers on the subject were collected after his death in a volume entitled *The Idea of History*, which appeared in 1945.

The views of Collingwood can be summarized as follows. The philosophy of history is concerned neither with "the past by itself" nor with "the historian's thought about it by itself," but with "the two things in their mutual relations." (This dictum reflects the two current meanings of the word "history"—the enquiry conducted by the historian and the series of past events into which he enquires.) "The past which a historian studies is not a dead past, but a past which in some sense is still living in the present." But a past act

2. The context of this celebrated aphorism is as follows: "The practical requirements which underlie every historical judgment give to all history the character of 'contemporary history,' because, however remote in time events thus recounted may seem to be, the history in reality refers to present needs and present situations wherein those events vibrate" (Benedetto Croce: *History as the Story of Liberty* [London: George Allen & Unwin, 1941], p. 19).
3. *Atlantic Monthly* (October 1928), p. 528.

is dead, *i.e.* meaningless to the historian, unless he can understand the thought that lay behind it. Hence "all history is the history of thought," and "history is the re-enactment in the historian's mind of the thought whose history he is studying." The reconstitution of the past in the historian's mind is dependent on empirical evidence. But it is not in itself an empirical process, and cannot consist in a mere recital of facts. On the contrary, the process of reconstitution governs the selection and interpretation of the facts: this, indeed, is what makes them historical facts. "History," says Professor Oakeshott, who on this point stands near to Collingwood, "is the historian's experience. It is 'made' by nobody save the historian: to write history is the only way of making it."[4]

This searching critique, though it may call for some serious reservations, brings to light certain neglected truths.

In the first place, the facts of history never come to us "pure," since they do not and cannot exist in a pure form: they are always refracted through the mind of the recorder. It follows that when we take up a work of history, our first concern should be not with the facts which it contains but with the historian who wrote it. Let me take as an example the great historian in whose honor and in whose name these lectures were founded. Trevelyan, as he tells us in his autobiography, was "brought up at home on a somewhat exuberantly Whig tradition"[5]; and he would not, I hope, disclaim the title if I described him as the last and not the least of the great English liberal historians of the Whig tradition. It is not for nothing that he traces back his family tree, through the great Whig historian George Otto Trevelyan, to Macaulay, incomparably the greatest of the Whig historians. Dr. Trevelyan's finest and maturest work *England under Queen Anne* was written against that background, and will yield its full meaning and significance to the reader only when read against that background. The author, indeed, leaves the reader with no excuse for failing to do so. For if, following the technique of connoisseurs of detective novels, you read the end first, you will find on the last few pages of the third volume the best summary known to me of what is nowadays called the Whig interpretation of history; and you will see that what Trevelyan is trying to do is to investigate the origin and development of the Whig tradition, and to roof it fairly and squarely in the years after the death of its founder, William III. Though this is not, perhaps, the only conceivable interpretation of the events of Queen Anne's reign, it is a valid and, in Trevelyan's hands, a fruitful interpretation. But, in order to appreciate it at its full value, you have to understand what the historian is doing. For if, as Collingwood says, the historian must re-enact in thought what has gone on in the mind of

4. Michael Oakeshott: *Experience and Its Modes* (Cambridge University Press, 1933), p. 99.

5. G. M. Trevelyan: *An Autobiography* (London: Longmans, Green & Company, 1949), p. 11.

his *dramatis personae,* so the reader in his turn must re-enact what goes on in the mind of the historian. Study the historian before you begin to study the facts. This is, after all, not very abstruse. It is what is already done by the intelligent undergraduate who, when recommended to read a work by that great scholar Jones of St. Jude's, goes round to a friend at St. Jude's to ask what sort of chap Jones is, and what bees he has in his bonnet. When you read a work of history, always listen out for the buzzing. If you can detect none, either you are tone deaf or your historian is a dull dog. The facts are really not at all like fish on the fishmonger's slab. They are like fish swimming about in a vast and sometimes inaccessible ocean; and what the historian catches will depend partly on chance, but mainly on what part of the ocean he chooses to fish in and what tackle he chooses to use—these two factors being, of course, determined by the kind of fish he wants to catch. By and large, the historian will get the kind of facts he wants. History means interpretation. Indeed, if, standing Sir George Clark on his head, I were to call history "a hard core of interpretation surrounded by a pulp of disputable facts," my statement would, no doubt, be one-sided and misleading, but no more so, I venture to think, than the original dictum.

The second point is the more familiar one of the historian's need of imaginative understanding for the minds of the people with whom he is dealing, for the thought behind their acts: I say "imaginative understanding," not "sympathy," lest sympathy should be supposed to imply agreement. The nineteenth century was weak in mediaeval history, because it was too much repelled by the superstitious beliefs of the Middle Ages and by the barbarities which they inspired, to have any imaginative understanding of mediaeval people. Or take Burckhardt's censorious remark about the Thirty Years' War: "It is scandalous for a creed, no matter whether it is Catholic or Protestant, to place its salvation above the integrity of the nation."[6] It was extremely difficult for a nineteenth-century liberal historian, brought up to believe that it is right and praiseworthy to kill in defense of one's country, but wicked and wrongheaded to kill in defense of one's religion, to enter into the state of mind of those who fought the Thirty Years' War. This difficulty is particularly acute in the field in which I am now working. Much of what has been written in English-speaking countries in the last ten years about the Soviet Union, and in the Soviet Union about the English-speaking countries, has been vitiated by this inability to achieve even the most elementary measure of imaginative understanding of what goes on in the mind of the other party, so that the words and actions of the other are always made to appear malign,

6. Jacob Burckhardt: *Judgments on History and Historians* (London: S. J.   Reginald Saunders & Company, 1958), p. 179.

senseless, or hypocritical. History cannot be written unless the historian can achieve some kind of contact with the mind of those about whom he is writing.

The third point is that we can view the past, and achieve our understanding of the past, only through the eyes of the present. The historian is of his own age, and is bound to it by the conditions of human existence. The very words which he uses—words like democracy, empire, war, revolution—have current connotations from which he cannot divorce them. Ancient historians have taken to using words like *polis* and *plebs* in the original, just in order to show that they have not fallen into this trap. This does not help them. They, too, live in the present, and cannot cheat themselves into the past by using unfamiliar or obsolete words, any more than they would become better Greek or Roman historians if they delivered their lectures in a *chlamys* or a *toga*. The names by which successive French historians have described the Parisian crowds which played so prominent a role in the French revolution—*les sans-culottes, le peuple, la canaille, les bras-nus*—are all, for those who know the rules of the game, manifestos of a political affiliation and of a particular interpretation. Yet the historian is obliged to choose: the use of language forbids him to be neutral. Nor is it a matter of words alone. Over the past hundred years the changed balance of power in Europe has reversed the attitude of British historians to Frederick the Great. The changed balance of power within the Christian churches between Catholicism and Protestantism has profoundly altered their attitude to such figures as Loyola, Luther, and Cromwell. It requires only a superficial knowledge of the work of French historians of the last forty years on the French revolution to recognize how deeply it has been affected by the Russian revolution of 1917. The historian belongs not to the past but to the present. Professor Trevor-Roper tells us that the historian "ought to love the past."[7] This is a dubious injunction. To love the past may easily be an expression of the nostalgic romanticism of old men and old societies, a symptom of loss of faith and interest in the present or future.[8] *Cliché* for *cliché*, I should prefer the one about freeing oneself from "the dead hand of the past." The function of the historian is neither to love the past nor to emancipate himself from the past, but to master and understand it as the key to the understanding of the present.

If, however, these are some of the sights of what I may call the Collingwood view of history, it is time to consider some of the dangers. The emphasis on the role of the historian in the making of

7. Introduction to Burckhardt: *Judgments on History and Historians*, p. 17.
8. Compare Nietzsche's view of history: "To old age belongs the old man's business of looking back and casting up his accounts, of seeking consolation in the memories of the past, in historical culture" (*Thoughts Out of Season* [London: Macmillan & Co., 1909], II, pp. 65-6).

history tends, if pressed to its logical conclusion, to rule out any objective history at all: history is what the historian makes. Collingwood seems indeed, at one moment, in an unpublished note quoted by his editor, to have reached this conclusion:

> St. Augustine looked at history from the point of view of the early Christian; Tillemont, from that of a seventeenth-century Frenchman; Gibbon, from that of an eighteenth-century Englishman; Mommsen, from that of a nineteenth-century German. There is no point in asking which was the right point of view. Each was the only one possible for the man who adopted it.[9]

This amounts to total scepticism, like Froude's remark that history is "a child's box of letters with which we can spell any word we please."[1] Collingwood, in his reaction against "scissors-and-paste history," against the view of history as a mere compilation of facts, comes perilously near to treating history as something spun out of the human brain, and leads back to the conclusion referred to by Sir George Clark in the passage which I quoted earlier, that "there is no 'objective' historical truth." In place of the theory that history has no meaning, we are offered here the theory of an infinity of meanings, none any more right than any other—which comes to much the same thing. The second theory is surely as untenable as the first. It does not follow that, because a mountain appears to take on different shapes from different angles of vision, it has objectively either no shape at all or an infinity of shapes. It does not follow that, because interpretation plays a necessary part in establishing the facts of history, and because no existing interpretation is wholly objective, one interpretation is as good as another, and the facts of history are in principle not amenable to objective interpretation. I shall have to consider at a later stage what exactly is meant by objectivity in history.

But a still greater danger lurks in the Collingwood hypothesis. If the historian necessarily looks at his period of history through the eyes of his own time, and studies the problems of the past as a key to those of the present, will he not fall into a purely pragmatic view of the facts, and maintain that the criterion of a right interpretation is its suitability to some present purpose? On this hypothesis, the facts of history are nothing, interpretation is everything. Nietzsche had already enunciated the principle: "The falseness of an opinion is not for us any objection to it. . . . The question is how far it is life-furthering, life-preserving, species-preserving, perhaps species-creating."[2] The American pragmatists moved, less explicitly and less wholeheartedly, along the same line. Knowledge is knowledge for some purpose. The validity of the knowledge depends on the validity of the purpose. But, even where no such theory has been

9. Robin G. Collingwood: *The Idea of History* (London: Oxford University Press; 1946), p. xii.
1. James Anthony Froude: *Short Studies on Great Subjects* (1894), I, p. 21.
2. Nietzsche: *Beyond Good and Evil*, Chapter 1.

professed, the practice has often been no less disquieting. In my own field of study, I have seen too many examples of extravagant interpretation riding roughshod over facts, not to be impressed with the reality of this danger. It is not surprising that perusal of some of the more extreme products of Soviet and anti-Soviet schools of historiography should sometimes breed a certain nostalgia for that illusory nineteenth-century heaven of purely factual history.

How then, in the middle of the twentieth century, are we to define the obligation of the historian to his facts? I trust that I have spent a sufficient number of hours in recent years chasing and perusing documents, and stuffing my historical narrative with properly footnoted facts, to escape the imputation of treating facts and documents too cavalierly. The duty of the historian to respect his facts is not exhausted by the obligation to see that his facts are accurate. He must seek to bring into the picture all known or knowable facts relevant, in one sense or another, to the theme on which he is engaged and to the interpretation proposed. If he seeks to depict the Victorian Englishman as a moral and rational being, he must not forget what happened at Stalybridge Wakes in 1850. But this, in turn, does not mean that he can eliminate interpretation, which is the life-blood of history. Laymen—that is to say, non-academic friends or friends from other academic disciplines—sometimes ask me how the historian goes to work when he writes history. The commonest assumption appears to be that the historian divides his work into two sharply distinguishable phases or periods. First, he spends a long preliminary period reading his source and filling his notebooks with facts: then, when this is over, he puts away his sources, takes out his notebooks, and writes his book from beginning to end. This is to me an unconvincing and unplausible picture. For myself, as soon as I have got going on a few of what I take to be the capital sources, the itch becomes too strong and I begin to write— not necessarily at the beginning, but somewhere, anywhere. Thereafter, reading and writing go on simultaneously. The writing is added to, subtracted from, re-shaped, cancelled, as I go on reading. The reading is guided and directed and made fruitful by the writing: the more I write, the more I know what I am looking for, the better I understand the significance and relevance of what I find. Some historians probably do all this preliminary writing in their head without using pen, paper, or typewriter, just as some people play chess in their heads without recourse to board and chess-men: this is a talent which I envy, but cannot emulate. But I am convinced that, for any historian worth the name, the two processes of what economists call "input" and "output" go on simultaneously and are, in practice, parts of a single process. If you try to separate them, or to give one priority over the other, you fall into one of two heresies. Either you write scissors-and-paste history without meaning or significance; or you write propaganda or historical fiction, and merely use facts of the past to embroider a kind of writing which has nothing to do with history.

Our examination of the relation of the historian to the facts of history finds us, therefore, in an apparently precarious situation, navigating delicately between the Scylla of an untenable theory of history as an objective compilation of facts, of the unqualified primacy of fact over interpretation, and the Charybdis of an equally untenable theory of history as the subjective product of the mind of the historian who establishes the facts of history and masters them through the process of interpretation, between a view of history having the center of gravity in the past and the view having the center of gravity in the present. But our situation is less precarious than it seems. We shall encounter the same dichotomy of fact and interpretation again in these lectures in other guises—the particular and the general, the empirical and the theoretical, the objective and the subjective. The predicament of the historian is a reflection of the nature of man. Man, except perhaps in earliest infancy and in extreme old age, is not totally involved in his environment and unconditionally subject to it. On the other hand, he is never totally independent of it and its unconditional master. The relation of man to his environment is the relation of the historian to his theme. The historian is neither the humble slave, nor the tyrannical master, of his facts. The relation between the historian and his facts is one of equality, of give-and-take. As any working historian knows, if he stops to reflect what he is doing as he thinks and writes, the historian is engaged on a continuous process of molding his facts to his interpretation and his interpretation to his facts. It is impossible to assign primacy to one over the other.

The historian starts with the provisional selection of facts and a provisional interpretation in the light of which that selection has been made—by others as well as by himself. As he works, both the interpretation and the selection and ordering of facts undergo subtle and perhaps partly unconscious changes through the reciprocal action of one or the other. And this reciprocal action also involves reciprocity between present and past, since the historian is part of the present and the facts belong to the past. The historian and the facts of history are necessary to one another. The historian without his facts is rootless and futile; the facts without their historian are dead and meaningless. My first answer therefore to the question, What is history?, is that it is a continuous process of interaction between the historian and his facts, an unending dialogue between the present and the past.

QUESTIONS

1. Carr begins with a question but does not answer it until the last sentence. What are the main steps of the discussion leading to his answer? The answer takes the form of a definition: which is the most important of the defining words?
2. If you were commissioned to write a history of the semester or of a particular group during the semester, what would be your most important "facts of history"?

On Science

KONRAD Z. LORENZ

The Taming of the Shrew[1]

Though Nature, red in tooth and claw,
With ravine, shrieked against his creed.
TENNYSON, *In Memoriam*

All shrews are particularly difficult to keep; this is not because, as we are led proverbially to believe, they are hard to tame, but because the metabolism of these smallest of mammals is so very fast that they will die of hunger within two or three hours if the food supply fails. Since they feed exclusively on small, living animals, mostly insects, and demand, of these, considerably more than their own weight every day, they are most exacting charges. At the time of which I am writing, I had never succeeded in keeping any of the terrestrial shrews alive for any length of time; most of those that I happened to obtain had probably only been caught because they were already ill and they died almost at once. I had never succeeded in procuring a healthy specimen. Now the order Insectivora is very low in the genealogical hierarchy of mammals and is, therefore, of particular interest to the comparative ethologist. Of the whole group, there was only one representative with whose behavior I was tolerably familiar, namely the hedgehog, an extremely interesting animal of whose ethology Professor Herter of Berlin has made a very thorough study. Of the behavior of all other members of the family practically nothing is known. Since they are nocturnal and partly subterranean animals, it is nearly impossible to approach them in field observation, and the difficulty of keeping them in captivity had hitherto precluded their study in the laboratory. So the Insectivores were officially placed on my program.

1. Chapter 9 of *King Solomon's Ring: New Light on Animal Ways*, 1952.

First I tried to keep the common mole. It was easy to procure a healthy specimen, caught to order in the nursery gardens of my father-in-law, and I found no difficulty in keeping it alive. Immediately on its arrival, it devoured an almost incredible quantity of earthworms which, from the very first moment, it took from my hand. But, as an object of behavior study, it proved most disappointing. Certainly, it was interesting to watch its method of disappearing in the space of a few seconds under the surface of the ground, to study its astoundingly efficient use of its strong, spade-shaped fore-paws, and to feel their amazing strength when one held the little beast in one's hand. And again, it was remarkable with what surprising exactitude it located, by smell, from underground, the earthworms which I put on the surface of the soil in its terrarium. But these observations were the only benefits I derived from it. It never became any tamer and it never remained above ground any longer than it took to devour its prey; after this, it sank into the earth as a submarine sinks into the water. I soon grew tired of procuring the immense quantities of living food it required and, after a few weeks, I set it free in the garden.

It was years afterwards, on an excursion to that extraordinary lake, the Neusiedlersee, which lies on the Hungarian border of Austria, that I again thought of keeping an insectivore. This large stretch of water, though not thirty miles from Vienna, is an example of the peculiar type of lake found in the open steppes of Eastern Europe and Asia. More than thirty miles long and half as broad, its deepest parts are only about five feet deep and it is much shallower on the average. Nearly half its surface is overgrown with reeds which form an ideal habitat for all kinds of water birds. Great colonies of white, purple, and grey heron and spoonbills live among the reeds and, until a short while ago, glossy ibis were still to be found here. Greylag geese breed here in great numbers and, on the eastern, reedless shore, avocets and many other rare waders can regularly be found. On the occasion of which I am speaking, we, a dozen tired zoologists, under the experienced guidance of my friend Otto Koenig, were wending our way, slowly and painfully, through the forest of reeds. We were walking in single file, Koenig first, I second, with a few students in our wake. We literally left a wake, an inky-black one in pale grey water. In the reed forests of Lake Neusiedel, you walk knee deep in slimy, black ooze, wonderfully perfumed by sulphureted-hydrogen–producing bacteria. This mud clings tenaciously and only releases its hold on your foot with a loud, protesting plop at every step.

After a few hours of this kind of wading you discover aching muscles whose very existence you had never suspected. From the knees to the hips you are immersed in the milky, clay-colored water characteristic of the lake, which, among the reeds, is populated by myriads of extremely hungry leeches conforming to the old pharmaceutical recipe, *"Hirudines medicinales maxime affamati."*[2] The rest of your person inhabits the upper air, which here consists of clouds of tiny mosquitoes whose bloodthirsty attacks are all the more exasperating because you require both your hands to part the dense reeds in front of you and can only slap your face at intervals. The British ornithologist who may perhaps have envied us some of our rare specimens will perceive that bird watching on Lake Neusiedel is not, after all, an entirely enviable occupation.

We were thus wending our painful way through the rushes when suddenly Koenig stopped and pointed mutely towards a pond, free from reeds, that stretched in front of us. At first, I could only see whitish water, dark blue sky and green reeds, the standard colors of Lake Neusiedel. Then, suddenly, like a cork popping up on to the surface, there appeared, in the middle of the pool, a tiny black animal, hardly bigger than a man's thumb. And for a moment I was in the rare position of a zoologist who sees a specimen and is not able to classify it, in the literal sense of the word: I did not know to which class of vertebrates the object of my gaze belonged. For the first fraction of a second I took it for the young of some diving bird of a species unknown to me. It appeared to have a beak and it swam on the water like a bird, not in it as a mammal. It swam about in narrow curves and circles, very much like a whirligig beetle, creating an extensive wedge-shaped wake, quite out of proportion to the tiny animal's size. Then a second little beast popped up from below, chased the first one with a shrill, bat-like twitter, then both dived and were gone. The whole episode had not lasted five seconds.

I stood open-mouthed, my mind racing. Koenig turned round with a broad grin, calmly detached a leech that was sticking like a leech to his wrist, wiped away the trickle of blood from the wound, slapped his cheek, thereby killing thirty-five mosquitoes, and asked, in the tone of an examiner, "What was that?" I answered as calmly as I could, "water shrews," thanking, in my heart, the leech and the mosquitoes for the respite they had given me to collect my thoughts. But my mind was racing on: water shrews ate fishes and frogs which were easy to procure in any quantity; water shrews were less subterranean than most other insectivores; they were the very insectivore to keep in captivity. "That's an animal I must catch and keep," I said to my friend. "That is easy," he responded. "There is a nest with young under the floor mat of my tent." I had slept that night in his tent and Koenig had not thought it worth-

2. "In medicine, the hungriest leech is best."

while to tell me of the shrews; such things are, to him, as much a matter of course as wild little spotted crakes feeding out of his hand, or as any other wonders of his queer kingdom in the reeds.

On our return to the tent that evening, he showed me the nest. It contained eight young which, compared with their mother, who rushed away as we lifted the mat, were of enormous size. They were considerably more than half her length and must each have weighed well between a fourth and a third of their dam: that is to say, the whole litter weighed, at a very modest estimate, twice as much as the old shrew. Yet they were still quite blind and the tips of their teeth were only just visible in their rosy mouths. And two days later when I took them under my care, they were still quite unable to eat even the soft abdomens of grasshoppers, and in spite of evident greed, they chewed interminably on a soft piece of frog's meat without succeeding in detaching a morsel from it. On our journey home, I fed them on the squeezed-out insides of grasshoppers and finely minced frog's meat, a diet on which they obviously throve. Arrived home in Altenberg, I improved on this diet by preparing a food from the squeezed-out insides of mealworm larvae, with some finely chopped small, fresh fishes, worked into a sort of gravy with a little milk. They consumed large quantities of this food, and their little nest-box looked quite small in comparison with the big china bowl whose contents they emptied three times a day. All these observations raise the problem of how the female water shrew succeeds in feeding her gigantic litter. It is absolutely impossible that she should do so on milk alone. Even on a more concentrated diet my young shrews devoured the equivalent of their own weight daily and this meant nearly twice the weight of a grown shrew. Yet, at that time of their lives, young shrews could not possibly engulf a frog or a fish brought whole to them by their mother, as my charges indisputably proved. I can only think that the mother feeds her young by regurgitation of chewed food. Even thus, it is little short of miraculous that the adult female should be able to obtain enough meat to sustain herself and her voracious progeny.

When I brought them home, my young watershrews were still blind. They had not suffered from the journey and were as sleek and fat as one could wish. Their black, glossy coats were reminiscent of moles, but the white color of their underside, as well as the round, streamlined contours of their bodies, reminded me distinctly of penguins, and not, indeed, without justification: both the streamlined form and the light underside are adaptations to a life in the water. Many free-swimming animals, mammals, birds, amphibians and fishes, are silvery-white below in order to be invisible to enemies swimming in the depths. Seen from below, the shining white belly blends perfectly with the reflecting surface film of the water. It is very characteristic of these water animals that the dark dorsal and the white ventral colors do not merge gradually into each other as is the case in "counter-shaded" land animals whose coloring is calculated to make them invisible by eliminating the contrasting shade on their undersides. As in the killer whale, in dolphins, and in penguins, the white underside of the watershrew is divided from the dark upper side by a sharp line which runs, often in very decorative curves, along the animal's flank. Curiously enough, this borderline between black and white showed considerable variations in individuals and even on both sides of one animal's body. I welcomed this, since it enabled me to recognize my shrews personally.

Three days after their arrival in Altenberg my eight shrew babies opened their eyes and began, very cautiously, to explore the precincts of their nest-box. It was now time to remove them to an appropriate container, and on this question I expended much hard thinking. The enormous quantity of food they consumed and, consequently, of excrement they produced, made it impossible to keep them in an ordinary aquarium whose water, within a day, would have become a stinking brew. Adequate sanitation was imperative for particular reasons; in ducks, grebes, and all waterfowl, the plumage must be kept perfectly dry if the animal is to remain in a state of health, and the same premise may reasonably be expected to hold good of the shrew's fur. Now water which has been polluted soon turns strongly alkaline and this I knew to be very bad for the plumage of waterbirds. It causes saponification of the fat to which the feathers owe their waterproof quality, and the bird becomes thoroughly wet and is unable to stay on the water. I hold the record, as far as I know hitherto unbroken by any other birdlover, for having kept dabchicks alive and healthy in captivity for nearly two years, and even then they did not die but escaped, and may still be living. My experience with these birds proved the absolute necessity of keeping the water perfectly clean; whenever it became a little dirty I noticed their feathers beginning to get wet, a danger which they anxiously tried to counteract by constantly preening themselves. I had, therefore, to keep these little grebes in crystal clear water which was changed every day, and I rightly assumed that the same would be necessary for my water shrews.

I took a large aquarium tank, rather over a yard in length and about two feet wide. At each end of this, I placed two little tables, and weighed them down with heavy stones so that they would not float. Then I filled up the tank until the water was level with the tops of the tables. I did not at first push the tables close against the panes of the tank, which was rather narrow, for fear that the shrews might become trapped underwater in the blind alley beneath a table and drown there; this precaution, however, subsequently proved unnecessary. The water shrew which, in its natural state, swims great distances under the ice, is quite able to find its way to the open surface in much more difficult situations. The nest-box, which was placed on one of the tables, was equipped with a sliding shutter, so that I could imprison the shrews whenever the container had to be cleaned. In the morning, at the hour of general cage-cleaning, the shrews were usually at home and asleep, so that the procedure caused them no appreciable disturbance. I will admit that I take great pride in devising, by creative imagination, suitable containers for animals of which nobody, myself included, has had any previous experience, and it was particularly gratifying that the contraption described above proved so satisfactory that I never had to alter even the minutest detail.

When first my baby shrews were liberated in this container they took a very long time to explore the top of the table on which their nest-box was standing. The water's edge seemed to exert a strong attraction; they approached it ever and again, smelled the surface and seemed to feel along it with the long, fine whiskers which surround their pointed snouts like a halo and represent not only their most important organ of touch but the most important of all their sensory organs. Like other aquatic mammals, the water shrew differs from the terrestrial members of its class in that its nose, the guiding organ of the average mammal, is of no use whatsoever in its underwater hunting. The water shrew's whiskers are actively mobile like the antennae of an insect or the fingers of a blind man.

Exactly as mice and many other small rodents would do under similar conditions, the shrews interrupted their careful exploration of their new surroundings every few minutes to dash wildly back into the safe cover of their nest-box. The survival value of this peculiar behavior is evident: the animal makes sure, from time to time that it has not lost its way and that it can, at a moment's notice, retreat to the one place it knows to be safe. It was a queer spectacle to see those podgy black figures slowly and carefully whiskering their way forward and, in the next second, with lightning speed, dash back to the nest-box. Queerly enough, they did not run straight through the little door, as one would have expected, but in their wild dash for safety they jumped, one and all, first onto the roof of the box and only then, whiskering along its edge, found the opening and slipped in with a half somersault, their back turned nearly vertically downward. After many repetitions of this maneuver, they were able to find the opening without feeling for it; they "knew" perfectly its whereabouts yet still persisted in the leap onto the roof. They jumped onto it and immediately vaulted in through the door, but they never, as long as they lived, found out that the leap and vault which had become their habit was really quite unnecessary and that they could have run in directly without this extraordinary detour. We shall hear more about this dominance of path habits in the water shrew presently.

It was only on the third day, when the shrews had become thoroughly acquainted with the geography of their little rectangular island, that the largest and most enterprising of them ventured into the water. As is so often the case with mammals, birds, reptiles, and fishes, it was the largest and most handsomely colored male which played the role of leader. First he sat on the edge of the water and thrust in the fore part of his body, at the same time frantically paddling with his forelegs but still clinging with his hind ones to the board. Then he slid in, but in the next moment took fright, scampered madly across the surface very much after the manner of a frightened duckling, and jumped out onto the board at the opposite end of the tank. There he sat, excitedly grooming his belly with one hind paw, exactly as coypus and beavers do. Soon he quieted down and sat still for a moment. Then he went to the water's edge a second time, hesitated for a moment, and plunged in; diving immediately, he swam ecstatically about underwater, swerving upward and downward again, running quickly along the bottom, and finally jumping out of the water at the same place as he had first entered it.

When I first saw a water shrew swimming I was most struck by a thing which I ought to have expected but did not: at the moment of diving, the little black and white beast appears to be made of silver. Like the plumage of ducks and grebes, but quite unlike the fur of most water mammals, such as seals, otters, beavers or coypus, the fur of the water shrew remains absolutely dry under water, that is to say, it retains a thick layer of air while the animal is below the surface. In the other mammals mentioned above, it is only the short, woolly undercoat that remains dry, the superficial hair tips becoming wet, wherefore the animal looks its natural color when underwater and is superficially wet when it emerges. I was already aware of the peculiar qualities of the waterproof fur of the shrew, and, had I given it a thought, I should have known that it would look, under water, exactly like the air-retaining fur on the underside of a water beetle or on the abdomen of a water spider. Nevertheless the wonderful, transparent silver coat of the shrew was, to me, one of those delicious surprises that nature has in store for her admirers.

Another surprising detail which I only noticed when I saw my shrews in the water was that they have a fringe of stiff, erectile hairs on the outer side of their fifth toes and on the underside of their tails. These form collapsible oars and a collapsible rudder. Folded and inconspicuous as long as the animal is on dry land, they unfold the moment it enters the water and broaden the effective surface of the propelling feet and of the steering tail by a considerable area.

Like penguins, the water shrews looked rather awkward and ungainly on dry land but were transformed into objects of elegance and grace on entering the water. As long as they walked, their strongly convex underside made them look pot-bellied and reminiscent of an old, overfed dachshund. But under water, the very same protruding belly balanced harmoniously the curve of their back and gave a beautifully symmetrical streamline which, together with their silver coating and the elegance of their movements, made them a sight of entrancing beauty.

When they had all become familiar with the water, their container was one of the chief attractions that our research station had to offer to any visiting naturalists or animal lovers. Unlike all other mammals of their size, the water shrews were largely diurnal and, except in the early hours of the morning, three or four of them were constantly on the scene. It was exceedingly interesting to watch their movements upon and under the water. Like the whirligig beetle, Gyrinus, they could turn in an extremely small radius without diminishing their speed, a faculty for which the large rudder surface of the tail with its fringe of erectile hairs is evidently essential. They had two different ways of diving, either by taking a little jump as grebes or coots do and working their way down at a steep angle, or by simply lowering their snout under the surface and paddling very fast till they reached "planing speed," thus working their way downward on the principle of the inclined plane—in other words, performing the converse movement of an ascending airplane. The water shrew must expend a large amount of energy in staying down since the air contained in its fur exerts a strong pull upwards. Unless it is paddling straight downwards, a thing it rarely does, it is forced to maintain a constant minimum speed, keeping its body at a slightly downward angle in order not to float to the surface. While swimming under water the shrew seems to flatten, broadening its body in a peculiar fashion, in order to present a better planing surface to the water. I never saw my shrews try to cling by their claws to any underwater objects, as the dipper is alleged to do. When they seemed to be running along the bottom, they were really swimming close above it, but perhaps the smooth gravel on the bottom of the tank was unsuitable for holding on to and it did not occur to me then to offer them a rougher surface. They were very playful when in the water and chased one another loudly twittering on the surface, or silently in the depths. Unlike any other mammal, but just like water birds, they could rest on the surface; this they used to do, rolling partly over and grooming themselves. Once out again, they instantly proceeded to clean their fur—one is almost tempted to say "preen" it, so similar was their behavior to that of ducks which have just left the water after a long swim.

Most interesting of all was their method of hunting under water. They came swimming along with an erratic course, darting a foot or so forward very swiftly in a straight line, then starting to gyrate in looped turns at reduced speed. While swimming straight and swiftly their whiskers were, as far as I could see, laid flat against their head, but while circling they were erect and bristled out in all directions, as they sought contact with some prey. I have no reason to believe that vision plays any part in the water shrew's hunting, except perhaps in the activation of its tactile search. My shrews may have noticed visually the presence of the live tadpoles or little fishes which I put in the tank, but in the actual hunting of its prey the animal is exclusively guided by its sense of touch, located in the wide-spreading whiskers on its snout. Certain small free-swimming species of catfish find their prey by exactly the same method. When these fishes swim fast and straight, the long feelers on their snout are depressed but, like the shrew's whiskers, are stiffly spread out when the fish becomes conscious of the proximity of potential prey; like the shrew, the fish then begins to gyrate blindly in order to establish contact with its prey. It may not even be necessary for the water shrew actually to touch its prey with one of its whiskers. Perhaps, at very close range, the water vibration caused by the movements of a small fish, a tadpole or a water insect is perceptible by those sensitive tactile organs. It is quite impossible to determine this question by mere observation, for the action is much too quick for the human eye. There is a quick turn and a snap and the shrew is already paddling shorewards with a wriggling creature in its maw.

In relation to its size, the water shrew is perhaps the most terrible predator of all vertebrate animals, and it can even vie with the invertebrates, including the murderous Dytiscus larva. It has been reported by A. E. Brehm that water shrews have killed fish more than sixty times heavier than themselves by biting out their eyes and brain. This happened only when the fish were confined in containers with no room for escape. The same story has been told to me by fishermen on Lake Neusiedel, who could not possibly have heard Brehm's report. I once offered to my shrews a large edible frog. I never did it again, nor could I bear to see out to its end the cruel scene that ensued. One of the shrews encountered the frog in the basin and instantly gave chase, repeatedly seizing hold of the creature's legs; although it was kicked off again it did not cease in its attack and finally, the frog, in desperation, jumped out of the water and onto one of the tables, where several shrews raced to the pursuer's assistance and buried their teeth in the legs and hindquarters of the wretched frog. And now, horribly, they began to eat the frog alive, beginning just where each one of them happened to have hold of it; the poor frog croaked heartrendingly, as the jaws of the shrews munched audibly in chorus. I need hardly be blamed for bringing this experiment to an abrupt and agitated end and putting the lacerated frog out of its misery. I never offered the shrews large prey again but only such as would be killed at the first bite or two. Nature can be very cruel indeed; it is not out of pity that most of the larger predatory animals kill their prey quickly. The lion has to finish off a big antelope or a buffalo very quickly indeed in order not to get hurt itself, for a beast of prey which has to hunt daily cannot afford to receive even a harmless scratch in effecting a kill; such scratches would soon add up to such an extent as to put the killer out of action. The same reason has forced the python and other large snakes to evolve a quick and really humane method of killing the well-armed mammals that are their natural prey. But where there is no danger of the victim doing damage to the killer, the latter shows no pity whatsoever. The hedgehog which, by virtue of its armor, is quite immune to the bite of a snake, regularly proceeds to eat it, beginning at the tail or in the middle of its body, and in the same way the water shrew treats its innocuous prey. But man should abstain from judging his innocently-cruel fellow creatures, for even if nature sometimes "shrieks against his creed," what pain does he himself not inflict upon the living creatures that he hunts for pleasure and not for food?

The mental qualities of the water shrew cannot be rated very high. They were quite tame and fearless of me and never tried to bite when I took them in my hand, nor did they ever try to evade it, but, like little tame rodents, they tried to dig their way out if I held them for too long in the hollow of my closed fist. Even when I took them out of their container and put them on a table or on the floor, they were by no means thrown into a panic but were quite ready to take food out of my hand and even tried actively to creep into it if they felt a longing for cover. When, in such an unwonted environment, they were shown their nest-box, they plainly showed that they knew it by sight and instantly made for it, and even pursued it with upraised heads if I moved the box along above them, just out of their reach. All in all, I really may pride myself that I have tamed the shrew, or at least one member of that family.

In their accustomed surroundings, my shrews proved to be very strict creatures of habit. I have already mentioned the remarkable conservatism with which they persevered in their unpractical way of entering their nest-box by climbing onto its roof and then vaulting, with a half turn, in through the door. Something more must be said about the unchanging tenacity with which these animals cling to their habits once they have formed them. In the water shrew, the path habits, in particular, are of a really amazing immutability; I hardly know another instance to which the saying, "As the twig is bent, so the tree is inclined," applies so literally.

In a territory unknown to it, the water shrew will never run fast except under pressure of extreme fear, and then it will run blindly along, bumping into objects and usually getting caught in a blind alley. But, unless the little animal is severely frightened, it moves in strange surroundings, only step by step, whiskering right and left all the time and following a path that is anything but straight. Its course is determined by a hundred fortuitous factors when it walks that way for the first time. But, after a few repetitions, it is evident that the shrew recognizes the locality in which it finds itself and that it repeats, with the utmost exactitude, the movements which it performed the previous time. At the same time, it is noticeable that the animal moves along much faster whenever it is repeating what it has already learned. When placed on a path which it has already traversed a few times, the shrew starts on its way slowly, carefully whiskering. Suddenly it finds known bearings, and now rushes forward a short distance, repeating exactly every step and turn which it executed on the last occasion. Then, when it comes to a spot where it ceases to know the way by heart, it is reduced to whiskering again and to feeling its way step by step. Soon, another burst of speed follows and the same thing is repeated, bursts of speed alternating with very slow progress. In the beginning of this process of learning their way, the shrews move along at an extremely slow average rate and the little bursts of speed are few and far between. But gradually the little laps of the course which have been "learned by heart" and which can be covered quickly begin to increase in length as well as in number until they fuse and the whole course can be completed in a fast, unbroken rush.

Often, when such a path habit is almost completely formed, there still remains one particularly difficult place where the shrew always loses its bearings and has to resort to its senses of smell and touch, sniffing and whiskering vigorously to find out where the next reach of its path "joins on." Once the shrew is well settled in its path habits it is as strictly bound to them as a railway engine to its tracks and as unable to deviate from them by even a few centimeters. If it diverges from its path by so much as an inch, it is forced to stop abruptly, and laboriously regain its bearings. The same behavior can be caused experimentally by changing some small detail in the customary path of the animal. Any major alteration in the habitual path threw the shrews into complete confusion. One of their paths ran along the wall adjoining the wooden table opposite to that on which the nest box was situated. This table was weighted with two stones lying close to the panes of the tank, and the shrews, running along the wall, were accustomed to jump on and off the stones which lay right in their path. If I moved the stones out of the runway, placing both together in the middle of the table, the shrews would jump right up into the air in the place where the stone should have been; they came down with a jarring bump, were obviously disconcerted and started whiskering cautiously right and left, just as they behaved in an unknown environment. And then they did a most interesting thing: they went back the way they had come, carefully feeling their way until they had again got their bearings. Then, facing round again, they tried a second time with a rush and jumped and crashed down exactly as they had done a few seconds before. Only then did they seem to realize that the first fall had not been their own fault but was due to a change in the wonted pathway, and now they proceeded to explore the alteration, cautiously sniffing and bewhiskering the place where the stone ought to have been. This method of going back to the start, and trying again always reminded me of a small boy who, in reciting a poem, gets stuck and begins again at an earlier verse.

In rats, as in many small mammals, the process of forming a path habit, for instance in learning a maze, is very similar to that just described; but a rat is far more adaptable in its behavior and would not dream of trying to jump over a stone which was not there. The preponderance of motor habit over present perception is a most remarkable peculiarity of the water shrew. One might say that the animal actually disbelieves its senses if they report a change of environment which necessitates a sudden alteration in its motor habits. In a new environment a water shrew would be perfectly able to see a stone of that size and consequently to avoid it or to run over it in a manner well adapted to the spatial conditions; but once a habit is formed and has become ingrained, it supersedes all better knowledge. I know of no animal that is a slave to its habits in so literal a sense as the water shrew. For this animal the geometric axiom that a straight line is the shortest distance between two points simply does not hold good. To them, the shortest line is always the accustomed path and, to a certain extent, they are justified in adhering to this principle: they run with amazing speed along their pathways and arrive at their destination much sooner than they would if, by whiskering and nosing, they tried to go straight. They will keep to the wonted path, even though it winds in such a way that it crosses and recrosses itself. A rat or mouse would be quick to discover that it was making an unnecessary detour, but the water shrew is no more able to do so than is a toy train to turn off at right angles at a level crossing. In order to change its route, the water shrew must change its whole path habit, and this cannot be done at a moment's notice but gradually, over a long period of time. An unnecessary, loop-shaped detour takes weeks and weeks to become a little shorter, and after months it is not even approximately straight. The biological advantage of such a path habit is obvious: it compensates the shrew for being nearly blind and enables it to run exceedingly fast without wasting a minute on orientation. On the other hand it may, under unusual circumstances, lead the shrew to destruction. It has been reported, quite plausibly, that water shrews have broken their necks by jumping into a pond which had been recently drained. In spite of the possibility of such mishaps, it would be shortsighted if one were simply to stigmatize the water shrew as stupid because it solves the spatial problems of its daily life in quite a different way from man. On the contrary, if one thinks a little more deeply, it is very wonderful that the same result, namely a perfect orientation in space, can be brought about in two so widely divergent ways: by true observation, as we achieve it, or, as the water shrew does, by learning by heart every possible spatial contingency that may arise in a given territory.

Among themselves, my water shrews were surprisingly good-natured. Although, in their play, they would often chase each other, twittering with a great show of excitement, I never saw a serious fight between them until an unfortunate accident occurred: one morning, I forgot to reopen the little door of the nest-box after cleaning out their tank. When at last I remembered, three hours had elapsed—a very long time for the swift metabolism of such small insectivores. Upon the opening of the door, all the shrews rushed out and made a dash for the food tray. In their haste to get out, not only did they soil themselves all over but they apparently discharged, in their excitement, some sort of glandular secretion, for a strong, musk-like odor accompanied their exit from the box. Since they appeared to have incurred no damage by their three hours' fasting, I turned away from the box to occupy myself with other things. However, on nearing the container soon afterwards, I heard an unusually loud, sharp twittering and, on my hurried approach, found my eight shrews locked in deadly battle. Two were even then dying and, though I consigned them at once to separate cages, two more died in the course of the day. The real cause of this sudden and terrible battle is hard to ascertain but I cannot help suspecting that the shrews, owing to the sudden change in the usual odor, had failed to recognize each other and had fallen upon each other as they would have done upon strangers. The four survivors quietened down after a certain time and I was able to reunite them in the original container without fear of further mishap.

I kept those four remaining shrews in good health for nearly seven months and would probably have had them much longer if the assistant whom I had engaged to feed them had not forgotten to do so. I had been obliged to go to Vienna and, on my return in the late afternoon, was met by that usually reliable fellow who turned pale when he saw me, thereupon remembering that he had forgotten to feed the shrews. All four of them were alive but very weak; they ate greedily when we fed them but died nonetheless within a few hours. In other words, they showed exactly the same symptoms as the shrews which I had formerly tried to keep; this confirmed my opinion that the latter were already dying of hunger when they came into my possession.

To any advanced animal keeper who is able to set up a large tank, preferably with running water, and who can obtain a sufficient supply of small fish, tadpoles, and the like, I can recommend the water shrew as one of the most gratifying, charming, and interesting objects of care. Of course it is a somewhat exacting charge. It will eat raw chopped heart (the customary substitute for small live prey) only in the absence of something better and it cannot be fed exclusively on this diet for long periods. Moreover, really clean water is indispensable. But if these clear-cut requirements be fulfilled, the water shrew will not merely remain alive but will really thrive, nor do I exclude the possibility that it might even breed in captivity.

QUESTIONS

1. Lorenz discusses a field trip and some other matters before he reports his laboratory observations. What is the effect of this organization?
2. What features of the shrew's behavior does Lorenz select for special emphasis? What conclusions does he draw about these features?
3. Though this is mainly a report of his observations, Lorenz includes matters which are not necessary to the report of strictly controlled observation of the shrew's habits. Indicate some of the places where his discussion moves beyond strict reporting. Characterize the roles he assumes in these passages. Do these other roles or revelations of personality compromise or support his claim to being a scientist?

NAOMI WEISSTEIN

Psychology Constructs the Female, or, The Fantasy Life of the Male Psychologist
(With Some Attention to the Fantasies of His Friends, the Male Biologist and the Male Anthropologist)

It is an implicit assumption that the area of psychology which concerns itself with personality has the onerous but necessary task of describing the limits of human possibility. Thus when we are about to consider the liberation of women, we naturally look to psychology to tell us what "true" liberation would mean: what would give women the freedom to fulfill their own intrinsic natures. Psychologists have set about describing the true natures of women with a certainty and a sense of their own infallibility rarely found in the secular world. Bruno Bettelheim, of the University of Chicago, tells us that

We must start with the realization that, as much as women want to be good scientists or engineers, they want first and foremost to be womanly companions of men and to be mothers.[1]

Erik Erikson of Harvard University, upon noting that young women often ask whether they can "have an identity before they know whom they will marry, and for whom they will make a home," explains somewhat elegiacally that

Much of a young woman's identity is already defined in her kind of attractiveness and in the selectivity of her search for the man (or men) by whom she wishes to be sought...[2]

Mature womanly fulfillment, for Erikson, rests on the fact that a woman's

... somatic design harbors an "inner space" destined to bear the offspring of chosen men, and with it, a biological, psychological, and ethical commitment to take care of human infancy.[3]

Some psychiatrists even see the acceptance of woman's role by women as a solution to societal problems. "Woman is nurturance ...," writes Joseph Rheingold (1964), a psychiatrist at the Harvard Medical School, " ... anatomy decrees the life of a woman ... when women grow up without dread of their biological functions and without subversion by feminist doctrine, and therefore

1. Bruno Bettelheim, "The Commitment Required of a Woman Entering a Scientific Profession in Present-Day American Society," *Woman and the Scientific Professions*, MIT Symposium on American Women in Science and Engineering, 1965 [Weisstein's note].

2. Erik Erikson, "Inner and Outer Space: Reflections on Womanhood," *Daedalus*, 93 (1964), 582–606 [Weisstein's note].

3. *Ibid*. [Weisstein's note].

enter upon motherhood with a sense of fulfillment and altruistic
sentiment, we shall attain the goal of a good life and a secure world
in which to live it."[4]

These views from men who are assumed to be experts reflect, in a
surprisingly transparent way, the cultural consensus. They not only
assert that a woman is defined by her ability to attract men, they
see no alternative definitions. They think that the definition of a
woman in terms of a man is the way it should be; and they back it
up with psychosexual incantation and biological ritual curses. A
woman has an identity if she is attractive enough to obtain a man,
and thus, a home; for this will allow her to set about her life's task
of "joyful altruism and nurturance."

Business certainly does not disagree. If views such as Bettelheim's
and Erikson's do indeed have something to do with real liberation
for women, then seldom in human history has so much money and
effort been spent on helping a group of people realize their true
potential. Clothing, cosmetics, home furnishings, are multi-million
dollar businesses: if you don't like investing in firms that make weap-
onry and flaming gasoline, then there's a lot of hard cash in "inner
space." Sheet and pillowcase manufacturers are concerned to fill
this inner space:

Mother, for a while this morning, I thought I wasn't cut out for married
life. Hank was late for work and forgot his apricot juice and walked out
without kissing me, and when I was all alone I started crying. But then
the postman came with the sheets and towels you sent, that look like
big bandana handkerchiefs, and you know what I thought? That those
big red and blue handkerchiefs are for girls like me to dry their tears
on so they can get busy and do what a housewife has to do. Throw open
the windows and start getting the house ready, and the dinner, maybe
clean the silver and put new geraniums in the box. *Everything to be ready
for him when he walks through that door.*[5]

Of course, it is not only the sheet and pillowcase manufacturers,
the cosmetics industry, the home furnishings salesmen who profit
from and make use of the cultural definitions of man and woman.
The example above is blatantly and overtly pitched to a particular
kind of sexist stereotype: the child nymph. But almost all aspects of
the media are normative, that is, they have to do with the ways in
which beautiful people, or just folks, or ordinary Americans, should
live their lives. They define the possible; and the possibilities are
usually in terms of what is male and what is female. Men and
women alike are waiting for Hank, the Silva Thins man, to walk
back through that door.

It is an interesting but limited exercise to show that psychologists
and psychiatrists embrace these sexist norms of our culture, that

4. Joseph Rheingold, *The Fear of Being a Woman* (New York: Grune & Strat-
ton, 1964), p. 714 [Weisstein's note].

5. Fieldcrest advertisement in the *New
Yorker,* 1965. My italics. [Weisstein's
note].

they do not see beyond the most superficial and stultifying media
conceptions of female nature, and that their ideas of female nature
serve industry and commerce so well. Just because it's good for business doesn't mean it's wrong. What I will show is that it *is wrong*;
that there isn't the tiniest shred of evidence that these fantasies of
servitude and childish dependence have anything to do with
women's true potential; that the idea of the nature of human possibility which rests on the accidents of individual development of
genitalia, on what is possible today because of what happened yesterday, on the fundamentalist myth of sex organ causality, has stran-
gled and deflected psychology so that it is relatively useless in
describing, explaining or predicting humans and their behavior.

It then goes without saying that present psychology is less than
worthless in contributing to a vision which could truly liberate—
men as well as women.

The central argument of my paper, then, is this. Psychology has
nothing to say about what women are really like, what they need
and what they want, essentially because psychology does not know.
I want to stress that this failure is not limited to women; rather, the
kind of psychology which has addressed itself to how people act and
who they are has failed to understand, in the first place, why people
act the way they do, and certainly failed to understand what might
make them act differently.

The kind of psychology which has addressed itself to these questions divides into two professional areas: academic personality
research, and clinical psychology and psychiatry. The basic reason
for failure is the same in both these areas: the central assumption
for most psychologists of human personality has been that human
behavior rests on an individual and inner dynamic, perhaps fixed in
infancy, perhaps fixed by genitalia, perhaps simply arranged in a
rather immovable cognitive network. But this assumption is rapidly
losing ground as personality psychologists fail again and again to get
consistency in the assumed personalities of their subjects.[6] Meanwhile, the evidence is collecting that what a person does and who
she believes herself to be, will in general be a function of what
people around her expect her to be, and what the overall situation
in which she is acting implies that she is. Compared to the influence
of the social context within which a person lives, his or her history
and "traits", as well as biological makeup, may simply be random
variations, "noise" superimposed on the true signal which can predict behavior.

Some academic personality psychologists are at least looking at
the counter evidence and questioning their theories; no such corrective is occurring in clinical psychology and psychiatry: Freudians

6. J. Block, "Some Reasons for the
Apparent Inconsistency of Personality," *Psychological Bulletin*, 70 (1968), 210–
212 [Weisstein's note].

and neo-Freudians, nudie-marathonists and touchy-feelies, classicists and swingers, clinicians and psychiatrists, simply refuse to look at the evidence against their theory and practice. And they support their theory and practice with stuff so transparently biased as to have absolutely no standing as empirical evidence.

To summarize: the first reason for psychology's failure to understand what people are and how they act is that psychology has looked for inner traits when it should have been looking for social context; the second reason for psychology's failure is that the theoreticians of personality have generally been clinicians and psychiatrists, and they have never considered it necessary to have evidence in support of their theories.

Theory without Evidence

Let us turn to this latter cause of failure first: the acceptance by psychiatrists and clinical psychologists of theory without evidence. If we inspect the literature of personality, it is immediately obvious that the bulk of it is written by clinicians and psychiatrists, and that the major support for their theories is "years of intensive clinical experience." This is a tradition started by Freud. His "insights" occurred during the course of his work with his patients. Now there is nothing wrong with such an approach to theory *formulation*; a person is free to make up theories with any inspiration that works: divine revelation, intensive clinical practice, a random numbers table. But he/she is not free to claim any validity for his/her theory until it has been tested and confirmed. But theories are treated in no such tentative way in ordinary clinical practice. Consider Freud. What he thought constituted evidence violated the most minimal conditions of scientific rigor. In *The Sexual Enlightenment of Children*,[7] the classic document which is supposed to demonstrate empirically the existence of a castration complex and its connection to a phobia, Freud based his analysis on the reports of the father of the little boy, himself in therapy, and a devotee of Freudian theory. I really don't have to comment further on the contamination in this kind of evidence. It is remarkable that only recently has Freud's classic theory on the sexuality of women—the notion of the double orgasm—been actually tested physiologically and found just plain wrong. Now those who claim that fifty years of psychoanalytic experience constitute evidence enough of the essential truths of Freud's theory should ponder the robust health of the double orgasm. Did women, until Masters and Johnson,[8] believe they were having two different kinds of orgasm? Did their psychiatrists badger them into reporting something that was not true? If so, were there other

7. Sigmund Freud, *The Sexual Enlightenment of Children* (New York: Collier Books, 1963) [Weisstein's note].

8. W. H. Masters and V. E. Johnson, *Human Sexual Response* (Boston: Little, Brown, 1966) [Weisstein's note].

things they reported that were also not true? Did psychiatrists ever learn anything different than their theories had led them to believe? If clinical experience means anything at all, surely we should have been done with the double orgasm myth long before the Masters and Johnson studies.

But certainly, you may object, "years of intensive clinical experience" is the only reliable measure in a discipline which relies for its findings on insight, sensitivity, and intuition. The problem with insight, sensitivity, and intuition, is that they can confirm for all time the biases that one started with. People used to be absolutely convinced of their ability to tell which of their number were engaging in witchcraft. All it required was some sensitivity to the workings of the devil.

Years of intensive clinical experience is not the same thing as empirical evidence. The first thing an experimenter learns in any kind of experiment which involves humans is the concept of the "double blind." The term is taken from medical experiments, where one group is given a drug which is presumably supposed to change behavior in a certain way, and a control group is given a placebo. If the observers or the subjects know which group took which drug, the result invariably comes out on the positive side for the new drug. Only when it is not known which subject took which pill, is validity remotely approximated. In addition, with judgments of human behavior, it is so difficult to precisely tie down just what behavior is going on, let alone what behavior should be expected, that one must test again and again the reliability of judgments. How many judges, blind, will agree in their observations? Can they replicate their own judgments at some later time? When, in actual practice, these judgment criteria are tested for clinical judgments, then we find that the judges cannot judge reliably, nor can they judge consistently: they do no better than chance in identifying which of a certain set of stories were written by men and which by women; which of a whole battery of clinical test results are the products of homosexuals and which are the products of heterosexuals,[9] and which, of a battery of clinical test results *and* interviews (where questions are asked such as "Do you have delusions?"[1]) are products of psychotics, neurotics, psychosomatics, or normals. Lest this summary escape your notice, let me stress the implications of these findings. The ability of judges, chosen for their clinical expertise, to distinguish male heterosexuals from male homosexuals on the basis of three widely used clinical projective tests—the Rorschach, the TAT, and the MAP—was *no better than chance*. The reason this is

9. E. Hooker, "Male Homosexuality in the Rorschach," *Journal of Projective Techniques*, 21 (1957), 18–31 [Weisstein's note].

1. K. B. Little and E. S. Schneidman,

"Congruences among Interpretations of Psychological Test and Anamnestic Data," *Psychological Monographs*, 73 (1959), 1–42 [Weisstein's note].

such devastating news, of course, is that sexuality is supposed to be of fundamental importance in the deep dynamic of personality; if what is considered gross sexual deviance cannot be caught, then what are psychologists talking about when they, for example, claim that at the basis of paranoid psychosis is "latent homosexual panic"? They can't even identify what homosexual anything is, let alone "latent homosexual panic."[2] More frightening, expert clinicians cannot be consistent on what diagnostic category to assign to a person, again on the basis of both tests and interviews; a number of normals in the Little and Schneidman study were described as psychotic, in such categories as "schizophrenic with homosexual tendencies" or "schizoid character with depressive trends." But most disheartening, when the judges were asked to rejudge the test protocols some weeks later, their diagnoses of the same subjects on the basis of the same protocol differed markedly from their initial judgments. It is obvious that even simple descriptive conventions in clinical psychology cannot be consistently applied; if clinicians were as faulty in recognizing food from non-food, they'd poison themselves and starve to death. That their descriptive conventions have any explanatory significance is therefore, of course, out of the question.

As a graduate student at Harvard some years ago, I was a member of a seminar which was asked to identify which of two piles of a clinical test, the TAT, had been written by males and which by females. Only four students out of twenty identified the piles correctly, and this was after one and a half months of intensively studying the differences between men and women. Since this result is below chance—that is, the result would occur by chance about four out of a thousand times—we may conclude that there *is* finally a consistency here; students are judging knowledgeably within the context of psychological teaching about the differences between men and women; the teachings themselves are simply erroneous.

You may argue that the theory may be scientifically "unsound" but at least it cures people. There is no evidence that it does. In 1952, Eysenck[3] reported the results of what is called an "outcome of therapy" study of neurotics which showed that, of the patients who received psychoanalysis the improvement rate was 44 percent; of the patients who received psychotherapy the improvement rate was 64 percent; and of the patients who received no treatment at all

2. It should be noted that psychologists have been as quick to assert absolute truths about the nature of homosexuality as they have about the nature of women. The arguments presented in this paper apply equally to the nature of homosexuality; psychologists know nothing about it; there is no more evidence for the "naturalness" of heterosexuality. Psychology has functioned as a pseudo-scientific buttress for patriarchal ideology and patriarchal social organization: women's liberation and gay liberation fight against a common victimization [Weisstein's note].

3. H. J. Eysenck, "The Effects of Psychotherapy: An Evaluation," *Journal of Consulting Psychology*, 16 (1952), 319–324 [Weisstein's note].

the improvement rate was 72 percent. These findings have never been refuted; subsequently, later studies have confirmed the negative results of the Eysenck study.[4] How can clinicians and psychiatrists, then, in all good conscience, continue to practice? Largely by ignoring these results and being careful not to do outcome-of-therapy studies. The attitude is nicely summarized by Rotter:[5] "Research studies in psychotherapy tend to be concerned more with pyschotherapeutic procedure and less with outcome. ... To some extent, it reflects an interest in the psychotherapy situation as a kind of personality laboratory." Some laboratory.

The Social Context

Thus, since we can conclude that because clinical experience and tools can be shown to be worse than useless when tested for consistency, efficacy, agreement, and reliability, we can safely conclude that theories of a clinical nature advanced about women are also worse than useless. I want to turn now to the second major point in my paper, which is that, even when psychological theory is constructed so that it may be tested, and rigorous standards of evidence are used, it has become increasingly clear that in order to understand why people do what they do, and certainly in order to change what people do, psychologists must turn away from the theory of the causal nature of the inner dynamic and look to the social context within which individuals live.

Before examining the relevance of this approach to the question of women, let me first sketch the groundwork for this assertion.

In the first place, it is clear[6] that personality tests never yield consistent predictions; a rigid authoritarian on one measure will be an unauthoritarian on the next. But the reason for this inconsistency is only now becoming clear, and it seems overwhelmingly to have much more to do with the social situation in which the subject finds him/herself than with the subject him/herself.

In a series of brilliant experiments, Rosenthal and his co-workers[7] have shown that if one group of experimenters has one hypothesis about what they expect to find, and another group of experimenters

4. F. Barron and T. Leary, "Changes in Psychoneurotic Patients with and without Psychotherapy," *Journal of Counseling Psychology,* 19 (1955); A. E. Bergin, "The Effects of Psychotherapy: Negative Results Revisited," *Journal of Counseling Psychology,* 10 (1963); R. D. Cartwright and J. L. Vogel, "A Comparison of Changes in Psychoneurotic Patients During Matched Periods of Therapy and No-therapy," *Journal of Counseling Psychology,* 24 (1960); C. B. Truax, "Effective Ingredients in Psychotherapy: An Approach to Unraveling the Patient-Therapist Interaction," *Journal of Counseling Psychology,* 10 (1963); E. Powers and H. Witmer, *An Experiment in the Prevention of Delinquency* (New York: Columbia University Press, 1951) [Weisstein's note].

5. J. B. Rotter, "Psychotherapy," *Annual Review of Psychology,* 11 (1960), 381–414 [Weisstein's note].

6. J. Block, *op. cit.* [Weisstein's note].

7. R. Rosenthal and L. Jacobson, *Pygmalion in the Classroom: Teacher Expectation and Pupil's Intellectual Development* (New York: Holt, Rinehart & Winston, 1968); R. Rosenthal, *Experimenter Effects in Behavioral Research* (New York: Appleton-Century Crofts, 1966) [Weisstein's note].

has the opposite hypothesis, both groups will obtain results in accord with their hypotheses. The results obtained are not due to mishandling of data by biased experimenters; rather, somehow, the bias of the experimenter creates a changed environment in which subjects actually act differently. For instance, in one experiment, subjects were to assign numbers to pictures of men's faces, with high numbers representing the subject's judgment that the man in the picture was a successful person, and low numbers representing the subject's judgment that the man in the picture was an unsuccessful person. Prior to running the subjects, one group of experimenters was told that the subjects tended to rate the faces high; another group of experimenters was told that the subjects tended to rate the faces low. Each group of experimenters was instructed to follow precisely the same procedure: they were required to read to subjects a set of instructions, and to say *nothing else*. For the 375 subjects run, the results showed clearly that those subjects who performed the task with experimenters who expected high ratings gave high ratings, and those subjects who performed the task with experimenters who expected low ratings gave low ratings. How did this happen? The experimenters all used the same words; it was something in their conduct which made one group of subjects do one thing, and another group of subjects do another thing.[8]

The concreteness of the changed conditions produced by expectation is a fact, a reality: even with animal subjects, in two separate studies,[9] those experimenters who were told that rats learning mazes had been especially bred for brightness obtained better learning from their rats than did experimenters believing their rats to have been bred for dullness. In a very recent study, Rosenthal and Jacobson (1968) extended their analysis to the natural classroom situation. Here, they tested a group of students and reported to the teachers that some among the students tested "showed great promise." Actually, the students so named had been selected on a random basis. Some time later, the experimenters retested the group of students: those students whose teachers had been told that they were "promising" showed real and dramatic increments in their IQs as compared to the rest of the students. Something in the conduct of the teachers towards those who the teachers believed to be the "bright" students, made those students brighter.

Thus, even in carefully controlled experiments, and with no outward or conscious difference in behavior, the hypotheses we start with will influence enormously the behavior of another organism.

8. I am indebted to Jesse Lemisch for his valuable suggestions in the interpretation of these studies [Weisstein's note].

9. R. Rosenthal and K. L. Fode, "The Effect of Experimenter Bias on the Performance of the Albino Rat," Harvard University, unpublished manuscript 1961; R. Rosenthal and R. Lawson, "A Longitudinal Study of the Effects of Experimenter Bias on the Operant Learning of Laboratory Rats," Harvard University, unpublished manuscript,1961 [Weisstein's note].

These studies are extremely important when assessing the validity of psychological studies of women. Since it is beyond doubt that most of us start with notions as to the nature of men and women, the validity of a number of observations of sex differences is questionable, even when these observations have been made under carefully controlled conditions. Second, and more important, the Rosenthal experiments point quite clearly to the influence of social expectation. In some extremely important ways, people are what you expect them to be, or at least they behave as you expect them to behave. Thus, if women, according to Bettelheim, want first and foremost to be good wives and mothers, it is extremely likely that this is what Bruno Bettelheim, and the rest of society, want them to be.

There is another series of brilliant social psychological experiments which point to the overwhelming effect of social context. These are the obedience experiments of Stanley Milgram[1] in which subjects are asked to obey the orders of unknown experimenters, orders which carry with them the distinct possibility that the subject is killing somebody.

In Milgram's experiments, a subject is told that he/she is administering a learning experiment, and that he/she is to deal out shocks each time the other "subject" (in reality, a confederate of the experimenter) answers incorrectly. The equipment appears to provide graduated shocks ranging upwards from 15 volts through 450 volts; for each of four consecutive voltages there are verbal descriptions such as "mild shock," "danger, severe shock," and, finally, for the 435- and 450-volt switches, a red XXX marked over the switches. Each time the stooge answers incorrectly, the subject is supposed to increase the voltage. As the voltage increases, the stooge begins to cry in pain; he/she demands that the experiment stop; finally, he/she refuses to answer at all. When he/she stops responding, the experimenter instructs the subject to continue increasing the voltage; for each shock administered the stooge shrieks in agony. Under these conditions, about 62½ percent of the subjects administered shocks that they believed to be possibly lethal.

No tested individual differences between subjects predicted how many would continue to obey, and which would break off the experiment. When forty psychiatrists predicted how many of a group of 100 subjects would go on to give the lethal shock, their predictions were orders of magnitude below the actual percentages; most expected only one-tenth of one per cent of the subjects to obey to the end.

But even though *psychiatrists* have no idea how people will

1. Stanley Milgram, "Some Conditions of Obedience and Disobedience to Authority," *Human Relations,* 18 (1965), 57–76; "Liberating Effects of Group Pressures," *Journal of Personality and Social Psychology,* 1 (1965), 127–134 [Weisstein's note].

behave in this situation, and even though individual differences do not predict which subjects will obey and which will not, it is easy to predict when subjects will be obedient and when they will be defiant. All the experimenter has to do is change the social situation. In a variant of Milgram's experiment, two stooges were present in addition to the "victim"; these worked along with the subject in administering electric shocks. When these two stooges refused to go on with the experiment, only 10 percent of the subjects continued to the maximum voltage. This is critical for personality theory. It says that behavior is predicted from the social situation, not from the individual history.

Finally, an ingenious experiment by Schachter and Singer[2] showed that subjects injected with adrenalin, which produces a state of physiological arousal in all but minor respects identical to that which occurs when subjects are extremely afraid, became euphoric when they were in a room with a stooge who was acting euphoric, and became extremely angry when they were placed in a room with a stooge who was acting extremely angry.

To summarize: If subjects under quite innocuous and non-coercive social conditions can be made to kill other subjects and under other types of social conditions will positively refuse to do so; if subjects can react to a state of physiological fear by becoming euphoric because there is somebody else around who is euphoric, or angry because there is somebody else around who is angry; if students become intelligent because teachers expect them to be intelligent, and rats run mazes better because experimenters are told the rats are bright, then it is obvious that a study of human behavior requires, first and foremost, a study of the social contexts within which people move, the expectations as to how they will behave, and the authority which tells them who they are and what they are supposed to do.

Biologically Based Theories

Biologists also have at times assumed they could describe the limits of human potential from their observations not of human, but of animal behavior. Here, as in psychology, there has been no end of theorizing about the sexes, again with a sense of absolute certainty surprising in "science." These theories fall into two major categories.

One category of theory argues that since females and males differ in their sex hormones, and sex hormones enter the brain,[3] there must

2. S. Schachter and J. E. Singer, "Cognitive, Social, and Physiological Determinants of Emotional State," *Psychological Review*, 63 (1962), 379–399 [Weisstein's note].

3. D. A. Hamburg and D. T. Lunde,

"Sex Hormones in the Development of Sex Differences in Human Behavior," in *The Development of Sex Differences*, ed. Maccoby (Stanford: Stanford University Press, 1966), pp. 1–24 [Weisstein's note].

be innate behavioral differences. But the only thing this argument tells us is that there are differences in physiological state. The problem is whether these differences are at all relevant to behavior.

Consider, for example, differences in levels of the sex hormone testosterone. A man who calls himself Tiger[4] has recently argued[5] that the greater quantities of testosterone found in human males as compared with human females (of a certain age group) determine innate differences in aggressiveness, competitiveness, dominance, ability to hunt, ability to hold public office, and so forth. But Tiger demonstrates in this argument the same manly and courageous refusal to be intimidated by evidence which we have already seen in our consideration of the clinical and psychiatric tradition. The evidence does not support his argument, and in most cases, directly contradicts it. Testosterone level does not seem to be related to hunting ability, dominance, or aggression, or competitiveness. As Storch[6] has pointed out, all normal *male mammals* in the reproductive age group produce much greater quantities of testosterone than females; yet many of these males are neither hunters nor are they aggressive (e.g. rabbits). And, among some hunting mammals, such as the large cats, it turns out that more hunting is done by the female than the male. And there exist primate species where the female is clearly more aggressive, competitive, and dominant than the male.[7] Thus, for some species, being female, and therefore, having less testosterone than the male of that species means hunting more, or being more aggressive, or being more dominant. Nor does having *more* testosterone preclude behavior commonly thought of as "female"; there exist primate species where females do not touch infants except to feed them; the males care for the infants at all times.[8] So it is not clear what testosterone or any other sex-hormonal difference means for differences in nature, or sex-role behavior.

In other words, one can observe identical types of behavior which have been associated with sex (e.g. "mothering") in males and females, despite known differences in physiological state, i.e. sex hormones, genitalia, etc. What about the converse to this? That is, can one obtain differences in behavior given a single physiological state? The answer is overwhelmingly yes, not only as regards non-sex-specific hormones (as in the Schachter and Singer experiment cited above), but also as regards gender itself. Studies of hermaphrodites

4. H. N. G. Schwarz-Belkin claims that the name was originally Mouse, but this may be a reference to an earlier L. Tiger (putative). See "Les Fleurs Du Mal," in *Festschrift fir Piltdown* (New York: Ponzi Press, 1914) [Weisstein's note].

5. Lionel Tiger, "Male Dominance? Yes. A Sexist Plot? No," *New York Times Magazine*, sec. N, Oct. 25, 1970 [Weisstein's note].

6. M. Storch, "Reply to Tiger," unpublished manuscript, 1970 [Weisstein's note].

7. G. D. Mitchell, "Paternalistic Behavior in Primates," *Psychological Bulletin*, 71 (1969), 399–417 [Weisstein's note].

8. *Ibid.* [Weisstein's note].

with the same diagnosis (the genetic, gonadal, hormonal sex, the internal reproductive organs, and the ambiguous appearances of the external genitalia were identical) have shown that one will consider oneself male or female depending simply on whether one was defined and raised as male or female:[9]

There is no more convincing evidence of the power of social interaction on gender-identity differentiation than in the case of congenital hermaphrodites who are of the same diagnosis and similar degree of hermaphroditism but are differently assigned and with a different postnatal medical and life history. (Money, 1970, p. 743).

Thus, for example, if out of two individuals diagnosed as having the adrenogenital syndrome of female hermaphroditism, one is raised as a girl and one as a boy, each will act and identify her/himself accordingly. The one raised as a girl will consider herself a girl; the one raised as a boy will consider himself a boy; and each will conduct her/himself successfully in accord with that self-definition.

So, identical behavior occurs given different physiological states; and different behavior occurs given an identical physiological starting point. So it is not clear that differences in sex hormones are at all relevant to behavior.

The other category of theory based on biology, a reductionist theory, goes like this. Sex-role behavior in some primate species is described, and it is concluded that this is the "natural" behavior for humans. Putting aside the not insignificant problem of observer bias (for instance, Harlow, of the University of Wisconsin, after observing differences between male and female rhesus monkeys, quotes Laurence Sterne to the effect that women are silly and trivial, and concludes that "men and women have differed in the past and they will differ in the future"[1]), there are a number of problems with this approach.

The most general and serious problem is that there are no grounds to assume that anything primates do is necessarily natural, or desirable in humans, for the simple reason that humans are not non-humans. For instance, it is found that male chimpanzees placed alone with infants will not "mother" them. Jumping from hard data to ideological speculation, researchers conclude from this information that *human* females are necessary for the safe growth of human infants. It would be reasonable to conclude, following this logic, that it is quite useless to teach human infants to speak, since it has been tried with chimpanzees and it does not work.

One strategy that has been used is to extrapolate from primate

9. J. Money, "Sexual Dimorphism and Homosexual Gender Identity," *Psychological Bulletin* 6 (1970), 425–440 [Weisstein's note].

1. H. F. Harlow, "The Heterosexual Affectional System in Monkeys," *American Psychologist*, 17 (1962), 1–9 [Weisstein's note].

behavior to "innate" human preference by noticing certain trends in primate behavior as one moves phylogenetically closer to humans. But there are great difficulties with this approach. When behaviors from lower primates are directly opposite to those of higher primates, or to those one expects of humans, they can be dismissed on evolutionary grounds—higher primates and/or humans grew out of that kid stuff. On the other hand, if the behavior of higher primates is counter to the behavior considered natural for humans, while the behavior of some lower primate is considered the natural one for humans, the higher primate behavior can be dismissed also, on the grounds that it has diverged from an older, prototypical pattern. So either way, one can select those behaviors one wants to prove innate for humans. In addition, one does not know whether the sex-role behavior exhibited is dependent on the phylogenetic rank, or on the environmental conditions (both physical and social) under which different species live.

Is there then any value at all in primate observations as they relate to human females and males? There is a value but it is limited: its function can be no more than to show some extant examples of diverse sex-role behavior. It must be stressed, however, that this is an extremely limited function. The extant behavior does not begin to suggest all the possibilities, either for non-human primates or for humans. Bearing these caveats in mind, it is nonetheless interesting that if one inspects the limited set of observations of existing non-human primate sex-role behaviors, one finds, in fact, a much larger range of sex-role behavior than is commonly believed to exist. "Biology" appears to limit very little; the fact that a female gives birth does not mean, even in non-humans, that she necessarily cares for the infant (in marmosets, for instance, the male carries the infant at all times except when the infant is feeding[2]); "natural" female and male behavior varies all the way from females who are much more aggressive and competitive than males (e.g. Tamarins[3]) and male "mothers" (e.g. Titi monkeys, night monkeys, and marmosets[4]) to submissive and passive females and male antagonists (e.g. rhesus monkeys).

But even for the limited function that primate arguments serve, the evidence has been misused. Invariably, those primates have been cited which exhibit exactly the kind of behavior that the proponents of the biological fixedness of human female behavior wish were true for humans. Thus, baboons and rhesus monkeys are generally cited: males in these groups exhibit some of the most irritable and aggressive behavior found in primates, and if one wishes to argue that

2. Mitchell, *op. cit.* [Weisstein's note].
3. *Ibid.* [Weisstein's note].
4. *Ibid.* (All these are lower-order primates, which makes their behavior with reference to humans unnatural, or more natural; take your choice.) [Weisstein's note].

females are naturally passive and submissive, these groups provide vivid examples. There are abundant counter examples, such as those mentioned above;[5] in fact, in general, a counter example can be found for every sex-role behavior cited, including, as mentioned in the case of marmosets, male "mothers."

But the presence of counter examples has not stopped florid and overarching theories of the natural or biological basis of male privilege from proliferating. For instance, there have been a number of theories dealing with the innate incapacity in human males for monogamy. Here, as in most of this type of theorizing, baboons are a favorite example, probably because of their fantasy value: the family unit of the hamadryas baboon, for instance, consists of a highly constant pattern of one male and a number of females and their young. And again, the counter examples, such as the invariably monogamous gibbon, are ignored.

An extreme example of this maiming and selective truncation of the evidence in the service of a plea for the maintenance of male privilege is a recent book, *Men in Groups* by Tiger.[6] The central claim of this book is that females are incapable of "bonding" as in "male bonding." What is "male bonding"? Its surface definition is simple: " . . . a particular relationship between two or more males such that they react differently to members of their bonding units as compared to individuals outside of it."[7] If one deletes the word male, the definition, on its face, would seem to include all organisms that have any kind of social organization. But this is not what Tiger means. For instance, Tiger asserts that females are incapable of bonding; and this alleged incapacity indicates to Tiger that females should be restricted from public life. Why is bonding an exclusively male behavior? Because, says Tiger, it is seen in male primates. All male primates? No, very few male primates. Tiger cites two examples where male bonding is seen: rhesus monkeys and baboons. Surprise, surprise. But not even all baboons: as mentioned above, the hamadryas social organization consists of one-male units; so does that of the gelada baboon.[8] And the great apes do not go in for male bonding much either. The "male bond" is hardly a serious contribution to scholarship; one reviewer for *Science* has observed that the book " . . . shows basically more resemblance to a partisan political tract than to a work of objective social science," with male bonding being " . . . some kind of behavioral phlogiston."[9]

In short, primate arguments have generally misused the evidence; primate studies themselves have, in any case, only the very limited function of describing some possible sex-role behavior; and at pres-

5. *Ibid.* [Weisstein's note].
6. Lionel Tiger, *Men in Groups* (New York: Random House, 1969) [Weisstein's note].
7. *Ibid.*, pp. 19–20 [Weisstein's note].
8. Mitchell, *op. cit.* [Weisstein's note].
9. M. H. Fried, "Mankind Excluding Women," *Science*, 165 (1969), 883–884 [Weisstein's note].

ent, primate observations have been sufficiently limited so that even the range of possible sex-role behavior for non-human primates is not known. This range is not known since there is only minimal observation of what happens to behavior if the physical or social environment is changed. In one study,[1] different troops of Japanese macaques were observed. Here, there appeared to be cultural differences: males in 3 out of the 18 troops observed differed in the amount of their aggressiveness and infant-caring behavior. There could be no possibility of differential evolution here; the differences seemed largely transmitted by infant socialization. Thus, the very limited evidence points to some plasticity in the sex-role behavior of non-human primates; if we can figure out experiments which massively change the social organization of primate groups, it is possible that we might observe great changes in behavior. At present, however, we must conclude that given a constant physical environment, non-human primates do not change their social conditions by themselves very much and thus the "innateness" and fixedness of their behavior is simply not known. Thus, even if there were some way, which there isn't, to settle on the behavior of a particular primate species as being the "natural" way for humans, we would not know whether or not this were simply some function of the present social organization of that species. And finally, once again it must be stressed that even if non-human primate behavior turned out to be relatively fixed, this would say little about our behavior. More immediate and relevant evidence, e.g. the evidence from social psychology, points to the enormous plasticity in human behavior, not only from one culture to the next, but from one experimental group to the next. One of the most salient features of human social organization is its variety; there are a number of cultures where there is at least a rough equality between men and women.[2] In summary, primate arguments can tell us very little about our "innate" sex-role behavior; if they tell us anything at all, they tell us that there is no one biologically "natural" female or male behavior, and that sex-role behavior in non-human primates is much more varied than has previously been thought.

Conclusion

In brief, the uselessness of present psychology (and biology) with regard to women is simply a special case of the general conclusion: one must understand the social conditions under which humans live if one is going to attempt to explain their behavior. And, to

1. J. Itani, "Paternal Care in the Wild Japanese Monkey *Macaca fuscata*," in *Primate Social Behavior*, ed. Southwick (Princeton: Van Nostrand, 1963) [Weisstein's note].

2. Margaret Mead, *Male and Female: A Study of the Sexes in a Changing World* (New York: William Morrow, 1949) [Weisstein's note].

understand the social conditions under which women live, one must understand the social expectations about women.

How are women characterized in our culture, and in psychology? They are inconsistent, emotionally unstable, lacking in a strong conscience or superego, weaker, "nurturant" rather then productive, "intuitive" rather than intelligent, and, if they are at all "normal," suited to the home and the family. In short, the list adds up to a typical minority group stereotype of inferiority:[3] if they know their place, which is in the home, they are really quite lovable, happy, childlike, loving creatures. In a review of the intellectual differences between little boys and little girls, Eleanor Maccoby[4] has shown that there are no intellectual differences until about high school, or, if there are, girls are slightly ahead of boys. At high school, girls begin to do worse on a few intellectual tasks, such as arithmetic reasoning, and beyond high school, the achievement of women now measured in terms of productivity and accomplishment drops off even more rapidly. There are a number of other, non-intellectual tests which show sex differences; I choose the intellectual differences since it is seen clearly that women start becoming inferior. It is no use to talk about women being different but equal; all of the tests I can think of have a "good" outcome and a "bad" outcome. Women usually end up at the "bad" outcome. In light of social expectations about women, what is surprising is that little girls don't get the message that they are supposed to be stupid until high school; and what is even more remarkable is that some women resist this message even after high school, college, and graduate school.

My paper began with remarks on the task of the discovery of the limits of human potential. Psychologists must realize that it is they who are limiting discovery of human potential. They refuse to accept evidence, if they are clinical psychologists, or, if they are rigorous, they assume that people move in a context-free ether, with only their innate dispositions and their individual traits determining what they will do. Until psychologists begin to respect evidence, and until they begin looking at the social context within which people move, psychology will have nothing of substance to offer in this task of discovery. I don't know what immutable differences exist between men and women apart from differences in their genitals; perhaps there are some other unchangeable differences; probably there are a number of irrelevant differences. But it is clear that until social expectations for men and women are equal, until we provide equal respect for both men and women, our answers to this question will simply reflect our prejudices.

3. H. M. Hacker, "Women as a Minority Group," *Social Forces*, 30 (1951), 60–69 [Weisstein's note].
4. Eleanor E. Maccoby, "Sex Differences in Intellectual Functioning," in *The Development of Sex Differences*, ed. Maccoby (Stanford: Stanford University Press, 1966), pp. 25–55 [Weisstein's note].

B. F. SKINNER
What Is Man?[1]

As a science of behavior follows the strategy of physics and biology, the autonomous agent to which we have traditionally attributed behavior is replaced by the environment—the environment in which the species evolved and in which the behavior of the individual is shaped and maintained.

Take, for example, a "cognitive" activity, *attention*. A person responds to only a small part of the stimuli impinging upon him. The traditional view is that he himself determines which stimuli are to be effective—by paying attention to them. Some kind of inner gatekeeper allows some stimuli to enter and keeps all others out. A sudden or strong stimulus may break through and "attract" attention, but the person himself is otherwise in control. An analysis of the environmental circumstances reverses the relation. The kinds of stimuli that break through by "attracting attention" do so because they have been associated in the evolutionary history of the species or the personal history of the individual with important—e.g., dangerous—things. Less forceful stimuli attract attention only to the extent that they have figured in contingencies of reinforcement.

We can arrange contingencies that insure that an organism—even such a simple organism as a pigeon—will attend to one object and not to another, or to one property of an object, such as its color, and not to another, such as its shape. The inner gatekeeper is replaced by the contingencies that the person has been exposed to and that select the stimuli he reacts to.

Face

In the traditional view a person perceives the world around him and acts upon it to make it known to him. It has even been argued that the world would not exist if no one perceived it. The action is exactly reversed in an environmental analysis. There would, of course, be no perception if there were no world to perceive, but we would not perceive an existing world if there were no appropriate contingencies.

We say that a baby perceives his mother's face and knows it. Our evidence is that the baby responds in one way to his mother's face and in other ways to other faces or other things. He makes this distinction not through some mental act of perception but because of prior contingencies. Some of these may be contingencies of survival. The face and facial expressions of the human mother have been

1. From *Beyond Freedom and Dignity*, 1971.

associated with security, warmth, food and other important things during both the evolution of the species and the life of the child.

The role of the environment is particularly subtle when what is known is the knower himself. If there is no external world to initiate knowing, must we not then say that the knower himself acts first? This is, of course, the field of consciousness or awareness which a scientific analysis of behavior is often accused of ignoring. The charge is a serious one and should be taken seriously.

Man is said to differ from the other animals mainly because he is "aware of his own existence." He knows what he is doing; he knows that he has had a past and will have a future; he alone follows the classical injunction, "Know thyself." Any analysis of human behavior that neglected these facts would be defective indeed. And some analyses do. "Methodological behaviorism" limits itself to what can be observed publicly; mental processes may exist, but their nature rules them out of scientific consideration. The "behaviorists" in political science and many logical positivists in philosophy have followed a similar line. But we can study self-observation, and we must include it in any reasonably complete account of human behavior. Rather than ignore consciousness, an experimental analysis of behavior has put much emphasis on certain crucial issues. The question is not whether a man can know himself but what he knows when he does so.

Skin

The problem arises in part from the indisputable fact of privacy: a small part of the universe is enclosed within a human skin. It would be foolish to deny the existence of that private world, but it is also foolish to assert that because it is private its nature is different from the world outside. The difference is not in the stuff that composes the private world but in its accessibility. There is an exclusive intimacy about a headache or heartache that has seemed to support the doctrine that knowing is a kind of possession.

The difficulty is that although privacy may bring the knower closer to what he knows, it interferes with the process through which he comes to know anything. As we have seen, contingencies under which a child learns to describe his feelings are necessarily defective; the verbal community cannot use the same procedures for this that it uses to teach a child to describe objects. There are, of course, natural contingencies under which we learn to respond to private stimuli, and they generate behavior of great precision; we could not walk if we were not stimulated by parts of our own body. But very little awareness is associated with this kind of behavior and, in fact, we behave in these ways most of the time without being aware of the stimuli to which we are responding. We do not attribute awareness to other species that obviously use similar private stimuli. To "know" private stimuli is more than to respond to them.

Help

The verbal community specializes in self-descriptive contingencies. It asks: What did you do yesterday? Why did you do that? How do you feel about that? The answers help persons adjust to each other effectively. And it is because such questions are asked that a person responds to himself and his behavior in the special way called knowing or being aware. Without the help of a verbal community all behavior would be unconscious. Consciousness is a social product. It is not only *not* the special field of autonomous man, it is not within the range of a solitary man.

And it is not within the range of accuracy of anyone. The privacy that seems to confer intimacy upon self-knowledge makes it impossible for the verbal community to maintain precise contingencies. Introspective vocabularies are by nature inaccurate, and that is one reason why they have varied so widely among schools of philosophy and psychology. Even a carefully trained observer runs into trouble when he studies new private stimuli.

Aware

Theories of psychotherapy that emphasize awareness assign a role to autonomous man that is the function of contingencies of reinforcement. Awareness may help if the problem is in part a lack of awareness, and "insight" into one's condition may help if one then takes remedial action. But awareness or insight alone is not always enough, and may be too much. One need not be aware of one's behavior or the conditions controlling it in order to behave effectively—or ineffectively.

The extent to which a man *should* be aware of himself depends upon the importance of self-observation for effective behavior. Self-knowledge is valuable only to the extent that it helps to meet the contingencies under which it has arisen.

Think

Perhaps the last stronghold of autonomous man is the complex "cognitive" activity called thinking. Because it is complex, it has yielded only slowly to explanation in terms of contingencies of reinforcement. We say that a person *forms a concept or an abstraction*, but all we see is that certain kinds of contingencies of reinforcement have brought a response under the control of a single property of a stimulus. We say that a person *recalls* or *remembers* what he has seen or heard, but all we see is that the present occasion evokes a response, possibly in weakened or altered form, acquired on another occasion. We say that a person *associates* one word with another, but all we observe is that one verbal stimulus evokes the response previously made to another. Rather than suppose that it is therefore autonomous man who forms concepts or abstractions, recalls or remembers, and associates, we can put matters in good order simply by noting that these terms do not refer to forms of behavior.

A person may take explicit action, however, when he solves a problem. The creative artist may manipulate a medium until something of interest turns up. Much of this can be done covertly, and we are then likely to assign it to a different dimensional system; but it can always be done overtly, perhaps more slowly but also often more effectively, and with rare exceptions it must have been learned in overt form. The culture constructs special contingencies to promote thinking. It teaches a person to make fine discriminations by making differential reinforcement more precise. It teaches techniques to use in solving problems. It provides rules that make it unnecessary to expose a person to the contingencies from which the rules derive, and it provides rules for finding rules.

Self-control or self-management is a special kind of problem-solving that, like self-knowledge, raises all the issues associated with privacy. It is always the environment that builds the behavior with which we solve problems, even when the problems are found in the private world inside the skin. We have not investigated the matter of self-control in a very productive way, but the inadequacy of our analysis is no reason to fall back on a miracle-working mind. If our understanding of contingencies of reinforcement is not yet sufficient to explain all kinds of thinking, we must remember that the appeal to mind explains nothing at all.

Inside

In shifting control from autonomous man to the observable environment we do not leave an empty organism. A great deal goes on inside the skin, and physiology will eventually be able to tell us more about it. It will explain why behavior indeed relates to the antecedent events of which we can show it to be a function.

People do not always correctly understand the assignment. Many physiologists regard themselves as looking for the "physiological correlates" of mental events. They regard physiological research as simply a more scientific version of introspection. But physiological techniques are not, of course, designed to detect or measure personalities, feelings, or thoughts. At the moment neither introspection nor physiology supplies very adequate information about what is going on inside a man as he behaves, and since they are both directed inward they have the same effect of diverting attention from the external environment.

Much of the misunderstanding about an inner man comes from the metaphor of storage. Evolutionary and environmental histories change an organism, but they are not stored within it. Thus we observe that babies suck their mothers' breasts and can easily imagine that a strong tendency to do so has survival value, but much more is implied by a "sucking instinct" regarded as something a baby possesses that enables it to suck. The concept of "human nature" or "genetic endowment" is dangerous when we take it in that sense. We are closer to human nature in a baby than in an adult, or in a primitive culture than in an advanced one, in the sense that environmental contingencies are less likely to have obscured the genetic endowment, and it is tempting to dramatize that endowment by implying that earlier stages have survived in concealed form: man is a naked ape. But anatomists and physiologists will not find an ape, or for that matter, instincts. They will find anatomical and physiological features that are the product of an evolutionary history.

Sin

It is often said too that the personal history of the individual is stored within him as a "habit." The cigarette habit is talked of as being something more than the behavior said to show that a person possesses it. But the only other information we have is about the reinforcers and the schedules of reinforcement that make a person smoke a great deal. The contingencies are not stored; they simply leave a person changed.

The issue has had a curious place in theology. Does man sin because he is sinful, or is he sinful because he sins? Neither question points to anything very useful. To say that a man is sinful because he sins is to give an operational definition of sin. To say that he sins because he is sinful is to trace his behavior to a supposed inner trait. But whether a person engages in the kind of behavior called sinful depends upon circumstances not mentioned in either question. The sin assigned as an inner possession (the sin a person "knows") is to be found in a history of reinforcement.

Self

It is the nature of an experimental analysis of human behavior to strip away the functions previously assigned to autonomous man and transfer them one by one to the controlling environment. The analysis leaves less and less for autonomous man to do. But what about man himself? Is there not something about a person—a self —that is more than a living body?

A self is a repertoire of behavior appropriate to a given set of contingencies, and a substantial part of the conditions to which a person is exposed may play a dominant role. Under other conditions a person may sometimes report, "I'm not myself today" or "I

couldn't have done what you said I did, because that's not like me."
The identity conferred upon a self arises from the contingencies
responsible for the behavior.

Split

Two or more repertoires generated by different sets of contingencies compose two or more selves. A person possesses one repertoire appropriate to his life with his friends and another appropriate to his life with his family. A problem of identity arises when
a person finds himself with family and friends at the same time.

Self-knowledge and self-control imply two selves in this sense. The
self-knower is almost always a product of social contingencies, but
the self that is known may come from other sources. The controlling self (the conscience or superego) is of social origin, but the
controlled self is more likely to be the product of genetic suscepti-
bilities to reinforcement (the id or the Old Adam). The controlling
self generally represents the interests of others; the controlled self
the interests of the individual.

Stranger

The picture that emerges from a scientific analysis is not of a
body with a person inside but of a body that *is* a person in the
sense that it displays a complex repertoire of behavior. The picture
is, of course, unfamiliar. The man we thus portray is a stranger, and
from the traditional point of view he may not seem to be a man at
all.

C. S. Lewis put it bluntly: "Man is being abolished."

There is clearly some difficulty in identifying the man to whom
Lewis referred. He cannot have meant the human species; far from
being abolished, it is filling the earth. Nor are individual men growing less effective or productive. What is being abolished is autonomous man—the inner man, the homunculus, the possessing demon,
the man defended by the literatures of freedom and dignity.

His abolition is long overdue. Autonomous man is a device we
use to explain what we cannot explain in any other way. We constructed him from our ignorance, and as our understanding
increases, the very stuff of which he is composed vanishes. Science
does not dehumanize man, it de-homunculizes him, and it must do
so if it is to prevent the abolition of the human species.

To man *qua* man we readily say good riddance. Only by dispossessing autonomous man can we turn to the real causes of human
behavior—from the inferred to the observed, from the miraculous
to the natural, from the inaccessible to the manipulable.

Purpose

It is often said that in doing so we must treat the man who survives as a mere animal. "Animal" is a pejorative term—but only because "man" has been made spuriously honorific. Joseph Wood Krutch argued that the traditional view supports Hamlet's exclamation "How like a god!" while Pavlov emphasized "How like a dog!" But that was a step forward. A god is the archetypal pattern of an explanatory fiction, of a miracle-working mind, of the metaphysical. Man is much more than a dog, but like a dog he is within range of a scientific analysis.

An important role of autonomous man has been to give direction to human behavior, and it is often said that in dispossessing an inner agent we leave man without a purpose: "Since a scientific psychology must regard human behavior objectively, as determined by necessary laws, it must represent human behavior as unintentional." But "necessary laws" would have this effect only if they referred exclusively to antecedent conditions. Intention and purpose refer to selective consequences, the effects of which we can formulate in "necessary laws." Has life, in all the forms in which it exists on the surface of the earth, a purpose? And is this evidence of intentional design? The primate hand evolved *in order that* the primate could more successfully manipulate things, but its purpose was to be found not in a prior design but rather in the process of selection. Similarly, in operant conditioning—when a pianist acquires the behavior of playing a smooth scale, for example—we find the purpose of the skilled movement of the hand in the consequences that follow it. In neither the evolution of the human hand nor in the acquired use of the hand is any prior intention or purpose at issue.

There is a difference between biological and individual purpose in that the latter can be felt. No one could have felt the purpose in the development of the human hand, but a person can in a sense feel the purpose with which he plays a smooth scale. But he does not play a smooth scale *because* he feels the purpose of doing so; what he feels is a by-product of his behavior and of its consequences. The relation of the human hand to the contingencies of survival under which it evolved is, of course, out of reach of personal observation; the relation of the behavior to contingencies of reinforcement that have generated it is not.

Control

As a scientific analysis of behavior dispossesses autonomous man and turns the control he has been said to exert over to the environment, the individual may seem particularly vulnerable. He is henceforth to be controlled by the world around him, and in large part by other men. Is he not then simply a victim? Certainly men have been victims, as they have been victimizers, but the word is too strong. It implies despoliation, which is by no means an essential consequence of interpersonal control. But even under benevolent control is the individual not helpless—"at a dead end in his long struggle to control his own destiny"?

It is only autonomous man who has reached a dead end. Man himself may be controlled by his environment, but it is an environment almost wholly of his own making. The physical environment of most persons is largely man-made—the walls that shelter them, the tools they use, the surfaces they walk on—and the social environment is obviously man-made. It generates the language a person speaks, the customs he follows, and the behavior he exhibits with respect to the ethical, religious, governmental, economic, educational and psychotherapeutic institutions that control him.

The evolution of a culture is in fact a kind of gigantic exercise in self-control. As the individual controls himself by manipulating the world he lives in, so the human species has constructed an environment in which its members behave in a highly effective way. Mistakes have been made, and we have no assurance that the environment man has constructed will continue to provide gains that outstrip the losses. But man as we know him, for better or for worse, is what man has made of man.

Roles

This will not satisfy those who cry "Victim!" C. S. Lewis protested: ". . . the power of man to make himself what he pleases . . . means . . . the power of some men to make other men what they please." This is inevitable in the nature of cultural evolution. We must distinguish the controlling self from the controlled self even when they are both inside the same skin, and when control is exercised through the design of an external environment, the selves are, with minor exceptions, distinct.

The person who, purposely or not, introduces a new cultural practice is only one among possibly billions it will affect. If this does not seem like an act of self-control, it is only because we have misunderstood the nature of self-control in the individual.

When a person changes his physical or social environment "intentionally"—that is, in order to change human behavior, possibly including his own—he plays two roles: one as a controller, as the designer of a controlling culture, and another as the controlled, as the product of a culture. There is nothing inconsistent about this; it follows from the nature of the evolution of a culture, with or without intentional design.

The human species probably has undergone little genetic change in recorded time. We have only to go back a thousand generations to reach the artists of the caves of Lascaux. Features bearing directly on survival (such as resistance to disease) change substantially in a thousand generations, but the child of one of the Lascaux artists transplanted to the world of today might be almost indistinguishable from a modern child.

Man has improved himself enormously in the same period of time by changing the world he lives in. Modern religious practices developed over a hundred generations and modern government and law developed in fewer than a hundred. Perhaps no more than 20 generations have been needed to produce modern economic practices, and possibly no more than four or five to produce modern education, psychotherapy, and the physical and biological technologies that have increased man's sensitivity to the world around him and his power to change that world.

Change

Man has "controlled his own destiny," if that expression means anything at all. The man that man has made is the product of the culture man has devised. He has emerged from two quite different processes of evolution: biological and cultural. Both may now accelerate because both are subject to intentional design. Men have already changed their genetic endowment by breeding selectively and by changing contingencies of survival, and for a long time they have introduced cultural practices as cultural mutations. They may now begin to do both with a clearer eye to the consequences.

Stage

The individual is the carrier of both his species and his culture. Cultural practices like genetic traits are transmitted from individual to individual. Even within the most regimented culture every personal history is unique. But the individual remains merely a stage in a process that began long before he came into existence and will long outlast him. He has no ultimate responsibility for a species trait or a cultural practice, even though it was he who underwent the mutation or introduced the practice that became part of the species or culture.

Even if Lamarck had been right in supposing that the individual could change his genetic structure through personal effort, we should have to point to the environmental circumstances responsible for the effort, as we shall have to do when geneticists begin to change the human endowment. And when an individual engages in the intentional design of a cultural practice, we must turn to the culture that induces him to do so and supplies the art or science he uses.

End

One of the great problems of individualism, seldom recognized as such, is death—the inescapable fate of the individual, the final assault on freedom and dignity. Death is one of those remote events that are brought to bear on behavior only with the aid of cultural practices. What we see is the death of others, as in Pascal's famous metaphor: "Imagine a number of men in chains, all under sentence of death, some of whom are each day butchered in the sight of others; those remaining see their own condition in that of their fellows, and looking at each other with grief and despair await their turn. This is an image of the human condition."

Some religions have made death more important by picturing a future existence in heaven or hell, but the individualist has a special reason to fear death: it is the prospect of personal annihilation. The individualist can find no solace in reflecting upon any contribution that will survive him. He has refused to be concerned for the survival of his culture and is not reinforced by the fact that the culture will long survive him. In the defense of his own freedom and dignity he has denied the contributions of the past and must therefore relinquish all claim upon the future.

Pictures

Science probably has never demanded a more sweeping change in a traditional way of thinking about a subject, nor has there ever been a more important subject. In the traditional picture a person perceives the world around him, selects features to be perceived, discriminates among them, judges them good or bad, changes them to make them better (or worse), and may be held responsible for his action and justly rewarded or punished for its consequences. In the scientific picture a person is a member of a species shaped by evolutionary contingencies of survival, displaying behavioral processes that bring him under the control of the environment in which he lives, and largely under the control of a social environment that he and millions of others like him have constructed and maintained during the evolution of a culture. The direction of the controlling relation is reserved: a person does not act upon the world; the world acts upon him.

It is difficult to accept such a change simply on intellectual grounds and nearly impossible to accept its implications. The reaction of the traditionalist is usually described in terms of feelings. One of these, to which the Freudians have appealed in explaining the resistance to psychoanalysis, is wounded vanity. Freud himself expounded, as Ernest Jones said, "the three heavy blows which narcissism or self-love of mankind has suffered at the hands of science. The first was cosmological and was dealt by Copernicus; the second was biological and was dealt by Darwin; the third was psychological and was dealt by Freud."

But what are the signs or symptoms of wounded vanity, and how shall we explain them? What people do about a scientific picture of man is to call it wrong, demeaning and dangerous, to argue against it, and to attack those who propose or defend it. These are signs of wounded vanity only to the extent that the scientific formulation destroys accustomed reinforcers. If a person can no longer take credit or be admired for what he does, then he seems to suffer a loss of dignity or worth, and behavior previously reinforced by credit or admiration will undergo extinction. Extinction often leads to aggressive attack.

Futility

Another effect of the scientific picture has been described as a loss of faith or "nerve," as a sense of doubt or powerlessness, or as discouragement, depression, or despondency. A person is said to feel that he can do nothing about his own destiny, but what he feels is a weakening of old responses that are no longer reinforced.

Another effect is a kind of nostalgia. Old repertoires break through as traditionalists seize upon and exaggerate similarities between present and past. They call the old days the good old days, when people recognized the inherent dignity of man and the importance of spiritual values. These fragments of outmoded behavior tend to be wistful—that is, they have the character of increasingly unsuccessful behavior.

Rainbow

These reactions to a scientific conception of man are, of course, unfortunate. They immobilize men of good will, and anyone concerned with the future of his culture will do what he can to correct them. No theory changes what it is a theory about. We change nothing because we look at it, talk about it, or analyze it in a new way. Keats drank confusion to Newton for analyzing the rainbow, but the rainbow remained as beautiful as ever and became for many even more beautiful.

Man has not changed because we look at him, talk about him, and analyze him scientifically. His achievements in science, government, religion, art and literature remain as they have always been, to be admired as one admires a storm at sea or autumn foliage or a mountain peak, quite apart from their origins and untouched by a scientific analysis. What does change is our chance of doing something about the subject of a theory. Newton's analysis of the light in a rainbow was a step in the direction of the laser.

Perils

The traditional conception of man is flattering; it confers reinforcing privileges. It is therefore easy to defend and difficult to change. It was designed to build up the individual as an instrument of countercontrol, and it did so effectively, but in such a way as to limit future progress.

We have seen how the literatures of freedom and dignity, with their concern for autonomous man, have perpetuated the use of punishment and condoned the use of only weak nonpunitive techniques. It is not difficult to demonstrate a connection between the unlimited right of the individual to pursue happiness and the catastrophes threatened by unchecked breeding, the unrestrained affluence that exhausts resources and pollutes the environment, and the imminence of nuclear war.

Physical and biological technologies have alleviated pestilence and famine and the painful, dangerous and exhausting features of daily life, and a behavioral techology can begin to alleviate other kinds of ills. In the analysis of human behavior it is just possible that we are slightly beyond Newton's position in the analysis of light, for we are beginning to make technological applications, and there are wonderful possibilities—all the more wonderful because traditional approaches have been so ineffective.

It is hard to imagine a world in which people live together without quarreling, maintain themselves by producing the food, shelter and clothing they need, enjoy themselves and contribute to the enjoyment of others in art, music, literature and games, consume only a reasonable part of the resources of the world and add as little as possible to its pollution, bear no more children than they can raise decently, continue to explore the world around them and discover better ways of dealing with it, and come to know themselves and the world around them accurately and comprehensively. Yet all this is possible. We have not yet seen what man can make of man.

QUESTIONS

1. What does Skinner say to indicate that he expects disagreement? Does he make any concessions in his address to his readers that would suggest an effort to win over those who disagree with him?
2. Is Skinner an optimist or a pessimist?
3. Is Skinner hard to read because his ideas are strange and disturbing or because his writing is bad? Does Orwell offer any help in answering this question?

THOMAS S. KUHN
The Route to Normal Science[1]

In this essay, 'normal science' means research firmly based upon one or more past scientific achievements, achievements that some particular scientific community acknowledges for a time as supplying the foundation for its further practice. Today such achieve-

1. From *The Structure of Scientific Revolutions*, 1962. (All notes are Kuhn's.)

ments are recounted, though seldom in their original form, by science textbooks, elementary and advanced. These textbooks expound the body of accepted theory, illustrate many or all of its successful applications, and compare these applications with exemplary observations and experiments. Before such books became popular early in the nineteenth century (and until even more recently in the newly matured sciences), many of the famous classics of science fulfilled a similar function. Aristotle's *Physica*, Ptolemy's *Almagest*, Newton's *Principia* and *Opticks*, Franklin's *Electricity*, Lavoisier's *Chemistry*, and Lyell's *Geology*—these and many other works served for a time implicitly to define the legitimate problems and methods of a research field for succeeding generations of paractitioners. They were able to do so because they shared two essential characteristics. Their achievement was sufficiently unprecedented to attract an enduring group of adherents away from competing modes of scientific activity. Simultaneously, it was sufficiently open-ended to leave all sorts of problems for the redefined group of practitioners to resolve.

Achievements that share these two characteristics I shall henceforth refer to as 'paradigms,' a term that relates closely to 'normal science.' By choosing it, I mean to suggest that some accepted examples of actual scientific practice—examples which include law, theory, application, and instrumentation together—provide models from which spring particular coherent traditions of scientific research. These are the traditions which the historian describes under such rubrics as 'Ptolemaic astronomy' (or 'Copernican'), 'Aristotelian dynamics' (or 'Newtonian'), 'corpuscular optics' (or 'wave optics'), and so on. The study of paradigms, including many that are far more specialized than those named illustratively above, is what mainly prepares the student for membership in the particular scientific community with which he will later practice. Because he there joins men who learned the bases of their field from the same concrete models, his subsequent practice will seldom evoke overt disagreement over fundamentals. Men whose research is based on shared paradigms are committed to the same rules and standards for scientific practice. That commitment and the apparent consensus it produces are prerequisites for normal science, i.e., for the genesis and continuation of a particular research tradition.

Because in this essay the concept of a paradigm will often substitute for a variety of familiar notions, more will need to be said about the reasons for its introduction. Why is the concrete scientific achievement, as a locus of professional commitment, prior to the various concepts, laws, theories, and points of view that may be abstracted from it? In what sense is the shared paradigm a fundamental unit for the student of scientific development, a unit that cannot be fully reduced to logically atomic components which might function in its stead? There can be a sort of scientific research without paradigms, or at least without any so unequivocal and so binding as the ones named above. Acquisition of a paradigm and of the more esoteric type of research it permits is a sign of maturity in the development of any given scientific field.

If the historian traces the scientific knowledge of any selected group of related phenomena backward in time, he is likely to encounter some minor variant of a pattern here illustrated from the history of physical optics. Today's physics textbooks tell the student that light is photons, i.e., quantum-mechanical entities that exhibit some characteristics of waves and some of particles. Research proceeds accordingly, or rather according to the more elaborate and mathematical characterization from which this usual verbalization is derived. That characterization of light is, however, scarcely half a century old. Before it was developed by Planck, Einstein, and others early in this century, physics texts taught that light was transverse wave motion, a conception rooted in a paradigm that derived ultimately from the optical writings of Young and Fresnel in the early nineteenth century. Nor was the wave theory the first to be embraced by almost all practitioners of optical science. During the eighteenth century the paradigm for this field was provided by Newton's *Opticks*, which taught that light was material corpuscles. At that time physicists sought evidence, as the early wave theorists had not, of the pressure exerted by light particles impinging on solid bodies.[2]

These transformations of the paradigms of physical optics are scientific revolutions, and the successive transition from one paradigm to another via revolution is the usual developmental pattern of mature science. It is not, however, the pattern characteristic of the period before Newton's work, and that is the contrast that concerns us here. No period between remote antiquity and the end of the seventeenth century exhibited a single generally accepted veiw about the nature of light. Instead there were a number of competing schools and sub-schools, most of them espousing one variant or another of Epicurean, Aristotelian, or Platonic theory. One group took light to be particles emanating from material bodies; for another it was a modification of the medium that intervened between the body and the eye; still another explained light in terms of an interaction of the medium with an emanation from the eye; and there were other combinations and modifications besides. Each of the corresponding schools derive strength from its relation to some particular metaphysic, and each emphasized, as paradigmatic observations, the particular cluster of optical phenomena that its own theory could do most to explain. Other observations were dealt

2. Joseph Priestley, *The History and Present State of Discoveries Relating to Vision, Light, and Colours* (London, 1772), pp. 385–90.

with by *ad hoc* elaborations, or they remained as outstanding problems for further research.[3]

At various times all these schools made significant contributions to the body of concepts, phenomena, and techniques from which Newton drew the first nearly uniformly accepted paradigm for physical optics. Any definition of the scientist that excludes at least the more creative members of these various schools will exclude their modern successors as well. Those men were scientists. Yet anyone examining a survey of physical optics before Newton may well conclude that, though the field's practitioners were scientists, the net result of their activity was something less than science. Being able to take no common body of belief for granted, each writer on physical optics felt forced to build his field anew from its foundations. In doing so, his choice of supporting observation and experiment was relatively free, for there was no standard set of methods or of phenomena that every optical writer felt forced to employ and explain. Under these circumstances, the dialogue of the resulting books was often directed as much to the members of other schools as it was to nature. That pattern is not unfamiliar in a number of creative fields today, nor is it incompatible with significant discovery and invention. It is not, however, the pattern of development that physical optics acquired after Newton and that other natural sciences make familiar today.

The history of electrical research in the first half of the eighteenth century provides a more concrete and better known example of the way a science develops before it acquires its first universally received paradigm. During that period there were almost as many views about the nature of electricity as there were important electrician experimenters, men like Hauksbee, Gray, Desaguliers, Du Fay, Nollett, Watson, Franklin, and others. All their numerous concepts of electricity had something in common—they were partially derived from one or another version of the mechanico-corpuscular philosophy that guided all scientific research of the day. In addition, all were components of real scientific theories, of theories that had been drawn in part from experiment and observation and that partially determined the choice and interpretation of additional problems undertaken in research. Yet though all the experiments were electrical and though most of the experimenters read each other's works, their theories had no more than a family resemblance.[4]

One early group of theories, following seventeenth-century prac-

3. Vasco Ronchi, *Histoire de la lumière*, trans. Jean Taton (Paris, 1956), chaps. i-iv.
4. Duane Roller and Duane H. D. Roller, *The Development of the Concept of Electric Charge: Electricity from the Greeks to Coulomb* ("Harvard Case Histories in Experimental Science," Case 8; Cambridge, Mass., 1954); and I. B. Cohen, *Franklin and Newton: An Inquiry into Speculative Newtonian Experimental Science and Franklin's Work in Electricity as an Example Thereof* (Philadelphia, 1956), chaps. vii-xii.

tice, regarded attraction and frictional generation as the fundamental electrical phenomena. This group tended to treat repulsion as a secondary effect due to some sort of mechanical rebounding and also to postpone for as long as possible both discussion and systematic research on Gray's newly discovered effect, electrical conduction. Other "electricians" (the term is their own) took attraction and repulsion to be equally elementary manifestations of electricity and modified their theories and research accordingly. (Actually, this group is remarkably small—even Franklin's theory never quite accounted for the mutual repulsion of two negatively charged bodies.) But they had as much difficulty as the first group in accounting simultaneously for any but the simplest conduction effects. Those effects, however, provided the starting point for still a third group, one which tended to speak of electricity as a "fluid" that could run through conductors rather than as an "effluvium" that emanated from non-conductors. This group, in its turn, had difficulty reconciling its theory with a number of attractive and repulsive effects. Only through the work of Franklin and his immediate successors did a theory arise that could account with something like equal facility for very nearly all these effects and that therefore could and did provide a subsequent generation of "electricians" with a common paradigm for its research.

Excluding those fields, like mathematics and astronomy, in which the first firm paradigms date from prehistory and also those, like biochemistry, that arose by division and recombination of specialties already matured, the situations outlined above are historically typical. Though it involves my continuing to employ the unfortunate simplification that tags an extended historical episode with a single and somewhat arbitrarily chosen name (e.g., Newton or Franklin), I suggest that similar fundamental disagreements characterized, for example, the study of motion before Aristotle and of statics before Archimedes, the study of heat before Black, of chemistry before Boyle and Boerhaave, and of historical geology before Hutton. In parts of biology—the study of heredity, for example—the first universally received paradigms are still more recent; and it remains an open question what parts of social science have yet acquired such paradigms at all. History suggests that the road to a firm research consensus is extraordinarily arduous.

History also suggests, however, some reasons for the difficulties encountered on the road. In the absence of a paradigm or some candidate for paradigm, all of the facts that could possibly pertain to the development of a given science are likely to seem equally relevant. As a result, early fact-gathering is a far more nearly random activity than the one that subsequent scientific development makes familiar. Futhermore, in the absence of a reason for seeking some particular form of more recondite information, early fact-gathering is usually restricted to the wealth of data that lie ready to hand. The resulting pool of facts contains those accessible to casual observation and experiment together with some of the more esoteric data retrievable from established crafts medicine, calendar making, and metallurgy. Because the crafts are one readily accessible source of facts that could not have been casually discovered, technology has often played a vital role in the emergence of new sciences.

But though this sort of fact-collecting has been essential to the origin of many significant sciences, anyone who examines, for example, Pliny's encyclopedic writings or the Baconian natural histories of the seventeenth century will discover that it produces a morass. One somehow hesitates to call the literature that results scientific. The Baconian "histories" of heat, color, wind, mining, and so on, are filled with information, some of it recondite. But they juxtapose facts that will later prove revealing (e.g., heating by mixture) with others (e.g., the warmth of dung heaps) that will for some time remain too complex to be integrated with theory at all.[5] In addition, since any description must be partial, the typical natural history often omits from its immensely circumstantial accounts just those details that later scientists will find sources of important illumination. Almost none of the early "histories" of electricity, for example, mention that chaff, attracted to a rubbed glass rod, bounces off again. That effect seemed mechanical, not electrical.[6] Moreover, since the casual fact-gatherer seldom possesses the time or the tools to be critical, the natural histories often juxtapose descriptions like the above with others, say, heating by antiperistasis (or by cooling), that we are now quite unable to confirm.[7] Only very occasionally, as in the cases of ancient statics, dynamics, and geometrical optics, do facts collected with so little guidance from pre-established theory speak with sufficient clarity to permit the emergence of a first paradigm.

This is the situation that creates the schools characteristic of the early stages of a science's development. No natural history can be interpreted in the absence of at least some implicit body of intertwined theoretical and methodological belief that permits selection, evaluation, and criticism. If that body of belief is not already implicit in the collection of facts—in which case more than "mere facts" are at hand—it must be externally supplied, perhaps by a current metaphysic, by another science, or by personal and historical accident. No wonder, then, that in the early stages of the develop-

5. Compare the sketch for a natural history of heat in Bacon's *Novum Organum,* Vol. VIII of *The Works of Francis Bacon,* ed. J. Spedding, R. L. Ellis, and D. D. Heath (New York, 1869), pp. 179–203.

6. Roller and Roller, *op. cit.,* pp. 14, 22, 28, 43. Only after the work recorded in the last of these citations do repulsive effects gain general recognition as unequivocally electrical.

7. Bacon, *op. cit.,* pp. 235, 337, says, "Water slightly warm is more easily frozen than quite cold." For a partial account of the earlier history of this strange observation, see Marshall Clagett, *Giovanni Marliani and Late Medieval Physics* (New York, 1941), chap. iv.

ment of any science different men confronting the same range of
phenomena, but not usually all the same particular phenomena,
describe and interpret them in different ways. What is surprising,
and perhaps also unique in its degree to the fields we call science, is
that such initial divergences should ever largely disappear.

For they do disappear to a very considerable extent and then
apparently once and for all. Furthermore, their disappearance is
usually caused by the triumph of one of the pre-paradigm schools,
which, because of its own characteristic beliefs and pre-conceptions,
emphasized only some special part of the too sizable and inchoate
pool of information. Those electricians who thought electricity a fluid
and therefore gave particular emphasis to conduction provide an
excellent case in point. Led by this belief, which could scarcely cope
with the known multiplicity of attractive and repulsive effects, several of them conceived the idea of bottling the electrical fluid. The
immediate fruit of their efforts was the Leyden jar, a device which
might never have been discovered by a man exploring nature casually or at random, but which was in fact independently developed by at least two investigators in the early 1740's.[8] Almost from
the start of his electrical researches, Franklin was particularly concerned to explain that strange and, in the event, particularly revealing piece of special apparatus. His success in doing so provided the
most effective of the arguments that made his theory a paradigm,
though one that was still unable to account for quite all the known
cases of electrical repulsion.[9] To be accepted as a paradigm, a theory
must seem better than its competitors, but it need not, and in
fact never does, explain all the facts with which it can be confronted.

What the fluid theory of electricity did for the subgroup that
held it, the Franklinian paradigm later did for the entire group of
electricians. It suggested which experiments would be worth performing and which, because directed to secondary or to overly complex manifestations of electricity, would not. Only the paradigm did
the job far more effectively, partly because the end of interschool
debate ended the constant reiteration of fundamentals and partly
because the confidence that they were on the right track encouraged
scientists to undertake more precise, esoteric, and consuming sorts
of work.[1] Freed from the concern with any and all electrical phe-

8. Roller and Roller, *op. cit.*, pp. 51–54.
9. The troublesome case was the mutual repulsion of negatively charged bodies, for which see Cohen, *op. cit.*, pp.
491–94, 531–43.
1. It should be noted that the acceptance of Franklin's theory did not end
quite all debate. In 1759 Robert Symmer
proposed a two-fluid version of that
theory, and for many years thereafter
electricians were divided about whether
electricity was a single fluid or two. But
the debates on this subject only confirm
what has been said above about the
manner in which a universally recognized
achievement unites the profession. Electricians, though they continued divided
on this point, rapidly concluded that no
experimental tests could distinguish the
two versions of the theory and that they
were therefore equivalent. After that,
both schools could and did exploit all
the benefits that the Franklinian theory
provided (*ibid.*, pp. 543–46, 548–54).

nomena, the united group of electricians could pursue selected phenomena in far more detail, designing much special equipment for the task and employing it more stubbornly and systematically than electricians had ever done before. Both fact collection and theory articulation became highly directed activities. The effectiveness and efficiency of electrical research increased accordingly, providing evidence for a societal version of Francis Bacon's acute methodological dictum: "Truth emerges more readily from error than from confusion."[2]

We shall be examining the nature of this highly directed or paradigm-based research in the next section, but must first note briefly how the emergence of a paradigm affects the structure of the group that practices the field. When, in the development of a natural science, an individual or group first produces a synthesis able to attract most of the next generation's practitioners, the older schools gradually disappear. In part their disappearance is caused by their members' conversion to the new paradigm. But there are always some men who cling to one or another of the older views, and they are simply read out of the profession, which thereafter ignores their work. The new paradigm implies a new and more rigid definition of the field. Those unwilling or unable to accommodate their work to it must proceed in isolation or attach themselves to some other group.[3] Historically, they have often simply stayed in the departments of philosophy from which so many of the special sciences have been spawned. As these indications hint, it is sometimes just its reception of a paradigm that transforms a group previously interested merely in the study of nature into a profession or, at least, a discipline. In the sciences (though not in fields like medicine, technology, and law, of which the principal *raison d'être* is an external social need), the formation of specialized journals, the foundation of specialists' societies, and the claim for a special place in the curriculum have usually been associated with a group's first reception of a single paradigm. At least this was the case between the time, a century and a half ago, when the institutional pattern of scientific

2. Bacon, *op. cit.*, p. 210.

3. The history of electricity provides an excellent example which could be duplicated from the careers of Priestley, Kelvin, and others. Franklin reports that Nollet, who at mid-century was the most influential of the Continental electricians, "lived to see himself the last of his Sect, except Mr. B.—his Eleve and immediate Disciple" (Max Farrand [ed.], *Benjamin Franklin's Memoirs* [Berkeley, Calif., 1949], pp. 384–86). More interesting, however, is the endurance of whole schools in increasing isolation from professional science. Consider, for example, the case of astrology, which was once an integral part of astronomy. Or consider the continuation in the late eighteenth and early nineteenth centuries of a previously respected tradition of "romantic" chemistry. This is the tradition discussed by Charles C. Gillispie in "The *Encyclopédie* and the Jacobin Philosophy of Science: A Study in Ideas and Consequences," *Critical Problems in the History of Science*, ed. Marshall Clagett (Madison, Wis., 1959), pp. 255–89; and "The Formation of Lamarck's Evolutionary Theory," *Archives internationales d'histoire des sciences*, XXXVII (1956), 323–38.

specialization first developed and the very recent time when the paraphernalia of specialization acquired a prestige of their own.

The more rigid definition of the scientific group has other consequences. When the individual scientist can take a paradigm for granted, he need no longer, in his major works, attempt to build his field anew, starting from first principles and justifying the use of each concept introduced. That can be left to the writer of textbooks. Given a textbook, however, the creative scientist can begin his research where it leaves off and thus concentrate exclusively upon the subtlest and most esoteric aspects of the natural phenomena that concern his group. And as he does this, his research communiqués will begin to change in ways whose evolution has been too little studied but whose modern end products are obvious to all and oppressive to many. No longer will his researches usually be embodied in books addressed, like Franklin's *Experiments . . . on Electricity* or Darwin's *Origin of Species,* to anyone who might be interested in the subject matter of the field. Instead they will usually appear as brief articles addressed only to professional colleagues, the men whose knowledge of a shared paradigm can be assumed and who prove to be the only ones able to read the papers addressed to them.

Today in the sciences, books are usually either texts or retrospective reflections upon one aspect or another of the scientific life. The scientist who writes one is more likely to find his professional reputation impaired than enhanced. Only in the earlier, pre-paradigm, stages of the development of the various sciences did the book ordinarily possess the same relation to professional achievement that it still retains in other creative fields. And only in those fields that still retain the book, with or without the article, as a vehicle for research communication are the lines of professionalization still so loosely drawn that the layman may hope to follow progress by reading the practitioners' original reports. Both in mathematics and astronomy, research reports had ceased already in antiquity to be intelligible to a generally educated audience. In dynamics, research became similarly esoteric in the latter Middle Ages, and it recaptured general intelligibility only briefly during the early seventeenth century when a new paradigm replaced the one that had guided medieval research. Electrical research began to require translation for the layman before the end of the eighteenth century, and most other fields of physical science ceased to be generally accessible in the nineteenth. During the same two centuries similar transitions can be isolated in the various parts of the biological sciences. In parts of the social sciences they may well be occurring today. Although it has become customary, and is surely proper, to deplore the widening gulf that separates the professional scientist from his colleagues in other fields, too little attention is paid to the essential relationship between that gulf and the mechanisms intrinsic to scientific advance.

Ever since prehistoric antiquity one field of study after another has crossed the divide between what the historian might call its prehistory as a science and its history proper. These transitions to maturity have seldom been so sudden or so unequivocal as my necessarily schematic discussion may have implied. But neither have they been historically gradual, coextensive, that is to say, with the entire development of the fields within which they occurred. Writers on electricity during the first four decades of the eighteenth century possessed far more information about electrical phenomena than had their sixteenth-century predecessors. During the half-century after 1740, few new sorts of electrical phenomena were added to their lists. Nevertheless, in important respects, the electrical writings of Cavendish, Coulomb, and Volta in the last third of the eighteenth century seem further removed from those of Gray, Du Fay, and even Franklin than are the writings of these early eighteenth-century electrical discoverers from those of the sixteenth century.[4] Sometime between 1740 and 1780, electricians were for the first time enabled to take the foundations of their field for granted. From that point they pushed on to more concrete and recondite problems, and increasingly they then reported their results in articles addressed to other electricians rather than in books addressed to the learned world at large. As a group they achieved what had been gained by astronomers in antiquity and by students of motion in the Middle Ages, of physical optics in the late seventeenth century, and of historical geology in the early nineteenth. They had, that is, achieved a paradigm that proved able to guide the whole group's research. Except with the advantage of hindsight, it is hard to find another criterion that so clearly proclaims a field a science.

4. The post-Franklinian developments include an immense increase in the sensitivity of charge detectors, the first reliable and generally diffused techniques for measuring charge, the evolution of the concept of capacity and its relation to a newly refined notion of electric tension, and the quantification of electro-static force. On all of these see Roller and Roller, *op. cit.*, pp. 66–81; W. C. Walker, "The Detection and Estimation of Electric Charges in the Eighteenth Century," *Annals of Science*, I (1936), 66–100; and Edmund Hoppe, *Geschichte der Elektrizität* (Leipzig, 1884), Part I, chaps. iii–iv.

Prose Forms: Parables

[When we read a short story or a novel, we are less interested in the working out of ideas than in the working out of characters and their destinies. In Dickens' Great Expectations, for example, Pip the hero undergoes many triumphs and defeats in his pursuit of success, only to learn finally that he has expected the wrong things, or the right things for the wrong reasons; that the great values in life are not always to be found in what the world calls success. In realizing this meaning we entertain, with Dickens, certain concepts or ideas that organize and evaluate the life in the novel, and that ultimately we apply to life generally. Ideas are there not to be exploited discursively, but to be understood as the perspective which shapes the direction of the novel and our view of its relation to life.

When ideas in their own reality are no longer the primary interest in writing, we have obviously moved from expository to other forms of prose. The shift need not be abrupt and complete, however; there is an area where the discursive interest in ideas and the narrative interest in characters and events blend. In allegory, for example, abstract ideas are personified. "Good Will" or "Peace" may be shown as a young woman, strong, confident, and benevolent in her bearing but vulnerable, through her sweet reasonableness, to the single-minded, fierce woman who is "Dissension." Our immediate interest is in their behavior as characters, but our ultimate interest is in the working out, through them, of the ideas they represent. We do not ask that the characters and events be entirely plausible in relation to actual life, as we do for the novel; we are satisfied if they are consistent with the nature of the ideas that define their vitality.

Ideas themselves have vitality, a mobile and dynamic life with a behavior of its own. The title of the familiar Negro spiritual "Sometimes I Feel Like a Motherless Child," to choose a random instance, has several kinds of "motion" as an idea. The qualitative identity of an adult's feelings and those of a child; the whole burgeoning possibility of all that the phrase "motherless child" can mean; the subtle differences in meaning—the power of context—that occur when it is a Negro who feels this and when it is a white; the speculative possibilities of the title as social commentary or psychological analysis; the peculiar force of the ungrammatical "like"—these suggest something of the "life" going on in and around the idea. Definition,

416

analogy, assumption, implication, context, illustration are some of the familiar terms we use to describe this kind of life.

There is, of course, another and more obvious kind of vitality which an idea has: its applicability to the affairs of men in everyday life. Both the kind and extent of an idea's relevance are measures of this vitality. When an essayist wishes to exploit both the life in an idea and the life it comprehends, he often turns to narration, because there he sees the advantage of lifelike characters and events, and of showing through them the liveliness of ideas in both the senses we have noted. Ideas about life can be illustrated in life. And, besides, people like stories. The writer's care must be to keep the reader's interest focused on the ideas, rather than on the life itself; otherwise, he has ceased being essentially the essayist and has become the short-story writer or novelist.

The parable and the moral fable are ideal forms for his purpose. In both, the idea is the heart of the composition; in both the ideas usually assume the form of a lesson about life, some moral truth of general consequence to men; and in both there are characters and actions. Jesus often depended on parables in his teaching. Simple, economical, pointed, the parables developed a "story," but more importantly, applied a moral truth to experience. Peter asked Jesus how often he must forgive the brother who sins against him, and Jesus answered with the parable of the king and his servants, one of whom asked and got forgiveness of the king for his debts but who would not in turn forgive a fellow servant his debt. The king, on hearing of this harshness, retracted his own benevolence and punished the unfeeling servant. Jesus concluded to Peter, "So likewise shall my heavenly Father do also unto you, if ye from your hearts forgive not every one his brother their trespasses." But before this direct drawing of the parallel, the lesson was clear in the outline of the narrative.

Parables usually have human characters; fables often achieve a special liveliness with animals. In March's "The Fisherman and the Hen," the old hen is clearly just a chicken, clucking, picking at worms, scratching the ground. But when the fisherman has struck her to steal her worm for bait, and the old hen, responding to his compassion for having wronged her, gets another worm in order to be struck and so to be fondled afterwards, the old hen is almost magically transformed into a peculiar psychological truth about human behavior. The story creates its own interest as a story, but by its end the reader realizes that the story exists for the sake of an idea—and that its relevance is a lesson about himself.

The writer will be verging continually on strict prose narrative when he writes the parable or fable, but if he is skillful and tactful, he will preserve the essayist's essential commitment to the definition and development of ideas in relation to experience.]

PLATO: The Allegory of the Cave[1]

And now, I said, let me show in a figure how far our nature is
enlightened or unenlightened: Behold! human beings living in
an underground den, which, has a mouth open towards the light
and reaching all along the den; here they have been from their childhood, and have their legs and necks chained so that they cannot
move, and can only see before them, being prevented by the chains
from turning round their heads. Above and behind them a fire
is blazing at a distance, and between the fire and the prisoners
there is a raised way; and you will see, if you look, a low wall
built along the way, like the screen which marionette players have
in front of them, over which they show the puppets.

I see.

And do you see, I said, men passing along the wall carrying all
sorts of vessels, and statues and figures of animals made of wood
and stone and various materials, which appear over the wall? Some
of them are talking, others silent.

You have shown me a strange image, and they are strange
prisoners.

Like ourselves, I replied; and they see only their own shadows, or
the shadows of one another, which the fire throws on the opposite
wall of the cave?

True, he said; how could they see anything but the shadows if
they were never allowed to move their heads?

And of the objects which are being carried in like manner would
they only see the shadows?

Yes, he said.

And if they were able to converse with one another, would they
not suppose that they were naming what was actually before them?

Very true.

And suppose further that the prison had an echo which came from
the other side, would they not be sure to fancy when one of the
passers-by spoke that the voice which they heard came from the
passing shadow?

No question, he replied.

To them, I said, the truth would be literally nothing but the
shadows of the images.

That is certain.

And now look again, and see what will naturally follow if the
prisoners are released and disabused of their error. At first, when
any of them is liberated and compelled suddenly to stand up and
turn his neck round and walk and look towards the light, he will
suffer sharp pains; the glare will distress him and he will be unable

1. From Book VII of *The Republic*.

to see the realities of which in his former state he had seen the shadows; and then conceive some one saying to him, that what he saw before was an illusion, but that now, when he is approaching nearer to being and his eye is turned towards more real existence, he has a clearer vision—what will be his reply? And you may further imagine that his instructor is pointing to the objects as they pass and requiring him to name them—will he not be perplexed? Will he not fancy that the shadows which he formerly saw are truer than the objects which are now shown to him?

Far truer.

And if he is compelled to look straight at the light, will he not have a pain in his eyes which will make him turn away to take refuge in the objects of vision which he can see, and which he will conceive to be in reality clearer than the things which are now being shown to him?

True, he said.

And suppose once more, that he is reluctantly dragged up a steep and rugged ascent, and held fast until he is forced into the presence of the sun himself, is he not likely to be pained and irritated? When he approaches the light his eyes will be dazzled and he will not be able to see anything at all of what are now called realities.

Not all in a moment, he said.

He will require to grow accustomed to the sight of the upper world. And first he will see the shadows best, next the reflections of men and other objects in the water, and then the objects themselves; then he will gaze upon the light of the moon and the stars and the spangled heaven; and he will see the sky and the stars by night better than the sun or the light of the sun by day?

Certainly.

Last of all he will be able to see the sun, and not mere reflections of him in the water, but he will see him in his own proper place, and not in another; and he will contemplate him as he is.

Certainly.

He will then proceed to argue that this is he who gives the season and the years, and is the guardian of all that is in the visible world, and in a certain way the cause of all things which he and his fellows have been accustomed to behold?

Clearly, he said, he would first see the sun and then reason about him.

And when he remembered his old habitation, and the wisdom of the den and his fellow-prisoners, do you not suppose that he would felicitate himself on the change, and pity them?

Certainly, he would.

And if they were in the habit of conferring honors among themselves on those who were quickest to observe the passing shadows and to remark which of them went before, and which followed after, and which were together; and who were therefore best able to draw conclusions as to the future, do you think that he would care for such honors and glories, or envy the possessors of them? Would he not say with Homer,

> Better to be the poor servant of a poor master,

and to endure anything, rather than think as they do and live after their manner?

Yes, he said, I think that he would rather suffer anything than entertain these false notions and live in this miserable manner.

Imagine once more, I said, such an one coming suddenly out of the sun to be replaced in his old situation; would he not be certain to have his eyes full of darkness?

To be sure, he said.

And if there were a contest, and he had to compete in measuring the shadows with the prisoners who had never moved out of the den, while his sight was still weak, and before his eyes had become steady (and the time which would be needed to acquire this new habit of sight might be very considerable) would he not be ridiculous? Men would say of him that up he went and down he came without his eyes; and that it was better not even to think of ascending; and if any one tried to loose another and lead him up to the light, let them only catch the offender, and they would put him to death.

No question, he said.

This entire allegory, I said, you may now append, dear Glaucon, to the previous argument; the prison-house is the world of sight, the light of the fire is the sun, and you will not misapprehend me if you interpret the journey upwards to be the ascent of the soul into the intellectual world according to my poor belief, which, at your desire, I have expressed—whether rightly or wrongly God knows. But, whether true or false, my opinion is that in the world of knowledge the idea of good appears last of all, and is seen only with an effort; and, when seen, is also inferred to be the universal author of all things beautiful and right, parent of light and of the lord of light in this visible world, and the immediate source of reason and truth in the intellectual; and that this is the power upon which he who would act rationally either in public or private life must have his eye fixed.

I agree, he said, as far as I am able to understand you.

Moreover, I said, you must not wonder that those who attain to this beatific vision are unwilling to descend to human affairs; for their souls are ever hastening into the upper world where they desire to dwell; which desire of theirs is very natural, if our allegory may be trusted.

Yes, very natural.

And is there anything surprising in one who passes from divine contemplations to the evil state of man, misbehaving himself in a ridiculous manner; if, while his eyes are blinking and before he has become accustomed to the surrounding darkness, he is compelled to fight in courts of law, or in other places, about the images or the shadows of images of justice, and is endeavouring to meet the conceptions of those who have never yet seen absolute justice?

Anything but surprising, he replied.

Any one who has common sense will remember that the bewilderments of the eyes are of two kinds, and arise from two causes, either from coming out of the light or from going into the light, which is true of the mind's eye, quite as much as of the bodily eye; and he who remembers this when he sees any one whose vision is perplexed and weak, will not be too ready to laugh; he will first ask whether that soul of man has come out of the brighter life, and is unable to see because unaccustomed to the dark, or having turned from darkness to the day is dazzled by excess of light. And he will count the one happy in his condition and state of being, and he will pity the other; or, if he have a mind to laugh at the soul which comes from below into the light, there will be more reason in this than in the laugh which greets him who returns from above out of the light into the den.

That, he said, is a very just distinction.

JONATHAN SWIFT: The Spider and the Bee[1]

Things were at this crisis, when a material accident fell out. For, upon the highest corner of a large window, there dwelt a certain spider, swollen up to the first magnitude by the destruction of infinite numbers of flies, whose spoils lay scattered before the gates of his palace, like human bones before the cave of some giant. The avenues of his castle were guarded with turnpikes and palisadoes, all after the modern way of fortification. After you had passed several courts, you came to the center, wherein you might behold the constable himself in his own lodgings, which had windows fronting to each avenue, and ports to sally out upon all occasions of prey or defense. In this mansion he had for some time dwelt in peace and plenty, without danger to his person by swallows from above, or to his palace by brooms from below, when it was the pleasure of fortune to conduct thither a wandering bee, to whose curiosity a broken pane in the glass had discovered itself, and in he went; where expatiating a while, he at last happened to alight upon one of the outward walls of the spider's citadel; which, yielding to the

1. From *The Battle of the Books.*

unequal weight, sunk down to the very foundation. Thrice he endeavored to force his passage, and thrice the center shook. The spider within, feeling the terrible convulsion, supposed at first that nature was approaching to her final dissolution; or else that Beelzebub,[2] with all his legions, was come to revenge the death of many thousands of his subjects, whom his enemy had slain and devoured. However, he at length valiantly resolved to issue forth, and meet his fate. Meanwhile the bee had acquitted himself of his toils, and posted securely at some distance, was employed in cleansing his wings, and disengaging them from the ragged remnants of the cobweb. By this time the spider was adventured out, when beholding the chasms, and ruins, and dilapidations of his fortress, he was very near at his wit's end; he stormed and swore like a madman, and swelled till he was ready to burst. At length, casting his eye upon the bee, and wisely gathering causes from events (for they knew each other by sight), "A plague split you," said he, "for a giddy son of a whore. Is it you, with a vengeance, that have made this litter here? Could you not look before you, and be d——nd? Do you think I have nothing else to do (in the devil's name) but to mend and repair after your arse?" "Good words, friend," said the bee (having now pruned himself, and being disposed to droll) "I'll give you my hand and word to come near your kennel no more; I was never in such a confounded pickle since I was born." "Sirrah," replied the spider, "if it were not for breaking an old custom in our family, never to stir abroad against an enemy, I should come and teach you better manners." "I pray have patience," said the bee, "or you will spend your substance, and for aught I see, you may stand in need of it all, towards the repair of your house." "Rogue, rogue," replied the spider, "yet methinks you should have more respect to a person, whom all the world allows to be so much your betters." "By my troth," said the bee, "the comparison will amount to a very good jest, and you will do me a favor to let me know the reasons that all the world is pleased to use in so hopeful a dispute." At this the spider, having swelled himself into the size and posture of a disputant, began his argument in the true spirit of controversy, with a resolution to be heartily scurrilous and angry, to urge on his own reasons, without the least regard to the answers or objections of his opposite, and fully predetermined in his mind against all conviction.

"Not to disparage myself," said he, "by the comparison with such a rascal, what art thou but a vagabond without house or home, without stock or inheritance, born to no possession of your own, but a pair of wings and a drone-pipe? Your livelihood is an universal plunder upon nature; a freebooter over fields and gardens;

2. The Hebrew god of flies. Pate MS.

and for the sake of stealing will rob a nettle as easily as a violet. Whereas I am a domestic animal, furnished with a native stock within myself. This large castle (to show my improvements in the mathematics) is all built with my own hands, and the materials extracted altogether out of my own person."

"I am glad," answered the bee, "to hear you grant at least that I am come honestly by my wings and my voice; for then, it seems, I am obliged to Heaven alone for my flights and my music; and Providence would never have bestowed on me two such gifts, without designing them for the noblest ends. I visit indeed all the flowers and blossoms of the field and the garden; but whatever I collect from thence enriches myself, without the least injury to their beauty, their smell, or their taste. Now, for you and your skill in architecture and other mathematics, I have little to say: in that building of yours there might, for aught I know, have been labor and method enough, but by woful experience for us both, 'tis too plain, the materials are naught, and I hope you will henceforth take warning, and consider duration and matter as well as method and art. You boast, indeed, of being obliged to no other creature, but of drawing and spinning out all from yourself; that is to say, if we may judge of the liquor in the vessel by what issues out, you possess a good plentiful store of dirt and poison in your breast; and, tho' I would by no means lessen or disparage your genuine stock of either, yet I doubt you are somewhat obliged for an increase of both, to a little foreign assistance. Your inherent portion of dirt does not fail of acquisitions, by sweepings exhaled from below; and one insect furnishes you with a share of poison to destroy another. So that in short, the question comes all to this—which is the nobler being of the two, that which by a lazy contemplation of four inches round, by an overweening pride, feeding and engendering on itself, turns all into excrement and venom, produces nothing at last, but flybane and a cobweb; or that which, by an universal range, with long search, much study, true judgment, and distinction of things, brings home honey and wax."

WILLIAM MARCH: The Unique Quality of Truth

When the old scholar heard that Truth was in the country, he decided to find her, as he had devoted his life to studying her in all her forms. He set out immediately, and at last he came upon the cottage in the mountains where Truth lived alone. He knocked on the door, and Truth asked what he wanted. The scholar explained who he was, adding that he had always wanted to know her and had wondered a thousand times what she really was like.

Truth came to the door soon afterwards, and the scholar saw that the pictures he had formed of her in his imagination were wrong. He had thought of Truth as a gigantic woman with flowing hair who sat nobly on a white horse, or, at the very least, as a sculptured heroic figure with a wide white brow and untroubled eyes. In reality, Truth was nothing at all like that; instead, she was merely a small shapeless old woman who seemed made of some quivering substance that resembled india rubber.

"All right," said the old lady in a resigned voice. "What do you want to know?"

"I want to know what you are."

The old lady thought, shook her head, and answered, "That I don't know. I couldn't tell you to save my life."

"Then have you any special quality that makes you an individual?" asked the scholar. "Surely you must have some characteristic that is uniquely yours."

"As a matter of fact, I have," said the old lady; then, seeing the question on the scholar's lips, she added, "I'll show you what I mean. It's easier than trying to explain."

The shapeless old woman began to bounce like a rubber ball, up and down on her doorstep, getting a little higher each time she struck the floor. When she was high enough for her purpose, she seized the woodwork above her door and held on; then she said, "Take hold of my legs and walk back the way you came, and when you know what my unique quality is, shout and let me know."

The old scholar did as he was told, racking his brains in an effort to determine what quality it was that distinguished Truth. When he reached the road, he turned around, and there in the distance was Truth still clinging to the woodwork above her door.

"Don't you see by this time?" she shouted. "Don't you understand now what my particular quality is?"

"Yes," said the old scholar. "Yes, I do."

"Then turn my legs loose and go on home," said Truth in a small petulant voice.

MATTHEW: Parables of the Kingdom[1]

Then shall the kingdom of heaven be likened unto ten virgins, which took their lamps, and went forth to meet the bridegroom.

And five of them were wise, and five *were* foolish.

They that *were* foolish took their lamps, and took no oil with them:

But the wise took oil in their vessels with their lamps.

While the bridegroom tarried, they all slumbered and slept.

And at midnight there was a cry made, Behold, the bridegroom cometh; go ye out to meet him.

Then all those virgins arose, and trimmed their lamps.

1. Matthew xxv.

And the foolish said unto the wise, Give us of your oil; for our lamps are gone out.

But the wise answered, saying, *Not so;* lest there be not enough for us and you: but go ye rather to them that sell, and buy for yourselves.

And while they went to buy, the bridegroom came; and they that were ready went in with him to the marriage: and the door was shut.

Afterward came also the other virgins, saying, Lord, Lord, open to us.

But he answered and said, Verily I say unto you, I know you not.

Watch therefore, for ye know neither the day nor the hour wherein the Son of man cometh.

For *the kingdom of heaven is* as a man travelling into a far country, *who* called his own servants, and delivered unto them his goods.

And unto one he gave five talents, to another two, and to another one; to every man according to his several ability; and straightway took his journey.

Then he that had received the five talents went and traded with the same, and made *them* other five talents.

And likewise he that *had received* two, he also gained other two.

But he that had received one went and digged in the earth, and hid his lord's money.

After a long time the lord of those servants cometh, and reckoneth with them.

And so he that had received five talents came and brought other five talents, saying, Lord, thou deliveredst unto me five talents: behold, I have gained beside them five talents more.

His lord said unto him, Well done, *thou* good and faithful servant: thou hast been faithful over a few things, I will make thee ruler over many things: enter thou into the joy of thy lord.

He also that had received two talents came and said, Lord, thou deliveredst unto me two talents: behold, I have gained two other talents beside them.

His lord said unto him, Well done, good and faithful servant; thou hast been faithful over a few things, I will make thee ruler over many things: enter thou into the joy of thy lord.

Then he which had received the one talent came and said, Lord, I knew thee that thou art an hard man, reaping where thou hast not sown, and gathering where thou hast not strawed:

And I was afraid, and went and hid thy talent in the earth: lo, *there* thou hast *that is* thine.

His lord answered and said unto him, *Thou* wicked and slothful servant, thou knewest that I reap where I sowed not, and gather where I have not strawed:

Thou oughtest therefore to have put my money to the exchanges, and *then* at my coming I should have received mine own with usury.

Take therefore the talent from him, and give *it* unto him which hath ten talents.

For unto every one that hath shall be given, and he shall have abundance: but from him that hath not shall be taken away even that which he hath.

And cast ye the unprofitable servant into outer darkness: there shall be weeping and gnashing of teeth.

When the Son of man shall come in his glory, and all the holy angels with him, then shall he sit upon the throne of his glory:

And before him shall be gathered all nations: and he shall separate them one from another, as a shepherd divideth *his* sheep from the goats:

And he shall set the sheep on his right hand, but the goats on the left.

Then shall the King say unto them on his right hand, Come, ye blessed of my Father, inherit the kingdom prepared for you from the foundation of the world:

For I was an hungred, and ye gave me meat: I was thirsty, and ye gave me drink: I was a stranger, and ye took me in:

Naked, and ye clothed me: I was sick, and ye visited me: I was in prison, and ye came unto me.

Then shall the righteous answer him, saying, Lord, when saw we thee an hungred, and fed *thee?* or thirsty, and gave *thee* drink?

When saw we thee a stranger, and took *thee* in? or naked, and clothed thee?

Or when saw we thee sick, or in prison, and came unto thee?

And the King shall answer and say unto them, Verily I say unto you, Inasmuch as ye have done *it* unto one of the least of these my brethren, ye have done *it* unto me.

Then shall he say also unto them on the left hand, Depart from me, ye cursed, into everlasting fire, prepared for the devil and his angels:

For I was an hungred, and ye gave me no meat: I was thirsty, and ye gave me no drink.

I was a stranger, and ye took me not in: naked, and ye clothed me not: sick, and in prison, and ye visited me not.

Then shall they also answer him, saying, Lord, when saw we thee an hungred, or athirst, or a stranger, or naked, or sick, or in prison, and did not minister unto thee?

Then shall he answer them, saying, Verily I say unto you, Inasmuch as ye did *it* not to one of the least of these, ye did *it* not to me.

And these shall go away into everlasting punishment: but the righteous into life eternal.

FRANZ KAFKA: Parable of the Law[1]

"Before the Law stands a doorkeeper. To this doorkeeper there comes a man from the country who begs for admittance to the Law. But the doorkeeper says that he cannot admit the man at the moment. The man, on reflection, asks if he will be allowed, then, to enter later. 'It is possible,' answers the doorkeeper, 'but not at this moment.' Since the door leading into the Law stands open as usual and the doorkeeper steps to one side, the man bends down to peer through the entrance. When the doorkeeper sees that, he laughs and says: 'If you are so strongly tempted, try to get in without my permission. But note that I am powerful. And I am only the lowest doorkeeper. From hall to hall, keepers stand at every door, one more powerful than the other. And the sight of the third man is already more than even I can stand.' These are difficulties which the man from the country has not expected to meet, the Law, he thinks, should be accessible to every man and at all times, but when he looks more closely at the doorkeeper in his furred robe, with his huge pointed nose and long thin Tartar beard, he decides that he had better wait until he gets permission to enter. The doorkeeper gives him a stool and lets him sit down at the side of the door. There he sits waiting for days and years. He makes many attempts to be allowed in and wearies the doorkeeper with his importunity. The doorkeeper often engages him in brief conversation, asking him about his home and about other matters, but the questions are put quite impersonally, as great men put questions, and always conclude with the statement that the man cannot be allowed to enter yet. The man, who has equipped himself with many things for his journey, parts with all he has, however valuable, in the hope of bribing the doorkeeper. The doorkeeper accepts it all, saying, however, as he takes each gift: 'I take this only to keep you from feeling that you have left something undone.' During all these long years the man watches the doorkeeper almost incessantly. He forgets about the other doorkeepers, and this one seems to him the only barrier between himself and the Law. In the first years he curses his evil fate aloud; later, as he grows old, he only mutters to himself. He grows childish, and since in his prolonged study of the doorkeeper he has learned to know even the fleas in his fur collar, he begs the very fleas to help him and to persuade the doorkeeper to change his mind. Finally his eyes grow dim and he does not know whether the world is really darkening around him or whether his eyes are only deceiving him. But in the darkness he can now perceive a radiance that streams inextinguishably from the door of the Law. Now his life is drawing to a close. Before he dies,

1. From the chapter, "In the Cathedral," of *The Trial* (1925).

all that he has experienced during the whole time of his sojourn condenses in his mind into one question, which he has never yet put to the doorkeeper. He beckons the doorkeeper, since he can no longer raise his stiffening body. The doorkeeper has to bend far down to hear him, for the difference in size between them has increased very much to the man's disadvantage. 'What do you want to know now?' asks the doorkeeper, 'you are insatiable.' 'Everyone strives to attain the Law,' answers the man, 'how does it come about, then, that in all these years no one has come seeking admittance but me?' The doorkeeper perceives that the man is nearing his end and his hearing is failing, so he bellows in his ear: 'No one but you could gain admittance through this door, since this door was intended for you. I am now going to shut it.' "

"So the doorkeeper deceived the man," said K. immediately, strongly attracted by the story. "Don't be too hasty," said the priest, "don't take over someone else's opinion without testing it. I have told you the story in the very words of the scriptures. There's no mention of deception in it." "But it's clear enough," said K., "and your first interpretation of it was quite right. The doorkeeper gave the message of salvation to the man only when it could no longer help him." "He was not asked the question any earlier," said the priest, "and you must consider, too, that he was only a doorkeeper, and as such fulfilled his duty." "What makes you think he fulfilled his duty?" asked K. "He didn't fulfill it. His duty might have been to keep all strangers away, but this man, for whom the door was intended, should have been let in." "You have not enough respect for the written word and you are altering the story," said the priest. "The story contains two important statements made by the doorkeeper about admission to the Law, one at the beginning, the other at the end. The first statement is: that he cannot admit the man at the moment, and the other is: that this door was intended only for the man. If there were a contradiction between the two, you would be right and the doorkeeper would have deceived the man. But there is no contradiction. The first statement, on the contrary, even implies the second. One could almost say that in suggesting to the man the possibility of future admittance the doorkeeper is exceeding his duty. At that time his apparent duty is only to refuse admittance and indeed many commentators are surprised that the suggestion should be made at all, since the doorkeeper appears to be a precisian with a stern regard for duty. He does not once leave his post during these many years, and he does not shut the door until the very last minute; he is conscious of the importance of his office, for he says: 'I am powerful'; he is respectful to his superiors, for he says: 'I am only the lowest doorkeeper'; he is not garrulous, for during all these years he puts only what are called 'impersonal questions'; he is not to be bribed, for he says in accepting a gift: 'I take this only to keep you from feeling that you have left something undone'; where his duty is concerned he is to be moved neither by pity nor rage, for we are told that the man 'wearied the doorkeeper with his importunity'; and finally even his external appearance hints at a pedantic character, the large, pointed nose and the long, thin, black, Tartar beard. Could one imagine a more faithful doorkeeper? Yet the doorkeeper has other elements in his character which are likely to advantage anyone seeking admittance and which make it comprehensible enough that he should somewhat exceed his duty in suggesting the possibility of future admittance. For it cannot be denied that he is a little simple-minded and consequently a little conceited. Take the statements he makes about his power and the power of the other doorkeepers and their dreadful aspect which even he cannot bear to see—I hold that these statements may be true enough, but that the way in which he brings them out shows that his perceptions are confused by simpleness of mind and conceit. The commentators note in this connection: 'The right perception of any matter and a misunderstanding of the same matter do not wholly exclude each other.' One must at any rate assume that such simpleness and conceit, however sparingly manifest, are likely to weaken his defense of the door; they are breaches in the character of the doorkeeper. To this must be added the fact that the doorkeeper seems to be a friendly creature by nature, he is by no means always on his official dignity. In the very first moments he allows himself the jest of inviting the man to enter in spite of the strictly maintained veto against entry; then he does not, for instance, send the man away, but gives him, as we are told, a stool and lets him sit down beside the door. The patience with which he endures the man's appeals during so many years, the brief conversations, the acceptance of the gifts, the politeness with which he allows the man to curse loudly in his presence the fate for which he himself is responsible—all this lets us deduce certain feelings of pity. Not every doorkeeper would have acted thus. And finally, in answer to a gesture of the man's he bends down to give him the chance of putting a last question. Nothing but mild impatience—the doorkeeper knows that this is the end of it all—is discernible in the words: 'You are insatiable.' Some push this mode of interpretation even further and hold that these words express a kind of friendly admiration, though not without a hint of condescension. At any rate the figure of the doorkeeper can be said to come out very differently from what you fancied." "You have studied the story more exactly and for a longer time than I have," said K. They were both silent for a little while. Then. K. said: "So you think the man was not deceived?" "Don't misunderstand me," said the priest, "I am only showing you the various opinions concerning that point. You must not pay too much attention to them. The scriptures are unalterable and the comments often enough merely express the commentators' despair. In this case there even exists an interpretation which claims that the deluded person is really the doorkeeper." "That's a farfetched interpretation," said K. "On what is it based?" "It is based," answered the priest, "on the simple-mindedness of the doorkeeper. The argument is that he does not know the Law from inside, he knows only the way that leads to it, where he patrols up and down. His ideas of the interior are assumed to be childish, and it is supposed that he himself is afraid of the other guardians whom he holds up as bogies before the man. Indeed, he fears them more than the man does, since the man is determined to enter after hearing about the dreadful guardians of the interior, while the doorkeeper has no desire to enter, at least not so far as we are told. Others again say that he must have been in the interior already, since he is after all engaged in the service of the Law and can only have been appointed from inside. This is countered by arguing that he may have been appointed by a voice calling from the interior, and that anyhow he cannot have been far inside, since the aspect of the third doorkeeper is more than he can endure. Moreover, no indication is given that during all these years he ever made any remarks showing a knowledge of the interior, except for the one remark about the doorkeepers. He may have been forbidden to do so, but there is no mention of that either. On these grounds the conclusion is reached that he knows nothing about the aspect and significance of the interior, so that he is in a state of delusion. But he is deceived also about his relation to the man from the country, for he is inferior to the man and does not know it. He treats the man instead as his own subordinate, as can be recognized from many details that must be still fresh in your mind. But, according to this view of the story, it is just as clearly indicated that he is really subordinated to the man. In the first place, a bondman is always subject to a free man. Now the man from the country is really free, he can go where he likes, it is only the Law that is closed to him, and access to the Law is forbidden him only by one individual, the doorkeeper. When he sits down on the stool by the side of the door and stays there for the rest of his life, he does it of his own free will; in the story there is no mention of any compulsion. But the doorkeeper is bound to his post by his very office, he does not dare go out into the country, nor apparently may he go into the interior of the Law, even should he wish to. Besides, although he is in the service of the Law, his service is confined to this one entrance; that is to say, he serves only this man for whom alone the entrance is intended. On that ground too he is inferior to the man. One must assume that for many years, for as long as it takes a man to grow up to the prime of life, his service was in a sense an empty for-

mality, since he had to wait for a man to come, that is to say someone in the prime of life, and so he had to wait a long time before
the purpose of his service could be fulfilled, and, moreover, had
to wait on the man's pleasure, for the man came of his own free
will. But the termination of his service also depends on the man's
term of life, so that to the very end he is subject to the man.
And it is emphasized throughout that the doorkeeper apparently
realizes nothing of all this. That is not in itself remarkable, since
according to this interpretation the doorkeeper is deceived in a
much more important issue, affecting his very office. At the end, for
example, he says regarding the entrance to the Law: 'I am now
going to shut it,' but at the beginning of the story we are told
that the door leading into the Law always stands open, and if it
always stands open, that is to say at all times, without reference to
life or death of the man, then the doorkeeper cannot close it.
There is some difference of opinion about the motive behind the
doorkeeper's statement, whether he said he was going to close the
door merely for the sake of giving an answer, or to emphasize his
devotion to duty, or to bring the man into a state of grief and
regret in his last moments. But there is no lack of agreement that
the doorkeeper will not be able to shut the door. Many indeed profess to find that he is subordinate to the man even in knowledge,
toward the end, at least, for the man sees the radiance that issues
from the door of the Law while the doorkeeper in his official position must stand with his back to the door, nor does he say anything
to show that he has perceived the change." "That is well argued,"
said K., after repeating to himself in a low voice several passages
from the priest's exposition. "It is well argued, and I am inclined
to agree that the doorkeeper is deceived. But that has not made
me abandon my former opinion, since both conclusions are to some
extent compatible. Whether the doorkeeper is clear-sighted or
deceived does not dispose of the matter. I said the man is deceived.
If the doorkeeper is clear-sighted, one might have doubts about that,
but if the doorkeeper himself is deceived, then his deception must
of necessity be communicated to the man. That makes the doorkeeper not, indeed, a deceiver, but a creature so simple-minded
that he ought to be dismissed at once from his office. You mustn't
forget that the doorkeeper's deceptions do himself no harm but
do infinite harm to the man." "There are objections to that,"
said the priest. "Many aver that the story confers no right on anyone
to pass judgment on the doorkeeper. Whatever he may seem to
us, he is yet a servant of the Law; that is, he belongs to the Law
and as such is beyond human judgment. In that case one must
not believe that the doorkeeper is subordinate to the man. Bound
as he is by his service, even only at the door of the Law, he is
incomparably greater than anyone at large in the world. The man

is only seeking the Law, the doorkeeper is already attached to it. It is the Law that has placed him at his post; to doubt his dignity is to doubt the Law itself." "I don't agree with that point of view," said K., shaking his head, "for if one accepts it, one must accept as true everything the doorkeeper says. But you yourself have sufficiently proved how impossible it is to do that." "No," said the priest, "it is not necessary to accept everything as true, one must only accept it as necessary." "A melancholy conclusion," said K. "It turns lying into a universal principle."

On Religion

ELDRIDGE CLEAVER
A Religious Conversion, More or Less[1]

Folsom Prison, September 10, 1965

Once I was a Catholic. I was baptized, made my first Communion, my Confirmation, and I wore a Cross with Jesus on it around my neck. I prayed at night, said my Rosary, went to Confession, and said all the Hail Marys and Our Fathers to which I was sentenced by the priest. Hopelessly enamored of sin myself, yet appalled by the sins of others, I longed for Judgment Day and a trial before a jury of my peers—this was my only chance to escape the flames which I could feel already licking at my feet. I was in a California Youth Authority institution at the time, having transgressed the laws of man—God did not indict me that time; if He did, it was a secret indictment, for I was never informed of any charges brought against me. The reason I became a Catholic was that the rule of the institution held that every Sunday each inmate had to attend the church of his choice. I chose the Catholic Church because all the Negroes and Mexicans went there. The whites went to the Protestant chapel. Had I been a fool enough to go to the Protestant chapel, one black face in a sea of white, and with guerrilla warfare going on between us, I might have ended up a Christian martyr—St. Eldridge the Stupe.

It all ended one day when, at a catechism class, the priest asked if anyone present understood the mystery of the Holy Trinity. I had been studying my lessons diligently and knew by heart what I'd been taught. Up shot my hand, my heart throbbing with piety (pride) for this chance to demonstrate my knowledge of the Word. To my great shock and embarrassment, the Father announced, and

1. From *Soul on Ice*, 1968.

it sounded like a thunderclap, that I was lying, that no one, not even the Pope, understood the Godhead, and why else did I think they called it the *mystery* of the Holy Trinity? I saw in a flash, stung to the quick by the jeers of my fellow catechumens, that I had been used, that the Father had been lying in wait for the chance to drop that thunderbolt, in order to drive home the point that the Holy Trinity was not to be taken lightly.

I had intended to explain the Trinity with an analogy to 3-in-1 oil, so it was probably just as well.

QUESTIONS

1. Why does Cleaver use the title he does, especially the word "conversion" in combination with a seeming contradiction in the qualification "more or less"?
2. How would Cleaver's account have differed in tone and style if he had been describing a "real" conversion?
3. What attitude does the phrase "sentenced by the priest" reveal? Does Cleaver use the phrase flippantly, objectively, seriously, humorously, or in some other way?
4. Explore the possibilities of Cleaver's analogy of the Trinity to 3-in-1 oil. Could it have been developed appropriately? Why does Cleaver say it was "probably just as well" he didn't use it?
5. From the way Cleaver describes his past attitude—"hopelessly enamored of sin myself, yet appalled by the sins of others"—what do you deduce his present attitude toward sin to be?

NICHOLAS OF CUSA
The Icon of God[1]

If I strive in human fashion to transport you to things divine, I must needs use a comparison of some kind. Now among men's works I have found no image better suited to our purposes than that of an image which is omnivoyant—its face, by the painter's cunning art, being made to appear as though looking on all around it. There are many excellent pictures of such faces—for example, that of the archeress in the market-place of Nuremberg; that by the eminent painter, Roger, in his priceless picture in the governor's house at Brussels; the Veronica in my chapel at Coblenz, and, in the castle of Brixen, the angel holding the arms of the Church, and many others elsewhere. Yet, lest ye should fail in the exercise, which requireth a figure of this description to be looked upon, I send for your

1. Preface to *The Vision of God.*

indulgence such a picture as I have been able to procure, setting forth the figure of an omnivoyant, and this I call the icon of God.

This picture, brethren, ye shall set up in some place, let us say, on a north wall, and shall stand round it, a little way off, and look upon it. And each of you shall find that, from whatsoever quarter he regardeth it, it looketh upon him as if it looked on none other. And it shall seem to a brother standing to eastward as if that face looketh toward the east, while one to southward shall think it looketh toward the south, and one to westward, toward the west. First, then, ye will marvel how it can be that the face should look on all and each at the same time. For the imagination of him standing to eastward cannot conceive the gaze of the icon to be turned unto any other quarter, such as west or south. Then let the brother who stood to eastward place himself to westward and he will find its gaze fastened on him in the west just as it was afore in the east. And, as he knoweth the icon to be fixed and unmoved, he will marvel at the motion of its immovable gaze.

If now, while fixing his eye on the icon, he walk from west to east, he will find that its gaze continuously goeth along with him, and if he return from east to west, in like manner it will not leave him. Then will he marvel how, being motionless, it moveth, nor will his imagination be able to conceive that it should also move in like manner with one going in a contrary direction to himself. If he wish to experiment on this, he will cause one of his brethren to cross over from east to west, still looking on the icon, while he himself moveth from west to east; and he will ask the other as they meet if the gaze of the icon turn continuously with him; he will hear that it doth move in a contrary direction, even as with himself, and he will believe him. But, had he not believed him, he could not have conceived this to be possible. So by his brother's showing he will come to know that the picture's face keepeth in sight all as they go on their way, though it be in contrary directions; and thus he will prove that that countenance, though motionless, is turned to east in the same way that it is simultaneously to west, and in the same way to north and to south, and alike to one particular place and to all objects at once, whereby it regardeth a single movement even as it regardeth all together. And while he observeth how that gaze never quitteth any, he seeth that it taketh such diligent care of each one who findeth himself observed as though it cared only for him, and for no other, and this to such a degree that one on whom it resteth cannot even conceive that it should take care of any other. He will also see that it taketh the same most diligent care of the least of creatures as of the greatest, and of the whole universe.

SIMONE WEIL
Spiritual Autobiography[1]

P.S. To Be Read First.

This letter is fearfully long—but as there is no question of an answer—especially as I shall doubtless have gone before it reaches you—you have years ahead of you in which to read it if you care to. Read it all the same, one day or another.

From Marseilles, about May 15 [1942]

Father,[2]

Before leaving I want to speak to you again, it may be the last time perhaps, for over there I shall probably send you only my news from time to time just so as to have yours.

I told you that I owed you an enormous debt. I want to try to tell you exactly what it consists of. I think that if you could really understand what my spiritual state is you would not be at all sorry that you did not lead me to baptism. But I do not know if it is possible for you to understand this.

You neither brought me the Christian inspiration nor did you bring me to Christ; for when I met you there was no longer any need; it had been done without the intervention of any human being. If it had been otherwise, if I had not already been won, not only implicitly but consciously, you would have given me nothing, because I should have received nothing from you. My friendship for you would have been a reason for me to refuse your message, for I should have been afraid of the possibilities of error and illusion which human influence in the divine order is likely to involve.

I may say that never at any moment in my life have I 'sought for God.' For this reason, which is probably too subjective, I do not like this expression and it strikes me as false. As soon as I reached adolescence, I saw the problem of God as a problem the data of which could not be obtained here below, and I decided that the only way of being sure not to reach a wrong solution, which seemed to me the greatest possible evil, was to leave it alone. So I left it alone. I neither affirmed nor denied anything. It seemed to me useless to solve the problem, for I thought that, being in this world, our business was to adopt the best attitude with regard to the problems of this world, and that such an attitude did not depend upon the solution of the problem of God.

This held good as far as I was concerned at any rate, for I never

1. From *Waiting for God*, 1951.
2. The Reverend Father Perrin, a Dominican who had endeavored to bring Simone Weil into the Roman Catholic Church.

hesitated in my choice of an attitude; I always adopted the Christian attitude as the only possible one. I might say that I was born, I grew up, and I always remained within the Christian inspiration. While the very name of God had no part in my thoughts, with regard to the problems of this world and this life I shared the Christian conception in an explicit and rigorous manner, with the most specific notions it involves. Some of these notions have been part of my outlook for as far back as I can remember. With others I know the time and manner of their coming and the form under which they imposed themselves upon me.

For instance I never allowed myself to think of a future state, but I always believed that the instant of death is the center and object of life. I used to think that, for those who live as they should, it is the instant when, for an infinitesimal fraction of time, pure truth, naked, certain, and eternal enters the soul. I may say that I never desired any other good for myself. I thought that the life leading to this good is not only defined by a code of morals common to all, but that for each one it consists of a succession of acts and events strictly personal to him, and so essential that he who leaves them on one side never reaches the goal. The notion of vocation was like this for me. I saw that the carrying out of a vocation differed from the actions dictated by reason or inclination in that it was due to an impulse of an essentially and manifestly different order; and not to follow such an impulse when it made itself felt, even if it demanded impossibilities, seemed to me the greatest of all ills. Hence my conception of obedience; and I put this conception to the test when I entered the factory and stayed on there, even when I was in that state of intense and uninterrupted misery about which I recently told you. The most beautiful life possible has always seemed to me to be one where everything is determined, either by the pressure of circumstances or by impulses such as I have just mentioned and where there is never any room for choice.

At fourteen I fell into one of those fits of bottomless despair that come with adolescence, and I seriously thought of dying because of the mediocrity of my natural faculties. The exceptional gifts of my brother, who had a childhood and youth comparable to those of Pascal, brought my own inferiority home to me. I did not mind having no visible successes, but what did grieve me was the idea of being excluded from that transcendent kingdom to which only the truly great have access and wherein truth abides. I preferred to die rather than live without that truth. After months of inward darkness, I suddenly had the everlasting conviction that any human being, even though practically devoid of natural faculties, can penetrate to the kingdom of truth reserved for genius, if only he longs for truth and perpetually concentrates all his attention upon its attainment. He thus becomes a genius too, even though for lack of talent his genius cannot be visible from outside. Later on, when the strain of headaches caused the feeble faculties I possess to be invaded by a paralysis, which I was quick to imagine as probably incurable, the same conviction led me to persevere for ten years in an effort of concentrated attention that was practically unsupported by any hope of results.

Under the name of truth I also included beauty, virtue, and every kind of goodness, so that for me it was a question of a conception of the relationship between grace and desire. The conviction that had come to me was that when one hungers for bread one does not receive stones. But at that time I had not read the Gospel.

Just as I was certain that desire has in itself an efficacy in the realm of spiritual goodness whatever its form, I thought it was also possible that it might not be effective in any other realm.

As for the spirit of poverty, I do not remember any moment when it was not in me, although only to that unhappily small extent compatible with my imperfection. I fell in love with Saint Francis of Assisi as soon as I came to know about him. I always believed and hoped that one day Fate would force upon me the condition of a vagabond and a beggar which he embraced freely. Actually I felt the same way about prison.

From my earliest childhood I always had also the Christian idea of love for one's neighbor, to which I gave the name of justice—a name it bears in many passages of the Gospel and which is so beautiful. You know that on this point I have failed seriously several times.

The duty of acceptance in all that concerns the will of God, whatever it may be, was impressed upon my mind as the first and most necessary of all duties from the time when I found it set down in Marcus Aurelius under the form of the *amor fati* of the Stoics. I saw it as a duty we cannot fail in without dishonoring ourselves.

The idea of purity, with all that this word can imply for a Christian, took possession of me at the age of sixteen, after a period of several months during which I had been going through the emotional unrest natural in adolescence. This idea came to me when I was contemplating a mountain landscape and little by little it was imposed upon me in an irresistible manner.

Of course I knew quite well that my conception of life was Christian. That is why it never occurred to me that I could enter the Christian community. I had the idea that I was born inside. But to add dogma to this conception of life, without being forced to do so by indisputable evidence, would have seemed to me like a lack of honesty. I should even have thought I was lacking in honesty had I considered the question of the truth of dogma as a problem for myself or even had I simply desired to reach a conclusion on this subject. I have an extremely severe standard for intellectual honesty, so severe that I never met anyone who did not seem to fall short of it in more than one respect; and I am always afraid of failing in it myself.

Keeping away from dogma in this way, I was prevented by a sort of shame from going into churches, though all the same I like being in them. Nevertheless, I had three contacts with Catholicism that really counted.

After my year in the factory, before going back to teaching, I had been taken by my parents to Portugal, and while there I left them to go alone to a little village. I was, as it were, in pieces, soul and body. That contact with affliction had killed my youth. Until then I had not had any experience of affliction, unless we count my own, which, as it was my own, seemed to me, to have little importance, and which moreover was only a partial affliction, being biological and not social. I knew quite well that there was a great deal of affliction in the world, I was obsessed with the idea, but I had not had prolonged and first-hand experience of it. As I worked in the factory, indistinguishable to all eyes, including my own, from the anonymous mass, the affliction of others entered into my flesh and my soul. Nothing separated me from it, for I had really forgotten my past and I looked forward to no future, finding it difficult to imagine the possibility of surviving all the fatigue. What I went through there marked me in so lasting a manner that still today when any human being, whoever he may be and in whatever circumstances, speaks to me without brutality, I cannot help having the impression that there must be a mistake and that unfortunately the mistake will in all probability disappear. There I received forever the mark of a slave, like the branding of the red-hot iron the Romans put on the foreheads of their most despised slaves. Since then I have always regarded myself as a slave.

In this state of mind then, and in a wretched condition physically, I entered the little Portuguese village, which, alas, was very wretched too, on the very day of the festival of its patron saint. I was alone. It was the evening and there was a full moon over the sea. The wives of the fishermen were, in procession, making a tour of all the ships, carrying candles and singing what must certainly be very ancient hymns of a heart-rending sadness. Nothing can give any idea of it. I have never heard anything so poignant unless it were the song of the boatmen on the Volga. There the conviction was suddenly borne in upon me that Christianity is pre-eminently the religion of slaves, that slaves cannot help belonging to it, and I among others.

In 1937 I had two marvelous days at Assisi. There, alone in the little twelfth-century Romanesque chapel of Santa Maria degli

Angeli, an incomparable marvel of purity where Saint Francis often used to pray, something stronger than I was compelled me for the first time in my life to go down on my knees.

In 1938 I spent ten days at Solesmes, from Palm Sunday to Easter Tuesday, following all the liturgical services. I was suffering from splitting headaches; each sound hurt me like a blow; by an extreme effort of concentration I was able to rise above this wretched flesh, to leave it to suffer by itself, heaped up in a corner, and to find a pure and perfect joy in the unimaginable beauty of the chanting and the words. This experience enabled me by analogy to get a better understanding of the possibility of loving divine love in the midst of affliction. It goes without saying that in the course of these services the thought of the Passion of Christ entered into my being once and for all.

There was a young English Catholic there from whom I gained my first idea of the supernatural power of the sacraments because of the truly angelic radiance with which he seemed to be clothed after going to communion. Chance—for I always prefer saying chance rather than Providence—made of him a messenger to me. For he told me of that existence of those English poets of the seventeenth century who are named metaphysical. In reading them later on, I discovered the poem of which I read you what is unfortunately a very inadequate translation. It is called "Love".[3] I learned it by heart. Often, at the culminating point of a violent headache, I make myself say it over, concentrating all my attention upon it and clinging with all my soul to the tenderness it enshrines. I used to think I was merely reciting it as a beautiful poem, but without my knowing it the recitation had the virtue of a prayer. It was during one of these recitations that, as I told you, Christ himself came down and took possession of me.

3. By George Herbert:

> Love bade me welcome: yet my soul drew back,
>   Guilty of dust and sin.
> But quick-eyed Love, observing me grow slack
>   From my first entrance in,
> Drew nearer to me, sweetly questioning
>   If I lacked anything.
>
> "A guest," I answered, "worthy to be here":
>   Love said, "You shall be he."
> "I, the unkind, ungrateful? Ah, my dear,
>   I cannot look on thee."
> Love took my hand, and smiling did reply,
>   "Who made the eyes but I?"
>
> "Truth, Lord; but I have marred them; let my shame
>   Go where it doth deserve."
> "And know you not," says Love, "who bore the blame?"
>   "My dear, then I will serve."
> "You must sit down," says Love, "and taste my meat."
>   So I did sit and eat.

In my arguments about the insolubility of the problem of God I had never foreseen the possibility of that, of a real contact, person to person, here below, between a human being and God. I had vaguely heard tell of things of this kind, but I had never believed in them. In the *Fioretti* the accounts of apparitions rather put me off if anything, like the miracles in the Gospel. Moreover, in this sudden possession of me by Christ, neither my senses nor my imagination had any part; I only felt in the midst of my suffering the presence of a love, like that which one can read in the smile on a beloved face.

I had never read any mystical works because I had never felt any call to read them. In reading as in other things I have always striven to practice obedience. There is nothing more favorable to intellectual progress, for as far as possible I only read what I am hungry for at the moment when I have an appetite for it, and then I do not read, I *eat*. God in his mercy had prevented me from reading the mystics, so that it should be evident to me that I had not invented this absolutely unexpected contact.

Yet I still half refused, not my love but my intelligence. For it seemed to me certain, and I still think so today, that one can never wrestle enough with God if one does so out of pure regard for the truth. Christ likes us to prefer truth to him because, before being Christ, he is truth. If one turns aside from him to go toward truth, one will not go far before falling into his arms.

After this I came to feel that Plato was a mystic, that all the *Iliad* is bathed in Christian light, and that Dionysus and Osiris are in a certain sense Christ himself; and my love was thereby redoubled.

I never wondered whether Jesus was or was not the Incarnation of God; but in fact I was incapable of thinking of him without thinking of him as God.

In the spring of 1940 I read the *Bhagavad-Gita*. Strange to say it was in reading those marvelous words, words with such a Christian sound, put into the mouth of an incarnation of God, that I came to feel strongly that we owe an allegiance to religious truth which is quite different from the admiration we accord to a beautiful poem; it is something far more categorical.

Yet I did not believe it to be possible for me to consider the question of baptism. I felt that I could not honestly give up my opinions concerning the non-Christian religions and concerning Israel—and as a matter of fact time and meditation have only served to strengthen them—and I thought that this constituted an absolute obstacle. I did not imagine it as possible that a priest could dream of granting me baptism. If I had not met you, I should never have considered the problem of baptism as a practical problem.

During all this time of spiritual progress I had never prayed. I was afraid of the power of suggestion that is in prayer—the very power for which Pascal recommends it. Pascal's method seems to me one of the worst for attaining faith.

Contact with you was not able to persuade me to pray. On the contrary I thought the danger was all the greater, since I also had to beware of the power of suggestion in my friendship with you. At the same time I found it very difficult not to pray and not to tell you so. Moreover I knew I could not tell you without completely misleading you about myself. At that time I should not have been able to make you understand.

Until last September I had never once prayed in all my life, at least not in the literal sense of the word. I had never said any words to God, either out loud or mentally. I had never pronounced a liturgical prayer. I had occasionally recited the *Salve Regina*,[4] but only as a beautiful poem.

Last summer, doing Greek with T——, I went through the Our Father word for word in Greek. We promised each other to learn it by heart. I do not think he ever did so, but some weeks later, as I was turning over the pages of the Gospel, I said to myself that since I had promised to do this thing and it was good, I ought to do it. I did it. The infinite sweetness of this Greek text so took hold of me that for several days I could not stop myself from saying it over all the time. A week afterward I began the vine harvest. I recited the Our Father in Greek every day before work, and I repeated it very often in the vineyard.

Since that time I have made a practice of saying it through once each morning with absolute attention. If during the recitation my attention wanders or goes to sleep, in the minutest degree, I begin again until I have once succeeded in going through it with absolutely pure attention. Sometimes it comes about that I say it again out of sheer pleasure, but I only do it if I really feel the impulse.

The effect of this practice is extraordinary and surprises me every time, for, although I experience it each day, it exceeds my expectation at each repetition.

At times the very first words tear my thoughts from my body and transport it to a place outside space where there is neither perspective nor point of view. The infinity of the ordinary expanses of perception is replaced by an infinity to the second or sometimes the third degree. At the same time, filling every part of this infinity of infinity, there is silence, a silence which is not an absence of sound but which is the object of a positive sensation, more positive than that of sound. Noises, if there are any, only reach me after crossing this silence.

Sometimes, also, during this recitation or at other moments,

Christ is present with me in person, but his presence is infinitely more real, more moving, more clear than on that first occasion when he took possession of me.

I should never have been able to take it upon myself to tell you all this had it not been for the fact that I am going away. And as I am going more or less with the idea of probable death, I do not believe that I have the right to keep it to myself. For after all, the whole of this matter is not a question concerning me myself. It concerns God. I am really nothing in it all. If one could imagine any possibility of error in God, I should think that it had all happened to me by mistake. But perhaps God likes to use castaway objects, waste, rejects. After all, should the bread of the host be moldy, it would become the Body of Christ just the same after the priest had consecrated it. Only it cannot refuse, while we can disobey. It sometimes seems to me that when I am treated in so merciful a way, every sin on my part must be a mortal sin. And I am constantly committing them.

I have told you that you are like a father and brother at the same time to me. But these words only express an analogy. Perhaps at bottom they only correspond to a feeling of affection, of gratitude and admiration. For as to the spiritual direction of my soul, I think that God himself has taken it in hand from the start and still looks after it.

That does not prevent me from owing you the greatest debt of gratitude that I could ever have incurred toward any human being. This is exactly what it consists of.

First you once said to me at the beginning of our relationship some words that went to the bottom of my soul. You said: "Be very careful, because if you should pass over something important through your own fault it would be a pity."

That made me see intellectual honesty in a new light. Till then I had only thought of it as opposed to faith; your words made me think that perhaps, without my knowing it, there were in me obstacles to the faith, impure obstacles, such as prejudices, habits. I felt that after having said to myself for so many years simply: "Perhaps all that is not true," I ought, without ceasing to say it —I still take care to say it very often now—to join it to the opposite formula, namely: "Perhaps all that is true," and to make them alternate.

At the same time, in making the problem of baptism a practical problem for me, you have forced me to face the whole question of the faith, dogma, and the sacraments, obliging me to consider them closely and at length with the fullest possible attention, making me see them as things toward which I have obligations that I have to discern and perform. I should never have done this otherwise and it is indispensable for me to do it.

But the greatest blessing you have brought me is of another order. In gaining my friendship by your charity (which I have never met anything to equal), you have provided me with a source of the most compelling and pure inspiration that is to be found among human things. For nothing among human things has such power to keep our gaze fixed ever more intensely upon God, than friendship for the friends of God.

Nothing better enables me to measure the breadth of your charity than the fact that you bore with me for so long and with such gentleness. I may seem to be joking, but that is not the case. It is true that you have not the same motives as I have myself (those about which I wrote to you the other day), for feeling hatred and repulsion toward me. But all the same I feel that your patience with me can only spring from a supernatural generosity.

I have not been able to avoid causing you the greatest disappointment it was in my power to cause you. But up to now, although I have often asked myself the question during prayer, during Mass, or in the light of the radiancy that remains in the soul after Mass, I have never once had, even for a moment, the feeling that God wants me to be in the Church. I have never even once had a feeling of uncertainty. I think that at the present time we can finally conclude that he does not want me in the Church. Do not have any regrets about it.

He does not want it so far at least. But unless I am mistaken I should say that it is his will that I should stay outside for the future too, except perhaps at the moment of death. Yet I am always ready to obey any order, whatever it may be. I should joyfully obey the order to go to the very center of hell and to remain there eternally. I do not mean, of course, that I have a preference for orders of this nature. I am not perverse like that.

Christianity should contain all vocations without exception since it is catholic. In consequence the Church should also. But in my eyes Christianity is catholic by right but not in fact. So many things are outside it, so many things that I love and do not want to give up, so many things that God loves, otherwise they would not be in existence. All the immense stretches of past centuries, except the last twenty are among them; all the countries inhabited by colored races; all secular life in the white peoples' countries; in the history of these countries, all the traditions banned as heretical, those of the Manicheans and Albigenses for instance; all those things resulting from the Renaissance, too often degraded but not quite without value.

Christianity being catholic by right but not in fact, I regard it as legitimate on my part to be a member of the Church by right but not in fact, not only for a time, but for my whole life if need be.

But it is not merely legitimate. So long as God does not give me the certainty that he is ordering me to do anything else, I think it is my duty.

I think, and so do you, that our obligation for the next two or three years, an obligation so strict that we can scarcely fail in it without treason, is to show the public the possibility of a truly incarnated Christianity. In all the history now known there has never been a period in which souls have been in such peril as they are today in every part of the globe. The bronze serpent[5] must be lifted up again so that whoever raises his eyes to it may be saved.

But everything is so closely bound up together that Christianity cannot be really incarnated unless it is catholic in the sense that I have just defined. How could it circulate through the flesh of all the nations of Europe if it did not contain absolutely everything in itself? Except of course falsehood. But in everything that exists there is most of the time more truth than falsehood.

Having so intense and so painful a sense of this urgency, I should betray the truth, that is to say the aspect of truth that I see, if I left the point, where I have been since my birth, at the intersection of Christianity and everything that is not Christianity.

I have always remained at this exact point, on the threshold of the Church, without moving, quite still, ἐν ὑπομένῃ[6] (it is so much more beautiful a word than *patientia*!); only now my heart has been transported, forever, I hope, into the Blessed Sacrament exposed on the altar.

You see that I am very far from the thoughts that H——, with the best of intentions, attributed to me. I am far also from being worried in any way.

If I am sad, it comes primarily from the permanent sadness that destiny has imprinted forever upon my emotions, where the greatest and purest joys can only be superimposed and that at the price of a great effort of attention. It comes also from my miserable and continual sins; and from all the calamities of our time and of all those of all the past centuries.

I think that you should understand why I have always resisted you, if in spite of being a priest you can admit that a genuine vocation might prevent anyone from entering the Church.

Otherwise a barrier of incomprehension will remain between us, whether the error is on my part or on yours. This would grieve me from the point of view of my friendship for you, because in that case the result of all these efforts and desires, called forth by your charity toward me, would be a disappointment for you. Moreover,

---

5. "And Moses made a serpent of brass, and put it upon a pole, and it came to pass, that if a serpent had bit-ten any man, when he beheld the serpent of brass, he lived" (Numbers xxi.9).

6. "To abide patiently."

although it is not my fault, I should not be able to help feeling guilty of ingratitude. For, I repeat, my debt to you is beyond all measure.

I should like to draw your attention to one point. It is that there is an absolutely insurmountable obstacle to the Incarnation of Christianity. It is the use of the two little words *anathema sit*.[7] It is not their existence, but the way they have been employed up till now. It is that also which prevents me from crossing the threshold of the Church. I remain beside all those things that cannot enter the Church, the universal repository, on account of those two little words. I remain beside them all the more because my own intelligence is numbered among them.

The Incarnation of Christianity implies a harmonious solution of the problem of the relations between the individual and the collective. Harmony in the Pythagorean sense; the just balance of contraries. This solution is precisely what men are thirsting for today

The position of the intelligence is the key to this harmony, because the intelligence is a specifically and rigorously individual thing. This harmony exists wherever the intelligence, remaining in its place, can be exercised without hindrance and can reach the complete fulfillment of its function. That is what Saint Thomas says admirably of all the parts of the soul of Christ, with reference to his sensitiveness to pain during the crucifixion.

The special function of the intelligence requires total liberty, implying the right to deny everything, and allowing of no domination. Wherever it usurps control there is an excess of individualism. Wherever it is hampered or uneasy there is an oppressive collectivism, or several of them.

The Church and the State should punish it, each one in its own way, when it advocates actions of which they disapprove. When it remains in the region of purely theoretical speculation they still have the duty, should occasion arise, to put the public on their guard, by every effective means, against the danger of the practical influence certain speculations might have upon the conduct of life. But whatever these theoretical speculations may be, the Church and the State have no right either to try to stifle them or to inflict any penalty material or moral upon their authors. Notably, they should not be deprived of the sacraments if they desire them. For, whatever they may have said, even if they have publicly denied the existence of God, they may not have committed any sin. In such a case the Church should declare that they are in error, but it should not demand of them anything whatever in the way of a disavowal of what they have said, nor should it deprive them of the Bread of Life.

7. "Let there be anathema" (a ban, curse, or excommunication).

A collective body is the guardian of dogma; and dogma is an object of contemplation for love, faith, and intelligence, three strictly individual faculties. Hence, almost since the beginning, the individual has been ill at ease in Christianity, and this uneasiness has been notably one of the intelligence. This cannot be denied.

Christ himself who is Truth itself, when he was speaking before an assembly such as a council, did not address it in the same language as he used in an intimate conversation with his well-beloved friend, and no doubt before the Pharisees he might easily have been accused of contradiction and error. For by one of those laws of nature, which God himself respects, since he has willed them from all eternity, there are two languages that are quite distinct although made up of the same words; there is the collective language and there is the individual one. The Comforter whom Christ sends us, the Spirit of truth, speaks one or other of these languages, whichever circumstances demand, and by a necessity of their nature there is not agreement between them.

When genuine friends of God—such as was Eckhart to my way of thinking—repeat words they have heard in secret amidst the silence of the union of love, and these words are in disagreement with the teaching of the Church, it is simply that the language of the market place is not that of the nuptial chamber.

Everybody knows that really intimate conversation is only possible between two or three. As soon as there are six or seven, collective language begins to dominate. That is why it is a complete misinterpretation to apply to the Church the words "Wheresoever two or three are gathered together in my name, there am I in the midst of them." Christ did not say two hundred, or fifty, or ten. He said two or three. He said precisely that he always forms the third in the intimacy of the tête-à-tête.

Christ made promises to the Church, but none of these promises has the force of the expression "Thy Father who seeth in secret." The word of God is the secret word. He who has not heard this word, even if he adheres to all the dogmas taught by the Church, has no contact with truth. The function of the Church as the collective keeper of dogma is indispensable. She has the right and the duty to punish those who make a clear attack upon her within the specific range of this function, by depriving them of the sacraments.

Thus, although I know practically nothing of this business, I incline to think provisionally that she was right to punish Luther.

But she is guilty of an abuse of power when she claims to force love and intelligence to model their language upon her own. This abuse of power is not of God. It comes from the natural tendency of every form of collectivism, without exception, to abuse power.

The image of the Mystical Body of Christ[8] is very attractive. But I consider the importance given to this image today as one of the most serious signs of our degeneration. For our true dignity is not to be parts of a body, even though it be a mystical one, even though it be that of Christ. It consists in this, that in the state of perfection, which is the vocation of each one of us, we no longer live in ourselves, but Christ lives in us; so that through our perfection Christ in his integrity and in his indivisible unity, becomes in a sense each one of us, as he is completely in each host. The hosts are not a *part* of his body.

This present-day importance of the image of the Mystical Body shows how wretchedly susceptible Christians are to outside influences. Undoubtedly there is real intoxication in being a member of the Mystical Body of Christ. But today a great many other mystical bodies, which have not Christ for their head, produce an intoxication in their members that to my way of thinking is of the same order.

As long as it is through obedience, I find sweetness in my deprivation of the joy of membership in the Mystical Body of Christ. For if God is willing to help me, I may thus bear witness that without this joy one can nevertheless be faithful to Christ unto death. Social enthusiasms have such power today, they raise people so effectively to the supreme degree of heroism in suffering and death, that I think it is as well that a few sheep should remain outside the fold in order to bear witness that the love of Christ is essentially something different.

The Church today defends the cause of the indefeasible rights of the individual against collective oppression, of liberty of thought against tyranny. But these are causes readily embraced by those who find themselves momentarily to be the least strong. It is their only way of perhaps one day becoming the strongest. That is well known.

You may perhaps be offended by this idea. You are not the Church. During the periods of the most atrocious abuse of power committed by the Church, there must have been some priests like you among the others. Your good faith is not a guarantee, even were it shared by all your Order. You cannot foresee what turn things may take.

In order that the present attitude of the Church should be effective and that she should really penetrate like a wedge into social existence, she would have to say openly that she had changed or wished to change. Otherwise who could take her seriously when they remembered the Inquisition? My friendship for you, which I

8. The Church as the community of those baptized into the life of Christ.

extend through you to all your Order, makes it very painful for me to bring this up. But it existed. After the fall of the Roman Empire, which had been totalitarian, it was the Church that was the first to establish a rough sort of totalitarianism in Europe in the thirteenth century, after the war with the Albigenses. This tree bore much fruit.

And the motive power of this totalitarianism was the use of those two little words: *anathema sit.*

It was moreover by a judicious transposition of this use that all the parties which in our own day have founded totalitarian regimes were shaped. This is a point of history I have specially studied.

I must give you the impression of a Luciferian pride in speaking thus of a great many matters that are too high for me and about which I have no right to understand anything. It is not my fault. Ideas come and settle in my mind by mistake, then, realizing their mistake, they absolutely insist on coming out. I do not know where they come from, or what they are worth, but, whatever the risk, I do not think I have the right to prevent this operation.

Good-by, I wish you all possible good things except the cross; for I do not love my neighbor as myself, you particularly, as you have noticed. But Christ granted to his well-beloved disciple, and probably to all that disciple's spiritual lineage, to come to him not through degradation, defilement, and distress, but in uninterrupted joy, purity, and sweetness. That is why I can allow myself to wish that even if one day you have the honor of dying a violent death for Our Lord, it may be with joy and without any anguish; also that only three of the beatitudes (*mites, mundo corde, pacifici*[9]) will apply to you. All the others involve more or less of suffering.

This wish is not due only to the frailty of human friendship. For, with any human being taken individually, I always find reasons for concluding that sorrow and misfortune do not suit him, either because he seems too mediocre for anything so great or, on the contrary, too precious to be destroyed. One cannot fail more seriously in the second of the two essential commandments. And as to the first, I fail to observe that, in a still more horrible manner, for every time I think of the crucifixion of Christ I commit the sin of envy.

Believe more than ever and forever in my filial and tenderly grateful friendship.

SIMONE WEIL

QUESTIONS

1. Weil's account is in the form of a letter to a Catholic priest. In what ways does that fact influence the organization, style, and tone

9. "The meek, the pure in heart, the peace-makers" (Matthew v. 5, 8, 9).

of the piece? Do you think the letter was originally meant to be published? Why or why not?

2. Weil describes "three contacts with Catholicism that really counted." How were these experiences different from each other? What effects of them can you find in attitudes described in other parts of the piece? Why didn't Weil join the Catholic Church?

4. What is Weil's objection to "the two little words anathema sit" ("let there be anathema")? What is the objection to the "image of the Mystical Body of Christ"? How are these objections related to Weil's other views?

5. Both Weil and Sartre (pp. 466–474) speak against some traditional religious ideas or beliefs. Are the bases for their objections to certain aspects of traditional religion in any ways the same? Explain.

6. Weil speaks of the differences between "the collective language and . . . the individual one," the "language of the market place" and "that of the nuptial chamber." What is the significance of these differences? Which kind of language does Weil appear to use most throughout the piece?

HENRY SLOANE COFFIN

What Crucified Christ?[1]

Some years ago a well-known British journalist, the late W. T. Stead, after witnessing the Passion Play at Oberammergau, came away saying to himself: "This is the story which has transformed the world." And he seemed to hear an echo from the Bavarian hills about him: "Yes, and will transform it."

Each generation stresses particular aspects of the Gospel; and it must be confessed that in our day, and especially in those circles where Christianity is interpreted in terms of contemporary thought, the cross does not hold the central place in preaching. With many men the Incarnation has taken the place formerly occupied by the Atonement, and the character of Jesus is proclaimed as the supreme revelation of God and the ideal for man. In other circles it has been the religious experience of Jesus which is oftenest preached, and men are bidden follow His way of life with God and man. In still other quarters it is His teaching which is dwelt on and men are enlisted as devotees of the Kingdom of God. But the cross, while it is mentioned as a significant unveiling of Jesus' character, or as the most draining ordeal for which He drew on spiritual resources, or as the climax of His devotion to His cause, is seldom preached as a redemptive act. Indeed few of those who have accepted the current

1. Chapter 1 of *The Meaning of the Cross*, 1931.

liberal theology devote many sermons to the cross of Christ. They feel themselves incapable of treating the theme.

There are various reasons for this. Our exaggerated individualism renders it difficult for us to think of One bearing the sins of others. Our easy optimism makes us think lightly of sin as an obsession of minds which hold unwholesome views of man and of God. Above all, the luxurious circumstances in which modern American Christians have found themselves have dulled our capacities for appreciating sacrifice. We have surrounded ourselves with conveniences and comforts, and we have tried to banish pain. The tortured form of One spiked on a beam of wood and done to death does not belong in our mental picture. Our ideals and manner of life are incompatible with this tragic and heroic symbol. Preachers have felt an unreality in attempting to explore with their people the meaning of the crucifixion.

This neglect of the cross has had something to do with the lack of transforming power in our message. No one can look complacently upon the present condition of our churches. Hundreds of them are barely holding on: they make no gains from the lives about them. In hundreds more, where there is bustle and stir, the activity is about trifles, and lives are not radically altered nor their communities made over. In very few does one find comrades of the conscience of Christ. In most the majority of communicants show no marks of the Lord Jesus in the purposes to which they devote themselves, in their attitudes towards their neighbors, in the opinions which they hold on public questions. Ministers can count on their fingers the number of their people ready to give themselves for an advance of the Kingdom. The wealth in Christian hands in this country is fabulous, but almost all Church Boards are crippled for want of support. More money is taken in at the gates of a single champion prizefight than a million Church members contribute in a whole year to the spread of the Gospel throughout the world. Above all repentance—a fundamental Christian experience— "repentance unto life" as the Westminster divines termed it—is a saving grace seldom seen. That which has most moved other centuries to repentance unto life has been the preaching of Christ crucified. Commenting upon Dwight L. Moody's insistence upon the efficacy of the sacrifice of Christ to do away with sin, Gamaliel Bradford writes:

To some of us, at any rate, whether we can accept this doctrine or not, it seems that the enormous, unparalleled growth and power and majesty of Christianity in the last nineteen hundred years depend upon it.

One would not harshly criticize brethren in the ministry who have shrunk from the word of the cross. We preachers are pitiable men, doomed to be haunted week after week with a sense of the insufficiency of our treatment of subjects obviously too high for us, and on which we are still constrained to speak. We become most abysmally aware of our incompetence when we attempt to set forth the meaning of the suffering and death of the Son of Man. John Milton, who had marvelously celebrated the birth of Jesus in the "Ode on the Morning of Christ's Nativity," attempted a sequel upon the Passion, but after a few exquisite stanzas he ceased in despair, and the fragment is published with the significant note:

This Subject the Author finding to be above the years he had when he wrote it, and nothing satisfied with what was begun, left it unfinished.

And years do not of themselves mature us to deal with this theme. Happily we discover that sermons which seriously try to interpret that supreme event possess a moving power out of proportion to the wisdom of their content.

How are we to preach Christ crucified? We want an interpretation of the cross for our generation which shall move to repentance and faith. In order to remain in close touch with reality, suppose we begin with two questions of history: First, How came it that the Life which subsequent centuries have looked up to as the best ever lived on our earth seemed so intolerable to the dominant groups of His day that they executed Him? Second, Why did Jesus force the issue that made His execution inevitable?

Let us attempt to answer the first question in this initial chapter remembering that we are not attempting a doctrine of the cross for classroom discussion, but for general presentation. How came it that He whom succeeding generations have revered as the best of men was put to death as a criminal? Who were the crucifiers of Christ?

First and foremost the religious leaders whom Church folk respected. It is a tribute to the force conferred by religious conviction that believing men are so often the prime movers in momentous occurrences, both in the blackest crimes and in the brightest triumphs of mankind. Faith, like fire, empowers its possessors whether for woe or for weal. We must not forget that there was ardent faith in God and conscientious loyalty to Him in the Pharisees who contrived the cruel death of our earth's divinest figure. Like one of their own school, they verily thought themselves under compulsion to act as they did.

That is why Church folk should study them carefully. Who were they? The successors of a brave and patriotic company of stalwart believers who had saved the Jewish faith when foreign conquerors attempted to compromise and wreck it by introducing their own customs and worship. They were known for that essential element in vital religion—detachment: they were called Separatists, Pharisees. They were the heirs of a noble army of martyrs. They knew and honored the Bible as the Law of God. They reverenced the scholars who had spent their lives in explaining it and applying it to life. They were the backbone of the synagogues throughout the land. They prayed; they believed in God's present government of His world and in His immediate control of events. They thought His angelic messengers spoke in the consciences of devout folk and watched for good over their steps. They looked forward to the resurrection of the righteous and their life in the Messiah's everlasting kingdom. They were intense lovers of home and country: in their households there was family religion, and boys, like Saul of Tarsus, were brought up to become devotees and leaders of the Church. They supplied the candidates for the ministry—the scribes who studied and interpreted the Torah. They furnished the missionaries who had enthusiasm to compass sea and land for a single proselyte, and had built up around the synagogues of the whole Mediterranean world companies of the God-fearing who had espoused the faith of Israel.

Men who sincerely try to order their lives by God's will usually work out a system of obligations, to which they hold themselves and seek to hold others. Now some matters can readily be embodied in rules—keeping the Sabbath, observing sacred festivals and fasts, adopting methodical times and habits of prayer, setting aside a tenth of one's gains for religious purposes. And some matters cannot be thus codified—having clean thoughts and generous sympathies, being conciliatory, honoring every human being, however unadmirable, as kin to God, serving him as his heavenly Father understandingly cares for him. And matters which can be incorporated in rules tend to be stressed above those which cannot be precisely defined. And when men have their beliefs and duties clearly stated, and are earnestly living by them, they are not apt to distinguish between more and less important items in their religious code: all of it is precious to them. They do not wish any of it changed. Sincere religion is inherently conservative. It deals with tested values.

Jesus scandalized them by disregarding practices which they considered God's Law. He broke the Sabbath shockingly. When asked to speak in the synagogues, His addresses upset many in the congregation. He associated with disreputable people—with loose women and with unpatriotic profiteering farmers of revenue. He touched the academic pride of their scholars: how should a carpenter correct their explanation of Scriptures which they had spent their lives in studying and for which they had the authority of recognized experts? Many of them had never heard Him for themselves, and at second or tenth hand, when the intervening hands are unfriendly, His sayings and doings appeared even more insufferable. From the outset He was surrounded in their minds with an atmosphere of suspicion. They sent spies to watch Him, and spies have a way of hearing what they fancy they are sent to hear. The Pharisees felt themselves guardians of the faith of Israel. Their fathers had fought and bled for it; their own lives were wrapped up in it; they were holding it in the dark days of Roman dominion for their children and children's children. Could they allow this Innovator, this Charlatan who made preposterous claims for Himself, to go on deceiving simple folk and perhaps wreck the Church? Quite apart from the embittering encounters Jesus had with some of them— encounters which may have been colored in our gospels by the subsequent strife between the Synagogue and the growing Christian Church, there was enough difference between His faith and life and theirs to rouse determined antagonism. In loyalty to God they must put an end to His mischievous career.

A second group were the inheritors of a lucrative commercial privilege—the aristocratic Sadducean priests who controlled the Temple area. They also were churchmen, but in comparison with the Pharisees, their religion was a subordinate and moderate interest. It was an inheritance which they cherished with an antiquarian's regard for its more primitive form. Their thought of Deity was of a remote and unaggressive Being, who left men to work out their own affairs, who certainly did not interfere or help by sending angelic spirits. God wished from Israel a seemly recognition in the maintenance of the time-honored ceremonies. For the rest they were broadminded. Their predecessors had welcomed the culture and customs of the Greeks, and they probably had a much more tolerant attitude in religion than the Pharisees. One might have picked up a Greek poem or drama in their homes; they were interested in the on-goings of the larger world; and after the manner of cultivated liberals they smiled in superior fashion on the narrow preoccupations of scribes with the details of the religious code. They were much more concerned with politics and finance than with religion. So long as Jesus remained in Galilee, they may never have heard of Him; or if some rumor of Him came to their ears, they would pay little attention to it. The alarm of the Pharisees over His teaching would have seemed to them a petty squabble which was no concern of theirs.

But when Jesus invaded the Temple precincts and created a commotion by overturning the tables of the money-changers, these gentlemen were roused. Here was a dangerous social Radical. Doubtless their leasing of space for booths in the outer court of the Temple had been criticized before, and there was popular talk over the prices of doves and lambs, and grumbling at the rate of exchange for the half-shekel. But this was the usual proletarian murmuring. Did they not provide a public convenience in these business arrangements? Were they not assisting worshippers in their religious duties? Did not the ancient Law clearly enjoin that the Temple tax should be paid in a particular coin? And must not someone supply facilities for exchanging the various currencies which pilgrims brought with them from all over the Empire for the proper silver piece? Was not four per cent a moderate broker's fee for such an exchange? The idea of this upcountry Agitator appearing and, without a word to anybody in authority, making this disturbance in the Temple court, and infecting the populace with the absurd notion that there should be no charge for perfectly legitimate ecclesiastical business! Where did He think animals for sacrifice would be procured? What did He consider a reasonable charge for exchange, if He called four per cent robbery? Who was He, anyhow, to take upon Himself to reform the financial methods of men whose forebears had derived their incomes unquestioned from these leases? His attack was a reflection not only upon them, but upon their honored fathers. Annas and Caiaphas had never seen the court of the Temple without booths and stalls; it was to them part of the natural order of things that cattle and doves should be sold there and money exchanged. Further they had been born to the tradition that the sacred area of the Temple belonged to the hereditary priesthood, and that they were to derive their support from its ceremonies. How could they understand the indignant feelings of Jesus? The charge, which the false witnesses brought, that He had threatened to destroy the Temple, may have had some slight basis in fact. Such statements are seldom made out of whole cloth. Jesus may have expressed the feeling that, if this Temple made with hands were destroyed, real religion might not lose much. That would disturb these gentlemen in their family sentiment, in their inherited faith, in their economic interests.

And they were politicians with a keen eye for the political situation. At the moment they were on fair terms with the Roman Empire and were allowed some freedom in the management of local affairs. A demagogue of this sort, as Caiaphas remarked, might stir up a political mess, and embroil them with the Roman authorities. Could they risk allowing Him to go on?[2]

A third figure among the crucifiers is the representative of imperialistic government. He seems to have been impressed by Jesus— more impressed than the scribes or the priests. We pity him as part of a system which our age feels to be inherently faulty. In theory at

2. Doctor L. P. Jacks has said of our contemporary churches: "The gravamen of the charge against the Church is not so much that there are definite abuses in its corporate life as that there is a general atmosphere of acquiescence in all that is worldly and conventional. No one knows exactly what ideal of life the Church stands for, unless it is that of a kindly and good-natured toleration of things as they are, with a mild desire that they may grow better in time, so far as that is compatible with the maintenance of existing vested interests." That is the position of the Sadducee; and Jesus touched it at its most sensitive point when He assailed vested interests [Coffin's note].

least we do not believe in one people governing another. It is bad for both peoples. It creates such attitudes as one sees in this scene—the priests fawning upon the governor and Pilate overbearing toward them and insulting the nation by the derisive title he orders nailed above the Victim on the cross. But among imperialistic peoples few have understood their business as well as the Romans. They probably kept Judaea in better order than any native leader could have kept it. They governed brutally, but there are still many who think that inferiors must be made to know their place. Jesus had been struck with their haughty attitude: "Ye know that the rulers of the Gentiles lord it." It may have been partially a patriot's unwillingness to speak against His own countrymen before an overlord which sealed His lips in the judgment hall.

All our narratives agree that the governor was most reluctant to execute this Prisoner. He suggested expedient after expedient to obviate it. He tried everything except the direct course of following his conscience and seeking to deal justly towards the Man before him. The system of which he was a part entangled him. Rome asked her procurators to keep the tribute flowing steadily from their provinces and to maintain quiet. No governor wished complaints lodged against him with his superiors. Pilate had to live with these priests, and in the end it seemed easier to let them have their way with this Peasant from Galilee. He was poor and insignificant, and to this day justice is never the same for the unfriended sons of poverty as for the wealthy and influential. Paul, claiming his rights as a Roman citizen, was to have days in court his Master could not command.

To the last Pilate was uncomfortable about the case. He did his best to shift responsibility—on Herod, on the crowd, on the priests. But the priests knew their man and played skillfully upon his loyalties and his fears. The fourth evangelist makes them say: "If thou release this man, thou art not Cæsar's friend." Fidelity to Cæsar was both a Roman's patriotism and his religion. They were appealing to Pilate's principles, and they won their point. Pilate washed his hands, but throughout the centuries his name has been coupled with this event as responsible for it on the lips of thousands who repeat "crucified under Pontius Pilate."

A fourth figure among crucifiers, although he is hardly a decisive factor, is a man of the gay world—Herod Antipas. A scion of an able family, born to wealth and position, brought up in Rome at the imperial court, admitted to the fashionable society of the capital in the golden age of Augustus, a member of the smart set, he knew all about the latest delicacies of the table, had a keen eye for a beautiful dancer, and surrounded by boon companions lived for pleasure. Like many in similar circumstances in contemporary America he had a shabby marital record, having become infatuated with his half-brother's wife, for whom he divorced his own wife and whom he stole from her husband. But divorces even of this sordid variety were not bad form then, any more than they are among ourselves today, and bad form was the only taboo Herod revered. He had a reputation for political shrewdness, and he had burnt his fingers in handling one prophet, John, and was wary of repeating the blunder. Jesus dreaded what He called "the leaven of Herod"—loose morals, lavish outlay, and sharp politics. He had spoken of this tetrarch as "that fox." Now these two were face to face.

Herod displayed a man-of-the-world's versatility in asking Him "many questions"—one wonders what they were. He was clever and was pleased to display his knowledge of religious fine points before his companions and before the priests. It was a chance to impress them. But Herod could make nothing of Jesus. And Jesus could make nothing of Herod. He had borne witness to His Messiahship before Caiaphas and the Sanhedrin; He had admitted His kingship to Pontius Pilate; but He had not a syllable to utter to Antipas. The tetrarch had heard of him as a wonder-worker and craved the chance to see Him do something startling. But Jesus' mighty works are not tricks to entertain and astonish. Herod had a conscience; could not Jesus appeal to that with some piercing story such as Nathan told adulterous David?[3] Did the Saviour ever confront a needier sinner? But He had not a word for him.

Herod was apparently "past feeling," and Jesus gave him up. This clownish roysterer and his cronies could think of nothing to do with their disappointing Prisoner but tog Him out in mock finery and make game of Him. Fancy the mind of Jesus while this went on! It cost Pilate some struggle to condemn Him; but when He was sent away from the tetrarch's palace, Herod had been laughing at Him as a buffoon, and was now smiling at his own shrewdness in outwitting the governor, and handing his awkward case back to him.

A fifth figure among the crucifiers is a disillusioned idealist. We have no reason to think that the man of Kerioth did not enlist in the cause of Jesus from the same high motives as the other disciples. If anything it was harder for him, the only Judaean in the group, than for Galileans. He heard all that they heard and he shared all that they shared, and, like them, he was disappointed. He had looked for a different issue. Jesus outdistanced his ideals; he fancied that Jesus did not measure up to his ideals and he grew critical. With many the attempt "to go beyond themselves and wind themselves too high" is followed by a reaction. What he had hoped for, and hoped for immediately, did not happen, and Judas became bitter. He felt himself duped. The confident attitude of Jesus as He set His face to what seemed to Judas folly and defeat, irritated him.

He was no longer the reasonable man he had been. It was that perhaps which led the disciples in retrospect to recall that the devil entered into him. They felt that he was at war with himself. And in such plight men not infrequently turn on those to whom they have been most warmly attached. Their disgust with themselves they are apt to vent on those who make them uncomfortable. Iago says of Cassio: "He hath a daily beauty in his life that makes me ugly." Jesus became hateful to Judas Iscariot. There may be a shred of truth in the theories which make his betrayal of the Master an attempt to force His hand, and compel Him to assume his power.

For what was it that Judas betrayed to the priests? Obviously not merely the spot where their police could arrest Jesus. That was not worth paying for. The police could follow him and find out His haunts. Probably Judas betrayed, as many modern interpreters think, the secret of Jesus' Messiahship, which was talked of in the inner circle but not published abroad. That was not clear to the priests or to the public even after the entry amid hosannas, for the shouts of a crowd are not evidence. Now they had a basis for trial, so Judas was in a sense forcing Jesus to declare Himself. But our narratives imply that Judas did it vindictively, not affectionately.

Disillusioned idealists become sour and cynical. And in cynicism conscience's unravel: Judas may easily have grown careless in handling the money in his custody. Avarice cannot have been the main motive in the betrayal, but greed has a place in most ignoble stories. Very trifling sums induce people still to hideous crimes. When a man is embittered, he is capable of anything, and it was a cynic who drove the shabby bargain with the chief priests and went out with thirty pieces of silver jingling in his purse and a betrayed Master on his conscience.

A sixth factor among the crucifiers is a crowd. The individuals who composed it were decent men, kind to their families and neighbors, and personally they would not have been cruel to this Prophet from Galilee. They had a prejudice against Him, and that prejudice was worked up until they were fused into a howling mob. In such a mass a man is lifted out of himself, loses control of his feelings, and his passions surge unchecked and augmented by the passions of the throng around him. He becomes a thousand times himself emotionally. Shakespeare's Bassanio speaks of

> The buzzing pleased multitude
> Whose every something being blent together
> Turns to a wild of nothing save of joy.

And the reverse is true when the crowd is prejudiced and their every something being blended together turns to a wild of nothing save of cruelty.

A crowd, being emotionally intense, is very suggestible. A catchword will set it off. Our propagandists and advertisers have taught us how we can be worked on in masses by names, phrases, pictures. And crowds are much more readily suggestible to the more primitive and coarser sentiments than to the finer. Man is a thinly varnished savage at best, lump him together in throngs and the varnish melts at the touch. When Pilate appeared unwilling to grant the priests' request, the crowd was swayed by nationalism; the priests were their own, and the governor the representative of the hated oppressor. They had a traditional right to claim clemency for a prisoner at the Passover. They will use it, and natural self-assertion impels them not to ask for One whom Pilate would gladly let them have. A suggestion is given them—Barabbas, a popular revolutionary of the crude type—a slogan for the emotions of a crowd.

Jesus can hardly have been popular. How much better "copy" for our own press Barabbas would be than the Teacher of Nazareth! Besides Barabbas is the nationalistic type Pilate would least like to release. Mobs feel and scarcely think. Could these men as individuals have calmly weighed Jesus and Barabbas, the result might have been different; but they were atingle with their cruder instincts. And a crowd which takes to shouting works itself to a violent pitch, and when thwarted can become fiendishly brutal. The spectators who packed the tiers of the Coliseum, turned down their thumbs at some fallen gladiator and yelled themselves hoarse demanding his death, would not have done anything of the sort by themselves. Each man in the crowd has lost his sense of personal responsibility. It is what men do in a social set, a political party, an economic group, a nation, a religious assembly, that is likely to be least moral and most diabolically savage. Pilate did his weak best not to execute Jesus; Herod found loutish amusement in Him, but showed no desire for His blood; Judas wished Him out of his way, but jail would have satisfied him; the crowd, with their tribal feelings roused—the instincts of the hunting pack—shouted "Crucify Him, crucify Him!"

A seventh factor among the crucifiers was a guard of soldiers. Jesus never spoke harshly of the military profession. One of His rare compliments was paid to an officer who had expressed his faith in terms of soldierly obedience. And probably it was in extenuation of the legionaries charged with the grim details of His execution that He prayed: "Father, forgive them, for they know not what they do." But it was by men prepared for their task by military discipline that He was done to death at Golgotha.

That system is deliberately planned to depersonalize those whom it trains. They are educated not to decide for themselves, but to give machine-like response to a command. Such a system, while it has noble associations with courage, loyalty, honor, and self-effacement, counteracts that which Christianity tries hardest to create—a reasoning conscience. The soldiers who scourged Jesus and spiked His hands and feet to the beams of the cross never thought what they were doing—they were victims of a discipline which had crucified their moral judgments.

Their occupation was held in high honor as the typical and most essential patriotic service. Rome ruled by physical might. She believed in awing inferior peoples and encouraged her soldiers to strike terror into them. The scourging which Pilate ordered—"the terrible preface," as it was called, to capital punishment—was forbidden for Roman citizens, but it was customary for provincials. A small guard was ordered to inflict on Jesus this appalling indignity in public—stripping Him, binding Him to a stake in a stooping position with hands behind Him, and beating Him with thongs at the ends of which were leaden balls or sharp-pointed bones.

And when that prostrating ordeal was over they took Him for further maltreatment to the privacy of the guardroom. Brutal mockery of the condemned was allowed the soldiers in order to maintain their *morale*. All the finer feelings must be overcome in those whose trade is iron and blood. And privacy seems to be an inevitable temptation to men with fellow-beings in their power. Schoolboys, jailors, keepers of the weak in mind or body, generation after generation, have to be watched against outbreaks of savagery to their victims. It was expected of the soldiers—a crude comic interlude of their rough day. But in fairness to these systematically hardened men let us recall that when the Prisoner was uplifted on the cross, slowly bleeding to death in agony, educated and revered religious leaders, professors of divinity, vented their detestation of Him with gibes. Theological animosity renders men as callous as professional hangmen.

Perhaps more so, for these soldiers had to restrain themselves from feeling by gambling at the foot of the cross. They had to sit by while the crucified writhed, and groaned, and cried, in their prolonged misery. It is not surprising that they resorted to the excitement of playing dice as a mental relief. They are typical representatives of callings into which men cannot put themselves—their minds and consciences and hearts. Such callings rob those who engage in them of moral vitality and make them fit agents of tragic occurrences like Calvary.

But there is still an eighth factor without which the crucifixion would not have taken place—the public. Behind the chief actors in the drama at Golgotha we see thousands of obscure figures—the populace of the city. One fancies them getting up in the morning and hearing rumors of a case on before the governor. The city, crowded with Passover pilgrims, would be more excitable and talkative than usual, and news of events at the palace, involving the Sanhedrin, would spread rapidly. Then, as people were in the midst of their morning's work, they would catch sight of that sinister procession tramping through the streets on the way to the place of execution outside the city wall. We can overhear such remarks as "Hello! another hanging today? Who's to be hung? Those two bandits? Who's the third prisoner? That Prophet from Galilee? Oh, they got Him very quickly, didn't they?" And as prisoners and guards filed past, the day's work was resumed.

Behind all earth's tragedies there is a public whose state of mind has much to do with the central event. Even under the least democratic government the authorities dare not go more than a certain distance without the popular will. The thousands of uncaring nobodies, to whom what was done with Jesus was a matter of indifference, gave scribes and priests and governor their chance. These obscure folk felt themselves without responsibility. What had they to do with this Prophet from the north country who had ridden into the city, hailed by a crowd of provincial pilgrims? Possibly it was of them that Jesus was thinking—the public of the capital city—when He said: "O Jerusalem, Jerusalem, that killeth the prophets."

The public is never of one mind; it represents various shades of opinion and feeling—sympathetic, hostile, indifferent; and all shades were there in Jerusalem. But if enough of its inhabitants had really cared about Jesus, He would never have been crucified. The chief handicap of the public is ignorance. The mass of the dwellers in Jerusalem knew next to nothing about the Prophet from Galilee. But Jesus did not weep over them merely because of their lack of information. Religious capitals, like cathedral towns, are proverbially hard to move. Religion was an old story to those who lived in the neighborhood of the venerable Temple and were familiar with the figures of the great doctors of the Law. They were complacent in sacred traditions of the past and not open to fresh incomings of the Most High. Jesus wept over their apathy. To Him it seemed that even unfeeling stones must respond to One who so manifestly represented God. They did not know the things which belonged to peace because they did not wish to know them. Jerusalem slew the Son of God not only because He had won the sharp ill-will of the powerful few, but also because the many did not want to be bothered with Him. And the public of Jerusalem, who thought the fate of this Stranger none of their business, had to bear the doom with their as-yet-unborn children; for judgment brings home social obligations and convinces us that by a myriad unsuspected cords men are tied up in one bundle of life in cities, in nations, in races, and in a world of men. These thousands of citizens of Jerusalem never went through the form of washing their hands, like Pilate. They were unaware of any accountability for this execution. But history with its destruction of the city rendered its verdict upon them.

Such a survey of the factors which crucified Jesus—and a course
rather than a single sermon is obviously necessary to treat them
with sufficient explicitness—forces men to think. This was the
world which executed the Life subsequent generations until this
hour revere as the best earth has seen. And plainly it is the world in
which we still live. All these forces are present and active in our
society—religious intolerance, commercial privilege, political expe-
diency, pleasure-loving irresponsibility, unfaithfulness, the mob
spirit, militarism, public apathy. These are perennial evils. They are
deep-seated in the very structure of human society. The forms of
political and economic and ecclesiastical organization may alter,
but these remain under all forms. We should find them in a socialist republic or a communist state, as surely as in an imperial despo-
tism or a capitalist regime. Moreover, they act and react upon each
other. The priests help Judas to his treachery and incite the mob;
Pilate stimulates the priests to play politics; the political methods
of both governor and religious leaders keep the public morally
indifferent; their sinister motives interweave into a corporate force
for evil. Together they make up what Jesus called "the power of
darkness," the satanic kingdom.

It is significant that the national and ecclesiastical capital is the
slayer of the prophets. Evil organizes itself with this inherent solidarity and possesses a group—a church, a nation, a race. These
forces were present in the villages and towns of Galilee, but they
came to a focus where the organization of the Jewish Church and
the Jewish nation had its seat, and where the representative of
imperial government exercised his power. Wickedness is a racial
force. It propagates itself generation after generation. Jesus recognized the unity of the factors with which He was struggling with
similar factors, which had always been present in the life of His
people, when He spoke of this generation which was crucifying
Him having upon it "all the righteous blood shed on earth," from
the blood of Abel on the first pages of the Jewish Bible to the
blood of Zachariah recorded on its last pages. Evil spreads itself
laterally, building up a corporate force of wickedness, and passes
itself on from age to age, linking the generations in a solidarity of
sin.

When we examine the factors which slew Jesus, we recognize
them at once as contemporaries. We can attach modern names to
them. There is nothing abnormal or unusual about these men who
rear the cross: they are acting true to type—a type which recurs
century after century throughout history. They are average folk.
We must not blacken their characters. John Stuart Mill, whose ethical judgments are singularly dispassionate, says of them:

They were not worse than men commonly are, but rather the contrary, men who possessed in a full, or somewhat more than a full meas-

ure the religious, moral, and patriotic feelings of their people; the very kind of men who in all times, our own included, have every chance of passing through life blameless and unspotted.

We can think of no more high-minded young man than the student of Gamaliel, Saul of Tarsus, and we know how cordially he approved the course taken by the leaders of Israel in putting Jesus out of the way.

We can easily multiply from history and literature men far more villainous—a Caesar Borgia or an Iago, for instance. Indeed we can find more depraved figures in almost any community, if we look for them. But the purpose of Jesus and the purposes of even good people clash. The inevitableness of the crucifixion is brought home to us. The issue between the motives of Jesus and those of the mass of mankind is thrown into light. They are irreconcilable. Life is a desperately real struggle between mutually destroying forces. If the motives of Jesus prevail, the factors that slew Him will cease to be. If the motives of Caiaphas and Pilate, of the mob, the soldiers, and the public prevail—there is an execution: "Away with such a fellow from the earth."

There are three crosses on Calvary: on two of them society is trying to rid itself of predatory bandits, on the third it placed One whom it considered also its enemy, perhaps a worse enemy since He was placed on the central cross. We level up with our standards of right, and we also level down. He who is above the conscience of the community is as likely to be slain as he who is below. This is our world; this is the society in which we move; these are the types of people with whom we associate; this is the public to which we belong. The slayers of Jesus are our relatives, kinsmen in thought and feeling. A sense of complicity in what they did comes upon us. We are bound up with them in this bundle of human life. The corporate evil which dominated first-century Palestine and moved these men to kill their Best dominates our world and is compassing similar fell results. Trails of blood lead to our doors. Wretched men that we are, who shall deliver us out of this social body of death?

And these factors are not only about us, they are also within us. As we scan these men who sent Jesus to His death—devout Pharisee and conservative Sadducee, Roman politician and false friend, emotional mob and unthinking soldiers, the host of indifferent or approving faces of the public behind them—their motives and feelings have been and are our own. You may recall in Hawthorne's *Mosses from an Old Manse* the scene where, going through the virtuoso's collection, he nearly falls over a huge bundle, like a peddler's pack, done up in sackcloth and very securely strapped and corded. " 'It is Christian's burden of sin,' said the virtuoso. 'O pray, let me see it,' cried I. 'For many a year I have longed to know its

contents.' 'Look into your own conscience and memory,' replied the virtuoso. 'You will there find a list of whatever it contained.' "
It is so with the motives of those who planned and carried out the death of Jesus. We do not need to ask: "Lord, is it I?" We are aware of belonging in this same realm of darkness, and of having dealt with His brethren very much as He was dealt with. As we think of ourselves, we shudder—"God, be merciful to me, a sinner."

Men speak of the absence of the sense of sin in our time. It has never been vigorous in any age, save as some judgment of history or the disturbing presence of the ideal has created it. We have witnessed a judgment on a colossal scale in the World War—a judgment upon our entire civilization. Some of us said to ourselves, feeling mankind in the grip of overmastering social forces of passion and greed and brutality: "Now is your hour and the power of darkness." And we know ourselves a long way yet from redemption from the motives which brought it on. Underneath the ease and comfort of our day there is restless discontent. Some of it is crassly materialistic—the common envy of the have-nots for the haves, the craving of the have-littles to have more. But souls are never satisfied with things. Life is in relationships, human and divine, in purposes. And men are dissatisfied with the quality of life. To take them to Calvary and show them the factors which nailed Jesus on the cross is to uncover for them a far more terrible world than they dreamed they were in, and to uncover for them themselves.

This gives us an inkling of Jesus' reason for putting Himself into men's hands and letting them do with Him as they would. His broken and bleeding body on the cross is the exposure of a murderous world. The Crucified becomes one with the unrecognized and misused and cruelly treated in every age. The nail-pierced Figure on Calvary haunts our race as a symbol of what is forever taking place generation after generation, and of what each of us has his part in.

Readers of Ibsen's drama *Emperor and Galilean* will recall how Julian is made to ask—

Where is He now? Has He been at work elsewhere since that happened at Golgotha?
I dreamed of Him lately. I dreamed that I had subdued the whole world. I ordained that the memory of the Galilean should be rooted out on earth; and it was rooted out. Then the spirits came and ministered to me, and bound wings on my shoulders, and I soared aloft into infinite space, till my feet rested on another world.
It was another world than mine. Its curve was vaster, its light more golden, and many moons circled around it. Then I looked down at my own earth—the Emperor's earth that I had made Galileanless—and I thought that all that I had done was very good.
But behold there came a procession by me on the strange earth where I stood. There were soldiers and judges and executioners at the head of

it and weeping women followed. And lo, in the midst of the slow-moving array, was the Galilean, alive and bearing a cross on His back. Then I called to Him and said, "Whither away, Galilean?" And He turned His face to me and smiled, nodded slowly and said, "To the place of the skull."

Where is He now? What if that at Golgotha, near Jerusalem, was but a wayside matter, a thing done as it were in passing! What if He goes on and on, and suffers and dies, and conquers, again and again, from world to world!

It is a vivid way of picturing the solidarity of the worlds of every generation, each offering its Golgotha. It is there that men come to themselves and realize their plight and the plight of society. Walter Pater said that "the way to perfection is through a series of disgusts." To let men see the factors which enact the tragedy outside the wall of Jerusalem is to disgust them with their world and with themselves. If some protest that this is not a wholesome state of mind, one may answer in the words of that robust thinker, Walter Bagehot: "So long as men are very imperfect, a sense of great imperfection should cleave to them." It is a necessary part of the process towards genuine healthy-mindedness. When they realize what caused the torture and execution of Jesus, they cry, "O not that! Such a world is intolerable!" And made conscious that they are builders of such worlds, and that their hands are stained, they hunger and thirst after righteousness.

QUESTIONS

1. Indicate each of the principal groups and figures who, by Coffin's account, contributed to the crucifixion of Christ. What leading motive does Coffin ascribe to each? How does Coffin show these motives to be perennial ones, operative now as then? Why does he do so?
2. Examine each of the transitions Coffin makes. How does he proceed from one part to another in his essay? How does he relate part to part? What order of progression is discernible in the essay?
3. Coffin accords the Pharisees considerable praise. Why? What does he imply to be the essential fault of the Pharisees? In what respects does he compare and contrast the Pharisees and Sadducees?
4. Coffin refers (p. 463) to the "motives of Jesus," but he does not delineate these or discuss them in full. To what extent has he indirectly indicated them in his account of the principal groups and figures contributing to the crucifixion?
5. Consider Coffin's title. Why has he asked precisely that question? Might he just as well have given as title "Who Crucified Christ?" Explain.

JEAN-PAUL SARTRE

Existentialism

Man is nothing else but what he makes of himself. Such is the first principle of existentialism. It is also what is called subjectivity, the name we are labeled with when charges are brought against us. But what do we mean by this, if not that man has a greater dignity than a stone or table? For we mean that man first exists, that is, that man first of all is the being who hurls himself toward a future and who is conscious of imagining himself as being in the future. Man is at the start a plan which is aware of itself, rather than a patch of moss, a piece of garbage, or a cauliflower; nothing exists prior to this plan; there is nothing in heaven; man will be what he will have planned to be. Not what he will want to be. Because by the word "will" we generally mean a conscious decision, which is subsequent to what we have already made of ourselves. I may want to belong to a political party, write a book, get married; but all that is only a manifestation of an earlier, more spontaneous choice that is called "will." But if existence really does precede essence, man is responsible for what he is. Thus, existentialism's first move is to make every man aware of what he is and to make the full responsibility of his existence rest on him. And when we say that a man is responsible for himself, we do not only mean that he is responsible for his own individuality, but that he is responsible for all men.

The word "subjectivism" has two meanings, and our opponents play on the two. Subjectivism means, on the one hand, that an individual chooses and makes himself; and, on the other, that it is impossible for man to transcend human subjectivity. The second of these is the essential meaning of existentialism. When we say that man chooses his own self, we mean that every one of us does likewise; but we also mean by that that in making this choice he also chooses all men. In fact, in creating the man that we want to be, there is not a single one of our acts which does not at the same time create an image of man as we think he ought to be. To choose to be this or that is to affirm at the same time the value of what we choose, because we can never choose evil. We always choose the good, and nothing can be good for us without being good for all.

If, on the other hand, existence precedes essence, and if we grant that we exist and fashion our image at one and the same time, the image is valid for everybody and for our whole age. Thus, our responsibility is much greater than we might have supposed, because it involves all mankind. If I am a workingman and choose to join a Christian trade union rather than be a Communist, and if by being a member I want to show that the best thing for man is resignation, that the kingdom of man is not of this world, I am not only involving my own case—I want to be resigned for everyone. As a result, my action has involved all humanity. To take a more individual matter, if I want to marry, to have children, even it this marriage depends solely on my own circumstances or passion or wish, I am involving all humanity in monogamy and not merely myself. Therefore, I am responsible for myself and for everyone else. I am creating a certain image of man of my own choosing. In choosing myself, I choose man.

This helps us understand what the actual content is of such rather grandiloquent words as anguish, forlornness, despair. As you will see, it's all quite simple.

First, what is meant by anguish? The existentialists say at once that man is anguish. What that means is this: the man who involves himself and who realizes that he is not only the person he chooses to be, but also a lawmaker who is, at the same time, choosing all mankind as well as himself, cannot help escape the feeling of his total and deep responsibility. Of course, there are many people who are not anxious; but we claim that they are hiding their anxiety, that they are fleeing from it. Certainly, many people believe that when they do something, they themselves are the only ones involved, and when someone says to them, "What if everyone acted that way?" they shrug their shoulders and answer, "Everyone doesn't act that way." But really, one should always ask himself, "What would happen if everybody looked at things that way?" There is no escaping this disturbing thought except by a kind of double-dealing. A man who lies and makes excuses for himself by saying "not everybody does that," is someone with an uneasy conscience, because the act of lying implies that a universal value is conferred upon the lie.

Anguish is evident even when it conceals itself. This is the anguish that Kierkegaard called the anguish of Abraham. You know the story: an angel has ordered Abraham to sacrifice his son; if it really were an angel who has come and said, "You are Abraham, you shall sacrifice your son," everything would be all right. But everyone might first wonder, "Is it really an angel, and am I really Abraham? What proof do I have?"

There was a madwoman who had hallucinations; someone used to speak to her on the telephone and give her orders. Her doctor asked her, "Who is it who talks to you?" She answered, "He says it's God." What proof did she really have that it was God? If an angel comes to me, what proof is there that it's an angel? And if I hear voices, what proof is there that they come from heaven and not from hell, or from the subconscious, or a pathological condition? What proves that they are addressed to me? What proof is there that I have been appointed to impose my choice and my conception of man on humanity? I'll never find any proof or sign to convince me of that. If a voice addresses me, it is always for me to decide that this is the angel's voice; if I consider that such an act is a good one, it is I who will choose to say that it is good rather than bad.

Now, I'm not being singled out as an Abraham, and yet at every moment I'm obliged to perform exemplary acts. For every man, everything happens as if all mankind had its eyes fixed on him and were guiding itself by what he does. And every man ought to say to himself, "Am I really the kind of man who has the right to act in such a way that humanity might guide itself by my actions?" And if he does not say that to himself, he is masking his anguish.

There is no question here of the kind of anguish which would lead to quietism, to inaction. It is a matter of a simple sort of anguish that anybody who has had responsibilities is familiar with. For example, when a military officer takes the responsibility for an attack and sends a certain number of men to death, he chooses to do so, and in the main he alone makes the choice. Doubtless, orders come from above, but they are too broad; he interprets them, and on this interpretation depend the lives of ten or fourteen or twenty men. In making a decision he cannot help having a certain anguish. All leaders know this anguish. That doesn't keep them from acting; on the contrary, it is the very condition of their action. For it implies that they envisage a number of possibilities, and when they choose one, they realize that it has value only because it is chosen. We shall see that this kind of anguish, which is the kind that existentialism describes, is explained, in addition, by a direct responsibility to the other men whom it involves. It is not a curtain separating us from action, but is part of action itself.

When we speak of forlornness, a term Heidegger was fond of, we mean only that God does not exist and that we have to face all the consequences of this. This existentialist is strongly opposed to a certain kind of secular ethics which would like to abolish God with the least possible expense. About 1880, some French teachers tried to set up a secular ethics which went something like this: God is a useless and costly hypothesis; we are discarding it; but, meanwhile, in order for there to be an ethics, a society, a civilization, it is essential that certain values be taken seriously and that they be considered as having an *a priori* existence. It must be obligatory, a *priori*, to be honest, not to lie, not to beat your wife, to have children, etc., etc. So we're going to try a little device which will make it possible to show that values exist all the same, inscribed in a heaven of ideas, though otherwise God does not exist. In other words—and this, I believe, is the tendency of everything called reformism in France— nothing will be changed if God does not exist. We shall find ourselves with the same norms of honesty, progress, and humanism, and we shall have made of God an outdated hypothesis which will peacefully die off by itself.

The existentialist, on the contrary, thinks it very distressing that God does not exist, because all possibility of finding values in a heaven of ideas disappears along with Him; there can no longer be an *a priori* Good, since there is no infinite and perfect consciousness to think it. Nowhere is it written that the Good exists, that we must be honest, that we must not lie; because the fact is we are on a plane where there are only men. Dostoievsky said, "If God didn't exist, everything would be possible." That is the very starting point of existentialism. Indeed, everything is permissible if God does not exist, and as a result man is forlorn, because neither within him nor without does he find anything to cling to. He can't start making excuses for himself.

If existence really does precede essence, there is no explaining things away by reference to a fixed and given human nature. In other words, there is no determinism, man is free, man is freedom. On the other hand, if God does not exist, we find no values or commands to turn to which legitimize our conduct. So, in the bright realm of values, we have no excuse behind us, nor justification before us. We are alone, with no excuses.

That is the idea I shall try to convey when I say that man is condemned to be free. Condemned, because he did not create himself, yet, in other respects is free; because, once thrown into the world, he is responsible for everything he does. The existentialist does not believe in the power of passion. He will never agree that a sweeping passion is a ravaging torrent which fatally leads a man to certain acts and is therefore an excuse. He thinks that man is responsible for his passion.

The existentialist does not think that man is going to help himself by finding in the world some omen by which to orient himself. Because he thinks that man will interpret the omen to suit himself. Therefore, he thinks that man, with no support and no aid, is condemned every moment to invent man. Ponge, in a very fine article, has said, "Man is the future of man." That's exactly it. But if it is taken to mean that this future is recorded in heaven, that God sees it, then it is false, because it would really no longer be a future. If it is taken to mean that, whatever a man may be, there is a future to be forged, a virgin future before him, then this remark is sound. But then we are forlorn.

To give you an example which will enable you to understand forlornness better, I shall cite the case of one of my students who came to see me under the following circumstances: his father was on bad terms with his mother, and, moreover, was inclined to be a collaborationist; his older brother had been killed in the German offensive of 1940, and the young man, with somewhat immature but generous feelings, wanted to avenge him. His mother lived alone with him, very much upset by the half-treason of her husband and the death of her older son; the boy was her only consolation.

The boy was faced with the choice of leaving for England and joining the Free French forces—that is, leaving his mother behind —or remaining with his mother and helping her to carry on. He was fully aware that the woman lived only for him and that his going off—and perhaps his death—would plunge her into despair. He was also aware that every act that he did for his mother's sake was a sure thing, in the sense that it was helping her to carry on, whereas every effort he made toward going off and fighting was an uncertain move which might run aground and prove completely useless; for example, on his way to England he might, while passing through Spain, be detained indefinitely in a Spanish camp; he might reach England or Algiers and be stuck in an office at a desk job. As a result, he was faced with two very different kinds of action: one, concrete, immediate, but concerning only one individual; the other concerned an incomparably vaster group, a national collectivity, but for that very reason was dubious, and might be interrupted en route. And, at the same time, he was wavering between two kinds of ethics. On the one hand, an ethics of sympathy, of personal devotion; on the other, a broader ethics, but one whose efficacy was more dubious. He had to choose between the two.

Who could help him choose? Christian doctrine? No. Christian doctrine says, "Be charitable, love your neighbor, take the more rugged path, etc., etc." But which is the more rugged path? Whom should he love as a brother? The fighting man or his mother? Which does the greater good, the vague act of fighting in a group, or the concrete one of helping a particular human being to go on living? Who can decide *a priori*? Nobody. No book of ethics can tell him. The Kantian ethics says, "Never treat any person as a means, but as an end." Very well, if I stay with my mother, I'll treat her as an end and not as a means; but by virtue of this very fact, I'm running the risk of treating the people around me who are fighting, as means; and, conversely, if I go to join those who are fighting, I'll be treating them as an end, and, by doing that, I run the risk of treating my mother as a means.

If values are vague, and if they are always too broad for the concrete and specific case that we are considering, the only thing left for us is to trust our instincts. That's what this young man tried to do; and when I saw him, he said, "In the end, feeling is what counts. I ought to choose whichever pushes me in one direction. If I feel that I love my mother enough to sacrifice everything else for her—my desire for vengeance, for action, for adventure—then I'll stay with her. If, on the contrary, I feel that my love for my mother isn't enough, I'll leave."

But how is the value of a feeling determined? What gives his feeling for his mother value? Precisely the fact that he remained with her. I may say that I like so-and-so well enough to sacrifice a certain amount of money for him, but I may say so only if I've done it. I may say "I love my mother well enough to remain with her" if I have remained with her. The only way to determine the value of this affection is, precisely, to perform an act which confirms and defines it. But, since I require this affection to justify my act, I find myself caught in a vicious circle.

On the other hand, Gide has well said that a mock feeling and a true feeling are almost indistinguishable; to decide that I love my mother and will remain with her, or to remain with her by putting on an act, amount somewhat to the same thing. In other words, the feeling is formed by the acts one performs; so, I cannot refer to it in order to act upon it. Which means that I can neither seek within myself the true condition which will impel me to act, nor apply to a system of ethics for concepts which will permit me to act. You will say, "At least, he did go to a teacher for advice." But if you seek advice from a priest, for example, you have chosen this priest; you already knew, more or less, just about what advice he was going to give you. In other words, choosing your adviser is involving yourself. The proof of this is that if you are a Christian, you will say, "Consult a priest." But some priests are collaborating, some are just marking time, some are resisting. Which to choose? If the young man chooses a priest who is resisting or collaborating, he has already decided on the kind of advice he's going to get. Therefore, in coming to see me he knew the answer I was going to give him, and I had only one answer to give: "You're free, choose, that is, invent." No general ethics can show you what is to be done; there are no omens in the world. The Catholics will reply, "But there are." Granted —but, in any case, I myself choose the meaning they have.

When I was a prisoner, I knew a rather remarkable young man who was a Jesuit. He had entered the Jesuit order in the following way: he had had a number of very bad breaks; in childhood, his father died, leaving him in poverty, and he was a scholarship student at a religious institution where he was constantly made to feel that he was being kept out of charity; then, he failed to get any of the honors and distinctions that children like; later on, at about eighteen, he bungled a love affair; finally, at twenty-two, he failed in military training, a childish enough matter, but it was the last straw.

This young fellow might well have felt that he had botched everything. It was a sign of something, but of what? He might have taken refuge in bitterness or despair. But he very wisely looked upon all this as a sign that he was not made for secular triumphs, and that only the triumphs of religion, holiness, and faith were open to him. He saw the hand of God in all this, and so he entered the order. Who can help seeing that he alone decided what the sign meant?

Some other interpretation might have been drawn from this series of setbacks; for example, that he might have done better to turn carpenter or revolutionist. Therefore, he is fully responsible for the interpretation. Forlornness implies that we ourselves choose our being. Forlornness and anguish go together.

As for despair, the term has a very simple meaning. It means that we shall confine ourselves to reckoning only with what depends upon our will, or on the ensemble of probabilities which make our action possible. When we want something, we always have to reckon with probabilities. I may be counting on the arrival of a friend. The friend is coming by rail or streetcar; this supposes that the train will arrive on schedule, or that the streetcar will not jump the track. I am left in the realm of possibility; but possibilities are to be reckoned with only to the point where my action comports with the ensemble of these possibilities, and no further. The moment the possibilities I am considering are not rigorously involved by my action, I ought to disengage myself from them, because no God, no scheme, can adapt the world and its possibilities to my will. When Descartes said, "Conquer yourself rather than the world," he meant essentially the same thing.

The Marxists to whom I have spoken reply, "You can rely on the support of others in your action, which obviously has certain limits because you're not going to live forever. That means: rely on both what others are doing elsewhere to help you, in China, in Russia, and what they will do later on, after your death, to carry on the action and lead it to its fulfillment, which will be the revolution. You even *have* to rely upon that, otherwise you're immoral." I reply at once that I will always rely on fellow-fighters insofar as these comrades are involved with me in a common struggle, in the unity of a party or a group in which I can more or less make my weight felt; that is, one whose ranks I am in as a fighter and whose movements I am aware of at every moment. In such a situation, relying on the unity and will of the party is exactly like counting on the fact that the train will arrive on time or that the car won't jump the track. But, given that man is free and that there is no human nature for me to depend on, I cannot count on men whom I do not know by relying on human goodness or man's concern for the good of society. I don't know what will become of the Russian revolution; I may make an example of it to the extent that at the present time it is apparent that the proletariat plays a part in Russia that it plays in no other nation. But I can't swear that this will inevitably lead to a triumph of the proletariat. I've got to limit myself to what I see.

Given that men are free and that tomorrow they will freely decide what man will be, I cannot be sure that, after my death, fellow-fighters will carry on my work to bring it to its maximum perfection. Tomorrow, after my death, some men may decide to set up Fascism, and the others may be cowardly and muddled enough to let them do it. Fascism will then be the human reality, so much the worse for us.

Actually, things will be as man will have decided they are to be. Does that mean that I should abandon myself to quietism? No. First, I should involve myself; then, act on the old saw, "Nothing ventured, nothing gained." Nor does it mean that I shouldn't belong to a party, but rather that I shall have no illusions and shall do what I can. For example, suppose I ask myself, "Will socialization, as such, ever come about?" I know nothing about it. All I know is that I'm going to do everything in my power to bring it about. Beyond that, I can't count on anything. Quietism is the attitude of people who say, "Let others do what I can't do." The doctrine I am presenting is the very opposite of quietism, since it declares, "There is no reality except in action." Moreover, it goes further, since it adds, "Man is nothing else than his plan; he exists only to the extent that he fulfills himself; he is therefore nothing else than the ensemble of his acts, nothing else than his life."

According to this, we can understand why our doctrine horrifies certain people. Because often the only way they can bear their wretchedness is to think, "Circumstances have been against me. What I've been and done doesn't show my true worth. To be sure, I've had no great love, no great friendship, but that's because I haven't met a man or woman who was worthy. The books I've written haven't been very good because I haven't had the proper leisure. I haven't had children to devote myself to because I didn't find a man with whom I could have spent my life. So there remains within me, unused and quite viable, a host of propensities, inclinations, possibilities, that one wouldn't guess from the mere series of things I've done."

Now, for the existentialist there is really no love other than one which manifests itself in a person's being in love. There is no genius other than one which is expressed in works of art; the genius of Proust is the sum of Proust's works; the genius of Racine is his series of tragedies. Outside of that, there is nothing. Why say that Racine could have written another tragedy, when he didn't write it? A man is involved in life, leaves his impress on it, and outside of that there is nothing. To be sure, this may seem a harsh thought to someone whose life hasn't been a success. But, on the other hand, it prompts people to understand that reality alone is what counts, that dreams, expectations, and hopes warrant no more than to define a man as a disappointed dream, as miscarried hopes, as vain expectations. In other words, to define him negatively and not positively. However, when we say, "You are nothing else than your life," that does not imply that the artist will be judged solely on the basis of his works of art; a thousand other things will contribute toward summing him up. What we mean is that a man is nothing else than a series of undertakings, that he is the sum, the organization, the ensemble of the relationships which make up these undertakings.

When all is said and done, what we are accused of, at bottom, is not our pessimism, but an optimistic toughness. If people throw up to us our works of fiction in which we write about people who are soft, weak, cowardly, and sometimes even downright bad, it's not because these prople are soft, weak, cowardly, or bad; because if we were to say, as Zola did, that they are that way because of heredity, the workings of environment, society, because of biological or psychological determinism, people would be reassured. They would say, "Well, that's what we're like, no one can do anything about it." But when the existentialist writes about a coward, he says that this coward is responsible for his cowardice. He's not like that because he has a cowardly heart or lung or brain; he's not like that on account of his physiological make-up; but he's like that because he has made himself a coward by his acts. There's no such thing as a cowardly constitution; there are nervous constitutions; there is poor blood, as the common people say, or strong constitutions. But the man whose blood is poor is not a coward on that account, for what makes cowardice is the act of renouncing or yielding. A constitution is not an act; the coward is defined on the basis of the acts he performs. People feel, in a vague sort of way, that this coward we're talking about is guilty of being a coward, and the thought frightens them. What people would like is that a coward or a hero be born that way. . . .

From these few reflections it is evident that nothing is more unjust than the objections that have been raised against us. Existentialism is nothing else than an attempt to draw all the consequences of a coherent atheistic position. It isn't trying to plunge man into despair at all. But if one calls every attitude of unbelief despair, like the Christians, then the word is not being used in its original sense. Existentialism isn't so atheistic that it wears itself out showing that God doesn't exist. Rather, it declares that even if God did exist, that would change nothing. There you've got our point of view. Not that we believe that God exists, but we think that the problem of His existence is not the issue. In this sense existentialism is optimistic, a doctrine of action, and it is plain dishonesty for Christians to make no distinction between their own despair and ours and then to call us despairing.

QUESTIONS

1. What are some of the methods or devices Sartre uses to define existentialism? Why does he use more than one method or device?
2. What is the significance of the words "if existence really does precede essence"? What does this mean? What is the force of "if"? Why does Sartre repeat the words later in the essay?
3. Why does Sartre use three separate terms—anguish, forlornness, despair? What, if any, are the differences among them?
4. Sartre makes a distinction between treating "any person as a means . . . [and] as an end" (p. 470). What are the implications of this distinction?
5. Sartre says that the "coward is responsible for his cowardice," since man "is defined on the basis of the acts he performs." Does this notion of responsibility agree with that of Henry Sloane Coffin in "What Crucified Christ?" (pp. 450–465)?

Notes on Composition

Saying Something That Matters

There is no point in the hard labor of writing unless you expect to *do* something to somebody—perhaps add to his store of information, perhaps cause him to change his mind on some issue that you care about. Determining just what that something is is half the battle; hence the importance of knowing your main point, your central purpose in writing, your **thesis**. It may seem that this step—perhaps in the form of a "thesis sentence" or exact statement of the main point—is inevitably prior to everything else in writing, but in actual practice the case is more complicated. Few good writers attain a final grasp of their thesis until they have tried setting down their first halting ideas at some length; to put it another way, you discover more precisely what it is you have to say in the act of trying to say it. Formulating and refining upon a thesis sentence as you work your way through a piece of writing helps you see what needs to be done at each stage; the finished piece, though, instead of announcing its thesis in any one sentence, may simply imply it by the fact of its unity, the determinate way the parts hang together. There is probably no single sentence in E. B. White's "Once More to the Lake" (p. 28) that will serve satisfactorily to represent the entire essay in miniature, yet clearly such a sentence could be formulated: The pleasure of recapturing the past is heavily qualified by an adult awareness of the inevitability of change. But whether you state the main point or leave it to be inferred, you need to decide what your piece is about, what you want to say about it, why, and to whom.

Sometimes a thesis will rest on a good many **assumptions**, related ideas that the writer may not mention but depends upon his reader to understand and agree to (if he is an honest writer) or to overlook and hence fail to reject (if his real purpose is to mislead). Machiavelli (p.276) appears to assume that it is more important for a prince to stay in power than to be a "good" man. We may feel that the question is highly ambiguous, or we may disagree sharply. But even if we decide, finally, that we can live with Machiavelli's assumption, we shall have acquired a fuller understanding of

477

what he is saying, and of our own relationship to it, for having scrutinized what is being taken for granted. The habit of scrutiny guards us against the careless or cunning writer whose unstated assumptions may be highly questionable. The same habit, turned on our own minds when we become writers, can save us from the unthinking use of assumptions that we would be hard pressed to defend.

Some theses lend themselves to verification by laboratory methods or the like; they deal with **questions of fact**. The exact order of composition of Shakespeare's plays could conceivably be settled finally if new evidence turned up. Whether or not the plays are great literature, on the other hand, is a **question of opinion**; agreement (though not hard to reach in this instance) depends on the weighing of arguments rather than on tests or measurements. Not that all theses can be neatly classified as assertions either of fact or of opinion (consider "Shakespeare's influence has been greater than Newton's"); still the attempt to classify his own effort can help a writer understand what he is doing.

Sometimes a writer addresses himself more specifically to his readers' **understanding**, sometimes he addresses himself chiefly to their **emotions**. Although the processes of thinking and of feeling are almost always mixed, still it is obvious that a description of a chemical process and a description of a candidate you hope to see elected to office will differ considerably in tone and emphasis. Accordingly you need to give some thought to the kind of result you hope to produce: perhaps simply an addition of information, perhaps a change of attitude, perhaps a commitment of the will to action.

The Means of Saying It

No worthwhile thesis comes without work, and the work of arriving at a thesis is much like the work of writing itself—developing, elaborating, refining upon an idea that is perhaps at first hazy. For convenience the process may be divided into setting bounds, or defining; marshaling evidence; and drawing conclusions.

DEFINING in a broad sense may be thought of as what you do to answer the question "What do you mean?" It sets bounds by doing two things to an idea: grouping it with others like it and showing how it differs from those others. "An island is a tract of land" (like a lot or prairie or peninsula) "completely surrounded by water and too small to be called a continent" (and therefore different from a lot, etç.). This process of classifying and distinguishing may take many forms, depending on the kind of thing you are dealing with and your reason for doing so. (Artifacts, for example, can hardly be defined without reference to purpose; a lock is a device *for securing* a door; a theodolite is an instrument used *to measure* horizontal or vertical angles.) **Some of** the standard methods are these: by giving **examples**, pointing to an instance as a short way of indicating class and individual characteristics ("*That* is a firebreak"; "A liberal is a man like Jefferson") ; by **negating**, explaining what your subject is *not*—i.e., process of elimination ("Love vaunteth not itself, is not puffed up"); by **comparing and contrasting**, noting the resemblances and differences between your subject and something else ("A magazine is sometimes as big as a book but differs in binding and layout") ; by **analyzing**, breaking down a whole into its constituent parts ("A play may be seen as exposition, rising action, and denouement"); by seeking a **cause** of the thing in question or an **effect** that it has produced ("Scurvy is the result of a dietary deficiency and often leads to anemia"); or by attributing to a thing an **end** or **means**, seeing it as a way of fulfilling purpose or as the fulfillment of a purpose ("Representation is the end of the electoral system and the means to good government").

When we turn to specimens of writing, we see immediately that the various methods of defining may serve not only for one-sentence "dictionary" definitions but also as methods of organizing paragraphs or even whole essays, where unfolding the subject is in a sense "defining" it, showing where its boundaries lie. Carl Becker (p.297) begins with a broad idea of democracy that would include virtually all governments, then by considering several negative examples refines his definition until all governments that are not democracies are excluded. W. E. B. Du Bois (p.245) explains two attitudes toward life through an extended comparison of Jacob and Esau. Edward Hallett Carr (p.347) sorts out the several ways in which historians have viewed and made use of facts, an analysis that leads to his answer to the question "What is history?" The choice of method in the above examples, it will be noted, is not random; each author selects according to his purpose in writing, and what suits one purpose exactly might be exactly wrong for another.

MARSHALING EVIDENCE. Once you have said what you mean, the next question is likely to be "How do you know?" Marshaling evidence may be thought of as what you do to answer that question. Where the matter at hand involves questions of fact, **factual evidence** will be most directly appropriate. (A diary, a letter—perhaps a cryptogram hidden in the text— might prove even to die-hard Baconians that Shakespeare himself did in fact write the plays which have been credited to him). Writers on scientific subjects inevitably draw chiefly on facts, often intricately arrayed, to support their conclusions. But it should not be assumed that factual evidence turns up mainly in scientific writing. Dee Brown's account (p.302) of the war for the Black Hills is obviously based on facts in the form of historical documents, and even the preacher Henry Sloane Coffin (p.450), arguing that the forces that crucified Christ are not merely historical but also contemporary, plainly appeals to facts with which most of us have become familiar.

Factual evidence is generally thought to carry more weight than any other kind, though the force of a fact is greatly diminished if it is not easily verifiable or attested to by reliable witnesses. Where factual evidence is hard to come by (consider the problems of proving that Bacon did not write Shakespeare's plays), the opinion of **authorities** is often invoked, on the assumption that the men most knowledgeable in a field are most likely to judge truly in a particular case. The testimony of authorities is relevant, of course, not only in questions of fact but also in questions of opinion. Francis Bacon (p.200), for example, invokes Solomon and Job to support his ideas about revenge. In general, however, the appeal to authority in matters of opinion has lost the rhetorical effectiveness it once had, perhaps because there is less agreement as to who the reliable authorities are.

As changes in the nature of the question draw in a larger and larger number of "authorities," evidence from authority shades into what might be called "the **common consent** of mankind," those generalizations about human experience that large numbers of readers can be counted upon to accept and that often find expression in proverbs or apothegms: "Risk no more than you can afford to lose" and "The first step toward Hell is halfway there." Such generalizations, whether proverbial or not, are a common ground on which writer and reader meet in agreement. The writer's task is to find and present the ones applicable to his particular thesis and then demonstrate that applicability.

DRAWING CONCLUSIONS. One of the ways of determining the consequences of thought—that is, drawing conclusions—is the process of applying generalizations (**deduction**): "If we should risk no more than we can afford to lose, then we had better not jeopardize the independence of our universities by seeking federal aid." Another way of arriving at conclusions is the process of **induction**, which consists in forming generalizations from a sufficient number of observed instances: "Since universities *A*, *B*, and *C* have been accepting federal aid through research grants for years without loss of independence, it is probably safe for any university to do so." Typically deduction and induction work reciprocally, each helping to supply for the other the materials upon which inference operates. We induce from experience that green apples are sour; we deduce from this generalization that a particular green apple is sour. A third kind of inference, sometimes regarded as only a special kind of deduction or induction, is **analogy**, the process of concluding that two things which resemble each other in one way will resemble each other in another way also: "Federal aid has benefited mental hospitals enormously, and will probably benefit universities just as much." An analogy proves nothing, although it may help the reader see the reasonableness of an idea and is often extremely valuable for purposes of illustration, since it makes an unknown clearer by relating it to a known.

Turning to our essays, we can see something of the variety of ways in which these three kinds of inference manifest themselves in serious writing: Samuel Johnson (p. 201) deducing from men's customary unwillingness to pay more than a thing is worth the conclusion that the pyramids are a monument to human vanity; Wallace Stegner arguing from a series of particular instances to the general conclusion that a community may be judged by what it throws away (p.1); a New Testament parable adumbrating the kingdom of heaven by likening it to ten virgins (p.424).

Such a list of examples suggests that in good writing the conclusions the writer draws, the consequences of his thought, are "consequential" in more than one sense: not only do they follow logically from the evidence he has considered, they are also *significant;* they relate directly or indirectly to aspects of our lives that we care about. To the questions suggested earlier as demands for definition and evidence, then, we must add a third. "What do you mean?" calls for precision yet admits answers vast in scope. "How do you know?" trims the vastness down to what can be substantiated but may settle for triviality as the price of certainty. The appropriate question to raise finally, then, is simply "So what?" and the conclusions we as writers draw need to be significant enough to yield answers to that question. We have come full circle back to the idea of saying something that matters.

And the Style

One theory of style in writing sees form and content as distinct: style is the way a thing is said, the thing itself an unchanging substance that can be decked out in various ways. Mr. Smith not only *died,* he *ceased to be,* he *passed away,* he *croaked,* he *was promoted to glory*—all mean "the same thing." According to a second theory, however, they are ways of saying different things: variations in **diction** imply variations in reference. To say that Smith *ceased to be* records a privative and secular event; to say that he *was promoted to glory* (a Salvation Army expression) rejoices in an event of a different order altogether. Content and form in this view are inseparable; a change in one is a change in the other.

In **metaphor** we can see that the two theories, instead of contradicting each other, are more like the two sides of a coin: when one idea is expressed in terms of another, it is the same and yet not the same. To view the passage from life to death as if it were a promotion from one military rank to a higher one is to see a common center of reference and widening circles of association at the same time. This seeing *as if* opens up a whole range of expression, since many meanings reside in the relationship between the two parts of a comparison rather than in either part by itself. Charles Lamb (p.201), ironically extolling borrowers over lenders, exclaims "What a careless, even deportment hath your borrower!" and then adds "what rosy gills!" His metaphor seems to suggest, approximately, that the borrower's healthy contentment depends on a certain fish-like obliviousness, yet no paraphrase captures the humorous aptness of the metaphor itself.

But style is by no means dependent on diction and metaphor alone. Grammatical relationships yield a host of stylistic devices, most of which can be described in terms of repetition and variation. Repetition may exist at every level; as commonly understood, its chief application is to the word (including the pronoun as a word-substitute), but the same principle governs the use of parallelism (repetition of a grammatical structure) within and between sentences, even between paragraphs. Failure to observe that principle—that similarity in idea calls for similarity in form—can be detected wherever a change in form implies that a distinction is being made when actually none is relevant to the context: "Their conversation was interrupted by dinner, but they resumed their discussion afterwards"; "She rolled out the dough, placed it over the pie, and pricked holes in it. She also trimmed off the edge." The corollary of the principle of appropriate repetition is the principle of appropriate variation—that difference in idea calls for difference in form. For every failure to repeat when repetition is called for there is a corresponding failure to vary when variation is called for: "Their discussion was interrupted when class discussion of the day's assignment began"; "It had been raining for many days near the river. It had been rising steadily toward the top of the levee." Failures of this sort, which suggest a similarity in idea or parallelism in thought where none exists, often strike the ear as a lack of euphony or appropriate rhythm: "A boxer must learn to react absolutely instantly"; "The slingshot was made of strips of inner tubes of tires of cars." The principle of appropriate variation applies, too, to sentences as wholes: if a separate sentence is used for each detail, or if every sentence includes many details, the reader may be given a false impression of parallelism or equality of emphasis. Here again variation may be a way to avoid misleading grammatical indications of meaning. In a writer like Samuel Johnson (p. 201), who works deliberately for a high degree of parallelism, correspondence between repetition and sameness of meaning, or variation and difference of meaning, is perhaps most conveniently illustrated.

All stylistic techniques come together to supply an answer to the question "Who is behind these words?" Every writer establishes an impression of himself—a persona—through what he says and the way he says it, and the quality of that impression obviously has much to do with his reader's willingness to be convinced. Honesty and straightforwardness come first—though the honesty of an ignoramus and the straightforwardness of a fool are unlikely to win assent. Some more sophisticated approaches to the adoption of a persona employ irony: the author assumes a character that the reader can see is at odds with his real intention. Whether direct or ironic, the chosen role must be suited to both the subject and the writer himself, who may want to try out several roles to see what each implies. Is he an expert or a humble seeker after truth, a wry humorist or a gadfly deliberately exacerbating hidden guilt? Even within the same general circumstances (in this case the schoolroom) Henry F. Ottinger (p. 63) and each of the teachers who reply to him are very different sorts of people. A self will be revealed in every phrase the writer sets down—even in details of spelling, grammar, and punctuation, which, if ineptly handled, may suggest to his readers a carelessness that destroys their confidence.

Authors

[*An* * *indicates the source of a selection in this anthology.*
Only a few of each author's works are cited.]

Maya Angelou (1924–   )
American actress, journalist, television script writer, and civil rights worker; author of *I Know Why the Caged Bird Sings, Just Give Me a Cool Drink of Water 'fore I Die*.

Sir Francis Bacon (1561–1626)
English politician, statesman, and philosopher; author of *Essays, Advancement of Learning, *New Organon, New Atlantis*.

Carl Becker (1873–1945)
American historian (Cornell); author of *Progress and Power, The Declaration of Independence, *Modern Democracy*.

Ronald Blythe (1922–   )
English historian and writer; author of *Akenfield: Portrait of an English Village, The Age of Illusion*.

Jacob Bronowski (1908–   )
British critic and statesman, senior fellow and trustee of Salk Institute for Biological Studies; author of *The Poet's Defence, The Common Sense of Science, Science and Human Values, The Identity of Man, Nature and Knowledge*.

Dee (Alexander) Brown (1908–   )
American historian and writer; author of *Bury My Heart at Wounded Knee, The Galvanized Yankees, Grierson's Raid*.

Jerome S. Bruner (1915–   )
American psychologist (Harvard University); author of *The Process of Education, Toward a Theory of Instruction, Processes of Cognitive Growth, The Relevance of Education*.

(John) Anthony Burgess (Wilson) (1917–   )
Author of *A Clockwork Orange, Re Joyce, The Novel Now, MF, Tremor of Intent, Enderby, The Long Day Wanes: A Trilogy, The Wanting Seed, Urgent Copy, The Worm and the Ring*.

H(erbert) J(ames) Campbell (1934–   )
English physiologist (Institute of Psychiatry at DeCrespigny Park); author of *Correlative Physiology of the Nervous System*.

Edward Hallett Carr (1892–   )
English historian (Cambridge), journalist, and statesman; author of *The Romantic Exiles; The Bolshevik Revolution, 1917–1923; *What Is History?*

(Arthur) Joyce (Lunel) Cary (1888–1957)
Anglo-Irish novelist, poet, and political philosopher; author of *Aissa Saved, The Horse's Mouth, Mister Johnson, The Captive and the Free* (novels), *A Case for-African Freedom, Power in Men, The Process of Real Freedom* (commentaries).

Sir Kenneth Clark (1902–   )
English art historian and critic; author of *Landscape into Art, The Nude, Leonardo da Vinci, Looking at Pictures, Civilisation*.

Eldridge Cleaver (1935–   )
Black American revolutionary, journalist, social critic; former Minister of Information of the Black Panther Party; currently in exile in Algeria; author of *Soul on Ice*.

Henry Sloane Coffin (1877–1954)
American clergyman and educator; president, Union Theological Seminary; author of *The Meaning of the Cross, Religion Yesterday and Today*.

Robert Coles (1929–   )
American psychiatrist (Harvard University); author of *Children of Crisis, Still Hungry in America, The*

Image Is You, The Wages of Neglect, Uprooted Children, Drugs and Youth, Erik Erikson: The Growth of His Work, *The Middle Americans, The South Goes North.

Bernadette Devlin (1947–)
Irish member of the British House of Commons and Catholic civil rights leader in Protestant-dominated Northern Ireland; author of **The Price of My Soul.*

Joan Didion (1934–)
American essayist, story writer, novelist, and journalist (*Life*); author of *Play It as It Lays, *Slouching Towards Bethlehem, Run River.*

W(illiam) E(dward) B(urghardt) Du Bois (1868–1963)
American author, editor, and teacher; a founder of the National Association for the Advancement of Colored People; relentless exponent of the complete equality of the Negro in America; author of *The Suppression of the African Slave Trade, The Souls of Black Folk, John Brown, Black Reconstruction, Dusk of Dawn, The Black Flame (A Trilogy).*

Ralph Ellison (1914–)
American novelist, story writer, social critic; author of *Invisible Man, *Shadow and Act.*

Erik H. Erikson (1902–)
German-born American psychoanalyst (Harvard University); author of *Young Man Luther, Identity and the Life Cycle, *Insight and Responsibility, Identity: Youth and Crisis, Childhood and Society, Gandhi's Truth* (Pulitzer Prize, 1970).

Robert Frost (1874–1963)
American poet, lecturer, teacher.

Christopher Fry (1907–)
English playwright and translator; author of the plays *The Boy with a Cart, The Dark Is Light Enough, The Lady's Not for Burning, Venus Observed, A Yard of Sun.*

Northrop Frye (1912–)
Canadian literary critic (University of Toronto); author of *Anatomy of Criticism, Design for Learning, *The Educated Imagination.*

Garrett James Hardin (1915–)
American biologist (University of California at Santa Barbara); author of *Nature and Man's Fate; Population, Evolution and Birth Control;*

Biology: Its Principles and Implications.

Eric Hoffer (1902–)
American longshoreman and social critic; author of *The True Believer, The Passionate State of Mind, The Ordeal of Change.*

John Caldwell Holt (1923–)
American educator; author of *How Children Fail, How Children Learn, Underachieving School, What Do I Do Monday?*

George Jackson (1942–1971)
American political revolutionary; 1960-1970, inmate of Soledad Prison (second-degree robbery); 1970, accused, with two other inmates, of killing a prison guard; 1971, killed in an alleged escape attempt; author of *Soledad Brother: The Prison Letters of George Jackson.*

Samuel Johnson (1709–1784)
English lexicographer, critic, moralist; journalist (*The Idler, *The Rambler*); author of *A Dictionary of the English Language, Lives of the Poets;* subject of Boswell's *Life.*

Franz Kafka (1883–1924)
Czech novelist and short-story writer; author of **The Trial, The Castle, Amerika.*

John F. Kerry (1943–)
American Yale University graduate and Vietnam veteran.

Thomas Kuhn (1922–)
American historian of science (Princeton University); author of *The Copernican Revolution, Planetary Astronomy in the Development of Western Thought, *The Structure of Scientific Revolutions.*

Charles Lamb (1775–1834)
English essayist, critic; author of **Essays of Elia* and, with his sister, Mary, *Tales from Shakespeare.*

Susanne K. Langer (1895–)
American philosopher and educator (Connecticut College); author of *The Practice of Philosophy, An Introduction to Symbolic Logic, Feeling and Form, *Problems of Art.*

Konrad Z. Lorenz (1903–)
Austrian-born German scientist; director of Max Planck Institute for Physiology of Behavior; author of **King Solomon's Ring* and *So kam der Mensch auf den Hund* (*Thus Came the Man to the Dog*).

Niccolò Machiavelli (1469–1527)
Florentine statesman and political philosopher during the reign of the Medici; author of *The Art of War, History of Florence, Discourses on Livy, *The Prince.*

William March (1893–1954)
Pseudonym of William Edward March Campbell; American businessman, novelist, short-story writer, fabulist; author of *Company K, The Little Wife and Other Stories, Some Like Them Short, *99 Fables.*

Matthew
One of the twelve Apostles of Christ, author of *The Gospel According to St. Matthew.

Toni Morrison (1931–   )
American writer; author of *The Bluest Eye.*

John Henry Newman (1801–1890)
English Catholic prelate and cardinal; author of *Tracts for the Times, *The Idea of a University, Apologia pro Vita sua.*

Huey P. Newton (1942–   )
Black American revolutionary; cofounder and Minister of Defense of the Black Panther Party.

Nicholas of Cusa (c. 1400–1464)
German Catholic prelate (bishop and cardinal) and philosopher, argued in favor of church councils over the pope and for the principle of consent as the basis of government; author of *De concordantia catholica, De docta ignorantia, *De visione Dei (The Vision of God).*

George Orwell (1903–1950)
Pseudonym of Eric Blair; English novelist, essayist, and social commentator, satirist of totalitarianism; author of *Down and Out in Paris and London, Homage to Catalonia, *Nineteen Eighty-Four, Animal Farm.*

Henry F. Ottinger (1941–   )
Instructor of English (University of Missouri).

Donald R. Pearce (1917–   )
Canadian professor of English (Santa Barbara); author of *Journal of a War: Northwest Europe, 1944-1945 and In the President's and My Opinion.*

Plato (427?–347 B.C.)
Greek philosopher, pupil and friend of Socrates, teacher of Aristotle, founder of the Academy, proponent of an oligarchy of intellectuals based on the assumption that virtue is knowledge; author of *The Republic.*

Adrienne Rich (1929–   )
American poet (City College of New York); author of *A Change of World, The Diamond Cutters, Necessities of Life, Snapshots of a Daughter-in-Law, Leaflets, The Will to Change.*

Stanley Sanders (1942–   )
American lawyer.

Jean-Paul Sartre (1905–   )
French philosopher, playwright, novelist, story writer, social and literary critic, Nobel Prize winner; author of *Existentialism, Existentialism and Humanism, No Exit, The Wall, Imagination, Of Human Freedom, The Problem of Method, The Words, The Transcendence of the Ego.*

Peter Schrag (1931–   )
German-born American editor and writer; author of *Voices in the Classroom, Out of Place in America, Village School Downtown.*

Chief Seattle (19th century)
American Indian, chief of the Duwampo tribe in Washington Territory.

B(urrhus) F(rederic) Skinner (1904–   )
American psychologist (Harvard); inventor of the Skinner box, an artificial environmental system for the control and study of behavior; author of *Science and Human Behavior, Walden Two, Beyond Freedom.*

Wallace Stegner (1909–   )
American essayist, novelist, professor of English (Stanford); author of *Remembering Laughter, The Women on the Wall, Beyond the Hundredth Meridian, A Shocking Star, *Wolf Willow, All the Little Live Things,* and *Gathering of Zion: The Story of the Mormon Trail.*

Jonathan Swift (1667–1745)
Irish satirist, poet, and churchman; author of *Gulliver's Travels, A Tale of a Tub, *The Battle of the Books.*

(Louis) Studs Terkel (1912–   )
American actor, interviewer, and writer; author of *Hard Times: An Oral History of the Great Depression, Division Street: America.*

Henry David Thoreau (1817–1862)
American philosopher, essayist, natu-

ralist, poet, disciple of Emerson, foremost exponent of self-reliance; author of *Walden,* "Civil Disobedience," **Journals.*

James Thurber (1894–1963)
American humorist, cartoonist, social commentator (*New Yorker*), playwright; author of *My Life and Hard Times; *Fables for Our Time; *Men, Women, and Dogs; The Beast in Me and Other Animals.*

John Updike (1932–   )
American novelist, story writer, poet; author of *Rabbit, Run; The Centaur; Of the Farm; Couples; Bech; Rabbit Redux* (novels); *The Same Door; Pigeon Feathers; The Music School* (stories).

Verta Mae (1938–   )
Black American writer; author of *Vibration Cooking* and *Thursdays and Every Other Sunday Off.*

Ian P(ierre) Watt (1917–   )
English-born American professor of English (Stanford University); author of *The Rise of the Novel.*

Simone Weil (1909–1943)
French essayist, poet, philosopher; author of **Waiting for God; Gravity and Grace; The Need for Roots;* *Oppression and Liberty; On Science, Necessity and the Love of God.*

Naomi Weisstein (1939–   )
American psychologist (Loyola University, Chicago); author of numerous papers on perception, cognition, information science, memory, and the psychology of differences between men and women.

Edward Weston (1886–1958)
American photographer; author of **The Daybooks.*

E. B. White (1899–   )
American essayist, journalist, editor (*New Yorker*); author of *One Man's Meat, *The Wild Flag, *The Second Tree from the Corner.*

Tom Wolfe (1931–   )
American essayist, story writer, social critic; author of **The Kandy-Kolored Tangerine-Flake Streamline Baby, The Pump House Gang, Radical Chic and Mau-Mauing the Flak Catcher.*

Virginia Woolf (1882–1942)
English novelist, essayist, and critic; author of *Mrs. Dalloway, To the Lighthouse* (novels), *The Common Reader, Granite and Rainbow, *The Second Common Reader* (essays).

Alphabetical Index